RACE AND THE *SUBJECT OF MASCULINITIES*

New Americanists   a series edited by Donald E. Pease

Harry Stecopoulos and Michael Uebel, Editors

RACE AND THE SUBJECT

OF MASCULINITIES

Duke University Press   Durham and London   1997

© 1997 Duke University Press
All rights reserved
Printed in the United States of America
on acid-free paper ∞
Typeset in Joanna by Tseng Information Systems, Inc.
Library of Congress Cataloging-in-Publication Data
appear on the last printed page of this book.

CONTENTS

IV. COMING AFTER

ACKNOWLEDGMENTS

First, we would like to thank our contributors for their infinite patience with a project that has taken far too long to complete. Their faith in the book has sustained us during this long process. Given the time-sensitive nature of their contributions, their commitment is all the more extraordinary.

We have also received sustenance from those friends at Virginia and elsewhere who have endured countless references to and discussions of the book over many years. Matt Brown, Nick Frankel, James Hurley, Brent Lanford, Andrea Levine, and Vance Smith have always been generous and wise interlocutors. Professors Eric Lott and Deborah E. McDowell of the University of Virginia provided us with important counsel; we thank them for their advice at virtually every stage of this project. Awards for patience and wisdom — above and beyond the call of duty — must also go to the wonderful people at Duke: Jean Brady, Richard Morrison, and, above all, our editor, Ken Wissoker. Ken shepherded this book through good times and bad; at times, he seemed more a collaborator than an editor.

Our parents have helped us weather graduate school in many ways; they have our appreciation.

Last here, but foremost in our thoughts, we want to thank Kathy Lavezzo and Debra Morris — partners whose deep investment in matters both intellectual and personal have made this book possible.

MEN IN COLOR

Introducing Race and the Subject of Masculinities

MICHAEL UEBEL

> Let's talk about identity-from-above as well as identity-from-below. That's
> something that is rarely stressed, rarely examined, rarely specified. We need
> to get a handle on how . . . whiteness, maleness, and straightness functions
> over time and space in relation to blackness or brownness or yellowness or
> womanness or gayness or lesbianness, etc.
> —Cornel West, "A Matter of Life and Death"

Identity politics has emerged in the past few years as the contemporary critical watchword. Recent special issues of *New Formations, Critical Inquiry, October,*
and *diacritics,*[1] along with a proliferating number of essays and books, attest to the explosion of interest in the politics of identity. Drawing on the
critical methods of gender studies, queer studies, film studies, ethnography,
and studies of colonialism, identity politics scrutinizes the effects of cultural
forces on identities and the forms in which identities are imagined. It describes a historical approach to subjectivity, attentive to the ways we understand individuals as products of a field of determinants, at once psychic,
institutional, interracial, bodily, homoerotic, homosocial, aesthetic, rhetorical, national. It deconstructs the opposition between the social and the psychic by obliging us, as Kaja Silverman famously puts it, "to approach history
always through the refractions of desire and identification, and to read race
and class insistently in relation to sexuality" and gender (*Male Subjectivity* 300).
And, most significantly, identity politics opens the way for describing identificatory practices as well as their products, for delineating ongoing processes
as well as "final" meanings.[2]

The present collection, subtended by the discourses and strategies of identity politics, debates the meanings of identities and the ethical questions
attending them from a relatively focused critical perspective. In order to
understand subjectivity as constituted by and constitutive of multiple positions, the contributors locate the subject at the intersection of race and mas-

culinity. Around the central question "How do men inhabit simultaneously their color and their gender?" others are elaborated: How is the imbrication of race and male subjectivity to be understood as a historically, culturally specific construct? What are the psychological and moral implications of transgression and identification for racial difference and masculine performance? What cultural limits define racial masculine identity and to what extent are they enforceable and finally transgressable? Which specific practices of representation are important to understanding race and the subject of masculinities? This last question in particular enlarges the scope of current identity inquiries and begs for a deeper understanding of gender and racial performativities. For while many practices of representation—such as blues, signifying, jazz, blackface minstrelsy, hairstyle, rap[3]—have been closely examined for the mechanics of racial identity, little attention has been given to their significance as racial masculine performance.

The essays collected here emphasize the provisional nature of racial masculine identities.[4] Although treating masculinities as varied as those of André Gide, Eddie Murphy, Malcolm X, and Bruce Lee, they are linked by the same assumption: racial maleness is the origin as well as the product of local transactions between the social and the psychic, of negotiations among popular forms of representation and political ideologies, and of technologies of performance. In other words, throughout this volume racial male subjectivity is read insistently in the context of the historical and cultural forces of which identity is both the result *and* the potential agent.[5] Reading men in the context of race is thus a dialectical intervention: an attempt to understand men at the (construction) site of specific power relations, each relation mediating the reproduction and transformation of another. Though the challenge to "race" masculinity is embraced collectively, each of the thirteen essays here answers that challenge in a unique way. Each provokes a reformulation of the critical terms with which gender and cultural theories usually map configurations of race and masculinities.

As a first step toward rethinking what Cornel West calls "identity-from-above"—signified for him by the concepts of masculinity, heterosexuality, patriarchy, and whiteness—the present essays explode the monolithic, homogeneous categories of dominance into their historically differentiated economies. Attention to the specific historicity and textuality of privileged, often ideologically invisible, categories such as whiteness prevents the acceptance of their uniformity and autonomy. Demystifying univocal, inevitable "myths" in a Barthesian fashion, the present essays maintain that categories such as whiteness and masculinity have no single "natural" or "objective" standing beyond the cultures they organize. But, of course, denying the cultural autonomy of whiteness, by asserting its particularity, does not amount to ignoring the power of its "autonomy-effects"—the ways in which it appears as a generality. Thus Richard Dyer, in his essay on the coupling of bodybuilding and colonialism, contends that white masculinities must be understood as historically specific constructions at the same time that they are recognized in their generality. "It is," he writes, "the ability to pass themselves off as not particular that allows them to go on being, within the regime of representation that they produce, 'invisible'" (289; this volume). Theorizing identity-from-above, then, necessitates an attention to the interplay of racial masculine particularities and generalities.

The criticism of racial masculinity in this volume thus demands this strategic assertion: that the opposition between identity-from-above and identity-from-below is a false one. The essays collected here reformulate this opposition as a vital, not always amiable, dialogue. Delineating the dominant or privileged depends upon analyzing the marginalized or colonized—and vice versa. As Christopher Looby, Eric Lott, and Gayle Wald demonstrate, whiteness is complexly structured by fantasies of blackness; and, as Herman Beavers argues, definitions of black masculine identity crucially hinge on investments in white male identity. Such interdependence shows that the formation of masculine identity is never strictly, so to speak, a black-and-white issue. The essays collectively refuse to suppress the crossing and uncrossing of central issues of race by the heterogeneity of masculine sex/gender interests and class/ethnic identities: Leerom Medovoi understands 1950s youth culture in terms of its masculinist challenge to the racial, generational, and class hegemonies of white America; Eric Lott reads Elvis impersonators as a reclamation of working-class machismo; Jonathan Dollimore argues for the political force of crossing lines of racial and sexual difference; and Yvonne Tasker interrogates Hong Kong and American martial arts films for what they reveal about nationalist and homoerotic masculine identifications.

Folding identity-from-above into identity-from-below, and vice versa, constitutes a refusal to reauthorize the historically and culturally dominant—whiteness, masculinity, straightness—a refusal that is not necessarily reducible to an opposition to the entangling of whiteness with blackness, masculinity with femininity, straightness with queerness. This volume attempts to theorize the dominant without endorsing, replicating, or valorizing it. Responding to the need for theorizing dominance, the collection seeks a way out of and beyond the dominion of identities-from-above: here it is precisely the "above" that is held for questioning. In the context of American history, as several contributors make clear, and in the recent context of pop singers Marky Mark or Vanilla Ice, the supersession of whiteness entailed ways into blackness. Yet "abolishing" whiteness is often only appropriation of and violence to blackness. A critical look at whiteness, enabled theoretically by a critical black perspective, not only will suggest that whiteness, too, is socially constructed (and therefore deconstructible), but also will condemn the dominance it risks erecting and concealing. Looby's and Dollimore's essays move toward a liberation from the dominance of whiteness through sexuality, an overcoming of race through same-sex desire. Lott's essay creates a space for the possibility of dismantling dominance through practices of impersonation, where claims of whiteness or class in relation to Elvis are always up for grabs. These essays insist on the links between practice and theory, as they try to push theory into its local, historical domain.

"Practice," Gilles Deleuze postulated, "is a set of relays from one theoretical point to another, and theory is a relay from one practice to another. No theory can develop without eventually encountering a wall, and practice is necessary for piercing this wall" (206). Together, the theories of racialized masculinities in this volume evoke practices aimed at transgressing the confining limits of theorizing only identities-from-above. *Masculinity* comes to designate a whole range of cultural forms and practices, and our use of the multiplex category *masculinities* in the title of this essay and volume signals our wish to account for the local diversities of the subject. The category *masculinities* is not meant to be a stable consolidation of historically specific subject-positions or a collective term for masculinity, but a polysemy denying the autonomy and stability of male identity as it claims to specify and interpret masculine self-perception, performativity, and existence. The term brings into play the recognition of the profound multiplicity and conditional status of the historical experience of male subjects. Masculinity becomes not the defining quality of men, of their fantasies and real experiences of self and other, but one coordinate of their identity that exists in a constant dialectical relation with other coordinates.

This dialectical constructionist view of racial and gender subjectivities directly challenges the dominant view of popular culture, described by Philip Cohen as "the mere effect of a collision between dominant and subordinate ideologies, or some kind of open space where discourses circulate" ("Tarzan" 25), merely to consolidate and invigorate a hegemonic discourse. Far from positing a static model of culture that forecloses the possibility of political progress, the contributors inscribe racial masculine existence and imagination within popular cultures that are constantly shifting the meanings that traditionally ground them. In the active production of new meanings, alliances such as the masculine with patriarchy or blackness with absolute otherness (and thus, whiteness with nondifference) betray their ideological flexibility. Such couplings reveal the contingency and fragility of their own encodings and the possibilities for altering their own terms of reference.

The essays in this collection suggest that the value of using *masculinities* as an active term in race- and gender-based criticism depends upon its inscription within a systematics of performance. Here racial and gender identities emerge as dynamic performances scripted, rehearsed, and (re)enacted in the presence of one another.[6] Yet any such insistence on the antiessentialist ontology of selfhood does not alone guarantee, as Robyn Wiegman's essay strikingly reminds us, that masculine identity will not be posited as a homogeneous subject category, construed wholly within a monolithic subjective function, an elision of crucial differences among men. Wiegman calls into question the idealizations of the male bond and its dream of masculine mutuality in the critical work of Leslie Fiedler and two of his contemporary adapters. The significance of race in representations of the male bond, she argues, has been displaced and silenced by the construction of a mythic white masculine subjectivity (Fiedler), the romanticization of male homosexuality as the radical potential of democracy (Robert K. Martin), and the figuring of a multiform self incorporating and effacing cultural difference (Joseph A. Boone). These configurations of maleness transmute racial *difference* into a model of masculine *sameness* by disavowing the complex interplay of racial and gender difference that crucially underwrites masculinities. Wiegman's metacritical treatment of interracial male bonding and quest narratives thus usefully contextualizes the critical stance employed by the other essays in this volume, by highlighting the interchange of race, gender, and sexuality in the construction of specific masculinities.

The central identity configuration posited throughout this collection, the dialectic between racial and gender difference, provides a fertile field for psychoanalytically charged accounts that reveal the especially competitive, contradictory sites of attraction and repulsion, desire and violence, and appropriation and disavowal occupied by racial masculinities. Dollimore's and Tasker's essays enlist Freudian and Lacanian accounts of colonialism, such as those of Frantz Fanon and Homi Bhabha, as well as psychoanalytic critiques of racial masculine politics, such as those of Kobena Mercer and Kaja Silverman,[7] to expose the racial dialectics of narcissism and aggression. The disavowal of difference (fetish) and its recognition (phobia), for instance, are two attitudes toward otherness that shape cross-racial identifications and the cultural production of masculinities. In the presence of the other, the subject is intensely ambivalent, poised between desire and fear, incitement and interdiction, mastery and anxiety.

Offering an incisive analysis of the psychomachia inherent in the position of mastery, Christopher Looby reads the memoir of Thomas Wentworth Higginson, white commander of an all-black Union Army regiment during the Civil War, in order to lay bare the sublimated fantasies inflecting his camaraderie with, and love for, his soldiers. Looby shows how Higginson's cross-racial identification depends on a logic of recognition and disavowal: the commander acknowledges his "racial envy" at the same time as he sanitizes his fetish objects under an aestheticizing gaze. Higginson thus retains the sovereignty of whiteness while indulging in a fantasy of blackness. Looby's reading complements Gayle Wald's in underscoring the social and psychological ramifications of "loving blackness,"[8] and, further, joins Richard Dyer's and Eric Lott's readings to address the conflictive construction and symbolic value of white masculinity.

The symbolic or metaphoric values of racial masculinities are rarely static. Several essays converge on a reading of racial masculinities as unstable icons marking mobile, shifting positionalities. The essays of José Muñoz, Gayle Wald, Harry Stecopoulos, Eric Lott, and Christopher Looby highlight the complex, culturally contingent construction of racial masculine identities as a function of not always coherent processes of self-fashioning. Muñoz reads Isaac Julien's film Looking for Langston and its allusions to the homoerotic photographs of Mapplethorpe and Van Der Zee as constructing shifting fantasies and communal identities against the social background of not only white, but heterosexist, supremacies in the age of AIDS. Wald analyzes the career of white jazz musician, hipster, and self-styled "voluntary Negro" Mezz Mezzrow, revealing how his racial passing is irrevocably coupled with mobile erotic, masculine, and aesthetic identifications. Stecopoulos explores the way in which turn-of-the-century white middle-class American men used "raced" cultural fantasies to prop up both their class identity and their sense of manhood during times of professional and financial failure. Stecopoulos demonstrates how texts such as the best-selling Tarzan of the Apes (1914) offer imperial fantasies of racial supremacy aimed at tenuously "resolving" moments of white male middle-class self-doubt by means of an uneasy fascination with and appropriation of black male physicality.

Discussing the symbolic value of racial identity, Richard Dyer and Herman Beavers turn to the gendered, raced body for its disclosures about the machinery of racism and colonialism. For both contributors, the racial male body manifests contradictory discursive practices and power investments. Dyer's richly suggestive reading of the white male body in Italian peplum films of the late 1950s and early 1960s treats skin color and muscle-contoured bodies as expressions of control, signifiers of colonial hegemony, where power derives from the simultaneous staging and transcending of hierarchies. The white male hero reigns supreme at the same time as he supersedes the system he rules; his power is at once particular and nonspecific, above the particular. In this way the hero can be hypermasculine *and* suprahuman, white *and* strikingly tanned, a conqueror of both primitive, non-white men *and* futuristic machine technology. At the heart of these paradoxical conditions, Dyer suggests, lies "perhaps the secret of all power."

Though the mechanism of power, the means by which racial masculinities signify specifically and unrestrictedly (invisibly), is transcultural—"the secret of *all* power"—the forms that it takes are culturally specific. Beavers investigates the "secret" of Eddie Murphy's power as a troubling icon of racial progress by situating his "coolness"—as sign of relief, control, *and* transgression—in the political context of racism, homophobia, and misogyny. He also situates Murphy's dialectical, cool pose in relation to Richard Pryor's radical appropriation of cool as a way of restoring the African American male "body in pain." Murphy's persona—consistent whether he plays himself or a character—allows him, like the heroic peplum bodybuilder, to cross the fixed lines of racial identity. Transcending the limits of race and body, Murphy and Pryor can reclaim, even transform, black experience.

In Robin D. G. Kelley's reading of Malcolm X's autobiographical account of his teenage years, the male body with its "fashionable ghetto adornments," to use Malcolm's own words, constitutes a forceful assertion of race, class, and gender prerogative. Malcolm's teenage years, Kelley suggests, coincided with a system of wartime cultural politics in which the cool hipster subculture of black males molded, for some, new identities relatively free of the constraints of patriotic fervor and petit bourgeois morality. The zoot suit, the conk, and the moves and language of the "hep cat" signified the ability to demystify the dominant ideology while remaining tied to it through gestures of appropriation. Recasting the male body and the ways it signifies is above all a political enterprise, aimed at producing new solidarities and exposing the bounds of the dominant and "normal" as fragile and subject to revision.

By mapping identities in terms of colonial fantasy and the iconography of racial masculine bodies, theoretical models emerge that are aimed at supplanting reductive accounts of identity formation at the intersection of race and masculinity. Critical paradigms that merely figure ambivalent fantasies of identification and the symbolic value of male racial bodies reproduce a false binarism of solidarity and transgression. Jonathan Dollimore, for example, argues persuasively for comprehending transgression in terms of solidarity, difference in terms of identification. Thus, the opposition always implied between difference and identification cannot be neatly described as contradictory. Part of the reason that the opposition cannot be contained, as Dollimore suggests, has to do with the category of difference itself. When Dollimore writes in Sexual Dissidence, "we are not all the same. We are differences which radically proximate" (229), he emphasizes the extent to which identity entails opposition and proximity. Difference itself challenges radical separation by foregrounding the contiguity of identities. By animating the play and friction of identities, the "struggle around positionalities," as Stuart Hall puts it ("New Ethnicities" 28), difference directs our attention to the "contact zone" of male subjectivity. As one useful paradigm for theorizing the embattled terrain of masculine identity formation, difference offers an important model for understanding how men inhabit their color.

Dollimore's critical treatment of marginalized histories, in which race and male homosexuality converge, showcases a larger project, as he puts it, "to think difference in terms of culture." Through the writings and life dramas of André Gide, Jean Genet, and Frantz Fanon, Dollimore radically redefines politics as inflected with desire, with "deviant" forms of sexuality and fantasy imbued with special knowledges of, and identifications with, an other. In Dollimore's view, crossing racial, class, and national boundaries, and, most significantly, the lines imposed by normative sexuality and erotic practice, is a vital, empowering act of social critique. By putting what might be called a queer spin on humanist discourses, he suggests that transgressive desire for the other displaces and potentially dismantles racism, colonialism, and imperialism. He reconstitutes the universal humanist discourses of alterity, which underwrite these nefarious isms, as humanist processes of difference and proximation, opposition and solidarity. Or, to quote a trenchant aphorism from his Sexual Dissidence: "To be against (opposed to) is also to be against (close up, in proximity to) or, in other words, up against" (229).

In Dollimore's political reformulation of difference there is no room for the sort of relativist claims that S. P. Mohanty recently has identified in contemporary critical idioms. The extreme relativist position, according to Mohanty, radicalizes difference in the attempt to proximate identities: if one posits separateness, two spaces, and then develops general interpretive criteria to account for both contexts, one ends up asserting "that all spaces are equivalent: that they have equal value, that since the lowest common principle of evaluation is all that I can evoke, I cannot—and consequently need not—

think about how your space impinges on mine, or how my history is defined together with yours" (67). Mohanty offers an antidote to the dangers of relativism: a historicizing approach to cultural practices that fully assesses human agency and the decisions constituting it. Relativist evaluations of culture and agency, this collection asserts, fall short of specifying, in order to adjudicate, the terms in which we might understand the intersection of race and masculinities at the level of human performativity.

Elaborating on the varieties of racial male cultural practice and the ways they are interpreted, these essays affirm the "radical proximation" of race and gender by taking advantage of recent philosophical discussions and feminist reformulations of gendered identity. The centrality of performance in these recent critiques of identity owes to the prevalent poststructuralist, Nietzschean belief that there is no psychological core in humans, no "ineffable interiority" of "true identity" (Butler, *Gender* 136)—put simply, you are constituted by what you do (and have done) and how you are interpreted doing what you do (and have done).[9] Basing gendered subjectivity on praxis suggests that bodies have "no ontological status apart from the various acts which constitute [their] reality" (Butler, *Gender* 136). We must formulate the cultural politics of race and masculinities in a turn away from defunct ontologies, toward the personal and political economies of performance and style.

Race, sexuality, gender, and nationality are increasingly defined less as fixed identities rooted in bodies, normative sexuality, nature, or geography, and more as dynamic and dramatic modes, the sum of one's cultural practices. Implicit in all the essays collected here is the assumption that racial masculinities are dynamic modes of cultural practice—shifting, repeating sets of performances denoting not a fixed or essential subject category but rather "a relative point of convergence among culturally and historically specific sets of relations" (Butler, *Gender* 10). Ralph Ellison's compelling view of blackness as "perpetual beginning"—a process, as Kimberly Benston puts it, subject to renewal and "generated from performance to performance" (173)—can help us, then, to investigate whiteness, or black or white maleness—in short, the *color of manhood*—as a revisionary process, a constitutive performance. Inscribing race and the subject of masculinities within the cultural politics of performativity generates an authentic ethics and politics of representation, a critique that accounts for the formative, not merely the expressive, roles of subjectivity in constituting social and political existence.[10]

Cultural practice, the per-formative aspect of identities, is inescapably bound up with *style*: gender is imagined as "corporeal style" (Butler, *Gender* 139); race is tied to "practices of stylization" (Mercer, "Black Hair" 51); and communities are distinguished "by the style in which they are imagined" (B. Anderson 15). Eric Lott and Gayle Wald locate style at the center of their inquiries into the tangled dynamics of gender, sex, and class underpinning racial impersonation. Wald shows how the subjective drama of Mezzrow's identity replaces a paradigm of fixed, essential identity with one of racial masculine style and performance. Lott applies the tools of cultural ethnography to popular appropriations of Elvis to interrogate the fantasies of black and white style, which are inescapably fantasies of class, animating masculine performance. In terms that overlap Looby's and Wald's accounts of whiteness, he shows how impersonation vitally depends upon a dialectical process of proximation: the lived proximity to an other, a proximity that at the same time is forgotten or disavowed. To "be" Elvis is to inhabit the conflicted terrain of his style, since it is finally style that enables proximation. Here, style manifests those racial and class subtexts structuring white working-class masculinity that it works so hard to enact and reclaim.

While this collection offers multiple readings of specifically contextualized racial male subjectivities, two essays in particular, those of Leerom Medovoi and Yvonne Tasker, enact larger strategies for performing disenchanting and juxtaposing interpretive readings. These essays suggest the extraordinarily intertextual nature of reading race and the subject of masculinities. Working in what he describes as a deconstructively informed cultural studies, Medovoi complicates Stuart Hall's notion of oppositional reading in order to interrogate the popular responses to, and social positionings of, the 1955 film *Blackboard Jungle*. He emphasizes the degree to which any site of opposition, or reading, is exclusionary: oppositionality and counterhegemonic solidarity depend on disavowing ideological difference. Yvonne Tasker, writing on the multiple racial discourses of masculine identity in Hong Kong and American martial arts films, acknowledges along with Medovoi the value of competing, oppositional readings. She traces the different fantasies of empowerment staged in three cinematic traditions: the macho nationalism of Bruce Lee in Hong Kong films; the performance and posing of hard white male bodies as the objects of a "homospectatorial look"[11] in American cinema; and the "fluid masculinity" of kung fu comedy.

Whether approached by a liberal humanist inquiry or by a decentering antiessentialism, the topics around which the essays organize themselves—dialectics/dialogics of identity, difference/identification, performativity/style—reflect what has been called "a renewed attention to ethics" (Harpham 7). The topics serve to mark points of intersection between the ways discourses of race are treated in this collection and the ethical commitments and descriptions attending them. Such points of intersection hinge on what might be termed an ethical "conceptual base" (17), one mediating between a notion of cultural identity as a matter of "being" and one of "becoming."[12] Racial masculine identities thus describe a process of positioning: they name the ways raced men position themselves in relation to the past that has shaped them and to the future they will shape. They possess a history, but also the power to perform, or transform, that history. The power of transformation, the ways in which power is exercised or undermined, and the choices power necessitates and depends upon, all require a postulation of what *ought* to be, a recognition of the obligation the future places on the individual subject.

In his recent book on ethical discourse and imperativity, Geoffrey Harpham reminds us of the significance of situating the *ought* "at the dead center of ethics" (18). *Ought* is a word, he puts it, "hovering between the 'constative' and the 'performative'" (18), between presence and praxis, between what is and what is to be. Ethics, in this dialogic description, describes a performative relation of identity to real and imaginative (ideal) conditions of existence.[13] Addressing this relation, then, marks an "ethical moment," the opportunity for both critical description and political intervention.[14] For if the categories race and masculinity crucially depend upon the dialectics of what *is* (bodies, the other, the past) and what *will be* or what is in process (desire, performance, the future), then we cannot, and ought not, disengage our readings of racial masculinities from an attention to the responsibilities and commitments demanded in the ethical moment.

This moment, which Dick Hebdige describes as the "yearning out towards something more and something better than this and this place now" ("Some sons" 38), compels us to the critical task of acknowledging the agency of masculinities and identifying the systems of meaning—race, sex, class, nation—that that agency constructs and potentially deconstructs. In their efforts to formulate the ambivalences resisting totalization, these essays locate racial male subjectivity not at the margins but in the contested space between the constative and the performative—that is, in the broad and broadly acknowledged territory of ethics. The ethical dimension to Dyer's historicism is clear: we must see systems of dominance such as whiteness as both agent and result of their historical moment of dominance, to the point that we recognize them as self-invented, and this prior to our forming any politics that would sabotage them. This collection, by offering multiple paradigms for reading the cultural intersections of race and masculinities, enriches our general understanding of identities as constructed and negotiated within and against a complex historical matrix of alterities, against a web of differences. It is the exclusion or privileging of these differences that raises important questions about reading strategies and political practice.

Notes

This essay (done in 1993) owes a great deal, except its imperfections, to the generosity and intellectual support of the following colleagues: John Foster, Deborah McDowell, Nick Frankel, Eric Lott, Laura Sanchez, Vance Smith, and Debra Morris.

1. See *New Formations* 5 (1988); *Critical Inquiry* 18 (summer 1992); *October* 61 (summer 1992); and *diacritics* 24 (summer–fall 1994).

2. The end of this paragraph calls for a footnote in the form of a "pocket bibliography" of writings on identity politics. Such a bibliography would not fit here, and probably need not since much of the work on identity politics is already absorbed into the critical mainstream. To take a shortcut, I refer the reader to the "references," "suggestions for further reading," "bibliography," and "notes" sections of the following collections: Grossberg, Nelson, and Treichler, eds., *Cultural Studies*; Ashcroft, Griffiths, and Tiffin, eds., *The Post-Colonial Studies Reader*; Abelove, Barale, and Halperin, eds., *The Lesbian and Gay Studies Reader*; Warner, ed., *Fear of a Queer Planet: Queer Politics and Social Theory*.

3. Here a cursory list must include Baker, *Blues, Ideology, and Afro-American Literature: A Vernacular Theory*; Gates, *The Signifying Monkey: A Theory of African American Literary Criticism*; Nero, "Toward a Black Gay Aesthetic: Signifying in Contemporary Black Gay Literature"; Lott, " 'The Seeming Counterfeit': Racial Politics and Early Blackface Minstrelsy" and *Love and Theft*; Mercer, "Black Hair/Style Politics"; Toop, *The Rap Attack: African Jive to New York Hip Hop*; Spencer, ed., *The Emergence of Rap and the Emergence of Black*; and Rose, *Black Noise*.

4. Those writing within the present-day politics of identity insist on the value of identity as a *strategic* term. Confining the term to its provisional use in order to complicate and question comprehensive, formulaic paradigms and to challenge their political validity, the politics of identity envisions the disenchanting of identity and its traditional forms of calculation. For example, Judith Butler prefers "to think about the invocation of identity as a strategic provisionality, using the term, but knowing when to let it go, living its contingency, and subjecting it to a political challenge concerning its usefulness" ("Discussion" 110). And Stanley Aronowitz writes: "A solution [to the problem of needing a generalized theoretical discourse of identity] is to offer theoretical formulations as *strategic*" ("Reflections" 103). In this spirit of disenchantment, Anthony Appiah and Henry Louis Gates Jr., in their editors' introduction to the "Identities" issue of *Critical Inquiry*, view identity politics as an emergent critique of the "cliché-ridden" (625) critical discourses of the 1980s and their 1990s incarna-

tions, discourses ruled by the triumvirate Race, Class, and Gender. The same spirit of disenchantment informs this collection of essays.

5. This treatment of identity in general—racial maleness specifically—harmonizes well with Joan W. Scott's recent call for the historicization of identities as a way of shifting the emphasis of political correctness, from a notion of stable identity as a cause of difference and discrimination to a notion of unstably proximate identities that are the "never-secured effect of a process of enunciation of cultural difference" ("Multiculturalism" 19). Scott continues: "it makes more sense to teach our students and tell ourselves that identities are historically conferred, that this conferral is ambiguous (though it works precisely and necessarily by imposing a false clarity), that subjects are produced through multiple identifications, some of which become politically salient for a time in certain contexts, and that the project of history is not to rectify identity but to understand its production as an ongoing process of differentiation, relentless in its repetition, but also—and this seems to me the important political point—subject to redefinition, resistance, and change" (19).

6. See Butler, *Gender Trouble* 1–25; *Bodies That Matter* 1–23; and "Critically Queer."

7. See, for starters, Fanon, *Black Skin, White Masks*; Bhabha, "The Other Question: The Stereotype and Colonial Discourse" and "Of Mimicry and Man: The Ambivalence of Colonial Discourse"; Mercer and Julien, "Race, Sexual Politics and Black Masculinity: A Dossier"; Mercer, "Skin Head Sex Thing: Racial Difference and the Homoerotic Imaginary"; and Silverman, "White Skin, Brown Masks: The Double Mimesis, or With Lawrence in Arabia."

8. "Loving blackness," bell hooks reminds us in *Black Looks*, cuts two ways: as revolutionary intervention, it decolonizes our minds, transmuting self-hatred and the devaluing of racial difference under white supremacy into the political resistance of self-love; as appropriation and fetishization of black culture, it commodifies difference as capital, objectifying cultural difference and perpetuating racism (see hooks, *Black Looks* 9–20).

9. As Nietzsche put it in *On the Genealogy of Morals*, "there is no 'being' behind doing, effecting, becoming; 'the doer' is merely a fiction added to the deed—the deed is everything" (45; qtd. in Butler, *Gender Trouble* 25).

10. Here, the idea of a "politics of representation" follows that of Stuart Hall, which I have paraphrased (see Hall, "New Ethnicities" 27).

11. I borrow the term from Diana Fuss's essay, "Fashion and the Homospectatorial Look," on the lesbian-looks encoded in women's fashion photography and advertising, homoerotic looks theorized generally "in terms of a visual structuring and identification that participates in organizing the sexual identity of *any* social object" (736).

12. I am applying here Stuart Hall's definition of cultural identity ("a matter of 'becoming' as well as 'being'") from his essay "Cultural Identity and Diaspora" to Harpham's notion of ethics conceived of as "a necessary, and necessarily impure and

unsystematic, mediation between unconscious or instinctual life and its cognitive and cultural transformation" (18).

13. The idea of an ethics of performativity traces its origins to Aristotle's *Nicomachean Ethics*, Book I, Chapter 7 (1098a 5ff.), where an analogy is drawn between man's relation to living the good life and a lyre-player's relation to playing the lyre well. Happiness, the good life, depends on performance, a notion that has been called Aristotle's "starting-point for ethical enquiry" (MacIntyre 58). See Aristotle 943.

14. The issue of the compatibility of the dual interventionist commitments in contemporary cultural studies—the goals of describing real conditions of existence and transforming them in the name of a less oppressive, more just society—is critiqued by Jennifer Daryl Slack and Laurie Anne Whitt from the standpoint of postmodernity and ecologically informed criticism. Slack and Whitt rightly contend that within cultural studies the end or destination of such interventionist commitments goes unarticulated and unspecified. I would like to suggest that inserting and emphasizing the performative basis of ethics within discussions of race and masculinities, or the objects of cultural studies more generally, moves toward specifying what they call "the normative bases of [cultural theorists'] theory and practice" (572).

READING MEN, READING RACE

DESIRE AND DIFFERENCE

Homosexuality, Race, Masculinity

JONATHAN DOLLIMORE

Theories of sexual difference notoriously disregard the erotics of other kinds of difference. As Mandy Merck observes, in such theories "no non-genital differences (of race, class, age, and so on) can signify such total Otherness, no genitally similar object can be legitimately eroticised" (5–6). But, of course, these other kinds of differences have always been erotically invested, not least in lesbian and gay cultures, where they are inflected by the crucial further difference of homosexuality as a difference/deviation from the norm. What sexual difference theorists see here is only desire-without-difference, that is, a desire for the *same* sex rooted in an alleged fear of the *other* sex. Beholden to an anatomically derived, heterosexual dualism, they tend to regard homosexuality as a disavowal of that very difference that is assumed to be fundamental to social, psychic, and sexual organization. In reply, it has been suggested that those adherents of sexual difference who repudiate or pathologize homosexual desire in this way may themselves be expressing a fear or disavowal of the same, or the proximate (Dollimore, *Sexual Dissidence*, ch. 17).

So should we seek to displace sexual difference by cultural difference? This could not exactly be a direct substitution: to attempt that would involve something like a category mistake. The suggestion to be explored is rather that, to think difference in terms of culture rather than hetero/sexuality, might be both more illuminating and more liberating. Attractive as that proposition has seemed in recent years, the form in which it has been pursued is fraught with difficulties. Most obviously, an ahistorical and mainly theoretical emphasis on cultural difference can perpetuate the imperialism it seeks to expose. As Ania Loomba puts it, in relation to colonialist studies, "the neglect of histories surrounding native insubordination either devalues or romanticises the latter, or worse, tends to read colonised subjects through linguistic or psychoanalytic theories which, for some of us at least, remain suspiciously and problematically shot through with ethnocentric assumptions whose transfer to all subalterns is unacceptable" (171).

Utopian Differences

No consideration of cultural and/or racial difference should ever neglect the sheer negativity, evil, and inferiority with which "the other" of such differences has been associated throughout history. In the wake of that history there is all the more to appreciate about the way progressive movements in our time have turned things around, positively embracing difference and otherness: "the emphasis on discontinuity, the celebration of difference and heterogeneity, and the assertion of plurality as opposed to reductive unities — these ideas have animated almost an entire generation of literary and cultural critics" (Mohanty 56–58).[1] Just one instance, especially relevant to what follows, is Roland Barthes's celebration of difference—so much difference, in fact, as eventually to subvert repression itself, producing a concept of desire wherein there would be, for instance, not homosexuality but homosexualities "whose plural will baffle any constituted, centred discourse" (*Roland Barthes* 69). Far from being an endorsement of discrimination, this excess of difference would disarticulate the very terms of discrimination.

The instance of homosexuality is not incidental here, since "perverse" desire figures crucially in Barthes's influential theories of difference and textuality. Like Wilde, Gide, and others, Barthes draws upon perverse desire to animate and inform his aesthetic and linguistic theories; further, it is in terms of language and art that such perversity would in part operate. In his inaugural lecture he imagines a utopian plurality of languages on which we would draw "*according to the truth of desire*": "This freedom is a luxury which every society should afford its citizens: as many languages as there are desires—a utopian proposition in that no society is yet ready to admit the plurality of desire. That a language, whatever it be, not repress another; that the subject may know without remorse, without repression, the bliss of having at his disposal two kinds of language; that he may speak this or that, according to his perversions, not according to the Law" (*Selected Writings* 467).

From within such a utopian perspective sexuality comes to be understood relationally—not as the internal relations of sexual difference, but the relations between the sexual and the nonsexual, as these both have been imagined and as they may now be radically envisioned. This would be related to a progressive sexual politics wherein the aim is not necessarily to liberate sexuality (the sexual drive), but to eroticize the social while at the same time releasing it from the grip of sexuality as conventionally conceived. Such theories have been plausibly criticized for their romantic and utopian strains, also for the way they echo and sometimes invoke a post-Freudian version of the polymorphous perverse. But often such criticisms laboriously misrepresent the utopian strain, not least by taking it too literally. Also, cultural context makes the crucial difference: the appropriation of the romantic, the utopian, and the polymorphous for what has hitherto been marginal to, and demonized and repressed by, the center, and perhaps internalized on the center's terms by the marginal, has quite different effects from, say, a more general (postmodern?) theory that "anything goes anywhere." For one thing, Barthes's perverse perspective on difference foregrounds a different history, one wherein there is no simple privileging of the marginal: the paradoxically perverse interrelationship between center and margins whereby the marginal returns to the center in a way that disarticulates the center-margin binary itself, is signified in this instance by his inaugurating his professorship with a lecture on the significance of perversity vis-à-vis language.

Since Barthes wrote that lecture in 1977, the affirmation of difference has become almost a new orthodoxy, and Mohanty's warning that this celebration may involve a sentimental charity concealing a more fundamental indifference is timely. So, too, is Homi Bhabha's skepticism about the way cultural theory uses the "Other" to deconstruct "the epistemological 'edge' of the West"; the problem being that "the 'Other' is cited, quoted, framed, illuminated, encased in the shot-reverse-shot strategy of a serial enlightenment," while at the same time losing "its power to signify, to negate, to initiate its 'desire', to split its 'sign' of identity, to establish its own institutional and oppositional discourse." Even as otherness is being affirmed it is also being foreclosed ("The Commitment to Theory" 16).

Interestingly, homosexuality has hardly ever been rehabilitated as a positive difference within and by those heterosexual discourses that hitherto constructed it as negative other. Progressives would willingly remove some of the stigma from homosexuality, and have often acknowledged the homosexual component within the heterosexually identified. But this is typically the at once honest and evasive acknowledgment of a troubling presence/absence. Put bluntly, to be identified positively outside of its own cultures, homosexuality usually has to be dissolved into androgyny. Or, alternatively, homosexuality might be called upon to loosen the rigid gender identities within heterosexuality: men are permitted a "feminine" component, and, less often, women a "masculine" one. But such acknowledgments of the "other" gender usually make for a fuller, more rounded, heterosexual identity. Hélène Cixous is an exception in this respect, and it is interesting that she becomes so by almost reversing the psychoanalytically inspired account of homosexuality as involving a fear of difference/desire of the same. Even though homosexuality as such remains muted, subsumed into an "other bisexuality," it is here nevertheless explicitly and exceptionally identified as a creative otherness: "This does not mean that in order to create you must be homosexual. But there is no invention possible, whether it be philosophical or poetic, without the presence in the inventing subject of an abundance of the other, of the diverse . . . there is no invention of other I's, no poetry, no fiction without a certain homosexuality (interplay therefore of bisexuality) making in me a crystallized work of my ultra subjectivities" (Cixous, "Sorties" 97).

Desiring the Different

The rarity of such positive conceptions of homosexuality within, or in relation to, otherness, is all the more significant given that homosexuals have been among those who have literally (rather than metaphorically or theoretically) embraced the cultural and racial difference of the "other." This history, addressed in what follows, is indispensable for current debates about difference.

Kobena Mercer and Isaac Julien are right to emphasize that the complexity that arises at the junction of race and sexuality is something that "some people simply *don't want to talk* about" (99). Of the convergence of homosexuality and race, fewer still are prepared to speak, and those who have spoken have often done so in racist and/or homophobic terms—and that, as Mercer and Julien show, includes people in both the black and gay communities.

A constructive, if brief, discussion of the problematic convergence of race and homosexuality occurs in Dennis Altman's now twenty-year-old pioneering study, *Homosexual Oppression and Liberation.* Altman discerns links between the oppression of blacks and homosexuals, and of the way that both are vulnerable to an internalization of their oppression. He considers that in America especially there has always been a strong cross-racial homosexual attraction, which is less restrained by social barriers than its heterosexual counterpart: "the very furtiveness and outlaw status of the gayworld has led to its greater integration across colour lines." Yet he refuses to sentimentalize the connection, recognizing that white homosexuals are not necessarily less racist than white heterosexuals,[2] and that the cross-racial attraction in question may, for both parties, be a consequence, rather than a repudiation, of their oppression. He suggests that blacks have been "at one and the same time both more accepting of and more hostile towards homosexuality," and that the hostility has often been extreme—as in the case of Eldridge Cleaver's notorious attack on James Baldwin (see Altman, esp. 192–207; Bergman). Despite this difficult history, crucial alliances have occurred. The gay movement learned greatly from black analysis and black political experience, and it was possible in 1970 for Huey Newton, joint founder of the Black Panther Party, to welcome alliance with the women's and gay movements. In this he made the Black Panthers the first significant radical group to recognize gay liberation as a valid political movement, and did so in terms that provoked hostility from some in his own party: "maybe I'm injecting some of my prejudices by saying that 'even a homosexual can be revolutionary'. Quite the contrary, maybe a homosexual could be the most revolutionary" (Newton, qtd. in Altman 204; see also Genet in Leyland, *Gay Sunshine Interviews*).

The relevance of this obscure and marginal history where race and homosexuality ambivalently converge is once again being recognized. Jonathan Rutherford finds something strangely relevant for British cultural politics in the 1990s in the cross-racial identifications of Lawrence of Arabia some seventy years before: "His identification with the Arabs and their culture displaced the centered position of his identity as a white man. The story is a compelling image of a postmodern world that is challenging so many of our own certainties and our cultural, sexual and political identities" (9). Rutherford cites Lawrence's own remark in *The Seven Pillars of Wisdom* to the effect that this identification "quitted me of my English self, and let me look at the West and its conventions with new eyes: they destroyed it all for me." [3] Significantly, Rutherford does not mention Lawrence's homosexuality, although this is, as Kaja Silverman shows, a crucial determinant in all this. Silverman explores the way Lawrence's homosexuality promotes an erotic identification that is itself crucial for his psychic participation in Arab nationalism; of how, in effect, he discovered himself within the Other. More generally, the case of T. E. Lawrence becomes an exemplary reminder that we are obliged "to approach history always through the refractions of desire and identification, and to read race and class insistently in relation to sexuality" ("White Skin, Brown Masks" 4, 10, 12).

This is especially so with writers such as Barthes and Genet, and Wilde and Gide before them, who, far from subordinating their outlawed sexuality to their radical politics or radical aesthetics, actively informed them with it. Of course, there were and are risks in doing that. From the vantage point of so-called postliberation, we know only too well the political blindnesses of sexual desire, and of how disastrous it can be to make sexuality the prime mover of a political vision. That holds true in principle for any sexuality. But, significantly, this is rarely, if ever, what those writers advocated. Arguably the blinder kinds of sexual radicalism, wherein sexuality is made the prime political mover, have tended to be mainly heterosexual, and in the case of Wilhelm Reich, overtly homophobic (see Weeks 160–70). What we learn from Wilde, Gide, Barthes, and others is that a conventionally understood politics, which ignores sexual desire, will quite possibly be as disastrous as one that makes that desire the prime mover—even, or especially so—in the age of so-called postliberation. But also, it is not exactly that they bring sexuality to politics (it was always already there); rather *deviant desire brings with it a different kind of political knowledge*, and hence inflects both desire and politics differently.

Desire and Strangeness

In 1920 Gide recalls walking the streets of Biskra with Dr. Bourget of Lausanne. The latter does not like what he sees: " 'Young men ought to be brought here to give them a horror of debauchery' exclaimed the worthy man, bursting with disgust." Gide's response nicely, if unawares, repudiates the sexual-difference view of homosexuality as solipsistic refusal of the other: "how little he knew of the human heart!—of mine at any rate. . . . Some people fall in love with what is like them; others with what is different. I am among the latter. Strangeness solicits me as much as familiarity repels" (If it Die 253). Seventy years on Michael Carson, writing of his own homosexual desire for the racially other, expresses a similar sentiment, though now with the addition of a revealing, probably necessary, and certainly crucial distinction: "I have always been sexually attracted to foreigners. *Foreignness for me provided a difference that moved me in a way that sexual difference never did*" (44).

But perhaps this celebration of the exotic cultural/racial other is merely the counterpart of the racist's demonizing of the other? Very possibly, and a remark of Michael Carson's explaining what it was that took him abroad in search of the other shows how the celebration may share the stereotypes of the demonized: "what I lacked was a foreign accent, almond eyes, straight or springy black hair, a black skin, a muscular physique, a mind full of difficult alphabets, a sense of rhythm, a pitiful history of slavery and oppression, and a massive member—though not necessarily in that order" (44).

But Carson is also suggesting how the fantasized desire for the "other" actually begins at home; how fantasy is ineradicably social and, as such, susceptible to stereotypes of all kinds, including racial and racist ones; how fantasy of and for the other exemplifies the mobilities of desire and identification. And a certain lack at the heart of both: what Carson actually finds in twenty years abroad is some oppressive sexual mores epitomized in a loveless fuck over the bonnet of a Chevy Impala. And his article is about the corollary of discovering that the other begins at home, namely disenchantment: "almost twenty years later I am not convinced that sexual love between men exists in places like Saudi Arabia" (45). Gide's experience, elsewhere and seventy years earlier, was very different, but, as we shall see, he too experiences the desire of the other as finally about disenchantment. Perhaps then, and in a way that recalls Freud, Carson and Gide are also writing about the strange impossibility of desire? Whether their accounts confirm, coincide with, or can substitute for the psychoanalytic account of desire as lack, is hard to say. But Gide's account especially does suggest how the vision of desire as loss is strangely inseparable from both the blindness of desire and its capacity to know more than it wants.

Taking Boys Home

I've described elsewhere Gide's chance meeting with Oscar Wilde in Algiers in 1895, and how, through Wilde, it led to a sexual encounter with a youth called Mohammed, which changed Gide's life and profoundly influenced his art (*Sexual Dissidence*, ch. 1). On that same occasion Gide befriends another Arab boy, Athman, and determines that Athman should accompany him when he returns to Paris. Gide's mother, aided by others, fiercely resists the proposal; with unprecedented tenacity Gide rebels against his mother but eventually loses the battle. Gide contends that he was virtually blackmailed into leaving Athman behind. There is an unforgettable description of their parting: "When, on the third morning I looked for Athman to say good-bye to him, he was nowhere to be found and I had to leave without seeing him again. I could not understand his absence; but suddenly, as I sat in the speeding train, a long way already from El Kantara, I caught sight of his white burnous on the banks of the oued. He was sitting there with his head in his hands; he did not rise when the train passed; he made no movement; he did not give a glance at the signs I made him; and for a long time as the train was carrying me away, I watched his little motionless, grief-stricken figure, lost in the desert, an image of my own despair" (If it Die 296). Gide had tried to persuade his mother, as he had persuaded himself, that bringing Athman to Paris was a "moral rescue," a question of the salvation of a boy through adoption. Even so his mother was appalled; she thought "that the desert and solitude had turned my brain" (If it Die, 293). She told him that he would cover himself with ridicule by bringing the boy back. After much argument Gide received a letter from a trusted household servant, Marie, who "swore she would leave the house on the day my 'negro' came into it. What would become of mamma without Marie? I gave in; I had to" (If it Die, 294).[4]

Epitomized in this struggle over Athman, and especially in Gide's correspondence with his mother,[5] is a hesitant yet certain knowledge of how sexual discrimination relates inextricably to other kinds of discrimination. In this one episode we find interconnections with race, class, colonialism, and (cultural) imperialism, and in ironic, domestic, tragically complex ways: witness Gide finally capitulating to the class, racial, and cultural prejudices of his own culture, *as voiced through his mother, who in turn speaks through her servant.* Discrimination descends through a hierarchy of the subordinate. Or more accurately, *hierarchies,* including those of class, race, and gender, and within each of which each subject is situated differently. Discrimination works through the asymmetry of subject positioning, and the plurality of hierarchies, as well as the brute fact of inequality institutionalized in hierarchy itself. That is partly what it means to speak of the interconnections of race, class, and gender. It suggests, too, why establishing personal culpability is not the issue; but since Gide has been criticized in this respect, it is something that needs to be addressed. In his personal relationships with Athman, and his political stance on colonial oppression, Gide could claim to have said and done more than most at that time. *Travels in the Congo* records his firsthand encounters with the brutalities of French colonialism. In an entry for October 1925 he states his determination to find out the full extent of these brutalities and to speak out against them (*Travels* 60). One of his biographers, Justin O'Brien, says Gide's awakening to social consciousness began here, when he saw the people of the Congo exploited, beaten, and killed by whites intent on quick profits (321). On his return to France Gide succeeded in publicizing the injustices he had witnessed, and with some effect at government level. His later siding with communism was undoubtedly influenced by this journey.[6]

Against that consider the following despicable episode that occurred during that same visit. It concerned Lord Alfred Douglas, who was on this occasion accompanied by Gide (but not Wilde, who had returned to England), and a boy called Ali, with whom, according to Gide, Douglas was in love. On discovering that Ali was also having an affair with a prostitute, Meriem, Douglas horsewhipped him: "his howls created a tumult among the people in the hotel." Gide, who disliked Douglas, adds: "I heard this uproar, but considered it wiser not to intervene, and remained shut up in my room" (If it Die 291).

Gide's account is at once critical and complicit and in a way that invites reflection. In the escape from sexual oppression and sexual repression, individuals have often, like Gide, crossed divisions of class and race. Potentially, both the experience of repression in their own culture and the experience of cultural difference on the other side of the divides they cross, contribute to a critique of repression that includes, but also goes beyond, its sexual forms. An identification consequent on a prior dislocation can make for a creative, empathetic partiality that is then the basis of a further identification and understanding of other kinds of discrimination. I have shown elsewhere how this is true of both Wilde and Gide (*Sexual Dissidence*, chs. 1, 3, 4). At the same time they remained, as we all remain, implicated in other kinds of discrimination of which they and we, originally and subsequently, are the agents rather than the victims, or maybe both agents and victims. If Douglas's brutality epitomizes racial, cultural, and sexual domination in its most callously direct form, Gide's self-description of remaining in the security of his room, considering it wiser not to intervene, becomes a resonant image of the hesitant complicities that most kinds of brutality and exploitation presuppose and in which most of us are implicated.[7]

So desire for, and identification with, the cultural and racial other brings with it a complicated, ambivalent history. Bronski, discussing the romanticizing of the non-Anglo by Edward Carpenter and others, declares: "the English fascination with the non-Anglo—and therefore more 'primitive' and 'natural'—cultures . . . was also based in and inseparable from deeply rooted standards of white British racism and political and cultural imperialism" (26–27; see also 15). Edward Said's pioneering *Orientalism* offers a more searching analysis of this phenomenon. With Gide and many others in mind, Said observes that virtually no European writer who wrote on or traveled to the Orient in the period after 1800 exempted himself or herself from a quest for sexual experience unobtainable in Europe: "What they looked for often—correctly I think—was a different type of sexuality, perhaps more libertine and less guilt-ridden; but even that quest, if repeated by enough people, could (and did) become as regulated and uniform as learning itself. In time 'Oriental sex' was as standard a commodity as any other available in the mass culture" (190). What makes the situation especially difficult in the case of homosexuality is that there are those who arm their homophobia by ignoring the first dimension described above—an exile that generates critique—insisting only on the second—the exile who flees one kind of discrimination only to perpetuate others, and who is seen to do so in virtue of the alleged "predatory" nature of the homosexual desire, now quintessentially defined as a desire that exploits the disadvantaged.

Decentering the Self in the Desire for the Other

For homosexuals more than most, the search for sexual freedom in the realm of the foreign has been inseparable from a repudiation of the "Western" culture responsible for their repression and oppression. For some, as indeed for T. E. Lawrence, this entailed not just the rejection of a repressive social order, but a disidentification from it requiring nothing less than the relinquishing of the self as hitherto constituted and inhabited by that order. In other words, precisely because of the coercive and normative alignments between subjectivity and sexuality in our culture, deviant sexuality becomes a refusal of certain kinds of subjectivity, as well as of certain kinds of normative desire. Of Pasolini's "growing passion for the Third World," Enzo Siciliano says, "He had the idea that 'Negritude . . . will be the way'. One might say that in him an old cultural dream—exoticism—donned progressive clothes. And it was true—progressivism was followed closely in his heart by the decadent enigmas of forgetfulness and oblivion" (263, 265). As so often, "decadent" is used here in such a way that it evades what it also gestures toward. But the connection of desire with forgetfulness and oblivion is important and follows in a long tradition: religious, mystical, romantic, or some combination of all these. It suggests, too, why the other of sexual fantasy may be fantasized in stereotypical or two-dimensional ways somehow at odds with the intensity and density of the desire which impels the fantasy. This fantasy may also register indirectly the resilience of the individual's own immediate cultural past: forgetfulness and oblivion are the means of escaping that past, but in a way that registers its continuing presence. The case of Gide, someone much attracted to African landscapes as places where "Western" consciousness is dissolved, is exemplary. At the very end of his life, writing again of the importance of how his experience as a homosexual had pushed him along the path of revolt, and recalling joyfully one of his lovers, Mala, Gide adds, "My most perfect memories of sensual delight are those enveloped in a landscape which absorbs it and in which I seem to be swallowed up. In the one I have just evoked of those transports with Mala, it is not only the beautiful swooning body of the child I see again, but the whole mysterious and fearful surrounding of the equatorial forest" (So Be It 42, 126–27; see also Dollimore, Sexual Dissidence, ch. 1).

Such experiences of sexual liberation bear witness to the socially constructed "nature" of identity with respect both to its contingency and its resilience: on the one hand, the self is experienced as radically different in the space of the other; it is here that Gide does begin to disentangle himself from a coerced, repressive subjectivity; on the other hand, if the extinction of self is the precondition of passing into the ecstasy with and through the other, it is an extinction that has to be replayed over and again *as a constitutive part of sexual ecstasy itself.* And if, as so often, ecstasy obliterates the specificity of the context that simultaneously enables and absorbs it, this is not only because ecstasy is potentially blind; it is also because what we repudiate remains with us as partial blindness to what we embrace in its stead.

Amyntas: *Desire and Loss*

Those of Gide's travel journals published as *Amyntas* are especially revealing of this process whereby loss of self becomes a discovery of self: both selves, the centered and the dispersed, are kept alive, both being necessary for the lyrical, unorthodox Western narrative that Gide maps onto the African landscape and his own illicit sexuality within it.

But if loss of self in the ecstatic union with the other entails a liberating loss of inhibition, by the very same fact it is then that Gide becomes, as it were, sublimely unaware of the plight of the other, especially when, as here, self, desire, and other are powerfully mediated through an exotic style of pastoral. *Amyntas* is a narrative of self-redemption in relation to, in the desire for, and in the space of, the other. But the other is without history; just as the loss of self is the precondition for the discovery of unconflicted, unrepressed, unfixed desire, so the precondition for this pastoral sublimity is the loss of history.[8] And again, the landscape that at once crystallizes and disperses desire, and in some remarkable images, is also effaced by it:

> I
> . . . a child's laughter at the water's edge—then nothing, no misgivings, no thoughts . . . What have I wanted until this day? What had I feared?

> III
> . . . The village stays the same: no one here wants more—no effort, no novelty. Within these narrow lanes, no luxury compels such poverty to know itself.

> V
> . . . Time passing here is innocent of hours, yet so perfect is our inoccupation that boredom becomes impossible.

VI

What have I sought till this day? Why did I strive? Now, oh now I know, outside of time, the garden where time comes to rest. A tranquil country, sealed away . . . Arcady! I have found the place of peace.

X

. . . No moving: Let time close over us like water . . . over this world, let the even surface of time close once again. . . .

XI

. . . Behind us, the patch of scorching crag that blocks the north winds; sometimes a cloud passes, a white tuft; hesitates, frays out until . . . absorbed by the blue air . . . And ahead of us, nothing—the desert's variegated void.

XII

. . . Here life is more voluptuous and more futile, and death itself less difficult. (Gide, *Amyntas* 3–11)

It is not for long that death is experienced as less difficult, the histories of self and other lost, and consciousness unconflicted. As the distilled purity of pastoral and the fullness of desire give way to the absences that constitute them, so the journals move toward disenchantment, the acknowledgment of loss, and a sense of the futility of returning in order to recover an original intensity of being:

> six times I have returned to that country, demanding the past from the present, flogging my emotions, requiring of them, still, that freshness they once owed to novelty, and from year to year finding in my ageing desires rewards ever less vivid. . . . Nothing compares to the first contact. (*Amyntas* 115)

> I have dreamed that I came back here—in twenty years. I passed by, and was no longer recognised by anyone; the unknown children did not smile at me; and I dared not ask what had become of those I had known, whom I feared to recognise in these bent men exhausted by life. (*Amyntas* 141)

The narrative suggests a movement into time that is also a fall into knowledge and loss (*Amyntas* 143), yet marked by brief moments of recovery, moments of gratified desire and a returning to life: "on this abandoned divan, I shall inhale for a long while still the earthy, vegetal smell which the faun left behind; then, in the morning, wakened at dawn, I shall fling myself into the delicious air" (*Amyntas* 104).

Occasionally he finds a transcendence of ardor, an equilibrium beyond desire—"the disappearance of desire and the renunciation of everything," a time innocent of hours, a perfect inoccupation in which boredom becomes impossible, a coming to life that is once more loss of consciousness: "I dissolve, I evaporate into blue air"; a being alive in a world where "death itself is less difficult" (*Amyntas* 101, 105, 107, 111). The most extraordinary moments traverse conventional divisions, occurring both in Edenic gardens (*Amyntas* 112, 146–47) and a drug-induced languor in darkened recesses of cafes: "to linger there . . . Abd'el Kader, leaning toward me, points to the sole ornament on the white wall, hanging in the center—a hideous, shapeless, childishly daubed doll, and says in a whisper: 'The Devil'. Time trickled by" (*Amyntas* 102).

The last travel journal ends with Gide back in Cuverville dreaming again of a loss of self—"to be rid of oneself, so that one blue breath, in which I am dissolved, might journey on"—a dissolution that would redeem loss, but now only by disavowing the recognition that what is most intensely desired is lost to the past. Redemption and disavowal are not compatible, and the final lines suggest the yet more severe knowledge that desire is of its nature the desire for what is lost:

> In Normandy's autumn, I dream of the desert spring . . .
>   The rattle of the palm fronds! Almond trees humming with bees! Hot winds, and the sugary savor of the air! . . .
>   The squalling north wind beats against my windows. It has been raining for three days.—Oh! how lovely the caravans were those evenings in Touggourt, when the sun was sinking into the salt. (*Amyntas* 155)

There is in these travel journals a movement toward the recognition that the most acute form of nostalgia is that which, in evoking the past as lost fullness, then faces it with the knowledge that the restless incompleteness felt so acutely now, in the present, was also a part of the imaginary fullness then; the truthfulness that aims to allay nostalgia only intensifies it.

Even with such insight it has to be said: we go to the exotic other to lose everything, including ourselves—everything except the privilege that enabled us to go in the first place. That privilege needs to be understood in diverse ways. Gide was, at least at that time, the sexual tourist of which Said and others have written, his opportunity to come and go enhanced by what is aptly and euphemistically called independent means. His privilege and independence might further be seen to confer the trappings of a "humaneness," which in truth was only a benign counterpart of the more brutal colonialism that appalled him. Further, what kind of indifference to (cultural) difference made Gide so confident Athman could survive in Paris? Was he really so unaware of those difficulties experienced by the person of color in white European culture—difficulties of which Frantz Fanon was to write so compellingly fifty years later in *Black Skin, White Masks*, and in relation to France specifically? The destructive psychic and social conditions Fanon describes would have been compounded in the case of Athman. It is all too revealing that, searching through the biographical work on Gide for further references to Athman in Europe, I came across hardly anything except the occasional derogatory, passing remark. When Athman did reemerge into visibility, it was once again as someone embroiled in the struggles of others, and, now along with Gide, subjected to the homophobic sneer. Consider, for instance, how Rupert Croft-Cooke, out to discredit Gide's account of Wilde's seduction of him (Gide) into a confirmed homosexuality, writes of Gide that he "picked up (among others) the Algerian boy prostitute Athman, who became known to other visiting Europeans, including Eugène Rouart and Francis Jammes, and was brought to Paris by Henri Ghéon" (7).[9]

I would remark yet a further factor relevant to race and colonialism, one which raises again the always ambiguous status of the aesthetic, and inseparably from its achievements: Gide is in Africa as a writer discovering and nurturing a creativity which itself is intrinsically exploitative. In retrospect, then, it is the final remark in that poignant description of Athman by the river that is the most telling: "for a long time, as the train was carrying me away, I watched his little motionless, grief stricken figure, lost in the desert, *an image of my own despair*" (emphasis added). It is an image encountered by Gide, but also projected by him, familiar and unforgettable as an evocation of the sadness that pervades the history of illicit love. It is also an image that tells us that if Gide's contribution to the liberation of the other was as a writer, that selfsame contribution exemplified an inevitably exploitative relation to those others on whose behalf he was writing, and that this exploitation persists as an aesthetic commitment long after the blindness or impossibility of desire was acknowledged. The "mature" writer not only survives those renunciations, they help constitute his art, an art that will always finally take priority over the plight of the other, even if, as was the case with Gide, it also succeeds in mitigating it.

But I would hope to reinscribe all of this knowledge within Gide's narratives of sexual liberation without surrendering or denying their affirmations—I was about to say tenderness—and to do that in part by the reminder that it is a knowledge implicit in or enabled by Gide's own transgressive crossing of some forbidden boundaries.

Fanon: Race and Sexuality

The example of Frantz Fanon here becomes instructive. Fanon's analysis of racism and "negrophobia," and his articulation of the predicament of the person of color living in, or in relation to, white culture, is also instructive for understanding sexual discrimination, especially homophobia, and the predicament of the gay person living in, or in relation to, heterosexual culture. My own study is indebted to Fanon's analysis of how discrimination is internalized psychically and perpetuated socially between subordinated groups, classes, and races—what, in relation to the latter, he calls "the racial distribution of guilt" (Black Skin, White Masks 103); also to his realization of the way the demonizing of the other is, above all, a mercurial process of displacement and condensation, so fluid, yet always with effects of a brutally material, actually violent kind.

Even so, there can be no facile equation of racist and sexual discrimination, and this for three main reasons, which, even as they preclude that equation, emphasize the significance of those points at which race and sexuality interconnect, and the particular importance of Fanon's work in this respect. First, as Mercer and Julien remind us, such an equivalence tends to obscure exactly those differences that need to be addressed if we are to understand not only each kind of discrimination separately but also their interconnections (99–100). Second, Fanon offers a kind of cultural critique that mostly preempts facile politics per se. Homi Bhabha, in a significant essay arguing the urgent need to reengage with Fanon in and for our own time, shows why. Bhabha writes of how Fanon "speaks most effectively from the uncertain interstices of historical change: from the area of ambivalence between race and sexuality, out of an unresolved contradiction between culture and class; from deep within the struggle of psychic representation and social reality" (foreword to Fanon, Black Skin, White Masks ix). From these uncertain interstices emerge Fanon's challenges to Enlightenment "Man," and indeed his challenge to the very idea of an essential human subject; Bhabha finds in Fanon a powerful and subversive sense of identity, which involves a split, precarious, contradictory relation to the Other, the upshot of which is a radical ambivalence, destructive but also potentially empowering.

The third reason why there can be no facile equation of racist and sexual discrimination via the appeal to Fanon concerns the place of sexuality, especially homosexuality, in his own writing. Fanon is surely right to stress the sexual component of racism, especially its destructive effects on (hetero)sexual relations across race. He stresses also the white person's fear of and fascination with the imagined sexual potency of the Negro: "For the majority of white men the Negro represents the sexual instinct (in its raw state). The Negro is the incarnation of a genital potency beyond all moralities and prohibitions" (Black Skin, White Masks 177). Further, Fanon remarks the ways in which, as a result, the Negro "has been fixated in terms of the genital" (165), with the corresponding displacement onto the person of color of inadequacies and fears intrinsic to the cultural, as distinct from the natural, formation of European sexuality.

Despite all this, Fanon deploys some of the worst prejudices that psychoanalysis has been used to reinforce: "All the Negrophobic women I have known had abnormal sex lives. . . . And besides there was also an element of perversion, the persistence of infantile formations: God knows how [Negroes] make love! It must be terrifying" (Black Skin, White Masks 158). Of the white woman's Negrophobic fear of rape by the black man, Fanon asks, "Basically does this fear of rape not itself cry out for rape? Just as there are faces that ask to be slapped, can one not speak of women who ask to be raped?" (156).

Fanon's ignorance and misrepresentation of women and their sexuality is apparent; less so his equally problematic representation of homosexuality, and the way he slides from the one to the other: "the Negrophobic woman is in fact nothing but a putative sexual partner—just as the Negrophobic man is a repressed homosexual" (Black Skin, White Masks 156). The homosexual is implicated all ways round, and according to some fairly crude psychoanalytic binaries. So, whilst in the foregoing passage repressed homosexuality is construed as a cause of a violent and neurotic racism, elsewhere Fanon regards manifest homosexuality as an effect of the same neurotic racism, though now in a masochistic rather than a sadistic form, and especially the masochistic relation of the white man to the black man: "There are, for instance, men who go to 'houses' in order to be beaten by negroes; passive homosexuals who insist on black partners" (177). He attributes an implied or assumed absence of homosexuality in Martinique to the absence of the Oedipus complex in the Antilles. Of certain transvestites there Fanon is anxious to assure the reader of their masculinity, and that they lead "normal sex lives." He adds, "In Europe, on the other hand, I have known several Martinicans who became homosexuals, always passive. But this was by no means a neurotic homosexuality: For them it was a means to a livelihood, as pimping is for others" (180n.44). Of the "Fault, Guilt, refusal of guilt, paranoia" that Fanon sees (surely correctly) as symptomatic of racism, he adds, "one is back in homosexual territory" (183). And in the process of contesting racist representations of the Negro's "sensuality," Fanon adds, "I have never been able, without revulsion, to hear a man say of another man: 'He is so sensual!' I do not know what the sensuality of a man is. Imagine a woman saying of another woman: She's so terribly desirable—she's darling" (201). In short, there are places in Fanon's writing where homosexuality is itself demonized as both a cause and an effect of the demonizing psychosexual organization of racism that Fanon elsewhere describes and analyzes so compellingly.

Such constructions of homosexuality in relation to race and racism are not specific to Fanon. The myth that homosexuality is "the white man's disease" persists today in some black communities, especially in certain kinds of political radicalism and nationalism. Cheryl Clarke cites from a leaflet distributed at a Black Liberation Movement meeting in 1981: "Revolutionary nationalists and genuine communists cannot uphold homosexuality in the leadership of the Black Liberation Movement. . . . Homosexuality is a genocidal practice. . . . Homosexuality does not birth new warriors for liberation . . . [it] is an accelerating threat to our survival as a people and as a nation." Clarke further remarks how here too this homophobia often connects with misogyny. She also makes the crucial point that it is wrong to attribute it to the mass of black people, finding it most marked among some intellectual and political leaders, who also obscure the central roles played by lesbians and gays in black communities. By contrast says Clarke, the poor and working class within those communities have often been more accepting of those "who would be outcast by the ruling culture—many times to spite the white man, but mainly because the conditions of our lives have made us empathic" (197–98, 205–6; see also Mercer and Julien 125, 139). The point made earlier about the potential empathy of the outcast is here made in reverse—about a community in relation to him or her. Those points of apparently incommensurable differences between groups, classes, nations, races, or whatever have been negotiated hesitantly and all too often anonymously by the outcasts and the deprived from either side. These are fragile empathies, too important to be either romanticized or ignored.

Another difficulty concerns the relations between politics and what has been called "Black Macho" (see Wallace, *Black Macho*). Again, the homosexual perspective is revealing. Jean Genet responded to an erotic charge in Arab and black masculinity inseparable from the recognition of its significance in a culture of resistance and the fight for liberation. As we shall see shortly, this is another point of identification between the different, one that suggests that the masculinities of any culture, black, Arab, or white, cannot always be grossed up as always and only homophobic. But if this "assumption of . . . manhood" (Fanon, *Black Skin, White Masks* 41) has constituted an agency of resistance — no small achievement when one recalls the crippling effects of domination and exploitation at the subjective level, effects that Fanon himself charts — it is one that perpetuates, in terms of sexual and gender relations, the very oppression being resisted at other levels. There is an analogy here with working-class culture, black and white, where masculinity has also been a source of resistance, but once again at the expense of ratifying a larger exploitative framework for men as well as women. As Jewelle Gomez has observed, homophobic prejudice is particularly dangerous for the black lesbian. Hers is a vulnerable yet crucial role as negotiator between difference: typically, she is one who refuses to outcast herself from the black community and family, because aware of its value and importance, yet by virtue of that same fact subjected within them to sexual discrimination: "we straddle the fence that says we cannot be uplifters of the race and lesbians at the same time" (Gomez and Smith 54).

Race and Humanism

The task Gomez envisages for the black lesbian returns us to radical humanism, and both Fanon and Gide as important points of reference. Homi Bhabha finds that Fanon most profoundly evokes the colonial condition not in his yearning for "the total transformation of Man and Society," nor in his appeal to the human essence (though "he lapses into such a lament in his more existential moment"), but in his understanding of the workings of "image and fantasy — those orders that figure transgressively on the borders of history and the unconscious" (foreword to Fanon, *Black Skin, White Masks* xiii). Perhaps the two interconnect more closely than this suggests — as they did with Gide.

Gide's narrative of a development from the desire for self-redemption in the space of the other, through the loss of self at the ecstatic height of this existential quest, to the unresolved sense of desire itself as a kind of loss, is amenable to a similar analysis; in Gide's case, image and fantasy do indeed figure transgressively on the borders of history and the unconscious. Even of that first ecstatic experience with Mohammed in 1895 he would write much later, "Every time since then that I have sought after pleasure, it is the memory of that night I have pursued" (If it Die 283). Nevertheless, those "most perfect memories of sensual delight" (So Be It 126–27) remained a strength, the impetus for a nonconformist humanism that, precisely because of its universalist aspirations, provides further identifications beyond sexuality. In their humanism, at least, Fanon and Gide may be compared. Bhabha is critical of Fanon's nonconformist humanism, especially its essentialist fantasies of the self and the yearning for total transformation that they partly enabled. On the penultimate page of Black Skin, White Masks Fanon declares that one of the things that he, the man of color, wants is "that it be possible for me to discover and to love man, wherever he may be." And he asks,

> Why not the quite simple attempt to touch the other, to feel the other, to explain the other to myself?
> Was my freedom not given to me then in order to build the world of You?
> At the conclusion of this study, I want the world to recognize, with me, the open door of every consciousness (231–32).

Homi Bhabha finds here an "existential humanism . . . as banal as it is beatific," adding, "there can be no reconciliation, no Hegelian 'recognition', no simple, sentimental promise of a humanistic 'world of the You' " (foreword to Fanon, Black Skin, White Masks xx–xxi). He suggests that such tendencies occur here as an overcompensation for the closed consciousness or "dual narcissism" to which Fanon attributes the depersonalization of colonial man; that "it is as if Fanon is fearful of his most radical insights" (xx). I would regard Fanon's humanism otherwise. Certainly it is quite different from the timid and time-serving humanism that Homi Bhahba and I are all too familiar with in "English Lit." It is also utterly different from, and indeed envisioned in direct opposition to, the colonial history of humanism.

A reassessment of Fanon's humanism has become necessary for reasons similar to my reconsideration of Gide's essentialism in sexual politics. Benita Parry argues that the most influential recent analysis of colonialist discourse encounters certain problems inseparable from its antiessentialism and antihumanism; in particular its tendency has been to obscure "the role of the native as historical subject and combatant, possessor of an-other knowledge and producer of alternative traditions," and to "limit native resistance to devices circumventing and interrogating colonial authority" (34). Parry sees the problem that Fanon addressed as precisely that of how to constitute self-identity in a way that validates native difference, and thereby empower the native to rebel. In the process Fanon might be said to have overestimated the extent to which, from subordination, it is possible to construct "a politically conscious, unified, revolutionary Self, standing in unmitigated opposition to the oppressor" (30). Or, put slightly differently, in imagining that self, he builds into it too much of the oppressor's culture—that is precisely what needs to be destroyed. Note how, in an utterly different context we encounter again some of the same charges brought against Gide and others with their sexual essentialism. But, as with them, so with Fanon: the criticisms underestimate the extent to which an oppositional humanism transforms in the process of appropriation. Likewise with his existential emphasis, which closely relates to that humanism. If, as Kobena Mercer suggests, white, middle-class sexual politics is overly preoccupied with the "self," with psychotherapy and psychology as its corollary (Mercer and Julien 123), Fanon offers an alternative whereby the existential dimension is rendered inextricably social, and on virtually every page.

The same existential emphasis made Fanon acutely aware that oppositional identities emerge not simply against, but from within, the terms of their oppression. Thus, Jean-Paul Sartre's dialectical relativizing of "Negritude" (see below) is passionately reproached but not refuted. Similarly, the self-evident fact that "*the racist creates his inferior*" gives rise to a complex history, and the equally complex, ambivalent, conflicted identity of the subordinated (Fanon, *Black Skin, White Masks* 83). So Fanon's oppositional humanism coexists with a demolition of one of the cornerstones of conventional humanism, the idea of a stable unified self. Yet, crucially, this painful awareness of the historically constituted "nature" of oppositional identities is not disavowed but itself reconstituted *within and as* the humanist universal affirmation: "The negro is not. Any more than the white man" (*Black Skin, White Masks* 93, 231). This is one of the several moves whereby, for Fanon, "a native contest initially enunciated in the invader's language, culminates in a rejection of imperialism's signifying system." As Parry adds, this is something that more recent colonialist discourse theory has not adequately considered (45).

Writing the preface to Fanon's *The Wretched of the Earth*, Jean-Paul Sartre remarked the violence and duplicity of European humanism in the colonial context; it had been, said Sartre, "nothing but an ideology of lies, a perfect justification for pillage; its honeyed words, its affectation of sensibility were only alibis for our aggressions" (21). In the conclusion to that book Fanon himself put it like this: "Let us waste no time in sterile litanies and nauseating mimicry. Leave this Europe where they are never done talking of Man, yet murder men everywhere they find them, at the corner of every one of their own streets, in all corners of the globe. For centuries they have stifled almost of the whole of humanity in the name of a so-called spiritual experience" (251). Against Mannoni's assertion to the contrary, Fanon insists that "European civilization and its best representatives *are* responsible for colonial racism" (90; emphasis added). Which means that the Third World's potential for transformation is crucially conditional on not imitating, or trying to "catch up with Europe" (252).

But, as *The Wretched of the Earth* and *Black Skin, White Masks* both indicate, the social and psychic realities from which transformation will come are also those that require transformation; the dominant that the emergent contests always already informs the emergent; in short, there is no outside from which a totally new start can be made. For Fanon this means that, despite Europe's crimes, which will not and cannot be forgotten, the Third World's "new history of Man" must "have regard to the sometimes prodigious theses which Europe has put forward" since "all the elements of a solution to the great problems of humanity have, at different times, existed in European thought" (*Wretched of the Earth* 253–54).

What is required in such a scenario is an insurrectionary appropriation so radical as to be also necessarily perverse: Fanon uses Hegel, Freud, and Sartre, but in each case simultaneously contests and perverts fundamental principles of their thought. Thus, to have application to the complexities of race the theories of Hegel and Freud must undergo radical critique and transformation; with some of Freud's followers, it is even the case of first having to discredit an overtly racist psychiatry (see, e.g., *Black Skin, White Masks* 63, 138, 151–52, 220; *Wretched of the Earth* 240–50). So with humanism more generally and more radically: it is not to be imitated, not modified, not simply borrowed from or differently applied; rather, its appropriation and transformation is conditional upon its negation, the using of it destructively against itself. What emerges from the space of humanism contradicts what once defined that space; in this sense Fanon can be said to have followed the path of the perverse: a negation of the dominant is made from a trajectory that emerged from it—a deviation from, which is also, simultaneously, a contradiction of. The radical interconnectedness of culture is redeemed for a radical politics.

This appropriation of European humanism was generous in a way inseparable from its shamelessness: the final manifesto of *The Wretched of the Earth* makes it clear that the vision for a new humanity that emerges from the appropriation is undertaken on behalf of Europe as well as the Third World. Both *The Wretched of the Earth* and *Black Skin, White Masks* close with affirmations made in the knowledge of exactly what threatens them—that being, after all, what both books are about, and what powerfully preempts the charge of humanist sentimentality: "I can already see a white man and a black man *hand in hand*" (*Black Skin, White Masks* 222). An image that suggests a provocative analogy: Fanon's perversion of humanism is not unlike the perversion of masculinity in the homoerotic imaginary.

Genet: "Risking a Sensibility" [10]

Obviously, the demonizing of the other is often inseparable from his or her exploitation. But, so too, may be identification with the other, as Charles Marowitz implies when he describes Genet's *The Blacks* as a play that champions blacks "not because they are socially downtrodden but because they personify two of [Genet's] favourite types: The Rebellious Outcast and The Splendid Primitive . . . Genet uses the blacks, the way a man who has just emptied his revolver reaches for the knife at his side" (175). Possibly, except that in homosexual culture it has rarely been, and certainly was not for Genet, quite that simple. Genet speaks of his own identifications across race and culture in an interview with Hubert Fichte in 1975: "I was invited by two revolutionary movements, the Black Panthers and the Palestinians. . . . these two groups have a very strong erotic charge. I wonder if I could have belonged to revolutionary movements, even if they were as just as—I find the Panthers' movement and the Palestinians' movement to be very just—but this belonging, this sympathizing with them is at the same time dictated by the erotic charge which the Arab world in its totality or the black American world represents to me, to my sexuality" (Leyland 79–80; cf. Hocquenghem, *Homosexual Desire* 126). Genet joined these movements because he was asked by them to do so. But he made it clear that, in these identifications, desire and politics were inseparable. That might plausibly be thought to take us no further than Wilde in Algiers in 1895: "The beggars here have profiles, so the problem of poverty is easily solved" (*More Letters* 129). In Genet's case it produced among other things *Prisoner of Love*, a record of the time he spent with the Black Panthers in the US and Palestinian soldiers in Jordan and Lebanon.[11] He began the book in 1983 and completed it shortly before he died, in 1986. It is an extraordinary poetic meditation on desire, politics, loving, and dying.

In the same 1975 interview Genet declares that he had no choice to identify with oppressed blacks since he too was black. What that identification involved becomes apparent in *Prisoner of Love* in a passage that renders the crucial difference not one of color, yet by the same criterion reinstates the distinction between blacks and whites: "What separates us from the Blacks today is not so much the colour of our skin or the type of our hair as the phantom-ridden psyche we never see except when a Black lets fall some joking and to us cryptic phrase. It not only seems cryptic; it is so. The Blacks are obsessionally complicated about themselves. They've turned their suffering into a resource" (46).

Throughout *Prisoner of Love* Genet again insists that his reasons for his identifications across race and culture were incorrigibly personal. He says he completely failed to understand the Palestinian revolution (3), that he could never completely identify with the nation or their movement (90), that he participated for fun (9), that his record of what happened is inaccurate (19), that writing itself is a lie (27), and memory unreliable (39). Even the revolution was unreal: "By agreeing to go first with the Panthers and then with the Palestinians, playing my role as a dreamer inside a dream, wasn't I just one more factor of unreality inside both movements?" (149). But this is not exactly the blindness of desire, nor even the selective vision of fantasy. First, because desire and fantasy seem to transform into a nonsublimated social identification; as he puts it in relation to one group of black students in America, "while I never desired any particular person, I was all desire for the group as a whole. But my desire was satisfied by the fact that they existed" (cf. 178–79). Second, because this is a kind of desire inseparable from an abundance of curiosity and attention; desire is curious, and attends in a way that renders *desire* itself an inappropriate word. Genet is inclined to speak rather of a love that alters perception and complicates judgment, especially in relation to masculinity and relations between men in the context of war and revolution. A range of issues recur throughout Genet's book; I concentrate on masculinity because of its problematic centrality in contemporary considerations of race, homosexuality, and gender more generally, and because Genet's relations to masculinity in *Prisoner of Love* often make these other considerations seem by comparison the simplistic and reductive pronouncements of a banal gender politics.

Genet regards the eroticism of the Black Panthers as manifest and inseparable from their politics and the challenge they presented to white America (*Prisoner of Love* 259–60). Moreover, despite their restraint, "the Black Panthers couldn't throw off their mutual attraction. Their movement consisted of magnetized bodies magnetizing one another." As for the fedayeen, they "observed a smiling rigour. But the eroticism was palpable. I could sense its vibrations, though I wasn't bothered by it" (126).

But this eroticism, and the masculinity of these men, frequently confounds the stereotypes. Thus he says of Ali, a member of Fatah, "He knew I loved him, but it didn't make him the slightest bit arrogant. It awakened his kindness" (*Prisoner of Love* 267). Genet speaks also of the kindness of the Panthers, which "brought me both real protection and education in affection" (83). Different again is the dancing of the Bedouin soldiers, at once chaste and erotic—"chaste because it takes place among men, mostly holding one another by the elbow or the forefinger . . . erotic because it takes place between men, and because it's performed before the ladies. So which sex is it that burns with desire for an encounter that can never be?" In their dancing, Genet detects a display, almost a confession, of the femininity that contrasted so strongly with their masculinity, and an acceptance of, even a desire for, annihilation.

Genet returns to this wish for death and martyrdom. He is admiring of the soldiers' courage but not persuaded by their beliefs: training people to sacrifice themselves produces not altruism but a fascinated following of others to death, not so much to help but merely to follow (*Prisoner of Love* 88). And looking at the Palestinian revolution "from a viewpoint higher than my own" he regards it as ultimately a revolt reaching to the limits of Islam, a "calling for a revision, probably even a rejection, of a theology as soporific as a Breton cradle" (88). Of the young Phalangists, "something halfway between monks and hoodlums," singing of the Immaculate Conception and marching toward immortality: "I was enchanted. I could calculate their cruelty from their stupidity" (32).

In others he finds both the impulse to self-sacrifice, and their masculinity, quite complex (*Prisoner of Love* 124). One of the men who most attracts him, Mubarak, is also one whose sexuality is most self-conscious, withdrawn, and complicated; Mubarak's masculinity is itself strung out across difference: he is a Sudanese African in Asia, fighting for a people who he does not understand and who regard him with a racist indifference (194–95); he speaks perfect French, but with a Parisian urban working-class accent. Genet describes him as "so obviously both a pimp—a barracks or red-light district ponce—and a whore that I could never make out what he was doing among the fedayeen" (153). Alternately ironic and sad, provocative and withdrawn, Mubarak shares Genet's gift for insightful reflection on the revolution and the sociopolitical forces at work within it and beyond. He also exhibited a flirtatiousness aimed at everyone and everything, "a desire to charm [that] prevented him from being sufficiently implacable" (152–53). Yet later, after Mubarak's death, Genet discovers that he didn't sleep with women or men; all of his sexuality was social: "the warmth of that voice had the shy yet imperious sureness of an erect penis stroking a beloved cheek. In that too I saw him as an obvious heir to the boys of the old Paris suburbs" (143). Perhaps that is also why Mubarak says, or at least why Genet recalls him saying, that if he wanted his book (*Prisoner of Love*) to be read he must write it in "a voice that's sweet but inexorable" (151).

With the fedayeen, love always at once complicates and simplifies the narrative. One of his most vivid memories is of three separate groups of fedayeen, each situated on a different hill, singing to each other just before dawn; it was a polyphony, "a great improvisation performed among the mountains, in the midst of danger," heedless of death, expressing and eliciting love (*Prisoner of Love* 36–40). Elsewhere Genet writes of a nineteen-year-old, washing the clothes of his friend who is shortly to go and fight, declaring that he loves the revolution and all the fedayeen, but his friend especially: "Yes. It is love. Do you think that at a time like this I am afraid of words? . . . if he dies tonight there will always be a gulf at my side, a gulf into which I must never fall" (87). More than two hundred pages later Genet writes, "out of the crowd a glance swifter than a wink reveals two fedayeen as two lovers. . . . Chaste, but so close that if one of them is sad the laughter of the other immediately fills the void in him" (330). These are Genet's reconstructions, and perhaps the gulf, the void, is his, not the soldiers'.

If Genet is seduced by the magnanimity of the fedayeen, their selflessness, courage, humor, and love for each other, he is also perplexed and disillusioned by the inseparability of these qualities from an "underlying desire for self-slaughter, for glorious death if victory was impossible" (*Prisoner of Love* 271–72). Surfacing from that perplexity, which is to say between, and sometimes within, the lyrical meditations on love, is that ambivalence of which Kobena Mercer has recently written (see "Skin Head Sex Thing") and a sense of the disturbing proximity of antagonists. Both are powerfully articulated in Genet's angry "fantasy" of the palace and the shanty town:

> one wonders which was real and which only a reflection. Anyhow, if the Palace was the reflection and the shanty town the reality, the reflection of the reality was only to be found in the Palace, and vice versa. Getting to know the other, who's supposed to be wicked because he's the enemy, makes possible not only battle itself but also close bodily contact between the combatants and between their beliefs. So each doctrine is sometimes the shadow and sometimes the equivalent of the other. . . . What sort of beauty is it these lads from the shanty town possess? When they're still children a mother or a whore gives them a piece of broken mirror in which they trap a ray of the sun and reflect it into one of the Palace windows. And by that open window, in the mirror, they discover bit by bit their faces and bodies. (58–62)

Desiring Difference

All the foregoing texts and histories suggest why theoretical or pseudopoliti-cal gestures toward difference are inadequate. As are (another recent develop-ment) separatist or essentialist "identity politics" wherein one group seeks its own advantage at the expense, or in ignorance, of others.[12] Still, I have no in-tention of prescribing a correct attitude toward difference, even less a correct theory of difference; I do not even know what the latter could possibly be. My consideration of difference originated in a turn to history in order to re-pudiate one such theory — specifically, that which construed homosexuality as an embrace of the same/fear of the different. It's a history that quite quickly produces that excess of difference that discredits the theory that ignored it but that also questions the theoretically and politically facile celebration of difference per se.

My task has been to reconsider some of those complicated but always sig-nificant histories wherein differences conflict and converge as desire itself. In doing so I wanted not to reduce, say, Gide's or Fanon's defense of difference to the limiting historical conditions of its articulation — the first as merely a (homo)sexual tourist, the second as developing a homophobic theory of Negrophobia. Rather, I've wanted to recover the history of each in relation to the other, finding in the process that Gide understood more than most about desire for the different, Fanon more than most about the ambivalence of dif-ference itself. As for Genet, someone whose involvement with the different has variously been repudiated as fascist, racist, and anarchistic, his Prisoner of Love is nothing less than an affirmation of the love that Fanon envisaged and that has sometimes given the dissident their courage. If I risk ending these thoughts on sexual dissidence by speaking of love, it is without apology and simply to acknowledge their inspiration.

Notes

A version of this essay first appeared in my Sexual Dissidence: Augustine to Wilde, Freud to Fou-cault (Oxford: Clarendon, 1991) and is reprinted here with permission of the publisher.

1. Mohanty goes on to argue that instead of sentimentally or vaguely celebrating cultural difference, we should search for that which unites us. In this respect he ar-gues for a conception "of agency as a basic capacity which is shared by all humans across cultures. And in understanding the divide between 'us' and 'them', it is this common space we all share that needs to be elaborated and defined" (71).

2. The racism of white gay male culture is both acknowledged and challenged by the contributors to M. Smith, *Black Men/White Men*; see especially Beame's interview with Smith, founder of BWMT (Black and White Men Together), and DeMarco, "Gay Racism."

3. But Lawrence adds, significantly, "I could not sincerely take on the Arab skin: it was an affectation only. . . . I had dropped one form and not taken on the other. . . . Sometimes these selves would converse in the void; and then madness was very near, as I believe it would be near the man who could see things through the veils at once of two customs, two educations, two environments" (*Seven Pillars* 10).

4. Delay suggests, with little evidence, that the arrest and trial of Wilde was also a factor, Gide now fearing the possibility of scandal if he took Athman to Paris. Delay also cites an unpublished letter of 6 March where Gide says: "My best to Marie—prepare Pauline for the idea of seeing a Negro near her" (404). Although he gave in on this occasion, four years later he did arrange for Athman to go to Paris.

5. Delay cites several of the unpublished letters in ch. 42, "Open Rebellion."

6. Others play down Gide's newfound political awareness; Guerard remarks that his move to communism was "indirect and hesitant" (25–26).

7. More vindictively, there are those who, even as they suffer or flee from one kind of discrimination, become agents of others in twisted proportion to the intensity of the one (or more) being fled. Mosse describes the case of Benedict Friedländer, who defended homosexuality as manly, respectable, and necessary to any well-functioning army, and who also believed the homosexual was especially capable of "transcending" sexuality. But Friedländer, himself a Jew, also used anti-Semitic arguments in defense of homosexuality, arguing that the attack on homosexuals was led by Jews "determined to undermine Aryan virility and self awareness." Mosse's comment is brisk but apposite: "the spectacle of one outsider attempting to buy his entrance ticket to society at the expense of another is common enough" (41).

8. Many years later, in his *Journal* for January 1933, Gide writes that he was not unaware of the political realities of colonialism at that time; it was a feeling of incompetence that prevented him from speaking. He adds, "It took the war to bring me to doubt of the value of 'competencies', to convince myself that . . . I had just as much right as anyone else, and even the duty, to speak."

The occluded political realities of the pastoral mode have been most effectively analyzed by Louis Montrose in relation to Renaissance literature, when the genre was at its height, and in ways suggestive for Gide; see especially Montrose, " 'Eliza,' " " 'The Place of a Brother,' " and "Of Gentlemen and Shepherds."

9. George Painter records that in 1904 Athman marries; in his *Journal* for 22 November 1905, Gide writes, "From Athman's latest letter I copy this sentence that Mardrus would not understand and that I should like not to forget: 'I love her very much' (he is speaking of his very young wife) 'and yet I have been able to make her sincere toward my mother and me; she is very good, and I only treat her very gently like how you treat a child' " (155; Gide's emphasis).

10. The phrase is Genet's; see Fichte, "Interview," in Leyland 76.

11. On Genet's reading of George Jackson's prison letters, see my *Sexual Dissidence* 98–100. On his involvement with the Black Panthers, see Gaitet.

12. For a critique of identity politics see Fuss, *Essentially Speaking*, ch. 6; and Mercer, "Welcome to the Jungle."

FIEDLER AND SONS

ROBYN WIEGMAN

When Leslie Fiedler's explosive reading of the American literary tradition as a drama "in which a white and a colored American male flee from civilization into each other's arms" (*Love* 12) appeared in 1960, Stanley Kramer's black-and-white classic, *The Defiant Ones* (1958), was the only cinematic version of interracial fraternity available to U.S. moviegoers. For the reader of Fiedler in the 1990s, this paucity of popular images is rather striking, as the decade of the 1980s featured one big box-office film after another modeled on the symbolic marriage among men, from *Stir Crazy* (1980) in the decade's opening year to *Lethal Weapon* 2 (1989) in its last. For some observers of U.S. culture, such a proliferation might confirm Fiedler's assertion of interracial male bonding as "the central myth of our culture . . . the most deeply underlying image of ourselves" (*Love* 182), providing as it does a now generic narrativity in which dark male and white confront and overcome the tableau of differences among them.

But rather than simply reading the reiteration of buddy images in the popular culture of the 1980s as definitive evidence of the literary critic's profoundly truthful rendering, Fiedler's turn in the early sixties to interracial male bonding figurations can be understood instead as a prototypical instance of the shift in the production of masculinities that characterizes the second half of the twentieth century more generally. The scene of racial differences among men emerges not simply as a primary social problem, but as this culture's most potentially violent and disruptive internal crisis—a crisis in which the tenuous interplay of race and gender is renegotiated in the broader transformation from segregation to integration. Where black feminists have critiqued the Civil Rights movement for its blindness to gender asymmetries, it is in the province of the popular that the final reduction of black liberation struggle to a kind of masculine quest narrative has been most effectively achieved.[1] In this province, the image of interracial fraternity comes to signify the "post–Civil Rights" era: the figure of the non-Eurocentric player serving to evince both multicultural difference and its shimmering egalitarian transcendence.

In this regard, Fiedler's challenge to the prevailing critical interpretation of the U.S. literary tradition as Adamic—his emphasis on Chingachgook, Queequeg, and Jim as key to the antisocial quests of Natty, Ishmael, and Huck—epitomizes the revisionist scenario finalized in the popular domain of the 1980s, as contemporary bonding narrations likewise displace myths of American singularity by heralding interracial fraternity.[2]

From the vantage point of this century's earlier segregationist ideal, the interracial male bond's emphasis on the "mutuality of gender," to use Joseph Boone's phrase ("Male Independence" 193), brings into powerful relief the antagonism that underlies the deployment of racial difference in U.S. culture, providing a means for inculcating the African American male into the cultural economy along the lines of a shared, "common" subjectivity. But the bond's reliance on gender sameness as the ground for fashioning the move toward integration is not unqualifiedly revolutionary, no matter how important the transgression of segregation may be. In the contemporary era, in fact, the alignment of the African American male with an overarching masculine sameness within the interracial bonding configuration betrays the cultural panic underwriting the move toward integration, where the specter of black male equality threatens the racial supremacy ensconced in U.S. patriarchal formations. By negotiating cultural fears around black male entitlement in the context of representational (as opposed to economic or political) inclusion, the difficult demands of 1960s civil rights discourses have been translated into strategies complicit not only with the expansion of capital's consumer needs, but with a shifting formation of white supremacy. In the deep disparity between the bond's image of loving interracial affection, then, and the social, political, and economic displacement of black men in late-twentieth-century America, we encounter one of the particularly problematic aspects attending integration and its rhetorical invocation as democracy's final achievement.

For Fiedler, the move away from definitive constructions of U.S. literature as coterminous with individual enhancement and solitary sojourning makes possible a less negating integrationist aesthetic, one that hopes to challenge white supremacy by offering images of collective political engagement across the divisive bounds of race. But his critical foregrounding of the bond begins in a curious place, linking as he does in his early, flamboyant piece, "Come Back to the Raft Ag'in, Huck Honey!" (1948), the "Negro and the homosexual" as the stock themes of interracial male bondings. As he writes, "the fact of homosexual passion contradicts a national myth of masculine love, just as our real relationship with the Negro contradicts a myth of that relationship; and those two myths with their betrayals are . . . one" (142). Through the figure of interracial fraternity, Fiedler builds a case for understanding the quintessential American myth as predicated on the "mutual love of *a white man and a colored*" (146), and it is precisely its homoerotic content, its love without lust, its disembodiment that constitutes its utopian telos. Why, if sexuality is repressed and denied, did Fiedler nonetheless begin by linking the Negro and the homosexual?

In the full-length treatment of this mythic American nexus, *Love and Death in the American Novel* (1960), it is significant that Fiedler replaces the "homosexual" with the concept of the "homoerotic." By 1966, in the revised edition, Fiedler would explain the shift: " 'Homoerotic' is a word of which I was never very fond. . . . But I wanted it to be quite clear that I was not attributing sodomy to certain literary characters or their authors, and so I avoided when I could the more disturbing word 'homosexual' " (*Love* 349 n). Clearly, the assumption of the homosexual as synonymous with sodomy is, to use his word, disturbing, but even this shift, he tells us, "has done little good" in garnering the "proper" reading of his text: "what I have to say on this score has been at once the best remembered and most grossly misunderstood section of my book" (*Love* 349 n). In his linking of the Negro and the homosexual as crucially intertwined in the male bonding narrative, it is the phantasmatic homosexual that continues to haunt the text long after Fiedler's attempt to make him disappear. But in the contemporary era, gay scholars have sought to reclaim the homosexual in the context of the bond's figuration, arguing for his presence, however oblique, in the narrative of male love. In this vein, Robert K. Martin reads *Moby-Dick* as an avowedly homosexual text, as is its author, though that homosexuality is spoken through symbolic and metaphoric articulations. For Boone, the homosexual possibilities of the interracial bond as radical political praxis counter the stifling conformities of compulsory heterosexuality.

And what of the Negro? That is, as they say, a much different story. Neither Martin nor Boone pay much attention to the interracial aspect of the bonding configuration, and, in this elision, they tend to repeat the asymmetries of race through which Fiedler reads the bond. But ultimately the imbrication of sexuality and race in all of these critical texts is too crucial and too complex to characterize in such simple and potentially dismissive terms, and I certainly don't want to discount the political project of bringing the issue of the homosexual back into critical view in the literary study of closely bonded men. The argument over the specificities of the bond and the particular frameworks through which the bond is read carry their own political portent in the 1990s, drawing us further into questions about the cultural crisis of the masculine and the negotiatory mechanisms that crisis has brought into play.

In citing the interracial scene of men together as the essence of an "American" literary tradition, Fiedler's *Love and Death in the American Novel* challenged the prevailing understanding of the literary tradition by extending the vision of the American hero as, in the words of R. W. B. Lewis, "an individual emancipated from history, happily bereft of ancestry, untouched and undefiled by . . . inheritances of family and race; an individual standing alone, self-reliant and self-propelling" (5). Where Lewis would appoint James Fenimore Cooper's Natty Bummpo as this quintessential "American Adam" (104)—a "figure of heroic innocence and vast potentialities" (1)—Fiedler focuses on Natty's relationship with his Indian soul mate, Chingachgook, examining how the white male's heroic escape from culture (and from the feminine that represents the "domestication" of culture) carries with it a longing for reconciliation with a (simultaneously eroticized and de-eroticized) dark brother.

Reading the literary text as a psychic symptom—the expression of our "deepest communal fantasies" (*Love* 14)—Fiedler hypothesizes a cultural unconscious whose meanings emerge most fully not in the singular work but in patterns of repetition traced across a range of texts, patterns he links to the psychic drama of the "American" context itself: "a world which had left behind the terror of Europe not for the innocence it dreamed of, but for new and special guilts associated with the rape of nature and the exploitation of dark-skinned people; a world doomed to play out the imaginary childhood of Europe" (*Love* 31). By structuring his inquiry around the figurations of love and death as they repeat themselves in sentimental fiction and its renegade offspring, the male bonding quest, Fiedler associates the guilt of betrayal with the psychic reversion to an imaginary innocence, a developmental inversion reflected in the fact that "the typical male protagonist of our fiction has been a man on the run, harried into the forest and out to sea, down the river or into combat—anywhere to avoid . . . the confrontation of a man and a woman which leads to the fall to sex, marriage, and responsibility" (*Love* 26). In the rejection of the heterosexual world for the "mythic" reconnection to the lost and betrayed other, "the great works of American fiction," Fiedler observes, echoing D. H. Lawrence, constitute a literature for boys, and hence "are notoriously at home in the children's section of the library" (*Love* 24).

In locating the tension of the literary tradition "between sentimental life in America and the archetypal image . . . in which a white and a colored American male flee from civilization into each other's arms" (*Love* 12), Fiedler's language seems to evoke the homosexual, suggesting that escape from the bonds of culture entails an unambiguous movement toward homosexual commitment. But this flight is no simple rejection of the heterosexual for the homosexual, but the very path of sublimated and conflicted desire, stranding the "typical protagonist" between two seemingly irreconcilable alternatives: innocent homoerotic bonding on one hand and "adult heterosexual love" (Love 12) on the other. Fiedler's formulation thus constructs a developmental narrative of sexual desire that locates the homoerotic in an imaginary, pre-symbolic realm, while casting the heterosexual on the side of uncontested Law, a formulation that reiterates the cultural compulsion toward maintaining heterosexuality as a simultaneously compulsory and natural psychic achievement.

It is this framing of the homoerotic that accounts for Fiedler's version of the bond's mythic innocence, its artifice of cultural disarticulation, and its romanticized presentation of masculine relations. By reading the homoerotic as the sublimated origin of a pure, pre-cultural, and preeminently preconscious desire, Fiedler shapes the particular instance of Natty and Chingachgook into this archetypal scene: "two lonely men, one dark-skinned, one white, bend together over a carefully guarded fire in the virgin heart of the American wilderness; they have forsaken all others for the sake of the austere, almost inarticulate, but unquestioned love which binds them to each other and to the world of nature which they have preferred to civilization" (Love 192). For Fiedler, the opposition between nature and culture forms the central allegory for the sexual,[3] necessitating that the bonds linking red man and white be forged literally in the wilderness where, in the absence of women and culture, differences of race and region can be rendered meaningless and the lofty, spiritual stability of an unquestioned and nonsexual love affirmed. In this world of men together, the "Holy Marriage of Males" provides the contrast to "mere heterosexual passion" and, in this, the U.S. literary tradition pivots on "a general superiority of the love of man for man over the ignoble lust of man for woman" (Love 382, 368, 369).

In this way, Fiedler establishes a binary opposition between the homoerotic—"a passionless passion, simple, utterly satisfying, yet immune to lust—physical only as a handshake is physical, this side of copulation" (Love 368)—and heterosexuality. But as Eve Kosofsky Sedgwick's work has so well demonstrated, the social relations of the homoerotic and the heterosexual are not antithetical but contiguous organizations within patriarchal cultures, constituting what she calls the "homosocial." As a term "obviously formed by analogy with 'homosexual,' and just as obviously meant to be distinguished from [it]" (*Between Men* 1), the homosocial locates the contradiction in patriarchal organization between the primacy accorded to relationships among men and the compulsory imperative of heterosexual reproduction. By reading both trajectories of social organization as mediated by the taboo against actual (as opposed to the culturally sanctioned innocent) homosexuality, Sedgwick reveals the path of heterosexual desire as deeply homosocial, for even within the heterosexual circuit, "we are in the presence . . . of a desire to consolidate partnership with authoritative males in and through the bodies of females. . . . [M]en's heterosexual relationships . . . have as their raison d'être an ultimate bonding between men" (*Between Men* 38, 50).[4] The heterosexual contract, contrary to Fiedler's representation, is not the source of a mature equality among men and women, nor is it the supersession of the homoeroticism underlying the "innocence" of the bond. Instead, it needs to be understood as a particularly powerful mechanism for the subvention of patriarchal relations. By failing to read both the heterosexual and the homoerotic as part of the complexities and asymmetries of gender relations, Fiedler's analysis falsely opposes male bonds to heterosexual normativity, casting homosexuality as the immaturity of arrested psychosexual development.

Fiedler, of course, is hardly alone in his homophobic panic, and it is not a particularly useful critical endeavor at this historical nexus to belabor the compulsory heterosexuality on which his criticism is founded. But it is important to register how his difficult negotiation of the sexual in interracial bonding narratives repeats, symptomatically, the ideological investments of the bond as it has been constituted as a cultural rhetoric. For to fantasize "not Little Rock but Hannibal" as the place where the "white man . . . ends up lying in the arms of the colored man" is to enter, as Fiedler quite rightly tells us, an old myth. But it is one that invests the interracial male bond with reproductive responsibilities, not the miscegenating kind, of course, but the spiritual and symbolic procreations that engender "America," in the face of a narrative recognition of differences among men, along an unambiguous masculine line. In his embrace of the nostalgic story of patriarchal paternity, Fiedler's critique begins to politically undo itself. As he writes of his text: "[it] does not spring to life unbegotten, unaffiliated and unsponsored. In one sense, it has been essentially present from the moment that I read aloud to two of my sons (then five and seven) for their first time *Huckleberry Finn*" (*Love* 13). This textual and textualized insemination, issued from father to son, culminates in the following equation: "the truth one tries to tell about literature is finally [no] different from the truth one tries to tell about the indignities and rewards of being the kind of man one is—an American, let's say, in the second half of the twentieth century, learning to read his country's books" (*Love* 16).

But to read his country's books is to be inscribed within a narrative of white paternity, one devoid of the very differences among men that define the "America" of Fiedler's American tradition. This elision, I would say, underwrites the cultural rhetoric of the interracial male bond in its most frequent incarnation, indicating not the dimensions of a mythic mass-mind, but the political, social, and economic tensions attending masculine relations in their various historical configurations. As such, it is no accident that we witness, over the course of the nineteenth century, the transformation of the bond from the friendship between white man and Indian to "the fugitive slave and the no-account boy" (*Love* 368), a transformation that evinces the bond's relation to broader social changes. It is in this sense, too, that Fiedler's own text, written in the late 1950s, can be read as mediating the historical conditions of its production, locating in the face of growing African American protest against segregation, the Adamic escape from women as an originary, pre-cultural compulsion toward the brown or black man. Such a reading of the literary tradition, of "the most deeply underlying image of ourselves," hinges on transfiguring the psychological terror of Little Rock into Hannibal, that place where "our dark-skinned beloved will rescue us . . . [and] comfort us, as if he knew our offense against him were only symbolic—an offense against that in ourselves which he represents—never truly *real*" (*Love* 182, 389). In Fiedler's critical universe, as in the bond's cultural deployment, the outrage against Jim Crow is recast as symbol of the white man's internal drama, where the image of "two lonely men, one dark-skinned, one white" replaces that specter of race war known as Little Rock.

In citing Natty, Ishmael, and Huck as sojourning not alone but in tandem with a dark brother, Fiedler's reinterpretation of the Adamic narrative of individual escape and alienation serves as one of the first integrationist responses to canonical literature and is, in this sense, a politically revisionary work. Its initial appearance in 1948 and its later reworking into *Love and Death in the American Novel* in 1960 straddle the most incendiary years of the McCarthy period, marking a relation to Cold War rhetoric (and hysteria) that cannot go unnoted. Here, in fact, is where we might locate the seemingly necessary terminological shift, that attempt by Fiedler to cleanse the bond even further of its potential homosexual implications, of the very fact that in his reading of male bonds the heterosexual is jettisoned and the homosocial literally superimposed onto it. But the move from Huck's childish affection to the constitution of a national masculine infatuation with the "Negro" is anxiety-inducing to the extreme, and in the various productions of cultural panic around potential otherness in the 1950s, Fiedler's challenge, even in its seemingly purged form, carries a threat of social and symbolic ruin. If the fairy is among us in the misogynist flight from home, if the turn away from women dissolves into homosexual innuendo, what becomes of locker room and boardroom, judicial and senate chamber?

And yet, it is also the case that Fiedler's figuration of homosexuality was itself subtended by heterosexist assumptions and patriarchal ideologies, as I have demonstrated, and that the obsessive response to the question of the homosexual had the effect of negating the Negro as anything other than white masculine meaning. In this regard, Fiedler's psychological universalism ironically reinscribes the centrality of the Adamic figure he seemed to argue against by defining literary encounters among racially differentiated men as both symbols and symptoms of the psychodrama of white masculinity. In founding this psychodrama on the betrayal of—and longed-for reconciliation with—other men, Fiedler's redefinition of the U.S. literary landscape simultaneously reads and encodes the transformation of the historic agency of African American protest into a sentimental male bonding relation. Such sentimentalization emerges as the definitive mark of white masculine subjectivity, integrating both "Negro and homosexual" as thematic concerns while negating their subjective positionalities as components not only of the category of "man," but of "America" as well.

While the effects of Fiedler's analysis finally make one skeptical of the political possibilities of this methodological emphasis (and of the politics of the male bond to sustain its challenge of social norms), it is interesting that recent critical readings of this literary configuration insist on the bond's subversive potential. Most importantly, these liberatory readings emerge from two of the leading gay studies scholars working in American literature and culture. For Robert K. Martin, whose comments are set in the context of a critical reevaluation of Melville's sea novels, the male bond's "democratic union of equals" (Hero 11) is capable of achieving "feminist goals." Masculine friendship, in short, challenges the appropriative and hierarchical gender structure of heterosexual coupling, which is viewed not as the culmination of mature development—what Fiedler calls "adult heterosexual love" (Love 12)—but as a social relation of domination "founded upon the inequality of partners" (Martin, Hero 7). By pointedly refashioning homosexuality as a political category of social identity *and* sexual practices, Martin critiques both Fiedler's linkage of homosexuality with "innocence" and his attention to "the sacred marriage [of males not] as an alternative to dominant social patterns but rather as an evasion of them" (*Hero* 9). In redrawing the political agenda around which images of masculine fraternity are critically approached, Martin's discussion is itself part of the growing emergence of lesbian and gay critical studies in the academy in the 1980s, an emergence that has produced broadscale rearticulations of the terrain of the sexual in U.S. culture.[5] Often in league with feminism, and in many ways made possible by it, lesbian and gay studies has furthered the understanding of sexuality as socially constructed, forging crucial distinctions between sexual identities, practices, and their differing relation to social forms of power.

Martin contributes to this body of scholarship not only by refusing to dismiss the centrality of masculine fraternity to Melville's oeuvre, but by insisting that the celebratory phallicism of Ishmael and Queequeg in *Moby-Dick*, nonaggressive and uneconomic in its production, constitutes a homosexual textuality central in Melville's time and our own to challenging the politics of the sex/gender system. Therefore, Martin rejects Fiedler's ascription of the novel in America as conjoining the homosexual with "the Negro," finding instead that "the proper model for an analysis of the condition of the homosexual is not the racial one but the sexual one: the situation of homosexuals in contemporary society is related to the situation of women" (*Hero* 13). While this shift discounts how the racial is itself sexualized in U.S. culture (the way blackness, for instance, has been aligned with the feminine), the figuration of homosexuality within a sexual paradigm assures the theoretical centrality of the discourse of sexual difference to images of closely bonded men. And yet, it also, paradoxically, establishes a heterosexual gendered paradigm as the vehicle for reading the homosexual: "A man entering into a homosexual relationship abdicates, in part, his role in the economy of power; no longer controlling women, he must therefore 'become' a woman" (Martin, *Hero* 14). Such a strict and seemingly incontrovertible binary opposition between (feminine) margin and (masculine) center maintains the logic of heterosexual coupling, even as Martin goes on to describe the force and power of homosexuality in Melville's universe as a transgression of patriarchal assumptions and social organizations.[6] Through the "affirmation of the values of nonaggressive male-bonded couples," he contends, "the power of the patriarchy can be contested and even defeated" (*Hero* 70).

For Martin, the quintessential Melvillean response to the possessive, de-

structive impulses of dominant masculinity can be found in the bond between Ishmael and Queequeg, whose coupling acts as the egalitarian antithesis to heterosexuality's hierarchical inscriptions:

> The destruction of the Pequod and its crew is a sign of the social disaster
> that for Melville followed upon the imposition of exclusive white male
> power in its search for control over all that is nature or nonself, while
> the survival of Ishmael is made possible only through the example, love,
> and self-sacrifice of Queequeg. Ishmael's return to the surface . . . is an
> indication, in one of the novel's symbolic patterns, of the . . . restoration
> of the feminine and maternal to a world that has forsworn all softness
> and affection. Ishmael survives the cataclysm of patriarchal aggression
> to be restored to the lost maternal principle from which he has been
> exiled. (Hero 70)

But what of the power relationship between dark man and white? After all, it
is Queequeg's coffin, literally scripted with the signs borne on his body, that
enables Ishmael's return from the depths of the sea—a sacrifice, as Martin
says, but one that heralds a protofeminist, antipatriarchal possibility? Why
this desire to transform femininity (as a maternal, soft, affectionate, self-
sacrificing, loving emblem) into a vehicle for and symbol of patriarchy's
transgression? Why gender as gender's transcendence? And why, in the process, such an evacuation of the significance of race and racial hierarchies?

Part of the answer to these questions lies in Martin's attempt to link the
political struggles of gay men with feminism as a way of forging a common-
ality of interests that can aid contemporary political struggle. But must gay
men become the feminine in order for feminism to understand the necessity
of forming political alliances within and across differences of sexuality and
sexual preferences? To be sure, Martin's use of gender to orchestrate gender's
transcendence is a provocative counter to the essentialized understanding of
bodies that underlies the script that heterosexuality offers. But when he asserts
that "Melville's work may be seen as a consistent appeal against the 'feminization' or domestication of American culture" and that "male homosexuality
is . . . a means of rejecting effeminacy" (Hero 15), the contradictions are arrest-
ing. If the homosexually bonded interracial couple in Melville's text functions
on the side of the feminine (evoking it, restoring it), how can homosexuality also be an appeal against feminization? A similar paradox resides in the
status of the phallus. On one hand, Martin claims that Melville's "insistence
on the presence of the phallus" (Hero 15) was a way of challenging the incipient feminization of nineteenth-century culture, a response to the (perceived)

domesticating features of (white) women's emergence into the public sphere. At the same time, Martin assures us that "the emphasis on the phallus of which I speak is directed toward the kind of celebration of its erotic potential that is characteristic of matriarchal cultures" (Hero 15–16). The primacy of the phallus as image and symbol is thus simultaneously an avenue for a masculine reinvigoration *and* a characteristic of matriarchal cultures, both a protest against feminization and an emblem of a female-centered world. And both of these significatory functions are found within narrative scenarios that take place at sea, in a context defined primarily by women's absence.

What is most striking here is the clear disjunction between the political agenda of a male homosexuality that can somehow be protofeminist and woman-centered, yet oppositional to feminization and situated in a world composed only of men. In one of his most stunning paradoxes, Martin thus envisions the exclusion of women from the social and symbolic order of the ship as the radical and necessary precondition for the transformation of patriarchal relations. By "eliminating the role of women in these novels," Martin claims that Melville can contrast the oppositional undercurrents within masculine sexuality: the "democratic eros" found in male friendship that reflects "the celebration of a generalized seminal power not directed toward control or production; and a hierarchical eros expressed in social forms of male power as different as whaling, factory-owning, military conquest, and heterosexual marriage" (Hero 4). The binary inscribed here reiterates the oppositional relation between homosexuality and heterosexuality, marking the homo as the site of a purified, committed male love and the hetero as its degraded counterpart. In both cases, the phallus functions as the primary signifier of the sexual, demonstrating not a transgression of patriarchal logic — that would, for instance, allow female desire(s) to be represented — but an appropriation of all erotic alternatives in the name of seminal power.[7]

While it is not impossible to imagine the realization of "some important feminist goals" (Martin, Hero 94) in a world without women (precisely because sexual difference does not require the scene of woman for its enactment or subversion), the desire to transform a romanticized male homosexual textuality into the framework for democratic union asks us to believe that love between men, as opposed to conquest and aggression, is the essential counterpoint to patriarchal dominations. This is clear in Martin's description of the ending of Moby-Dick, where amongst the chaotic destruction forged by patriarchal excess there exists "a pastoral vision of a restored harmony that might be achieved if only men would learn to love each other (individually and socially)" (Hero 94). While it would be deeply problematic to disparage relationships "based on the principles of equality, affection, and respect for the other" (*Hero* 94), it is nonetheless unclear how a noncompetitive masculine love for one another can translate into the kind of broad social transformation necessary for the abatement of patriarchy. To transgress the order of compulsory heterosexuality is not in and of itself a transformation of the symbolic and cultural laws that encode and enforce its centrality as normative. Indeed, Martin's singular scripting of masculinity as either patriarchal or antipatriarchal might finally obscure more than it reveals about masculinity, sexuality, and the social production of power in U.S. culture.

In this kind of oppositional logic, Martin forges an image of the social that depends not only on the spatial conceptions of margin and center, but on a privileging of the margin as inherent locus of subversion. In the wake of a variety of poststructuralist teachings and in the context of contemporary political crises, such a position has become nearly impossible to maintain, inscribing as it does a deterministic understanding of power and marking subjective positionalities as uncontradicted, nonconflicted domains. It is this that finally undermines Martin's interpretive strategy, for in the idealization of the margins, he both rigidifies relations of sexual domination and comes to equate all marginal positions (of gender, race, class, sexuality) as the same. In positing, for instance, that "[t]he marriage of Queequeg and Ishmael is a vision of a triumphant miscegenation that can overcome the racial and sexual structures of American society" (*Hero* 94), Martin suspends close scrutiny of the implications of this metaphoric miscegenation—its culmination in the dark man's sacrifice for the white man's rebirth—in favor of an elevated praise for the loving bond of undifferentiated and seemingly equal men. "[P]oor Ishmael survives alone," Martin laments, "only symbolically supported by Queequeg; even there, it seems, Melville was not to able to imagine what it might have been like for two men to love each other *and survive*" (*Hero* 7). The clear repression of the significance of race as a determining factor in the narrative's solution is a striking reinscription of the asymmetrical power that structures relations among men.

But while I may challenge Martin's dismissal of race in an interpretive framework that overtly seeks feminist goals, it is finally some of feminist theory's own paradigmatic elisions that his critical perspective encodes.[8] In offering an understanding of the social positionality of "man" along lines marked primarily by the hierarchical relations of sexual difference, Martin seems stranded within that earlier moment in feminist theorizations of the social when female homosexuality served as the first wave of difference to question the monolithic sanctity of "woman." Martin's attempt to clear the ground of the masculine same by inserting sexuality as difference in relations among men rehearses this necessary gesture, but it too uniformly constructs the realm of social positionality within the sex/gender system, displacing other formations (here, most notably race) that not only condition the very shape and substance of sexual difference, but that also challenge its theoretical logic and stability. That there is no realm in which masculinity or femininity can be fractured off from their determination in relation to other axes of difference necessitates an approach to issues of interracial male bonding attentive not only to normative sexual and gendered dimensions, but importantly to those of race as well.

The kinds of issues I have raised in connection to Martin's exploration of fraternity perhaps circulate most coherently within broader critical discussions about the political and theoretical relationship of men to feminism, discussions that are almost always difficult and antagonistically formed.[9] Certainly a great amount of this difficulty involves the pressure such issues impose on feminism's historical reliance on female identity as the founding framework for its political articulation. In the context of a growing number of men trained in feminist academic discourses as well as the rise of lesbian and gay studies and other recent investigative turns toward masculinities within the sex/gender system, the epistemological assurance of feminism as a collective "voice" or identity forged in the name of women has begun to give way. Add to this feminism's own dawning emphasis on women's multiple and non-commensurate subjective figurations in terms of race, class, sexuality, and nation, and one recognizes the broadscale internal critique and transformation around "identity" that feminism currently engages. The contemporary debate over men and/in feminism must thus be seen not as an issue imposed by men, but as a response to political arguments and challenges that feminism has elicited, a struggle that both encompasses and exceeds "men and feminism" by importantly challenging the very epistemological security of "women's" relationship to feminism itself.

Interracial male bonding narratives and their critical canon are particularly interesting from this perspective, where identities in crisis comprise not only the cultural context governing their deployments, but the political and theoretical problematic that feminism brings to bear. If it is true that feminism has in many ways drawn its organizational sustenance from a counter identity formation (locating in "woman" and "women" that which is excluded from patriarchy and therefore, as the logic goes, that which can most effectively undermine it), it is equally true that the identity of "man" and "men" has provided feminism with the definitional relation underpinning its understanding of patriarchy: as the central locus of the patriarchal, masculine identity has served as the cohesive term through which feminism has mapped the psychological and political determinations of the social itself.

Under these conditions, it is not altogether bizarre to suggest that the mythology of masculine fraternity functions, in a way akin to feminist invocations of sisterhood and common oppression, as the instantiation of both a complicitous and potentially resistant rhetoric. In the contemporary popular realm, as in canonical literary formations, interracial male bonding narration obsessively replays mythic male union as a counter to the fragmentation and historically shifting "nature" of masculine identities within the social. The proliferation of these images attests to the ongoing crisis of identity in U.S. culture and points to the incoherency that contemporary representations of the masculine simultaneously foreground and allay. As in feminist theory's current attention to the limitations of identity and in the context of postmodern understandings of subjectivity as multiple and contradictory, it is the significance of this incoherency that has emerged as central to rethinking both the political as a category and its epistemological foundation for struggle.[10] Therefore it is particularly interesting that critical discussions of masculine fraternity, drawing on feminist theory and its political commitment to patriarchal disruptions, would so forcefully insist on the achievement of cohesion within the interracial male bond, an achievement that tends to recontain differences among men within a rather singular and monolithic subjective function.

Joseph A. Boone's discussion of the male bond in *Tradition Counter Tradition* (1987) is most telling in this regard. While it offers a sophisticated understanding of the theoretical issues involved with linking masculine relations to feminist goals, it curiously reinscribes the centrality of the white male by defining his attainment of a coherent, self-affirming identity as the culmination of a radical social critique. As we shall see, this possibility is contingent on displacing power asymmetries between racially differentiated men in a narrative focus on the male bond's encodement in quest literature where "the outward voyage to confront the unknown . . . simultaneously traces an inner journey toward a redefinition, a 'remaking' of self that defies, at least partially, social convention and sexual categorization" (*Tradition* 228–29). By ascribing the dynamics of this inner journey to the protagonists of such classic bonding novels as *Moby-Dick* and *Huckleberry Finn*, Boone charts a "counter-tradition" to the "courtship and wedlock plotting" of the literature of sentimental romance (*Tradition* 226). Here, in language that recalls, alternately, Lawrence,

Lewis, Fiedler, and Martin, a "single or unattached protagonist existing outside the boundaries of matrimonial definition or familial expectation" is able
to discover "an affirming, multiform self that has begun to break through the
strictures traditionally imposed on male social identity" (*Tradition* 226, 228).

Boone's emphasis on "self" and "identity" signals his critical paradigm's
most foregrounded assumption: that the problematic of masculine domination necessitates the "reintegration of [men's] often fragmented identity, a
leveling of the reductively constructed hierarchies of heart and mind as well
as those severed 'halves' of personality associated . . . with the two sexes" (*Tradition* 229). Such reintegration heralds the complete and "true self" (*Tradition*
229), one that exceeds the bifurcation of masculine and feminine constituted
in the social script of gender and reiterated by the traditional marital relation
itself. In this process, the feminine as a category of personal qualities and at-
tributions can be incorporated into the male quester's identity as a way of
challenging "society's constitution of 'the feminine' as a specifically female
and hence 'inferior' category" (*Tradition* 239). Significantly, Boone recognizes
the potential appropriative gesture inherent in notions of integrating the
feminine into man where the feminine's incorporation can simply reinscribe
the dualism of gender. Instead, he "envision[s] a male subjectivity for which
the 'feminine' is never 'other' because it is already an intrinsic, integral aspect of a dynamically multiform self" (*Tradition* 239). And it is this vision that
he charts in the work of Melville and Twain, where the traditional conflict
between masculine and feminine subjective formations is unhinged from its
biologized essentialism and explored in worlds that are devoid of women,
but indebted to the expansive possibilities of the feminine nonetheless.

Even if we consider the linguistic straitjacket imposed by gender—the
very difficulty of defining alternative modes of sexual "identities" that do not
reiterate the oppositional logic of sexual difference—can feminism risk the
assumption that the male incorporation of the feminine as a non-other relation will necessarily lead to a transformation of women's economic, social,
and political *positions* in U.S. culture? Is there not a difference, a deeply important political difference, between the realms of the individual psychosexual
and the structural relations of which patriarchal domination is only a part?
Most importantly, what political effect do we imagine from the equation that
occurs in Boone's discourse between male disidentification with the masculine on the one hand, and male identification with the feminine on the other?
These questions seem to me central to the kind of critical paradigm offered by
Boone's analysis, where the individual drama of masculinity emerges as the
landscape/seascape of potential revolutionary praxis and thereby inscribes a

masculine quest toward subjective wholeness as the precondition for patriarchal transcendence. That this "wholeness" is defined not in antagonism to the feminine but as an embrace of its potentially threatening alterity signals for Boone its radical redefinition, but I am struck by the formulation of such a social vision: where notions of "true self," "independent self," "fluid identity," "inclusive, unlimited identity," "complete sense of self," "autonomous selfhood" circulate as the teleology of political struggle (*Tradition* 229, 243, 247, 251, 253, 252). This replication of the individualism and mythology of self-definition that heralds capitalist subjective formations fails to register the complexities not only of the subject's relation to the social, but of the social itself.

Boone is able to chart this replication as an emancipatory agenda, in part, through the formalist aspect of his reading, where the relationship of the quest's narrative plot and textual structure to its protagonist's psychological struggle are intertwined. Ishmael's rejection of socially restrictive roles, for instance, is formally cast as Melville's rejection of traditional textual organization and plotting. As in *Moby-Dick*, Boone contends, the quest novel eschews the symmetrical narrative models of romance literature—which typically feature conflict-separation-resolution—by moving toward open-form, multifaceted textual voices, and disparate representational modes. In this way, "the reader gains the sense not merely of several types of narrative strung together, but of one mode after the other being left behind, traveled beyond, as the evolving quest carries both reader and protagonist into increasingly uncharted and heteroglossic realms of discourse and plot" (*Tradition* 240). In defining the form of the quest as an intrinsic aspect of the quest itself, Boone locates a new narrative rhythm, "a counter-traditional geography of male desire in fictional form" (*Tradition* 241). At the heart of such a counter-tradition is a revolutionary mode of characterization, one that defies the linear model of psychological development for a variated pattern. Here, "as 'voices' and subjects of their texts' ever-shifting registers, Ishmael and Huck . . . attest to a construction of personality that embraces the fullness of contradiction and difference" (*Tradition* 241). In the process, their individuality and self-definition are affirmed, as a wholeness of identity emerges through the confrontation and incorporation of contradiction and difference.

Unification through contradiction. Difference as the vehicle for an expansive, fluid self. It is at the level of these figurations of identity that my skepticism about the accumulative logic of subjective wholeness is particularly engaged, since it is here that the white masculine protagonist of the quest genre encounters the racially differentiated masculine "other" and is most fully liberated from his struggle with self-division and internal chaos by moving toward "inclusive, unlimited identity" (*Tradition* 251). Such inclusiveness pivots on an unacknowledged transformation of all social differences into the protagonist's internalized order of completion, allowing him an inclusive, affirming, and socially transgressive identity that is significantly achieved by no one else. What does it mean, for instance, that Huck's "multiple roles, identities, and fabricated biographies . . . give him the figurative space within which to develop a more complete sense of self" (*Tradition* 253), when the very framework of such figurative space is made possible by the social scripting of race and gender—of white masculinity—that he enjoys? For Boone, these movements into unknown identities are enabled by the protagonist's narrative positioning as outside the realm of culture. But it seems to me that very specific aspects of his cultural coding underwrite the possibilities of transgression from the outset, aspects of cultural coding that do not cease to function merely because the narrative takes us downriver or out to sea. It is not a great surprise that the transgressive image of masculine completion resides within a textual body defined, implicitly if not altogether explicitly, by white skin.

The fact is: the multiform self that Boone heralds as evidence of a new rhythm of masculine desire is transgressive only when we remain within the narrative logic of a romantic counter-tradition, where the image of a socially nonconformist masculinity—nonaggressive, fluid, encompassing—can subvert the dynamic of domination linked to patriarchal manifestations.[11] By thinking only through the paradigm of sexual difference, and understanding it primarily as an oppositional relation between masculine/feminine and male/female, the presence of an interracial male bonding configuration in quest literature can become the primary vehicle for gender's transcendence.[12] As Boone writes, "the male bond opens the way to an undivided identity, once Ishmael learns to overcome his initial prejudices and recognize in this seemingly racial 'other' a mutual companion, an equal spirit, and an equivalent, mirroring self. And because this bond ultimately rests on equality and a mutual recognition of independent identities, it encodes, as Baym has observed, a set of values directly 'opposite . . . the usual female-male association'; it affirms one's individuality without halving it" (*Tradition* 245). The language of "*one's* individuality" betrays the singular trajectory of identity's articulation, not only in Boone's criticism or the canonical literature he draws his observations from, but in the contemporary deployment of interracial male bonds as well. The seeming equality and mutual recognition made possible by the bond constitutes the "racial 'other'" as a "mirroring self," a constitution that incorporates difference into the affirmation of a now singular (one's) individuality. This reinscribes, in ways that are quite familiar, the confrontation of differences into a rhetoric of cultural sameness where the "racial 'other'" (the term itself signifying the asymmetry I am examining) serves as the textual body across which the subversive recasting of "the usual female-male association" can play. "Above all else," Boone asserts, "it is Huck's loving relationship with the slave, Jim, that measures his status as a cultural misfit and his unretraceable deviation from a traditional standard of manhood" (*Tradition* 253).

The slippage from the racial to the gendered, evident in the various quotes used in the preceding paragraph, occurs repeatedly in Boone's discussion, marking the status of the "racial 'other'" not only as stand-in for the feminine, but as the white male protagonist's symbolic transcendence of the logic of gender altogether. The "racial 'other'" thus exists as the definition of white masculine multiplicity, a definition that reads the male bond solely through an individualized white masculine perspective. When Boone writes that "[i]f Huck's identity cannot be fitted to one role, neither does this bond conform to a single need" (*Tradition* 256), it is Huck's identity that founds the descriptive contours and political possibilities of the interracial male bond itself. The analytic refusal to recognize the narrative disparity between Huck and Jim (the recognition, for instance, that Jim does not have access to the multiplicity of roles available to Huck) is the precondition for crafting their relationship as "a mutuality of spirit that, over time, becomes genuine, reciprocal, and nonpossessive: as such it at least partially transcends the hierarchies defining the relation of man and wife, parent and child, white and black, in American society" (*Tradition* 256). By finding in the interracial male bond an image of fraternity seemingly devoid of the hierarchical consequences of the heterosexual contract, Boone marks the transgression of the sexual as simultaneously a transgression of all hierarchical relations. But while the discourse of sexual difference thus functions to negotiate differences among men by veiling internal hierarchies through an image of masculine mutuality and independent identity, Boone's qualification—the "at least partially"—significantly evokes the disavowed but frequently returning suspicion that this critical paradigm, as Jim says to Huck, is just "too good for true" (88).

While the proliferation of interracial male bonding narratives in the popular arena is certainly unmatched, in number if not in philosophical scope, by their presence in canonical literature, critical discussions of the American tradition have nonetheless debated, for almost half a century, the meaning, centrality, and utopian possibilities inherent in the image of closely bonded men. But instead of locating the interracial male bond along the double axes of race and gender, we have seen how the critical heritage more frequently focuses on the radical displacement of heterosexual romance as precondition to (and symbolic enactment of) the nostalgic dream of racial transcendence. From this perspective, the bond's defiance of the history of enslavement, lynching, and segregation through narratives that posit the similarities and compatibilities among black and white men subverts the heterosexual model of social interaction by translating alienation and differentiation into mutuality and sameness. Too often, this reading of subversion belies the complexities of cultural productions of interracial male bonds, enabling the defiance of one historical nexus (gender) to symbolically mark the defiance of a number of others (race, class, sexuality) as well. In reading the social and psychosexual dynamics of gender through a binary figuration of masculine/feminine, this critical discourse not only rigidifies gender's meaning and mode of inscription, but it also suspends the significance of other formations of power in a limited account of social relations.

In transmuting the narrative of racial difference into a scenario of the mutuality of gender, the critical discourse demonstrates, at its deepest level, the integrationist ideal in twentieth-century U.S. culture: where the deployment of sexual difference in the scene of relations among men turns away from the imposition of a highly sexualized difference — as evinced in lynching and castration rituals or in images of the African American male as bumbling, feminized "coon" — toward an incorporation based on the contours of a masculine sameness. Here, the powerful seduction (and historically shifting articulation) of the discourse of sexual difference functions as the primary means for framing and negotiating power relations among black and white men. By understanding the deployment of sexual difference as operating in those narrative and cultural scenarios devoid of the presence of woman, we approach an underlying assumption of my text: that the implication of sexual difference always exceeds the biologizing foundation of its discursive encodement as woman, functioning instead across categories of identity to inscribe, reinforce, and overdetermine hierarchical arrangements, even (indeed especially) those among men. In its articulation as masculine mutuality, the discourse of sexual difference operates quite impressively to disavow the impact of racial difference in interracial male bonding narration, both in the contemporary popular realm and that of canonical literature as well. As such, the interracial male bond's vision of gender and racial transcendence, heralded as emblem of equality, does not necessarily encode broad social transformation, no matter how evocative and seemingly innocuous the central image of men can be.

In rejecting the universalized vision of men together as symbol of cultural freedom, I am not negating in total the potential for interracial male configurations to challenge social arrangements, for antiracist struggle does necessitate forging alliances across categories of identity. And yet, by calling into question the idealization of the bond and its relation to discursive and social relations of race and gender, I want to emphasize the historically located productions of both interracial male bonding narratives and their critical discourse—productions bound together in the increasing cultural struggle over the content and contextual parameters constituting "America." That this struggle is not simply a quest for a more real or true America (or even one more faithful to its purported ideals), but a contestation over the political and discursive grounds of its very existence demonstrates that America is, above all, a rhetorical figure, defined by its excessive performance, and constituted by the logic that establishes not only its geographical but its metaphysical borders.[13] In the context of the 1980s' popular explosion of interracial male bonding configurations, we witness a further instance of the performance of "America," one that not only marks its incessant productivity, but underscores the logic of specular integration that informs its contemporary narration. Through this logic, the symbolic investment of "America" as locus of democratic achievements is rearticulated in the face of racial hierarchies, and its tenuousness under segregation newly secured by representational circuits that do not simply posit inclusion, but equate that inclusion with social, political, and economic reform.

As this essay has discussed, the interracial male configuration provides an important opportunity for such a translation: in the contemporary critical canon as in its popular filmic deployment, the image of interracial male bonds calls "America" back from its segregationist past to the new possibilities attending integration, where it can be hailed in the context of "democratic possibility," its founding narrative and ideological trope. As Houston A. Baker Jr. writes, it is the very idea of America (in his text, AMERICA)[14] that provides the unification through which the shifting and contentious identities within the United States can be yoked to a seemingly stable and inclusive governing sign: "Black and white alike have sustained a literary-critical and literary-theoretical discourse that inscribes (and reinscribes) AMERICA as immanent idea of boundless, classless, raceless possibility in America. The great break with a Europe of aristocratic privilege and division has been filled by virtuoso rifts on AMERICA as egalitarian promise, trembling imminence in the New World" (65). While the context of Baker's discussion—"a literary-critical and literary-theoretical discourse"—points to a rather small enclave within the broader deployment of America, it is significant that the contextual parameters of discussions about the form, shape, and substance of the literary have historically revolved around the definition of America, finding within its scope the framework for appeals to canonical visibility and theoretical inclusion.

Baker's suspicion of integrationist logic hinges on the fact that the key players in literary-critical performances of America have been "founding (white) fathers, or black men who believe there are only a few more chords to be unnot(ted) before Afro-American paternity is secure" (65). This is a telling figuration, not simply because it marks the domain of America's inscription as masculine, but more importantly because it recognizes the asymmetrical distribution of power among racially differentiated men that underwrites that masculine domain as well. But the most stunning rhetorical aspect of Baker's figuration is its use of the paternal metaphor to describe both the asymmetry among men and the "egalitarian promise" of its transcendence. Here, the founding white fathers can confer upon the disinherited black sons the symbolic position of paternity, "'initiat[ing]' [them] into American Democracy" for the first time as "'contributors' to American civilization" (65). In this integrationist (initiation) narrative, black men gain access to America's signification by providing symbolic proof of their issue (contribution), joining the white fathers in an interracial configuration that upholds both the idea of trembling imminence and its implicit logic of the white father's civilizing conquest. Significantly, national collective identity is thus constituted in a paternal relation, one in which the white father begets the black son who, in turn, can beget America as symbolic proof and performative invocation of this patriarchal reproductive relation. Patriarchal paternity, negotiated across the body of racial difference, heralds "America" itself.

The focus on paternity as the metaphorical relation underpinning America's rhetorical enactment suggests the kind of anxieties attending reproduction that feminists have long linked to patriarchal productions. And it is in the context of the reproductive anxieties propelling America's obsessive desire for repetition that we are ushered, once again, into the symbolic heart of closely bonded men, where the generative stakes involved in collecting differences into a unified, autonomous, undivided whole are revealed. Boone's descriptive terminology for the quest protagonist's self-defining internal goal returns as the rhetorical topos of America, depicting a logic of paternal creation that, contrary to Boone's contention, seems quite far from revolutionary, protofeminist ideals. But where Baker describes a birthing process in which white man generates black, it is important that the narrative structure Fiedler, Martin, and Boone describe is marked by an inversion: the black male serves as the enabling figure for the white male's traumatic re-birth. This critical inversion bears the mark of integration's ideological subversion, allowing the white masculine figure to be healed, in his painful voyage through the psychological or physical domain of the social margins, by the now loving black male he has misjudged, hated, or feared. In the process of this reconfiguration of hierarchical arrangements, a voice of authority and integrated wholeness emerges—a voice now both singular and multiple— that can narrate past, present, and future for an America, trembling beacon, of democratic ideals.

This reconfiguration is contingent, as I have demonstrated, on the incipient reduction of the African American male to a highly commodified construction—captured in an economy of visibility defined and specified by the specular relations of late-twentieth-century cultural production. That academic discourse replays, in various ways, the specularity of the popular domain is evinced by its rhetorical pretense toward visibility and inclusion, where the circulation of an eccentric, "different" body is heralded as the prevailing sign of its emancipatory, postsegregationist appeal. But while we may applaud the stretch toward a new and different signification, both popular and academic discourse converge at a point of critical, non-transgressive return, lighting out not toward an unknown territory but ensconcing us perhaps more fully within the complexities and asymmetries the theoretical escape was to have healed. And it is here, as well, that my own discourse, reading the returns and elisions of the interracial male bonding configuration, cannot wholly transcend its consumptive logic of specular appeal. While I might try to contain the white masculine's quest for self-definition, the bond's other male figure is offered, in the end, no narrative, theoretical, or social release. Even in critique, some meaningful presence—some subjective weight—is inadvertently suspended, as the bond's powerful inscription of sameness and difference continues its work along the fault line of race and gender tensions.

Notes

1. See Wallace, *Black Macho*, for a cogent analysis of sexual difference within Civil Rights and black power discourses and organizations.

2. For the classic discussion of the Adamic tradition, see Lewis.

3. For a more extended discussion of the sexual mapping of the nature/culture binarism in U.S. literary production, see Baym and Kolodny.

4. Sedgwick's reading of the homosocial nexus of masculine bonds provides an important rethinking of Luce Irigaray's rather transhistorical account of the homosexual economy underpinning patriarchal relations. For Sedgwick, Irigaray's transmutation of the homosocial into the homosexual displaces the force and power of the heterosexual imperative, and makes the understanding of homophobia and misogyny difficult to apprehend. See in particular Sedgwick, *Between Men* 26–27.

5. See Fuss, *Inside/Out*, for a wide-ranging and useful bibliography of this important body of work.

6. This evacuation arises in part from the way Martin interprets Fiedler's discussion of homosexuality in *Love and Death* as "the situation of homosexuals in contemporary society" (*Hero* 13). "[H]ow painful it has been," Martin writes, "to see homosexuals' lives and artistic creations so abused. . . . *Love and Death* was important for gay people . . . it announced that we were there. . . . [but] it instantly . . . said, in effect, that we must be cured" (*Hero* 9). In reading *Love and Death* as evoking the presence of "gay people," Martin credits Fiedler with a conceptualization of sexual identity virtually absent from Fiedler's discussion of the bond, thereby too neatly packaging homosexual tensions, homoerotic desires, and homosocial masculine relations.

7. This revision of the closed economy of the phallic signifier is perhaps best demonstrated by Martin's graphic insistence that "[s]urely no one can read Melville without rejoicing in the verbal exuberance, in the sheer delight of handling words, of touching them, of rolling them around in the mouth, almost as if they were globules of sperm" (11–12). To contest patriarchal inscriptions of the phallus as instrument of domination and conquest is obviously a necessary political deployment, but Martin's equation of a benign masculinity with democracy's most radical potential, represented by the phallus as non(re)productive sexuality, offers a less aggressive but nonetheless wholly masculine representational body for the signification of America.

8. In an earlier piece, "Melville's Geography of Gender," I take Martin to task for his "failure" to adequately articulate the male bond in relation to feminist goals. That reading now strikes me as not simply faulty, but overly committed to constructing the masculine as a homogeneous entity. Martin's desire to begin to isolate differences among men, while needing to be further textured, does indeed have important consequences for feminism—as my own text has set out to explore. My rethinking of this earlier critique of critical discussions of interracial male bonding extends, as well, to Boone, whom I discuss shortly.

9. While the relationship of men and feminism did not simply appear in 1987 with the publication of *Men in Feminism*, edited by Alice Jardine and Paul Smith, this text has provided a focal point for many discussions in subsequent years. See Boone's response to this anthology, "Of Me(n) and Feminism," as well as the bibliography provided there. See also Robbins.

10. In "Ethnicity: Identity and Difference," Stuart Hall reviews the various developments in Western intellectual thought that have provided important challenges to the logic of identity, with its pretense toward a true or autonomous self. From Marx, we

understand "that there are always *conditions* to identity which the subject cannot construct" (11); from Freud, that the unconscious "destabilizes the notion of the self, of identity, as a fully self-reflective entity" (11); from Saussure, "that one is always inside a system of languages that partly speak us, which we are always positioned within and against" (12); and from Nietzsche, that "the end of the notion of truth" (12) implicitly decenters the tradition of Western rationality, undermining the possibility of identity as the product of an essential, logical truth.

11. Newfield's "The Politics of Male Suffering" offers an important rethinking of the singular association between aggressivity and patriarchal domination by analyzing the masochistic passivity of masculinity in Hawthorne's *The Scarlet Letter*. Such masochism he reads as supportive of patriarchal structures.

12. In his subsequent work on men's relation to feminism and to antipatriarchal politics, Boone overtly seeks out relations of power discrepancies among men as a way of circumventing the dire binary of sexual difference that underlies both his reading of quest literature and much feminist theory itself. In "Of Me(n) and Feminism," for instance, he critiques the ways in which "man" has been constituted "as a homogeneous entity" (18). While he makes no reference to his earlier work on the romantic counter-tradition, he does offer insights into the theorization of "man" that move in importantly new directions.

13. The very preoccupation in this country with the definitional contours of an American cultural or literary tradition in the past two hundred years attests to the ongoing struggle over the content of the sign that most invests us, as social subjects, with meaning. That this sign is a political as well as rhetorical production—and not simply a matter of essential being—is the theoretical framework governing recent debates in U.S. education around issues of multiculturalism. Here, the contestation over "America" is most vivid, as the debate pointedly questions the identifications and systems of economic and political alliance through which the narrative of America is being told. In a similar way, critical discussions about the literary canon pressure its historical point of view, questioning the subsumption of a variety of texts and cultural contexts into a unified and singular understanding of tradition. See especially Craige.

14. In *Blues, Ideology, and Afro-American Literature*, Baker explains, "Writing AMERICA in captials [sic] enables one to distinguish between an *idea* and what Edmundo O'Gorman describes . . . as a 'lump of cosmic matter.' As an idea . . . the sign AMERICA is a willful act which always substitutes for a state description. The substitution imposes problematical unity and stasis on an ever-changing American scene" (66).

WHITE LIKE WHO?

"AS THOROUGHLY BLACK AS THE MOST FAITHFUL PHILANTHROPIST COULD DESIRE"

Erotics of Race in Higginson's *Army Life in a Black Regiment*

CHRISTOPHER LOOBY

Nat Austern, In Memoriam

Camp-life was a wonderfully strange sensation . . .
—Thomas Wentworth Higginson, *Army Life in a Black Regiment*

War feels to me an oblique place . . .
—Emily Dickinson, *Letters of Emily Dickinson*

The "Bare Sight"

In war a society's constructions of its norms of manhood may be observed in their most vivid forms.[1] The American Civil War has the additional critical advantage of providing a context in which the crucial role of race in the construction of American masculinity is evident in all its complexity. Manhood in America is crucially dependent upon a dialectic of racial difference; categories of gender and sexuality are inextricably entangled with racial identities.[2] As the case of Thomas Wentworth Higginson, the abolitionist minister and radical activist who became the commander of the pioneer regiment of ex-slaves in the Civil War, will show, normative white manhood in particular is dependent upon a complex doubleness of attitude toward black manhood.[3] Black males, in white cultural discourses, are often feminized by virtue of their status subordination and by a host of racist denegations (stereotypes of childishness, simplemindedness, etc.), but at the same time, paradoxically, a hyperbolic masculinity is attributed to them by virtue of their mythic investment with phallic enormity, savage and uncontrollable lusts, and so forth.[4] This complex of projective fantasies, an imputed combination of masculine lack and masculine excess, constructs the black man as the contradictory Other of white masculine identity.[5]

The working-out of this masculine racial dialectic is powerfully present, in a particularly heightened form, in the experience of the black regiments of the Union Army during the Civil War, and it is dramatically legible in Thomas Wentworth Higginson's autobiographical account in *Army Life in a Black Regiment* (1869)[6] of his experiences as colonel of the First South Carolina Volunteers (later 33rd U. S. Colored Infantry). The United States Colored Troops enlisted free Northern blacks, freedmen, and escaped slaves under the command of white officers, and thus brought men of the different races into new and highly charged forms of intimate homosocial camaraderie:[7] what before had been, for most of these men, a matter of unconscious projection from a distance—the psychic intertwining of achieved masculine identity with racial fantasy—became now a matter of familiar contact in the physically energized all-male context of military order.

Opposition in the North to the use of black troops in the Union cause was, it is evident, basically an effect of deep racial prejudice, but the factor of gender anxiety in this prejudice should not be underestimated.[8] To admit black men into the army would be to concede them the status of *men*, to grant their manhood by virtue of their admissibility to the male homosocial institution that had the most direct indicative relation to male identity of all such institutions. Corporal James Henry Gooding, a volunteer in the Massachusetts 54th, one of the first regiments of free Northern blacks, wrote a series of letters to the New Bedford (Massachusetts) *Mercury* during 1863 and 1864, giving a first-hand account of his military experience. In one letter he quoted with evident approval a speech by Massachusetts Governor John A. Andrew, who claimed, at the ceremonial presentation of flags to the 54th, that "Today we recognize the right of every man in this Commonwealth to be a MAN and a citizen. . . . They go to vindicate a foul aspersion that they were not men" (Gooding 21). William Wells Brown, reporting on another speech by Governor Andrew, likewise emphasized the tribute Andrew had paid to the "manly" character of the black soldiers, the "qualities of manhood" they had evinced (149). In a late diary entry Higginson recorded a sermon given by Private Thomas Long of his regiment, who recalled the skepticism and hostility that they felt from white soldiers at the start of their enterprise, but which they had honorably "whipped down": "we lived it down by our naturally manhood . . . we have showed our energy & our courage & our naturally manhood" (WD Mar. 27, 1864).[9] Higginson's own final words in the "Conclusion" to *Army Life in a Black Regiment* similarly foreground this "gender moment": "It was their demeanor under arms that shamed the nation into recognizing them as men" (AL 251).

Frederick Douglass implicitly acknowledged that these were the stakes of the issue in a notable August 1861 editorial entitled "Fighting Rebels with Only One Hand," in which he decried the government's stubborn refusal to enlist black troops, even after four months of war and no major Northern victory. "Why does the government reject the negro? Is he not a man?" Douglass demanded. He went on to develop an unusual image of biracial national male embodiment that touched upon exactly the reason for the white resistance to black military enlistment:

> If persons so humble as we can be allowed to speak to the President of the United States, we should ask him if this dark and terrible hour of the nation's extremity is a time for consulting a mere vulgar and unnatural prejudice? . . . We should tell him that this is no time to fight with one hand, when both are needed; that this is not time to fight only with your white hand, and allow your black hand to remain tied. . . . While the Government continues to refuse the aid of colored men, thus alienating them from the national cause, and giving the rebels the advantage of them, it will not deserve better fortunes than it has thus far experienced. (qtd. in McPherson 164)

Douglass's radical fantasy of the nation's collective militarized male body is of a *corps* partly black and partly white (one hand belongs to one race, one hand to the other) and gaining *esprit* as an effect of such racial duality: the figure literalizes, as it were, the truth of American manhood as a structure essentially comprising both white and black, the races conjoined in a necessary mutual dependence.[10] When the War Department, a year after Douglass's editorial, finally authorized General Rufus Saxton, military governor of the Sea Islands in South Carolina, to raise five regiments of black troops there, a halting process was begun that would bring normative white masculinity into repeated crisis: its hidden foundation upon the denial of manhood status to black men would now be subverted, at least intermittently, although restored by a chronic panicked attempt to deny the black man's entitlement to masculinity.[11]

When President Lincoln, having reconciled himself to the military necessity of black enlistment, wrote in March 1863 to Andrew Johnson, War Governor of Tennessee, that the "colored population is the great *available* and yet *unavailed of* force for restoring the Union," he (unlike Douglass) had no thought of black men and white men sharing, as it were, a figurative national masculine body. On the contrary, he pictured the massed ranks of black troops as fearsomely Other, as fearsome *because* other—their dramatic *visual* difference (their color) constituting a large part, it seems, of their potential terroristic force: "The bare sight of 50,000 armed and drilled black soldiers upon the banks of the Mississippi would end the rebellion at once. And who doubts that we can present that sight if we but take hold in earnest?" (qtd. in McPherson 171). Douglass already agreed that blackness was a fearsome weapon. "One black regiment would be, in such a war," he wrote in May 1861, "the full equal of two white ones. The very fact of color in this case would be more terrible than powder and balls" (qtd. in Cornish 5).

Sharing Lincoln's and Douglass's fascination with the fearsome aesthetic of armed blackness—the expected military efficacy of colored troops' *visual* impact—was Thomas Wentworth Higginson, the New England abolitionist recruited by General Saxton to command the First South Carolina Volunteers. Higginson was a brilliant literary observer of the encounter between white men and black men in the context of military life's exacerbation of the contradictory structure of interracial masculine interdependence, and his memoir, *Army Life in a Black Regiment*, powerfully condenses what it seems necessary to call his proto-Mapplethorpean scopophilic attachment to the militarized black male body. Higginson's text takes great pleasure in the "bare sight" of black masculinity; like Robert Mapplethorpe's controversial photographs of black male nudes, collected in *Black Book* (1986), Higginson's representations engage in a compelling dramatization of the explosive combination of desire, identification, and scopic fascination that characterizes the white male gaze at the black male object.[12] By invoking Mapplethorpe in this connection, I hope to foreground the issues of race, politics, and the erotic gaze that are present in such a controversial fashion in the *Black Book* photographs, in the interest of making similar issues evident in Higginson's writing. Although it will be impossible here to do justice to the intricacies of these issues as they are present in Mapplethorpe's work,[13] I will come back to them explicitly at the end of the present essay, risking meanwhile (for the heuristic purpose stated) the anachronism and tendentiousness latent in my labeling Higginson "proto-Mapplethorpean."

I will be assuming, for the purposes of interpreting Higginson's black book, a modified Freudian account of the social structuration of erotic desires. The basic assumption is that men's sexual desires are originally relatively inchoate and indiscriminate, and may be directed toward either male or female objects (not to say nonhuman or inanimate objects). Socialization into normative manhood entails an elaborate erotic pedagogy, by virtue of which men's desires for women are permitted overt expression, even incited and rewarded, while their homosexual desires are variously prohibited and stigmatized, but also redirected in transformed fashion toward overtly nonsexual aims. Among the institutional venues of critical importance for this sublimation of homosexual desire is the military, where the *esprit de corps* or *ca-maraderie* of the group effectively absorbs and redirects the homoerotic energy that otherwise might find direct sexual expression.[14]

The military, among all such sublimating homosocial organizations in the general institutional apparatus of sublimation, enforces the most extreme, conflicted form of the structure of homosocial incitement/homosexual repression: the military context coercively *prescribes* the intensification of male-homosocial affective attachments, while at the same time it punishingly *proscribes* the physical expression of homosexual desires. It thus excites male-male emotional bonding to the highest pitch of intensity short of avowed homosexual love, and does so in circumstances of domestic intimacy, physical proximity, and a near total deprivation of privacy; but it exerts also the most punitive homophobic controls upon those incited attachments.[15] Into this volatile homosocial/homosexual environment—into the midst, as it were, of the grounding of masculine military valor in the dynamics of homosexual panic—the alliance of black soldiers and white officers in the United States Colored Troops overtly introduced the matter of race, which was, in fact, already covertly structuring those dynamics.

Higginson usually receives only a footnote in American literary history, for he is remembered today mostly for his dubious role as Emily Dickinson's "preceptor."[16] He deserves better, however, for he was a politically engaged intellectual and artist at the forefront of radical antislavery, labor, and feminist causes.[17] Born in 1823 into a formerly wealthy New England Brahmin family descended from first-generation Puritans, Higginson entered Harvard in 1837, just after Emerson delivered his famous and controversial address on "The American Scholar" to the Phi Beta Kappa Society. Higginson imbibed transcendentalism from, among others, his freshman Greek tutor, Jones Very; he also studied French with Henry Wadsworth Longfellow. Upon graduation he first became a tutor in a suburban school, then private tutor to three children of a widowed cousin whose somewhat advanced ideas of social reform began Higginson's moral and political radicalization. The next few years saw him immersed in philosophy and romantic literature as a nonmatriculated scholar at Harvard, and gradually drifting (with some resistance of his own, and some assistance from his second cousin Mary Channing, later to be his wife) toward social reform movements such as temperance, female suffrage, and, especially, abolitionism. Entering divinity school in 1844, he left it in despair the next year, but returned in 1846 with renewed hope that writing, preaching, and social action could be combined in a productive and satisfying career. He was forced to resign from the first pulpit he occupied after ordination, in

Newburyport, Massachusetts, having offended members of his congregation with his ardent abolitionism and his undisguised Free-Soil political work.

Continuing to speak, write, and campaign for Free-Soil politics following his resignation from Newburyport in 1849, he accepted the pulpit of a Free Church in Worcester, Massachusetts, in 1852 after much pleading from the congregation; having married Mary Channing soon after his ordination, he also supported her in her chronic invalidism. Mary did not disguise her lack of desire for children, and her preference, combined with her husband's solicitousness of her delicate health, probably led them to conduct their marriage relatively chastely. At the same time, Higginson was given to intense romantic friendships with other men, relationships that approached the limits of socially acceptable male-male attachment. This is just to say that Higginson's relationship to the normative institution of heterosexual marriage was not an entirely unremarkable one.[18]

Higginson had, of course, been deeply dismayed by the terms of the Compromise of 1850 and by the Fugitive Slave Act, in particular, and he was therefore prepared to undertake prompt action when, in 1854, the fugitive Anthony Burns was seized in Boston at the behest of his pretended owner, Col. Charles T. Suttle of Alexandria, Virginia. While a public meeting of anti-slavery activists was being held in Faneuil Hall and police attention was on that crowd, Higginson bought handaxes and led an assault on the courthouse to free Burns forcibly. The attempt failed, and Higginson suffered injury from a courthouse guard's cutlass, while another guard was killed by a bullet. But Higginson's militancy only increased following this failed rescue. The year 1856 found him in Kansas promoting free-soil emigration in the attempt to forestall that territory's emergence as another slave state. In 1858 he enlisted as one of the so-called Secret Six who backed John Brown's plan for inciting violent slave insurrection in the South. When the Harper's Ferry raid failed, Higginson was the only one of the six backers to admit and even proclaim his assistance to Brown's effort, resolved to face the consequences of his participation in the illegal scheme rather than flee or disclaim responsibility.

In 1860 Higginson began the serious study of military science, and formed a series of drill clubs, as well as taking fencing lessons and frequenting the gymnasium, in order to prepare himself for the coming conflict. Around this time, he also contributed numerous essays to the *Atlantic Monthly*, many of them treating the related subjects of male health, bodily fitness, and military heroism ("Saints, and their Bodies," "Physical Courage," "A Letter to a Dyspeptic" and its sequel, "The Murder of the Innocents," "Barbarism and Civilization," "Gymnastics," "The Ordeal by Battle"). Throughout these essays

Higginson worried that American men had become feminized and had suffered physical decay as a result of their civilization; he looked to athletics
and war as means of masculine reinvigoration. He also worried that "we pale
faces" lacked the courage naturally possessed by "Africans" ("Physical Courage" 732), and claimed that athletic exercise would restore to the overcivilized
white man "a little of the zest of savage life" possessed also by the "South-Sea
Islander" and the "Indian" ("Gymnastics" 285).

The racial envy characterizing Higginson's discourse of the male body
links it to another series of essays he published in the *Atlantic* at the same
time, which concerned the history of slave insurrections ("The Maroons of
Jamaica," "The Maroons of Surinam," "Denmark Vesey," "Nat Turner's Insurrection," "Gabriel's Defeat"). Higginson here made disparaging comparisons
between, for instance, the "effeminate, ignorant, indolent white community"
and the "infinitely more hardy and energetic" black population in Jamaica
("Maroons of Jamaica" 214), and he was plainly fascinated by the Scotsman
John Gabriel Stedman's love affair and marriage with the slave girl Joanna,
whom he met when sent as an officer of the Scots Brigade of the Dutch Army
to restore rebel maroons to slavery. Higginson noted that one result of Stedman's erotic encounter with the colonized Other was that he found upon his
return to Europe that white people's "complexions were like the color of foul
linen . . . when compared to the sparkling eyes, ivory teeth, shining skin,
and remarkable cleanliness" of the blacks he had left behind ("Maroons of
Surinam" 557).[19] The eroticization and aestheticization of the racial Other to
which Higginson responded in Stedman, and the invidious racial distinctions
he made between black manhood and white, as well as the general anxiety
he felt about masculine vigor and the general interest he took in male bodily
condition and appearance, were all densely compacted in his immediately
subsequent military adventures. Enlisting in the (white) Fifty-First Massachusetts regiment in 1862, he was appointed to the rank of captain; but just as this
group was about to receive its marching orders, Higginson accepted a surprise invitation to assume the command, with rank of colonel, of the (black)
First South Carolina Volunteers, the group that Higginson was later at pains
to establish as the first regiment of freedmen "mustered into the service of
the United States" (AL 263).

"A Divertisement of Men Alone"

An essential component of Higginson's affective response to army life was captured in a letter he wrote to his mother on October 13, 1862, when he described the all-male dancing that took place in the barracks at Camp John E. Wool near Worcester, Massachusetts, where companies of the Massachusetts 51st were drilling. It serves to remember how much of Higginson's adult life he chose to invest in one or another of the foundational homosocial institutions of his masculinist and largely patriarchal society (e.g., in addition to the army, all-male Harvard College, the exclusively male ministry, and abolitionist organizations that were rife with barely sublimated same-sex love)[20] following his adolescence and young adulthood in an otherwise all-female household. As we have seen, it is precisely these homosocial organizations, according to psychoanalytic theory, that function to convert potentially homosexual erotic desire into good fellowship, social feeling, benevolence, and cooperation. But as subsequent analysts have pointed out, the homosocial structure of patriarchy is forever congruent with, dependent upon, and at some risk of relapsing into its pre-sublimated, potentially genital-erotic form (Sedgwick, *Between Men* 83–96, *Epistemology* 182–88). And it is precisely in such institutions as the military barracks, the school dormitory, and the seminary that it is known to relapse in this way with some frequency and with occasional scandal.

When Higginson describes the men-only military balls at Camp Wool, then, it is only too easy to see the machinery of sublimation imperfectly at work:

> Camp Wool. Oct 13. 1862
>
> Dearest Mother
> One of the richest things we have here in the barracks is the dancing. About once a week the men have a regular ball; the bunks at the middle of the building are moved on one side, candles are stuck about the rafters, one or two kerosene lamps suspended, two fiddlers hoisted on a top bunk, with Stuart Brown our Adjutant in a red jockey cap to call the figures; & all take partners to the extent of 30 or 40 couples. The ladies are distinguishable by a handkerchief tied to the arm, & conduct themselves with much propriety, & as the younger & more delicate are naturally selected to act in this capacity, they sometimes acquit themselves with much grace especially in the rare intervals when a waltz or polka is permitted. But these airy side dishes seldom come in—the bulk

of the entertainment consisting of country dances of the very solidest description, thorough heel-&-toe work, & no flinching—as you wd.
think could you hear them over my head at this moment. I can remember nothing but the remotest of the Brattleboro public balls which can
in the least rival the amount of work accomplished; these perhaps being
even more concentrated since they not only begin at 7. but close at 9. The
men not yet being uniformed exhibit every variety of shirts and jackets,
while here & there the shoulderstraps of some lively young Lieutenant
flash through the struggling mass. My young Lieutenant Bigelow after
looking on for a while was swept away by the charms of the prettiest of
the Sergeants, named Fairweather, & I last saw him winding through the
"Portland Fancy" with her. (WL 760; LJ 174–75)

There is a kind of cautious obeisance paid here—in the text and, evidently,
in the army camp itself—to heterosexual convention: some of the soldiers
play women's roles and some play men's, so that each dancing couple is puta-
tively a cross-gender pair. Those chosen to act the female parts are "naturally"
the ones subordinate by virtue of youth or "more delicate" physical being
("delicate" may refer either to beauty or to relatively small stature). There is
no elaborate transvestism employed to create the cross-gender pretense, but
rather a single conventional marker of assumed gender difference, handker-
chiefs knotted to the arms of the feminized dance partners. These "ladies" are
said to "conduct themselves with much propriety" and to "sometimes acquit
themselves with much grace," which seems to hint at a certain amount of
mincing and flouncing (army "camp"?). Such theatrical femininity is only
intermittent, however, whether because the "younger & more delicate" are
resisting their coerced feminization or, alternatively, because the men, collectively, are less thoroughly committed to the masquerade of cross-gender
propriety than it might seem. The latter possibility is suggested by Higginson's claim that such "airy side dishes" as the waltz or polka are mostly
eschewed, the men preferring "country dances of the very solidest description," in which gendered partnering is less conspicuous and all the men can
dance energetically and athletically.

The curious reference to the "work accomplished" in these vigorous dances
is clearly a figure for the expenditure of physical energy by the soldiers in
their preferred athletic exertions. But it is also, possibly, a dissimulation of
the recreational and unproductive character of same-sex eros—a pretense
that homosex is, like heterosex, at least potentially a productive practice, a
form of "work." We may also read it as a metaphorical acknowledgment of

the socio-erotic work being done by this ceremonial conversion of homo-erotic potential into proper masculine camaraderie.[21]

Although Higginson, as he writes to his mother, claims to be hearing the noise of such a dance "over [his] head at this moment," that is, only at a near remove, he has obviously been a delighted eyewitness to this occasion only a moment before. His account of Lieutenant Bigelow's enchantment by "the charms of the prettiest of the Sergeants, named Fairweather" is very likely a displacement of Higginson's own fascinated stance toward the spectacle, for, as we will see, he is always exceptionally attentive to the beauty and charm of his soldiers, individually and collectively (see, e.g., WL 761, LJ 171, 173). The assumed innocence of Higginson's description of the erotic masquer-ade almost gives way, in the sentences that follow in the letter, to a more knowing, less dissimulating attitude toward the homoerotic potential of the scene, and to a more frankly libidinal investment in it on his own part, an investment betrayed textually (if not overtly acknowledged) by an infusion of excitement in the language he employs:

> Up aloft, on all the cross timbers of the roof along the upper row of bunks, are perched the spectators, all masculine; the dim lights glimmer on dusky figures & particolored caps, while the floor rocks with the per-petual surge of motion. Without the excitement of love or wine, with simply the pent up physical energy of two days inaction during a storm, they dance like Maenads or Bacchanals, their whole bodies dance, in the pauses between the figures they throb & tremble all over, as they keep time to the music; sometimes solitary uncouth men who are not danc-ing begin to whirl & frisk alone by themselves in corners, unnoticed & unnoticing. In each set there are mingled grim & war-worn faces, look-ing old as Waterloo, with merely childish faces from school, & there is such an absorption, such a passionate delight that one would say danc-ing must be a reminiscence of the felicity of Adam before Eve appeared, never to be seen in its full zest while a woman mingled in it. It is some-thing that seems wholly contrary to all theories of social enjoyment — & then to think that these New Englanders are called grave & unenjoying! In all the really rustic entertainments I have ever seen, from Katahdin to Kansas, there has been a certain stiffness wh. I supposed inherent & in-evitable; I remember a ball of lumbermen at *South Moluncus* or *Number Three* in Maine that was as joyless as Beacon St: & yet here in these barracks I have beheld a scene where the wildest revelry absorbed every person,

& yet without woman or drink. There is no swearing or vulgarity, they are too much absorbed for that; it is all perfectly real to them; they look forward to it & back upon it as any other young men might look on any other ball & no one could dream to hear them speak of it, that it is all a divertisement of men alone. (WL 760; LJ 175–76)

Higginson's immediate fascination with these surging, throbbing, and trembling men—with the contagious vibration of masculine bodily excitation—is for him at once a cause for some mild alarm (the "solitary uncouth men" who "whirl & frisk alone by themselves in corners" seem to register the possibility of illicit sexuality, solitary masturbation being the age's most familiar example of male erotic dissolution, although one whose danger lies as much in the other forms of depravity to which it may lead as in its own excess [Barker-Benfield 135–226; Moon 19–25]) and, conversely, for an answering reassurance (the dancing, faux-heterosexual couples properly ignore the solitary perverts).[22] But what of this "absorption" and "passionate delight," "zest" and "revelry" that are reminiscent, to Higginson's humming imagination, "of the felicity of Adam before Eve appeared," this elated dancing that would be spoiled by the intrusion of a woman? A "certain stiffness" is recalled as inherent in the usual heterosexual scenario; the "wildest revelry" is possible only in women's absence (and note the incidental linking of women and drink, as if both were artificial stimulants that interfered with the pure mutual absorption and ecstatic communion of the all-male carnival). Higginson's pleasure in discovering that, "wholly contrary to all theories of social enjoyment," men have more fun dancing among themselves, is patent.

Men-only dances are not guaranteed always to be so wonderful; other all-male dances previously observed by Higginson had been joyless, like rustic entertainments in general. But the male-female dance is written off entirely as hopelessly staid, not even potentially enjoyable. A few years earlier in an essay for the *Atlantic Monthly* recounting his first trip abroad (to the Portuguese island of Fayal, in the Azores), Higginson had described with unconcealed dismay the deadliness of the dancing at an evening party he attended: "The company perform their dancing with the accustomed air of civilized festivity, 'as if they were hired to do it, and were doubtful about being paid' " ("Fayal" 538). The later army-camp dance, however, was by contrast captivating in its ecstatic release of "pent-up physical energy." The unacknowledged transgressive potential of the all-male entertainment, alluded to in the admission that the dance's euphoria "seems wholly contrary to all theories of social enjoyment," is again hinted at in Higginson's claim that the event "is all perfectly real to them"—an assertion seemingly offered against an anticipated derogation of a same-sex dance as unreal, a derivation or simulation of the real, cross-sex event.

Higginson's final sentence in the letter is a model of ambiguous syntax: "no one could dream to hear them speak of it, that it is all a divertisement of men alone." Does this mean that when the soldiers speak of their dancing they no longer make any reference to the anomaly of its all-male composition—that their ordinary discourse no longer registers the absence of women as a lack, or betrays any sense that their amusement is different from and/or lesser (less "real") than a presumed norm of heterosexual sociability? Or, quite to the contrary, do the men, in the pronominal diction of their everyday conversations, so completely carry on the sustained fiction of heterosociability (as Higginson briefly did earlier in the passage with his single substitution of a feminine pronoun—"her"—for a masculine one in the reference to pretty Sergeant Fairweather, charmer of young Lieutenant Bigelow) that anyone who overheard them talking about it *would think*, not knowing the facts, that they *were* talking about male-female dancing?[23] Higginson's language allows either reading—that the men habitually preserve or discard the heterosocial alibi—and the textual ambiguity measures his own suspension between the alternatives.[24]

Higginson loved the army in part precisely for its approximation to a fantasized Eden before Eve intruded (although the logic of this astonishing figure is certainly opaque: Adam was, after all, *alone* before Eve came, and he wouldn't have had *any* partner—male or female—for his waltz; he would have necessarily danced like one of the solitary, uncouth men, "unnoticed & unnoticing"). At the same time, Higginson is acting out, here and elsewhere, a compulsion to reintroduce women into male homosocial/homosexual fantasies: in 1863, having transferred to the black regiment in South Carolina, he writes in his journal one day that he "tea'd with three schoolmistresses and it is quite bewildering; I had forgotten that there were so many women in the world" (LJ 185). Bewilderment shades into dismay: even three women seems like "so many," and the forgetfulness from which they have roused him registers as a dream from which he wasn't entirely happy to be awakened.

"The Color of Coal"

"I believe I have a constitutional affinity for undeveloped races," Higginson wrote on November 21, 1863, adding, however, that his fondness for those in this category was unmixed with "any of Thoreau's anti-civilization hobby" (WD 865; LJ 213–14). The affinity in question was, of course, chiefly with black folk, the "unsophisticated Africans" (WD 867; LJ 215) with whom he was in close daily contact. This "constitutional affinity"—its emotional character and deep affective charge—was evidently obscure to him, and difficult to conceptualize. Here, he frames it as simply one aspect of a more general attraction to all undeveloped, unsophisticated peoples—and adds, to buttress his implied claim that it's not a specific attraction to blacks, "I always liked the Irish & thought them brilliant" (WD 865; LJ 214). And he is at pains to distinguish his own affinity for blacks from what he implies is a romantic primitivism, a fixed prejudice against the forms of cultural development or sophistication associated with the civilizing process, a prejudice he attributes to Thoreau. It is plain that Higginson is hard pressed to know exactly how to think about his own xenophilia; hard put to find a way both to avow his love for the race to whose cause he devoted himself *and* disavow the erotic investment that informed that love.[25]

Higginson begins his memoir by appealing to darkness of skin color to establish the claim that the First South Carolina Volunteers were "the first slave regiment mustered into the service of the United States during the late civil war" (AL 27). There *had* been some colored troops previously raised in New Orleans by Major-General Butler, he concedes, but those were recruited from among that city's free population and were very light-skinned. "'The darkest of them,' said General Butler, 'were about the complexion of the late Mr. Webster,'" Higginson recounts with satisfaction (AL 27). Higginson's own regiment, on the contrary, "contained scarcely a freeman, [and] had not one mulatto in ten" (AL 27). Describing his responses upon first encountering some of his soldiers when he arrived in South Carolina, he writes that they "all looked as thoroughly black as the most faithful philanthropist could desire; there did not seem to be so much as a mulatto among them. Their coloring suited me . . ." (AL 33; this line does not, in fact, appear in Higginson's diary [see WD Nov. 24, 1862], although in *Army Life* it is quoted as part of a diary excerpt). The dark coloring of the soldiers continued to fascinate Higginson, and his remarkably candid recurrences to the topic of epidermal blackness are often revealing of his own largely stereotypical beliefs:

> Already I am growing used to the experience, at first so novel, of living among five hundred men, and scarce a white face to be seen,—of seeing them go through all their daily processes, eating, frolicking, talking, just as if they were white. Each day at dress-parade I stand with the cus-

tomary folding of the arms before a regimental line of countenances so
black that I can hardly tell whether the men stand steadily or not; black
is every hand which moves in ready cadence as I vociferate, "Battalion!
Shoulder arms!" nor is it till the line of white officers moves forward,
as parade is dismissed, that I am reminded that my own face is not the
color of coal. (AL 34–35; rather heavily emended from the original diary
[see WD Nov. 27, 1862])

This is a peculiar and crucial moment in the text of Army Life in a Black Regiment
and in Higginson's experience of the everyday phenomenology of visible
racial difference. He records the novelty of the encounter, the unfamiliarity
to him of the massed array of dark faces and hands, the strange and somewhat disorienting effect of the sight—so disorienting that he somehow can't
register it very accurately, can't even tell if the black soldiers are standing still
or not, as he could do with white soldiers. This seems to be because he sees
them only as a mass; at first, he says, "They all looked just alike; the variety
comes afterwards, and they are just as distinguishable, the officers say, as so
many whites" (AL 35). And soon enough it turns out to be true: "I find, first
their faces, then their characters, to be as distinct as those of whites" (AL 53).

The process of learning to distinguish one black face from another begins
with making distinctions between degrees of darkness: "some companies,
too, look darker than others, though all are purer African than I expected"
(AL 35). This initial discrimination between the darker and the not-so-dark,
however, is still not a distinction between individuals, but between one mass
of soldiers and another, between two companies with different average skin
tones. The explanation Higginson offers for the overall darkness of these men
is that the Confederates, when they evacuated the region, took with them the
house servants, among whom were most of the mixed-race slaves, "so that
the residuum seems very black" (AL 35). Degree of blackness soon enough
begins to help him to distinguish one individual soldier from another, but
this is evidently only because the lighter they get, the more the differences
in their features are visible to his eyes: although among his best soldiers—
those he distinguished as the bravest and most daring—many were mulattos,
as some (including Higginson himself, initially) might have expected, there
were still "others [who] were so black you could scarcely see their features"
(AL 232). The premium Higginson places on visible uniformity for purposes
of military spectacle thus leads him to prefer the darkest soldiers precisely for
(what is to his eyes) their indistinguishability.[26]

Higginson's increasing ability to make distinctions between lighter and darker skins (within what he takes to be the very restricted range of color among this "residuum") is always constrained, therefore, by his acknowledged *desire* ("philanthropi[c]") that they *be* "thoroughly black." He is a connoisseur of dark skin tones, and his tendency toward hyperbole when he lavishes adjectives on those skins is remarkable. The "extreme blackness" (*AL* 29) of one soldier's skin is exceeded by the "jet-black, or rather, I should say, *wine-black*" color of one Sergeant Prince Rivers, about whose complexion Higginson rhapsodizes: it is "like that of others of my darkest men, having a sort of rich, clear depth, without a trace of sootiness, and to my eye very handsome" (*AL* 73–74). Higginson's preference for his darkest men was, it appears, well known to his family: after his first brief visit to South Carolina to inspect the situation before accepting the offered commission in the black regiment, he returned home to announce his affirmative decision, whereupon a niece is reported to have exclaimed, "Will not Uncle Wentworth be in bliss? A thousand men, every one as black as a coal!" (*WL* 768; *WD* Jan. 19, 1863; cf. *AL* 74).

The bliss with which blackness filled him—blackness "blacker than ink" (*AL* 135), deep "inky" and "ebony" blackness (*AL* 167) especially—extended even to the fantasy of being blackened himself, losing his whiteness and becoming dark black. His claim, quoted above, that at daily dress-parade he routinely forgets "that my own face is not the color of coal" echoes his letter to his mother on November 28, 1862, in which he admonished her, "if I don't come home jet black you must be very grateful" (*WL* 770). Higginson's desires that his soldiers be as black as possible, that he forget (when among them) that he's not black, and that he might somehow actually become black himself, are all particular variations on a kind of fantasy upon which military *esprit de corps* thrives, a fantasy of selfless absorption into a powerful collective body. Like Robert Gould Shaw, colonel of the Massachusetts 54th, who reported in a letter that in choosing his subordinate white officers, their merits were discussed by asking "'does any one know whether he has enough nigger to him' or 'are his heels long eno' for this work?'" and whose self-reference in this context was to "I as a Nigger Col[onel]" (Duncan 289–90, 292), Higginson's decision to assimilate himself to the cause of black militarization was underwritten by a comparable nervously thrilled sense of racial assimilation (he, too, records that he and his fellow officers "commonly speak of ourselves as colored officers" [*WD* Apr. 6, 1863]). This desire has, no doubt, many obscure psychosocial sources, but the only one that is frequently and openly acknowledged by Higginson is an aesthetic preference: for purposes of military pageantry, precision drilling, and parading, visual uniformity is the effect he especially wants, and an indistinguishable array of dark bodies is particularly useful to Higginson's "seemingly fastidious interest in drill and discipline" (Edelstein 285) as a means toward achieving this effect.[27]

When, upon visiting the camp of a white regiment after about five weeks in his own camp, he "by good luck happened upon a review and drill of the white regiments," his happiness at chancing upon one of his favorite aesthetic gratifications was quashed by seeing among the white soldiers "that same absence of uniformity, in minor points" that he had noticed also among the white officers of his own black regiment (AL 64). He recalls that "it has cost much labor to bring [his white officers] to any uniformity in their drill" (AL 64), in contrast to his black enlisted men, who more readily drill with great uniformity of action. "It needs an artist's eye to make a perfect drill-master" (AL 64), but it also, it seems, needs soldiers whose innate talent for drilling is attributable to a racial character that paradoxically marks them as superior to whites in some inferior ways. "I have never yet heard a doubt expressed among the officers as to the *superiority* of these men to white troops in aptitude for drill and discipline, because of their imitativeness and docility, and the pride they take in the service" (AL 51). Since three-fourths of drill, on Higginson's account, "consist of attention, imitation, and a good ear for time," his docile, naturally mimetic, and intrinsically rhythmic black soldiers have a certain "superiority" in these respects; he concedes, however, that the other one-fourth of the practice of drill—"The application of principles, as, for instance, performing by the left flank some movement before learned by the right"—finds the black soldiers "perhaps slower than better educated men" (AL 52). Higginson qualifies his judgment ("perhaps"), and the ground of his invidious racial discrimination is explicitly the relative degree of *education* (rather than native intelligence) of black soldiers versus whites, but the implication that higher-level cognitive operations (such as abstract spatial manipulation) may exceed the native intellectual capacities of blacks is decidedly present nevertheless.

Higginson's patronizing attitude toward his "young barbarians" (AL 34) is manifest everywhere in the text: they are "this mysterious race of grown-up children with whom my lot is cast" (AL 41), they "seem the world's perpetual children, docile, gay, and lovable, in the midst of this war for freedom in which they have intelligently entered" (AL 51). Even when describing in retrospect, after his life with the black soldiers has ended, the ways in which his prejudices and expectations had been exploded and disappointed upon intimate contact with the racial object of his philanthropy, his love for them and his increased knowledge are mixed thoroughly with condescension. He had previously written an article "to show the brutalizing influences of slavery," and so "[he] was constantly expecting to find male Topsies, with no notions of good and plenty of evil. But [he] never found one" (*AL* 239, 232).[28] But if he now professes that he "cannot conceive what people at the North mean by speaking of the negroes as a bestial or brutal race" (*AL* 239) it is, patronizingly, only because of the "childlike absence of vices" among the blacks (*AL* 232). A rhetorical gesture of humility—"We, their officers, did not go there to teach lessons, but to receive them. There were more than a hundred men in the ranks who had voluntarily met more dangers in their escape from slavery than any of my young captains had incurred in all their lives" (*AL* 233)—and a flat claim of racial equality—"As to the simple fact of courage and reliability I think no officer in our camp ever thought of there being any difference between black and white" (*AL* 237)—do not erase the exoticizing racial fantasy that pervades the book. Plainly Higginson "had a kind of sahib complex," as one historian has written, adding that in general "an aura of pseudocolonial paternalism surrounded the 'Negro soldier cause' in New England" (Frederickson 171).[29]

The psychodynamics of desire and identification across racial lines are among the most interesting and vexing features of the book: Higginson's attempts to transpose himself, as it were, into the subject positions of the slave, the freedman, and the black soldier are often breathtaking, and just as often (or sometimes simultaneously) painfully awkward. For instance, Higginson writes, "I often asked myself why it was that, with this capacity of daring and endurance, they had not kept the land in a perpetual flame of insurrection. . . . It always seemed to me that, *had I been a slave*, my life would have been one long scheme of insurrection. But I learned to respect the patient self-control of those who had waited till the course of events should open a better way. When it came they accepted it" (*AL* 235; emphasis added). The blacks' patience must be made compatible with their courage; it must be made itself a form of courage. (This was a tall order: "if the truth were told," Higginson had written in 1861, "it would be that the Anglo-Saxon habitually despises the negro because he is *not* an insurgent, for the Anglo-Saxon would certainly be one in his place. Our race does not take naturally to non-resistance, and has far more spontaneous sympathy with Nat Turner than with Uncle Tom" ["Ordeal by Battle" 94].) So Higginson attributes the slaves' patience to a rational calculation of their chances of success given their penniless and unarmed condition; but he also attributes it to "the peculiar temperament of the races" (AL 235). And this vague racial essentializing around the questions of patience and courage brings him to this egregious (albeit ambiguous) passage:

> But side by side with this faculty of patience, there was a certain tropical element in the men, a sort of fiery ecstasy when aroused, which seems to link them by blood with the French Turcos, and made them really resemble their natural enemies, the Celts, far more than the Anglo-Saxon temperament. To balance this there were great individual resources when alone, —a sort of Indian wiliness and subtlety of resource. Their gregariousness and love of drill made them more easy to keep in hand than white American troops, who rather like to straggle or go in little squads, looking out for themselves, without being bothered with officers. The blacks prefer organization. (AL 236–37)

But for every such unfortunate, racially essentializing passage in the text, there is another deeply honorable one, like the scene in which Higginson leads an expedition up the Edisto River to Wiltown Bluff in enemy territory, where the landing party first sees "black dots" appearing in the meadows, which turn out to be the "human heads" of masses of slaves coming toward their "prospective freedom" (AL 166–67). With a modest confession of the inaccessibility (to him) of these black subjectivities, Higginson writes, "I wish that it were possible to present all this scene from the point of view of the slaves themselves" (AL 167). But he does not here attempt to occupy their point of view, or to speak for them; rather, he tactfully concedes that privilege to an aged black man whose recollections of a comparable scene of freedom Higginson had once recorded while the old man told his tale in Higginson's tent. This man's account, Higginson says, was "by far the best glimpse I have ever had, through a negro's eyes, at these wonderful birthdays of freedom" (AL 168). The scene is powerful, especially as the white officer's narrative voice fades, and it is then "the apparition of a black soldier" as the agent of liberation that creates in the old slave "an ecstasy of admiration" (AL 168). "'De black sojers so presumptious!'" the old man says three times. To which Higginson rejoins, "I inwardly vowed that my soldiers, at least, should be as 'presumptious' as I could make them" (AL 168). The arming of black regiments was a large-scale attempt to grant to members of the enslaved race some agency in their own liberation; Higginson's narrative is a similar experiment on a smaller scale, underwritten likewise by a belief that black agency was, at least initially, a gift conferred upon them by whites— "presumptious" blacks made so only by white authority.

"I Always Like to Observe Them When Bathing"

I want you to feel, as I, the sensation of being seen. For the white man has enjoyed for three thousand years the privilege of seeing without being seen. It was a seeing pure and uncomplicated; the light of his eyes drew all things from their primeval darkness. The whiteness of his skin was a further aspect of vision, a light condensed. The white man, white because he was man, white like the day, white as truth is white, white like virtue, lighted like a torch all creation; he unfolded the essence, secret and white, of existence. Today, these black men have fixed their gaze upon us and our gaze is thrown back in our eyes; black torches, in their turn, light the world and our white heads are only small lanterns balanced in the wind.
— Jean-Paul Sartre, Black Orpheus

Army Life in a Black Regiment is a somewhat discomposed book, with alternating stretches of retrospective narration (dating from 1869), edited diary entries from days in camp (Nov. 24, 1862, to Feb. 29, 1864), a discourse on and an anthology of Negro spirituals (chapter 9), and a series of various appendices. What formal coherence the book has is due to thematic continuities, and to some striking symmetries between different passages. One particular symmetry is of special relevance to the issues of the erotics of race and of the possible transpositionality of racial identities in Army Life in a Black Regiment. In chapter 2 Higginson writes in a diary entry of his accustomed voyeurism with regard to his soldiers:

> January 14. [1863]
> In speaking of the military qualities of the blacks, I should add, that the only point where I am disappointed is one I have never seen raised by the most incredulous newspaper critics, — namely, their physical condition. To be sure they often look magnificently to my gymnasium-trained eye; and I always like to observe them when bathing, — such splendid muscular development, set off by that smooth coating of adipose tissue which makes them, like the South-Sea Islanders appear even more muscular than they are. Their skins are also of finer grain than those of whites, the surgeons say, and certainly are smoother and far more free from hair. But their weakness is pulmonary; pneumonia and pleurisy are their besetting ailments; they are easily made ill — and easily cured, if promptly treated: childish organizations again. Guard-duty injures them more than whites, apparently; and double-quick movements, in choking dust, set them coughing badly. But then it is to be remembered that this is their sickly season, from January to March, and that their healthy season

will come in summer, when the whites break down. Still my conviction
of the physical superiority of more highly civilized races is strengthened
on the whole, not weakened, by observing them. (AL 72; rather heavily
emended from WD Jan. 13, 1863)

His disappointment with the black soldiers' physical being has to do with
their lessened military utility: their lungs are prone to illness, their suscepti-
bility attributed to "childish organizations." But if Higginson's belief in the
superior physical strength and endurance of "more highly civilized races"
is reconfirmed, his belief in the (possibly superior) beauty of black men is
evident. Their "splendid muscular development" is exaggerated to the eye
(and imaginarily to the touch) by the "smooth" fatty tissue that they, like the
South-Sea Islanders, are supposedly endowed with. The tactility implied by
the adjective "smooth" is involved with the simile that compares these black
men to another colored race, one that in the writings of some of Higginson's contemporaries (Herman Melville and Charles Warren Stoddard, for instance) had acquired and would continue to acquire associations with erotic
disorientation. Pacific Islanders, in nineteenth-century American literature,
were emblems of an innocent (childlike) homoerotic freedom.[30] Higginson's
fetishization of the blacks' skin here is notable not only for its sensual tactility
("smooth," "smoother," "free from hair"), but also for the way his failure at
this moment of close-up examination to attend to the *color* of their skin re-
focuses attention on its *texture*: for once, although he is obviously gazing from
a distance in rapt aesthetic/erotic contemplation, he does *not* concentrate on
the way color figures in the spectacle of their bodies, but focuses instead on
imaginary touch sensations (even while displacing his knowledge of these
sensations onto vicariating "surgeons").[31] The soldiers "look magnificently"
but they evidently feel even better.

    This scene is obviously one in which a version of the phenomenon we have
come to denominate the "male gaze" is operating:[32] Higginson's scopic agency
renders these black men the passive objects of surveillance, their implicit
feminization as objects of the gaze reinforced by the notation of their relative
hairlessness and by their attributed childlikeness. And having likened them
to Pacific island races he goes on, in the next paragraph, as he does elsewhere
also, to invoke another racial simile: their talent for warfare is due in part
to "an Indian-like knowledge of the country and its ways" (AL 73). Higginson will subsequently invert this scenario of the racial gaze in chapter 6, "A
Night in the Water," where, as we will see, *he* is now naked in the water and
his white body is looked over by a black soldier. This later chapter will find

him compared, in turn, to an Indian—a Choctaw—as if the fantasy of black-white racial transposition needed a third, intermediary term to effect it.

The inverted symmetry between the scene of Higginson gazing at the naked bodies of his bathing black soldiers and the later scene (to which I wish now to give extended attention), in which Higginson's wet, naked, white body becomes the object of the gaze of one of his black soldiers, is the most strikingly chiasmic realization in this book of the effort at imaginary racial transposition, at what might be called rhetorical blackface.[33] "A Night in the Water" is Higginson's account of a "personal reconnaissance by swimming" across the river toward a rebel camp in order to "ascertain the numbers and position of the picket on the opposite causeway" (AL 152, 153). His emergence from the river an hour or so later, his white body glowing in the moonlight, is a scene that culminates this strange, intense narrative of watery immersion and bodily transcendence.

The chapter begins with a striking, dreamlike image: "In the retrospect I seem to see myself adrift upon a horse's back amid a sea of roses," Higginson writes (AL 151). The scenic quality of this memory-phantasm is in keeping with his frequent return to the "picturesque" elements of his military experience (AL 32, 33, 138, 139, 163). The spectatorial attitude toward the soldiers is no doubt dictated, in part, simply by the circumstance of Higginson's often-mounted point of view: elevated above his soldiers on horseback, as well as by military rank and a host of other social distinctions (class, race, education, etc.), the collective mass of soldiers no doubt ordinarily appeared to him at some distance in stark patterned formations. The gaze in this opening sentence is notably doubled: the memoirist phantasmically "see[s]" his earlier self upon horseback, from which prior vantage point he was (implicitly) seeing the scene then before him, the "sea of roses."

The impacted visual thematics in the sentence are matched by its lamination of the visual with two other characteristically Higginsonian thematics, the fluid and the floral. The "sea of roses" here (another proto-Mapplethorpean detail) links up with the many exotic blooms that decorate this chapter and the entire text.[34] A military officer on horseback obviously does not usually survey a field of roses; he ordinarily surveys a field of soldier's bodies, the arrayed ranks of his subordinates. The substitution in this sentence of "a field of roses" for "array of black bodies" condenses the volatile and racialized erotic/aesthetic economy characterizing *Army Life in a Black Regiment*, an economy in which exotic flowers and black male bodies are transposable as objects of a fetishizing gaze. Racialist theory in Higginson's day ascribed "color" only to particular non-white races, and contemporary floricultural discourses, with their interest in the breeding of flowers for more and deeper color, likewise spoke of plant species as races that were to be eugenically bred. Higginson's substitution of "roses" for "black men" is thus the displacement of one type of race by another, one form of color by another, and (not incidentally) an illegitimate object of desire by a permissible one. It is thus not surprising that Higginson, having decided to undertake the swimming expedition that will be a sensual adventure as much as a military one, notes that when he rode out to the causeway "which thrust itself far out across the separating river, — thus fronting a similar causeway on the other side," along the way some "dewy Cherokee roses brushed my face" (AL 153): the erotically and racially charged sensual detail should alert us to the densely invested nature of the ensuing narrative of somatic exaltation and dissolution.

The water he then faced was "pale, smooth, and phosphorescent" (AL 153), and in order to keep his nocturnal mission secret, he told his soldiers, who stood guard like "black statues," that he was only going for a swim:

> I do not remember ever to have experienced a greater sense of exhilaration than when I slipped noiselessly into the placid water, and struck out into the smooth, eddying current for the opposite shore. The night was so still and lovely, my black statues looked so dreamlike at their posts behind the low earthwork, the opposite arm of the causeway stretched invitingly from the Rebel main, the horizon glimmered so low around me, — for it always appears lower to a swimmer than even to an oarsman, — that I seemed floating in some concave globe, some magic crystal, of which I was the enchanted centre. With each little ripple of my steady progress all things hovered and changed; the stars danced and nodded above; where the stars ended the great Southern fireflies began; and closer than the fireflies, there clung round me a halo of phosphorescent sparkles from the soft salt water. (AL 154)

During this swim Higginson seems suspended between intensified sensations of embodiment and disorienting effects of bodilessness, of dissolution into the "concave globe" or "magic crystal" of which he feels himself, in Emersonian fashion, to be the "enchanted centre."[35] Uncanny sensations are reported: "when some floating wisp of reeds suddenly coiled itself around my neck, or some unknown thing, drifting deeper, coldly touched my foot, it caused that undefinable shudder which every swimmer knows, and which especially comes over one by night" (AL 155). As he approached the opposite shore, the surface of the river "became smoother and smoother, and nothing broke the dim surface except a few clumps of rushes and my unfortunate head" (AL 156). The salience of his head distresses him, not only because it could betray his presence to Rebel guards who may be watching, but also because in these peculiar circumstances it becomes a metonym for embodiedness:

> The outside of this member [his conspicuous head] gradually assumed to its inside a gigantic magnitude; it had always annoyed me at the hatter's from a merely animal bigness, with no commensurate contents to show for it, and now I detested it more than ever. A physical feeling of turgescence and congestion in that region, such as swimmers often feel, probably increased the impression. I thought with envy of the Aztec children, of the headless horseman of Sleepy Hollow, of Saint Somebody with his head tucked under his arm. Plotinus was less ashamed of his whole body than I of this inconsiderate and stupid appendage. (AL 156)

This passage of, as it were, hyperembodiment (with its evident phallic-erectile and masculinist associations and its weird castrato fantasy) is quickly followed, after Higginson's brief approach to the enemy shore, by a seem-ingly thorough reversal, a fantasy of utter disembodiment.[36] Leaving the Rebel side, and fearful of observation, he "sank slowly below the surface, and swam as far as [he] could under the water" (AL 157). As a result of "absorbed at-tention first, and this immersion afterwards" (AL 157), when he rises to the surface he finds he has lost his sense of spatial orientation, and also his sense of time. He tries to navigate by the stars, and to aim for the causeway back on the Union side, but has no confidence in his sense of direction: "everything appeared to shift and waver, in the uncertain light" (AL 158).

The head here may also be taken as a metonym for the rational indepen-dence that is supposed to underwrite the white male's unique claim to civic individualism, his investiture with a share of political sovereignty—an in-vestiture powerfully reiterated in Higginson's case by his military office's obvious racial distinction. The fantasy of headlessness may thus register obliquely, with a particular racial inflection (cf. "my head is hard; I was fitted by nature to command a colored regiment" [WL 884; LJ 220–21]), something like the longing for ecstatic human communion (loss of separate selfhood) that Georges Bataille emblematized by the acephalic figure ("Sacred" 180).[37] The watery immersion here also figures an immediacy of bodily continuity with the physical world, a renunciation of the segregation of consciousness and animality that founds the classical conception of humanity: Bataille's aphorism, "every animal is in the world like water in water" (Theory 19) is an apt summary of the strategy governing Higginson's reclamation of the body, the somatic experiences, and the sexuality that he was required to renounce by a culture that equated white masculinity with disembodiment.[38] The excited crescendo of ethnographic, literary, and religious-historical associations — Aztec sacrificial rites, Washington Irving's headless American, and various martyred Christian saints conventionally represented iconographically by head held in hands (Denys, Oswald, Sidwell, Sigfrid, et al.) — emphasizes the mood of frenzied dissolution of identity.

Higginson's account of this disorienting passage — out of space, out of time — is also characterized intermittently by relative sensationlessness. But just as he begins to feel deeply worried by his somatic dislocation, he is abruptly returned to his body: "Suddenly I felt a sensation as of fine ribbons drawn softly down my person, and I found myself among some rushes" (AL 158–59). This return to embodiment and locatedness is in some ways deceptive, however: he fears he has drifted far above or below the causeway he was aiming for on the Union side (he can't even tell which it might have been — above or below) and will now be "compelled to flounder over half a mile of oozy marsh" to reach the shore (AL 158). (Reembodiment seems to mean dragging through muck.)[39] Worse, he fears for a moment that he may even have inadvertently turned and swum back to the Rebel shore.[40] Looking at the stars, he eliminates that possibility; but the alternative of crossing the "treacherous expanse of mud" with its "miry embrace" is to his mind only marginally preferable (AL 159):

> I can distinctly remember that for about one half minute the whole vast universe appeared to swim in the same watery uncertainty in which I floated. I began to doubt everything, to distrust the stars, the line of low bushes for which I was wearily striving, the very land on which they grew, if such visionary things could be rooted anywhere. Doubts trembled in my mind like the weltering water, and that awful sensation of having one's feet unsupported, which benumbs the spent swimmer's heart, seemed to clutch at mine, though not yet to enter it. I was more absorbed in that singular sensation of nightmare, such as one may feel equally when lost by land or by water, as if one's own position were all right, but the place looked for had somehow been preternaturally abolished out of the universe. At best, might not a man in the water lose all his power of direction, and move in an endless circle until he sank exhausted? It required a deliberate and conscious effort to keep my brain quite cool. I have not the reputation of being of an excitable temperament, but the contrary; yet I could at that moment see my way to a

condition in which one might become insane in an instant. It was as if a fissure opened somewhere, and I saw my way into a mad-house; then it closed, and everything went on as before. Once in my life I had obtained a slight glimpse of the same sensation, and then, too, strangely enough, while swimming,—in the mightiest ocean-surge into which I had ever dared plunge my mortal body. (AL 159–60)

The sudden appearance of a light gleaming from a ruined plantation building where his pickets were headquartered returns him quickly to sanity and reorients him to reality. Emerging from the river—in a passage that seems to recall Homer's account of Odysseus's naked supplication before Nausikaa, his need to establish his friendly intentions in order to receive clothes (vi)—he is immediately accosted by one of his statuesque black sentries, armed and wary:

> Suddenly, like another flash, came the quick, quaint challenge,—
> "Halt! Who's go dar?"
> "F-f-friend with the countersign," retorted I, with chilly, but conciliatory energy, rising at full length out of the shallow water, to show myself a man and a brother.
> "Ac-vance, friend, and give de countersign," responded the literal soldier, who at such a time would have accosted a spirit of light or goblin damned with no other formula.
> I advanced and gave it, he recognized my voice at once. And then and there, as I stood, a dripping ghost, beneath the trees before him, the unconscionable fellow, wishing to exhaust upon me the utmost resources of military hospitality, deliberately presented arms!
> Now a soldier on picket, or at night, usually presents arms to nobody; but a sentinel on camp-guard by day is expected to perform that ceremony to anything in human shape that has two rows of buttons. Here was a human shape, but so utterly buttonless that it exhibited not even a rag to which a button could by any earthly possibility be appended, buttonless even potentially; and my blameless Ethiopian presented even to this. Where, then, are the theories of Carlyle, the axioms of "Sartor Resartus," the inability of humanity to conceive "a naked duke of Windlestraw addressing a naked House of Lords"? Cautioning my adherent, however, as to the proprieties suitable for such occasions thenceforward, I left him watching the river with renewed vigilance, and awaiting the next merman who should report himself.
> Finding my way to the building, I hunted up a sergeant and a blanket, got a fire kindled in the dismantled chimney, and sat before it in my single

garment, like a moist but undismayed Choctaw, until horse and clothing could be brought round from the causeway. It seemed strange that the morning had not yet dawned, after the uncounted periods that must have elapsed; but when the wardrobe arrived I looked at my watch and found that my night in the water had lasted precisely one hour. (AL 161–62)

The "rising at full length out of the shallow water, to show myself as a man and a brother," that is, a male human being, draws the reader's attention to his nakedness and the visible genital evidence of his maleness. This sentence also alludes unmistakably to the utterance of the archetypal slave who appeared on countless abolitionist documents—posters, medals, etcetera. On these texts, the enchained, pleading slave is represented as asking, "Am I not a man and a brother?" (Yellin 58). Higginson thus subtly characterizes the moment of his emergence from the water and display of white maleness as, contradictorily, an assumption of solidarity with the black slaves and with the black soldier on guard who met him with the challenge.

If his naked body guarantees his return to recognized human status, and his emergence from the water is figured as an accession to a weird racial hybridity, visibly very white but rhetorically black-identified, Higginson's recognizable voice returns him to his proper identity and particular military status. His mock outrage at the sentry's performance of the ceremony of presenting arms is curious; it is at once calculated to demonstrate that, even in his dripping naked state, his charismatic presence compelled the soldier to acknowledge ritually his authority, but it is also crafted to give him an excuse to linger over his "utterly buttonless" condition.[41] Having "not even a rag to which a button could by any earthly possibility be appended," as he tells us with delicious redundancy, he finds that clothes do not make the man; having divested himself of clothes for his swim, and having had an uncanny out-of-body experience in the water, Higginson is anxious to reassure himself that his rank, race, and other features of his identity are inherent in his person after all, not detachable like clothes. After the experience of radical ontological insecurity—"that awful sensation of having one's feet unsupported"—Higginson is relieved to have his white man's body back again, a ground or support for the racial and social identity (not to mention its presumed ontological ground) that he had temporarily alienated.

Reaching the building in his naked state, he finally covers himself with a blanket, and waits there "in my single garment, like a moist but undismayed Choctaw, until horse and clothing" are returned to him. The panicky desperation of his claim to a natural, inherently superior, embodied identity coexists here with a last fleeting fantasy of identification with the Other (Choctaw), as if his whiteness and rank were not only a satisfaction he was happy to recover but also a burden he was reluctant to take up again immediately. The white officer who condescended to his black soldiers here fantasizes a radical trans-position of identities: himself as supplicant black slave, or as naked Indian. Higginson's particular white male body (recognized here by its Other) is pre-cisely his ticket back to the universal civic subjecthood reserved for members of his race, with its privilege of disembodiment; but in a nostalgic gesture toward the embodiment he was now shedding, as it were, he vicariously tries on the racial bodies of those debarred from the ambiguous privilege of bodily suppression. His willed self-divestiture, imaginary blackface masquer-ade, and antiphallic somatic adventure dramatize in intricately related ways the troubled, unstable construction of white masculine sovereignty.[42]

Higginson/Mapplethorpe

Under what conditions does eroticism mingle with political solidarity?
—Kobena Mercer, "Skin Head Sex Thing"

I have alluded to Robert Mapplethorpe's photographs of black male nudes sev-eral times in the course of this discussion of the erotics of race in Higginson's *Army Life in a Black Regiment* for several reasons: on the basis of the uncanny repe-tition in Mapplethorpe's pictures, more than a century later, of something like Higginson's construction of his soldiers as eroticized objects of a racialized and gendered gaze; because of the photographs' vigorous desublimation of the homoerotic subtext of Higginson's account of interracial male homosoci-ality; and also (more particularly) on the basis of their similar conjoining and metonymic substitution of exotic flowers and black nudes.[43] Mapplethorpe's pictures of black male nudes have been controversial. Kobena Mercer and Isaac Julien have argued that the images in *Black Book* "appropriate[d] elements of commonplace racial stereotypes to prop-up, regulate, organise, and fix the aesthetic reduction of the black man's flesh to a visual surface charged and burdened with the task of servicing a white male desire to look and, more im-portantly, assert mastery and power over the looked-at" (145). What Mercer and Julien found compelling but unsettling about these images was "the way they facilitate the public projection of certain erotic fantasies about the black male body" (141). More recently, Judith Butler has cited as "[p]erhaps the most offensive dimension of Mapplethorpe's work" its "engage[ment with] a certain racist romanticism of Black men's excessive physicality and sexual readiness," and she appears to regret that Jesse Helms attacked Mapplethorpe not for this offense but for his homoeroticism and obscenity ("The Force of Fantasy" 118–19). Peggy Phelan observes that "Mapplethorpe's aestheticization of and love for black men is complex," but she avers that he "makes use of a racist mythos which exploits the tropes of black male virility and appropriates the history of slavery" (45), and finally she judges that his "treatment of the racially marked body replicates the operative power of whiteness, politically and psychically" (47). If this were unequivocally true, one might, after all, expect Jesse Helms to like the pictures. Several years after the Mercer and Julien critique, when Mercer returned to the subject in another essay, he modified (and moderated) his criticism crucially, still holding that the photographs "inscribe a process of objectification in which individual black male bodies are aestheticized and eroticized as objects of the gaze," but arguing that they also possess a "radically polyvocal quality" that allows them both to "reinscribe the fixed beliefs of racist ideology" *and* to perform a "subversive deconstruction of the hidden racial and gendered axioms of the nude in dominant traditions of representation" ("Skin Head Sex Thing" 171, 181, 179, 181). Mercer achieves this ambivalence of judgment by virtue of having decided that it is not the case simply "that fetishism is necessarily a bad thing" (181). In other words, the objectification of the black body that once seemed baldly racist now seems ambivalently suspended between a gaze that despises its object and one that beholds it with reverence, awe, envy, and desire.

Mercer argues that in Mapplethorpe's photographs of black men "all references to a social, political or cultural context are ruled out of the frame," thus abstracting their images from history and fixing them essentialistically—and this judgment he has not revised (Mercer and Julien, "Race" 143; cf. "Skin Head Sex Thing" 171, "all references to a social or historical context are effaced by the cool distance of the detached gaze"). Contra Mercer, Thomas Yingling calls attention to the ways in which Mapplethorpe's pictures—by including explicit visual references to the history of racism and racial violence, as in *Untitled*, 1980, for instance (*Black Book* 54), in which the hooded figure seems to allude to lynching—"encod[e] some awareness of [their] own fetishistic practice" and are therefore not simply racist, but self-consciously *address* racism (20–21). The pictures of black men with flowers (e.g., in blackand-white, *Dennis Speight*, 1983 and *Ken Moody*, 1984 [*Black Book* 45, 85]; see also, in color, *Ken Moody*, 1984 and *Dennis Speight with Calla Lilies*, 1983 [*Perfect* 44, 45]) might be said to do the same thing: they critically *refer* to (rather than merely repeat) the history of orientalizing or exoticizing of black men, the customary assimilation of them to the natural and—by virtue of acknowledging that history without pretending that it is possible utterly to disown or transcend it—make it available for critique and transformation. Black Book is a catalogue of stereotypes, and in cataloguing the stereotypes it recognizes them as such (i.e., *as stereotypes*). In its formal composition (its sequencing of images, its juxtaposition of certain images, its repetition and modulation of certain kinds of images), it dramatically draws attention to the received conventions governing the representation of black men, and in doing so it does not merely promulgate such conventions but thematizes them and defamiliarizes them in ways that have made many people who have a stake in those conventions strikingly uncomfortable.

The claim that Mapplethorpe's pictures have a critical political dimension, however diffidently it is offered here, needs an extended analysis of Black Book to be made persuasive.[44] A brief comparison might be helpful here, however. The theatrical artifice of Mapplethorpe's Isaiah, 1980 (Black Book 23), a model posed in a studio holding a bamboo spear and with an animal skin draped over his shoulder (Figure 1), *thematizes* the racialist fantasy that (for instance) merely *informs* the uncannily similar 1841 portrait of Cinque (Honour 158; also McElroy 34), painted on commission by Nathaniel Jocelyn for the abolitionist leader Robert Purvis (Figure 2). The depiction of Cinque, who led the slave mutiny on the Amistad in 1839, places him in an imaginary West African landscape, renaturalizing him (as it were) by taking him away from the American scene of his political rebellion. Certainly it locates him in a "context" of the kind that Mercer finds missing in Mapplethorpe's photographs, and perhaps it anticipates Cinque's eventual return to Africa following his acquittal by the United States Supreme Court. In Jocelyn's painting, the spear is presented as an authentic native African implement; in Mapplethorpe's photograph it is plainly a studio prop in a white fantasy. I would say that it is precisely the *decontextualization* of "Isaiah" and his weapon that makes Mapplethorpe's critical point: this image is and avows itself to be a product of conditions of artistic and ideological production that obtain in New York City in 1980, rather than an image that pretends to record a figure and circumstances that belong naturally together in any real historical setting.[45]

I would emphasize the phenomenon of interpellated desire that characterizes these pictures: Mapplethorpe's photographs coercively install the viewer in the position of the xenophilic white male homosexual desiring subject, whose attraction to the black male body cannot help but be a guilty one—a desire contaminated in some degree by the white supremacist imaginary's construction of that object. (The way Mapplethorpe's photographs turn the

Figure 1. Isaiah, 1980. (Copyright 1980 by The Estate of Robert Mapplethorpe)

viewer gay is probably an important source of their shattering power and scandalous odor.) It may seem bleak to hold such contamination of desire to be inevitable, but this strikes me as a necessary implication of the under-standing that erotic desire is socially and historically constructed. But if the white male subject's desire for black male flesh cannot ever escape entirely from the ideological inscriptions of the history of white racism, that doesn't render such desire useless for more utopian purposes. The whole history of the dependence of American white male identity upon an ambivalent structure of fantasy with regard to black men—the simultaneous overestima-tion/denigration of black manhood—is sedimented in the intimate experi-ence of white men's (homoerotic) desires for and (homophobic) disowning of their desires for black men. That history is certainly one to be regretted in many respects, but it cannot be easily dismantled (and certainly won't be

Figure 2. Cinque, by Nathaniel Jocelyn, c. 1840, oil on canvas. (New Haven Colony Historical Society)

dismantled if left unexamined), and therefore we must hope that it may be transformed and redeemed.

It is obvious enough that while Higginson's enchanted scopophilic relationship to his soldiers nourished his radical political commitment to the cause of their emancipation, the gaze embodied in Mapplethorpe's photographs has no such directly political translation. As Arthur Danto has put it, "It is difficult to suppose that Mapplethorpe had any particularly well-formed political views. He was not an activist" (325). It is easily supposed, on the contrary, that one view Mapplethorpe might well have had was that sex ought not to be held to any very strict standards of political virtue.[46] His photographs of black men cumulatively amount to a brazen refusal to submit his own erotic predilections to any political censorship, or to apologize for an organization of sexual desire that found racial difference to be one of its key structuring elements. Mapplethorpe's *Self-Portrait*, 1981, of himself giving a blow job to a black penis (*Mapplethorpe* 123), like the more famous *Self-Portrait*, 1978, of himself with a bullwhip up his ass (*Mapplethorpe* 47), sufficiently manifests his unrepentance. In drawing attention to the similarities between Higginson and Mapplethorpe, I am not trying to confer on Mapplethorpe the political virtue that Higginson exhibited in his courageous antislavery activism, nor am I seeking to justify or forgive Higginson's erotic gaze at the black male body by showing (in an ends-justify-the-means fashion) that it issued in progressive political commitments. That gaze needs no justification or forgiveness; in itself it is ethically and politically neutral. On the contrary, its condemnation (in my view) would need, like the ostensibly antiracist condemnation of Mapplethorpe's purported "racism," something more than the hasty moralistic appeal that has largely underwritten the latter.

Higginson's deeply felt and politically effectual desire for/identification with his black male subordinates was certainly grounded in habits of objectification and aestheticization of their bodies. (It's worth asking how objectification got such a uniformly bad reputation. Desire intrinsically depends upon it.[47] In any case, I agree with Victor Burgin that it is a critical mistake "to equate a putative 'masculine gaze' [or, I would add, a 'white gaze'] with 'objectification'" and that it is unfortunate that so often in the wake of Mulvey "'objectification' is named only in order to be denounced" [220].) Under the conditions of crisis in the period of the Civil War, Higginson shows us not only how eroticism mingles with cross-racial political solidarity. *Army Life in a Black Regiment* illustrates, more importantly, the "operative continuities between political sympathies on the one hand and, on the other, fantasies connected with sexual pleasure," "the extremely obscure process by which sexual pleasure *generates* politics" (Bersani 206, 208). Higginson shows us how political solidarity across racial boundaries may be grounded in an erotics of race that we can trace, ironically, to sources that are colored, as it were, by the history of racial oppression.

Notes

1. For an acute feminist account of the Western philosophical construction of warfare as a manly pursuit see Lloyd; also Pateman 49–51. Theweleit's *Male Fantasies* is relevant, and has been richly suggestive for the present essay; the task of discriminating those aspects of his analysis that are generalizable to all military formations

and those that are specific to German fascism cannot be undertaken here. See also Barker-Benfield 207.

2. Hernton writes in his study of the "sexualization of racism in the United States" that "from the era of slavery to the present . . . all race relations tend to be, however subtle, sex relations" (6). Berlant (citing Spillers) suggests that "American genders are always racially inflected" (111).

3. My central concern in the present essay is with Higginson's experience of his whiteness and maleness in relation to his black soldiers, so my emphasis is consequently on the meaning of blackness for white men. I share with Richard Dyer a wish "to try to make some headway with grasping whiteness as a culturally constructed category" (141), and especially masculine whiteness, rather than assuming it as an unmarked norm. Of course, the risk here is that such a focus may inadvertently reinstate the norm and remarginalize women and people of color. Toni Morrison's essay on "whiteness and the literary imagination" is exemplary in the direction it gives to the attempt to understand whiteness, its emergence from a web of "longing" and "terror" in the face of "an Africanist other" (17, 16). See also Michaels. In this connection it is worth noting also Allan Gurganus's remarkable collection of stories, White People. Since I have so far found no documents that represent in any depth the perspectives of the black soldiers in Higginson's regiment themselves, I'd like at least to direct attention to the remarkable collection of letters from black soldiers in other regiments recently edited by Redkey. And Susie King Taylor, a former slave who served as a laundress in Higginson's regiment, provides in her memoir Reminiscences of My Life in Camp with the 33rd U. S. Colored Troops, Late 1st South Carolina Volunteers (1902), to which Higginson wrote a brief introduction, what may be the only extant account, however elliptical, by an African American of the First South Carolina Volunteers.

4. Fanon's is, of course, the classic exposition. This contradictory fantasy is instantiated, in a particular manner that is relevant to Higginson, in the stereotypical nineteenth-century figure of the black urban dandy, familiar on the blackface minstrel stage, in lithographs, and in other public media. This "effete but potent" (Lott, Love and Theft 25) dandy figure, representing (attempted) cultural assimilation, and commonly called Tambo, was contrasted with the emasculated rural plantation Negro figure of Sambo. If the dandy, as I argue elsewhere, eventually forms a constituent part of the emerging social type of the homosexual in America, in a long process of accretion that joins together the bachelor, the masturbator, and other sex- and gender-dissident types into a composite figure (Looby, "Bachelorhood"), then it is crucial to my argument about the central role of race in the construction of American masculinity that the most conspicuous version of the dandy in American popular culture was the black dandy, whose race and class transgressions (his peculiar appeal had to do with the comedy of a black man's dressing and acting like an upper-class white person) seem to represent, metonymically, a vague sexual transgression. That the black dandy was nominally coded as heterosexually aggressive (inclined to think he could pursue white women) only, to my mind, makes explicit in a displaced fashion the

specifically *sexual* danger he embodied. Thus when Higginson in *Army Life in a Black Regiment* credits his soldiers with possessing a "very courteous" demeanor toward one another, but immediately qualifies this observation by adding that their courteous manners possess "none of that sort of upstart conceit which is sometimes offensive among free Negroes at the North, the dandy-barber strut" (50–51), he is calling upon a familiar stereotype with its salient racial-erotic connotations and manifestly defending against its appeal. "This is an agreeable surprise, for I feared that freedom and regimentals would produce precisely that," he continues (51). Regimentals are dress uniforms; it is as if Higginson feared that giving them fancy clothes would induce in them the kind of attitudes that Stowe represented notably in the character of Adolph ("a highly-dressed young mulatto man, evidently a very *distingué* personage, attired in the ultra extreme of the mode, and gracefully waving a scented cambric handkerchief in his hand" [254]), the uppity and vaguely homoerotic manservant of the "poetical voluptuary" (253) Augustine St. Clare (on this see Foreman). Another such defensive moment in *Army Life*, which links up with the invocation of the black dandy figure via the trope of dress, comes when Higginson suddenly catches himself fussing too much about prissy details of camp housekeeping, how he likes to keep his men all "perfectly *soigné* in all personal proprieties" and so forth, and concludes abruptly that "[o]f course, if you dwell on them only, military life becomes millinery life alone" (218). An 1829 etching depicting the black dandy can be seen in Honour (Part 2, 59). See also Pieterse 134 and Lott, *Love and Theft* 131–35.

5. Bhabha's is now a standard account of the process of constructing the Other as "a complex, ambivalent, contradictory mode of representation, as anxious as it is assertive" ("The Other Question" 22). For a brief genealogy of the term *Other* and its prestige in current academic discourse see Harpham 6–9.

6. Citations to Higginson's *Army Life in a Black Regiment* will be abbreviated *AL*.

7. On "homosocial" see Sedgwick, *Between Men* 1–5.

8. A valuable study of white working-class racism in the North, one of the few works to examine critically the "construction of identity through otherness" in the culture of "whiteness" (Roediger, *Wages of Whiteness* 14, 13), admirably details the mutual determinations of class and racial identities, but doesn't say much (as one reviewer pointed out [Glickman 209]) about the co-determination of both by gender categories. See Cullen for an account of African American men's gendered stake in the Civil War and military service.

9. Where I have been able to examine Higginson's War Diary in manuscript I will quote the text from that source, identifying it by the abbreviation *WD* with the Houghton Library's stamped reference number for those parts that are extant in Higginson's autograph manuscript leaves, and the date of the entry for those parts that are available only in his sister's copy.

10. "Totality of existence comes for the army only at the moment in which it links to its destiny the life of each of those whom it unites into a single aggressive body and a single soul" (Bataille, "Structure" 142).

11. The available histories of the black army regiments (I. Berlin, W. W. Brown, Cornish, Glatthaar, Quarles) detail the ongoing problems between Negrophobic officers and their colored troops, and between white army regiments and the black soldiers they despised but were sometimes forced to cooperate with. These historians are not, as a rule, alert to the gender issues involved.

12. Important statements on race and the politics of the gaze may be found in Gaines, "White Privilege"; hooks, *Black Looks*; Mercer and Julien, "Race, Sexual Politics"; and Mercer, "Skin Head Sex Thing."

13. I take up these issues in a fuller way in "Race and Eros in Mapplethorpe's *Black Book*."

14. In *Group Psychology and the Analysis of the Ego* Freud argues that artificial groups such as the church and the army are held together by love relationships, emotional ties that derive from (are an expression of) "sexual love with sexual union as its aim" (29); in such groups, however, instinctual libidinal impulses are "diverted from this aim or are prevented from reaching it, though always preserving enough of their original nature to keep their identity recognizable (as in such features as the longing for proximity, and self-sacrifice)" (29–30). "It seems certain," he later specifies, "that homosexual love is far more compatible with group ties [than heterosexual love], even when it takes the shape of uninhibited sexual impulses—a remarkable fact, the explanation of which might carry us far" (95). These are the elements of the psychoanalytic theory of sublimation, a theory that, as Laplanche and Pontalis point out, only exists in a "somewhat undeveloped" state in Freud's writings (*Language* 432). One would wish to quarrel first off with the biologistic assumption that sexual energy is original and its desexualized form a secondary derivation from the original form; Freud's description of the "plasticity" of the sexual instincts, "their capacity for altering their aims, their replaceability" (*New* 86) hints at a better theory, one that doesn't privilege one expression of desire (genital, object-directed, "sexual" in the narrow sense) over any others but treats them as all potentially transmutable into one another. Thus, since Higginson's homosexual love for his soldiers probably (I conjecture on the basis of his evident prudery and the cultural taboo on same-sex and interracial physical sexual practices) did not find a narrowly sexual (genital) expression, it therefore likely contributed in sublimated form (in the manner Freud described in other texts) to his "particularly active share in the general interests of humanity" ("Psychoanalytic" 164). The suggestion in *Group Psychology* that uninhibited, physically expressed homosexual love is compatible with strong group ties is somewhat at odds with Freud's usual claim that it is precisely the *sublimation* of such desires—their deflection from sexual objects, diversion to fresh uses—that enables them to contribute their energy to "the normal social relationships of mankind" ("Psychoanalytic" 164). (On homosexual sublimation see also Freud, "'Civilized'" 28 and "Certain" 169–70.)

15. Sedgwick's analysis of the homophobic structuring of relations between men in public heterosexual-normative society is assumed here *tout court*. See *Between Men* and *Epistemology*. See especially her brief remarks on the armed services in *Epistemology* 186.

See also Theweleit (2: 339): "thou shalt love men, but thou shalt not be a homosexual."

16. Despite his contemporary reputation and his central institutional role as editor and journalist, Higginson is mentioned in a recent authoritative survey of New England literary culture almost without exception only in conjunction with Dickinson (see Buell). On Higginson's role in Dickinson's life see Wolff, especially 249–59; see also St. Armand, Emily Dickinson 181–217 and "Fine." Biographical information in the following paragraphs and throughout is derived from Edelstein, M. T. Higginson, Meyer, Wells, and E. Wilson.

17. Higginson turned after the war decisively from antislavery to feminist reform causes, and suffered a different sort of stigma as a result; William Dean Howells in a letter to Charles Dudley Warner in 1874 referred derisively to Higginson (who had in 1872–73 been an associate editor of the Woman's Journal, a publication supporting the principles of the American Woman Suffrage Association, and with whom Howells had long had an edgy relationship) as "Lady Wentworth Higginson." See Howells 54.

18. Higginson's second wife observes in her biography that the letters (from which she prints excerpts) between her husband and his college friend, the South Carolinian William Henry Hurlbut, were "more like those between man and woman than between two men" (M. T. Higginson 125). In a letter to his mother in 1848, Higginson said Hurlbut was "like some fascinating girl," and he frequently praised Hurlbut's appearance: "a true Southerner, the best sort—slender, graceful, dark, with raven eyes and hair," "so handsome in his dark beauty that he seemed like a picturesque oriental" (qtd. in Edelstein 81, 64, 313). Referring to Hurlbut, Higginson observed, "I never loved but one male friend with passion—and for him my love had no bounds—all that my natural fastidiousness and cautious reserve kept from others I poured on him; to say that I would have died for him was nothing" (M. T. Higginson 126). Martin discusses Hurlbut's fascination for the novelist Theodore Winthrop, who fictionalized him in Cecil Dreeme (as Higginson also did in his only novel Malbone), in the context of nineteenth-century ideas of romantic friendship ("Knights-Errânt" 179–80). For more on male romantic friendship in nineteenth-century America, see Crowley.

19. Stedman was a frequent reference point for Higginson during his army life. As he approached the Sea Islands he wrote in his diary, "The shores were soft, though low & as we steamed up to Beaufort on the flood tide this morning, it seemed almost as fair as the canal between whose banks Captain Stedman floated into lovely Surinam" (WD Nov. 24, 1862). Quoting this passage in Army Life Higginson edited it slightly (AL 33). Pratt discusses Stedman's transracial love affair as "a romantic transformation of a particular form of colonial sexual exploitation" (95) in a section of her aptly titled chapter on "Eros and Abolition" (90–102). Compare Higginson in a 26 June 1863 letter to his mother: "All white soldiers look dirty, whether they are or not, from the sunburn & the beard, whereas my men's complexions are the best possible to hide it; a shiny black skin always looks clean. . . . Then the artistic effect of the line of white officers against the sombre & steady background is very good. Any artist would prefer to hv. his soldiers black" (WL 809; LJ 208). Where I have been able to examine Higgin-

son's letters in manuscript I will quote the text from that source, identifying the War Letters by WL with the Houghton Library's stamped reference number (as I did with the War Diary; see note 9 above). Where a passage has also appeared in the selective edition of Higginson's *Letters and Journals* I will give a citation for convenience to that source also, abbreviated LJ.

20. Yacovone's discussion of romantic friendship among male abolitionists is pertinent here, although marred by its nervous attempt to establish the purity of such relationships, to preserve them from "the suspicion of homoerotic intent" (94). His polemic against gay studies for its willingness to consider the homosocial and the homosexual as overlapping on a continuum leads him to claim even that it is a mistake to "assum[e] homoerotic desire or intent" in *Whitman* (239 n. 40)! Hatt's brief remarks on Higginson are interesting: "It would be easy to overlook the sexual resonances of, say, Higginson's remarks about the pleasures of watching his black bathing beauties; it would be similarly easy, and similarly historically mistaken, to predicate an erotic charge in looking that represents homosexuality, whether latent or not" (28). Hatt prefers to "avoid the trap of discussing homosexuality" (31)—although he claims not to "subscribe to the radical social constructionist view of homosexuality as historically incoherent before the rise of sexology in the late nineteenth century" (35 n. 33)—by sticking to the term *homoerotic*, which designates for him "a desire between men that can be conceived as something other than an ostensible self-evident homosexuality" (31). I don't entirely follow Hatt's reasoning.

21. For an account of another Union Army ball featuring cross-dressing, held by some Massachusetts troops stationed at Brandy Station, Virginia, see Mitchell 71–72. One soldier's letter home reported that the "boy girls" (soldiers, particularly drummer boys, dressed as women) were "so much better looking" than the few "real women" present that the latter left the ball. The feminized men in fact "looked almost good enough to *lay* with and I guess some of them did get layed with," he continued. "I know I slept with mine." Mitchell avers that this probably referred "not to some homosexual activity" (72), but homosexual activity does seem to be the plain sense of the thing.

22. Near the very end of his service, Higginson wrote in his diary of "the most tumultuous 'shout' I ever remember," so enthralling that "every white spectator's foot came soon into play," for "it is impossible for any one who has an ear not to partake the rhythmical excitement." In this case, "[i]n all corners of the room the people who were squeezed out of the circle were jerking & footing it by themselves," but no stigma here attaches to their solitary dancing (*WD* 926).

23. Higginson's exchange of gendered pronouns makes him a practitioner of what he elsewhere identified as his comical soldiers' "usual head-over-heels arrangement of their pronouns" (*AL* 192), particularly noticeable to him in their spirituals; registered also, however, when one of his men appealed to him for approval of a marriage that the soldier's captain had advised against on the grounds that the woman had seven children whose father was also a member of the regiment. " 'Cap'n Scroby [Trow-

bridge] he acvise me not for marry dis lady, 'cause she hab seben chil'en. What for use? Cap'n Scroby can't lub for me. I mus' lub for myself, and I lub he.' I remember on this occasion 'he' stood by, a most unattractive woman, jet black, with an old pink muslin dress, torn white cotton gloves, and a very flowery bonnet, that must have descended through generations of tawdry mistresses" (*AL* 243). Higginson's intermittent misogyny seems to coalesce here with his momentary enchantment with the prospect of a marriage between he and he. The cross-gendering of pronouns also draws his attention on 7 Jan. and 25 May 1863; he remarks at the latter place, "I get so accustomed to hearing the use of he & his for she & hers that I insensibly fall into it myself." This is a complicated moment in Higginson's career of imaginary racial relocation and this career's intersection with questions of gender, for here assimilating to black consists in falling into racial habits of gender confusion.

24. This dance took place in the white camp in Massachusetts, but amateur transvestite entertainments were not absent from Higginson's social life in camp in South Carolina. An excerpt from his entry for 28 Dec. 1863:

> On Christmas Evening there was a little party at Gen. Saxton's which went off very pleasantly.—charades, games, music, jugglery &c. It was odd in the charades to see what I have often noticed, the impossibility of judging who possess dramatic ability. Capt. Saxton the mildest & timidest of men was more free & easy in his own, while Mrs. Lander who never before saw a charade, but was bred to the stage from childhood, was seriously embarrassed by timidity— though awkward she never could be. This interested me for I remember in my essay on Physical Courage to have chronicled the same thing about some eminent English actress.—Another surprise was the success of Gen. Saxton & wife in interchanging characters. She the smallest woman I ever saw, almost, appearing as a Lilliputian officer & he as a strong minded wife. Their costuming or "make-up" was admirable & when she [he] finally caught him [her] up in her [his] arms for protection & ran out of the room the applause was enthusiastic. (*WD* 870; brackets present in original)

In the mentioned essay on "Physical Courage," in illustration of his claim that many people's courage is dependent upon habit, and is utterly lost in the face of novel dangers, Higginson had indeed mentioned "that Mrs. Inchbald, the most fearless of actresses, was once entirely overcome by timidity on assuming a character in a masquerade" (731). That is, she could readily learn a role and play it in public on stage, but in private company when asked to improvise she was overcome by stage fright. The implicit analogy here between stage acting and the performance of military bravery is one that links up with Higginson's general interest in military spectacle, and his sense of the army as a venue for role-switching. The possibility of transvestism seems to be on all minds: Higginson records a "droll" moment during his occupation of Jacksonville when his soldiers are aroused because "a white man, in woman's clothes, has been seen to enter a certain house,—undoubtedly a spy. Further evidence discloses the Roman Catholic priest, a peaceful little Frenchman, in his professional apparel" (*AL* 117). In a prewar essay Higginson had published anonymously in *Putnam's*, he wrote in the voice of a woman who sought to reclaim her physical health by undertaking a hiking trip—a "feminine expedition" in "Bloomer dresses"—in Maine ("Going" 242). In a letter of Mar. 20, 1864, Higginson reports that the previous night the Adjutant "came in with a handsome young officer in new uniform—really very handsome—who turned out after a while to be Mrs. Dewhurst. . . . Almost all were entirely deceived & I shld. certainly hv. been, but for a hint I overheard" (*WL* 885). He writes in his diary that one day he and another officer were reminiscing about "some of the funny things" they remembered from their Edisto expedition, among them "the little [slave] boy with no rag of clothing except the basque waist of a lady's dress, wrong side before, with long whalebones perceptible" (*WD* 922), and very casually he mentions in a diary entry from near the end of his service that one night they had "a dance in the parlor, with a capital fiddler from the regiment & one officer acting as lady" (*WD* 923). One of the more enigmatic episodes of identity-switching recorded in Higginson's diary occurs in Apr. 1864, when the quartermaster's wife came to his door dressed as "an elderly black lady in large cap & bonnet," who "began to talk wildly" and run at the black servants, some of whom "thought her a ghost, some an insane woman & some a secesh spy" (*WD* 924).

25. I take the convenient concept of "xenophilia" from Bailey (30), although unlike Bailey, who wants the term to designate a simple and politically suspect relationship to the Other—"simple xenophilia, an overvaluing of the 'authenticity' of black culture and a concomitant desire to possess and contain it"—I would not like the term automatically to designate a predominantly patronizing, aggrandizing, condescending, or imperialistic attitude toward its object. Higginson's desire for and love of African Americans (at least the men; he often—though with striking exceptions—found black women "repulsive" [qtd. in Edelstein 259]) certainly has elements of such suspect qualities, but since it obviously reworks such affective detritus into a life-risking political commitment it ought not to be dismissed with a formula. See also Mercer and Julien's statement that "alongside 'negrophobia,' the fear of blacks among whites, there is a sort of 'negrophilia' manifest in the commonplace white fascination with black skin" (150).

26. In his journal Higginson wrote in 1863: "I am conscious of but little affection for individuals among them, if a man dies in hospital or is shot down beside me, I feel it scarcely more than if a tree had fallen, of course if the tree is a fine one I am sorry; but over their *collective* joys & sorrows I have smiles & tears" (*WD* 858; also qtd. in Edelstein 281). In his account in *Army Life* of the regiment's first regular battle, he writes that when a man fell beside him he "felt it no more than if a tree had fallen,—I was so busy watching my own men and the enemy, and planning what to do next" (*AL* 86). In his journal he tries to justify this callousness by writing "Probably it is like the love of animals for their young; they cannot count, do not subdivide affection into fractions. Brute mothers will die for their collective progeny, but you may take them

one by one, without notice; no bird cares for a single egg, only for the eggs. I like to go round the tents of an evening & hear them purring & know that they are happy, and happier for seeing me pass" (WD 858). If the only way he can justify his moral insensitivity to the individual suffering of his men is to figure them as unhatched bird eggs, Higginson seems equally willing to animalize and feminize himself in order to carry out the metaphor's implications. Curiously, in this same passage, he recurs to the topic he addressed in the journal passage on transvestite charades (cited above in note 24), the relation between vicarious role-playing and physical courage: he doesn't care if an individual soldier dies in battle, but "I shrink from exposing them [collectively] to danger, I cannot fling them away, they suggest emotions of cowardice for them which I could not personally feel." That is, when he identifies himself with them, Higginson permits himself to feel fear (to lack physical courage) on behalf of his black soldiers collectively.

27. "The army has an aesthetic all its own," Bataille writes; drilling and pageantry are the means of forming the "single aggressive body" of the military collectivity ("Structure" 141, 140). As this essay is going to press I find that McNeill in an intriguing work accords to dance and drill—"keeping together in time" and the "muscular bonding" (1ff.) it promotes—a decisive role in the creation of human communities in the West. According to one possible figural logic, a biracial army could be imagined as a mulatto body; but Higginson's aversion to mulatto skins disqualifies such a figure for his purposes. He prefers a pattern of racial alternation—"white, black, white"— of the kind he first saw when his regiment deployed for the first time in conjunction with two white regiments: "For the first time I saw the two colors fairly alternate on the military chessboard; it had been the object of much labor and many dreams, and I liked the pattern at last" (AL 126, 127).

28. The essay he refers to is "The Moral Results of Slavery." A few pages after citing Stowe's Topsy as a sign of his own previous ignorant stereotypical expectations of black character, Higginson describes the delicacy with which it was necessary to discipline his soldiers, since a too severe punishment "found them as obstinate and contemptuous as was Topsy when Miss Ophelia undertook to chastise her" (AL 244). They were not like Topsy; they were just like Topsy. "I used to think that I should not care to read 'Uncle Tom's Cabin' in our camp; it would have seemed tame" (AL 234). Cf. note 30 below.

29. On the "orientalism" of Army Life see Worley 161, 165–68, 170–71, 176.

30. See Martin, "Knights-Errant" 171. Stoddard corresponded with Higginson, among others, in 1869 (as the latter was finishing Army Life) about his wish to bring with him, on a lecture tour devoted to the Sandwich Islands, "a couple of little Native boys who should at the close of the evening, sing, dance and entertain the people with some of their picturesque and grotesque mannerisms" (qtd. in Austen 45).

31. Dr. Seth Rogers, Surgeon of the First South Carolina Volunteers under Higginson, in letters to his daughter that Higginson later published in the Proceedings of the

Massachusetts Historical Society, rhapsodized Higginsonianly (here, in a letter of 5 Feb. 1863) about the physical being of the black soldiers:

> I never look at Robert Sutton without feeling certain that his father must have been a great Nubian king. I have rarely reverenced a man more than I do him. His manners are exceedingly simple, unaffected and dignified, without the slightest touch of haughtiness. Voice, low, soft and flooding, as if his thoughts were choking him. He is tall straight and brawny muscled. His face is all of Africa in feeling and in control of expression. By this I do not mean cunning, but manly control. He seems to me kingly, and oh! I wish he could read and write. He ought to be a leader, a general, instead of a corporal. I fancy he is like Toussaint l'Ouverture and it would not surprise me if some great occasion should make him a deliverer of his people from bondage. Prince Rivers, — just as black as Robert Sutton, — has a peculiar fineness of texture of skin that gives the most cleanly look. He is agile and fleet, like a deer, in his speed and like a panther in his tread. His features are not very African and his eye is so bright that it must "shine at night, when de moon am gone away." His *manners* are not surpassed on this globe. I feel my awkwardness when I meet him. This because an officer ought to be as polite as a soldier. (357)

32. For the canonical account of the "male gaze" see Mulvey, "Visual Pleasure." Gaines attempts to articulate Mulvey's account of the gendering of looking with racial categories, and calls for "more work" on, among other subjects, "the interracial intermingling of male 'looks', and other visual taboos related to sanctions against interracial sexuality" ("White Privilege" 21). bell hooks offers suggestive speculations along these lines, and refers intriguingly to an essay I have been unable to track down with the promising title "The Miscegenated Gaze" by "black male artist Christian Walker" (*Black Looks* 7). Carol Clover's explorations of the oscillation between a phallic/assaultive/sadistic gaze and a vulnerable/reactive/introjective gaze in the viewing experience of male horror film fans would provide a useful set of terms for characterizing Higginson's absorption in/of the spectacle of the black male body.

33. Higginson's familiarity with northern blackface minstrel entertainment is evident (see note 5 above). And when he regrets that his black men are "growing more like white men, — less naive and less grotesque," it seems clear that the standard of blackness he invokes, as that from which they are falling away, is that of the stage minstrel — a white man's impersonation of a negro (*AL* 224). In a journal entry from his earliest days in camp, he observed, apropos of a turkey shoot in which a young man "fired his piece into the ground at half cock," that there was "such infinite guffawing & delight, such rollings over in the grass, such dances of ecstacy, that made the Ethiopean minstrelsy of the stage appear no caricature" (*WD* Nov. 27, 1862). That is, he previously would have thought that stage minstrelsy was a distortion or exaggeration of actual African American merriment, but after firsthand observation Higginson

judges that there was no distortion. This passage is later adapted for *Army Life* with some interesting emendations: now when he observes the soldiers clowning around at target practice, he judges their merriment to be "such guffawing and delight, such rolling over and over on the grass, such dances of ecstasy, as made the 'Ethiopian minstrelsy' of the stage appear a feeble imitation" (*AL* 36). Having once (on the spot, in the army camp) judged the remembered minstrel show to have been, after all, and despite his prior skepticism, an adequate copy of the original ("no caricature," i.e., not an exaggeration), he now claims that, far from being an exaggeration, it is a diminished or reduced copy ("feeble imitation") of the original. That is, the white entertainer's blackface minstrel performance wasn't essentially an *inaccurate* imitation, only an inferior one, lacking in performative energy. While this emendation seems to promote actual black performance to the status of an inimitable object, one that a white copy can't touch, at the same time it confers upon the black soldiers a recognized talent for the ludicrous and the grotesque, a talent that (of course) no white man could match. The blacks are naturally such caricatures that a white imitation can't help but be feeble. Lott's discussion of the gender politics of blackface minstrelsy is acute; see especially "The Seeming Counterfeit," 233–34.

34. The brief account of the relationships between racial and floricultural discourses that follows is condensed from my essay "Flowers of Manhood."

35. Higginson's "concave globe" no doubt alludes to Emerson's famous "transparent eye-ball" in *Nature* (10). But it registers also, I believe, something of his own somatic experience, a kind of relationship to his body that is different from that usually represented in the aggressive, bounded phallic schema his culture (and ours) promotes and enforces; something like what Paul Smith calls "a masculinity for which the hysterical desire for somatic loss, the death of the body in an efflux of substance, is a paramount element of its constitutive reality" (107), an inner experience of the male body that contests the rigid, circumscribed imperative. Higginson's pleasure in the swimmer's sensations of unboundedness is manifest in other writings: "Swimming has also a birdlike charm of motion. The novel element, the free action, the abated drapery, give a sense of personal contact with Nature which nothing else so fully bestows. No later triumph of existence is so fascinating, perhaps, as that in which the boy first wins his panting way across the deep gulf that severs one green bank from another, (ten yards, perhaps,) and feels himself thenceforward lord of the watery world" ("Saints" 593). In Higginson's novel *Malbone*, Hope, left "in the water alone, her feet unsupported by any firm element" (171), finds that "her head was hot and her ears rang," she felt "a vacant cavity within" and "her life seemed boiling up into her head; queer fancies came to her, as, for instance, that she was an inverted thermometer with the mercury all ascending into a bulb at the top" (172). Just as she loses consciousness—"as when ether brings at last to a patient, after the roaring and tumult in his brain, its blessed foretaste of the deliciousness of death" (173)—she is fortunately rescued.

36. If Pateman is correct that the universal civil individual in the liberal polis is fashioned implicitly after the male body, but that to preserve the fiction of univer-

sality the civil individual must then be abstracted even from his masculinity, to suppress all traces of "the mundane world of necessity, the body, the sexual passions and birth" and thereby construct an artificial, disembodied, purely rational political subject (45ff.); and if Berlant is right that "American women and African-Americans have never had the privilege to suppress the body" and have thereby been debarred from access to political sovereignty (113); then it might be argued that Higginson's oscillation in the water between embodiment and disembodiment is merely a rehearsal of that "privilege to suppress." While not wishing to deny that political enfranchisement is a privilege in relation to disenfranchisement, I also want to notice (as I believe Higginson does) the pathos of the fate that makes alienation from the body and its pleasures a "privilege."

37. On the secret society of "Acephale" organized by Bataille see Stoekl xix–xxiii.

38. A remarkable anonymous essay in *Putnam's* in 1854 (when Higginson was an occasional contributor) called "Bathing and Bodies" gives an account of the experience of the "thrills of the purest physical pleasure" available in a bath house in Damascus, characterized generally by different forms of exquisite passivity and abject submission to the "dexterous hands" of the attendant. The result of the elaborate rituals of the bath is that "[t]he world vanishes; sight, hearing, smell, taste (unless we open our mouth), and breathing, are cut off; we have become nebulous" (533).

39. Theweleit's account of the way images of dirt, mire, morass, slime, pulp, shit, etc., function in the fascist soldier male's imaginary is suggestive: they are what threaten the male body's integrity, what it must be defended against (1: 385ff.). Plainly for Higginson the "miry embrace" carries a freight of psychic associations, but he seems generally to *equate* embodiment with ooze, mud, and mire: at this moment, for him to *reacquire* his local body would be to be stuck in mud, while his disorientation allows him to transcend the flesh.

40. This chiasmic reversal—the Rebel side is the Union side, and the Union side is the Rebel side—seems to register subliminally Higginson's recognition of an essential similarity between Northern and Southern men's investments in the lure of disembodiment and reembodiment offered them by imaginary identification with black men, a lure to which in this nighttime swim Higginson was succumbing and resisting.

41. Judith Butler's claim that "recognition is not conferred on a subject, but forms that subject" (*Bodies* 226) is to the point here. Higginson's claim to original possession of authority, authority inherent in his person, appears here to depend strictly upon its recognition by the black soldier. Higginson abjectly recognizes that he needs the black soldier's recognition in order to resume his superior subject position. Amy Kaplan has made the intriguing suggestion to me that the black sentry's elaborate performance of the ceremony of presenting arms may be an act of signifying—that he may be playing with Higginson at this moment. If so, his exaggerated and unnecessary performance of military ceremony at this awkward moment would be a brilliant satire on Higginson's very claim to possess commanding authority despite his nakedness. On "signifying" in African American culture see Gates. It is plain enough

from Higginson's diary and letters that the soldiers frequently engaged in some very pointed satire on their white officers, satire that he sometimes recognized and sometimes didn't. One occasion when he did was when the soldiers, resentful that they were not being paid the amount they had contracted for, devised a song, "sung sarcastically," which was "really quite a daring reference to dignitaries," as Higginson acknowledged, in which they declared they were "Gwine to Washington / To fight for Linkum's darter." Higginson observes that "their nonsense is as inscrutable as children's, you can never get behind it & find where they get the combination of ideas," but it seems clear enough that the song involved a humorous threat to seek compensation for their reduced pay in the form of what they evidently knew well to be the reward that would set white men's teeth on edge, namely white female flesh (*WD* 864). Another example: Higginson thinks it is only "unconscious satire" when the laborers call F. A. Eustis, a plantation owner, "Mr. Useless" (*WD* Aug. 26, 1863).

42. Other accounts of race, masculinity, and the homoerotic are Silverman's on T. E. Lawrence (*Male Subjectivity* 299–338) and Dollimore's on Gide, Genet, and others (17–42; this volume). Moon discusses the way racial difference plays out in Whitman's discourse of masculine fluidity and translatability in *Leaves of Grass* (*Disseminating* 80–83). Sánchez-Eppler's claim, that "Whitman's concept of embodiment is delimited by the body of the slave," that "throughout Whitman's poetry, to a significant degree the fundamental image of the body remains for Whitman that of the slave: one central example of the completely corporeal person" (926), is suggestive for Higginson as well: the reduction of the slave to a mere sellable body stripped of social personhood makes that body available as an object of identification for those (like Whitman or Higginson) who desire to recover a somatic being from which their privileged whiteness has alienated them. Ironically, Higginson was phobically averse to recognizing his similarity to the poet in this respect (or any other), consistently disparaging Whitman's poetry of embodiment as "malodorous" ("Walt Whitman" 262), "unmanly" ("Unmanly Manhood" 33), and "nauseating" ("Recent Poetry" 476), and charging him with evasion of military service during the Civil War ("Unmanly Manhood" 33; Letter to [Sylvester] Baxter).

43. The metonymic logic of substitution of exotic flowers and nude black males (as two signifiers of taboo eroticism) is discussed in detail in my "Flowers of Manhood."

44. See my "Race and Eros in Mapplethorpe's *Black Book*."

45. Melody Davis's remarks on "Isaiah" are telling, for in spite of striving to indict Mapplethorpe's *Black Book* generally for being "racist and fetishizing" (85), her errant syntax allows itself to be read against her own polemic: "Swathed in leopard skin, bamboo pole in hand, Isaiah poses in a New York studio as a white man's African fantasy, the stereotypical 'native,' seen in countless colonial photographs" (72). Davis wants to say that Mapplethorpe is stereotyping Isaiah as an African native, but her sentence equally well says that it is a photograph *of the stereotype.*

46. See Morrisroe (233–39, 242–49, 252, 318) and Fritscher (96, 172, 214–18, 239–40) for information (some of it dubiously reliable) on Mapplethorpe's personal attrac-

tion to black men and fondness for racist epithets. There is a fascinating photograph in Morrisroe (following 176) of Mapplethorpe and friends as children in Floral Park, Long Island, in Halloween costume; one child wears blackface and has a sign reading "Topsy." This gives, perhaps, a small but telling clue as to the acceptable practices of racial masquerade in the suburban community in which Mapplethorpe's psyche was formed.

47. Although I can't find it in me absolutely to celebrate, as Bersani does, the banishment of ethical personhood from sexuality.

MEZZ MEZZROW AND THE VOLUNTARY NEGRO BLUES

GAYLE WALD

> And I was going to learn their music and play it for the rest of my days. I was going to be a musician, a Negro musician, hipping the world about the blues the way only Negroes can. I didn't know how the hell I was going to do it, but I was straight on what I had to do.
> —Mezz Mezzrow, *Really the Blues* (1946)

As he recounts in his 1946 autobiography *Really the Blues*, becoming "a Negro musician" and "hipping the world about the blues" were the related life-long ambitions of Milton "Mezz" Mezzrow (1899–1972)—the flamboyant jazz clarinetist, prolific weed pusher, and prototypical "white Negro" hipster whose name itself was evocative of "jazz." Born Milton Mesirow to Russian-Jewish immigrant parents who hoped that their son would one day take over the family drugstore business, Mezzrow managed to realize the second of these ambitions—disseminating blues—through a lifelong immersion in African American musical cultures, especially the Chicago-style music that he first encountered as a teenager. For more than half a century Mezzrow "hipped the world about the blues" through his musical performance, his work as an arranger and producer, his encouragement of other performers, and, not least, his memoirs, which double as an extended paean to the music of his idols, Sidney Bechet and Louis Armstrong. Written in the wake of the emergence of bebop, a style that would eventually displace many of the jazz performers of Mezzrow's generation, *Really the Blues* champions "real" blues with the special fervor of a disciple for whom blues is not primarily a cultural "birthright" but rather an object of worshipful and enthusiastic devotion. "Hipping the world about the blues" was indeed the central preoccupation of Mezzrow's life, leading him in the 1950s and '60s to devote his energies to organizing all-star blues reunion concerts throughout Europe, where the audience for music of the 1920s and '30s remained strong.

But if "hipping the world" about blues was a rather straightforward ambition that defined the trajectory of Mezzrow's varied and erratic career, then becoming "a Negro musician"—the first of Mezzrow's stated ambitions—was more complicated and less easily realized, implying a radical transformation (if not transcendence) of personal history, social identity, and racial ideology. The obvious if unstated question that lies behind Mezzrow's explicit desire to "be" a "Negro musician"—namely, what exactly is a "Negro musician?"—raises a series of additional and pressing concerns that *Really the Blues* brings to the fore: How are racial identities constituted and experienced? To what degree do individuals exercise volition over racial identity, or how is volition over the terms of identity itself a function of, and a basis for, racial identity and identity-formation? Why would someone who is the ostensible beneficiary of white skin privilege (and patriarchal gender privilege) want to "cross the color line," and to what degree is such imagined racial or cultural mobility itself predicated upon a correspondingly rigid and immobile conception of "blackness?" What sorts of interests (not to mention fantasies about masculinity, sexuality, and race) are served by such an "innocent" and apparently harmless desire to "be" black?

Such questions are the implicit subtext of "Case History of an Ex-White Man," a somewhat sensational, promotional feature story that *Ebony*, then in its infancy, devoted to Mezzrow the year his memoirs were published. Timed to coincide with the release of *Really the Blues* and titled in punning reference (apparently at the urging of Richard Wright) to both the Freudian case history and the title of James Weldon Johnson's 1912 novel *Autobiography of an Ex-Colored Man*, the article touts Mezzrow as an object of bemusement, curiosity, and somewhat guarded appreciation. In melodramatic language that echoes the histrionics of *Really the Blues*, the article describes Mezzrow, who was living in Harlem at the time, as "one of the few whites" to have "passed through the Jim Crow portals of Negro life to live on equal terms with its harried inhabitants" (11). According to Bernard Wolfe, a writer who helped Mezzrow with the manuscript of his memoirs, Mezzrow over his lifetime came to believe not only that he had crossed a geographical or social threshold, but that "he had actually, physically, turned black" ("Ecstatic" 398). *Ebony*, of course, disagreed with this eccentric notion: "Physically speaking," the magazine wryly notes, Mezzrow "couldn't pass for Negro by any stretch of the imagination; his skin is too white." Instead, the article continues, his "conversion to 'the race' has taken place largely within himself. In psychological makeup, he is completely a black man and proudly admits it" (11).

Skin tones notwithstanding, as *Ebony*'s audience was well aware, there was little to stop Mezzrow from claiming African ancestry and thereby joining the

Figure 1. Milton "Mezz" Mezzrow and Sidney Bechet. (Institute for Jazz Studies, Newark, NJ)

ranks of African Americans whose forebears, like those of their "white" compatriots, were predominantly European. Anecdotally, most of the magazine's readers could have cited examples of relatives or acquaintances whose skin, like Mezzrow's, was ostensibly too white to allow them to "pass for Negro" but who nevertheless lived comfortably and without apparent contradiction or confusion as African American: the blue-eyed, blond-haired Walter White, a longtime leader of the NAACP, was a well-known and highly visible example. Moreover, throughout the early twentieth century, black newspapers had often taken note of a sort of circumstantial and informal "passing" among white women who, by establishing new social identities within black communities, bypassed some of the stigma attached to marriage across the color line. As the *Ebony* article recognizes, however, Mezzrow's was not primarily a biological claim, despite his assertions of having undergone actual physical transformation. Instead, his status as a "voluntary Negro" (to use the parlance of the day) depended upon a series of complex and often contradictory identity-claims that were grounded in a cultural, rather than a biological, racial essentialism: in particular, a belief that blues, arguably the most privileged form of black musical expression, contained within it the "essence" of black racial difference, so that by mastering the form and the spirit of blues one could also master "blackness." With its desperate enthusiasm and forced joviality, *Really the Blues* bears witness to the central conundrum of (implicitly male) "white Negro" self-fashioning: that while he is attempting to "be" a "Negro musician," Mezzrow is in fact engaging in a self-defeating and ultimately self-referential venture to appropriate the very qualities that he himself has (romantically) ascribed to black masculinity.

This essay uses the specific example of Mezzrow's autobiography to theorize the emergence of "white Negro" masculinity within the context of early blues and jazz music cultures. *Really the Blues*, in this account, is not primarily a narrative about finding a self in the Other—a standard interpretation of stories of cross-racial desire, especially where the subjects in question are already invested with social authority by virtue of race or gender.[1] Instead, I read *Really the Blues* as a narrative in which the "self" in question is not "discovered" but actively produced through a mimetic performance of Otherness as it is conceived within the colonial imagination of the white Negro. Such a reading implies that white Negro masculinity cannot be understood simply or unproblematically as an antihegemonic choice to "identify," politically or otherwise, with a racially marginalized population. On the contrary, while it may seem to stem from antihegemonic impulses, such a choice is not inherently at odds with—and may even depend upon—a corresponding wish to preserve the racial authority of white masculinity. This is not to discount the averred sincerity of such choices, but rather to point out that even the sincerest emulation of the qualities with which one invests an Other is not itself necessarily free of self-interest; certainly, in Mezzrow's case, it is not free of the objectifying or exoticizing proclivities endemic in the sort of racist representation that, in other contexts, he would have vigorously repudiated.

Really the Blues attests to the paradoxes of white Negro masculinity insofar as it is a conversion narrative about the impossibility of conversion. At bottom, in other words, Mezzrow's quixotic narrative of black masculinity documents how discourses of racial and sexual authenticity are fundamentally and inevitably self-contradictory, and how fantasies of white racial self-transformation, to the extent that they are predicated upon the preservation of romantic and ultimately racist fantasies of the Other, remain fixed within the terms of racial essentialism, notwithstanding their seeming commitment to a notion of the "flow" of identities across social boundaries (of race, class, gender, and sexuality).[2] In particular, the more that Mezzrow seeks to fix "blackness" as the idealized object of his own mercurial racial and sexual identifications, the more he experiences himself as unalterably fixed within the terms of a "white" masculinity that he seeks to renounce.

Really the Blues is broadly relevant to the study of race and masculinity because it shows how the presumed white male authority to appropriate the cultural production of racially marginalized populations is predicated upon the relative immobility of those who are most marginalized (i.e., fixed) by racial discourse. On the other hand, Really the Blues also demonstrates that notions of stable or essential racial difference (such as those necessary to Mezzrow's own "voluntary Negro" fantasies) may ultimately interfere with, or impose limits upon, attempts to appropriate the culture and knowledge of the Other. Indeed, because it is an idealizing and essentializing formulation, Mezzrow's desire to play blues "the way only Negroes can" establishes within his text a dynamic of perpetual hope and perpetual frustration—an ongoing wish to "be black" that is necessarily and continually hindered by his belief in the innateness and inviolability of "blackness" for black people.

Mezzrow may have treated his claims to black citizenship with a kind of reverential earnestness that was itself an invitation to parody, but the Ebony article, along with other accounts of Mezzrow's career, suggest that black observers were apt to take him less seriously. With Really the Blues just hitting the bookstands, Ebony predicted that Mezzrow's story would make "an amazing raw and racy saga that [would] shock the book reading public [and] . . . send the book soaring into the best seller class." Mezzrow's black colleagues viewed his cross-racial posturing as a mild annoyance, since ultimately white clubowners, booking agents, and producers posed more of a threat and since, in the long run, Mezzrow's flamboyant style was secondary to his music. As clarinetist and soprano saxophonist Bechet once confided to a friend, "Mezz should know that race does not matter—it's hitting the notes right that counts" (Chilton 178). In fact, in his own autobiography, Treat It Gentle, Bechet suggested that Mezzrow's exquisitely self-conscious "Negro" stylizations may actually have interfered with the quality of his playing. "Mezzrow, he'd had this rage of being King of Harlem for a while and that was wearing out some," he wrote. "When a man is trying so hard to be something he isn't, when he's trying to be some name he makes up for himself instead of just being what he is, some of that will show in his music, the idea of it will be wrong" (Bechet 168–69).

Capitalizing upon the opportunity Mezzrow presented for entertaining visual spectacle, Ebony packed its pages with photographs of Mezzrow, not only in the company of black musicians, but also in various prosaic poses at home with his second wife, a black woman named Johnnie Mae Berg, and their son and Mezzrow's namesake, Milton Jr. One photograph depicts Mezzrow at the dinner table with his family, another shows him teaching his son how to play the clarinet as Johnnie Mae looks on. *Ebony*'s insistence on Mezzrow's bourgeois ordinariness (an ordinariness intended to resonate with *Ebony*'s middle-class African American readers) contradicted the eccentricity and extraordinariness of his self-representation. In other respects, however, Mezzrow's experience closely mirrored that of other young white jazzmen who came of age in Chicago in the 1920s. Like Eddie Condon, Jimmy McPartland, Bud Freeman, Pee Wee Russell, and Dave Tough, young white musicians associated with the Austin High School "gang," Mezzrow grew up emulating a New Orleans idiom that he first heard played in North Side clubs by white groups such as the New Orleans Rhythm Kings, Bix and the Wolverines, and the Original Dixieland Jazz Band (LeRoi Jones 149–50; Mezzrow 341–43). Self-taught on the clarinet and saxophone, Mezzrow followed jazz when it moved east in the late 1920s from Chicago to New York, performing and recording with various groups, some of his own making, for nearly two decades. In 1937, he gained notoriety outside of the jazz world for forming the Disciples of Swing, one of the earliest interracial bands and the first to play a gig in Manhattan's prestigious Savoy Ballroom. The peak of Mezzrow's career as a performer came during his collaboration with Bechet in a series of now-famous recording sessions organized by French jazz aficionado Hughes Panassié in which Mezzrow played second clarinet to Bechet's lead on songs such as "Weary Blues" and even Mezzrow's original composition "Really the Blues." [3]

A notorious drug dealer, by some accounts better known in Harlem jazz circles for the quality of his weed than for the quality of his playing, Mezzrow honed his street cachet serving time on Riker's Island in the early 1940s on drug possession and trafficking charges. Prison also marked a critical turning-point in Mezzrow's career, a shift away from musical performance and toward other modes of deliberate self-mythologizing. Soon after his release, Mezzrow met Wolfe, a Jewish intellectual with an interest in black popular culture, whose initial interest in doing a magazine article on Mezzrow eventually flowered into the idea for a full-length book.[4] Ironically, perhaps, *Ebony*'s hyperbolic premonitions of Mezzrow's literary success eventually panned out: a quick best-seller, *Really the Blues* went through at least six hardbound reprintings and was reissued in paperback (with a preface by Henry Miller) in 1963, 1974, and most recently 1990.[5] In contrast to *Ebony*, which harbored fewer illusions about Mezzrow's authenticity, the white press greeted *Really the Blues* as the "real" thing—in the words of the *Saturday Review*, the first jazz history by "an insider" (Gehman 26). Calling it an "intense, sincere and honest book," the *New Republic* wrote that Mezzrow's autobiography "makes all the novels with jazz backgrounds seem as phony as an Eddie Condon concert" (B. Moon 605), apparently unconcerned with the fact that Condon, although a rival, was also one of Mezzrow's original Chicago compatriots. A *Newsweek* review went so far as to venture to compare Mezzrow to Bessie Smith, asserting that whereas Smith merely "sang the blues," Mezzrow "lived them, brutally" ("Vipers, Tea, and Jazz," 88)—a claim even more outrageous in the light of Smith's tragic and premature death in 1937 after being denied admittance to a white hospital. The book was also fundamental to the development of the bohemian sensibilities of young whites, including Jack Kerouac, Allen Ginsberg, who read it at the counter of the Columbia bookstore in the mid-1940s, and Norman Mailer, who used Mezzrow as the prototype for his infamous 1957 "White Negro" essay. Bob Wilber, a white student of Bechet's, wrote that for aspiring white jazz musicians of a later generation, *Really the Blues* was a "bible" in which they immersed themselves and from which they drew inspiration (15).

"A friend once remarked," wrote British jazz critic G. E. Lambert, "that everything Mezz touched turned to gold except his clarinet" (11). In the mid-1940s, around the time when *Really the Blues* was published, Mezzrow took on a series of more conventional roles, arranging gigs and even founding his own short-lived record label, King Jazz, whose payroll included Bechet, Sam Price, Cousin Joe, Lips Page, Danny Barker, Pops Foster, Sid Catlett, Fitz Weston, Kaiser Marshall, Sox Wilson, Coot Grant, Wellman Braud, and Baby Dodds (Lambert 11). Yet as King Jazz folded and the 1940s waned, Mezzrow became increasingly disillusioned by the eclipse of New Orleans–style jazz by commercialized big-band swing and studiously introverted "modernist" bebop. The appearance of bebop presented a golden opportunity for Mezzrow, a staunch traditionalist, to assert that New Orleans was the true, original, and authentic musical form—the complementary discourse to that of the avant-garde, who contended that bebop merely distinguished those who could play it from those who could not (that is, Mezzrow). Well aware, in any case, that modernist trends rendered him obsolete as a paid performer in the United States, Mezzrow moved to Paris in 1951 to become a "classic" blues impresario.

Assessments of the significance of Mezzrow's contributions to jazz vary. Whereas to champions of the avant-garde, Mezzrow symbolized traditionalist incompetence, to black musicians amused by his self-appointed role as black musical guardian, he was just another white clarinetist, tolerated by jazz luminaries such as Louis Armstrong, because he could be relied upon to supply a steady stream of high-quality marijuana. Perhaps the most famous put-down came from (then) *Down Beat* columnist Nat Hentoff, who once sardonically dubbed Mezzrow the "Baron Munchausen" of jazz, accusing him of being "so consistently out of tune that he may have invented a new scale system" ("Counterpoint" 5).[6] On the other hand, especially for those who shared Mezzrow's narrow musical tastes, he was the music's "greatest white musician" (Lambert 10), a traveling "jazz ambassador" and a champion of New Orleans–style music before it became adulterated by the mainstream or reappropriated by beret-wearing young black artistes.[7]

To have come from the "other side of the tracks" was a late-nineteenth-century colloquialism that connoted that one had lower-class origins. Meaningful as the phase was for describing class differences, it possessed even greater cultural significance for blacks, for as Paul Oliver once noted, "the poorest sectors [of the major American cities] were those that back on to the railroad tracks, where the great locomotives as they gathered speed on leaving the immense railroad terminals of Chicago, Kansas City, or St. Louis caused the poor frame houses to shudder to their inadequate foundations, blackening their walls with grime and smoke, cracking the ceilings and killing the vegetation. When Jack Ranger sang of seeing his woman pass his door as the Texas-Pacific train took her away, he was speaking literally, not metaphorically" (67). The photograph on the title page of the *Ebony* article picks up on these historical junctions between blues, railroads, transience, and mobility. In the photograph, Mezzrow poses at the corner of West 132nd Street and Seventh Avenue in Harlem with his young son (at whom he is looking, face downturned) and musicians Bechet, Red Allen, and Baby Dodds.[8] A "ONE WAY" sign pointing away from Mezzrow's head toward Bechet seems to suggest that Mezzrow's destination lies in the direction of his jazz hero, or at least somewhere down West 132nd. As urban intersections act as switchboards, the place where people from different walks of life converge, so the intersection of the *Ebony* photograph evokes a kind of "meeting-place of the races," a convergence literally embodied in the figure of Mezzrow's young mulatto son. The image of the intersection is particularly evocative of Mezzrow's deeply held conviction that jazz was a cultural medium that could connect people across seemingly insurmountable lines of race, class, and Jim Crow. "I believe very strongly," he once told a British interviewer, that jazz "can do a lot to help crash the color barriers of bias and hatred"; it "can help evolve a new civilisation and culture . . . for to understand jazz you don't need to be technically minded, and it's evident wherever I've been that people from all walks of life and colours of skin enjoy jazz" (Palmer 5).

Such comments were not merely idealized, romantic posturing on Mezzrow's part; jazz, after all, had been the conduit of his own initiation into black subculture, the form into which he channeled his musical talents, and the means by which he formed friendships and broke color barriers that were rarely ever penetrated. His commitment to jazz performance—something that was not just incidental to his white Negro self-fashioning—gave him access to new cultural styles, a new language (jive), and antihegemonic, minoritarian sensibilities. Whereas for blacks the jazz life represented a step up, a means of professionalizing and honing black musical creativity, for whites like Mezzrow it represented open rebellion, the creation of alternative social spaces in which one could reject deeply ingrained American social customs (such as segregation) and scorn bourgeois mores. Hentoff has suggested that, given the comprehensiveness of Jim Crow, it was only by means of extravagant or radical gestures of white social and cultural divestment that young white men could ever mingle on what was, more or less, an equal footing with their black male peers (The Jazz Life 14). Hentoff brackets this imagined social parity of white and black jazz musicians within the larger context of often shameless commercial exploitation and theft of black talent. Yet his argument—based as it is in liberal ideas of social mobility and social opportunity—sidesteps the question of how white masculinity accrues the authority for such "divestment" and whether, within a context in which racism is the condition of social relations, it may ever be a radical gesture after all, particularly if it leaves intact the very circumstances that allow for, and even encourage, the exercise of such volition.

In Really the Blues Mezzrow codes his defiance of his family and their traditions as a transgressive redistribution of cultural "wealth"—what he calls "stealing good, like Robin Hood." Such devotion to the hipster ethic gave Mezzrow the possibility of forging an identity that was culturally and geographically distinct from the world of his parents and sister. In one crucial scene from the book, Mezzrow represents this process of self-invention in terms that resemble the familiar "I've got a woman at home who treats me bad / I've got a woman in town who's good to me" blues lyric, in which women figuratively embody either male enslavement to, or freedom from, the demands of domestic life. In particular, Mezzrow uses Bessie Smith as a personification of authenticity, spontaneity, primitivism, and unschooled innocence to stage a rebellion against his sister Helen, who by contrast represents domestic entrapment, artistic suffocation, and middlebrow indifference to everything that Mezzrow finds exciting and transgressive about jazz. In the scene, Mezzrow asks Helen, a stenographer, to transcribe the lyrics from a Smith recording, but then becomes enraged with "her fancy high-school airs" (54). Helen, he writes, "kept 'correcting' Bessie's grammar, straightening out her words and putting them in 'good' English until they sounded like some stuck-up jive from McGuffy's Reader instead of the real down-to-earth language of the blues" (54). As an act of revenge, Mezzrow steals Helen's fur coat, sells it to a madam, and uses the money to purchase his first alto saxophone. If Helen figures what Mezzrow must give up in order to "become" a black man, then Smith represents the cathected enabler of his self-invention, the means by which he invests himself with innocence, bravery, and liberty. "I had to cut loose some way," he explains, "to turn my back once and for all on that hincty, killjoy world of my sister's and move over to Bessie Smith's world body and soul." After the robbery "I began to breath easier — my sister had paid for her fine-lady act and put me in a business where they said 'ain't' all day long and far into the night. Great deal" (54).

"The important thing about white jazzmen," jazz critic Gary Giddins once remarked, "is not that they appropriated the black American's music — a narrow and paranoid sentiment that denies the individuality of all jazzmen, white and black — but that so many of them chose a black aesthetic as the best possible source for self-examination" (254). While Giddins perhaps overstates the point about jazz as an equal-opportunity music available to everyone on identical terms, his observation about jazz as a mirror of white identity helps to make sense of Mezzrow's own checkered career. In particular, Mezzrow's dedication to a hipster ethic was complicated by the fact that he used hipsterism to stave off a gnawing fear that he was part of the very structures he despised; "black" identity was thus merely the antithesis, or most nearly, of what he wanted to repudiate. Such an observation sheds light on Mezzrow's characteristic boastfulness, which was simultaneously his paraphrase of the African American tradition of playing the dozens and a measure of his own anxious self-disparagement. Even his colorful use of jazz jive, the means by which he performatively enacts "blackness" in his book, reflected Mezzrow's apprehension that he lacked his own resources of creativity, comedy, and play.

As the scene of cultural trade-off demonstrates, jazz was both a metaphor and a music for Mezzrow, both a portal to black experience and a form of artistic expression. In this regard, Mezzrow's discourse of musical and cultural authenticity shared more in common with the viewpoint represented by LeRoi Jones (Amiri Baraka) in his 1963 book Blues People, than with that voiced by Ralph Ellison in his well-known response to Jones. Whereas Jones believed blues to be an "inviolable" black music and "a kind of ethno-historic rite as basic as blood" (148), Ellison wanted to see black music, even the hallowed tradition of blues, "first as poetry and as ritual," which could transcend its social and political context (257). Whereas Jones viewed the "mainstream"—in which he included middle-class blacks—with undisguised contempt, Ellison contended that black idioms had always shaped "white" musical culture, no matter how much whites had sought to discredit, disguise, or repress these influences, and no matter how much middle-class blacks had chosen to disown them.

Like Jones, Mezzrow harbored decidedly unbending beliefs in black musical authenticity, convictions that were merely the analog to his romanticization of "authentic" black masculinity. As the title of his autobiography suggests, Mezzrow defined jazz narrowly, cultivating on the one hand a disdain for the assimilationist ethos of swing and on the other a loathing for the antiassimilationism of what was alternatively called bebop, "cool" jazz, or "progressive" music (LeRoi Jones 81–88). In fact, Mezzrow maintained that the term "modern jazz" was oxymoronic, that rock and roll bore a clearer manifestation of jazz influences than the sounds of a Dizzy Gillespie or Charlie Parker. "Nobody today knows the standards," he waxed nostalgic in 1964; "now these musicians who go to college, Juilliard, Boston and Chicago Conservatory, come out with mathematical equations that to me reeks of intellectual stench and is not jazz, period" (Palmer 5).

Such a sentiment might be read merely as a reflection of Mezzrow's fidelity to the cult of the self-taught, non-reading black musician among young, romantically minded white jazz artists (LeRoi Jones 152; Stearns 129). But Mezzrow's hostility to certain kinds of swing and bebop was also, as I have begun to suggest, a reflection of his essentialism and a strategy for carving out a distinct and protective niche for his own artistry. Mezzrow's musical fundamentalism sprang from a variety of sources, including the centrality of Chicago-style blues in his own artistic formation, but it was informed throughout by Mezzrow's own desperate need to place himself at the center of 1930s and 1940s jazz history, alongside virtuosos such as Bechet and Armstrong. In other words, Mezzrow used an authenticist discourse to elevate himself above the crowd—as much to signal his resistance to dominant values and to assert independence from a certain preordained narrative of his life as to distinguish himself among white jazz musicians.

The fervency of Mezzrow's belief in the real, the natural, and the authentic set him apart from his white peers, but it also consigned him to a life of perpetual and unabated frustration. To the degree that he could find talent worthy of emulation among white as well as black artists, Mezzrow was not a banal proponent of the notion that only blacks could play jazz; nevertheless, he staked his own claims of black identity upon the shoulders of "real" black people. In his preface to white rhythm-and-blues musician Johnny Otis's memoirs *Upside Your Head!: Rhythm and Blues on Central Avenue*, George Lipsitz compares Otis's transformative immersion in black culture to that of Europeans held in captivity by Native American tribes, where the convert typically defended his or her adopted community with exemplary zeal (Lipsitz xix). But the idea of "captivity" only begins to capture the complexity of Mezzrow's situation. While Mezzrow's discourse of the natural was ironically one way that he reinforced the artificiality of his own identity-claims, it was also emblematic of jazz's own ethic of improvisation, which demanded of its practitioners a self-conscious effort to appear unself-conscious (Sidran 54). The fact that he had to work at seeming unaffected did not stop Mezzrow from representing his initial efforts at playing the saxophone (he later switched to clarinet) as instinctual and effortless—"The blues," he wrote, "came so natural . . . to me" (12)—but neither was such an assertion of spontaneity unique to Mezzrow; indeed, it was conventional. Even the fact that Mezzrow, in using jazz as a mark of self-distinction, had relegated himself to a kind of perpetual need to recreate himself was characteristic of jazz, which in its parody and defiance of the cultural "mainstream" continually engaged in a renegotiation of the boundaries between "insiders" and "outsiders." At the same time, however, blues was quite literally a "discipline" for Mezzrow—not only a particular branch of musical knowledge, but an authority to which he felt compelled to submit, body and soul. The irony, or perhaps the tragedy, of Mezzrow's "case history," as *Really the Blues* makes abundantly clear, is that ultimately he would become enslaved, and even defeated, by his own authenticist ideals.

Really the Blues bears out its formal relation to blues most pointedly in its trope of repetition—specifically, in Mezzrow's repeated avowal of having "crossed the line" to become a black jazzman. The underlying paradox of these assertions is that while each lays claim to a certain finality (as when the phrase "to cross a line" indicates irrevocability, the burning of bridges), none ultimately fulfills its promise of permanence, of absolute and irreversible transformation. Mezzrow names these critical turning-points in his jazz life "millennial moments," a phrase that evokes epiphany, apocalypse, and rebirth through conversion. Sent at sixteen to reform school, where he listens to the black kids in an adjacent Jim Crow cell block sing the blues, Mezzrow is literally re-formed, converted, reborn, metamorphosed: "The tonal inflections and the story they told, always blending together like the colors in an artist's picture, the ways the syllables were always placed right, the changes in the words to fit the music—all this hit me like a millennium would hit a philosopher" (14). Mezzrow may have gone into reform school "green," but, he writes, "I came out chocolate brown" (18).

From this story of Mezzrow's reform-school rebirth in *Really the Blues* emerge several crucial observations, the first of which is that Mezzrow is simultaneously participating in the process of lending "blackness" associative value and reaping the benefits of appropriating this value as his own (Morrison 52). The "hipster" persona that Mezzrow cultivates through his relationships with black jazz musicians thus represents the flowering, at least in part, of his own projective fantasies. Yet because these fantasies are themselves "in process," subject to change based upon Mezzrow's own shifting emotional needs, Mezzrow must continually chase after his "millennium." (Another way of putting this would be to say that "authenticity" is itself an unstable commodity.) Thus, every adversity that Mezzrow faces—every obstacle to the attainment of the fantasmatic object of his identificatory desires—gets transformed into an occasion, retrospectively, for renewed affirmation of the realizability of these desires. For example, Mezzrow's addiction to opium, a dependency that almost costs him his life, becomes merely another opportunity for singing the blues. This explains why for Mezzrow the event of racial passing perpetually remains in the realm of fantasy, where he is fated continually to rehearse rather than realize desire. The formal expression of this fantasy, *Really the Blues* is not just a caricature of white Negro hipness, but a literary blues performance, one whose circularity and repetition echoes the circularity and repetition of blues. Much as a musical phrase is recapitulated and yet transformed through each iteration in blues, so each subsequent repetition of Mezzrow's "arrival" builds upon and modifies the paradigm for conversion set forth in reform school.[9]

The imperative of repetition in his own self-fashioning notwithstanding, Mezzrow equates jazz with freedom—both from the formal requirements of classical music and from the "neuroses" associated with bourgeois white male (hetero)sexuality. Indeed, Mezzrow projects onto black masculinity the improvisational qualities of blues itself, for just as "true" blues, in his account, are produced spontaneously, without the mediation of a written text, so Mezzrow imagines black men as possessing immediate and improvisational access to desire and its fulfillment. In Harlem, he writes, "they didn't build any brick walls between wanting and doing, the urge and the act. People up there . . . weren't walking skinfuls of repressions and they didn't mope around having sex flashes every hour on the hour. They never had to sneak like emotional pickpockets into show and movie-houses to get their erotic kicks second-hand. . . . In our 'culture,' between the urge and the act come the foot lights, or anyhow a movie projector" (204–5). Here jazz serves as the explicit metaphor of Mezzrow's fantasy of tearing down the cultural and psychological barriers that inhibit sexual gratification. If the "movie projector" in his narrative figures representation itself, the process that mediates in a symbolic economy between desire and the real, then Mezzrow conceives his own particular white racial "lack" in terms of an imperative to experience gratification secondhand. Black men, by contrast, are liberated from the *need for fantasy* itself; for them, nothing intervenes between urge and act, longing and reality.

Fantasizing about the other's enjoyment is always a fraught venture for Mezzrow, however, because it is so interwoven with his fears of not possessing autonomous means of experiencing pleasure. Within this conflicted libidinal economy, black masculinity functions as the mirror of Mezzrow's fantasies *and* his terrors, the bearer of what he simultaneously wants *and* dreads. It is precisely this ambivalence, Slavoj Žižek argues, that underlies all racisms or xenophobias, in which the "other" is both deified and demonized, at once admired and feared.[10] Thus Mezzrow, like Mailer's "White Negro," can associate himself, in explicitly homoerotic fashion, with the disruptive quality he imaginatively projects onto black male heterosexuality, while also acting out of a certain homophobia and racism. Because this ambivalence is one of the defining conditions of Mezzrow's identification, every attempt he makes to "become" black, is tinged by a corresponding revulsion from blackness, a need to effect distance between "self" and "other" by reinstating difference. In analogous fashion, Eric Lott sees a complex dialectic between "love and theft" as a force that informs the articulation of blackface minstrelsy. Minstrelsy was not merely a representation of an aversion to black culture or black people, but a means by which whites signaled their (repressed) "investiture in black bodies," their "desire to try on the accents" of "blackness" (*Love and Theft* 6). Such ambivalent cross-racial desire, he writes, "coupled a nearly insupportable fascination and self-protective division with respect to black people and their cultural practices, and . . . made blackface minstrelsy less a sign of absolute white power and control than of panic, anxiety, terror, and pleasure" (6).[11]

In Mezzrow's text, this ambivalence makes itself felt most strongly in Mezzrow's use of jazz jive as a way of asserting his identity with authentic black masculinity. Like all autobiography, *Really the Blues* is an act of self-mythologizing, but in distinction from other narratives, Mezzrow heavily stakes his identity-claims on linguistic performance, through which he codes himself as a black man addressing the black masses (Ross, *No Respect* 80). "I think [*Really the Blues*] was a success because I wrote in plain, simple language that anybody could understand," he once told an interviewer, adding, paradoxically, that he "wanted the book to be read and understood by the most illiterate Negro in the states" (Bruynoghe 9). Thus, it is all the more ironic that Mezzrow's jive style served as a useful marketing gimmick that helped to sell the book to white readers, an idea supported by the fact that *Really the Blues* has, as an appendix, an extensive "glossary of terms" that recalls Cab Calloway's 1938 *Hepsters Dictionary* (an oxymoron, since no "real" hepster would ever be caught dead with, let alone need, a dictionary). Most amazingly, the book also features a brief "Jive Section," in which Mezzrow demonstrates his linguistic virtuosity, and a translation of the "Jive Section" in an appendix. However, although Mezzrow's jive talk is intended to demonstrate his mastery of a black lexicon—and thus presumably his authenticity as a white Negro—it ultimately disrupts the illusion it works so assiduously to create. In fact, Mezzrow's excruciatingly affected performance of black talk reveals precisely the disparities or discrepancies it wants to repress or forget.

Mezzrow may profess an awareness of jive as parody and social critique, one that mocks "the game and the rule-makers too . . . the whole idea of eloquence, and the idea that words are anything but hypes and camouflage" (225), but he possesses little distance from his own appropriation of "black talk." While he writes that the hipster "stays conscious of the fraud of language" unlike "ofays" who "hold forth pompously, like they had The Word" (227), quite often Mezzrow's disparaging description of other whites comes back to haunt him. The best demonstration of how this tension plays itself out is in the "Jive Section" of *Really the Blues*, which Mezzrow constructs with an eye toward impressing white readers with a performance of his insider's fluency. Written in dramatic rather than narrative form, the "Jive Section" attempts to camouflage Mezzrow's difference from the other characters in his text, but paradoxically the "sameness" of his performance ends up reinforcing it. Here, for example, Mezzrow is on a Harlem street corner selling marijuana, when one of his regular customers (Fourth Cat) walks up with a friend, who is so impressed by Mezzrow's fluency that he asks whether Mezzrow has any black "blood":

> FOURTH CAT (*Coming up with a stranger*): Mezz, this here is Sonny Thompson, he one of the regular cats on The Avenue and can lay some iron too. Sonny's hip from way back and solid can blow some gauge, so lay an ace

on us and let us get gay. He and Pops [Louis Armstrong] been knowin'
each other for years.
ME: Solid, man, any stud that's all right with Pops must really be in there.
Here, pick up Sonny, the climb's on me.
SONNY (To his friend): Man, you know one thing? This cat should of been
born J.B. [jet black], he collars all jive and comes on like a spaginzy.
(Turning to me.) Boy, is you sure it ain't some of us in your family way
down the line? Boy you're too much, stay with it, you got to git it.
FIFTH CAT: Hey Poppa Mezz! Stickin'?
ME: Like the chinaberry trees in Aunt Hagar's backyard. (217)

Although the "Jive Section" asserts Mezzrow's linguistic identity with other
black men, its effect is ultimately double-edged; while it affirms Mezzrow's
status as an insider, it does so at the risk of exposing his black identity as
ridiculously staged, merely theatrical and hyperbolic. Even Mezzrow's fellow
white musicians found his black talk laughable: Condon nicknamed Mezzrow "Southmouth," and Wilber wrote that it was "ridiculous to hear this
Jewish guy from Chicago coming out with a rich southern drawl" (40).

If Mezzrow is able to sustain the fantasy of his own authenticity through
the display of jive, despite the ways in which he clearly fails to master the
"excess" such a performance inevitably produces, then artistic collaboration
serves as the means by which Mezzrow unwittingly and unwillingly must
"face the music"—that is, the limitation of his fantasy, the difficulty of crossing a line that stays always one step ahead. Collaborative work affords Mezzrow both physical proximity to black artists (important because it violates
bourgeois social taboos and provides fertile ground for his homoerotic fantasies) and the opportunity to hone his own performance of black masculinity
through a process of eroticized mirroring. Yet collaboration is also disruptive,
the means by which Mezzrow re-faces the eruption of irreconcilable difference. This is particularly the case in Mezzrow's description of his work with
Bechet during the Panassié sessions when they recorded "Really the Blues."
Although Mezzrow represents their collaboration as harmonious, a marriage
of minds and musical temperaments—"We fitted together like pieces of a jig-
saw puzzle" (367), he writes—Mezzrow's enthusiasm is dampened by a nag-
ging consciousness of his own mediocrity, which comes to light in contrast
with Bechet's genius. Bechet's playing titillates Mezzrow, his musical flour-
ishes leaving Mezzrow "all trembling inside" (367), but Bechet's virtuosity also
has the power to shame Mezzrow, because in the reflection of Bechet's playing he clearly recognizes the absurdity of his fantasy of their compatibility.

It is during moments of such proximity that Mezzrow perhaps unintentionally reveals how easily his pleasure in identification with black masculinity dissolves into a fear of the failure of his own masculinity. At one point he admits, "The race made me feel inferior, started me thinking that maybe I wasn't worth beans as a musician or any kind of artist, in spite of all my big ideas. The tremendous inventiveness, the spur-of-the-moment creativeness that I saw gushing out in all aspects of Harlem life, in the basketball games, the prize-fights, the cutting contests, the fast and furious games of rhyming and snagging on The Corner—it all dazzled me, made me doubt if I was even in the running with these boys" (239).

Mezzrow's despair at moments such as this one—moments of the most intense identification and hence the deepest disappointment—suggest that his "white Negro" fantasy is psychically enabling, insofar as it defends him both from an internalized self-hatred and from the necessity of facing his own feelings of shame and inadequacy. Having erected a certain fantasy of "authentic" blackness as the sole standard of his own self-worth, Mezzrow measures himself against his ideal and (not surprisingly) finds himself unworthy. Mezzrow's self-loathing explicitly irrupts into his autobiography in a scene in which, locked up on Riker's Island, he projects self-hatred onto the other white inmates, reacting to them like Gulliver upon returning to England after his travels. Face-to-face with junkies, derelicts, and drunks—symbols of "the dying white-man's world" (304)—in the prison receiving room, Mezzrow longingly recalls Harlem, "where the people [are] real and earthy" (306). "I could hardly listen to the talk of my [white] cellmates," he says, "their language and mannerisms and gestures were so coarse and brutal, they spoke with their lips all twisted up, in harsh accents that jarred on my nerves" (306). Like Gulliver's revulsion at his family's smells and sounds, Mezzrow's revulsion at the white prisoners marks his disgust with white society, of which he is still, albeit unwillingly, a part. But whereas in Swift, political satire opens up a space for autocritique, Mezzrow's lack of self-consciousness at this moment precludes or discourages self-ironizing gestures. Having looked to the jazz life for liberation, here he is instead enslaved by his own master-ideal.

Mezzrow's inability to indulge in self-parody on Riker's Island marks the imminent breakdown of his fantasy. Instead of coming to a more mature recognition of the politics of white passing, or even realizing the limitations of his identity-claims, Mezzrow resigns himself to the impossibility of ever "crossing over" by representing an epiphanic episode of spiritual possession by the spirits of his jazz heroes. This moment of literal blues inspiration occurs, like the scene above, on Riker's Island, where Mezzrow is playing

with the prison's Ninth Division jazz band. In distinction from prior millennial moments, this one, with its overtones of religious rapture, replaces
the emphasis on Mezzrow's self-conscious resolve to play in an "authentic"
style with its corollary—submission to unconscious impulses. The result is
an idealized picture of blues improvisation, in which Mezzrow transcends
musical memory and influence, indeed transcends agency altogether:

> And then, Jesus, I fell into a queer dreamy state, a kind of trance, where
> it seemed like I wasn't in control of myself any more, my body was run-
> ning through its easy relaxed motions and my fingers were flying over the
> keys without any push or effort from me—somebody else had taken over
> and was directing all my moves, with me just drifting right along with it,
> feeling it was all fitting and good and proper. . . . And it was exactly, down
> to a T, the same serene exaltation I'd sensed in New Orleans music as a
> kid, and that had haunted me all my life, that I'd always wanted to recap-
> ture for myself and couldn't . . . and my clarinet and the trumpet melted
> together in one gigantic harmonic orgasm, and my fingers ran every
> whichaway. . . . And all of a sudden, you know who I was? I was Jimmy
> Noone and Johnny Dodds and Sidney Bechet . . . they were inside my
> skin, making my fingers work right so I could speak my piece. (321–24)

As the recapturing of previously felt rapture, the very rapture that early
in the narrative led Mezzrow to dedicate himself to blues, the moment also
marks a homecoming, the completion of a circuit. Like the wandering Jew
of the parable, "I had," Mezzrow writes, "been wandering for twenty years,
looking for this fine fabled place, and suddenly I made it, I was home" (323).
In contrast to the first millennium, in which Mezzrow comes out of reform
school "chocolate brown," on Riker's Island he is again reborn, restored to
a previous greenness. "The rest of my life spread out in front of me smooth
and serene," he writes, "because I not only knew what I had to do, I knew
I could do it. . . . The millennium was one me—a small-size, strictly one-
man millennium, but still a millennium" (324). Through his rehearsal of this
"final" millennial moment, in other words, Mezzrow enables his narrative to
arrive at a tentative closure, in defiance of a blues economy marked by infinite variation on a single theme.

I want to close by suggesting that Mezzrow's inability to engage in self-
parody is what set him apart, not only from his white peers in the 1930s, but
from the very blues aesthetic that he emulated—one that privileges double
entendre, ribald sexual punning, and shrewd political satire. Although *Really
the Blues* effects a tone of exuberant playfulness, ultimately Mezzrow's auto-

biography is weighted down by the impossibly high stakes by which he defines his entire "white Negro" enterprise. Given that authenticity is such a stern master, it is not hard to see how Mezzrow's pleasure at "acting black" was also at times overshadowed by displeasure at the inevitable intrusion of difference. One is left to wonder, moreover, at the level of Mezzrow's self-involvement, the degree to which he was (and is in *Really the Blues*) always performing and always his own audience. Finally, it is ironic that Mezzrow's very obsession with "crossing over" left him little energy to devote to the very radical politics that came to be associated, at least superficially, with the tradition of white hipsterism in the 1950s and 1960s.

The "naturalness" question so crucial to Mezzrow's authenticist jazz discourse additionally reinforces the notion of the difficulty of black identity for blacks themselves. This is precisely the point that ghostwriter Bernard Wolfe takes up in two essays he wrote in response to the experience of writing *Really the Blues*, essays that he later combined for the book's afterword. "The truth about the Negro performer," he argued in these, "is that he is required to be a *Negro impersonator*" ("Ecstatic" 396)—the idea for Wolfe being that through "the tyranny of expectancy," dominant American cultural stereotypes shape and create the very images that are later disparaged, emulated, or both. Black cultural styles, Wolfe argues, are largely the product of the majority's "wish-fulfilled images," which in turn produce the need for further innovation, a redrawing of the line that separates "insiders" from "outsiders." Wolfe's notion that black performers are called upon to "act black" and that black performance styles reflect the need to produce "blackness" as a constantly shifting, unstable commodity eventually found its way into Fanon's *Black Skin, White Masks*, especially the chapter on "The Negro and Psychopathology." For Fanon, Wolfe's work demonstrates the connection between the deceptive smile of B'rer Rabbit and the "white mask" of the black Antillean, between the subversive tales passed on among African American slaves and the subversive mimicry of colonial subjects outside of the United States. In the reworked version of the article that Fanon cites, Wolfe returns the compliment (at least implicitly) by punningly renaming Mezzrow's book *White Skin, Black Masks*. As Wolfe's comparison suggests, Fanon's text represents an inversion of *Really the Blues*, an ironizing and oppositional "response" to Mezzrow's "call." Whereas Mezzrow represents the process by which he becomes a "voluntary Negro," Fanon analyzes the colonial subject's "voluntary servitude" to a hegemonically instituted ideal; whereas Mezzrow narrates his own problematic efforts to internalize a black mask, Fanon is concerned with reinterpreting black men's relation to white cultural hegemony in terms of masquerade or disguise.

The point of Fanon and Wolfe's intellectual exchange is that "black" identity (especially "authentic" blackness) may be no less difficult for blacks to perform and that white cultural imperatives impose a heavy and unrelenting burden. Or, to return to the example of Mezzrow: while white male jazz musicians may have had to negotiate the appropriation or adaptation of black performance styles, black performers must also always concern themselves with a certain white cultural mandate to perform—especially to perform "blackness." Of gangstas and divas, the "two polarities" of black male "fierceness" currently raging in black popular culture, Andrew Ross has recently observed that "whether underplayed or overplayed, these theatrical versions of black masculinity are as much methods of deflecting or neutralizing white disapproval as modes of expressing black traditions" ("Gangsta and Diva" 191). In his "passionate love affair with the ghetto" (Wolfe, "Ecstatic" 389), his romance with black male authenticity, Mezzrow remained largely oblivious to this possibility.

For Mezzrow, racial passing was predicated upon a fantasy of the stability of the color line, but what his autobiography unwittingly demonstrates is the instability of race, insofar as difference depends upon constantly shifting conditions of identification (Bhabha, "Interrogating Identity" 193). The tension between Mezzrow's embrace of authenticity and his recurring failure ever to live up to his own jazz standards underscores the pathos governing his entire enterprise. Certain assertions, such as Mezzrow's avowal that he had suffered under Jim Crow, additionally point to the potential danger (and not least the disingenuousness) of claims of white ownership of black experience. Forever professing to have "crossed over" the color line and yet always tragically conscious of the hollowness of this claim—of the fact, in other words, that black cultural citizenship (what lay on the "other" side of the line) consistently eluded him—Mezzrow's life thus played itself out as a series of desperate and harried improvisations, his own Voluntary Negro Blues.

Notes

This essay is an expanded version of a paper delivered at the Unnatural Acts Conference held at the University of California, Riverside, in February 1993. A revised version of this paper will form part of a chapter in my forthcoming book Crossing the Line: Racial Passing in Twentieth-Century American Literature and Culture.

1. I explore the relation between gender and "white Negro" performance in " 'I'm a Loser, Baby'."

2. See Coco Fusco, *English Is Broken Here: Notes on Cultural Fusion in the Americas*, especially pages 25–36 and 65–77. Fusco's book appeared after this essay had already been submitted for publication.

3. None of Mezzrow's recorded music is easily available today, although his collaboration with Bechet on "Really the Blues" can be found on *The Legendary Sidney Bechet* (RCA, 1988).

4. By his own account, Mezzrow drafted *Really the Blues* in longhand and then submitted the manuscript to Wolfe for editing and revising (Hennessey 25). Mezzrow also claimed that 365,000 words were cut from the original manuscript, but, he said, the material was later lost.

5. Long out of print, *Really the Blues* was reissued in 1990 by Citadel Underground, in an edition that contains Wolfe's undated afterword. Mezzrow's claim that the book was translated into "every language except Spanish" is one, not surprisingly, that I have been unable to verify, although *Really the Blues* did meet with some success in France.

6. Mezzrow had already "done jazz a considerable disservice in this country with the publication of his book on space cadets [*Really the Blues*]," Hentoff wrote in 1953, adding that upon Mezzrow's return from France he hoped that Mezzrow would be honored "with the Order of Invincible Ignorance, First Class" ("Counterpoint" 5).

7. Ironically, Mezzrow's greatest fan was neither an American nor black, but the French jazz critic Panassié, who not only wrote frequently about Mezzrow for the *Bullean du Hot Club de France*, but who even penned a 1952 monograph titled *Quand Mezzrow enregistre* [When Mezzrow Records]. Panassié was among those who believed Mezzrow the greatest living white jazz musician. See *Bulletin de Hot Club de France*, n. 132, 3e serie (November 1969) and n. 196, 3e serie (March 1970) for Panassié tributes to Mezzrow.

8. There is also a second boy in the photograph, standing behind Milton Mesirow Jr., but he is unidentified in the caption. Like the article, the photograph is unattributed.

9. Laplanche and Pontalis draw related connections between fantasy and desire, mimesis and performance in *The Language of Psychoanalysis*, their explication and elaboration of the Freudian lexicon. Fantasy, they argue, is not the willful expression of a desiring subject, but a series of scenarios in which one is both a participant and an observer, much as through autobiography Mezzrow constitutes himself as both author and subject. "Even where they can be summed up in a single sentence," they write, "phantasies are still scripts (*scenarios*) of organised scenes which are capable of dramatisation—usually in visual form" (318). Fantasy is thus related to performance through its primary function, which is the mise-en-scène or mimesis of desire. Yet "in so far as desire is articulated in this way through phantasy, phantasy is also the locus of defensive operations," in which "what is *prohibited* is always present" (318). The expression of a wish in fantasy is thus, according to Laplanche and Pontalis, inevitably attended by the expression of a prohibition.

10. For a cogent discussion of this dynamic, see Žižek, "Eastern Europe's Republic of *Gilead*."

11. In a footnote, Lott goes on to speculate: "It may be that by the 1920s an imaginary proximity to 'blackness' was so requisite to white identity and to the culture industry which helped produce that entity—witness the sudden vogue of the suntan—that the signifier of blackface had become redundant; the apposite development of forceful public black cultural production in the Harlem Renaissance also made itself felt" (*Love and Theft* 240 n. 13). Lott's observations suggest that there may be more than an incidental connection between the demise of minstrelsy as a professional entertainment staple in the 1920s and the creation of a "new" breed of white person—the white Negro—as exemplified in Mezzrow.

READING THE BLACKBOARD
Youth, Masculinity, and Racial Cross-Identification

LEEROM MEDOVOI

Reading the Writing on the Blackboard

One could hardly find a more pronounced foreshadowing of postwar American youth's politicization than *The Blackboard Jungle*. Starring Glenn Ford, Sidney Poitier, and Vic Morrow in a tale of high-school delinquency, *Blackboard*, a Hollywood feature film of 1955, thematized emerging conflicts between adults and teenagers over the meaning of generational and racial difference. By the sixties, these conflicts would begin to enter more explicitly political arenas. Today, however, *Blackboard* is remembered, along with *Rebel without a Cause*, as one of Hollywood's founding teenpics, and in particular as the world's first rock-and-roll film. Though it lacked the full soundtrack sported by many subsequent teenpics, the film used as its title song Bill Haley's then obscure "Rock Around the Clock." An enormous success, *Blackboard* launched Haley's career and accelerated the insurgent popularity of rock (then a Southern black musical form) among teenagers.

These two characterizations of the film are quite compatible; indeed, one might suppose that it is *The Blackboard Jungle*'s precise status as Hollywood's first rock-and-roll teenpic that enabled it to voice for young people an incipiently political articulation of their resistance to the America of their parents. This tempting synthesis, however, relies upon an oversimplification of *The Blackboard Jungle* at both the textual and contextual levels. In his historical survey of the teenpic, Thomas Doherty has properly pointed out that *Blackboard* is actually a liminal example of the genre, produced before the film industry had fully developed the concept of a distinct teenage market (75). Like *Rebel without a Cause*, *The Blackboard Jungle* was still expected by its producers to succeed as an "adult film" with only secondary appeal to teenagers, though as Doherty explains, this expectation quickly proved misguided as both films were "embraced enthusiastically by the nation's young. (A 1956 survey . . . found that *Blackboard Jungle* was the favorite film of high school students . . .)" (75). Indeed

The Blackboard Jungle's surprise draw and unexpected box-office windfall were instrumental in convincing financially strapped Hollywood studios, steadily losing their general family audience to the new medium of television, that one route to sizable profits might lie in producing low-budget films specifically targeting the lucrative youth audience (75).[1]

Nevertheless, unlike the juvenile delinquent and rock-and-roll films that followed, *The Blackboard Jungle* also appealed greatly to adult viewers. The film succeeded, in other words, both as a social problem film and as a teen-pic, drawing an audience deeply divided along generational lines. Given this bifurcated audience, *Blackboard's* historical significance is far less transparent than often supposed by fifties rock-and-roll enthusiasts.

Stuart Hall's early essay, "Encoding/Decoding," provides a critical vocabulary well suited for approaching such multivalent moments in social signification as the reception of *Blackboard*. I would like to use Hall's terms here as analytical tools for reinterpreting *Blackboard's* mark on postwar America's cultural landscape. In the process, however, I will also be confronting certain limitations of these terms, limitations, I would argue, that share a common history with the film to which I am applying them.

In "Encoding/Decoding," Hall argues that power differentials within or between audiences will fissure a popular text's meanings along political lines. Mapping a Marxist understanding of ideology onto reader-response criticism, Hall proposes a useful analytic distinction between three types of popular reading: dominant, oppositional, and negotiated.[2] A dominant reading will identify and decode a popular text's preferred meanings, by which Hall means those interpretive results that both "have the institutional/political/ideological order imprinted in them" and "have themselves become institutionalized" (134).

By contrast, an oppositional reading of a popular text occurs only when a viewer systematically "refuses" the meanings preferred by dominant ideology, and instead "decode[s] the message in a *globally* contrary way. He/she de-totalizes the message in the preferred code in order to retotalize the message within some alternative framework of reference. This is the case of the viewer who listens to a debate on the need to limit wages but 'reads' every mention of the 'national interest' as 'class interest'" (S. Hall, "Encoding" 137–38). Between these two extremes lies the negotiated reading. Typically performed by viewers or readers who are ambiguously situated within power relations, negotiated readings accept a popular text's preferred meanings at the general level, but modify them "at a more restricted situational (situated) level," often by positing exceptions and alternatives (S. Hall, "Encoding" 137).[3]

Today, the dominant/oppositional polarity deployed in Hall's 1979 essay may seem somewhat mechanical. Nevertheless, as a corrective to both *Screen* and Frankfurt School varieties of the popular culture–as–ideological apparatus thesis, the reception-directed argumentation of "Encoding/Decoding" still guides much of contemporary popular culture studies. In *Television Culture*, for example, John Fiske uses Hall's theory of reading as a point of departure, arguing that the specification of a text's ideological dimension is only the first step in assessing how it signifies for readers. Using Hall's terms to stress the radical diversity of meanings that might be generated out of a single episode of the TV show *Hart to Hart*, Fiske speculates that

> a dominant reading of the . . . segment [discussed] in chapter 1 would be made by a white, middle-class, urban, northern male, and would conform to the dominant ideology as it is encoded in the text. An oppositional reading might be made by a Hispanic member of the working classes, who would reject the dominant meanings and pleasures offered by the program because they opposed his interests; he might support the crimes of the Hispanic villain as revolutionary acts against white capitalism. A woman, however, might produce a negotiated reading, which accepted the ideological framework of the narrative, but negotiated within it a special significance for the heroine, her actions, and the values she embodies. (64)

Well aware of the reductive causality he is risking here, Fiske quickly points out that Hall tended to "overemphasize class in relation to other social factors" and cautions that "there are very few perfectly dominant or purely oppositional readings." Nevertheless, Fiske embraces Hall's underlying argument that the political valence of popular culture inheres not in its texts, but rather in the negotiation between socially positioned viewers and the codes that structure the texts (Fiske 64). Like Hall, Fiske contends that popular texts lack any intrinsic ideological closure. Closure instead becomes an effect intermittently imposed by dominant ideologies that, by leading subjects to prefer certain semiotic processes over others, will tend to limit the play of meaning in their readings of popular texts. Indeed, a dominant reading can be defined as an instance where that tendency has won out: the reader has successfully decoded the text in an ideologically coherent manner, and repressed any textual contradictions of that coherency.

A generally unacknowledged corollary of Hall's school of thought, however, is that oppositional readings must also constitute their own ideological closures of popular texts. Like someone who reads "dominantly," Hall's oppositional debate listener, who systematically substitutes "class interest" for "national interest" performs politically coherent work. So too does Fiske's oppositional TV viewer, who reads for "revolutionary acts against white capitalism." Like dominant readings (and decisively unlike the fragmented, contradictory, negotiated ones), both oppositional readings are guided by ideology (though to be sure a "counterideology" such as socialism, nationalism, or anti-imperialism) to prefer certain meanings. And therefore they too must repress certain other meanings that threaten to disrupt their counterideology.

What Fiske considers to be the negotiated feminine (and potentially feminist) meanings of Hart to Hart, for example, are entirely absent from the Hispanic male's oppositional reading, just as they are from the dominant reading of the white male. Somehow in the process of creating the ideological closure of "revolutionary acts against white capitalism," the "oppositional reading" posed by Fiske has excluded oppositionality in terms of gender. If less overtly, Hall's oppositional viewer, while systematically substituting every utterance of "nation" with "class," precludes the alternative replacement of "nation" with "male."

These exclusions illustrate not only that several oppositional readings of a popular text are possible; they indicate, I argue, that the counterideological closure (or, as Hall puts it, the "retotalization") of oppositional reading can itself be understood as a hegemonic process, one that in these two examples has repressed possible decodings of gender oppression for the sake of decoding class and racial struggle instead. My point here is that the Gramscian notion of counterhegemony, so central to recent cultural studies theorizations of resistance, needs to be taken in a double sense; a "counterhegemony" refers to the formation of a political adversary to an existing hegemony, but also attests to that adversary's status as *a local hegemony in its own right*, with its own means of "manufacturing consent" for the sake of collective struggle.

Though neither Hall nor Fiske ever pursues this line of argument, the commonalities they implicitly draw between oppositional and dominant readings indicate the theoretical viability of second-order oppositional readings, informed by counter-counterideologies, if you like, that oppose the hegemonic hierarchization of meaning imposed by the "original" oppositional readings. Such would be the case with feminist rereadings of either the socialist reception of Hall's wage debate, or the Marxist/anti-imperialist reception of Fiske's Hart to Hart episode. Of course, these second-order oppositional readings could then be countered by a third, and from here we move into an infinite regression, or to put it in deconstructive terminology, into an infinite displacement of political difference.

To assert that further oppositional readings of a text are always possible, however, reveals nothing about whether such readings have ever been performed, let alone become widespread practices in the reception history of a given text. Here I propose that we might draw a useful methodological distinction between deconstruction as pure textual analysis and a cultural studies informed by deconstruction. The former's work ends when it has demonstrated the formal possibilities for the destabilization of any hermeneutic closure. The latter, however, in the spirit of cultural studies' concern with the production of meaning by audiences, remains fundamentally concerned with the historical status of these destabilizations, whether, how, and why they were (or were not) mobilized by viewers, and what we can infer about the cultural moment(s) during which the text circulated.

Brown vs. the Blackboard of Education: A Dominant Reading

As we shall see, the teenage audience's response to The Blackboard Jungle can be usefully analyzed in terms of such a deconstructive cultural studies framework. The film allowed teenagers to read with pleasure for certain oppositional meanings that threatened to disrupt the hegemony of white middle-class adults as it evolved alongside important changes in mid-fifties American racial politics. In this sense, the readings performed by teenage viewers of The Blackboard Jungle were counterhegemonic. However, as I will also suggest, the oppositionality of these meanings was structured by a masculinist ideology that, by the late fifties, would itself become hegemonic within youth culture and politics, and not be systematically challenged until the late sixties.

That the film occasioned any disruption of the adult social order, however, might surprise a present-day viewer. The Blackboard Jungle tells the seemingly conservative story of a white teacher named Richard Dadier (Glenn Ford) — just out of the Navy and newly recruited by all-male, inner-city North Manual Arts High School — who struggles to wrest the allegiance of a black student, Gregory Miller (Sidney Poitier), away from an interracial gang of juvenile delinquents led by an Irish boy, Artie West (Vic Morrow).

Artie and Mr. Dadier struggle against one another throughout the film, particularly after Dadier catches and turns in another boy for attempting to rape a new woman teacher, Miss Hammond. While Dadier wields his classroom authority against Artie, Artie employs various covert forms of attack: avenging his friend by beating up Dadier (and another teacher) in a dark alley, anonymously accusing him of using racist epithets in class, and even sending unsigned notes to his pregnant wife, Anne, accusing her husband of cheating on her with Miss Hammond.

In the end Dadier wins Gregory over from the gang, though before he does, the teacher must himself be taught a lesson in liberal racial politics. Dadier had overhastily assumed that the black student, Gregory, was his anonymous accuser, and learns to regret this mistake. When he apologizes to Gregory, Dadier proves his commitment to the democratic principle of racial justice. Only at the very end of the film does Dadier (along with the viewer) learn for certain that Artie has been the real culprit. In the final scene, as Artie pulls a switchblade on Dadier during class, Gregory finally sides with the teacher, towing all but one of the other boys along with him.

In narrating a white man's effort to shoulder the burden of civilizing a denizen of the "blackboard jungle," the film depicts a racial cross-identification (of a black boy with a white man) that serves white interests. Furthermore, Dadier constructs this identification on the ideological terrain of masculinity, winning Gregory over by teaching him that maturation into manhood requires abandoning the gang and siding with the educational system. Gregory here stands in for the majority of Dadier's ethnically and racially diverse students, who, as I noted, will join Gregory in finally rallying to his side against Artie and his one remaining crony, Belazi. As Peter Biskind has argued, this ending sacrifices the two genuine "bad apples" so that the film's other boys can be redeemed into a liberal intergenerational consensus on the need for students to cooperate with an understanding school system (216). Thus far, The Blackboard Jungle appears to articulate unambiguously the intersections of dominant racial, gender, and generational ideology: the film's "message" is that even those few young people (white and non-white) seemingly fated for economic and racial hardship can still alter their future if they make a constructive moral commitment to respect, obey, and identify with the middle-class white men who will show them the road to success. Otherwise, they are doomed.[4]

This reading approximates Hall's "dominant reading" not only because of its ideological import, but also because the reading is strongly encouraged by certain structures in the text itself, which take great pains to provide normative guidelines for reception. Perhaps the most explicit and powerful of these guidelines is the bombastic, discursive preface that frames the narrative, declaring The Blackboard Jungle's socially responsible purpose of informing citizens. As the preface reminds the viewer, "We, in the United States, are fortunate to have a school system that is a tribute to our communities and to our faith in American youth." However, the preface continues, "today we are concerned with juvenile delinquency—its causes—and its effects." This concern justifies the film, the preface implies, because, "we believe that public awareness is a first step toward a remedy for any problem." Not private profit then but public welfare, not exploitation but education, is alleged to motivate this film's depiction of such sordid subject matter.

The preface's clever slide in the subject position of the personal pronoun, from its explicit "We the citizens of the United States" (the decoders of the film) to its implicit "We who have produced this film" (its encoders) marks a rhetorical effort to align author and spectator as equally responsible citizen-subjects: both take seriously their public duty to inform and become informed about political questions of the day. Within this preface at least, the implied producers and the implied viewers are also unmistakably adults. The film is not for youth, but only about them.

In this respect, the film claims for itself the same pedagogical value as does the Evan Hunter novel upon which it is based; both texts aim to provide adults with the social knowledge they require in order to tackle the problem of juvenile delinquency effectively. However, Hunter's naturalistic novel actually sticks far more closely than the film to its professed informational function. Depicting teacher Rick Dadier's harrowing first semester on the job at North Manual Arts High School in the Bronx, the novel documents for its reader an urban ecology of the blackboard jungle. It methodically analyzes the desperate situation of those who live in the "trash can of the school system," explains why they behave as they do, and demonstrates the naïveté of middle-class faith in the public educational system as an engine for social mobility. In so doing, the sensationalism of Hunter's novel actually functions to subvert comfortable American assumptions about prospects for economic uplift among the urban underclass.

By contrast, the film would appear to serve dominant ideological interests far more loyally than the novel, whose grim thematics of political economy it replaces with a moral economy, in which the reformable delinquents are actually saved in the end while the unredeemable are treated to their just deserts. Unlike the novel's more ambiguous ending, in which Dadier wins only a limited victory against the worst of the delinquents, the film version concludes with Dadier's triumphant transformation of Manual High, showing its viewer how the integrity and dedication of a single good teacher can save the educational system by leading his non-white students to cross-identify with him as the embodiment of the authority of whiteness and maturity.

The film's ideological divergence from the novel is clearly revealed in one of the few scenes it appends to Hunter's original narrative. After a series of failures in his classroom, and indeed after he and another teacher have been beaten up in an alley after hours, a downcast Rick Dadier finds new inspiration by visiting Professor A. R. Kraal, the man who had once trained him to teach. Kraal, now a principal, gives Dadier a tour of his school, the luxurious, suburban norm from which Manual High deviates: a lily-white campus of docile teenagers who learn Latin, chemistry, and proudly sing the national anthem. Reinspired by this vision of what might be, Mr. Dadier returns to Manual High, puts his shoulder back to the wheel, and single-handedly succeeds in steering his kids onto the right track.

The contrast sketched between Kraal's school and Manual High is only a brief addition to Hunter's narrative of 1954, but it indicates a sharpening of the story's engagement with perhaps the most unavoidable of all political contexts of its day: racial desegregation. The film's release in March of 1955 came some ten months after the Supreme Court's first ruling in its landmark *Brown v. Board of Education* case on the unconstitutionality of segregated schools, and only two months prior to a widely anticipated second decision in which the Court determined that desegregation must be implemented "with all deliberate speed" (Oakley 191–93).

If in the mid-fifties a reformed political hegemony in the U.S., inclined to accept the Supreme Court's verdict for desegregation, was beginning to coalesce, the legal decision was, for white moderates and liberals near the center of that hegemony, acceptable as a political goal only under very specific terms and conditions. By and large, even the most liberal white opinion could only affirm racial integration by imagining interracial schooling taking place through the piecemeal admission and assimilation of non-whites who could then be brought to cross-identify racially with the primarily white and white-staffed schools. To conceive of "minority majority" or nonassimilationist integrated education, seemed tantamount to accepting the collapse of the racial order. "It's all very well to talk about school integration—if you remember that you may also be talking about social disintegration," President Eisenhower himself remarked privately in 1956, one year before reluctantly ordering the use of federal troops to escort a mere nine black students to all-white Central High School in Little Rock, Arkansas (Oakley 194).

In portraying a "wild," fully integrated high-school student body, both

Figure 1. Professor Kraal's all-white, coed school is a vision of social order.

the film and book versions of Blackboard engage these racial fears, collapsing juvenile delinquency and desegregation into the representation of a singular "social problem." The film version of Blackboard Jungle, however, marks its racial position even more explicitly by stressing the contrast between Kraal's school and Manual High. The former becomes a model institution that Manual High must emulate if Dadier is to make integrated schooling a positive success rather than a debacle. In Kraal's school, students are patriotic, obedient, and loyal to white, middle-class American values as embodied by teachers and principal. At Manual High, racial integration at first seems to be accompanied by a loss of patriotism, obedience, and general social order. With the exception of one cowed, good boy in an early scene, Manual High's white students are as unruly and disrespectful as their non-white peers. In the one scene where Dadier and Artie Shaw speak in private, Artie explicitly voices his cynical contempt for patriotism, explaining proudly how he will refuse to play the sap and fight for his country if called upon.

Though Kraal tempts Dadier with a job offer at his school, Dadier reluctantly turns it down, feeling that his students deserve opportunity too, and that his duty therefore lies with them. By the end of the film, that duty has been discharged. Through his perseverance, Mr. Dadier manages to convert his integrated classroom's attitude and behavior into something very much

Figure 2. Integrated, all-boy Manual High is in utter chaos.

akin to Kraal's all-white classrooms. The moment of truth, of course, comes in the final scene when all but one student abandon Artie as he brandishes his knife at Mr. Dadier. Indeed, the fate of the one exception, Belazi, is coded symbolically to reflect the school's shift toward obedience and patriotism. As Belazi makes a move to join Artie's attack on Mr. Dadier, another student grabs an American flag and rams Belazi against the blackboard. This act signals the end of juvenile delinquency's reign at Manual High, and the beginning of the school's rebirth as a successful democratic experiment in integration, institutional proof that the white teacher's authority can survive in a multiracial classroom.

The Blackboard Erased?: A Brief Reception History

The dominant reading of The Blackboard Jungle presented above stresses a particular conjunction of generational, racial, and nationalist ideologies from the mid-fifties. If, however, meanings are produced only in the readerly encounters of subjects and texts, then one might expect that Blackboard's preferred meanings were refracted, inverted, rejected, reconsidered, or in some other way negotiated by its contemporary audiences, activating other, less preferred but structurally available, meanings as the film circulated.[5] This applies not only to the film's teenage viewers, but to adults as well, who, as the historical evidence suggests, were unevenly compliant with *Blackboard's* preferred meanings. Far from achieving general acceptance as a means of adult edification regarding the social problem of juvenile delinquency in integrated schools, *The Blackboard Jungle*, in fact, became a highly controversial movie that rocked the film industry.

To a considerable extent, adult disagreement over *Blackboard* derived from uncertainty regarding the nature of its unexpected appeal to teenagers. Although, as I have suggested, *Blackboard* resolves its narrative by vanquishing the widely feared "multiracial delinquency" problem and reestablishing white adult authority, the film's original teenage audiences seem to have pointedly ignored the "moral" of the story, revoking in the process the premature closure between implied producer and viewer asserted in the film's preface.

The concern with teenage viewers began even before the film's release, when a New York City schoolteacher was stabbed to death by a student (McGee and Robertson 31). This incident immediately foregrounded the basic question that would consume adult debates over the film. Would *The Blackboard Jungle* help the public tackle juvenile delinquency by telling the truth about it, as MGM claimed, or would the depiction of youth violence on-screen simply exacerbate the problem? Even though the murderer could not yet have seen the film, his crime's uncanny parallel to *Blackboard's* final scene, in which Artie slashes and threatens to kill Mr. Dadier in their Bronx high-school classroom, provided ammunition for those critics of the film who believed in the deleterious effects of screening such subject matter.

Subsequent media reports on the responses of teenagers were far from reassuring. James Gilbert relates that, "[a]ttending a preview of the film, producer Brooks was surprised, and obviously delighted, when young members of the audience began dancing in the aisles to the rock and roll music. This occurred repeatedly in showings after the film opened" (184–85). Other adults, however, were less than delighted to learn that teenagers were sitting quietly through the careful guidelines of the moralistic preface, but erupting wildly as soon as it gave way to "Rock Around the Clock." Their suspicions, as Gilbert notes, were further confirmed by "other reactions [that] were more threatening. For example in Rochester, New York, there were reports that 'young hoodlums cheered the beatings and methods of terror inflicted upon a teacher by a gang of boys' pictured in the film" (184–85).[6] One Toronto alderman, upon witnessing local teenagers' response to a showing of *The Blackboard Jungle*, told a local newspaper that " 'Hollywood has succeeded, as usual, in glorifying in the minds of teenagers just the things it claims to attack.' [Alderman] Dennison claimed he would lead in the ban efforts. . . . He said the great applause in the film came when a 'tough guy' pupil told a teacher to 'go to hell' and then drew a knife and stabbed the teacher" ("Toronto Hubbub"). In the weeks following the film's release, the press also reported several scattered incidents of juvenile delinquency allegedly "linked" to the film. In a column titled "Police Seek to Finger 'Blackboard Jungle' As Root of Hooliganism," for example, *Variety* reported that the film, "was blamed by Schenectady police for prompting several teen-agers last week to form a gang, which proposed to wage a battle with an Albany group. Other juvenile outbreaks were [also] attributed to the motion picture. . . . Sergeants Joseph Monaco and Patricia Wellman of the Youth Aid bureau said that several teenagers, picked up by police for questioning, 'admitted' they banded together after seeing *The Blackboard Jungle*" ("Police Seek"). Even in Memphis, where the film was licensed on an "adult only" basis, teenage girls gathered after the movie to burn down a local barn. According to the *Motion Picture Daily*, a local juvenile court judge had determined that "the leader of the group, organized just a few hours before the fire, is a 14-year-old who said she got the idea after seeing *The Blackboard Jungle* which finished a three-week run at Loew's state here on Thursday. She [Judge McCain] said the girls said, 'We wanted to be tough like those kids in that picture.' The leader said, although the picture was labeled 'for adults only,' she and her date had no difficulty gaining admittance and that there were others there even younger than she" ("Girls Burn"). Incidents such as these only deepened public concern that young people were seeking out *The Blackboard Jungle* because it encouraged misreadings that glorified teenage violence and terrorism.[7]

Nevertheless, MGM, the studio responsible for *Blackboard*, could hardly afford to pull the film from distribution since the box-office receipts quickly revealed it to be a smash hit by any measurement (Gilbert 185). Within one year of its release, *The Blackboard Jungle* had grossed nearly seven million dollars, "holding over for a third week in some areas where a one-week run is normal," and becoming "the company's top money-making new film of nearly the past couple of years" ("'Blackboard Jungle'").

MGM was further reassured by the fact that, though the film was under attack in some publications and even banned in certain cities, it also had well-respected defenders who were satisfied by the film's professed intentions, and by what they believed to be the moral force of its preferred reading. Most notable of the film's proponents was then Screen Actors Guild president Ronald Reagan, who at the Kefauver hearings on delinquency, lauded the positive role model presented by Mr. Dadier, and the indisputable villainy of Artie West: " 'Any juvenile seeing it would have to have a feeling of disgust for the bad boy,' Reagan told the committee. 'And I got something else out of it. I found in it a great tribute to a group of persons who seldom get much credit—the schoolteachers of this country' " (McGee 47). For the most part, adult institutional voices agreed with Reagan. As *Variety* reported, "nine of the twelve civic, religioso and parents-teachers groups which appraise films in the so-called green sheet praised *Jungle*, rating it 'outstanding' for a pic of its type" (" 'Blackboard Jungle' ").

In the end, *The Blackboard Jungle* survived the onslaught of criticism to become a smashing commercial success and eventually the model for an entire subgenre of delinquent teenpics. Some reviewers nonetheless remained certain that, far from assisting adult social authority, MGM's film was instead subverting it by allowing its youth audience pleasures that differed radically and dangerously from those admitted by the dominant reading. But what exactly were these pleasures? And in particular, what generational, racial, and gendered meanings were eliciting them?

The Blackboard's Jungle: Reading Oppositionally

Curiously, the text of *The Blackboard Jungle* seems to comment on these very questions by proposing a model for its own subversive uses. In a film-within-a-film scene, *Blackboard* explicitly depicts a fragmentary moment of oppositional youth reading. When he first arrives on the job at Manual High, Mr. Dadier employs tough tactics in an effort to coerce discipline from his sullen, rebellious students. When the stick fails, Dadier tries a carrot instead, attempting to win their interest by bringing a tape recorder into class. Artie and the other students mischievously manage to subvert the taping session, so Dadier tries again by screening an animated cartoon of *Jack and the Beanstalk*. This time, Dadier succeeds. The students enjoy watching the movie, and afterward are pleased to discuss it.

Over the course of their discussion, Dadier proposes a reading consonant with his own liberal paternalism. He wants the students to identify with Jack, but on very specific terms. The giant from whom Jack steals the harp and goose, as it so happens, had himself killed Jack's father long ago. As a loyal son who slays his father's murderer, Jack is judged by Dadier to be a laudable figure. However, in keeping with his liberal notion of racial tolerance, Dadier increasingly stresses that it must not be the giant's *difference* that excuses Jack's violence; an attack on someone justified through prejudice alone is immoral.

Gregory, meanwhile, is reluctant to identify with Jack. To begin with, Jack is lazy and inconsiderate of his poor mother, thoughtlessly selling the family cow for a "mess of beans." But even more importantly, Gregory is disturbed by the fact that Jack kills without any knowledge—let alone any proof—that the giant is his father's murderer. Recognizing the absence of any formal procedure for ascertaining the giant's guilt, Gregory grows somewhat skeptical that the giant got only what he deserved, suspecting that he was scapegoated merely because of his physical difference.

Though he distrusts Dadier's reading, Gregory's eventual desertion of the gang for the educational system is portended by the broad possibilities for co-optation built into his own reading: if Jack's laziness alienates Gregory, then Gregory is grasping firmly onto a masculine bread winner ethos, something Dadier actually encourages in Gregory as a way of getting him to buckle down in the classroom. If Gregory wants a trial, he is calling for liberal judgment, the putative impartiality of which legitimates institutional violence, as it will by the end of the film, when the revelation of Artie's guilt sanctions Dadier's right to smash the delinquent boy repeatedly against the blackboard. Indeed, if Jack has managed to avenge his father, then by the end of the cartoon he has begun to take on his father's own masculine responsibility. Gregory's reading thus portends the implication by the end of the film that, with this change of heart, Gregory is now following in Dadier's footsteps and will someday himself become the new bearer of paternal authority.[8]

Gregory may be far more willing than Dadier to believe that the giant's death has been made acceptable by his otherness. Nevertheless, he ultimately accepts Dadier's insistence that Jack's deed would be ethical and laudable if the giant's criminality could be proven. Gregory, in his concern for the possible victim of a racial injustice, flirts with the giant, but ultimately accepts Jack as the proper object of his identification. In Hall's terms, Gregory's reading is a paradigmatically negotiated one, disinclined to accept dominant ideology in local situations when it victimizes him in terms of his racial position, but inclined to play along at a more global level.

Artie West's reading, however, is very different and bears close scrutiny. At first Artie, the boy who turns out to be the villainous gang leader, refuses to join the other boys in enjoying the movie (an anticipation of his eventual isolation). Artie recognizes that Dadier is trying to shift the class's identification with *Jack and the Beanstalk*. Any pleasure they take is ultimately not theirs, but Dadier's. "It's a phony," snarls Artie. To enjoy the cartoon is already to be co-opted by the teacher's game, to accept the hierarchy of white/professional/adult/teacher over non-white/poor/young/student.

Figure 3. Artie is left out of the fun when Dadier screens "Jack and the Beanstalk."

For one brief instant, however, Artie does something else. Idly speaking his own pleasures of the text, Artie announces to the class that (like Dadier) he identifies with Jack. Unlike Dadier, however, Artie likes him because Jack proves that crime pays, getting away as he does both with theft and murder. Artie here describes a criminal identification process directly parallel to that which adults feared teenagers were engaging in with *The Blackboard Jungle*, namely identifying with Artie rather than with Dadier.

Dadier's effort after Artie's comment to win sympathy for the giant as a possible victim of intolerance is as much a response to Artie's generational threat as it is a moral lesson on racism. Jack, after all, is a boy who victimizes a giant man, a juvenile delinquent who kills an oversized adult. "Is it right to dislike somebody because he's different?" asks Dadier. "There are a lot of us right here in this classroom who are different than anyone else." In fact, Dadier is the only one who is marked as different from anyone else; he is the only adult in a room full of boys, and for that matter an adult who has twice been the scapegoat of what he considers to be a bad rap, first for getting the cold shoulder after catching the rapist, and then for being victimized by a violent hate crime.

The fairy-tale cartoon conveniently speaks to Dadier's experience, since Jack is pursued by the giant only after he snatches the magic harp, which is personified as a woman screaming for help. Should Dadier be attacked simply because he is an adult who tried to stop a juvenile rapist? In its generational register, Dadier is reacting to what he fears is a real possibility that Artie's reading may be embraced by his classmates.[9] Gregory, for one, is deeply affected by Dadier's plea, turning half toward Artie and half toward Dadier after class to warn, "That giant, if he done wrong, at least I think he should've had a trial."

Dadier's discursive maneuver in this scene parallels that of adults in relation to The Blackboard Jungle itself. Acknowledging the dominant meanings preferred by the text, but also the fact that these were not the meanings that teenagers seemed to derive, Estes Kefauver's U.S. Senate committee report, Motion Pictures and Juvenile Delinquency, articulated the conflicted reading that many adults had negotiated with The Blackboard Jungle:

> While the committee recognizes and appreciates the artistic excellence of this film, it feels there are valid reasons for concluding that the film will have effects on youth other than the beneficial ones described by its producers. . . . It is felt that many of the type of delinquents portrayed in this picture will derive satisfaction, support, and sanction from having made society sit up and take notice of them. Although the tough individual portrayed by Artie West is used to show the crime-does-not-pay requirement by the end of the film, even the producer . . . agreed that the type of individual portrayed by Artie West upon viewing this film will in no way receive the message purportedly presented in the picture and would identify with him no matter what the outcome of the film. (U.S. Senate 46–47)

Artie's reading of Jack and the Beanstalk, that crime does pay, the committee suspects, threatens to overwhelm the preferred reading of criminality in The Blackboard Jungle, namely that it does not. Of course, the rather small number of violent juvenile delinquents were not the committee's only concern any more than Artie represents Dadier's sole concern. The rowdy success of the film with a wide teenage audience fed an even deeper anxiety—namely, that alienated but heretofore obedient teenagers might also choose to identify with Artie and his gang.

The Blackness of the Board: Cross-Racial Identification
and Oppositional Reading

In addition to identifying with Jack both as juvenile and as delinquent, Artie takes his pleasure in a way that also has submerged cross-racial implications, though they may not be obvious at first glance. Race, as we saw in Dadier and Gregory's readings, is a central issue in the class's discussion of *Jack and the Beanstalk*. Artie's identification with Jack, however, would seem also to imply his identification with whiteness. In fact, this is not so simple. If Artie's Jack is a thief, then so is the giant: both of them steal the goose. And if his Jack is a murderer, then again so is the giant, who killed Jack's father. If criminality, if taking what one wants and getting away with it, grounds Artie's identification, then the giant is as promising a candidate as Jack. Jack, in fact, follows in the giant's footsteps, much as the "hipster" would emulate the "Negro" in Norman Mailer's controversial essay, "The White Negro."

Originally just "half a page about what I thought of integration in the schools," Mailer's essay on the "hows" and "whys" of the postwar hipster subculture grew out of his contention that "the white loathes the idea of the Negro attaining equality in the classroom because the white feels that the Negro already enjoys sensual superiority" (299). For Mailer, the "White Negro" is someone who, in a suffocating postwar age that demands stringent conformity even as it threatens nuclear annihilation, has chosen to drop out of the white race and become a hipster. The hipster, abandoning the sterile privilege of white "classroom superiority," self-consciously models his life on the "Negro," pursuing instead the black man's "sensual superiority." The "Negro," in turn, serves as a figure whose racial marginalization and terrorization have led him to an existential, even psychopathic, creed of acting on his desires without regard to the law. Mailer, ironically enough given his essay's original intent, thus ends up accepting mainstream white concern with juvenile delinquency as a potential consequence of racial integration, though he valorizes, rather than condemns, that result.[10] Like Jack for Artie, the White Negro for Mailer is someone who proves to the world that crime pays after all, most of all in a conformist era like the fifties.

By scrutinizing *The Blackboard Jungle*, we can find possibilities for "White Negro" modes of criminal identification similar to those Artie West picks out in *Jack and the Beanstalk*. For example, by using Bill Haley's anthem, "Rock Around the Clock," to fade from the film titles (superimposed on a blackboard) into the opening diegetic shot of delinquent students dancing in the schoolyard, *The Blackboard Jungle* could interpellate its "youth-cultured" specta-

Figure 4. The multi-raced boys of Manual High rock around the clock with one another.

tors into their rebellion by explicitly identifying rock and roll, the increasingly preferred music of *Blackboard's* actual youth audience, with the film's depiction of black, Puerto Rican, and white youth's unified antagonism toward the white adult-controlled educational institution. The musical reference is oblique, requiring an inference similar to Artie's in the case of the cartoon. Bill Haley and his Comets, like Elvis or Jerry Lee Lewis, are white. Yet their rock-and-roll music is clearly an appropriation of Southern black culture. The use of the title song thus indirectly solicits a youth spectator to identify not with the white adult Mr. Dadier, but with the racially mixed and threatening body of students.

Up to this point, I have used primarily textual evidence to reconstruct an oppositional reading, a strategy that, by locating structures of meaning in the text agreeable to youth rebelliousness, helps to explain why *The Blackboard Jungle* was so amenable to oppositional appropriations. That these meanings were so readily activated by teen moviegoers, however, indicates that these meanings were already entering into general discursive circulation. This is why Mailer's "The White Negro," which explicitly calls the new hipster sensibility a "menage a trois" between the bohemian, the juvenile delinquent, and the Negro, proves so helpful in elucidating the racial dimension of Artie's identification with Jack (305–6). In effect, Mailer's essay discursively restates and affirms the same mode of rebellion mobilized by The Blackboard Jungle for teenagers.

As a way of confirming that these oppositional youth pleasures and meanings were growing in power and importance from the mid-fifties onward, I have chosen two additional intertexts from the late sixties. Both were widely read essays that, like Mailer's, explicitly theorize racial cross-identifications among white youth. Mailer had already discussed the oppositionality of the "White Negro" in terms of generational conflict, arguing that the language of hip is one "most adolescents can understand instinctively, for the hipster's intense view of existence matches their experience and their desire to rebel" (308–9). An essay from Eldridge Cleaver's 1968 collection, Soul on Ice, foregrounds generational conflict even more prominently. The best-seller of the Black Power movement, Soul on Ice was published by Dell as a mass-market paperback, which sold two million copies within four years, particularly among young people involved in the counterculture and the New Left.

In the essay entitled "The White Race and Its Heroes," Cleaver begins by referring to himself as an "Ofay Watcher," one of the colored people of the world who view their white oppressors from the shadows of colonialism. Since entering Folsom Prison in 1954, only one year prior to Blackboard's release, Cleaver tells us he has witnessed a remarkable development among young Ofays, "who are experiencing the great psychic pain of waking into consciousness to find their inherited heroes turned by events into villains. Communication and understanding between the older and younger generations of whites has entered a crisis. . . . So thoroughgoing is the revolution in the psyches of white youth that the traditional tolerance which every older generation has found it necessary to display is quickly exhausted, leaving a gulf of fear, hostility, mutual misunderstanding, and contempt" (72–73).

Cleaver suggests that white adults cannot admit that young people no longer deify such heroic father-figures of the race as George Washington and Thomas Jefferson, who for all their high-sounding rhetoric owned hundreds of slaves and were thus important players in the crimes of colonialism: "The elders do not like to give these youngsters credit for being able to understand what is going on and what has gone on. When speaking of juvenile delinquency, or the rebellious attitude of today's youth, the elders employ a glib rhetoric. They speak of the 'alienation of youth,' the desire of the young to be independent, the problem of 'the father image' and 'the mother image' and their effect upon growing children who lack sound models upon which to pattern themselves. But they consider it bad form to connect the problem of

the youth with the central event of our era—the national liberation movements abroad and the Negro revolution at home" ("The White Race" 74).

Cleaver's words here seem to speak almost directly to the preface of *The
Blackboard Jungle* discussed earlier, whose assertion that "today we are concerned with the problem of juvenile delinquency," decenters racism as the
film's social problem even as it implicitly connects the two issues. As Cleaver's
argument would suggest, the film's dominant meanings repudiate the possibility that racial oppression (as opposed to racial mixing) could motivate
juvenile delinquency. Indeed, the narrative structure itself, in which it is a
white youngster, Artie, who is the embittered, adversarial, delinquent leader,
and not Gregory, also serves to undercut the valorization of youth criminality as an appropriate response to white racism. Instead, the film presents
Dadier as a champion of liberal values, and stigmatizes Artie as an opportun-
ist who cynically uses the issue of racism to create a wedge between Dadier
and his other students.

But while this particular structuring of the characters in the film bolsters
the dominant reading, it cannot entirely repress the semiological alternatives.
Cleaver notes in the same essay that America has always had two conflicting
images of itself, images that are effectively captured by Frederick Douglass's
famous speech, "What to the American Slave is the Fourth of July?" Cleaver
quotes Douglass: "To him your celebration is a sham; your boasted liberty, an
unholy license; your national greatness, swelling vanity; your sounds of rejoicing are empty and heartless; your denunciation of tyrants, brass-fronted
impudence; your shouts of liberty and equality, hollow mockery" (qtd. in
"The White Race" 78). From the perspective of a racially oppositional reading
of *The Blackboard Jungle*, Douglass's "you" could well be referring to Dadier and
his liberal rhetoric. In fact, the film gives no indication that the students have
at all experienced any racial tensions among themselves until Dadier attempts
to teach them lessons in liberal tolerance. In other words, the film permits
a reading that reverses Artie's and Dadier's moral standing in the dominant
reading: it is *Dadier* who cynically exploits racism, using it to divide the students who have united against him.

Cleaver argues that "Because there is no common ground between these
contradictory images of America, they had to be kept apart" ("The White
Race" 79). Of course, in *The Blackboard Jungle* it is precisely these images that are
not kept apart, but instead allowed to coexist textually. Depending on how
one reads, Dadier is either a heroic father-figure or a racist tyrant. The school
system is an institution serving either democracy or white supremacy. And

Artie West is either a savage criminal or one of the emerging new breed of Ofays described by Cleaver, born in the fallout of *Brown v. Board of Education*, who prefers to identify, and even to organize, with his racially oppressed cohorts rather than with their colonizers ("Convalescence" 177). Little wonder that to overcome these threatening meanings it has set in motion, *The Blackboard Jungle* must break the cross-racial alliance between Artie and Gregory, particularly via racial antagonism, so that Gregory can freely choose to assist Dadier in defeating the threat of the juvenile gang.

I would here like to introduce my second intertext from the late sixties: Jerry Farber's widely circulated essay, "The Student as Nigger." Like Cleaver's *Soul on Ice*, Farber's essay is a piece of radical political writing that was quickly picked up by a mass-market paperback company, Pocket Books. Highly influential in the generational political thinking of young sixties radicals, especially on high-school campuses, Farber explains his essay's popularity in the preface to the paperback edition: "Early in 1967 I wrote 'The Student as Nigger' and published it in the *Los Angeles Free Press*. . . . When 'The Student as Nigger' appeared, I hoped that a few other underground papers would pick it up but I had no idea that it would arouse the interest that it did. The article, particularly its central metaphor, embodied ideas and feelings that had been around for a long time but were then working their way rapidly to the surface. I don't know exactly how often it has been reprinted; I would guess about 500 times. It has appeared in several magazines, in a book, in almost all of the underground papers and, most frequently, in student newspapers and pamphlets on hundreds of campuses in the United States and Canada" (13).

Farber, at the time a teacher at L.A. State College, is referring, of course, to his essay's sustained analogy between white-black and teacher-student hierarchy. He begins with a series of specific observations: the separate but unequal student dining facilities, the policing of student sexuality, the encouragement in students of obsequious deference and obedience. Farber concludes: "What school amounts to, then, for white and black alike, is a 12-year course in how to be slaves. What else could explain what I see in a freshman class? They've got that slave mentality: obliging and ingratiating on the surface but hostile and resistant underneath. As do black slaves, students vary in their awareness of what's going on. Some recognize their own put-on for what it is and even let their rebellion break through to the surface now and then. Others—including most of the "good students"—have been more deeply brainwashed. They swallow the bullshit with greedy mouths" (93). Farber's argument adds something to Cleaver's. While Cleaver assumes that white youth actually step beyond their own privileged interests to disidentify with their elders and to identify instead with their colored peers, Farber offers another mechanism, in which young whites draw an analogy between the authoritarianism of white supremacy and their own subordination within adult-controlled institutions.

However problematic it may be, Farber's analogy heuristically provides an explanation for the initial solidarity of the students at Manual High, and does so without attributing transcendent ideals to the white students. The oppositional viewer need not consider Artie's lead in classroom rebellion to be inspired by some implausible vision of a beloved community. Rather, Artie has merely gathered together his classmates, who are disciplined and abused by the school as "niggers," regardless of their race.

In the scene where Dadier attempts to win the class's cooperation by bringing a tape recorder to school, for example, Artie and the class cleverly insist that Dadier give the microphone to Morales, because they realize that the teacher's gimmick, which requires obedience to institutional language, cannot tolerate Morales's repeated use of the word "stinking" (or "f——cking" in the novel) to comment on how he spent his morning. Dadier tries to claim this as a racist abuse of Morales rather than an attack on his own authority. "I can see you're really good friends to Morales," he scolds. But the students know better. As Gregory puts it, "sure are, too bad you can't say the same, Teach."

Dadier, whose liberal understanding of racism as personal intolerance disallows a "Student as Nigger" analogy, cannot imagine this incident as a metaphor for institutional subordination. Hence his profound offense when the principal tells Dadier that an anonymous student has accused him of using racist language in the classroom. Dadier justifies his use of racial epithets, "spic," "mic," and, of course, "nigger," as part of a lesson in the need for tolerance in an integrated classroom. However, for Artie, who reported him, they function to splinter the class's generational solidarity along racial lines, and thereby make it easier for Dadier to reimpose the teacher-student hierarchy. While Dadier's gambit fails here, next time he has better luck (as we have already seen) with the *Jack and the Beanstalk* discussion.

Boyhood in Blackboard: The Masculinist Negotiation of "Oppositional" Reading

I have now elaborated a second coherent reading of the film, one marked this time by an oppositional relation to the increasingly powerful liberal ideology of assimilationist white-identified integration. But to paraphrase Fiske, there is no such thing as a purely oppositional reading. What I would like to do now is to sketch out the nature of this "oppositional" reading's negotiation with dominant ideology, and thereby reveal its hegemonic face. As I have already hinted, this negotiation is played out in relation to the problematics of gender, and in particular, with the masculine gendering of generational opposition.

Let us return for a moment to Farber's "Student as Nigger." After he draws his racial-generational analogy, Farber tries to explain why it is that teachers would treat their students like "niggers." This part of his argument relies upon yet another analogy, between domination and emasculation: "their [teachers'] most striking characteristic is timidity. They're short on balls. . . . In California state colleges, the faculties are screwed regularly and vigorously by the Governor and Legislature and yet they still won't offer any solid resistance. They lie flat on their stomachs with their pants down, mumbling catch phrases like 'professional dignity' and 'meaningful dialogue.' . . . the classroom offers an artificial and protected environment in which they can exercise their will to power. Your neighbor may drive a better car; gas station attendants may intimidate you; your wife may dominate you; the State legislature may shit on you; but in the classroom, by God, students do what you say—or else" (95). To stand up for oneself, to refuse to be dominated, is understood by Farber as a masculine act of refusing to be raped or screwed. The refusal to be dominated indicates that one "has balls," that one is a man who has not yet been castrated. The misogynistic implication of Farber's rhetoric is not difficult to see: only those "with balls" (men) are not "screwed" (penetrated as an act of domination). Those "without balls" (women) get "screwed." The homophobic corollary follows that "men who are screwed" (gays) are dominated, castrated, and thus not real men at all.[11]

Farber's sexual metaphor is hardly original, but rather a central trope of patriarchal language. As Catharine MacKinnon has emphatically pointed out, we all know what it means to get "fucked." But while MacKinnon analyzes the metaphor in order to critique patriarchy, Farber makes uncritical use of it for its counterhegemonic potential. And while coding generational opposition as a struggle against emasculation may serve as a strong rhetorical foundation for counterhegemony, it will do so by privileging heterosexual masculinity (and the straight men who can reclaim it) as the normative site of opposition.

The oppositional meanings of The Blackboard Jungle structure the students' rebellion against the teacher according to just this masculinist logic. In the boys' eyes, Rick Dadier's manhood is tenuous and highly suspect: he is soft spoken; his wife has lost a baby; he lacks sufficient interest in his attractive colleague, Miss Hammond. As Farber might have put it, Dadier "lacks balls." At several points, the students question his heterosexuality. The day after Artie's boys successfully beat up Dadier in a dark alley, Gregory teases him for using makeup to hide the bruises: "That's okay Teach, I know lots of men who wear makeup." Dadier doesn't help matters with such banter as, "I came back to school today because I missed you so much, Artie." Even Dadier's role as disciplinarian problematizes his masculinity. Dadier received his accreditation as a teacher at a women's college. If his mission is to convert Manual High (an all-boys school) into something like the suburban ideal represented by Kraal's coed high school, then Dadier's duty would seem to require importing the feminine and its castrated obedience to Manual High.

If Dadier is emasculated in the oppositional reading of The Blackboard Jungle, then what of the students themselves? How can they be represented? Farber is suggestive on this matter too, for in addition to applying his sexual metaphor to teachers, he also engages it in his description of students. Still pursuing the question of authoritarianism in the classroom, Farber finally reaches what he considers the darkest reason of all for the master-slave approach to education: "The less trained and the less socialized a person is, the more he constitutes a sexual threat and the more he will be subjugated by institutions, such as penitentiaries and schools. Many of us are aware by now of the sexual neurosis which makes white men so fearful of integrated schools and neighborhoods, and which makes the castration of Negroes a deeply entrenched Southern folkway. We should recognize a similar pattern [of castration] in education. . . . It begins . . . with parents' first encroachments on their children's free unashamed sexuality and continues right up to the day when they hand you your doctoral diploma with a bleeding, shriveled pair of testicles stapled to the parchment" (96). To rebel against the school system, however, is to ward off this threat of castration, to stand up to the teacher's efforts at subordination and emasculation, which for Farber are analogous terms.

Keeping Farber's phallic mode of rebellion in mind, let us return to Blackboard's opening scene, in which students dance in the schoolyard to Bill Haley's "Rock Around the Clock." I suggested earlier that this scene may interpellate its young viewers into interracial rebellion against white adults' authority. Indeed, the scene's rock-and-roll soundtracking makes it one of the most subversive in the film, a moment when the implied viewer is most distinctly a youth who rocks to the music of delinquency, and thus where oppositional meanings seem most privileged over dominant meanings.[12] Shortly after screening the schoolyard dancing, however, the camera pans along the sidewalk until it reaches a group of delinquent boys behind the "bars" of the schoolyard, crudely appreciating a passing woman.

Figure 5. The boys hoot and whistle at her.

This masculinization of opposition, I argue, is itself a compromise, a negotiation with dominant gender ideology that qualifies and problematizes the
scene's potential oppositionality. How is this so? First, it is significant that
the students dancing together in the opening scene are all boys. As previously noted, aptly named Manual Arts is an all-boys school. This opening
scene, like several others that follow, makes available an unusually explicit
homoerotic (third) reading where boys take sensual pleasure in one another.
However, in having already heterosexualized and masculinized youth rebellion, the previously discussed "oppositional" reading, in which the students
of Manual High do not want to be "screwed" by Dadier, cannot tolerate any
implication that they may indeed want to be "screwed" by him or even one
another. The threatened eruption of homoerotic meaning is repressed by extending the shot so that it concludes with a representation of the delinquents'
heterosexual desire. The shot thereby restores phallic oppositionality to the
boys: their desire to "screw" marks them as rebellious, as refusing to submit
to the school authority that intends to castrate them.

In general, the rebellious, integrated schoolboys of Manual High tend to
control the heterosexual male gaze of the camera throughout the film. In
addition to the opening sequence, for example, another scene soon follows
where the entire auditorium of boys at the school's orientation meeting
whistle at Miss Hammond. The camera dwells with emphasis on the colored

Figure 6. Dadier watches
the boys as they eye Miss
Hammond.

Figure 7. But it's a white
boy who tries to rape her.

faces staring at her legs, then cuts to their gaze, tightly following her legs as Miss Hammond climbs the stairs to the podium. This scene is soon followed by the attempted rape itself. While the attacker is white, these racially marked shots setting up the boys' desire for Miss Hammond "color" the incident with the American myth of the black rapist.[13]

In the dominant reading, Dadier's fortunate discovery and thwarting of the rape attempt establishes his credibility as a role model. The delinquent's expression of uncontrolled, violent desire is criminal, requiring Dadier's intervention as agent of institutional law. The narrative is thus structured along lines parallel to American racial mythology, where the lust of black men for white women requires the political dominance and vigilance of white men. And in this scene, that white man is Dadier. However soft spoken and not quite classically heroic he may be, Dadier is man enough to stop a crazed delinquent from sexually assaulting a respectable white woman.

This lesson is not only for the viewer's benefit, but also for the students within the film, who must respect Dadier's ability to fight, however furious they are at the consequences for their friend, who will probably go to prison.

When they take revenge on Dadier later, by ambushing him and another teacher in an alley, Artie's gang will be sure to outnumber them by three or four to one. Dadier, in other words, is rendered as a genuine Hollywood hero fighting against enormous odds. Ultimately he must win because, though the street toughs he takes on may seem macho on the outside, they are really cowards who fight only when the odds are in their favor. In the final scene, when he can square off one-on-one with Artie, Dadier proves that he is more a man than the delinquent punk who has tormented him.

In the oppositional reading of the attempted rape scene, however, the delinquent's sexual violence is legitimated as an act of rebellion against the repressive domination of school authority; Dadier's interference becomes an act of institutional violence that martyrs the boy. Here, normative identification-structures have been reversed, interpellating the spectator to identify with the (masculine) rapist against the female victim's (desexualized) male defender. Though unmistakably a threat to dominant masculine ideology, then, these "oppositional meanings" clustered around the rape scene misogynistically present women as objects that the boy rebels can sexually dominate as a means of combating their own oppression at the hands of institutional authority.

Why Read the Blackboard?

What does the struggle between these readings tell us? In theoretical terms, the case of The Blackboard Jungle provides a detailed case study of how, in order to perform an "oppositional" reading at all, other oppositional meanings must be repressed or denied. My point here is somewhat analogous to Gayatri Spivak's argument that the subaltern cannot speak, because in order to do so, some other axis of alterity, such as that of woman, must be silenced. In a similar fashion, I would argue that any "oppositional" reading is premised upon the denial of other oppositional readings, that any counterhegemonic practice is founded upon the repression of political difference.

The opening scene, in which possible homoerotic meanings to rock-and-roll dancing must be repressed, is potentially revealing here. Could there be a queer reading of The Blackboard Jungle in which homosexual desire threatens both the institutional authority of the school and the machismo of the gang? The scattered moments of banter between Dadier and Artie strongly suggest this possibility. Dadier and Artie do play out their struggle, after all, through a battle for the affection of Gregory that could plausibly allow Blackboard to be read as a tale of triangulated gay desire.

Alternatively, one could elaborate another possible reading also denied by the oppositional youth reading, this time centering on Anne Dadier. I have hardly mentioned Dadier's pregnant wife in this essay, primarily because her scenes are narratively separated from the conflict at the school. Trapped for the most part at home in the Dadier apartment or later in the maternity ward at the hospital, Anne enters the conflict primarily as yet another, off-site object of struggle between her husband and Artie, who sends her letters asserting her husband's infidelity. Given that her isolation is what allows her to be emotionally devastated by the letters, Anne's story suggests other meanings, critical of the gendered boundary between public and private, that could enable another kind of oppositional reading. Both the queer and the feminist readings, however, are buried by the masculinist "oppositional" reading, which cannot allow hegemonic masculinity, the rhetorical basis of its oppositionality, to be subverted.

This Spivakian sort of theoretical argument, that counterhegemony must itself always be locally hegemonic, has yet to be assimilated by British cultural studies in its analyses of ideological resistance. As Angela McRobbie has persuasively argued, British cultural studies has had a long love affair with masculinist youth culture, romanticizing the tough rebelliousness of working-class boys at the expense of asking difficult questions about the situation of subcultural girls.[14] McRobbie might also have added that the same is true regarding the status of gays in youth subcultures; inquiries into female and gay experiences of domination and resistance within youth subcultures would lead to less straightforwardly affirmative, and hence less ideological, evaluations of youth cultural oppositionality.

Of course, it is hardly coincidental that British cultural studies and the youth reading of *The Blackboard Jungle* both valorize masculinist rebellion. Cultural studies after all was itself born out of the New Left of the sixties, and the centrality of its concern with resistant youth cultures can be traced back quite compellingly to the generational antagonisms that first developed in the United States and in Britain during the fifties. Cultural studies' own repertoire of oppositional images, in other words, draws heavily from the likes of Artie West. The case of *Blackboard*'s oppositionality should therefore have a special poignancy for cultural studies practitioners.

The submerged histories of these generational antagonisms and the popular images through which they were played out are in need of scholarly excavation, since today the young people of the fifties are largely remembered as the conservative elder siblings of their brothers and sisters who grew up during the sixties. While youth in the fifties, mainstream pop history tells us, accepted the social complacency of their parents, it was only the next decade that witnessed a rupture in generational harmony. However, as the case of *The Blackboard Jungle* indicates, generational rifts over the meaning of youth rebellion—and especially in connection to racial integration—can be discerned far earlier.

Specifically, *Blackboard* reveals how the historical moment of *Brown v. Board of Education* posed the cultural possibility that white American youth might racially cross-identify with their non-white generational peers. The film thereby anticipates the political activism of certain young whites in the sixties who would enthusiastically support SNCC's efforts, form SDS, volunteer to go south for Freedom Summer, and join Berkeley's free-speech movement (itself born out of student solidarity work for Southern civil rights). It also anticipates the writing of a book like Hebdige's *Subculture*, with its deep interest in the references and allusions of punk style to black culture.

At the same time, this tradition of racial and generational radicalism has deployed a masculinist discourse that, far from opposing or even questioning gender and sexual hierarchies, negotiates their attendant ideologies as a means of articulating rebellion against the institutions of white adult power. Assertions of hegemonic phallic sexuality against an emasculating social order have been uncritically privileged in both youth politics and cultural studies as oppositional practices. What I have termed the "oppositional" reading of *The Blackboard Jungle*, then, typifies the emergent hegemony in the fifties of a masculinist mode of generational rebellion, also discernible in rock and roll itself, the hipster subculture, and in such popular analyses as Mailer's "The White Negro" and Paul Goodman's *Growing Up Absurd*.[15]

The masculinist mode of protest carried on into the sixties, promoted by figures such as Farber, who programmatically called for a youth politics "with balls," and Cleaver, who advocated the "rape-on-principle" of white women and denounced James Baldwin as a sexual traitor to his race. The generational and racial radicalism made available by *The Blackboard Jungle*, then, structured into its opposition a misogynistic and homophobic protest that made it extremely difficult for the New Left to address gender and sex issues. By the late sixties, this masculinist coding of rebellion had become so oppressive that it would help to precipitate a splintering of the youth movement.[16]

The case of *The Blackboard Jungle*, then, speaks to our present cultural situation on several registers. First, it debunks our historical myth of the fifties as an age of consensus; even the decade so vigorously eulogized by neoconservatives was a time of considerable social struggle, as we can see in the deeply conflicting meanings of racial integration that were read from the film. The ideologically negotiated "oppositionality" that Blackboard obtained for youth of the fifties also illuminates the historical logic of a growing movement toward the independent articulation of feminist and gay liberationist oppositions in the United States. Finally, the film also directs us to the roots of cultural studies' own romanticization of youthful masculine rebellion. Most generally, these various histories suggest the need for a more self-consciously deconstructive method of evaluating the political valence of oppositional culture. Adversarial identities, resistant reading practices, counterhegemonies, and coalition politics are all as much political problems as they are solutions. The adequacy of struggles against domination depends upon continuous self-critique, upon never-ending efforts to answer the question: *Who or what have "we" left out?*

Notes

I would like to express my gratitude to those who helped me with this essay: Regenia Gagnier, Robert Latham, my editors, Michael Uebel and Harry Stecopoulos, and two anonymous readers at Duke University Press. Special thanks go to Marcia Klotz for her invaluable advice and editing skills.

1. Thomas Doherty's book, *Teenagers and Teenpics*, painstakingly details Hollywood's economic motives for trying to tap the youth market in the fifties. See particularly 17–70.

2. In effect, "Encoding/Decoding" aims to politicize Umberto Eco's notion of the "aberrant decoding," a situation that results when addresser and addressee of a message do not share the same codes. Hall uses Eco's concept to explain the dynamics that underlie what mass-media studies have traditionally called communication "misunderstandings" or "failures." The discipline, Hall insists, must accept the fact that the interpretive (decoding) moment is not simply individual and idiosyncratic, but on the contrary, just as social as the production (encoding) moment. When different classes in mass-mediated societies share a popular culture but apply different codes to it, this means that they are in a state of ideological contradiction that *potentially* may lead to overt social conflict.

3. Hall's theory of reading is deeply indebted to Gramsci's modification, through his theory of hegemony, of the Marxist theory of the state as instrument of the ruling class. Indeed, Hall's model of the popular text can best be understood as a semiotic hegemony (again as opposed to ideological instrument of the ruling class). For Gramsci, political hegemony involves manufacturing general consent to state power by way of its incorporation of the interests of classes and class factions other than

those of the "ruling" class (the coalition forming what he calls a "historical bloc"). Similarly, Hall's popular text produces widespread semiotic consent to its preferred meanings by allowing most viewers to negotiate their own social position with them.

4. The middle-class discourse on the Los Angeles "riots" functioned very similarly. Without actually denying that unrelieved frustration with poverty, political disenfranchisement, and police brutality, might have motivated the lawbreaking, it nevertheless bemoaned an absence of "maturity" and "personal responsibility" among the perpetrators, and especially among minority youth gang members. In both the dominant readings of The Blackboard Jungle's juvenile delinquency and of the civil unrest in L.A., tolerating social inequality becomes a sign of one's maturity, adulthood, and even manhood.

5. This is the basic limitation of Peter Biskind's critique of The Blackboard Jungle as a liberal tale of intergenerational consensus-formation. While the reading is highly persuasive in its own terms, it turns the film's reception history into an aberrant footnote to its "real" political significance.

6. These teenage responses to The Blackboard Jungle, and the controversies over the film's meaning to which they gave rise, continue today in such recent examples as the public debates over films like Colors and Menace 2 Society. In this respect, Blackboard is the progenitor of a significant post–rock 'n' roll film cycle playing off of adults' class- and race-based fears of urban youth gang violence.

7. James Gilbert's A Cycle of Outrage is the best study to date of adult anxiety in the fifties that mass media were encouraging juvenile delinquency. See especially 162–95 for a discussion of the debates over whether to censor Hollywood teenpics.

8. Sidney Poitier would literally take on Glenn Ford's role later in his career, playing the part of the schoolteacher in To Sir with Love.

9. Peter Biskind interprets Artie's reading in very similar generational terms, describing it as a threat to Dadier, who "can't allow the kids to heroize him [Jack] in these terms, to make him over into a juvenile Dillinger" (213). Artie's delinquent reading, also bears a racial significance, just as Dadier's response (apparently a lesson on racism) includes a generational dimension. Racial and generational antagonism in this scene, in other words, are always being articulated together, as they are throughout the film.

10. In different ways, both James Baldwin and Lorraine Hansberry compellingly criticized Mailer's romanticization of what is, in effect, the very segregationist's stereotype of the black man that he had presumably set out to demolish. Baldwin objected to the sexualization of Mailer's romance, yet another use of black men as "walking phallic symbols" by someone who should have known better ("The Black Boy" 172). Hansberry protested more generally to the wholesale reduction of black America to the marginal life of the street hustler. Yet at bottom, their critiques share a dismay at the potential costs for black people of Mailer's obsessive masculinization of cross-racial rebellion, a dismay I share when I critique the "oppositional reading" of Blackboard.

11. Barbara Ehrenreich discusses the pervasiveness of this masculinist ideology during the fifties in the second chapter of her book, *The Hearts of Men* (14–28).

12. A similarly oppositional scene occurs when Dadier's fellow teacher, Joshua Edwards, is enticed into playing his jazz records for the students. Mocking the wimpy Bix Beiderbecke record, Artie puts on a fast-paced tune, then proceeds to break the entire collection while the other boys dance. The music is bop rather than rock, but the boys' wild dance is similarly linked with their delinquency, and contrasted with Edwards's impotence.

13. Once again the film cautiously mediates its more dangerous racial meanings, using white characters (Jack in the cartoon, Bill Haley and the Comets for rock and roll, the rapist in this scene), to signify a racial threat. This allows the film to engage white fears of integration, but maintain its liberalism by avoiding overt racial demonization in the reactionary tradition of *Birth of a Nation*.

14. McRobbie's critique is leveled at the canonical cultural studies texts on youth subcultures: Paul Willis's *Learning to Labour*, Dick Hebdige's *Subculture*, and the *Resistance through Ritual* anthology coedited by Stuart Hall and Tony Jefferson.

15. I have written on rock and roll as masculinist rebellion in another essay, "Mapping the Rebel Image."

16. See Sara Evans' *Personal Politics* for a detailed history of how the women's movement emerged from the limitations of the New Left. See Dennis Altman's *Homosexual* for a meditation on the relationship of gay political consciousness to the counterculture and New Left. Particularly useful are chapters 5 and 6, where Altman elaborates his own metaphor of the "faggot as nigger" (152–226).

THE WORLD ACCORDING TO NORMAL BEAN

Edgar Rice Burroughs's Popular Culture

HARRY STECOPOULOS

In 1911 Edgar Rice Burroughs sent his first adventure romance, *Under the Moons of Mars*, to *All-Story Magazine* under the unusual pseudonym "Normal Bean." *All-Story* accepted and published Burroughs's narrative, but his odd pen name never made it into print. Assuming that the name was no more than a mistake, an overzealous editor changed "Normal" to "Norman," thus ruining the new writer's desired authorial persona. Burroughs would make his pulp magazine debut as "Norman Bean" and, angry over the editorial error, would revert to his legal name in his next publication, the extraordinarily popular *Tarzan of the Apes*. If Burroughs couldn't assume the identity of "Normal Bean" for his pulp writing career, he did not, it seems, want any pen name at all.[1]

Although considered little more than an amusing anecdote by Burroughs enthusiasts, the story of this peculiar pseudonym encapsulates how one of the century's most popular adventure writers began his career with profoundly ambivalent feelings about his identity and his medium. Burroughs's desire to begin his pulp writing career with the identity of "Normal Bean," slang for "normal head," suggests that becoming a popular cultural producer offered him an opportunity to assert publicly a phrenologically inflected "average" American identity that denoted his membership in the status quo.[2] Yet the defensive literalness of the pseudonym "Normal Bean"—the demand that the author of *Under the Moons of Mars* be affirmed as a member of the dominant order—implies Burroughs's uneasy recognition that, while certain aspects of his first pulp publication jibed with his culture's white bourgeois ideals, other aspects of his new popular venture stood, at best, in marginal relation to those "norms." Rather than simply bolstering Burroughs's sense of the stability and value of his white middle-class male identity, his new job producing adventure tales also threatened his sense of identity. The fact that

All-Story accepted Burroughs's romance but found his pseudonym so odd as to require correction would only have intensified Burroughs's worry that producing popular pulp romances had decidedly uncertain consequences for his identity as a "normal" American man.

By arguing that Burroughs felt somewhat estranged from the status quo at the beginning of his pulp writing career, I don't mean to excuse or ignore the prejudice that so often characterizes his romances. Instead, I want to suggest that Burroughs's failed deployment of the pseudonym "Normal Bean" testifies to how his investment in popular cultural production both reflected and produced a peculiarly middle-class crisis of white male identity. W. E. B. Du Bois, David Roediger, and Eric Lott have argued that whiteness for European-American working men often constitutes a form of racist compensation, whereby feelings of superiority to people of color (as well as women) enable the men to accept, even celebrate, a capitalist system that denigrates and exploits them.[3] According to these thinkers, crises of racial identity have historically unsettled white working-class men whenever this system of psychosocial compensation foundered. A similar, if often less visible, dynamic has also informed the history of European-American middle-class males such as Burroughs. Insofar as white bourgeois men have traditionally imagined their whiteness as mutually constitutive with a certain property-based social position, periodic socioeconomic challenges to that sense of self-esteem—feminism, the Great Depression, affirmative action—often have had important implications for these males' sense of racial identity. However established he may appear to be, whiteness for the average European-American middle-class man has never been as coherent an identity as we might think it is.

Burroughs's anxiety-ridden beginnings as a pulp adventure writer constitute one middle-class male's cultural response to the instability of white identity.[4] Faithful to a highly individualistic, even heroic model of Anglo-Saxon bourgeois manhood, Burroughs found intolerable a new standardized middle-class world that often seemed more white collar than white. The frustrated bourgeois turned to the possibilities of popular cultural production, I argue, in an attempt to recover a sense of his whiteness in an incorporated, postfrontier America. Producing adventure tales of disenfranchised but noble white men who regain their "rightful" identity offered Burroughs a way of celebrating a traditional proprietary conception of white male identity in defiance of modernity. Yet Burroughs's uneasy fascination with his own position as a vulgar cultural producer and his often eroticized representation of his heroes' racial cross-identifications suggests that writing adventure romances didn't so much resolve his crisis of whiteness as intensify it. Dramatizing throughout his early romances the slippage between normalcy and fantasy, self and other, Burroughs appears to have taken just as much pleasure in dissolving white male identities as he did in fortifying them. At once predictably elitist and flamboyantly transgressive, the odd story of this adventure writer's first pulp experiences offers us nothing less than a glimpse of how the turn-of-the-century bourgeoisie used "raced" popular culture to transform their anxiety over modernity into the uneasy pleasure of making and unmaking white subjectivity.

Burroughs's Beginnings

Before we turn to Burroughs's cultural production, some discussion of the adventure writer's earlier life is in order.[5] Edgar Rice Burroughs was born into a bourgeois home in Chicago in 1875. His parents, Mary and George Burroughs, were typical Victorian Americans. Mary Burroughs served as homemaker, while George Burroughs, a former Union major, ran his own business. By most accounts, the Burroughs home appears to have been dominated by the pater familias's dictatorial attitude rather than by a more nurturing maternal presence. Accustomed to giving orders to both soldiers and employees, the elder Burroughs maintained his home in an autocratic fashion; he was, according to one relative, "very much the patriarch" and demanded obedience from his wife and four sons (qtd. in Porges 778). George Burroughs exercised a similarly dictatorial attitude toward people of color and the working class—acting paternalistic toward "well-behaved" African Americans while rejecting absolutely the labor rebellions typical of this era.[6] Whether at home or in the marketplace, the authoritarian Burroughs "took it for granted that he knew best what was to be done" (qtd. in Porges 778).

For all his power as a white bourgeois male, however, the stern and militaristic Burroughs patriarch could not convince his youngest son, Edgar, to behave. While Edgar initially found his father's military career and entrepreneurial spirit exemplary, in his mid-teens he began rebelling. Sent to visit his older brothers in frontier Idaho during a summer vacation, Burroughs returned to Chicago unwilling to accept the strictures of school and home. Chafing under his father's commands to study, Edgar would ignore his assignments for the Harvard School, move on to Phillips Andover only to suffer dismissal a semester later, and develop a reputation as a disciplinary problem at the Michigan Military Academy where he eventually matriculated. The future pulp writer's subsequent failure to pass the entrance exam for West Point established all the more his resistance to his father's desires.

Such filial conflicts were hardly unusual among white middle-class families during the turn of the century. Michael Rogin has argued that this era witnessed a "general crisis of patriarchy" that often emerged in a rebellion of white middle-class sons against their fathers (198). These generational clashes often reflected the fading of traditional proprietary conceptions of bourgeois work and the rise of new white-collar images of middle-class labor. In the case of the Burroughs family, Edgar's defiance of his father soon crystallized into an anachronistic commitment to the autonomy promised by a mythic frontier, while his father responded by demanding that his son accommodate himself to the demands of a bureaucratic modern workplace.[7] Sensitive to the vagaries of business ownership from his own experience with the economic recession of the 1890s, Edgar's father was wary of the proprietary conception of middle-class employment and sensitive to the way in which a new white-collar redefinition of middle-class employment might provide greater security. We might imagine that for the elder Burroughs, events such as the closing of the frontier and the creation of enormous corporations such as U.S. Steel were, while unsettling, less anxiety-producing than the possibility of personal economic disaster.[8] The elder Burroughs appears to have emulated the father in George Horace Lorimer's bestselling *Letters of a Self-Made Merchant to His Son* (1904), insisting that Edgar accept the fact that "there isn't any such thing as being your own boss" in the new bureaucratized workplace (82).

Yet if the elder Burroughs viewed the new white-collar conception of middle-class employment in neutral terms, Edgar found it hard to accept the idea that his life's work would consist of what C. Wright Mills so famously described as "the handling of paper and money and people" (65). Refusing to accept his father's dictates, Edgar insisted on creating his future in terms of a fantasized past of unlimited land and multiple opportunities. He appears to have wanted what he imagined his father had: access to the unlimited territorial and entrepreneurial opportunities represented by an era before the closing of the frontier and the growth of enormous corporations. As his adult job history displays, Burroughs found it difficult to accept the notion that he would have to understand his white-male middle-class identity not in terms of property and power, but in terms of a salary, a bureaucracy, and female coworkers. He would abandon a clerk position at his father's battery factory in favor of a military career and then soon quit that. Several years later, Burroughs would quit a low-level managerial position at Sears Roebuck to start a number of businesses, none of which succeeded. Committed to an outdated conception of white middle-class male identity, determined to regain his rightful wages of whiteness, Burroughs demonstrated repeatedly to his father and the world that he would not accept the white-collar ethos.

The "Popular" as (Fantastic) Frontier

Having failed "at every enterprise [he] had ever attempted," by age thirty-six Burroughs found himself a frustrated man unable to support his wife and children (qtd. in Heins 11). Yet despite the poverty that both he and his family endured in the uneasy years following the economic panic of 1907, Burroughs didn't change his attitude toward the white-collar world. Instead of finding and keeping a clerical or low-level managerial job in order to support his family, Burroughs continued to pursue his own fantasy of white male autonomy, if in a new manner. At the end of the decade, Burroughs turned his attention away from the more predictable options he had been exploring—the West, entrepreneurial schemes, even imperialist military ventures—toward the world of working-class-oriented popular culture. Burroughs was hardly unusual among the white bourgeoisie in this period as he became interested in the "popular" as a field of opportunity. Shortly before Burroughs's turn to the popular, respectable white men such as Owen Wister had appropriated the dime-novel Western and turned it into a middlebrow form. Men of similar social position such as Cecil B. DeMille would soon turn to film and, through the use of middlebrow theatrical properties and performers, help legitimate what had been in large part a working-class medium.[9]

Much of this middle-class interest in the popular combined ostensible reform of the demimonde with the expropriation of working-class culture. But for cultural producers invested in the revitalization of white manhood such as Wister, Burroughs, and Jack London, the zone of the popular proved appealing as well because it suggested an arena seemingly antithetical to an overly gentrified, emasculated, white bourgeoisie. For example, in an early comic poem written for the *Chicago Tribune*, Burroughs depicts the "vulgar" sport of boxing as offering the white middle classes a new model of virile white masculinity. Celebrating prize fighting over and against the more elite sport of auto racing, Burroughs claims that "the highbrowed gent ... can learn a lesson from the dope of lowbrow's game, of white man's hope," despite the fact that the working-class or petit bourgeois male does not have "a massive dome" (qtd. in Porges 201–2). By using the phrase "white man's hope," Burroughs refers to the typical contemporary description of a white boxer talented enough to defeat black heavyweight champion Jack Johnson. Singing the praises of lowbrows and their pastimes in this way doesn't so much suggest Burroughs's identification with these "abnormal beans" as reflect his marked interest in the popular as a means of defending white supremacist and patriarchal ideologies. Colonizing the arena of the popular offered Burroughs and other white men a way to promote virile white manhood in the face of the emasculating influence of a white-collar modernity.

Yet even as this marginal pop culture functioned for very different types of white middle-class men as a zone of new opportunity—a new sort of frontier—its marginal qualities no doubt worried downwardly mobile white men such as Burroughs.[10] Evocative of his class disenfranchisement, the popular's marginality to the white middle-class disturbed as much as it appealed to him. This anxiety manifested itself when he turned from defending the popular in comic lyrics to becoming a writer of pulp adventure stories. Sensitive to the fact that he was writing for periodicals far less respectable than magazines such as the *Atlantic Monthly* or the *Saturday Evening Post*, Burroughs's first experience writing adventure romances for the pulps is characterized by the recognition that he is entering a field that produces "rotten" stories— valueless narratives far removed from the English Renaissance and Latin texts assigned in the prep schools he attended.[11] Worse still, choosing to become a pop-culture producer reminded Burroughs that he hadn't relinquished his childish desire for a new frontier. Thus, while pulp work was thrilling, it also reminded him of his inability to fulfill his responsibilities as a man and support his family through white-collar work: "I was very much ashamed of my new vocation," wrote Burroughs of his first experience producing an adventure romance. "It seemed a foolish thing for a full grown man to be doing—much on a par with dressing myself in a boy scout suit and running away from home to fight Indians" (qtd. in Porges 4). While drawn to the popular because its aura of the margins suggested a new and decidedly non-bourgeois frontier—a space of freedom and economic opportunity— Burroughs's desire for that new frontier also distressed him.

This turn to the new frontier of the popular proved upsetting to the failed white-collar man not only because it suggested an inability to accept office-work and live up to his responsibilities as the head of a household, but also because this desire licensed his articulation of disturbingly outrageous fantasies of alien lands, races, and species. In looking to the pulp popular as a new frontier of economic possibility and freedom through the production of science fiction stories, Burroughs feared he had inadvertently accessed a profoundly transgressive part of his imagination. The contemporary status of pulp science fiction and science fantasy—Burroughs's typical genres of choice—no doubt helped inspire his fears. While other popular adventure genres such as the Western and the sea story had acquired some middle-brow legitimation, and other popular mediums such as film were highly visible sites of contestation between the working class and the bourgeoisie, pulp science fiction and science fantasy represented an unknown and thus potentially more disturbing cultural phenomenon in the years before World War I. Americans were not accustomed to the realistic portrayal of such scientifically-inflected adventures and experiences in their cheaper periodicals.[12] Indeed, in the 1920s, pulp writer Robert Howard, the creator of Conan the Barbarian, would find himself ostracized by his Texas neighbors due to the outrageous stories he wrote for pulps such as *Weird Tales*.[13] By turning to the pulp popular as a new site of possibilities, Burroughs found himself drawn to a subgenre so odd, so outrageous, that it did not even qualify for a position on the contemporary cultural hierarchy.

Burroughs's sense of himself as a figure possessed of an abnormal imagination—of an imagination linked with some fantastic otherworldly frontier—so affected him that, as we have seen, it necessitated the authorial persona with which he began his pulp writing career. Burroughs felt compelled to assert his normalcy, or better, his whiteness, when publishing his first science fantasy romance in a pulp magazine. And this anxiety over producing the "'improbable' variety of tale," as Burroughs would soon refer to his cultural productions, would continue to trouble the new pop-culture producer long after his initial experience with *All-Story Magazine*. For the first three years of his career, Burroughs would often label his adventure romances as "foolish" (qtd. in Porges 4). In 1913, for example, he would tell his editor: "I probably lack balance . . . a well-balanced mind would not turn out my kind of stuff" (qtd. in Porges 150). The pop-culture "frontier" that Burroughs had chosen to settle led repeatedly to moments of self-doubt for the already-anxious, failed, white-collar man. The promise the popular offered could not be separated from the tensions it provoked.

Not Like Other Men

Yet the intensity of these worries also proved emblematic of the pulp writer's special attraction to pop-culture production. Even as he articulated his anxieties over his new occupation, Burroughs would also admit, however obliquely, that he enjoyed abandoning familial and bourgeois norms for the strange pleasures of the popular. In a 1912 letter to his editor at *All-Story Magazine*, for example, Burroughs acknowledges his cathexsis to the alterity of a truly alien pop-culture form in a manner that suggests pride, even pleasure. He first describes *Tarzan of the Apes*, then a work in progress, as the story of a "scion of a noble English house . . . brought up among a band of fierce anthropoids," and then comments self-consciously on his own interest in writing fantastic romances: "I seem," claims Burroughs, "especially adapted to the building of the 'damphool' species of narrative" (qtd. in Porges 123–24). In this remarkable admission, Burroughs acknowledges his own connection to a form of popular fiction so alien as to suggest another, less intelligent species. Science fantasy narratives, Burroughs suggests, are in certain ways the cultural equivalent of the "anthropoids" who raise Tarzan; they are, to push the parallel a bit further, recognizably "lowbrow." In admitting that he is "especially adapted to the building" of such a "'damphool' species" of cultural product, Burroughs acknowledges both the social otherness of his cultural productions and the extent to which he recognizes—even enjoys—his own easy relation to them. For Burroughs, producing these alien species of cultural production both confirms his unsettling distance from the world of "normal beans" and at the same time testifies to his delight in standing apart from that world. And while that pleasure stems in part from the knowledge that his willingness to brave the vulgar popular may prove lucrative, it also stems, I would argue, from a delight in transgressing the cultural divide that the novice pulp writer can barely articulate. For Burroughs, the popular proved to be a frontier that thrilled by allowing him to ponder his own otherness.

To suggest that Burroughs enjoyed the alterity of his new position as a pop-culture producer isn't to deny that his cultural productions took as their main subject the experience of white male heroes triumphing (often violently) over people of color, women, and the working class—over any figure that might represent difference. These conquests of the Other are in fact central to Burroughs's use of popular culture to resolve personal and social crises, for they typically enable his white male heroes to recover the wealth, standing, and even identity they have lost. Yet even as Burroughs's early romances focus on white male heroes triumphing, they also represent his heroes' attraction to difference. By representing how his heroes' encounters with alterity not only affirm but also pleasurably dissolve their white subjectivities, Burroughs acknowledges his own transgressive attraction to an "othered" pop sphere.

The most obvious way Burroughs inscribes a sense of a "divided mind" in his romances is by emphasizing how his heroes want to inhabit simultaneously two different worlds.[14] Both John Carter and Tarzan, Burroughs's most well known protagonists, are famously torn in their attachment to different spheres—the one exotic, if brutal (Mars or the African jungle), the other civilized, if, at times, hypocritical (U.S. society or royal English society).[15] This spatial metaphor should suggest to us any number of binary oppositions in U.S. culture and society during this era, but it directs us most powerfully to the way that Burroughs uses issues of race and racial identity to explore his heroes' contradictory consciousnesses. As is so often the case in American popular culture, the metaphor of the color line enables the representation of separate, even oppositional attachments. In constructing scenes where his white male heroes uneasily identify with, desire, and even masquerade as a "dark" male Other, Burroughs uses racial discourse to allegorize his own anxiety-ridden fascination with the vulgar, marginal world of pop-culture production. Attempting to represent the pleasure he received from constructing "'damphool' narratives," the pulp writer displaced his investment in the alterity of the popular onto his romances' fantastic racial tableaux.

Burroughs's use of race to at once resolve and express his heroes' social contradictions plays an important role in his first romance *Under the Moons of Mars*. The romance begins with John Carter "masterless, penniless," without a "livelihood," adrift in the postbellum world (12). As a Virginian who fought for the Confederacy, Carter represents someone who, like Burroughs, has lost a way of life.[16] Carter has no illusions about recreating the antebellum plantation tradition, but he does hope to restore his finances and make a new life for himself. Burroughs makes clear from the outset that race and racial conflict will provide our hero with the opportunity to recover his many losses. Thus the romance opens in the Southwest with Carter and his white buddy looking for gold and fighting off Apaches in time-honored Western fashion. Yet, when the action shifts to Mars, the predictable racial politics of the Western give way to more fantastic racialist situations involving many-limbed green warriors, huge white apes, and lithe red Martians. Bill Brown has argued that the racial confusion in Burroughs's Mars offers the ex-Confederate officer an opportunity to restore racial order, if in another world, and thus triumph over the threat of interracial contact in a manner worthy of Thomas Dixon ("Science Fiction"). The social contradictions ex-Confederate officer John Carter faces at the beginning of the romance are indeed resolved through his role as racial savior on Mars; however this new role also places him in situations that make his contradictions palpable in terms of species/racial impersonation and masquerade. Over the course of the romance, the ex-Confederate captain cross-dresses in the military clothing of a green Martian (56), "anoints" his entire body with "a reddish oil" in order to pass for a "full-fledged red Martian," and, most transgressive of all, falls in love with a red Martian princess (90). Racial confusion doesn't so much lead to racial segregation as it leads to racial (and species) transgression.

For Michael Denning, no doubt, these masquerades and moments of cross-identification would function less as transgressive performances than as examples of Carter's desire to surveil, infiltrate, and then control various Martian communities. Describing the Nick Carter detective stories that preceded Burroughs's adventure romances during the turn of the century, Denning warns scholars against taking moments of disguise seriously as evidence of subversion (204–5). Yet in having John Carter perform a "redface" act—a fairly transparent version of playing a Native American—Burroughs has his hero take on the species identity of Dejah Thoris, the red Martian princess he loves. Carter doesn't simply masquerade as the Other in order to better control an alien environment; he masquerades as the Other in order to express his libidinal investment in the other—in a red female who, within the world of the romance, hails from another planet and, within the world of Burroughs's allegory, represents a Native American woman. Ironically enough, then, in resolving his own earthly social contradictions by responding to the racial confusion of Mars, John Carter ends up figurally transgressing the Native American/European-American color line that structures the world of the Western he has just left behind. And Carter continues to desire his red Martian beloved and Mars itself after he has returned to earth and restored his sense of wealth and identity in a postplantation world. Recovery of his whiteness—of his whiteness as property—does not preclude Carter's continued desire to cross the line and undo his identity once more. Little wonder, then, that in an early draft of the romance, Burroughs informed the reader that his hero was "not like other men," thereby implying that John Carter was, in effect, something of an abnormal bean.[17]

The Family Tree

In *Under the Moons of Mars*, Burroughs displays the contradictions that underlie his hero's identity through a number of oppositions—alien and human, Native American and European American, "mother earth" and "beloved Mars" (*Gods* vi)—yet he never represents Carter in terms of his class identity (1). The exploration of species, planetary, and, above all, racial difference in Burroughs's first romance gives way in *Tarzan of the Apes* to a more slippery investigation of the relationship between the axes of race, species, and class.[18]

The introduction of class into Burroughs's popular production comes with a new emphasis on the family romance. Usually defined as a child's fantasy of having noble, wealthy, or famous parents, the family romance provides Burroughs with a structured way of imagining how a disenfranchised English boy might rediscover his whiteness. Yet what proves unusual about Burroughs's use of the family romance is his interest in obstructing the flow of the plot with various scenes of racial cross-identification and cross-dressing. Burroughs seems as interested in having his hero be an ape, even a black man, as he does in having him fulfill the family romance trajectory. In part, Burroughs's emphasis on his hero's fascination with otherness reflects the famed primitivism of the novel. Yet Burroughs's interest in lingering on his hero's "dark" encounters also suggests that he may be more interested in using his narrative to explore his own experiences with alterity than he is in producing an efficient, orderly family romance of white aristocracy.

Burroughs begins by foregrounding the very subaltern groups typically associated with "vulgar" culture by the contemporary bourgeoisie: people of color and the working class. The plot begins with Tarzan's father, Lord Greystoke, receiving orders to travel to Africa in order to investigate the impressment of black British subjects into the work gangs of another imperial power. People of color thus first appear in this narrative as workers, not simply as "natives." Yet this "racing" of labor hardly has occurred and the plot hardly gotten underway when Burroughs offers us yet another instance of oppressed labor: the mistreatment of the multiracial crew aboard the Greystokes' vessel. Not only does the proximity of the two representations ask the reader to connect the plight of black African workers and the plight of Western workers, but Burroughs further emphasizes the link between the two by naming the white leader of the oppressed sailors "Black Michael," a designation that, as Eric Cheyfitz has noted, links categories of racial and class identity (347).

These two linked opening sequences suggest a populist sympathy for the downtrodden and hostility toward the powerful. Yet even as he occasionally turns populist, Burroughs sidesteps any serious investment in such a politics by emphasizing that both oppressed groups, the black natives and the Western sailors, are repulsive and bestial.[19] Here and elsewhere in the romance, the narrator describes Western sailors as "motley" (18) and "villainous" (19), and the African blacks as "low" and "brutish" (85). *Tarzan of the Apes*, thus represents the "white" working class in almost the same negative racial terms that are applied to the African natives. Even Black Michael, the one working-class character on the ship characterized in somewhat positive terms, constitutes a profoundly equivocal figure—at once responsible for saving the Greystokes' lives and producing the circumstances that lead to their violent deaths and their son's desperate plight. Burroughs's racism will hardly come as a shock, but neither should his demonization of the working-class sailors surprise us, given the novice pulp writer's anxieties over his new intimacy with the vulgar pop-culture sphere.[20]

The common demonization of the black Africans and the Western sailors also performs important structural work for Burroughs at this early point in the romance. If the romance's opening events link working-class and black men through a rhetoric of bestiality, the novel soon establishes a material referent for that rhetoric in the figure of the ape. Sensitive to the pejorative association of the word "ape" and related terms such as "lowbrow" with subaltern males, Burroughs deploys eugenicist thinking to bind the "raced" class conflicts with which the romance begins to the ape drama that stands at the heart of his romance.[21] And if the use of evolutionary slurs isn't enough of a common thread, Burroughs also offers plot parallels—the apes, for example, attack the Greystokes' cabin in much the same way that the sailors attack the officers in a mutiny (39). Rhetorically and structurally, Burroughs asks us to understand apes in this romance as an allegory for people of color and the working class.

Yet if apes constitute a bestial and offensive allegory of blackness and working-classness, they represent an allegory with a difference. In chronicling his young aristocratic hero's fantastic adventures in the African jungle, Burroughs offers a radically ambivalent portrayal of the apes. The apes may be dark, violent, and threatening to Tarzan, but they are also loyal, simple, and powerful—nature's noble primitives. They thus represent the worst aspects of the bestiality ascribed by Burroughs to people of color and the working class and at the same time offer a way of suggesting the more appealing aspect of the "natural" Other. It is by characterizing the apes as mediated signs of ambivalence that Burroughs uses his white hero to articulate and explore his own contradictory feelings about the alterity of his new pop-culture enterprise. The narrative about an orphaned white aristocratic boy living among the apes, in other words, allows Burroughs to comment on his own feelings about being estranged from the white middle class and pursuing a new career in what a later commentator would call "the pulp jungle." Uneasily identifying with and becoming a part of the lowbrow or ape world, Tarzan reflects and refracts Burroughs's own unsettling identification with the lowbrow world of pop culture.

Therefore, when we examine the moments of xenophilia that tinge Tarzan's adventures with the apes, we witness Burroughs's self-exploration of his own feelings about the new marginal cultural production in which he has invested—and the working class and people of color that this cultural field invariably suggests. Burroughs's self-exploration involves, moreover, the recognition of the black African as an object of desire. Working-class people, as we have already seen, only figure as exotic early in the romance—in the figure of Black Michael—yet black Africans prove fascinating, as well as horrible, throughout the narrative. While Burroughs it seems cannot tolerate the thought of representing the working class in an alluring manner, he can use his ape-man—a man already proximate to the other—to explore his uneasy interest in black Africans and blackness. The appeal of blackness to Tarzan, like his own apeness, proves central to Burroughs's reconstruction of the meaning of white identity.

Beyond the Pale

We see particularly dramatic evidence of Burroughs's investment in otherness when his English upper-class hero, whose very name means "white-skin" in ape language, both identifies with and at times impersonates male apes and black African warriors (*Tarzan* 52). In one early scene, Tarzan regrets the fact that he lacks the hairy skin, large features, and red eyes of his ape "cousin." The scene constitutes Burroughs's attempt at comic relief, yet it also inadvertently suggests that in envying an ape, Tarzan, "the aristocratic scion of an old English house" (53), not only violates what we might call the species line, but he also crosses lines of race and class, if only metaphorically. When Tarzan envies "the mighty lips and powerful fangs," "the beautiful broad nostrils," and "generous nose," of the ape (53), we sense white anxiety and white desire emerging in the face of otherness. If the ape features are "mighty" and "powerful," "broad" and "generous," human features are represented in precisely the opposite fashion. Tarzan considers his mouth "a tiny slit," his teeth "puny," and his nose "pinched" and "half-starved" (53). Instead of celebrating whiteness by thoroughly ironizing "poor little Tarzan's" admiration of the apes, this passage represents the white man's identification with and desire for a virile, powerful, dark other. This portrayal of whiteness as scarcity and apeness as plenitude suggests nothing so much as white male fear of and desire for what Slavoj Žižek would call the Other's enjoyment—an enjoyment that always stands in for that which can be castrated ("Eastern Europe's"). Burroughs represents his hero's envy of ape features in language that reflects the white middle-class male's traditional jealousy over the supposedly better endowed working-class or, better, African American, male. The young Tarzan's fascination with the inflated, even phallic, facial features of the ape recalls turn-of-the-century white middle-class male's anxious interest in the mighty musculature of bodybuilders and boxers.

Tarzan's ape-envy displays the degree to which Burroughs's ambivalent attitude toward the "lower" classes and their culture both reflects and produces a more specific fascination with the fantasized rough physicality of the subaltern human. *Tarzan* reveals Burroughs's pleasure in describing the well-toned bodies of men who rely on physical strength for survival; we see this in his frequent descriptions of the ape-man's well-proportioned muscular body. For Burroughs, Tarzan has a "straight and perfect figure, muscled as the best of the ancient Roman gladiators must have been muscled, and yet with the soft and sinuous curves of a Greek god" (122).[22] We also witness Burroughs's fascination with the muscular male body in moments when he attributes a similar scopophilic desire to his hero. Tarzan's fascination with male apes constitutes an important example of his voyeuristic activity, but African warriors are by far his favorite object of visual pleasure. Consider, for example, Tarzan's first encounter with a black African male. The scene begins with Tarzan observing Kulonga, the black African warrior who has killed his ape foster mother. His immediate response is one of fascination rather than anger: "Tarzan looked with wonder upon the strange creature beneath him— so like him in form and yet so different in face and color. His books had portrayed the *negro*, but how different had been the dull, dead print to this sleek and hideous thing of ebony, pulsing with life" (90).[23] Tarzan, like the turn-of-the-century white reader, already "knows" the image of "the negro" from prejudiced images and literature he has found among his dead parent's things, but this image does not do justice to the black African warrior. The "dull, dead print," the racist stereotype, cannot contain the fact that Tarzan finds the black man fascinating, sublime. The African warrior simultaneously suggests the erotic, even phallic ("sleek," "pulsing with life"), and the terrible (a "hideous thing of ebony"). Tarzan finds him at once fearful and attractive. Or, as Burroughs puts it in a later retelling of the ape-man's youthful adventures: "Although he hated [the blacks], Tarzan derived considerable entertainment in watching them" (*Jungle* 13).

However, such moments of homoerotic fascination with the "dark" male other hardly constitute the extent of Tarzan's interest in alterity. Burroughs's hero not only identifies with, envies, and even desires the "dark" male Other, he cross-dresses as the Other as well. Thus, when the young ape-boy finds ape identity more desirable than human identity, we see Tarzan trying to simulate dark, hairy, ape skin "by plastering himself from head to foot with mud" (*Tarzan* 53). Invoking the spectacle of blackface minstrelsy here, Burroughs returns once again to the theme of racial cross-dressing he had used in his first Martian narrative. Wearing mud in order to approximate the skin of an ape serves as a sign of young Tarzan's desire to transgress social hierarchies and take on the identity of the Other.

This moment of minstrel humor should alert us, moreover, to the logic of blackface at work in the hero's name itself. A translation of the ape-words "white-skin," according to the narrator, the name "Tarzan" not only denotes the hero's white skin and his marvelous white qualities, but like Burroughs's pen name "Normal Bean," serves to mask a more problematic identification with the marginal. While the ape word "zan" means "skin"—suggesting nothing more than a fictive vocabulary—the ape word "tar" means "white," surely a more telling translation in the context of U.S. racialist culture. For "tar" to mean "white" in what has typically been understood to be a white supremacist romance raises the possibility of racial trouble in this world. Tarzan, our exemplary "white" man, our Anglo-Saxon *übermensch*, is also a "Tar"-man, a man of blackness. Just as in the mudface scene, the irony built into Tarzan's name suggests that white skin cannot emerge without an invocation of blackness. Burroughs himself suggests the possibility of Tarzan constituting a Tarman when he has the apes call him "Tarmangani," a nonsense word that makes still more manifest the notion that this hero's whiteness cannot be trusted. A character representative of "whiteness," Burroughs's hero suggests nothing less than the contradictions and ironies to which such a totalizing notion inevitably gives rise.

In other respects, of course, the ape man's appropriation of blackness hardly proves as innocuous as it does in the double entendre of a name or in the blackface humor of the pool scene. The ape-man's appropriation of black African male clothing, in particular, proves far more disturbing. From the moment of his first encounter with Kulonga to the end of the romance, Tarzan's interaction with black African males results in their deaths and his theft of their clothing and jewelry. In these savage moments of Ku Klux Klan-like vigilantism, we witness Burroughs's racism at its most repulsive. Yet these moments of lethal violence against black people are also moments for the white ape-man to appropriate black identity:

> Tarzan dispatched his prisoner quickly and silently; removed the weapons and ornaments, and—oh, the greatest joy of all—a handsome doeskin breechcloth, which he quickly transferred to his own person.

> Now indeed was he dressed as a man should be. None there was who
> could now doubt his high origin. (123)

In this scene, racist murder licenses racial cross-dressing which carries with
it a powerful suggestion of interracial homoerotic desire. Tarzan covers his
own penis in a garment no doubt still warm from the black man's body.
One wonders if the ape-man's "joy" may have more to do with his uneasy
desire for the black man than with his desire for the black man's breechcloth. More paradoxically still, the African's clothing provides the ape-man
with a new sense of prestige; cross-dressing in a black man's "breechcloth"
doesn't threaten Tarzan's sense of himself as a well-bred individual, as one
might expect given the racist tenor of the romance; instead it underwrites
his feeling of prestige and power and proclaims his "high origin." By demonstrating how his hero feels assuredly upper class when clad in a black African
costume, Burroughs inadvertently demonstrates how white male fantasies of
racist violence do not only imaginatively resolve lived social contradictions,
but also produce fantasies that are themselves contradictory. Instead of only
demonstrating his white aristocratic power, the murderous ape-man offers
us an image of himself as a dark, rough hero.

Becoming white for Tarzan thus seems to involve staging again and again
the pleasure and pain he experiences in standing beyond the pale. And this
logic continues to inform the novel even when Burroughs shifts into the
plot's denouement and moves toward the expected rediscovery of the ape-
man's white aristocratic "origin." When Jane, her middle-class friends and
family, and their captors arrive in Tarzan's part of Africa—a turning point in
the plot—we see repeated attempts by the ape-man to demonstrate that the
white respectable visitors are, in Burroughs's words, "his own kind" (121).
Nowhere else in the romance does Tarzan make as concerted an effort to
recover his whiteness. Yet no matter how valiantly Tarzan defends Jane and
her compatriots from black Africans, apes, and the mutinous working-class
men, these members of "his own kind" still find him somehow Other. Clayton Greystoke, Tarzan's cousin, assumes the ape-man has affiliations with the
local black African tribe (218), while even Jane cannot ignore the fact that
the seemingly noble man who has captivated her has the manners of an
untutored working-class beast (219). Indeed, even after Tarzan has received
training in spoken language and good manners from a French mentor, Jane
still considers him only moderately better than "white trash" (164). In the last
pages of the romance, Jane decides that she cannot tolerate the thought of

marrying the jungle man, and informs him that she plans to marry Clayton, his genteel relative and current heir to the Greystoke fortune.

Jane's rejection of the ape-man sets up the romance's last dramatic moment: fully conscious at this point of his "true" identity, Tarzan insists on his ape-ness and in so doing allows his newly betrothed cousin to inherit the massive Greystoke estate. The scene represents our protagonist as a figure so noble he willingly gives up his money, even his identity, for the woman he loves. Yet while this reading of the romance's last scene seems a likely sentiment with which to conclude a popular adventure romance, perhaps we should ask ourselves whether Tarzan may be getting precisely what he wants when he insists on his apeness (288). Or, perhaps we should ask ourselves whether Burroughs derived more satisfaction from making Tarzan remain something of an Other than from making the jungle man affirm his white aristocratic origin and end the romance in a triumphant manner. While an affluent adventure writer such as Owen Wister concludes The Virginian (1904) by leaving the titular hero upwardly mobile and romantically involved, the downwardly mobile, ever-anxious Burroughs leaves his hero in limbo, positioned between the jungle and civilization, between apes and humans, between blackness and whiteness.[24] It should hardly surprise us, given Burroughs's difficult relationship with his own father and the new middle-class status quo, that Tarzan does not at the end of the novel accept the paternal name and fortune, but chooses, like his creator, to seek his own path. Yet what is striking about Tarzan's choice is that he uses otherness—his apeness, his "Africanness"— to construct, in effect, a whiteness alternative to that of the paternal legacy and the dominant middle-class society. We may speculate that Tarzan's last moment mirrors that of his creator when he started writing for the pulps, anxious over his identity, fascinated by his connection to the Other, worried about the future. The fact that Tarzan articulates his divided sensibilities at the end of the romance in a Wisconsin middle-class home, a setting socially and geographically proximate to Burroughs's own family home, only underscores this reading. Torn between his white middle-class upbringing and a new, pop-culture world, Burroughs leaves his hero as divided as himself.

Whiteness Regained?

If Burroughs began his pulp career with profound anxieties over his position in a changing white middle-class world, several extraordinarily successful years of adventure romance sales eliminated much of his self-doubt and social anxieties. Burroughs's string of pulp publications during his first four years in business ensured that he could make a living writing adventure romances. The enormous popularity of his writings with increasingly respectable readers certainly should have reassured him of his normalcy. Yet even as he grew comfortable once again in the world of "normal beans," Burroughs still resisted the ways of a new bureaucratic middle-class society. Burroughs's insistence on living according to the principles of an earlier middle-class culture characterized both his personal decisions and his business decisions for a long time to come. In 1919, Burroughs created a frontier-like experience for himself when he and his family moved to a large ranch in what is now suburban Los Angeles.[25] The proprietary feeling the ranch offered Burroughs would extend into his writing career. In 1923, Burroughs would incorporate himself as a writer, thus turning the basis for the white-collar revolution into a personal strategy. And in 1931, Burroughs would begin publishing his books himself, once again insisting upon the proprietary, autonomous nature of his labor.

By turning to the new frontier of the popular, Burroughs had succeeded in emulating, even surpassing, his father's example and created for himself a valuable family business on the traditional model. Yet it is important to recognize that in turning to the popular to regain the "landed" white bourgeois manhood that history seemed intent on denying him, Burroughs also discovered the unsettling thrill of experiencing the dissolution of a white identity, if only through the fantastic transgressions of pop-culture production. The popular offered Burroughs a way to regain a sense of manly, proprietary, white-male identity, yet at the same time the popular forced him to recognize, however fleetingly, however uneasily, that he enjoyed the experience of having a "divided mind"—of experiencing a contradictory, hybrid sense of self.

Indeed, if the bulk of Burroughs's career presents us with many offensive examples of his investment in whiteness and property, it also provides us with glimpses of his continuing interest in the pleasure of difference and the place of that interest in his cultural construction of whiteness. One may cite his continued fascination with writing scenes of racial cross-identification and cross-dressing, of course, or, odder still, his use of a drawing of an African warrior on the cover of the official guide to the unfortunately named *Tarzan Clans of America*.[26] But perhaps a more fitting conclusion would involve turning to another illustration of Burroughs's interest in alterity—and another instance when the pulp writer's use of pseudonyms ends up revealing more than he would like. In 1941, Burroughs, anxious over marital issues and health problems, writes a humorous story and chooses to sign the story's preface with a name far more surprising than "Normal Bean"—the name "Joe Louis" (Porges 678). In this appropriation of the great black boxer's name we see an act of expropriation, but we also witness the creator of Tarzan willing to identify himself with—indeed, even assume the identity of—an African American boxer. Here we see, as it were, an inadvertent recognition by the aging Burroughs that, in turning to the popular as a new frontier, he hadn't only championed what he called the white man's hope—entertainments celebratory of a racist, white, working class. He had also revealed his fascination with, even his desire for, the black man's hope—the muscular, virile body of the black warrior. By using the name "Joe Louis" as his own pseudonym, Burroughs offers one last reminder of how one of the century's most influential creators of white fictions could never escape the sense that his successful writing emerged in large part from a willingness to allow his whiteness to become momentarily undone. Burroughs may have begun writing pulp adventure romances in the hopes of shoring up his identity as "Normal Bean," as a white middle-class man, but his popular production led him to admit, however inadvertently, that the very idea of wanting to be "Normal Bean" had everything to do with wanting to be "Joe Louis."

Notes

Many thanks are due Andrea Levine, Eric Lott, Michael Uebel, and Ken Wissoker, all of whom proved to be wise auditors. Above all, however, I am indebted to Kathy Lavezzo: her faith and wisdom sustained me during the writing process.

1. *Under the Moons of Mars* (later retitled *A Princess of Mars*) appeared attributed to "Norman Bean" in six consecutive issues of *All-Story* (Feb. 1912–July 1912). Burroughs's next published romance, *Tarzan of the Apes* (1912) appeared in *All-Story Magazine* attributed to "Edgar Rice Burroughs (Norman Bean)." From then on each of Burroughs's published adventure romances appeared under the name "Edgar Rice Burroughs." Porges describes the editor's error and Burroughs's responses to it in his mammoth biography of the pulp author (7, 128, 136). We should also note that Burroughs used the pen name "Normal Bean" in writing an (unpublished) article on managing a business (Porges 111) and, more importantly, in writing and publishing a series of comic verses about Southern California in the *Chicago Tribune* between 1913 and 1915 (Porges 199–202). Burroughs attempted to use a few other pen names later in his career, but he never succeeded in having this material published. All subsequent biographical material in this essay will be drawn from works by Fenton, Heins, Lupoff, and Porges.

2. The vast majority of scholars who have written on Burroughs tend to assess him as a fairly uncomplicated supporter of white supremacy and patriarchy. See Fanon,

Black Skin, White Masks 146; Cheyfitz; Easthope; and Bederman. Boscaglia's reading of male masochism in *Tarzan of the Apes* complicates the usual reading of Burroughs in an interesting fashion, but only Marianna Torgovnick offers a counterintuitive interpretation of Burroughs's most famous romance, arguing that the text begins by having the English orphan question the binary oppositions that structure Western society (nature/culture, male/female, black/white), only to accept the usual hierarchical structure of these oppositions by the end of the narrative. No one has explored Burroughs's experience of class, although Philip Cohen's important gloss on white working-class male response to Tarzan as a pop icon serves as something of a complement to my reading of the class politics underwriting Burroughs's pop cultural production. See Cohen, "Tarzan."

3. See Du Bois's *Black Reconstruction*, Roediger's *The Wages of Whiteness*, and Lott's *Love and Theft*. Needless to say, these three seminal works are only some of the many books and articles that offer a variety of investigations of whiteness.

4. In a future article I hope to examine the reception of Burroughs's first romances among 1910s cultural consumers.

5. The following biographical discussion is drawn mainly from Porges.

6. George Burroughs helped an African American Confederate soldier procure employment after the Civil War (Porges 779). He later made his feelings toward the working class known by attending the execution of the Haymarket martyrs in 1887 (Porges 777).

7. My sense of white middle-class life at the turn of the century owes a great deal to Aron, Filene, Higham, Hofstadter, Kocka, Lears, and Macleod. Christopher Wilson's important book, *White Collar Fictions: Class and Social Representation in American Literature, 1885–1925*, has proven an invaluable source on the crisis of middle-class identity during this era and on the need to avoid a nostalgic representation of nineteenth-century middle-class life.

8. Cindy Aron argues that during the late nineteenth-century "many members of the old entrepreneurial and professional middle class faced . . . crises severe enough to bring them to the verge of economic disaster" (8–9).

9. For an important discussion of Wister and the middlebrow Western, see Saxton. Higashi's recent book on DeMille offers a fascinating account of the director's gentrification of a vulgar pop medium.

10. I have been influenced by Erik Olin Wright's thoughts on "contradictory class location." See Wright 19–63.

11. I quote here from one of Burroughs's memories of his pulp origins: "I had gone thoroughly through some of the all-fiction magazines," Burroughs recalls, "and I made up my mind that if people were paid for writing rot such as I read, I could write stories just as rotten" (qtd. in Heins 12). For the history of U.S. magazines during this period, see Peterson; McCann; and Mullen. For an interesting attack on the dangerous vulgarity of adventure magazines see Mathiews.

12. While versions of fantasy literature or science fiction have played a role in U.S.

literary culture from Brocken Brown and Poe onward, ostensibly realist versions of such fictions were new at the turn of the century. See Franklin (1966) and Brown (1993).

13. Server provides a useful discussion of Howard's problems with his neighbors (44–45).

14. I take the phrase "divided mind" from the title of Peter Conn's book on American literature and culture from 1898 to 1918.

15. In his recent informal ethnographic exploration of English working-class boys' interest in the ape-man, however, Philip Cohen makes readily apparent how the contradictions inherent in the figure of Tarzan spoke to the social contradictions the boys endured in everyday life. Cohen first points out the secret fascination these white working-class boys have with black people. He then argues that "playing at Tarzan on the streets of their inner-city neighborhoods licensed [the boys] to 'behave like savages' whilst maintaining their supremacy as 'Lords of the Urban Jungle' over and against both the black presence *and* the civilizing mission. In this way they succeed in turning a code which puts them down into a device for affirming the superior patrimony of being not only white and male but also working-class 'born and bred'" ("Tarzan" 28–29).

16. The extraordinary popularity of plantation romances, plantation parks, and plantation musicals during this period suggests that the white middle classes of the North and Midwest found some satisfaction in comparing the changes they were enduring to the changes white southerners had experienced during and after the war.

17. A reproduction of this page may be found in Porges, 109. In the published version, Burroughs replaced this all-too-revealing statement with the line "I have not aged as other men."

18. Burroughs wrote *The Outlaw of Torn*, a neomedieval romance, between the two published works, but revised it continuously until its publication in 1914.

19. We might consider Burroughs's use of populism in the midst of demonizing the subaltern a typical instance of bourgeois Progressivist contradiction—at once inheriting a populist perspective from the great working-class movements of the turn of the century and, at the same time, reifying predictable white middle-class stereotypes of the Other.

20. The first film version of *Tarzan of the Apes* (1918) significantly alters the representation of white working-class males in the narrative by introducing a new character, the loyal white sailor Binns, who watches over the orphaned noble infant in Africa until he is enslaved by Arab traders.

21. From the late nineteenth century to our own period, the word "ape," like the word "gorilla," has often served as an insulting evolutionary metaphor for what the white middle class often understands as the biological backwardness of people of color and the white working class. In the *Dictionary of American Slang*, the word "ape" is defined as both "a derogatory word for [a] Negro" and "a hoodlum or strongarm man" in American slang. *The Random House Dictionary of American Slang* provides much the

same definition. The eugenic discourse that conflated racial and class otherness in the pejorative term "lowbrow" extends to the polyvalence of the term "ape."

22. The first film version of *Tarzan of the Apes* warrants mention here because its star, ex-fireman and *Biograph Pictures*–extra Elmo Lincoln, had such a large body that he horrified Burroughs. By this point a wealthy and socially established man, Burroughs found Lincoln's massive chest and large musculature repulsive. No doubt skittish over the way Lincoln's enormous body suggested a working-class identity, Burroughs wanted his hero played by a white man with a more well-proportioned, which is to say refined, build. D. W. Griffith, the star director at *Biograph*, had no such problem with Lincoln's build. Indeed, legend has it that it was the ex-fireman's massive "pecs" which first attracted the famous director's eye. See Porges 315–16; Essoe 23–28.

23. Given that this is the first time that Tarzan has seen a human being, his fascination may seem less racially motivated than I argue here. Yet, as we shall see, Burroughs uses language that emphasizes the racial dimensions of the confrontation, thus forcing us to read the scene as one that has to do more with race and less with species.

24. See Bold for an interesting reading of Wister's conclusion within the context of the popular Western.

25. Burroughs would eventually break up the ranch and turn it into the suburb of Tarzana. The man who'd resisted the white-collar revolution would thus end up building a town for white-collar workers.

26. Heins offers a duplication of the guide cover, p. 110.

ALL THE KING'S MEN

Elvis Impersonators and White Working-Class Masculinity

ERIC LOTT

I haven't figured out why Detroit has this attraction [to] Elvis. But this is a
blue-collar town with down to earth people, the kind Elvis liked.
—Danny Vann, Elvis impersonator

something in their psyche insists on elvis
—Lucille Clifton, "us and them"

As the plane touched the tarmac of McCarran Airport, a nearby passenger, as
if on cue, sang out: "Viva, Las Vegas!" And how could he not, since Elvis now
occupies as central a place in Vegas's mythology as Vegas does in Presley's. It
was all part of the script, one in which my own inquiring mind fit all too
well. No room here for academic-renegade posturing: my desire to attend the
fifth annual Elvis Presley International Impersonators Association convention in the interest of pinning down the purpose of Elvis impersonation only
confirmed my status as interloping voyeuristic outsider, or as fan—even as it
suggested my resemblance to the culture-industry vampires (from talk shows
to magazine segments to camp cinema) who had made Elvis impersonators
such a hot commodity of late. Nonetheless, what I found largely contradicts
the scripted scenarios and easy critiques of Elvis impersonation that circulate so smugly through academe and pop life both. The truly numberless
performers of Presley give eerie and perhaps dubious body to the shade of
Elvis; they inhabit and prolong the irradiating afterglow that is the lingering
cultural presence of Elvis Presley. Yet an initial approach to the meaning of
that habitation lies in the fact that the great majority of these impersonators
are working-class white men who stress the Pelvis's route from rags to king
of rock and roll. Like baseball and the Statue of Liberty, the figure of Elvis
guards the way into America.

Not, of course, to everyone's satisfaction. The lines of critique are familiar enough. For fin-de-millennium doomsayers, Elvis impersonators confirm

the cretinizing powers of "mass" culture. In an America of simulation and deceit, a Joe Elvis or Elvis Little may seem another instance of the chronic ache of "hyperreality," as Umberto Eco has called it, being one more fake in a land without qualities.[1] William McCranor Henderson's novel *Stark Raving Elvis* (1984), as its title implies, tells the story of an Elvis impersonator lost to madness because of his overinvestment in the fiber-optically–circulated image of Elvis. However, for black pop groups like Public Enemy or Living Colour, fakery in this case means (at best) a performer who got more from black culture than he gave. For too many, Elvis has been mistakenly coronated. As Chuck D and Flavor Flav of Public Enemy rap:

> Elvis was a hero to most
> But he never meant shit to me
> Straight up racist that sucker was
> Simple and plain
> Motherfuck him *and* John Wayne!

Living Colour's spectacular "Elvis Is Dead" aims for a similar effect while, in accord with the peculiarly meiotic logic to which dead Elvis has given rise, keeping his image in circulation.[2] Still another, though more adoring, critique of Elvis's apotheosis emerges in camp appropriations of him. Marjorie Garber has written of Elvis impersonators' "unmarked transvestism," and strong whiffs of camp sensibility hover around such phenomena as the film *Honeymoon in Vegas* (1992), with its skydiving Elvises, or Elvis impersonator/parodist El Vez, the Mexican Elvis, who is rather more marked in the transvestite sources of his travesty (Garber 363–74).[3]

I am not specifically concerned here with any one of these critiques, but taken together they define the territory I want to occupy. The phenomenon of Elvis impersonation, I will argue, is worth looking at for what it reveals about the racial and class unconscious of contemporary white working-class masculinity. The influence of the culture industry on the formation of the white Imaginary, the "white-Negro" resonance of Elvis's image, and the cross-dressing aura of his impersonation all, of course, bear importantly on this unconscious, and all have a place in my account. In some respects, however, these emphases have bequeathed us terms of dismissal rather than of analysis. If I rely on such emphases only for the purpose of broad orientation it is because I want, by way of the Elvis impersonator, to know how working-class white men currently live their whiteness. Elvis impersonation in essence constitutes a series of popular appropriations of Elvis, and attests to the kinds of meanings that are presently constructed in his name. As the impersonators themselves by and large take this mode of performance seriously, it seems to me to deserve not supercilious irony nor mere censure, but an attempt at critical investigation.

Toward this end I interviewed a cohort of Elvis performers and impersonators, as well as their fans, and called on their representation (and self-representation) in various contemporary media.[4] The discourse around and my own conversations with these people yielded the information on which I draw. My undertaking has been made easier by the consolidation of the aforementioned Elvis Presley International Impersonators Association (EPIIA), a "clearing house for information regarding activities of Elvis performers *worldwide*," and by the publication of American Graphic Systems, Inc.'s *I Am Elvis: A Guide to Elvis Impersonators.*[5] The EPIIA convention, which brings together a multitude of performers and codifies its parent organization's cultural politics, is a fascinating affair—somewhat of a cross between a Moose Lodge gathering's hearty camaraderie and an academic conference's meeting of stars, minds, "experts," rivals, and paraphernalia-hawkers. The *Guide* is an apparently sober document recording the biographies and vital statistics— birth date, height/weight, astrological sign, and agent's phone number—of sixty-five performers of varying resemblance to the King. There are heavily bearded Elvises, four-year-old Elvises, and Elvis duos; Italian Elvises, Greek Elvises, Jewish Elvises, a Lady Elvis, even a Black Elvis. Impersonator impresario Ed Franklin boasts, "We've had every type of Elvis there is in the world."[6] As ethnographic study has lately hosted some of the richest work in cultural studies, what follows owes as well to the methodological and practical explorations by writers such as Philip Cohen, Paul Willis, Janice Radway, Donna Gaines, and others.[7] My broadest—and most fiercely held—assumption is summed up in Paul Willis's remark that cultural forms, however idiosyncratic or marginal, "may not say what they know, nor know what they say, but they mean what they do" (*Learning* 125–26), and in so doing legitimate the attention we give them. Such forms are part of larger, shared patterns of life, and the logic of their practice extends to broader relations of feeling and practice. And there is a point to them. Impersonating Elvis may seem a tad bizarre, but it has a human rationale that deserves articulation. I do not mean, of course, that such performance is mystified and inarticulate without the help of the heroic cultural inquirer. Nothing could be further from the truth. It might be more exact to say that mine is an effort of translation, submitting the gestures of the impersonators to another set of codes or social area of language. I only follow what the impersonators themselves intimate about their work. As EPIIA president and impersonator Rick Marino (a veritably Clintonian figure of political smoothness, intergenerational bonding, and showbiz smarts) told me of the impersonators' (literal) investments in Elvis: "When you're growing up, sometimes, you know, if you're a man, you need somebody to look at, to get a guidance or some kind of direction for the type of man you want to be. . . . A lot of the guys, you know, maybe their dad didn't quite do it for 'em and so they look to Elvis and in a kind of an offbeat way, maybe, he kind of like, you know, made 'em feel good."

Just how Elvis makes them feel good will, I hope, become clear—cultural forms mean what they do. First, a few words about this form's historical and cultural contexts are in order. For one thing, working-class men's traditional gender self-definition, despite glimmers of its recuperation in Hollywood and elsewhere, has for some time been under siege amid what Barbara Ehrenreich calls the "androgynous drift" of the last three decades (*Hearts* 99–116). That self-definition, a well-known persona of hard-bitten manliness, has since the onset of the industrial revolution been a gendered response to class oppression.[8] Substituting physical resourcefulness and strength for power in the workplace, valorizing and in some subjective sense choosing a life of manual labor that only oppresses them, working-class men have developed a compensatory way of being in the world. In *Learning to Labour*, Paul Willis describes the formation of this dynamic in the context of the contemporary school, where working-class kids' refusal of middle-class culture and its overinvestment in mental labor entails a corollary celebration of truancy and manual work—the result of which is, of course, to slot them, for good, into working-class jobs. Willis demonstrates the extent to which this refusal—often expressed in the most imaginative if unruly ways—is extremely clearheaded in its suspicion that the credentials the school offers are bogus and that the work it promises for even the most "behaved" working-class student will be boring and utterly meaningless. This affirmation of manly mastery, to be sure, also depends on a commonsense sexism that is extremely oppressive to women in the workplace as well as the home, and which certainly qualifies its clarity. And it often depends as well on an extreme ambivalence toward working-class black men, whose social proximity and cultural difference make them useful Others for white group solidarity but whose masculinist self-definition (and cultural difference) also earn the fascination and respect of white working-class males. We can expect to see these important differentiations again shortly.

This white working-class self-conception perhaps had its heyday in the 1960s, when the subjective sense of physical power was, for once, matched by the so-called *embourgeoisment* of American workers. The extent to which this *embourgeoisment* occurred remains a matter of debate, and it was in any case to erode rather precipitously (with the auto and related industries) in the following decades.[9] Changes in the ideologies of manhood, including the 1960s counterculture's embrace of androgyny, the encroaching obsolescence of anticommunist machismo, and the looming attractiveness of the "sensitive man," were undergirded by a massive shift in political economy.[10] Simply put, this was a shift from "Fordism" to "post-Fordism," from an industrial regime of mass assembly-line production to a halting and low-wage service economy in which, moreover, the sexual division of labor was blurred. Economy and identity came together in working-class men's felt inability to *provide*—a masculine ideal the social script increasingly disdained anyway.[11] As the service sector fully emerged, so too did "office" styles of manhood in which class prejudices were physically encoded. Certainly older modes of working-class masculine self-styling persist, but they find no sanctioned place in the corridors of what Michael Dukakis in his 1988 presidential campaign blandly and speciously termed "good jobs at good wages." This is not, of course, to lament their passing, nor to claim that many of the worst effects of that older conception of masculinity no longer exist, much less to suggest that those effects do not extend even now to middle-class men. If anything, male physical violence and abuse, for instance, have redoubled in hysterical fashion in the face of troubled self-definition.

The resulting situation of "embattled" masculinity has dovetailed with another context—that of "identity politics." Whether it is known by its antagonistic popular representation as affirmative action and "quotas" or in its academic guise as pluralizing syllabi and multicultural identities, this development has seemed to put the squeeze on even a reconstructed category of straight-white-male. For many working-class white men, however wrongly, "preferential" treatment for victims of historical injustice has seemed a great betrayal of the American worker, facilitating an already-insistent migration of jobs to foreign locales and bodies. In this context the rhetoric of multiculturalism hovers with great belittling force. Meanwhile, the virtual absence of good work on white class identities in current cultural debate suggests that white working-classness doesn't really rate as a fashionable identity, and that no one is serious about investigating the class commitment of current left sloganeering.[12] Some historians' recent studies of the whiteness of the white working class, while certainly salutary developments, in fact put forward fairly bleak views of working-class tastes and attitudes, and help gird an intellectual community for whom the working-class white male is the most backward and least regenerable portion of the population today, writer of no

"great" books, perpetrator of Howard Beach and Bensonhurst, and personally responsible for the rise of Reagan/Thatcher "authoritarian populism." [13]

For this reason the perils of an unapologetically academic undertaking like
this one ought to be plainly and frankly acknowledged. Given the standard
run of attempts on the part of the academy to represent working-class culture, there is plenty of room to worry about the class effects of rendering
working-class interests and desires for (mostly) other academics. My own
sense is that left intellectuals, though inevitably caught up in economies of
prestige and therefore subject to various class disidentifications, are not necessarily doomed from the start when they try to investigate working-class
life. Surely there are massive dangers involved in their attempts to do so, ones
that stem directly from their social location in the academy both as producers
of a certain kind of class-based knowledge and as credentializers willy-nilly
committed to the partial reproduction of social hierarchy. Just as surely are
attempts by erstwhile working-class people to live and identify themselves
as working class within the academy up against the most hideous pressures
to declass and disidentify themselves. But I don't think those disidentifications completely corrupt imaginative acts of working-class cultural reconstruction. The air may be fouled with commonsense definitions of working
people as inbred, bloated, bigoted fools, but these definitions exist on precisely the plane one occupies with different definitions in order to combat
them. This plane may be worlds away from working-class culture proper, but
that does not invalidate its capacity for clarity or militancy—though it does
entail a necessary intellectual vigilance on the part of the cultural critic. Confronted with the uncertainty and instability of audience response to papers
like mine—the impossibility of guaranteeing that discourse will be received
as it was intended to be—there is always the potential for political disaster,
but the hazard seems worth courting in the interest of the little good such
work might do, and—who knows?—wayward responses of sadism and embarrassment could themselves be more edifying than we imagine. At the very
least they open to view class feelings that usually remain masked by genteel
academic or, conversely, "progressive" decorum.

I will argue that the purpose of Elvis impersonation is to provide "magical" resolutions of these social pressures confronting contemporary white
working-class masculinity. [14] Buffeted by an era of post-white-male politics,
based on an economy of labor that is well-nigh obsolete in these post-Fordist
times—in every respect a relic of the postwar working class's better days—
blue-collar machismo is produced and reclaimed in the Elvis impersonator
but in appropriately damaged and partial form. The fate of working-class

masculinity in a postwar era of *embourgeoisment* followed by scarcity seems subtly encoded in the arcana and trajectory of Elvis's career, in which most of the impersonators are wholly versed: his meteoric rise in the mid-1950s, the long (if banal) holiday of silly movies in the 1960s, the shattering 1968 comeback, the late concert tours before the sad decline to death in 1977. While some of the impersonators perform a whole range of Presley music, the raw 1950s Elvis and the kitschy 1970s Elvis are the favorites, according to the two principal myths that give "imaginary" form to white working-class masculinity. These myths are less discrete than their historical sources might suggest, sometimes overlapping in a given performer and sometimes not. In any case I take Diana Fuss's point that the identity they help construct owes to the processes of mimicry and identification I'm studying here.[15] If the outward signs of working-class affiliation are less and less "given" or inevitable because of the confusing disarticulation of laboring identities in our time—if they now derive much more from the realm of culture than that of work—the two chief Elvis performance styles exist as a place where working-classness may be adopted, confirmed, or secured, even if unconsciously. The first of these, the younger Elvis, is a fantasy of working-class "blackness," and invokes a long American tradition of cultural impersonation. The second, the Vegas Elvis, is a fantasy of "whiteness," which is to say class in displaced form. Both fantasies are rooted in styles of masculine embodiment that owe in turn to the dynamic at the heart of Elvis impersonation—a constant shuttling between looking like a fan and feeling like a king.

The Man Who Would Be King

The art of impersonation is built on a contradiction. Appreciation, deference, spectatorship, and emulation compete with inhabitation, aggression, usurpation, and vampirism. In Elvis impersonation, as in other kinds of impersonation, there is an unsteady but continual oscillation between these stances. Elvis impersonators' remarks about their idol reflect a remarkably schizophrenic movement from prostration to megalomania and back again. Bert Hathaway, like a great many of these performers, calls Elvis "the greatest person that has ever walked the face of the earth" (*Guide* 62); Ron Dye remarks with casual seriousness that Elvis was "sent by God for a purpose—to help during troubled times" (*Guide* 43); and several impersonators credit Elvis and his music with helping them through severe personal traumas. Yet even as they recognize the uniqueness and special power of Elvis Presley, these

Figure 1. "They thought I was the real thing": Ray Kajkowski and bodyguards. (photo courtesy of Ray Kajkowski)

performers yearn in often unconscious ways to unseat the master. Former construction worker and logger Clayton Benke-Smith claims that he is able to wear custom-made jumpsuits made from patterns bequeathed by Elvis's seamstress to their maker, B&K Enterprises, which are "Elvis' *exact size*" (*Guide* 13). Elvis impersonators typically indulge this sort of fortuitousness with trinitarian fervor. On an August 1992 segment of the CBS magazine program *48 Hours* devoted to Elvis impersonators, former car salesman Dennis Wise spoke of impersonating Elvis as "my calling for the last fifteen years. . . . You can't teach somebody to be Elvis—you either have it or you don't." And the impersonator Michael alleges that during one of his recreations of Elvis's 1973 *Aloha from Hawaii* TV special, a woman gave him a red lei at *precisely the same moment* Elvis received one in the original show (*Guide* 84). These near-Oedipal fantasies of replacing the father appear again in Henderson's *Stark Raving Elvis* ("He was the King. . . . *Beat that, Elvis!*" [67]) and, of course, in the several performers, like Dennis Wise himself, who have undergone plastic surgery in their quest for authenticity. Yet impersonators are equally happy to make baldly regicidal connections: "The crowds went crazy. They thought I was the real thing," says trucker Ray Kajkowski. On *48 Hours* Dennis Wise remarked, "When people come up to me and say, 'Man, I shut my eyes and I swore it was

Elvis up there'—that's when you know you've *got* it." For electronics worker Mike Moat, the "ultimate compliment" would be to have "Elvis fans think of me when they hear Elvis songs"—a peculiar enough inversion of the usual relation of mimic to star to suggest a revealing confusion of motives (*Guide* 91).

This confusion in Elvis's most loyal fans might be understood as a mixing-up of two kinds of looking at Elvis. Laura Mulvey famously codified these (in regard to the movies) as fetishistic scopophilia and voyeurism. The first stems from the pleasure of using someone as an object of sexual stimulation through sight, and is a function of the sexual instincts; the second comes from identification with the projected image, and is a function of ego libido (Mulvey, *Visual* 18). While in film these looks are essentially spread across differently gendered actors—the woman there to be looked at in a sexual way and the man taking on the male spectator's identification as his perfect or ideal ego—the body of Elvis bears both looks in the arena of Elvis impersonation. Sometimes, as we have seen, he is the fetishized object of impersonators' fascination; at others he is the ideal ego they seek to inhabit or even replace. To be Elvis or to have him—that is the (unacknowledged) question. Of course, the issue isn't nearly so clear-cut as this since, as Diana Fuss argues (contra Freud and Lacan), "the desire to be *like* can itself be motivated and sustained by the desire to *possess*: being can be the most radical form of having" (Fuss, "Fashion" 737). As impersonator James Wallace says:

> *James Wallace:* It's like, I'm James first and Elvis second, and when I'm on the stage, you know, I can be the Elvis side of me, and when I'm off-stage I'm James, definitely. It gives me an opportunity to be a fan in the front row, like I said, in the sense that the excitement is in the air for me, similar to what he was able to enjoy himself. . . .
> *Eric Lott:* What's it feel like to be Elvis?
> *JW:* Sometimes it feels real powerful and exhilarating and other times it's, uh, kind of scary in the similarities that I have when you visually look at me. Some people have taken it to the extreme of thinking, like, it's the ghost, or the brother, or, you know, things like that.

The oscillation between—or conflating of—Elvis as a source of identification and as a source of contemplation accounts for the impersonators' schizophrenic response to their idol. Here, though, the two kinds of looking are acted out, white masculinity performed, putting the impersonator at much greater risk than the average cinematic spectator.

For while the ideal ego of a larger-than-life Elvis might seem an attractive

counter to the life of forklift and shop floor, the fact is that it may also implicate the performer in something to which he is never adequate—a confirmation, in psychoanalytic terms, of castration.[16] There may, in other words,
be elements of masochism built into the imaginary projection of the ego that
Elvis impersonation seems to hold out for its practitioners. So much is suggested by the impersonators' repeated assertions that, as Bill Cochran puts
it, "Nobody can ever be another Elvis so to copy him exactly would be virtually impossible" (Guide 28). Such disavowals not only confess failure, they
let impersonators off the hook, and perhaps account for the number of performers who claim not really to impersonate Elvis so much as recall his aura.
"I don't impersonate Elvis, I put on a show," says Rick Marino; telephone
worker Danny Vann concedes, "I know I'm not Elvis, nobody can replace
him . . . I don't consider myself an impersonator—I consider myself an inter-
preter" (Guide 113); Donn Jett prefers to think of himself as an impressionist
rather than an impersonator, perhaps a distinction without a difference (Guide
67). The inherent inability to live up to Elvis's image presents a great problem for this mode of performance, and produces the peculiar situation in
which self-apotheosizing results in simultaneous self-damage. Elvis's image
is in this sense a kind of fetish that, as Christian Metz writes, enables a phallic self-inflation but also exposes the insufficiency that requires it: "the fetish
signifies the penis as absent, it is its negative signifier; supplementing it, it
puts a 'fullness' in place of a lack, but in doing so it also affirms that lack"
(71). Perhaps this is another reason why landscaper James Wallace finds in-
habiting Elvis "kind of scary," a word several impersonators use to describe
the experience of being placed on Elvis's pedestal by awestruck fans. In any
case, those impersonators who feel this pressure most strongly displace feelings of inadequacy into Elvis-like humility. "They didn't come to see me,"
says Bob Erickson of his most memorable performance; "they came to see an
Elvis show" (Guide 52). The irony of all this, of course, is that imaginary self-
assertion has in practice become a kind of fan-like deference.

Similar reversals attend the other kind of looking at Elvis embodied in his
impersonation. Dennis Wise's perfectly innocent remark that "I loved [Elvis]
with all my heart" and have "dedicated my life to him" suggests an erotic
agenda underlying the fascinated spectatorship of Elvis that returns with
potentially disrupting force (Guide 123; 48 Hours, August 1992). Impersonators'
enthusiastic accounts of their makeup and apparel ("when I feel like a red
night," said Wise on 48 Hours, "I wear my red one here") perhaps suggest
nothing more than the variety of purposes that lie behind transvestism—

or as Australian ambulance supervisor Ken Welsh, who personally spent one hundred forty hours embossing his jumpsuit with jewelry, asks defensively, "Who said men can't sew?" (Guide 120). But the widespread embarrassment and innuendo surrounding Elvis impersonation points more directly to the homoerotic implications built into such acts. "He's a fag, you know," says a cowboy of Byron Bluford, the impersonator in Stark Raving Elvis (36); or as EPIIA head Ron Bessette says of the men who could finally "sing like Elvis, walk like Elvis, be Elvis" once they hooked up with his organization: "A lot of these guys have been in the closet for so long" (Abramowitz C9). Often contemplation of the figure of Elvis threatens to become fascination with Elvis's literal figure, as in Clayton Benke-Smith's boast that he and Elvis wear the exact same size of jumpsuit.[17] This must account for former Ford worker and impersonator Marc Roberts's steady disavowal of such intentions: "I loved the guy, but, you know, it's not like a . . . sort of like a homosexual type deal, it's more like how you would love your brother, or a family member, something like that." One feels a bodily fascination with Presley everywhere in conversations with impersonators, but it is true that it comes to the surface in the most displaced ways. These often take the form of curiously adjusted matrimonial scenarios, as in Port Arthur, Texas, entertainer Sammy Stone Atchison's remark that his ultimate fantasy would consist of being recognized as the only good Elvis impersonator, or "the King's best man in music" (Guide 11). The role of court counselor puts one close enough to the King's person; but how much more so fantasies of taking his place in the marriage bed: ad agent Craig MacIntosh's wife on occasion dresses up as Elvis's onetime wife, Priscilla, while Darrin Race fantasizes about marrying whomever might be found to impersonate Ann-Margret in the role she played in Viva Las Vegas! I hope I may be forgiven if this proliferation of impersonations, recalling the Elvis impersonator's own, strike me as displacements of homoerotic attention to Elvis himself.[18] All of this is submerged in the act of performance, of course, but it also typically disguises itself as the concern we have seen with sartorial display, where any too specific homoerotic charge is buried in a sublimated admiration for Elvis spectacle, the lure of the image. The irony of such spectacle, and of the other displacements, is plainly that the admiring spectatorial contemplation of Elvis becomes a mode of one-upping self-assertion.

Such contradictions and cross-cuttings of feeling and desire in the art of Elvis impersonation make it a highly unstable form, where intended gestures and effects constantly threaten to turn into their opposites. Even before one enters onto the terrain of race and class, the predicament of masculine performativity has unsettled the whole affair. This instability traverses the structures of feeling that so insistently connect Elvis impersonation with the unconscious of working-class white men, to which we must now begin to turn.

The White Negro

Perhaps one of the most curious things about the cult of Elvis is that no fan club or subcultural stylistic affectation will suffice; the body of Elvis must be inhabited. Behind this seemingly bizarre demand lies a history of imitation in which Elvis figures quite centrally. Himself an alleged impostor, the historical referent of Norman Mailer's 1957 "The White Negro," Elvis inherited a blackface tradition that lives a disguised, vestigial life in his imitators.[19] Nobody who thinks with their ears can dismiss Elvis as merely a case of racial rip-off, but the legacy of blackface does lie behind both Elvis and the need for his impersonation. If only as a performative signifier of racial difference through which everyday cross-racial interest was at once facilitated and denied, blackface designates the complex cultural mix that inspired Elvis Presley's music. Given what Robert Cantwell calls the "deep Afro-American hues" of country music's Grand Ole Opry, there was a certain logic, however questionable, behind Opry performers' occasional practice, in the 1930s and after, of playing in blackface (Cantwell 254–56). If Elvis's early country songs recalled this practice (Opry star Bill Monroe wrote Presley's hit, "Blue Moon of Kentucky"), his early blues songs especially wore a blackface hue. As Presley's guitarist Scotty Moore exclaimed (in a kind of blackvoice falsetto) after a sensual Elvis performance of "Blue Moon" in an early recording session: "*Damn, nigger!*" (Marcus, *Mystery* 196). Presley's not-quite and yet not-white absorption of black style was inevitably indebted to a musical tradition of racial impersonation.[20] Mimicking him, Elvis impersonators impersonate the impersonator, a repetition that nearly buries this racial history even as it suggests a preoccupation with precisely the blackface aura of Elvis (as do, more literally, impersonators' renditions of Dan Emmett's 1859 blackface standard, "Dixie," in the context of Presley's "American Trilogy"). In any case, this double mimicry everywhere implies that Elvis's "otherness" is a partial motive for his impersonators.

Chicago impersonator John Paul Rossi puts a familiar spin on this idea:

> Eric Lott: You have this really interesting remark [in the I *Am Elvis* guide], "Like Elvis, I think I am a black man wrapped in white skin." Can you say more about that? Because I think people do have this sense that he was kind of a racial crossover figure.

John Paul Rossi: Ultimately, yeah, I think he was, pretty much—rhythmically, you know, and timing-wise—it's just that rhythm thing of his, right. And like a James Brown, too, he had a lot of that James Brown schtick in there too, and the way he went about singing.

EL: So you really see his music and his whole mode of performing to be indebted to black sounds.

JPR: Definitely, sure, but for that he would have never made it. . . .

EL: Do you get your moves from—do you listen to black records, or watch black performance?

JPR: Yeah, I've bought now, in a row, about six blues CDs, in the last month or so! I'm pretty much indebted to that early blues sound from the '30s, '40s, '50s—Muddy Waters' stuff, Howlin' Wolf, yeah.

Surely Rossi's remark about being a "black man wrapped in white skin" resorts to the dubious and essentialist racial signifiers whose gradual withering away allowed Elvis Presley not to wear blackface. As John Szwed has put it, the fact that white-Negro performers like Presley can communicate "blackness" without blackface illustrates the at least partial detachment of culture from color and the increasing interpenetration of black and white styles (28). However, rhetorical figures like Rossi's ought not be dismissed too grandly, for they rightly register the degree to which "racial" cultures still exist in the face of Elvis's transgressions, and gesture toward some of the more urgent questions raised by Elvis impersonation. Reversing the metaphor of blackface and positing a fundamental "blackness" about Presley, Rossi's words indicate that part of the drama of his impersonation is indeed a racial crossing over. There is no way to partake of an embodied, not to say hidden, "blackness" ("wrapped in white skin") without becoming that body. The problem is how to *represent* this crossing into "blackness" without blackface, and it is here that Elvis impersonation comes to the rescue. It is as though such performance were a sort of second-order blackface, in which, blackface having for the most part overtly disappeared, the figure of Elvis himself is now the apparently still necessary signifier of white ventures into black culture—a signifier to be adopted bodily if one is to have success in achieving the intimacy with "blackness" that is crucial to the adequate reproduction of Presley's show. Eric "Elvis" Domino says that rather than duplicate Elvis's technique, he calls on moves inspired by James Brown, Michael Jackson, Jackie Wilson, and Prince: "In order to do it, you have to *feel* it inside" (*Guide* 39). To feel it inside without betraying it outside is to become Elvis Presley; "blackness" is both an indis-

Figure 2. Fear of a black Elvis: Clearance Giddens. (photo courtesy of Clearance Giddens)

pensable and invisible part of Elvis impersonation. Blackface minstrelsy has here given way to its iconic, nearly vaporous, suggestion.

The scandal of the black Elvis impersonator makes this fact perfectly clear. His aura of transgression indicates, first, that the image of Elvis is founded on a usually unspoken racial crossing and a phantom evocation of "blackness." Consider a remark from the entry in I Am Elvis on house painter Clearance Giddens, a black Elvis: "Fans . . . don't seem to mind that Clearance doesn't look the part because he certainly *sounds* like Elvis" (Guide 58). And no wonder, since he's the "source" of Elvis's "act," or at least its goal. While we will see that black meanings do get effaced in the cult of Elvis, it is important to note the sort of racial rapprochements that may also occur in its midst. One *Geraldo* show of August 1992, for example, devoted itself to Elvis impersonators (with, incidentally, Geraldo himself in impersonator garb and at key moments—usually while talking to black audience-members—in black-voice). Black Elvis Giddens (who does sound astonishingly like Presley) was a focus of both controversy and extreme fascination, garnering almost as many questions as all of the white impersonators combined. With Geraldo offering little but gawking unease, Giddens both acknowledged the irony of his own position and sought to turn it to the account of interracial solidarity — a desire reciprocated by both the mostly white audience and the white impersonators (and confirmed by the white impersonators I have interviewed).

Following Geraldo's smirking query regarding the typical reception of Giddens's act came this exchange:

> *Clearance Giddens:* When I started out, it was unreal, you know . . .
> *Geraldo:* What does "unreal" mean?
> CG: Well, they kept saying, "What is a black Elvis?" you know, and uh, then they got to see the show they say, "OK, we can deal with it, it's happenin'."

To this perhaps overly sunny assessment of white racial feeling, Giddens added that his audience at first "was an all-white crowd — now, over the years, it's a mixed crowd now — it's lookin' good!" This upbeat perspective was soon interrupted by the sort of charged moment Geraldo has become notorious for manufacturing. A black audience-member stood up and attacked Giddens for betraying his race by mimicking a white entertainer, and a revealing set of exchanges occurred:

> *Black man:* I'd like to say to the guy in red [Giddens] . . . I think that it's very disrespectful for you to be as a black man, you're supposed to represent us, running around tryin' to be somebody you could never be.

> *White woman* [shouting]: He's got my vote, he's very good and I like him, as a black Elvis I like him because Elvis dealed a lot with black people, and he's very good!

> *Giddens:* What folks gotta understand is music don't have a color to it, you know . . . [applause]

> *White man:* Elvis used to listen to gospel music and he's also in effect part black because he did listen to gospel and his musical background is from the black heritage.

> *White Elvis impersonator Russ Howe:* . . . What he's doing is beautiful. [shakes Giddens's hand, to loud applause]

Handshake and applause both, be it noted, were (at least in intention) unpatronizing. No doubt this occurrence came off with an air of rebuke toward black impatience with the figure of Elvis; it also displayed a remarkable ease with the literal return of Presley to his "roots." So does the EPIIA's recent showcasing of C. J. Charlton, an excellent Cherokee/African American performer and a ringer for James Brown whose prominent place on the 1994 Las Vegas program advertised a certain, if exceptional, commitment to interracial appropriations of Elvis. For their part, black impersonators seem to see Elvis performance as a route of assimilation without an abandonment of cultural complexity; Charlton told me he thought Elvis's meaning could be summed up in one word—"U.S.A."—giving it an inclusive spin that probably exceeds that of most white impersonators.[21]

For the black Elvis's scandal also says that the only legitimate crossing over is from white to black—that for a black man to become Elvis is an implicit humiliation or exposure or ironizing of Presley, a telling form of sacrilege. In comments such as the one I just quoted from the I Am Elvis guide, the oscillation between black Elvises' resemblance and non-resemblance to Presley points up an anxiety about the adequacy of Elvis's own impersonation of black cultural practices—indeed an anxiety about his needing (or taking) them in the first place—and an implicit desire to keep him securely this side of the racial divide. This is perhaps the meaning of the necessary hiddenness of "blackness" in Elvis and especially his impersonators; more than simply laying claim to a sort of omni-racial cultural power, subsuming the "blackness" on which you depend may just be self-protection—a defense against accusations of theft or inadequacy. Though it seems peculiar for impersonators to access black practices by mimicking a white man, it really is safer that way. In this sense the Elvis impersonator recalls the Joker of the film Batman (1989), who, as Andrew Ross has observed, evokes a threatening racial subtext (his movements underwritten by the Prince soundtrack, he speaks in a sort of rap-rhyming and schemes to spike commercial beauty products with skin-altering substances) that is, however, "wholly occluded" (Ross, "Ballots" 30–31). Like the Joker, Elvis and (even more) his impersonators are in whiteface. Of course, the effect of this is, in the end, to bypass the rich play of cultural sources behind Presley's music. Getting a feel for Elvis's black "inside" through his white "outside" ends with the erasure of black culture. Thus the real achievement of Elvis impersonators is to both glorify and repress the white working-class fascination with "blackness." In the largest sense, impersonating Elvis is a way of living the proximity of one's working-class whiteness to black culture while aggressively forgetting that proximity.

Impersonator Danny Vann emphasizes just this spatial dimension of the matter in his remarks on Elvis's estate, Graceland: "To me, Elvis didn't hold to no race. I mean in fact, if you look where Graceland is, it is now and has always been in the ghetto of Memphis. He was surrounded by more black people than he was white." This imagines Elvis, properly I think, in a geography of racial-cultural adjacency even as it leaves Elvis lording over—and obscuring, at least in white fans' eyes—the scene of which he became the musical representative. This is a situation, in other words, of extraordinary ambivalence, in which black working-class masculinity both aids and threatens white working-class male self-definition. The popularity of Elvis and his impersonators suggests that the assumption of white working-class codes of masculinity in the United States is partly negotiated through an imaginary black interlocutor, but that the latter must remain only dimly acknowledged.[22] Moreover, if white male fantasies of black men partially structure white "manliness," the consequences of this affair are quite complex. As Philip Cohen has observed, the threat of "blackness" may call forth vehement disavowals; but the subterranean accents of desire for and envy of black men and their imagined physical adeptness and grace may always return, a return that implies a recognition that black and white both inhabit the same proletarian public realm (Cohen, "Tarzan" 27; see also Hall, "New" 29). The relation of these lived outcomes to racist violence on the one hand and organized radicalism on the other is itself complex and variable, though the pinched class context I have outlined surely tilts these complicated and ambivalent feelings in a less than liberatory direction. Yet the very form of Elvis impersonation suggests the great mistake of ignoring its racial complexity, and that of working-class white men generally. Recent studies of working-class racial attitudes and racial politics, it seems to me, unnecessarily close down the logical possibility of radicalism located in white working-class racial ambivalence. David Roediger's brilliant study of the racism of the nineteenth-century working class, The Wages of Whiteness, ends up circumscribing the chances for cross-racial solidarity in the name of tough-mindedness and honesty. Certainly the book is a necessary corrective to the old slogan, "black and white, unite and fight." But with such a straitened view of working-class racial politics, one is hard pressed to explain even the most fleeting instant of interracial solidarity or cross-racial interest, let alone exploit such instances for truly resistant uses.[23] If Elvis impersonation is any indication, white racial ambivalence is the unwitting host of certain generous impulses as well as of an inability to acknowledge the fascination with racial difference on which they are partly based. Such performance may indeed be saying that constrictions of material circumstance have exiled white workingmen's complexity of racial feeling from everyday life into fantasy about the figure of Elvis Presley.

To the extent that black cultural resonances are suppressed even in Elvis impersonation, the masculine problematic I discussed earlier reveals just how this occurs. In approximating Elvis's assumed "blackness," approaching his "otherness," the impersonators, I would suspect, fear coming up short. The threat of inadequacy in the identification with an Elvis ego-ideal is perhaps traceable less to the figure of Elvis in this case than to the black cultural components upon which his image absolutely depends, and which lie behind the substitution of Elvis for the black interlocutor—James Brown, say. (This substitution may, in fact, speak to moments on the street of white male working-class racial hostility born of "castration anxiety.") Imaginary self-projection may quickly deflate when it is held up to the black "source," particularly when this is overlaid with white male fantasies of black men's enormous potency, and so perhaps requires black invisibility—and fetish-Elvis's replacement of this (b)lack—to be fulfilled. Of course, it may be that the longing to replace one's performative ideal, whether Elvis or his black alter-ego, is already a displacement (if not a component) of one's desire for it; we have seen how easily the spectatorial admiration on which Elvis impersonation depends can flip over into homoerotic interest—the presence of which may well indicate another reason for the disavowal of black maleness in this mode of performance. (One need only think here of the self-conscious banter concerning same-sex desire between Mel Gibson and Danny Glover in those demotic favorites, *Lethal Weapon* I, II, and III, the banter both raising and dissolving the specter of interracial male desire.) But certainly the conventional displacement of homosex into male identification is in turn liable to cast into doubt one's ability to outdo the "original."[24] Therefore, many Elvis impersonators circumvent "blackness" altogether in their performances, eclipsing an imagined set of attributes to which they are, in fact, powerfully attracted and indebted. Their solution to the felt embattlement of white masculinity is an assumption of the figure of Elvis, which to a great extent buries his "blackness" and at the same time appropriates its power.

What white impersonators are up against was demonstrated on the *Geraldo* show that featured the impersonators *en bloc*. After they had all had a chance to perform during the course of the show, the audience was asked (by way of applause) to pick the best impersonator of Elvis—or as Geraldo put it, the "most authentic Elvis." The winner: Clearance Giddens, the black Elvis. Proving that the attractiveness of "blackness" lies hidden in the skin of Elvis and his impersonators, this upset also revealed the reason for its constant, anxious suppression—a haunting sense of inadequacy expressing in distorted "dream-work" form the diminished options of white working people today.

Class Act

Loftier ideals surround "late Elvis," and give an extra twist to the term. A few impersonators credit themselves with sparking rumors of an Elvisian afterlife—"Elvis Alive and Well in Kalamazoo"—but more than a few have been touched by his posthumous presence. Janice K, the Lady Elvis, experienced an Elvis visitation that left a nearby tree "scorched and singed" (*Guide* 71). Mystical testimony abounds among Elvis impersonators. "In the beginning there was the word and the word was Elvis," says Clayton Benke-Smith (*Guide* 12). Sammy Stone Atchison remarks that "Elvis was the most charismatic person ever on earth except for Jesus" (*Guide* 10). Full-time impersonator Dave Carlson describes his audiences as "lonely people who are looking for someone to save them—and that's what Elvis was all about." Impersonators and their audiences aren't crackpots and hallucinators; rather they prove the force of V. S. Naipaul's view of Elvis in *A Turn in the South* (1989) as a sort of beatified redneck, with Graceland a version of the New Jerusalem (Naipaul 225; Spigel 177–94). The last shall be first, says this saint of the people.

It is indeed the class profile of the carpenter from Galilee that inspires the impersonators. Sammy Stone Atchison, the man who compares Elvis's charisma to that of Jesus, also provides him a more secular gloss:

> Eric Lott: [Elvis] is a pretty large figure, at this point, in the annals of American culture—what do you think he stands for, what does this figure mean in the larger sense, as a kind of myth, almost?
> Sammy Stone Atchison: It's like what I've been hearing recently on some of these programs on Elvis that pretty well have described it. It was the American Dream—that if this man that had nothin' could go to that plateau in his life in America, well, then other people could and that's what set all that off in the '50s and it's still happening. They think about how he persisted and he made it and he had nothin' as far as any finances, and so they figure well, there's a chance for all of us. It was a rags to riches story and that doesn't happen very much and it's just something they saw happenin' and could happen.
>
> Elvis is a symbol of what America stands for, the choice to start from the bottom and rise to the top—and remain there. (*Guide* 10)

On the surface, at least, Elvis seems to embody an age-old tale about the romance of rising in America. If the clinching phrase here strikes one as a little odd—neither Jesus nor Elvis remained safely at the top—its very overstatement is interesting. This is Elvis being willed into the American Dream, or vice versa, the effort coming through in the insistence that one *can* remain at the top even though one *chooses* to start at the bottom . . . *what?* How is it that Elvis's success gave people like him the idea that "there's a chance for all of us" if this rags-to-riches story "doesn't happen very much"? The cracks in Atchison's mightily overdetermined and heartfelt reading of Elvis indicate that another chief reason for his impersonation is to provide an imaginary triumph over the working-class circumstances for which he continues to stand.

Full-time impersonator E. P. King sums this up well: "What I think of is a country boy that didn't have nothin', that started out with nothin', and just made it and made himself the greatest thing since popcorn, you know what I mean? I mean, anyone that didn't have nothin', that lived in a *shack*, to go to the heights that Elvis did—you've gotta give a man credit for that, you know." Impersonator Danny Vann's remarks suggest that this class revenge-fantasy, apparently a significant aspect of Elvis's image among the impersonators, depends by definition on Elvis's inwardness with working-class life:

> In my opinion, Elvis represented, to the people that grew up with him and to the people today, a person who could feel what they felt. He was a character that was bigger than life, that was able to get up there and *feel* his songs. If you listen to the way he sang the songs, he *lived* those songs he sang, and he reached out and touched people through those songs. He sang about life—you know, "Love Me Tender," "Don't Be Cruel," "I'm All Shook Up," "Burning Love"—you know, that's what country-western has been throughout all the years, too, is singing about life, but they always pick on the negative side; Elvis looked on the beautiful side . . .

Here is a version of what T. S. Eliot (of all people), in his obituary of working-class music-hall singer Marie Lloyd, called the "collaboration" between artist and audience "which is necessary in all art and most obviously in dramatic art." Eliot's rather untypical remarks about Lloyd quite resemble Danny Vann's about Elvis and his audience (which, of course, includes his impersonators, and *their* audiences): "It was, I think, this capacity for expressing the soul of the people that made Marie Lloyd unique, and that made her audiences, even when they joined in the chorus, not so much hilarious as happy. . . . it was her understanding of the people and sympathy with them, and the people's recognition of the fact that she embodied the virtues which they genuinely most respected in private life, that raised her to the position she occupied at her death" (Eliot 172–74). Or, as young-Elvis impersonator Ray Guillemette puts it, "to me, you could see that he sang and he lived and he existed for

those people that put him where he was." Elvis called (and still calls) forth
working-class allegiances from audiences who, in Danny Vann's terms, know
about "life." Elvis was, Vann's remarks intimate, one of "us," he felt what "we"
felt, was bigger than life but still lived it. And in the living came a victory
over toil and limit (country-western's "negative side of life") that provides
an imaginary victory ("the beautiful side") to this day for his impersonators
and their followers. It is important to note that this imaginary victory does
not deny or finesse but rather confirms and celebrates a particular kind of
working-class cultural sensibility, a sensibility, moreover, that is less some
immediate expression of any clearly defined U.S. working-class world than
an achieved product of Elvis impersonators and their audiences.

Turning to the historical significance of this sensibility, Vann adumbrates
what we might call the Cadillac connection. Vann's remarks not only stress
the centrality of Elvis's class triumph to Elvis impersonation, they powerfully
link a number of seemingly unrelated historical elements—Presley's popularity in the North, the auto industry, working-class structures of feeling, and
the peculiar density of Elvis sightings and Elvis impersonators in Michigan,
particularly the Detroit area:

> *Danny Vann:* For those who grew up with him, [Elvis] was the kid next
> door, you know, rags to riches type thing, everyone can relate to that as
> well. We're a compassionate society, and when we see somebody who
> had it rough who made it big, our heart goes out to him, you know, and
> we're behind him. . . . I felt moved by what he sang, otherwise I don't
> think I could keep singing the same songs myself for twenty-five years
> and still enjoy them. . . . And I feel there are times when I'll do a song
> like "My Way," or something like that, that I even get choked up, even
> singing it, let alone, you know, what it does to the crowd. It's just that
> the whole atmosphere, the audience—having the opportunity to get up
> there and move an audience to their feet is just an unparalleled thrill,
> you know. So I really feel grateful for the opportunity.
> *Eric Lott:* . . . You say there are more than three dozen Elvis impersonators
> in the [Detroit] area—this is really interesting to me. . . .
> *DV:* A lot of auto-workers migrated from the South. There's a lot of coun-
> try folk here. They have a suburb of Detroit called Taylor, Michigan, and
> its nickname is "Taylortucky," there are so many people from Kintuck
> there, you know. I've done several shows there, and of course I have to
> do "Kentucky Rain," and it brings the house down! Detroit's a melting-
> pot city.[25]

A central fact of twentieth-century American social history is, I believe, encoded in the odd practice of Elvis impersonation. If, as so many have suggested, the decline of the auto industry is part and parcel of the constriction of working-class life today (the central episode in the erosion of working-class *embourgeoisment* and the masculine "pride of place" that accompanied it), it would be hard to overstate the significance of the Motor City's embrace of Elvis—mythologizer, owner, and bestower of pink Cadillacs. Apparently condensed in the figure of Elvis are a whole range of social facts and facts of feeling. To reclaim and embody Elvis is to recall the moment in U.S. history when auto workers drove an American prosperity and an empowered masculinity that they believed would shortly be their own. (A friend of mine who had worked all his life in State of Illinois warehouses and shop floors used to tell me over and over that when he retired he was going to buy himself a Cadillac.) The figure for this power and success is Elvis himself, who Danny Vann notes "had it rough [and] made it big" and whose example provides a similar kind of "opportunity" for Vann the impersonator and implicitly his audiences. The connection of "Kintuck" with the Detroit auto industry makes available a host of affective alliances and lends this triumphant mode of performance its air of working-class solidarity.[26] Vann's own intense emotion as he sings that ode to manly autonomy, "My Way," gives us a sense of its singular power as a working-class *cri de coeur* in addition to its singular kitschiness as a bleat of overstated individualism; and it's this class resonance Vann invokes when he says that "our heart goes out to" the poor-boy-made-good who could represent a "melting-pot" constituency so victoriously.

Much is made, in fact, of the royal excesses that crowned Elvis's rise to the top—not only the Cadillacs but also the sideburns, the polyester, the sheer physical outwardness—by impersonators of the later, Vegas Elvis. These entertainers display the propensity of working-class men to resist their class subjection in and through the body, enacting rituals of self-assertion and imaginary beneficence. Simple pleasures become exorbitant emblems. We have already seen the great investment in costume; one of the impersonators on *Geraldo*, Mike Memphis, claimed that his jewelled cape alone cost eleven hundred dollars. Dave Carlson performs as part of his act an "Elvis in a Dream" sequence in which, as he explains it, "the guy who looks like the M.C. of the show, he says he fell asleep watching an old Elvis movie and he dreamed that Elvis was performing the show—then all of a sudden the 2001 music starts and the lights go down and smoke comes up and I appear out of that—it's like a dream." To a man, the impersonators capitalize on the theatrics of excess. The striving for enlarged and fantastical embodiment behind the accoutrements of Elvis

Figure 3. Elvis in a dream: Dave Carlson. (photo courtesy of Dave Carlson)

spectacle calls to mind Georg Simmel's analysis of "adornment." "The radiations of adornment, the sensuous attention it provokes, supply the personality with . . . an enlargement or intensification of its sphere: the personality, so to speak, *is* more when it is adorned." Thus, according to Simmel, is *having* transformed into *being* (340). In Elvis impersonation one acquires not only the majestic treasures of Elvis's person but, in a sense, Elvis's person too. This in turn *makes* more, as Simmel would have it, of the person of the impersonator. Onstage, aided by late Elvis's karate kicks, sweaty scarves, and myriad superfluous physical feats, the impersonators undergo an achieved, sometimes prosthetic, self-enlargement. As Ray Kajkowski says of his first Elvis performance:

> They had a '50s dance at the bowling alley, and they had an Elvis impersonator contest there—I didn't look anything like Elvis. . . . They only had one other contestant in it and the prize was fifty dollars, and I'd drank a couple three beers, I guess, and decided I was able to do it. . . . I got up there, and I don't remember what song I did, it was kind of a fast-moving song, you know I was wiggling the microphone and carrying on. And I watched this other guy . . . he just stood there with a guitar, I think he sang "That's Alright, Mama" or something, but you know, he didn't move or nothin', he just stood there and sang. So I says "No, Elvis *moved*," you know, 'cause I watch those TV specials. So that's what I did.

At the end of the song I dropped down on one knee, and there was this table of about eight gals old enough to appreciate Elvis, I dropped down on one knee and kissed this gal's hand. For two, two and a half minutes of stupidity I made fifty dollars! I decided if I could do that I might as well go into doing it. . . . That was in October of '87 and in January of '88 I did my first show. So it just started growing from that. Now I've got two limousines, and I take bodyguards, and all that.

From his sense that Elvis *moved* to his hiring of limos and bodyguards, Kajkowski here calls on precisely the physical bigness that translates into personal power: out of the bowling alley and into the showroom.[27]

Ron George says he sought such self-enlargement in concert performances as opposed to small clubs or dance halls:

When I started doing this, I was doing, like, the cabaret thing in Nevada, and all of them are not like nightclubs . . . they're showrooms, and they hold anywhere from three hundred to five hundred people, but they're still basically a showroom, you don't go dancing or anything, you go in, sit down, and you're entertained. So it's an entertainment concert, is what it is. Where if you took it into a small place—one time I was talked into doing one in a nightclub . . . people dancing, and that. And I just hated it, because that wasn't what he was about; he was about—like I said, it was a big, it was a spectacle. I mean, it might sound funny, the first time I ever saw him was when he came out in 1969, Oakland Coliseum in California, and I would say that—and I saw him six times afterwards—sitting in the audience with the people that are around you, and watching everybody in that place, 20,000 people, I would not be surprised that if Jesus walked out onstage that he would get any more attention than Elvis did. It was that amazing—it was like you didn't believe that was a real person actually coming out and doing that. . . . Nobody even comes close—*except* for Neil Diamond.

If the modern sports arena was the only venue capable of featuring Elvis's enormity, the impersonator's showroom seems necessary to help call that enormity back. No surprise, then, that impersonator Marc Roberts's favorite performance memory is a pre-game gig in Cleveland Stadium for forty-five to fifty thousand baseball fans that was covered by all three major networks, CNN, ESPN, and the Sports Channel. The important point about all of these instances of performative self-aggrandizement is that their rootedness in the spectacle of the body is no mistake, more a cause than an effect of the vogue of Elvis impersonation. It is an extension of a working-class male dynamic of social puissance through physical assertion.

And this emphasis on the body is, I would insist, a cultural handling of class opposition—not the mindless flash or entertaining distraction that most are quick to assume working-class audiences want. That very assumption, in fact, was treated with great disdain by the impersonators with whom I spoke. "A lot of the media . . . [ask] really dumb questions," Dave Carlson told me. "They would say, 'So, you guys all sittin' around eating cheeseburgers?' stuff like that. And I'd say, 'If you're gonna talk to me like that I won't even talk to you, if you're gonna ask something serious, I'll be glad [to talk].'"[28] This from the man who does the immaculately tasteful "Elvis in a Dream" act! It may well be in direct antagonism to the popular view of late Elvis and his impersonators that Elvis performers embrace the overblown, stress the kitsch, wear it like a badge of honor. What reads to many as "bad taste" may just be a refusal to conform to middle-class dictates on such matters: and when impersonators are called on their excessive behaviors they retort with a pointed fuck-you. If class is indeed a "relational" category, as E. P. Thompson taught us a generation ago, then the working-class habits and tastes to which Elvis impersonators give one form arise at least partly in response to—against—middle-class expectations and observations (Thompson 9–11; Ehrenreich, Hearts 135). In Elvis impersonation, I would argue, the middle-class (academic no less than corporate media) gaze is forcefully returned, and many of the impersonators seem to be aware of the fact. John Paul Rossi admits that he occasionally visits the supermarket dressed as Elvis:

> Eric Lott: Lots of jokes are always made about Elvis impersonators, and my sense is that people like you are a lot more serious about it than these jokes suggest. Do you ever treat it as a joke? Or are you treated like a joke by some people? Do you get wisecracks or anything?
>
> John Paul Rossi: Some of the times when I'm seen, like, in a supermarket, 'cause sometimes I wear my hair long with the sideburns, people will look at me kind of cross-eyedly, you know. "Why do you look like that?" "Well," I tell 'em, "I do the Elvis thing, you know." And they'll kind of start laughing. That's really about the only time when I'm looked upon as a negative. . . .
>
> EL: It's interesting to me, though, that you go out to the grocery store looking like that. I mean, that's cool. Why do you do that—it's just, you feel like it, or it's after a performance, or it's before a performance, or what?

JPR: I guess it's kind of like a psych-out thing. I do it a lot before a per-formance. I'll let my hair out and the sideburns, and all that there. Just to see if I can get any attention, too—sometimes I like to be the center of attention.

Dick Hebdige once read punk fashion as a violent working-class negation of the middle-class look (Subculture 113–27); I read the investment in Elvis as a more "traditionalist" version of this resistant sense of stylistic difference. As impersonator Joe Paige says of his seventh-grade mimicry of Elvis: "It was the age of Elton John and Led Zeppelin, and liking Elvis was a little differ-ent" (Abramowitz C1). Impersonator Ron George stresses (again) the physical, "manly" dimension of this class feeling. "Of all the guys that were in the business, [Elvis] was the rough-and-tumble asskicker. . . . All of the others, the Ricky Nelsons, and Fabian, and Pat Boone, and all—they were all kind of, you know, the little sissy kind of guys; Elvis was a street kid, kick-ass. All the guys could relate to that." [29]

The finale of impersonator Tony Grova's version of Presley's "American Trilogy" at the 1994 EPIIA convention makes plain the working-class tra-ditionalism of Elvis impersonators' cultural politics. At once embarrassing and stirring, Grova's emphatic bended-knee, back-turned presentation of an eagle-embossed sequined cape announced a twin devotion to American nationalism (the eagle in flight) and to the sequin implicit in this form's ag-gressive stylistic heroics. The performance of determined class self-respect as "American Trilogy's" masculine, kitschy, and frankly nationalist theatricality, however, ought to be marked as a working-class statement of the firmest sort. If the impersonators suggest this persona equally rejects the liberated sexual ethos of Elton John and the middle-class reactionary persona of Pat Boone, this is because there is here a popular investment in reclaiming American nation-alism from its perceived usurpers—however similar their politics may seem on the face of it—and dissenting from their unearned, complacent jingoism. Tony Grova's "American Trilogy" communicated something close to a spell-binding working-class rendition of "America the Beautiful" I once heard— a confounding spectacle, it would seem, of some of American nationalism's main victims celebrating (with feeling) the sentiments used to exploit their labor at home and their bodies in wars abroad. Not so confounding, in fact. The vehemence of this crowd's collective shout, like certain Elvis imperson-ators' overblown finales, momentarily took back the nation and gave it to some of the people on whose backs it had been built.

The fantasies of Elvisian excess, then, mean anything but upward mobility;

imperial selfhood, rather, not class envy but self-validation. I read Sammy Stone Atchison's fantasia of mobility, which I have quoted, as a trope of triumph rather than a longing to enter a higher class. Even in Atchison's idea that you can choose to start at the bottom there is a muted identification with people *down here* rather than *up there*. Henderson's *Stark Raving Elvis* makes the case: "Here was a man who made pure style out of being white trash. He was dazzling. He didn't apologize for anything. He turned it into gold. With Elvis as your guide, there was no need to hide your bush-hog status in front of rich kids—you strutted it right in their faces. . . . Being Elvis was being *somebody*" (12). The flip side of this self-conscious class will is a collective ethos affirming a commitment to working-class mutuality and solidarity. For example, the EPIIA conventions significantly refuse to mount impersonator competitions; the collective, celebratory "showcase" is the chosen form. Moreover, a few performers do only charity work, and nearly all of them consider such work an important part of their schedules.[30] Illinois impersonator Rick Ardisano prizes Elvis's image as a "humanitarian, you know, giving things to people no matter what race, creed, or color, you know, it didn't matter to him. . . . they were a human being like everybody else, he treated everybody the same—and that's what I like about him"; Pittsburgh impersonator Dave Atkins says the figure of Elvis stands for "helping people . . . and that's what I enjoy doing"; Bobby Erickson dreams of doing a "show for charity that would generate millions of dollars for many needy children" (*Guide* 52). This impulse appears in other impersonators as a desire to bestow on friends the sudden extraordinary gifts of which Elvis was capable.[31] Louie Michael Bunch Jr. says he "would love to be able to go into a dealership and order a fleet of cars for my friends and family" (*Guide* 22). Talking to the impersonators, one gets the idea that Elvis went wrong not because of his famed indulgences but because, in the end, the signs of collectivity—the exorbitantly outfitted party spaces, the handsome gifts—substituted for the social relations they were meant to cement. Thus EPIIA president Rick Marino lovingly recalled to me the camaraderie that attended waiting all day in line for Elvis tickets and then, three months later, seeing the show. And Ray Kajkowski stresses Elvis's "tender-hearted, easy-going" side:

> You see [Elvis] played up a lot as a bad temper, and all that. Well, I think he probably had a little temper; I do too, you know. But, you know, I care about somebody standing there with a sign that says "I'll work for food," too, you know, I care about those people. I think some of my feelings are on the same lines, as far as I care about people. I certainly'll

never be anything like he was, you know, as far as a big name or nothing. . . . But I think, you know, because of the type of person—he cared
for people and their needs, their real needs, not just givin' 'em money
and saying, "here, here you go."

Real needs, not just money: the bottom line is human connection. This is a
rather striking emphasis in a mode of performance known for its glitter and
monomania.

It is nevertheless significant that, as far as I have been able to make out,
this elemental collective urge is manifested only in ideologies of charity.
No overtly political persona of a distinctly working-class kind obstructs the
purity of the Elvis impersonator's emphasis on style (in this, as in so many
other ways, the impersonators are true to Presley himself). The summer I
visited Vegas, the forty-thousand-member Culinary Workers Local 226, affili-
ate of the Hotel and Restaurant Employees International, happened to be engaged in pitched rhetorical and often sidewalk combat with the 5,005-room
mega-resort MGM Grand Hotel and Themepark, which had refused to sign a
union contract for its eight thousand union-eligible workers. This struggle,
involving protest gatherings (to the blared music of Elvis's fellow "traditionalist" Bruce Springsteen) and routine picketing (one picketer confidently as-
sured me a union victory), emblematized Las Vegas's status as the "last great
union town in America" and MGM Grand's place in that town as a possible
"River Rouge of gambling" (Davis, "Armageddon" 46–50). Not one of the
impersonators I spoke to at the convention had even heard of the struggle.
Post-Fordism in a nutshell, I thought; the CIO is dead, and with it any sense of
national political solidarity to accompany the impersonators' working-class
nationalist cultural politics. But this was overhasty: such cultural politics,
in precisely post-Fordist fashion, are a key place where erstwhile political
solidarities are outlined and affirmed, the historical template through which
class is now often defined. This is why Bill Clinton in 1992 won partially on
what we might call an Elvis slate (an impersonator gigged at the inaugural
ball), and why his abandonment of that slate in his politically transparent
"middle-class bill of rights" has been so dispiriting ("Bill").

Elvis impersonators work their cultural solidarities to create something
beyond the hype: a *promesse de bonheur* that embodies the group good time of a
liberated Saturday night.[32] Recall T. S. Eliot's words about Marie Lloyd making
her audiences "not so much hilarious as happy." This collective principle of
hope shows up in the utopian strain in many impersonators' remarks. Over
and over the performers told me that they helped recall for Elvis's fans a

better, happier time—what we have seen Danny Vann call the "beautiful side" of life. Rick Marino put it like this: "Seems like everybody thinks about when they were young when they think about Elvis. It takes a lot of people back to an earlier time in their life, where we didn't have all the problems we have today. . . . Things just seemed to be, you know, going to a Dog 'n' Suds and using the phone, and—it just seemed to be more fun. I don't think that people today have fun and I think that Elvis is a real large symbol of that." Ron George, who concurs nearly verbatim with this view, concludes: "And the people, of course, that look at it, the media, they want to make fun of it because they don't understand it." The elements of escapism in these remarks are balanced by the sense that Elvis's fans understand something that the media and other outsiders don't—that "cunning and high spirits," as Walter Benjamin wrote, best equip one to meet the world (102). Impersonator Dave Carlson remarks that Elvis "made us happy, made us feel good, and that obviously is the goal of every entertainer, that's what we're hired for, is to make people happy." Jordanian-American impersonator Nazar Sayegh told me that his purpose in performance is to "try to give back as much as possible the euphoria that this man had left behind." No trivial affair, this: for all wish-fulfillment, as Ernst Bloch wrote, even fairy tales and pulp fiction, may be "castle in the air par excellence, but one in good air and . . . the castle in the air is right." Speaking of the pulp fiction hero, who bears an unmistakable resemblance to Elvis Presley, Bloch writes:

> [He] does not wait, as in the magazine story, for happiness to fall into his lap, he does not bend down to pick it up either like a bag thrown to him. Rather [he] remains related to the poor thickskin of the folk-tale, the bold boy who sets corpses on fire, who takes the devil for a ride. . . . The romanticism of the robber thus shows a different face, one which has appealed to poor folk for centuries, and colportage [pulp fiction] knows all about it. . . . Here there is immature, but honest substitute for revolution. (367–68)

It bears keeping in mind that this is the best moment of the working-class wish-fulfillment visible in Elvis impersonation. For its collective *esprit* does depend on male physical prowess and includes women only insofar as they become fans, admirers, and passive gazers—hands for the impersonators to kiss. Impersonator Bert Hathaway's wife Linda makes a virtue of this particular "necessity": "It is exciting seeing the women go after [Bert] like that" (*Guide* 62). Throughout my analysis we are firmly in the realm of male aggrandizement and self-definition, the mundane, bruising privileges of patriarchy, which is only partially redeemed by its class ethos. In Lillian Rubin's *Worlds of Pain* there is ample documentation of working-class women's struggle to be something more than mere dependencies, subordinate to the male "provider" (who, as often as not, is not the sole provider). As one young repairman remarked of his wife, "She doesn't want there to be a king in this household" (176). King onstage, then, if not within the family. Impersonator Ron George concedes point-blank that Elvis was "a sexist," and most impersonators play to predominantly female working-class audiences whose particular investment in Elvis impersonators deserves some comment.

What I found in talking to female fans of the impersonators was a volatile mixture of apparent devotion, frankly spectatorial desire, and a healthy dose of ironic distance. Las Vegas fan Ruth Madeiras and California fan Jana Stanford conveyed the respectful ruling tone of female audience-members in averring that their role was (in Madeiras's words) "keeping him alive" and (in Stanford's words) supporting the men who "keep the legend alive." But I caught other accents as well. Stanford is herself a sometime impersonator, and thus struck me as a more self-conscious member of the audience than might have appeared to be the case: she was an implicit rival as well as admirer, perhaps taking full stock of the performers beneath her official fealty to them; and she knew from their vantage point what they needed from an audience, perhaps performing that role as on other occasions she performs its opposite number. It is hard to believe, watching the seemingly spontaneous combustion of female adoration for the Elvis performer (quite a spectacle in its own right, as women line up to kiss the performer and receive a sweated scarf), that some such self-consciousness is entirely absent from the public erotic indulgence that is at any rate given free rein by many female fans. Nor is outright irony banished from the audience though it may be repressed onstage. I spoke with two women attending the EPIIA convention together who were perfectly capable of laughing it up about the flying Elvises in *Honeymoon in Vegas* even as they made fine and serious distinctions among the performers they liked at the convention. They too had seen *Geraldo*'s impersonators show, and made merciless fun of his masculine pretensions: "maybe people should impersonate Geraldo." The culture of impersonation itself seemed the brunt of some buried amusement here, a hunch that was confirmed by a remark that followed. Geraldo, said one of the women, is "probably an Elvis wannabe and he's just jealous." As Geraldo goes, of course, so go the impersonators — none of the King's men is immune to the feminist deflations that may occur in the demanding and audacious audience that Elvis performers try to regard as one more prop. We underestimate the female fans of Elvis's performing male fans if we miss their complex ensemble of motives and impulses, including not only selfless celebration but also self-conscious theatrics, not only love but unspoken identification, frank sexual objectification, and severe ironic humor.

Of course, the needy ambience of Elvis performing—its requiring fawning women spectators who at any moment may ridicule or dump you—suggests the sense of inadequacy that haunts it; a built-in hidden injury returns to dampen the working-class transcendence of Elvis shows. As Byron Bluford, *Stark Raving Elvis*'s working-class impersonator protagonist, complains: "There's no way to rest, you never go far enough." This is what beats him in the end: "Colonel Parker [Elvis's manager] didn't need him, didn't need a new Elvis. There would be no heir to the King, no such thing, none of them would take his place, nobody. . . . Kneel down and eat your fantasy, boy! And who the hell were we even talking about now? Byron. Byron. Byron. Who the hell was that now?" (Henderson 181, 203–4). The literally masochistic configuration of this scene, in which the performer's inability to replace or reproduce Elvis becomes prostration before the master and then an emptying of the self, is the fabulist version of the everyday highwire act that Elvis impersonators perform. This drama of inferiority is obviously played out both in gender and class terms; the masculine anxiety that requires Elvis performers' self-verifying self-projection overdetermines its proletarian struggle for self-validation. The "secondary identification" (to borrow from Freud) with Elvis through which self-projection occurs seems something like a theatricalized Oedipal introjection of him—necessary to the achievement of identity but never securely accomplished. Byron Bluford's dazed repetition of his own name to himself, a name that seems to verge on the meaningless and so requires repetition, is the perfect picture of this dilemma.[33] More impersonators than fictional Byron Bluford have betrayed this problem to us, safe to say; but I would stress that it suffuses the class drama of Elvis impersonation as a sort of performative requirement rather than a group psychological profile: because it sums up something about the achieved working-classness of the disparate impersonators and their audiences rather than expresses in any given or direct way their immediate social or psychological circumstances. By the same token, this deep sense of inadequacy is not simply a hazard or by-product of impersonating Elvis Presley. I would argue that amid this feeling of being unable to fully capture or represent Elvis is a subjective recognition of oppression. The structure of Elvis impersonation perfectly grasps working-class structures of masculine class feeling because the failures and embarrassments that shadow it are homologous with working-class "injured dignity," as Richard Sennett and Jonathan Cobb call it. Sennett and Cobb's notion of the "hidden injuries of class," while it underestimates the clarity about class possessed by the popular classes, aptly describes one moment of working-class subjectivity wherever it lives: the resort to self-blame in a context of American individualism that "reminds" white workingmen that the class position they have inherited and resist in so many ways is ultimately their own fault (79, 95–96, 151–88, 256).

This is not to parrot the conventional wisdom about working-class people lacking in self-esteem because they have "failed," a pitying and condescending view that carries with it more than a whiff of blame. It is, rather, to note the working-class resonance of a performance in which the "star" strives to be somebody—Elvis—that, in the end, he can't be. Elvis impersonating results in an apt scene of abjection: it surely is every man for himself, sawing the air and getting nowhere but doing it with style. Impersonator James Wallace's moving remarks on Elvis's decline, so unlike the glibly cynical renderings of both academe and TV, illustrate, I think, a sense of the injury Elvis seems to represent and that the impersonators, for class reasons, appear to want to claim:

> And as for his later years and his downfall, you know, as a lot of people tend to call it, I don't know—I mean, if he wasn't Elvis Presley out there in the world he'd be another person who had some bad things hit him in his life and he wasn't able to handle it and he had a downfall trying to handle it, you know. If any other person had their mother fall away from him, and that was the closest thing to his heart, and then his replacement was Priscilla and she left him, and he had a lot of problems with his physical stature because of the hours he was living and the life he was leading, it'd be quite depressing and hard to keep. . . . If it was you or I we wouldn't hear about it, but it's him and he's a public figure where the world sees it in a negative light. . . .

> He was very insecure about doing anything that he was doing, 'cause he didn't think he had the magnetism he did. But when he got out there, he almost kind of was giddy about it 'cause he'd just laugh like, "Why they acting like that?" you know, "What am I doing?" One guy said to him, I don't remember who it was, "Just get out there and do it again, boy, you're doing great." . . .

> You can look at a man and you can degrade a man, but he's the one who's gonna have to be makin' the decision on his own self, and he did whatever decisions he had to make.

It is the tragic view of Elvis that links him with "you or I" in Wallace's remarks—just another person "who had some bad things hit him." The blind-sided victimization of that phrase is as surely a language of class as the sense of insecurity Wallace attributes to Elvis and by implication to his impersonators is its performative analogue. And yet responsibility for one's own fate is here laid at the doorstep of workingmen everywhere—not only a (perhaps contradictory) assertion of one's own agency and humanity in the face of overwhelming odds but an echo of shame about that fate that is best depicted in the impossibility of impersonating Elvis Presley.

Elvis, then, as metaphor: a retro fantasy in postmodern garb; an imaginary resolution of a historical predicament that working-class white men can neither fully face nor forget. No doubt Elvis functions in working-class life as a sort of cultural herald, something to rally round and reclaim. What else are all the tabloid stories, all the impersonations in so many VFW's and Moose Lodges, but a momentary reclamation of something "they" are imagined to have taken from "us"? Impersonating Elvis is in this sense a sustained and intense moment of performative working-class self-creation or -production. We have seen the ambivalences and compromises of that production, the embattled racial and gender postures, the haunting sense of insufficiency, themselves telling and somewhat depressing summations of working-class feeling in our moment. While reports of Elvis Presley's death, as the tabloids remind us, may be greatly exaggerated, the "King" is, in the ways I have sketched, surely ailing. And yet in the realm of the spirit, Elvis, for better and worse, is more alive than ever.

Notes

Some early notes toward the present essay were published in the *Nation* (8 July 1991) and are incorporated here. Many thanks to Ruth DeJauregui of American Graphic Systems, Inc., for various tips and inside information on Elvis impersonators; to the impersonators and fans themselves for sharing their thoughts and ideas so generously; to friends and audiences at Rutgers University, the University of Michigan, the University of Southern Maine, Wesleyan University, the University of Chicago, the University of Delaware, George Mason University, the University of Washington, Columbia University, and the University of Virginia Junior Faculty Reading Group; to Steve Arata, Karen Bock, Lisa Brawley, Lucinda Cole, Rita Felski, Rick Livingston, Greil Marcus, Sean McCann, Jahan Ramazani, and Caroline Rody for critical suggestions on early drafts and for useful information of various kinds; and to Brian Lott for helping me learn from Las Vegas.

1. Eco himself isn't nearly so doomy; see Eco. A similar (though too cynical) view may be found in Kroker, Kroker, and Cook.

2. For splendid coverage of Elvis's afterlife, see Marcus, *Dead Elvis* and Rodman, *Elvis After Elvis*.

3. Impersonator Ron George told me that he (among others) was offered a part in *Honeymoon in Vegas* but turned it down because he was wary of being "bunched in" with "a bunch of other idiots out there"—his opinion of the general run of Elvis impersonators, like that of the corporate media, tending toward disgust and disavowal. For El Vez, see American Graphic Systems, Inc. (48–51) (hereafter, parenthetically cited in the text as *Guide*).

4. Besides interviewing impersonators and fans and watching the performances at the 1994 Elvis Presley International Impersonators Association convention, I conducted telephone interviews with impersonators and related people (managers, agents, organizers, etc.) from May 1992 to September 1993; all information and quotations are drawn from my personal interviews and observations unless otherwise noted.

5. The EPIIA was formed in 1989 by Ron and Sandy Bessette and is a "non profit organization dedicated to the preservation and continuing art form, style, and music of Elvis Presley thru Elvis performers and fans; to maintain professionalism, ethics, and standards for those performers who continue Elvis's creative and continuing art form" (quotations from EPIIA membership brochure). In addition to publishing a bimonthly newsletter, the Bessettes organize impersonator "mini-showcases," multi-impersonator shows, and the annual EPIIA convention, a massive affair now in its sixth year (1995) formerly held in Chicago and now held in Las Vegas. Ron Bessette told me that (as of May 1993) the EPIIA sports approximately two hundred performer-members (though there are vastly more impersonators in the United States and abroad) and four hundred fan-members (one of whom is myself).

6. *Geraldo*, August 1992.

7. I refer here to Cohen, "Subcultural Conflict"; Willis, *Learning* and "Notes"; Radway, *Reading* and "Reception Study" 361; Gaines; Hall, "Encoding/Decoding"; Morley; Modleski 35–58; and Spigel, the pathbreaking precursor to my essay.

8. See, for example, Tolson 63–64; Willis, "Shop Floor Culture"; Chodorow 96–97; Montgomery 13–14; Wilentz passim; Stansell 77–78, 81, 95–96, 137–41; Denning, ch. 9.

9. See Aronowitz, *False Promises*; Braverman; Davis, *Prisoners*.

10. For an interesting treatment of the cinematic fate of white masculinity in this period of industrial decline, see Ross, "Cowboys."

11. Ehrenreich, *Hearts* 173–75; see also the special issue on post-Fordism of the *Socialist Review* 21.1 (1991).

12. Namely the "class" part of that oft-invoked portmanteau, gender-race-and-class. This is strikingly evidenced, for example, in recent issues of journals devoted to the matter of "Identities"; see *Critical Inquiry* 18.4 (1992) and *October* 61 (1992). Stanley Aronowitz's brief, acute remarks in the latter about white male working-class politi-

cal sympathies only highlight the dearth of such commentary here as elsewhere (36).

13. Historians who have taken up the formation of American working-class white-ness include Saxton and Roediger; see also Lott, *Love*. For an analysis of 1980s "authoritarian populism" see Hall, *Hard Road* 123–60. Nice ripostes to the alleged backwardness of working-class men may be found in Ehrenreich, *Hearts* 134–36; Sennett and Cobb 217–18.

The mostly sheepish appearance of "whiteness" in a variety of recent media (e.g., Jim Belushi and Alex Karras's early-1980s "white man's rap" on *Saturday Night Live*, Martin Mull's *History of White People in America*, etc.) seems a transparent response to its perceived—not actual—marginalization or devaluation, as does the far less sheepish male rampage film. For the notable contradictions even in the latter see Pfeil.

14. I am indebted here to the pioneering work on performance cultures in Hall and Jefferson; Hebdige. See Rubin 161 for a sense of the autonomy and fulfillment such activities might provide for men who are radically constricted on the job.

15. "Identity, because it is never in a moment of critical repose, because it resists the forces of suspension or negation, and because it neither begins nor ends at a point of total immobility, draws its very life-blood from the restless operations of identification, one of the most powerful but least understood mechanisms of cultural self-fashioning" (Fuss, "Fashion" 716).

16. See Neale 7–8 and Safouan 85–87. I have also profited from reading Modleski, ch. 4.

17. For a similar argument regarding male spectators looking at men in film, see Rodowick 8.

18. Henderson's *Stark Raving Elvis* depicts a loaded scene in which impersonator Byron Bluford is fellated by a woman named Elvis who wears white satin-and-rhinestone jumpsuits and her hair slicked back—scarcely even a disguise for the same-sex erotics I detect generally in Elvis impersonation. "Byron's eyes closed and his face became a mask of domination. He grasped her head and held it in place. 'Stay there, Elvis,' he muttered. It was half speech, half grunt. 'Right there, baby'" (179). One might incidentally note here Byron's urge to invert the balance of power between Elvis and impersonator as well as the possible sham quality of that inversion ("mask of domination"). This captures the impersonators' quandary precisely.

19. In some ways the most explicit, and most misleading, of the charges of Elvis's impersonation of black cultural figures is Alice Walker's story "Nineteen Fifty-five."

For more on the social relations encoded in modern instances of blackface see Lott, "White" and Rogin.

20. Here I am appropriating the terms of Bhabha, "Of Mimicry and Man" 132.

21. For Alice Walker's own interesting spin on her earlier charge of Elvis's cultural expropriation of black material see *Temple* 187–89, in which one character deems Elvis Native American (thanks to Caroline Rody for bringing this to my attention).

22. For a fuller statement of this argument, see Lott, *Love*, chs. 2 and 5.

23. See Michael Rogin's excellent review of Roediger, "Black Masks"; see also Sen-

nett and Cobb 68–69, 136–37 for some acute remarks dispelling the myth of the racist, nationalist "hard hat." Ross, *No Respect* 229–32 has some interesting things to say on the possibilities of exploiting moments of working-class ambivalence for emancipatory ends.

24. See Sedgwick, *Epistemology* 211 for a powerful analysis of the way same-sex desire may be transmuted into safer forms of male envy and identification.

25. Impersonator Marc Roberts, a former Cleveland Ford worker originally from Selma, Alabama, confirmed this connection for me.

26. On "affective alliances" see Grossberg 79–87.

27. Impersonator Ray Guillemette, who specializes in the young Elvis, amusingly remarked to me, "No matter how much you move, you'll always find somebody . . . you get off the stage, drenching wet, and they'll say, 'you gotta *move* more!' "

28. The April 1991 EPIIA newsletter carried an exasperated critique of the Oprah Winfrey Show for making Elvis fans and impersonators "look like fanatics and crazy people."

29. Cf. Rubin 179.

30. The EPIIA vocally supports charity work by performer-members and fan-members alike; see, for example, the April 1991 EPIIA newsletter.

31. Marc Roberts spoke approvingly to me of Elvis's "down home" persona and his readiness to let fly with impressive acts of economic redistribution.

32. It may be worth noting that I tried one Saturday night to reach performers by phone for this project: none were home.

33. I draw this emphasis from Fuss, "Fashion" 718; for detailed remarks on the kind of masochistic moments I sense in Elvis impersonation, see also Silverman, *Male* 299–338.

 **VISUALIZING RACE AND THE
SUBJECT OF MASCULINITIES**

THE RIDDLE OF THE ZOOT

Malcolm Little and Black Cultural Politics during
World War II

ROBIN D. G. KELLEY

But there is rhythm here. Its own special substance:
I hear Billie sing, no good man, and dig Prez, wearing
    the Zoot
suit of life, the pork-pie hat tilted at the correct angle,
through the Harlem smoke of beer and whiskey, I
    understand the
mystery of the signifying monkey,
in a blue haze of inspiration, I reach to the totality
    of Being.
I am at the center of a swirl of events. War and death.
rhythm. hot women. I think life a commodity
    bargained for
across the bar in Small's.
I perceive the echoes of Bird and there is a gnawing in
    the maw
of my emotions.
—Larry Neal, "Malcolm X—An Autobiography"

Much in Negro life remains a mystery; perhaps the zoot suit conceals profound political meaning; perhaps the symmetrical frenzy of the Lindy Hop
conceals clues to great potential power—if only Negro leaders would solve
this riddle.
—Ralph Ellison, 1943

"Like hundreds of thousands of country-bred Negroes who had come to the
Northern black ghetto before me, and had come since," Malcolm X recalled in
his autobiography, "I'd also acquired all the other fashionable ghetto adornments—the zoot suits and conk that I have described, the liquor, cigarettes,

the reefers—all to erase my embarrassing background" (56). His narrative is familiar: the story of a rural migrant in the big city who eventually finds social acceptance by shedding his country ways and adopting the corrupt lifestyles of urban America. The big city stripped him of his naïveté, ultimately paving the way for his downward descent from hipster to hustler to criminal. As Malcolm tells the story, this period in his life was, if anything, a fascinating but destructive detour on the road to self-consciousness and political enlightenment.

But Malcolm's narrative of his teenage years should also be read as a literary construction, a cliché that obscures more than it reveals.[1] The story is tragically dehistoricized, torn from the sociopolitical context that rendered the zoot suit, the conk, the lindy hop, and the language of the "hep cat" signifiers of a culture of opposition among black, mostly male, youth. According to Malcolm's reconstructed memory, these signifiers were merely "ghetto adornments," no different from the endless array of commodities black migrants were introduced to at any given time. Of course, Malcolm tells his story from the vantage point of the Civil Rights movement and a resurgent Pan-Africanism, the early 1960s when the conk had been abandoned for closely cropped hairstyles, when the zoot had been replaced with the respectable jacket and tie of middle-class America (dashikis and Afros from our reinvented mother country were not yet born), and when the sons and daughters of middle-class African Americans, many of whom were themselves college students taking a detour on the road to respectability to fight for integration and equality, were at the forefront of struggle. Like the movement itself, Malcolm had reached a period of his life when opposition could only be conceived of as uncompromising and unambiguous.

The didactic and rhetorical character of Malcolm's *Autobiography*—shaped by presentist political concerns of the early 1960s and told through the cultural prism of Islam—obscures the oppositional meanings embedded in wartime black youth culture. And none of Malcolm's biographers since have sought to understand the history and political character of the subculture to which he belonged.[2] The purpose of this essay is to rethink Malcolm's early life, to reexamine the hipster subculture and its relation to wartime social, political, economic, and ideological transformations.

World War II was a critical turning point not only for Malcolm but for many young African Americans and Latinos in the United States. Indeed, it was precisely the cultural world into which Malcolm stepped that prompted future novelist Ralph Ellison to reflect on the political significance of the dance styles and attire of black youth. Ironically, one would think that

Malcolm, himself a product of wartime black youth culture, was uniquely situated to solve the riddle posed by Ellison in 1943. Nevertheless, whether or not Malcolm acknowledged the political importance of that era on his own thinking, it is my contention that his participation in the underground subculture of black working-class youth during the war was not a detour on the road to political consciousness but rather an essential element of his radicalization. The zoot suiters and hipsters who sought alternatives to wage work and found pleasure in the new music, clothes, and dance styles of the period were "race rebels" of sorts, challenging middle-class ethics and expectations, carving out a distinct generational and ethnic identity, and refusing to be good proletarians. But in their efforts to escape or minimize exploitation, Malcolm and his homies became exploiters themselves.

"I Am at the Center of a Swirl of Events"

The gangly, red-haired young man from Lansing looked a lot older than fifteen when he moved in with his half-sister Ella, who owned a modest home in the Roxbury section of Boston. Little did he know how much the world around him was about to change. The bombing of Pearl Harbor was still several months away, but the country's economy was already geared up for war. By the time U.S. troops were finally dispatched to Europe, Asia, and North Africa, many in the black community restrained their enthusiasm, for they shared a collective memory of the unfulfilled promises of democracy generated by the First World War. Hence, the Double V campaign, embodied in A. Philip Randolph's threatened march on Washington to protest racial discrimination in employment and the military, partly articulated the sense of hope and pessimism, support and detachment, that dominated a good deal of daily conversation. This time around, a victory abroad without annihilating racism at home was unacceptable. As journalist Roi Ottley observed during the early years of the war, one could not walk the streets of Harlem and not notice a profound change. "Listen to the way Negroes are talking these days! ... [B]lack men have become noisy, aggressive, and sometimes defiant" (306).[3]

The defiant ones included newly arrived migrants from the South who had flooded America's Northeastern and Midwestern metropolises. Hoping to take advantage of opportunities created by the nascent wartime economy, most found only frustration and disappointment, because a comparatively small proportion of African Americans gained access to industrial jobs and training programs. By March of 1942, black workers constituted only 2.5 to 3 percent of all war production workers, most of whom were relegated to low-skill, low-wage positions. The employment situation improved more rapidly after 1942: by April of 1944, blacks made up 8 percent of the nation's war production workers. But everyone in the African American community did not benefit equally. For example, the United Negro College Fund was established in 1943 to assist African Americans attending historically black colleges, but during the school year of 1945–46, undergraduate enrollment in those institutions amounted to less than 44,000. On the other hand, the number of black workers in trade unions increased from 150,000 in 1935 to 1.25 million by the war's end. The Congress of Industrial Organizations's (CIO) organizing drives ultimately had the effect of raising wages and improving working conditions for these black workers, though nonunion workers, who made up roughly 80 percent of the black working class, could not take advantage of the gains. The upgrading of unionized black workers did not take place without a struggle; throughout the war white workers waged "hate strikes" to protest the promotion of blacks, and black workers frequently retaliated with their own wildcat strikes to resist racism.[4]

In short, wartime integration of black workers into the industrial economy proceeded unevenly; by the war's end most African Americans still held unskilled, menial jobs. As cities burgeoned with working people, often living in close quarters or doubling up as a result of housing shortages, the chasm between middle-class and skilled working-class blacks, on the one hand, and the unemployed and working poor, on the other, began to widen. Intraracial class divisions were exacerbated by cultural conflicts between established urban residents and the newly arrived rural folk. In other words, demographic and economic transformations caused by the war not only intensified racial conflict but led to heightened class tensions within urban black communities.[5] For Malcolm, the zoot suit, the lindy hop, and the distinctive lingo of the hep cat simultaneously embodied these class, racial, and cultural tensions. This unique subculture enabled him to negotiate an identity that resisted the hegemonic culture and its attendant racism and patriotism, the rural folkways (for many, the "parent culture") that still survived in most black urban households, and the class-conscious, integrationist attitudes of middle-class blacks.

"The Zoot Suit of Life"

Almost as soon as Malcolm settled into Boston, he found he had little tolerance for the class pretensions of his neighbors, particularly his peers. Besides, his own limited wardrobe and visible "country" background rendered him an outsider. He began hanging out at a local pool hall in the poorer section of Roxbury. Here, in this dank, smoky room, surrounded by the cracking sounds of cue balls and the stench of alcohol, Malcolm discovered the black subculture that would ultimately form a crucial component of his identity. An employee of the poolroom, whom Malcolm called "Shorty" (most likely a composite figure based on several acquaintances, including his close friend Malcolm Jarvis), became his running partner and initiated him into the cool world of the hep cat (see Perry 48–49; Malcolm X, *Autobiography* 38–41; Wolfenstein 154–57).

In addition to teaching young Malcolm the pleasures, practices, and possibilities of hipster culture, Shorty had to make sure his homeboy wore the right uniform in this emerging bebop army. When Malcolm put on his very first zoot suit, he realized immediately that the wild sky-blue outfit, the baggy punjab pants tapered to the ankles, the matching hat, gold watch chain, and monogrammed belt were more than a suit of clothes. As he left the department store he could not contain his enthusiasm for his new identity. "I took three of those twenty-five-cent sepia-toned, while-you-wait pictures of myself, posed the way 'hipsters' wearing their zoots would 'cool it'—hat dangled, knees drawn close together, feet wide apart, both index fingers jabbed toward the floor" (52). The combination of his suit and body language encoded a culture that celebrated a specific racial, class, spatial, gender, and generational identity. East Coast zoot suiters during the war were primarily young black (and Latino) working-class males whose living spaces and social world were confined to Northeastern ghettos, and the suit reflected a struggle to negotiate these multiple identities in opposition to the dominant culture. Of course, the style itself did not represent a complete break with the dominant fashion trends; zoot suiters appropriated, even mocked, existing styles and reinscribed them with new meanings drawn from shared memory and experiences.[6]

While the suit itself was not meant as a direct political statement, the social context in which it was created and worn rendered it so. The language and culture of zoot suiters represented a subversive refusal to be subservient. Young black males created a fast-paced, improvisational language that sharply contrasted with the passive stereotype of the stuttering, tongue-tied Sambo; in a world where whites commonly addressed them as "boy," zoot suiters made a fetish of calling each other "man." Moreover, within months of Malcolm's first zoot, the political and social context of war had added an explicit dimension to the implicit oppositional meaning of the suit; it had become an explicitly un-American style. By March 1942, because fabric rationing regulations instituted by the War Productions Board forbade the sale and manufacturing of zoot suits, wearing the suit (which had to be purchased through informal networks) was seen by white servicemen as a pernicious act of anti-Americanism—a view compounded by the fact that most zoot suiters were able-bodied men who refused to enlist or found ways to dodge the draft. Thus when Malcolm donned his "killer-diller coat with a drape-shape, reat-pleats and shoulders padded like a lunatic's cell" (Cosgrove 78), his lean body became a dual signifier of opposition—a rejection of both black petit bourgeois respectability and American patriotism.[7]

The urban youth culture was also born of heightened interracial violence and everyday acts of police brutality. Both Detroit and Harlem, two cities in which Malcolm spent considerable time, erupted in massive violence during the summer of 1943. And in both cases riots were sparked by incidents of racial injustice (see Capeci, *Race Relations* and *Harlem Riot*; Sitkoff, "Detroit"; Shapiro 310–37). The zoot suiters, many of whom participated in the looting and acts of random violence, were also victims of, or witnesses to, acts of outright police brutality. In a description of the Harlem Riot, an anonymous zoot suiter expresses both disdain for and defiance toward police practices:

> A cop was runnin' along whippin' the hell outa [sic] colored man like they do in [the] slaughter pen. Throwin' him into the police car, or struggle-buggy, marchin' him off to the jail. That's that! Strange as it may seem, ass-whippin' is not to be played with. So as I close my little letter of introduction, I leave this thought with thee:
>
> Yea, so it be
> I leave this thought with thee
> Do not attempt to fuck with me. (Clark and Barker 146)[8]

The hipster subculture permeated far more than just sartorial style. Getting one's hair straightened (the "conk" hairdo) was also required. For Malcolm, reflecting backward through the prism of the Nation of Islam and Pan-Africanism, the conk was the most degrading aspect of the hipster subculture. In his words, it was little more than an effort to make his hair "as straight as any white man's." Malcolm writes, "This was my first really big step toward self-degradation: when I endured all of that pain, literally burning my flesh to have it look like a white man's hair. I had joined that multitude of Negro men and women in America who are brainwashed into believing that the black people are 'inferior'—and white people 'superior'—that they will even violate and mutilate their God-created bodies to try to look 'pretty' by white standards" (*Autobiography* 54).

Malcolm's interpretation of the conk, however, conveniently separates the hairstyle from the subculture of which it was a part, and the social context in which such cultural forms were created. The conk was a "refusal" to look like either the dominant, stereotyped image of the Southern migrant or the black bourgeoisie, whose "conks" were closer to mimicking white styles than those of the zoot suiters. Besides, to claim that black working-class males who conked their hair were merely parroting whites ignores the fact that specific stylizations created by black youth emphasized difference—the ducktail down the back of the neck, the smooth, even stiff look created by Murray's Pomade (a very thick hair grease marketed specifically to African Americans), the neat side parts angling toward the center of the back of the head.

More importantly, once we contextualize the conk, considering the social practices of young hep cats, the totality of ethnic signifiers from the baggy pants to the coded language, their opposition to war, and emphasis on pleasure over waged labor, we cannot help but view the conk as part of a larger process by which black youth appropriated, transformed, and reinscribed coded oppositional meanings onto styles derived from the dominant culture. For "the conk was conceived in a subaltern culture, dominated and hedged in by a capitalist master culture, yet operating in an 'underground' manner to subvert given elements by creolizing stylization. Style encoded political 'messages' to those in the know which were otherwise unintelligible to white society by virtue of their ambiguous accentuation and intonation" (Mercer, "Black Hair" 49).[9]

"But There Is Rhythm Here"

Once properly attired ("togged to the bricks," as his contemporaries would have said), sixteen-year-old Malcolm discovered the lindy hop, and in the process expanded both his social circle and his politics. The Roseland Ballroom in Boston, and in some respects the Savoy in Harlem, constituted social spaces of pleasure free of the bourgeois pretensions of "better-class Negroes." His day job as a soda fountain clerk in the elite section of black Roxbury became increasingly annoying to him as he endured listening to the sons and daughters of the "Hill Negroes," "penny-ante squares who came in there putting on their millionaires' airs." Home (his sister Ella's household) and spaces of leisure (the Roseland Ballroom) suddenly took on new significance, for they represented the negation of black bourgeois culture and a reaffirmation of a subaltern culture that emphasized pleasure, rejected work, and celebrated a working-class racial identity. "I couldn't wait for eight o'clock to get home to eat out of those soul-food pots of Ella's, then get dressed in my zoot and head for some of my friends' places in town, to lindy-hop and get high, or something, for relief from those Hill clowns" (Malcolm X, *Autobiography* 59–60).

For Malcolm and his peers, Boston's Roseland Ballroom and, later, Harlem's Savoy, afforded the opportunity to become something other than workers. In a world where clothes constituted signifiers of identity and status, "dressing up" was a way of escaping the degradation of work and collapsing status distinctions between themselves and their oppressors. In Malcolm's narrative, he always seemed to be shedding his work clothes, whether it was the apron of a soda jerk or the uniform of a railroad sandwich peddler, in favor of his zoot suit. At the end of his first run to New York on the Yankee Clipper rail line, he admitted to having donned his "zoot suit before the first passenger got off" (*Autobiography* 72). Seeing oneself and others "dressed up" was enormously important in terms of constructing a collective identity based on something other than wage work, presenting a public challenge to the dominant stereotypes of the black body, and reinforcing a sense of dignity that was perpetually being assaulted. Malcolm's images of the Roseland were quite vivid in this respect: "They'd jampack that ballroom, the black girls in wayout silk and satin dresses and shoes, their hair done in all kinds of styles, the men sharp in their zoot suits and crazy conks, and everybody grinning and greased and gassed" (*Autobiography* 49).

For many working-class men and women who daily endured backbreaking wage work, low income, long hours, and pervasive racism, these urban dance halls were places to recuperate, to take back their bodies. Despite opposition from black religious leaders and segments of the petite bourgeoisie, black working people took the opportunity to do what they wished with their own bodies. The sight of hundreds moving in unison on a hardwood dance floor unmistakably reinforced a sense of collectivity as well as individuality, as dancers improvised on the standard lindy hop moves in friendly competition, like the "cutting sessions" of jazz musicians or the verbal duels known as "the dozens." Practically every Friday and Saturday night, young Malcolm experienced the dual sense of community and individuality, improvisation and collective call-and-response: "The band, the spectators and the dancers, would be making the Roseland Ballroom feel like a big rocking ship. The spotlight would be turning, pink, yellow, green, and blue, picking up the couples lindy-hopping as if they had gone mad. 'Wail, man, wail!' people would be shouting at the band; and it would be wailing, until first one and then another couple just ran out of strength and stumbled off toward the crowd, exhausted and soaked with sweat" (Malcolm X, *Autobiography* 51).[10]

It should be noted that the music itself was undergoing a revolution during the war. Growing partly out of black musicians' rebellion against white-dominated swing bands, and partly out of the heightened militancy of black urban youth—expressed by their improvisational language and dress styles, as well as by the violence and looting we now call the Harlem Riot of 1943—the music that came to be known as "bebop" was born amid dramatic political and social transformations. At Minton's Playhouse and Monroe's Uptown, a number of styles converged; the most discerning recognized the wonderful collision and reconstitution of Kansas City big band blues, East Coast swing music, and the secular as well as religious sounds of the black South. The horns, fingers, ideas, and memories of young black folk (most, keep in mind, were only in their early twenties), such as Charlie Parker, Thelonius Monk, Dizzy Gillespie, Mary Lou Williams, Kenny Clarke, Oscar Pettiford, Tadd Dameron, Bud Powell, and a baby-faced Miles Davis, to name only a few, gave birth to what would soon be called "bebop."

Bebop was characterized by complex and implied rhythms frequently played at blinding tempos, dissonant chord structures, and a pre-electronic form of musical "sampling" in which the chord changes for popular Tin Pan Alley songs were appropriated, altered, and used in conjunction with new melodies. While the music was not intended to be dance music, some African American youth found a way to lindy hop to some remarkably fast tempos, and in the process invented new dances such as the "apple jack."

Although the real explosion in bebop occurred after Malcolm began his stay at Charleston State Penitentiary, no hip Harlemite during the war could have ignored the dramatic changes in the music or the musicians. Even the fairly conservative band leader Lionel Hampton, a close friend of Malcolm's during this period, linked bebop with oppositional black politics. Speaking of his own music in 1946, he told an interviewer, "Whenever I see any injustice or any unfair action against my own race or any other minority groups 'Hey Pa Pa Rebop' stimulates the desire to destroy such prejudice and discrimination." [11] Moreover, while neither the lindy hop nor the apple jack carried intrinsic political meanings, the social act of dancing was nonetheless resistive—at least with respect to the work ethic (see Gilroy, "One Nation" 274; T. Hunter 92–93; Hazzard-Gordon).

"War and Death"

From the standpoint of most hep cats, the Selective Service was an ever-present obstacle to "the pursuit of leisure and pleasure." As soon as war broke out, Malcolm's homeboys did everything possible to evade the draft (Malcolm was only sixteen when Pearl Harbor was attacked, so he hadn't yet reached draft age). His partner Shorty, a budding musician hoping to make a name for himself stateside, was "worried sick" about the draft. Like literally dozens of young black musicians (most of whom were drawn to the dissonant, rapid-fire, underground styles of bebop), Shorty succeeded in obtaining 4F status by ingesting something that made "your heart sound defective to the draft board's doctors"—most likely a mixture of benzadrine nasal spray and coke.[12] When Malcolm received notice from the draft board in October of 1943, he employed a variety of tactics in order to attain a 4F classification. "I started noising around that I was frantic to join . . . the Japanese Army. When I sensed that I had the ears of the spies, I would talk and act high and crazy. . . . The day I went down there, I costumed like an actor. With my wild zoot suit I wore the yellow knob-toed shoes, and I frizzled my hair up into a reddish bush conk." His interview with the army psychiatrist was the icing on the cake. In a low, conspiratorial tone, he admitted to the doctor, "Daddy-o, now you and me, we're from up North here, so don't you tell nobody. . . . I want to get sent down South. Organize them nigger soldiers, you dig? Steal us some guns and kill up crackers [sic]!" (Malcolm X, *Autobiography* 104–7).[13] Malcolm's tactic was hardly unique, however. Trumpeter John "Dizzy" Gillespie, a pioneer of bebop, secured 4F status and practically paralyzed his army recruitment officer with the following story: "Well, look, at this time, at this stage in my life here in the United States whose foot has been in my ass? The white man's foot has been in my ass hole buried up to his knee in my ass hole! . . . Now you're speaking of the enemy. You're telling me the German is the enemy. At this point, I can never even remember having met a German. So if you put me out there with a gun in my hand and tell me to shoot at the enemy, I'm liable to create a case of 'mistaken identity,' of who I might shoot" (Gillespie 119–20).

   Although these kinds of "confessions" were intended to shake up military officials and avoid serving, both Malcolm and Dizzy were articulating the feelings of a great majority of men who shared their inner cultural circle—feelings with which a surprisingly large number of African Americans identified. The hundreds, perhaps thousands, of zoot suiters and musicians who dodged the draft were not merely evading responsibility. They opposed the war altogether, insisting that African Americans could not afford to invest their blood in another "white man's war." "Whitey owns everything," Shorty explained to Malcolm. "He wants us to go and bleed? Let him fight" (Malcolm X, *Autobiography* 71). Likewise, a Harlem zoot suiter interviewed by black social psychologist Kenneth Clark made the following declaration to the scholarly audience for whom the research was intended: "By [the] time you read this I will be fighting for Uncle Sam, the bitches, and I do not like it worth a dam [sic]. I'm not a spy or a saboteur, but I don't like goin' over there fightin' for the white man—so be it" (Clark and Barker 145). We can never know how many black men used subterfuge to obtain a 4F status, or how many men—like Kenneth Clark's informant—complied with draft orders but did so reluctantly. Nevertheless, what evidence we do possess suggests that black resistance to the draft was more pervasive than we might have imagined. By late 1943, African Americans comprised 35 percent of the nation's delinquent registrants, and between 1941 and 1946, over two thousand black men were imprisoned for not complying with the provisions of the Selective Service Act (see Gill 164–68; Flynn).[14]

While some might argue that draft dodging by black hipsters hardly qualifies as protest politics, the press, police, and white servicemen thought otherwise. The white press, and to a lesser degree the black press, cast practically all young men sporting the "drape shape" (zoot suit) as unpatriotic "dandies" (see Tyler 34–39). And the hep cats who could not escape the draft and refused to either submerge their distaste for the war or discard their slang faced a living nightmare in the armed forces. Zoot suiters and jazz musicians, in particular, were the subject of ridicule, severe punishment, and even beatings. Civilian hipsters fared no better. That black and Latino youth exhibited a cool, measured indifference to the war, as well as an increasingly defiant posture toward whites in general, annoyed white servicemen to no end. Tensions between zoot suiters and servicemen consequently erupted in violence; in June 1943, Los Angeles became the site of racist attacks on black and Chicano youth, during which white soldiers engaged in what amounted to a ritualized stripping of the zoot. Such tensions were also evident in Malcolm's relations with white servicemen. During a rather short stint as a sandwich peddler on the Yankee Clipper train, Malcolm was frequently embroiled in arguments with white soldiers, and on occasion came close to exchanging blows.[15]

"I Think Life a Commodity Bargained For"

Part of what annoyed white servicemen was the hipsters' laissez-faire attitude toward work and their privileging of the "pursuit of leisure and pleasure." Holding to the view that one should work to live rather than live to work, Malcolm decided to turn the pursuit of leisure and pleasure into a career. Thus after "studying" under the tutelage of some of Harlem's better-known pimps, gangsters, and crooks who patronized the popular local bar Small's Paradise, Malcolm eventually graduated to full-fledged "hustler."

Bruce Perry and other biographers who assert that, because Malcolm engaged in the illicit economy while good jobs were allegedly "a dime a dozen," we should therefore look to psychological explanations for his criminality, betray a profound ignorance of the wartime political economy and black working-class consciousness.[16] First, in most Northeastern cities during the war, African Americans were still faced with job discrimination, and employment opportunities for blacks tended to be low-wage, menial positions. In New York, for example, the proportion of blacks receiving home relief *increased* from 22 percent in 1936 to 26 percent in 1942, and when the Works Progress Administration shut down in 1943, the percentage of African Americans employed by the New York WPA was higher than it had been during the entire depression (Greenberg 198–202; Fusfeld and Bates 45–46). Second, it was hard for black working people not to juxtapose the wartime rhetoric of equal opportunity and the apparent availability of well-paying jobs for whites with the reality of racist discrimination in the labor market. Of the many jobs Malcolm held during the war, none can be said to have been well-paying and/or fulfilling. Third, any attempt to understand the relationship between certain forms of crime and resistance must begin by questioning the dominant view of criminal behavior as social deviance. As a number of criminologists and urban anthropologists have suggested, "hustling" or similar kinds of informal/illicit economic strategies should be regarded as efforts to escape dependency on low-wage, alienating labor.[17]

The zoot suiters' collective hostility to wage labor became evident to young Malcolm during his first conversation with Shorty, who promptly introduced the word "slave" into his nascent hipster vocabulary. A popular slang expression for a job, "slave" not only encapsulated their understanding of wage work as exploitative, alienating, and unfulfilling, but it implies a refusal to allow *work* to become the primary signifier of identity. (This is not to say that hustlers adamantly refused wage labor; on the contrary, certain places of employment were frequently central loci for operations.) Implied, too, is a rejection of a work ethic, a privileging of leisure, and an emphasis on "fast money" with little or no physical labor. Even Shorty chastised Malcolm for saving money to purchase his first zoot suit rather than taking advantage of credit (Malcolm X, *Autobiography* 44, 51; Wolfenstein 157).[18]

Malcolm's apprenticeship in Boston's shoeshine trade introduced him to the illicit economy, the margins of capitalism where commodity relations tended to be raw, demystified, and sometimes quite brutal. Success here required that one adopt the sorts of monopolist strategies usually associated with America's most celebrated entrepreneurs. Yet, unlike mainstream entrepreneurs, most of the hustlers with whom Malcolm was associated believed in an antiwork, anti-accumulation ethic. Possessing "capital" was not the ultimate goal; rather, money was primarily a means by which hustlers could avoid wage work and negotiate status through the purchase of prestigious commodities. Moreover, it seems that many hustlers of the 1940s shared a very limited culture of mutuality that militated against accumulation. On more than one occasion, Malcolm gave away or loaned money to friends when he himself was short of cash, and in at least one case "he pawned his suit for a friend who had pawned a watch for him when he had needed a loan" (Wolfenstein 155; Perry 72).[19]

Nevertheless, acts of mutuality hardly translated into a radical collective identity; hustling by nature was a predatory act that did not discriminate by color. Moreover, their culture of mutuality was a male-identified culture limited to the men of their inner circle, for, as Malcolm put it, the hustler cannot afford to "trust anybody." Women were merely objects through which hustling men sought leisure and pleasure; prey for financial and sexual exploitation. "I believed that a man should do anything that he was slick enough, or bad and bold enough, to do and that a woman was nothing but another commodity" (Malcolm X, *Autobiography* 134). Even women's sexuality was a commodity to be bought and sold, though for Malcolm and his homeboys selling made more sense than buying. (In fact, Bruce Perry suggests that Malcolm pimped gay men and occasionally sold his own body to homosexuals [77–78, 82–83]).[20]

At least two recent biographies suggest that the detached, sometimes brutal manner with which Malcolm treated women during his hipster days can be traced to his relationship with his mother (Perry 51–52; Wolfenstein 162–63). While such an argument might carry some validity, it essentially ignores the gendered ideologies, power relationships, and popular culture that bound black hipsters together into a distinct, identifiable community. Resistance to wage labor for the hep cat frequently meant increased oppression and exploitation of women, particularly black women. The hipsters of Malcolm's generation and after took pride in their ability to establish parasitical relationships with women wage earners or sex workers. And jazz musicians of the 1940s spoke quite often of living off women, which in many cases translated into outright pimping.[21] Indeed, consider Tiny Grimes's popular 1944 recording featuring Charlie Parker on alto:

> Romance without finance is a nuisance,
> Mama, mama, please give up that gold.
> Romance without finance just don't make sense,
> Baby, please give up that gold.
>
> You're so great and you're so fine,
> You ain't got no money, you can't be mine,
> It ain't no joke to be stone broke,
> Honey you know I ain't lyin'.
> (Parker, "Romance without Finance")

Furthermore, the hustler ethic demanded a public front of emotional detachment. Remaining "cool" toward women was crucial to one's public reputation and essential in a "business" that depended on the control and brutal exploitation of female bodies. In the words of black America's most noted pimp scribe, Iceberg Slim, "the best pimps keep a steel lid on their emotions" (vi).

These gendered identities, social practices, and the discursive arena in which pimping and hustling took place were complicated by race. As in the rest of society, black and white women did not occupy the same position; white women, especially those with money, ranked higher. Once Malcolm began going out with Sophia, his status among the local hipsters and hustlers rose enormously: "Up to then I had been just another among all the conked and zooted youngsters. But now, with the best-looking white woman who ever walked in those bars and clubs, and with her giving me the money I spent, too, even the big important black hustlers and 'smart boys' . . . were clapping me on the back, setting us up to drinks at special tables, and calling me 'Red'" (Malcolm X, *Autobiography* 68). As far as Malcolm and his admirers were concerned, "Detroit Red" conquered and seized what he was not supposed to have—a white woman. Although some scholars and ordinary folk might view Malcolm's dangerous liaison as an early case of self-hatred, the race/gender politics of the hustling community and the equally cool, detached manner with which they treated white women suggests other dynamics were operating as well. White women, like virtually all women (save one's mama), were merely property to be possessed, sported, used, and tossed out. But unlike black women, they belonged to "Charlie," the "Man," "whitey," and were theoretically off-limits. Thus, in a world where most relationships were "commodified," white women, in the eyes of hustlers at least, were regarded as stolen property, booty seized from the ultimate hustle.

Hustling not only permitted Malcolm to resist wage labor, pursue leisure, and demystify the work ethic myth, but in a strange way the kinds of games he pulled compelled him to "study" the psychology of white racism. Despite the fact that members of this subaltern culture constructed a collective identity in defiance of dominant racist images of African Americans, the work of hustling "white folks" often required that those same dominant images be resurrected and employed as discursive strategies. As a shoeshine boy, for example, Malcolm learned that extra money could be made if one chose to "Uncle Tom a little," smiling, grinning, and making snapping gestures with a polishing rag to give the impression of hard work. Although it was nothing more than a "jive noise," he quickly learned that "cats tip better, they figure you're knocking yourself out." The potential power blacks possessed to manipulate white racial ideologies for their own advantage was made even clearer during his brief stint as a sandwich salesman on the Yankee Clipper commuter train: "It didn't take me a week to learn that all you had to do was give white people a show and they'd buy anything you offered them. . . . We were in that world of Negroes who are both servants and psychologists, aware that white people are so obsessed with their own importance that they will pay liberally, even dearly, for the impression of being catered to and entertained" (Malcolm X, *Autobiography* 75). Nevertheless, while Malcolm's performance enabled him to squeeze nickels and dimes from white men who longed for a mythic plantation past where darkies lived to serve, he also played the part of the model Negro in the watchful eye of white authority, a law-abiding citizen satisfied with his "shoeshine boy" status. It was the perfect cover for selling illegal drugs, acting as a go-between for prostitutes and "Johns," and a variety of other petty crimes and misdemeanors.[22]

In some respects, his initial introduction to the hustling society illumined the power of the trickster figure or the signifying monkey, whose success depended not only on cunning and wiles, but on knowing what and how the powerful thought. Yet the very subculture that drew Malcolm to the hustling world in the first place created enormous tension, as he tried to navigate between Sambo and militant, image and reality. After all, one of the central attractions of the zoot suiters was their collective refusal to be subservient. As Malcolm grew increasingly wary of deferential, obsequious behavior as a hustling strategy, he became, in his words, an "uncouth, wild young Negro. Profanity had become my language" (Malcolm X, *Autobiography* 77). He cursed customers, took drugs with greater frequency, came to work high, and copped an attitude that even his coworkers found unbecoming. By the war's end, burglary became an avenue through which he could escape the mask of petty hustling, the grinning and Tomming so necessary to cover certain kinds of illicit activities. Although burglary was no less difficult and far more dangerous than pulling on-the-job hustles, he chose the time, place, and frequency of his capers, had no bosses or foremen to contend with, and did not have to submit to time clocks and industrial discipline. Furthermore, theft implied a refusal to recognize the sanctity of private property.

Malcolm's increasingly active opposition to wage labor and dependence upon the illicit economy "schooled" him to a degree in how capitalism worked. He knew the system well enough to find ways to carve out more leisure time and autonomy. But at the same time it led to a physically deleterious lifestyle, reinforced his brutal exploitation of women, and ensured his downward descent and subsequent prison sentence. Nevertheless, Malcolm's engagement with the illicit economy offered important lessons that ultimately shaped his later political perspectives. Unlike nearly all of his contemporaries during the 1960s, he was fond of comparing capitalism with organized crime and refused to characterize looting by black working people as criminal acts—lessons he clearly did not learn in the Nation of Islam. Just five days before his assassination, he railed against the mainstream press's coverage of the 1964 Harlem riot for depicting "the rioters as hoodlums, criminals, thieves, because they were abducting some property." Indeed, Malcolm insisted that dominant notions of criminality and private property only obscure the real nature of social relations: "Instead of the sociologists analyzing it as it actually is . . . again they cover up the real issue, and they use the press to make it appear that these people are thieves, hoodlums. No! They are the victims of organized thievery" (Malcolm X, "Not Just an American Problem" 161).

"In a Blue Haze of Inspiration, I Reach the Totality of Being"

Recalling his appearance as a teenager in the 1940s, Malcolm dismissively observed, "I was really a clown, but my ignorance made me think I was 'sharp'" (Malcolm X, *Autobiography* 78). Forgetting for the moment the integrationist dilemmas of the black bourgeoisie, Malcolm could reflect: "I don't know which kind of self-defacing conk is the greater shame—the one you'll see on the heads of the black so-called 'middle class' and 'upper class,' who ought to know better, or the one you'll see on the heads of the poorest, most downtrodden, ignorant black men. I mean the legal-minimum-wage ghetto-dwelling kind of Negro, as I was when I got my first one" (Malcolm X, *Autobiography* 55). Despite Malcolm's sincere efforts to grapple with the meaning(s) of "ghetto" subculture, to comprehend the logic behind the conk, the reat pleat, and the lindy hop, he ultimately failed to solve Ralph Ellison's riddle. In some ways this is surprising, for who is better suited to solve the riddle than a former zoot suiter who rose to become one of America's most insightful social critics of the century?

When it came to thinking about the significance of *his own* life, the astute critic tended to reduce a panoply of discursive practices and cultural forms to dichotomous categories—militancy versus self-degradation, consciousness versus unconsciousness. The sort of narrow, rigid criteria Malcolm used to judge the political meaning of his life left him ill-equipped to capture the significance of his youthful struggles to carve out more time for leisure and pleasure, free himself from alienating wage labor, survive and transcend the racial and economic boundaries he confronted in everyday life. Instead, "Detroit Red" in Malcolm's narrative is a lost soul devoid of an identity, numbed to the beauty and complexity of lived experience, unable to see beyond the dominant culture he mimics.

This is not at all to suggest that Malcolm's narrative is purposely misleading. On the contrary, precisely because his life as a pimp, prostitute, exploiter, addict, pusher, and all-purpose crook loomed so large in his memory of the 1940s, the thought of recuperating the oppositional meanings embedded in the expressive black youth cultures of his era probably never crossed his mind. Indeed, as a devout Muslim recalling an illicit, sinful past, he was probably more concerned with erasing his hustling years than reconstructing them. As bell hooks surmises, Malcolm's decision to remain celibate for twelve years probably stems from a desire to "suppress and deny those earlier years of hedonistic sexual practice, the memory of which clearly evoked shame and guilt. Celibacy alongside rigid standards for sexual behavior may have been Malcolm's way of erasing all trace of that sexual past" (*Yearning* 84).

In the end, Malcolm did not need to understand what the zoot suit, bebop, lindy, or even hustling signified for black working-class politics during the war. Yet his hipster past continued to follow him, even as he ridiculed his knob-toed shoes and conked hair. His simple but colorful speaking style relied on an arsenal of words, gestures, and metaphors drawn in part from his street-corner days. And when he lampooned the black bourgeoisie before black working-class audiences, he might as well have donned an imaginary zoot suit, for his position had not changed dramatically since he first grew wary of the "Hill Negroes" and began hanging out in Roxbury's ghetto in search of "Negroes who were being their natural selves and not putting on airs" (Malcolm X, *Autobiography* 43). There, among the folks today's child gangstas might have called "real niggaz," fifteen-year-old Malcolm Little found the uniform, the language, the culture that enabled him to express a specific constellation of class, racial, generational, and gendered identities.

What Malcolm's narrative shows us (unintentionally, at least) is the capacity of cultural politics, particularly for African American urban working-class youth, to both contest dominant meanings ascribed to their experiences and seize spaces for leisure, pleasure, and recuperation. Intellectuals and political leaders who continue to see empowerment solely in terms of "black" control over political and economic institutions, or who belittle or ignore class distinctions within black communities, or who insist on trying to find ways to quantify oppression, need to confront Ellison's riddle of the zoot suit. Once we situate Malcolm Little's teenage years squarely within the context of wartime cultural politics, it is hard to ignore the sense of empowerment and even freedom thousands of black youth discovered when they stepped onto the dance floor at the Savoy or Roseland ballrooms, or the pleasure young working-class black men experienced when they were "togged to the bricks" in their wild zoot suits, strolling down the avenue "doin' the streets up brown."

Whatever academicians and self-styled nationalist intellectuals might think about Malcolm Little's teenage years, the youth today, particularly the hip-hop community, are reluctant to separate the hipster from the minister. Consider, for example, W. C. and the MAAD Circle's sampling of Malcolm's voice to open their lyrical recasting of the political economy of crime, "If You Don't Work, U Don't Eat," in which Los Angeles rapper Coolio asserts, "A hustle is a hustle, and a meal is a meal / that's why I'm real, and I ain't afraid to steal." Or consider Gangstarr's video, "Manifest," in which the lead rapper, "Guru," shifts easily between playing Malcolm—suit, rimmed glasses, and all—rapping behind a podium before a mosque full of followers, to rollin' with his homeboys, physically occupying an abandoned, deteriorating building, which could have easily been a decaying Roseland Ballroom. Not coincidentally, beneath his understated tenor voice switching back and forth between sexual boasting and racial politics, one hears the bass line from Dizzy Gillespie's bebop classic, "A Night in Tunisia." Through an uncanny selection of music, an eclectic mix of lyrics, and a visual juxtaposing of young black men "hanging out" against Malcolm the minister, Guru and D. J. Premier are able to invoke two Malcolms, both operating in different social spaces but sharing the same time—or, rather, timelessness. While some might find this collapsing of Malcolm's life politically and intellectually disingenuous, it does offer a vehicle for black (male) youth to further negotiate between culture as politics and culture as pleasure.

But "collapsing" the divisions Malcolm erected to separate his enlightened years from his preprison "ignorance" also compels us to see him as the product of a *totality of lived experiences*. As I have tried to suggest, aspects of Malcolm's politics must be sought in the riddle of the zoot suit, in the style politics of the 1940s that he himself later dismissed as stupidity and self-degradation. This realization is crucial for our own understanding of the current crisis of black working-class youth in urban America. For if we look deep into the interstices of the postindustrial city, we are bound to find millions of Malcolm Littles, male and female, whose social locations have allowed them to demystify aspects of the hegemonic ideology while reinforcing their ties to it. But to understand the elusive cultural politics of contemporary black urban America requires that we return to Ellison's riddle posed a half century ago and search for meaning in the language, dress, music, and dance styles rising out of today's ghettos, as well as the social and economic context in which styles are created, contested, and reaccented. Once we abandon decontextualized labels like "nihilism" or "outlaw culture" we might discover a lot more Malcolm Xs—indeed, more El Hajj Malik El Shabazzes—hiding beneath hoods and baggy pants, Dolphin earrings and heavy lipstick, Raiders' caps and biker shorts, than we might have ever imagined.

Notes

This essay originally appeared in *Race Rebels: Culture, Politics, and the Black Working Class* (New York: Free Press, 1994), and is reprinted here with permission of the publisher.

1. A number of scholars, from a variety of different disciplines and standpoints, have illustrated the extent to which the *Autobiography* depended on various rhetorical strategies and literary devices (i.e., conversion narrative). See especially Benson; Berthoff; Clasby; Demarest; Ohmann; Hodges; Whitfield.

2. Part of the reason for this, I believe, has something to do with the unusual proclivity of most Malcolm biographers to adopt a psychobiographical approach in place of an analysis that places the subject within specific historical and cultural contexts. Examples include Perry, *Malcolm*, "Malcolm X in Brief: A Psychological Perspective," "Malcolm X and the Politics of Masculinity," "Escape from Freedom, Criminal Style";

Goodheart; Harper; C. J. Robinson; Wolfenstein. The worst example thus far is clearly Bruce Perry's massive psychobiography. Ignoring African American urban culture in general, and black politics during World War II in particular, enables Perry to treat Malcolm's decisions and practices as manifestations of a difficult childhood, thus isolating him from the broader social, cultural, and political transformations taking place around him. Throughout the book Perry betrays an incredible ignorance of black culture and cultural politics, and the fact that standard works are omitted from the notes and bibliography further underscores this point. On the other hand, Wolfenstein makes some reference to black politics during the war, but his very thin discussion focuses almost exclusively on organized, relatively mainstream black politics such as A. Philip Randolph's March on Washington Movement. The cultural politics of black zoot suiters, for all its contradictions and apparent detachment from social struggle, is ignored. See also, Breitman, *The Last Year of Malcolm X: The Evolution of a Revolutionary* and *Malcolm X: The Man and His Ideas*; Clarke; Cone; Goldman; Moore.

3. On black politics during the war, see Dalfiume, *Fighting on Two Fronts* and "The 'Forgotten Years' of the Negro Revolution"; Garfinkel; Finkle; Kellogg; Wynn; Modell, Goulden, and Sigurdur; Sitkoff, *A New Deal for Blacks* 298–325 and "Racial Militancy and Interracial Violence"; Korstad and Lichtenstein; Shapiro 301–48.

4. See Marable 14–17; Foner 239, 243; Fusfeld and Bates 48; Harris 113–22; Lipsitz 14–28; Lichtenstein 124–26.

5. Wolfenstein (175–76) makes a similar observation about the intensification of intraracial class divisions, although we disagree significantly as to the meaning of these divisions for the emergence of black working-class opposition. Besides, I am insisting on the simultaneity of heightened intraracial class struggle and racist oppression.

6. I'm making a distinction here between African American zoot suiters and the Chicano zoot suiters in the Southwest. In predominantly Mexican American urban communities, especially Los Angeles, the zoot suit emerged about the same time, but it also has its roots in the *pachuco* youth culture, an equally oppositional style politics emerging out of poverty, racism, and alienation. They reappropriated aspects of their parents' and grandparents' Mexican past in order to negotiate a new identity, adopting their own hip version of Spanish laced with English words and derived from a very old creolized dialect known as Calo. For more on Chicano zoot suiters and pachuco culture, see Cosgrove; Mazon; Sanchez-Tranquilino and Tagg; Sanchez-Tranquilino; Turner and Surace; Paz 5–8; Madrid-Barela. The best general discussions of the zoot in African American culture are Cosgrove 77–91; Tyler 32–38; Chibnall 56–81. Malcolm's own description of his zoot suits can be found in *Autobiography* 52, 58.

7. See Cosgrove 78, 80; LeRoi Jones 202; Lott, "Double V" 598, 600; Sidran 110–11; Tyler 31–66.

8. See Clark and Barker 146; and for a broader discussion of police brutality in Harlem during the late 1930s and 1940s, see Greenberg 193–94, 211.

9. See also Levine, *Black Culture and Black Consciousness* 291–92. For a general discussion

of the ways oppositional meaning can be reinscribed in styles that are essentially a recasting of aspects of the dominant culture, see Hebdige, *Subculture* 17–19. Although Wolfenstein does not completely accept Malcolm's description of the conk as an act of self-degradation, he reduces his transformation to hipster entirely to a negation of waged work, ignoring the creative construction of an ethnic identity that celebrates difference as well as challenges the hegemonic image of the black male body. In Wolfenstein's schema, oppositional identity becomes merely caricature. Thus he writes, "he was trying to *be* white, but in a black man's way" (157).

10. For a description of the Savoy in Harlem, see J. Anderson 307–14.

11. Qtd. in Lott, "Double V" 603. Lott's essay is by far the best discussion of the politics of bebop. See also Gitler, *Swing to Bop*; Chambers; Gitler, *Jazz Masters of the 1940's*; LeRoi Jones 175–207; Kofsky, chapter 1; Reisner; Sidran 78–115; J. Wilson.

12. See Malcolm X 71; Gill 166–67; Gitler 115–16; Tyler 34–35. It is interesting to note that in Germany a subculture resembling black hipsters emerged in opposition to "Nazi regimentation." They wore zoot suits, listened to jazz, grew their hair long, and spent as much time as possible in the clubs and bars before they were closed down. The "swing boys," as they were called, faced enormous repression; jailings and beatings were common merely for possessing jazz records. See Beck 45–53; "Hans Massaquoi" 500–501; Kater, "Forbidden Fruit? Jazz in the Third Reich" and *Different Drummers*.

13. Malcolm's later speeches returned to this very theme. The military was initially reluctant to draft African Americans, Malcolm explained to his audiences, because "they feared that if they put us in the army and trained us in how to use rifles and other things, we might shoot at some targets that they hadn't picked out. And we would have" (Malcolm X, *Malcolm X Speaks* 140; "Not Just an American Problem, but a World Problem" 176).

14. Ironically, one of the most widely publicized groups of black conscientious objectors happened to be members of the Nation of Islam. About one hundred of its members were arrested for resisting the draft, including its spiritual leader Elijah Muhammad. Yet, despite the fact that a number of jazz musicians had converted to Islam and even adopted Arabic names (e.g., Sahib Shihab, Idris Sulieman, and Sadik Hakim) during the war, Malcolm claims complete ignorance of the Nation prior to his prison stint. On the Nation of Islam during the war, see Gill 156–57; Essien-Udom 80–81; Sidran 82.

15. See Tyler 38; Mazon 54–77; Cosgrove 80–88; James et al. 254–55; Malcolm X, *Autobiography* 77.

16. For example, Bruce Perry (who characterizes Malcolm's entire family as a bunch of criminals) not only suggests that theft is merely a manifestation of deviant behavior rooted in unfulfilled personal relationships, but he naturalizes the Protestant work ethic by asserting that Malcolm's resistance to "steady employment" reflected a reluctance to "assume responsibility" (57–61).

17. See Stack; Valentine. For comparative contemporary and historical examples

from Britain, see the brilliant book by Linebaugh; Box; Ditton; Hollinger and Clark; and for a general discussion of the informal economy and working-class opposition, see C. Robinson.

18. For a discussion of the "hustler's ethic" as a rejection of the "Protestant work ethic," see Hudson 414–16.

19. Cayton and Drake found numerous examples of poor black residents in Chicago's South Side mutually supporting one another while simultaneously engaged in the illicit economy (570–611).

20. The evidence Perry provides to make this assertion (which includes simplistic Freudian interpretations of later speeches!) is slim, to say the least. But even if the hearsay Perry's informant passed on is true, it would not contradict my argument. For the manner in which Malcolm allegedly exploited gay men positioned them as Other, and in the cases Perry cites obtaining money was far more important than sexual pleasure. He apparently did not identify with an underground gay community; rather, it was merely another "stunt" in the life of a hustler.

21. See, for example, Davis with Troupe 87–189; Mingus; and for some postwar examples beyond the jazz world, see Liebow 137–44; Milner and Milner.

22. A number of scholars have suggested that pimps and hustlers, at least in black folklore, were more like modern-day tricksters than "bad men." See, for example, Levine 381–82; Milner and Milner 242.

"THE COOL POSE"

Intersectionality, Masculinity, and Quiescence in the
Comedy and Films of Richard Pryor and Eddie Murphy

HERMAN BEAVERS

"Black will make you . . . or black will un-make you."
"Ain't it the truth, Lawd?"
—Ralph Ellison

A 1992 edition of the *Philadelphia Inquirer* ran a front-page story describing a woman who thought she saw an "armed intruder lurking motionless at the top of [a set] of dimly lit steps." Responding to her fright, police officers dispatched to the scene arrived expecting the worst. With guns drawn (.357 Magnums, no less) the officers entered the hallway, which was above a video store, and warned the "perpetrator" to drop his gun. After moving to a different angle, one of the officers, Larry Kirk, "noticed something familiar about the face."

The "armed intruder" turned out to be a life-sized, cardboard promotional poster of actor-comedian, Eddie Murphy, used to advertise the video release of his film, *Another 48 Hours.*[1] Rather than informing the reader that the officer had come upon the Murphy poster, the writer relates the story as though the officers had come upon Eddie Murphy in the flesh. It is at this point that the reporter chooses to inform the reader that what both the officers and the female caller have perceived as an "intruder" is Murphy's cardboard likeness.

While the humor of this situation is obvious, what I want to call attention to is the cultural machinery at work underneath. The headline of the article, "Gun Play," signals the reporter's tongue-in-cheek approach to the incident. However, the title masks a drama of symbols and reactions that, in their turn, generate new symbols and implicate the reader within a web of socially charged assumptions. The manner in which the story is organized as a reading event attempts to recapture the scenario, to present it dramatically. The reader of the story is not immediately informed that the officers have encountered a

life-sized cardboard cutout. Rather, this information is withheld. The reporter
leads the reader to reckon, as the police do, that "[i]t was Eddie Murphy." As
the story suggests, it is recognition of Murphy's face—as icon rather than as
cardboard figure done in his likeness—that eliminates the danger. And it is on
this note that we are then informed that the "perpetrator" is a "gun-wielding"
likeness of Murphy. There are several items that make the reporting of this
incident of such great cultural consequence. The first is that the reporter leads
the reader to experience the same form of tension as the police officers; there
is an undeniable drive toward mimesis that involves the manipulation of information and detail to recreate the incident itself. But we must consider
within this mimetic process the underlying assumptions that make it possible.

This leads to the second item, namely that the manner in which the incident is reported involves a trajectory that moves from tension to relief to humor. The story utilizes a kind of racial titillation to accomplish its ends. In the
actual event, one can assume that the result of the scenario is the officers' public embarrassment. At the time this article appeared in the Inquirer, Murphy's
appeal was so powerful, he could disarm the police officers, thwart the violent response reserved for armed intruders.[2] As that moment's potent symbol
of Hollywood's love for the depiction of irreverent, virile, and nonconformist heroes, his "presence" on the darkened stairwell generated the acceptable.

The story attempts to create the same illusion manifested by the cardboard
figure and it suggests that Eddie Murphy, as Hollywood icon, enjoyed the
luxury of criminal trespass. He can act, in accordance with the roles in which
he is most easily recognized, as transgressive figure. On both the situational
and ideological fronts, Eddie Murphy, as source of relief, can just as easily
be seen as a source of "cool." Not only does he defuse a potentially violent
confrontation, the familiarity he evokes and the racially transcendent status
he holds mean that the proper association has been made. As comedian, even
striking a violent pose, he means no harm.

Iconographic power transforms, contravenes threat. This makes it important to read the incident and its journalistic account as complementary texts.
Race is so implicitly embedded in the article's discursive scheme we can infer
that the story's position on the front page speaks to its purpose as a social release valve. As such, the story functions as a referent for instances where real
black men with real weapons—whose names we do not know—hurt, maim,
and kill or, conversely, are themselves the victims of violence either from
their peers or the police. It recapitulates our paranoia and makes it a source
of laughter, rather than a source of fear. Moreover, the occlusion of race deflects attention away from a perception of the police as vehicles of excessive

force; this owes to the fact that the story's humor comes at police expense, casting them as bumbling rather than dangerous, amusing rather than lethal.

What makes this possible is Murphy's status as a comedic figure. But this points to the third item of the story: though the reporter never directly references the race of the supposed intruder, Murphy's "presence" brings it to the fore. By withholding the actual nature of the situation, the journalist suggests that what prevents the "gun play" from occurring is that Murphy possesses the status necessary to defuse a situation between a black man and the police. The fact that the story makes use of an African American who has mass appeal suggests that the racial situation in America is manageable given his ability to allay the sense of threat. The placement of the story as a front-page item refers to its importance as a quiescent device.[3] Thus, even as one can read the article as a surrogate for stories describing acts of violence involving black men, what nullifies this conceptual jump is the fact that Eddie Murphy, as humorous icon, makes fearful rumination an inappropriate response. For he is so thoroughly removed from racial specificity, having "transcended" that form of categorization, that the writer of the story need not make any mention of race. What appears to be the case here is that the narrative of racial conflict, often a source of mass arousal, has been deactivated; in actuality it has rigged for silent running: the reader can't see for laughing.

One wonders how this story would have been presented—and where—had the cardboard figure been Clint Eastwood, whose films reflect the "rugged individualism" of the expansionist phase of nineteenth-century America. Indeed, he often plays a cowboy, even when his films are set in the twentieth century. His characters are violent and unorthodox, serving to restore order and protecting the status quo, even if, as the *Dirty Harry* films suggest, force must be used to protect the polity from itself.[4]

African American males have no historical or cultural niche as patriarchal protectors by which to contextualize violence. Hence, rebellion is delegitimized as a form of resistance. Riots are singularly viewed as the collapse of order rather than the perception of hegemonic menace that evokes a violent response. Thus, the presentation of African American men in the public sphere manifests issues of security. Where Murphy, as cardboard figure, must travel from threat to joke, Eastwood is solidly ensconced as an icon of protection, of reason and order.

But how do we arrive at this oasis of quiescence? How does the African American male body construct or contribute to that quiescence? What is it about Eddie Murphy's cinematic presence that can create such universal familiarity and relief? In discussing Murphy's early films, Manthia Diawara points out, "Murphy's character[s are often] deterritorialised from a black milieu and transferred to a predominantly white world" (71). But this explains only partially why Murphy's characters have such great appeal to white audiences. It resolves the racial dynamics involved, but I wish to explore the manner in which gender is also imbricated in such an analysis.

Diawara's observation that black male characters are "made less threatening to whites . . . by white domestication of black customs and culture" indicates that Murphy's stardom can be justified on grounds that extend beyond the discourse of race (71). A deeper interrogation leads me to conclude that his popularity is generated by the manner in which it dramatizes the intersectionality of race and gender. The way, that is, that he manifests, not only a racial identity, but an identity foregrounded within the assumptions that surround masculinity.

African American feminist thought has articulated the manner in which black women can be marginalized within the space of both race and gender.[5] The underlying assumptions that underscore notions of African American maleness offer a slightly different configuration. Despite the fact that African American men struggle to exercise power in the racial sphere, as men, they are quite capable of both manifesting and exercising power.[6] What this demonstrates is that black masculinity (as an interstice) is often emblematic of an intersection of deficiency and effaceable power, which takes on numerous formulations (e.g., power over women, other men, nature). Moreover, when sexuality is configured into this matrix, heterosexuality is the paradigmatic site for black men to manifest issues of race and gender. Thus, the exercise of black masculinity is organized around the redress of deficiency in the racial sphere, power that is manifested in highly visible formulations, with heterosexuality becoming the site at which these come together.

Hence, the dilemma of black men is most often discussed in terms of race. As one essay devoted to "The Challenge of Black Males," begins, "The challenge, not to mince words, is racism." While this assessment is by no means incorrect, neither is it totally accurate, for it, like many of the articles one reads devoted to the plight of the black male, does not build an analysis based on intersectionality. Rather it elides the difference between the discourses of race and gender.[7] Few essays written from a "racial perspective" articulate strategies that intervene, not only in terms of providing viable (and variable) models of male behavior, and valorize a plurality of black masculinities, but that also challenge the assumptions upon which masculinity is based. Rarely does one see discussions of black masculinity that dismantle, if only temporarily, the race/gender matrix; there are few essays that relate, for example, the "crisis" of black men to a larger crisis of masculinity that cuts across lines of race, class, or sexual preference.[8] Nor do we find much in the way of how black men exercise power and the arenas in which this occurs. The myth of black masculinity is that racism leads to a total fragmentation of self, the embodiment of total powerlessness.[9] And finally, one finds that issues of black masculinity are synecdochical; that is, black males are often configured as "the race." The challenge to rescue black males is, likewise, a totalized effort that will lead to the survival of the whole of African American people.

In a talk entitled "Sexuality and Intersectionality: When Race and Gender Stop Making Sense," Kimberlé Williams Crenshaw points to the manner in which the discourse of antiracism functions in the black community. Crenshaw observes: "Patriarchy and sexism are not simply subordinated to racism within Black political discourse; frequently it is normatively embraced. The clearest articulations of antiracism's investment in patriarchy are reflected in efforts to conceptualize racial domination solely in terms of the emasculation of the Black community." [10] What this indicates is that antiracist discourse, in the various forms it assumes, places black male experience at the center and deploys patriarchy and heterosexuality as the normalized paradigms of black masculinity.

Important in this discussion is what Richard Majors describes as the "cool pose." Cool, as Majors delineates it, is a dialectical phenomenon. On the one hand, it issues from the ways black men have learned "to mistrust the words and actions of dominant white people [and thus], black males have learned to make great use of 'poses' and 'postures' which connote control, toughness, and detachment." Conversely, however, Majors indicates that cool can also represent a problem when "cool suppres[ses] the motivation to learn, accept, or become exposed to stimuli, cultural norms, aesthetics, mannerisms, values, etiquette, information or networks that could help them overcome problems caused by white racism." [11]

The purpose of this essay, then, is to examine Richard Pryor's and Eddie Murphy's comedy, which manifests "cool" as an attempt, in the former, to restore the injured African American male body and, in the latter, to protect it from injury. Pryor's comedy (most notably his stand-up) relies on a black nationalist posture that is often explicitly articulated, while Murphy's is more implicit, embedded in a presentation of the self under attack. In light of this, both comedians force us to examine more closely the manner in which the disenfranchisement of black men is constructed and addressed—not only inside the black community, where commentators rely so heavily on a racial critique that frequently diminishes or ignores altogether issues of gender, but also outside the community, where black men function in the public sphere as metonyms of familiarity and progress (instruments of quiescence). Here the African American male body undergoes a transformative procedure where orality displaces corporeality and transgression becomes aligned with progress.[12] Cool becomes an important weapon because it represents an ideological consensus in the black community that cuts across socioeconomic lines, and it allows black men to address the issue of style as it likewise stands as a safeguard against outside threat (Scarry 86). It is important to the mainstream because its postulation of a style of resistance is easily transformed, in advertising for example, into the consumption of goods and services that signify nonconformist behavior, a refusal to be co-opted by the mainstream.[13]

The reasons for this can be partially explained in Foucault's observation that, "[T]he social body is the effect . . . of the materiality of power operating on the . . . bodies of individuals" ("Body/Power" 55). If a consumer culture is, as Cornel West has asserted, driven by acts of stimulation, we can see the alternative strategies (e.g., drug culture, gangs, or random violence) that black men enact as attempts to manifest power, make it visible, to create a new material state and thus feel themselves to be part of an alternative social body.[14] However, the mainstream makes visibility and participation synonymous. And participation is for those individuals who can effect changes in their lives (or the lives of others) and turn those changes into material benefits. It is these individuals who become actors in the symbolic drama of black masculinity, because if one is able to control how one becomes visible, one is indeed imbued with power.

It is with this in mind that I want to turn my attention to Eddie Murphy, his representations of power, and their ability to render the black male body recognizable, familiar. The twelve films in which Eddie Murphy has performed to date are conjoined by the fact that, in each, he portrays figures of transgression. In this respect, his characters are often at the crossroads of criminality and legality and, through a series of turns, they wind up in the service of restoring order. Unlike Eastwood, who performs this task with a reserve that sometimes borders on the catatonic, Murphy's characters possess a style that embodies the cool pose as it functions in the public sphere (Majors 85). For example, when the 48 Hours films are juxtaposed against the Beverly Hills Cop series, Murphy moves from a criminal who winds up protecting and enforcing the law to a law enforcement officer who transgresses the law to restore order and white, male authority.[15] In all four films, however,

Murphy's characters engage in the same forms of wisecracking and flamboyance that represent a black cultural signature.

To grasp the full significance of Eddie Murphy's fiction films, as opposed to his two concert films, one must first understand the assumptions that foreground his style of comedy. What makes Murphy's comedy so intriguing is that he intends it as an antiracist discourse that reflects a high degree of influence from an earlier comedian: Richard Pryor. As Murphy himself has asserted, "My [comedy] roots are back inside his [Pryor's] stuff, his style."

I suggest that Murphy's publicly recognized work, beginning on *Saturday Night Live*, represents a neonationalist posture that takes the form of individual license. However, Pryor's black nationalism takes very overt forms. As Donald Bogle asserts, Pryor's sensibility reflects nationalism because he demonstrates black solidarity (258–64). For instance, in *Richard Pryor Live in Concert*, there is a moment when Pryor asks for the house lights to be brought up so that he can introduce former Black Panther leader, Huey P. Newton. During his second concert film, *Richard Pryor Live in the Sunset Strip*, there are audience reaction shots intercut with Pryor's stage performance, one of which reveals Jesse Jackson in the audience.[16] These events, which disrupt the mimetic flow of the comedy routines, insert Pryor's work into a political context: his comedy also performs serious cultural labor and the proof of this is that he is the object of the nationalist gaze. Both of these instances demonstrate Pryor's commitment to a nationalist posture, one where "cool" is not only a stylistic posture but a political one as well.

Murphy's interpretation of the impact of the Black Power movement in the 1960s and 1970s leads him to position himself as a comedian vis-à-vis American culture in ways that both reflect and revise Pryor's influence. He does not exhibit Pryor's racial solidarity, nor is his work necessarily political. As I will elaborate below, Murphy is a solitary figure. His comedy mediates American mainstream responses to race; where the 1960s brought images of an angry black mass, by the 1980s, Murphy was often either alone (as in the concert films), or he was the lone black figure in a sea of white faces. Indeed, there is the moment in the film *Trading Places* where Murphy's character, having become upwardly mobile, abruptly breaks ranks with blacks as he settles into a more upscale lifestyle.[17]

This implies that there are very pronounced differences in the respective impact of Pryor's and Murphy's work. The most profound distinction, which I want to take up below, obtains in their manifestations of the black male body. As an instrument of expressivity, the black male body, when presented by African American performers, often represents potency and control; it is the manifestation of cool. To see the effect of this I want to look, first, at Richard Pryor's concert films. There, we find a comedian whose material is generated by his life experience. Hence, Pryor's comedy reflects the personal catastrophes he has survived, which include nearly dying of burns after setting himself on fire, the breakup of four marriages, several heart attacks, and drug addiction. But Pryor's gift as a comedian is his ability to resurrect himself through his comedy. His concert films, as opposed to the fiction films in which he co-stars with whites, allow the viewer to see the wages of mainstream success for black males.[18] He sends the message to black men that one can have success and acclaim, but these things are not without their costs.[19]

Pryor's comedy, particularly after 1972, has a very strong political foundation whose purpose is to valorize black male energy. In contrast to Murphy, his style has a self-reflexive component where the point of origin for his comedy is his experiences: his concert films are instances where he turns his gaze upon himself. Just as the nineteenth-century slave narrative allowed the black subject to talk about him or herself, to bring pain and suffering into the public space of utterance (with the quest for freedom serving as the ultimate healing force), Pryor's concert films are examples of a conflation of pain and self-rumination. Pryor's comedy often depicts the events that surround his own social faux pas. Further, he interrogates at least in cursory fashion, issues of masculinity through examinations of his own behavior that black men rarely articulate among themselves. Pryor has manifested negative social behaviors—for example, fear of intimacy, violent tendencies, and self-centeredness—but it is his awareness of this that creates the niche from which he speaks. In taking his own behavior and subjecting it to a comedic critique, he also places that behavior into a social context based on the notion that black men are not allowed, in a racist society, to act in openly threatening ways. The concert films are oriented around establishing very clear issues of African American maleness. When Pryor launches into a routine on why he was shooting at his own car (the result of a domestic dispute), he concludes that the police "don't kill cars, they kill niggahs" and then begins to joke about police brutality against African American men.

The results of this, as his second concert film illustrates, is that the humor of Pryor's material is to be found in the ways he emphasizes the significance of events as they pertain to both a personal and social milieu. Thus, Pryor comes to us as a figure who is always in process, with that process projected against the backdrop of the nation's cycle of societal failure. He turns the idea of the "macho man" inside out to reveal an often desperate, confused individual. While a racist society makes it necessary to be able to confront threat,

Pryor's comedy also works out the dilemma of cool, which Majors sees as the cause of severe problems: "In many situations a black man won't allow himself to express or show any form of weakness or fear or other feelings and emotions. He assumes a facade of strength, held at all costs, rather than 'blow his front' and thus his cool" (86). In other words, his comedy insists that the attempt to manifest masculinity, in a racist society, is not only a source of humor, but finally a source of delusion and danger. His comedy must be understood, in fact, as a comedy that has a very fixed notion of what constitutes legitimate forms of masculinity — for example, the ability to be visible and in control — and thus it demonstrates that black masculinity is concerned with the attempt to reach such an ideal state.

Pryor's comedy is indicative of his ability to be in a constant state of revision, but that process has to be considered in light of the fact that his comedy never dislodges male supremacy. Antony Easthope's view, that we can view masculinity as a collective attempt to master threat, is what provides insight into Pryor's comedic presence. For what he brings into performative space are repeated instances where he has attempted to master the assaults on his ego. Pryor makes it very clear that he is doing this; he manifests a subjectivity that is always destabilized by its attempt to maintain the sovereignty of its boundaries. He locates the masculine project at the center; his stand-up works out the tension between trying to be a heterosexual black male in a racist society and the dilemmas of identity that this project ensures.[20] The male ego, in Pryor's comedy, is therefore "defined by its perimeter and the line drawn between what is inside and what is outside. To maintain its identity it must not only repel external attack but also suppress treason within" (Easthope 40). His concert films work out the failures that arise from his attempts to protect his ego. "I was just on the Today show," Pryor related in an interview, "and they were telling me how wonderful I was and I walk out into the reality of America and I can't get a cab." The implication is that his addictions and other antisocial behaviors are the results of the self-hatred precipitated in a racist society; his attempts to loose himself from its demons are often driven by his embrace of other demons: violence, addictive behavior, and infidelity. Here, there is a strong correlation to be made between addiction and national contradiction. As we learn from his concert films, at no time can we read Pryor's performances as promises that he will alter his lifestyle to reflect a total transformation, because his comedy contends that America has made no strides toward a corresponding type of transformation.

There is a relationship between body and nation here, one that invokes the body as social mirror. Pryor's body, lying in a hospital badly burned is, symbolically speaking, a result of how hard it is to be a black man in America. There is an unspoken confluence between his injury and black men burned alive in the Jim Crow South. His experience with freebasing is the measure of his failure to "live up to" the adult responsibility of controlling his life,[21] with the ultimate control being control of one's body. Thus, by personifying the crack pipe or the vodka bottle, imbuing both with voices that evoke demonic power, Pryor locates the source of his fall outside the body. Comedy, then, is his way of reclaiming his body.[22] Here, control of the body falls within the discourse of cool. When he performs the routine describing the injuries he sustained from freebasing, Pryor asserts that he "dipped a cookie in condensed milk and the shit blew up." This is an important act of signifying on American society, for it suggests that the illusion of "making it," of being integrated, "condensed" into the mainstream, is a volatile concept that contributes to his injuries. He moves into the routine, which describes his addiction, injury, and recovery in full. What finally makes Pryor's performance so affecting is that it asserts, "I am willing to do with myself something that the nation in which I live has failed to do: admit my failures."

This is not to suggest that Pryor's manifestation of black masculinity is not without its problems. His attempts to articulate and destabilize the social death of racism maintain static notions of masculinity. This can be seen as he relates the discovery that certain women do not have orgasms or that, in fact, they have their own standards of what constitutes pleasurable sexual experiences. While the humor in the routine arises out of Pryor's ability to evoke the fear of failure men experience in heterosexual encounters, the notion that men mediate the quality of a sexual encounter is never challenged.[23]

In this instance and others, Pryor suggests that women are activities to be engaged in (literally, given his many marriages), not individuals with whom to share experiences or who offer insight. They are canvases against which he projects his quest for a viable—or perhaps even a not so viable—self. However, the fact that Pryor's concert films all present instances where he makes comedy out of the exorcism of his demons, suggests a protoradicalism as it pertains to masculinity and race that offers a hint to the possibility of revising notions of the black male subject.

Pryor's resurrective posture can be contrasted to Eddie Murphy's posture of license. What distinguishes Murphy's brand of comedy is that, as a child of the sixties and early seventies, he is a product of television. As Todd Gitlin has observed, this has its consequences, namely in light of the way "television lets us see only close up: shows us only what the nation already presumes, focuses on what the culture already knows—or more precisely, enables us to gaze upon something the appointed seers think we need or want to know" (3). Hence, one sees that he draws his comedy routines from characters and processes familiar to us because we have already seen them. His ability to mimic Ricky Ricardo or Ralph Kramden is endearing because he manifests an aura of revisionist familiarity.

Murphy's career must be understood, then, in light of his beginnings in television, where his comic style emanates as an intervention into racist stereotypes. But this intervention is foregrounded in his acceptance of the idea that the 1960s and early 1970s produced forms of racial mobility that enabled racial stereotypes to be destabilized. Murphy's comedy is cast against this conceptual backdrop. Thus, where Pryor makes jokes about whites using a distinctly black idiom that, in their most extreme form led to his banishment from series television, Murphy makes jokes about blacks to largely white audiences by mimicking white racism, fusing black and white icons (his Little Richard Simmons character is an example of this melding), often tapping into the homophobia that crosses racial lines, all of which are simultaneously signs of racial progress and emotional distance. Murphy's middle-class upbringing betrays American notions of "the black experience" as one that is poverty-driven and full of violence and neglect. His repeated presentations of a "black man [who is] quick-witted and sharp-tongued, undaunted and unconquerable," speak to the manner in which his body is beyond rupture. The Buckwheat character that Murphy resurrected on Saturday Night Live was intended to capture its absurdity, to suggest that its stupidity was also a signal of its harmlessness. What makes this problematic, though, is that it suggests that American society has evolved past this form of representation and the ideology that produces it, which makes it a legitimate source of comedy.

Where Pryor's notion of the comic subject is based on almost total instability, Murphy's comedy centers him within a popular-culture milieu that arranges his subject matter around him, as if he were engaged in a kind of social spectatorship where society is the object of the gaze. This means that he is positioned to look at people looking at him. During the concert film Delirious he comments on the manner in which he is the object of a hostile (read here, homoerotic) gaze. What creates the hostility, however, is that the homoerotic gaze is a force capable of disrupting Murphy's sexual potency, thus collapsing his cool posture. In his leather suits, Murphy represents the essentialized black male body, a body that is invincible with its signifying armor surrounding it. Thus, when he refers to the leather suit he wears for the performance as "faggot leather shit," he is not engaging in self-deprecating humor; rather he articulates the leather's protective significance, as it protects him from the homoerotic gaze. This form of the gaze, as he conceptualizes it, is a threat because it attempts to breach the boundaries the male body establishes (Easthope 51–54).

Murphy's stand-up material is generated, therefore, by his portrayal of the obstacles to sexual performance. In *Delirious*, Murphy proclaims that "These are the fuck years for me . . . I fuck." He establishes a much more concrete sense that his is an ego under assault. Thus, in *Raw*, Murphy's routine is based on the manner in which he is confronted by hostile figures: hostile women who want to exploit Murphy, hostile fans, both black and white, who want to take away the body of material acquisitions that comedy has allowed him to amass, and family who do not understand his needs. *Raw* expresses Murphy's fear of being exploited by any and all and articulates the fear that they will emasculate him. When we consider the fictional skit, where the young Eddie Murphy tells a joke that none of his family understands, which actually transgresses the boundaries of familiar propriety, we can see that Murphy is moved to construct a masculinity that foregrounds solitude as a response to the exterior threat of rejection.

Murphy's fiction films seem to redress this fear, to make retaliation (against women and gay men, for example) not only likely but appropriate and natural because the cool posture calls for this kind of delineation of maleness. In comparing Murphy and Pryor, the difference comes in Pryor's ability, as mime, to act out his dilemma as a black man with his body; when he reclaims the body, it becomes comic instrument. Murphy, whose talent lies in imitating voices, is more mobile. He is able to make incursions into the bodies of others because he can occupy their voices. His is a comedy that could only occur in a post-1960s milieu, largely because he works out the nationalist idea that the black male body could destabilize the society by displacing white maleness. Where Pryor's body is a text onto which the impact of racism is mapped (as the burns on his body articulate), Murphy's voice becomes a means by which to disrupt those forces that threaten to ignore or undermine black male power.

In an age of talking heads and cardboard bodies, Murphy represents a break from the physical. This is exemplified by a comment made by one of the producers of *Saturday Night Live*, who noted: "[T]he whole black-and-white thing works because of his eyes. He never loses the charm in his eyes. In his eyes he never stops smiling. His eyes tell the audience he's laughing. . . . Eddie's eyes are the eraser for misunderstanding." What the producer evokes is a reductive model of the classic coon figure. Indeed, the implication is that Murphy's ability to avoid "misunderstanding," is grounded in the fact that his style defuses threat, displaces anger. But consider, again, the manner in which this message is conveyed. The eye, the instrument of the gaze (both literally and as a social device), does not create, rather it obliterates. As a container for comedy, the eye, as Murphy utilizes it, is either a visionary tool capable of seeing beyond distinctions of black and white, or it is a crucible that burns away the impurity of racial confrontation (e.g., "the whole black-and-white thing"), leaving the pure product of humor (the signal of racial understanding). The deeper implication here is that Murphy's comedic style is successful because of his ability to control parts of his body. But here, that control is not used in the service of aggressiveness or dispute, or even critique, but as a palliative gesture that creates quiescence. And that control truncates the body, fragments it into usable parts. Thus, in order to discern that Murphy's comic tone is not one tinged with threat, one has to break up the body, focus on the part that evokes security.

What I describe above needs to be contrasted to the posture Murphy has assumed as co-producer, writer, or director. While his other films have been successful, what makes them noteworthy are his characters' relationships to the status quo. The three films that have seen Murphy stationed at a different point in the means of production—Raw, Coming to America, and Harlem Nights—represent a conceptual unit of a different sort. What distinguishes them is that each film valorizes the reification of masculine energy as an agency that never interrogates itself, that situates self-referentiality as a condition of male normalcy, capable of reproducing itself.[24]

Thus, when Murphy makes jokes about Africa in Raw, he does so with the apparent assumption that the Black Power movement situated a conception of Africa in the public mind during the 1960s and 1970s, which emblematizes manhood and political control. Further, it is a concept that it seems Murphy expects his audience to engage within the comedic transaction. However, when one compares Murphy's vision of Africa—in Coming to America and Raw—to Pryor's notion of Africa, which he espouses in Live in the Sunset Strip, one sees very profound differences. In the former, Africa is either the site of a fairy tale (Coming to America) or it is a revocation of a primitive and precapitalist space that, in Raw, is synonymous with submissive women. Murphy asserts that he wants to go to Africa and find Umfufu, the "bush-bitch." But in doing so he works out a contemporary version of the Triangle Trade: he goes to find a woman who lacks the wherewithal to resist or emasculate him. As a black man who performs the cultural labor of entertaining the masses, Murphy's African woman serves the same purpose as the African American woman in slavery: as breeder and economic entity subject to his whim. In exchange, he receives artistic and economic kudos, signified by the icons of success (he arrives in a limousine) and the "fan interviews" at the beginning of Raw, symbols of his crossover status.

Pryor's Africa, conversely, is a site of personal transformation, a site where he comes to eschew the use of the word "nigger." In a touching moment, Pryor articulates the inner symbolism of the word "as a sign of our own wretchedness." While both men provide images of Africa that are, in their respective fashions, romantic, it is Pryor's image that is the more empowering of the two because it deconstructs racist language as an instrument of oppression.

But it is precisely because of this that Murphy's comedy must be read as a comedy that falls into a tradition. His awareness of his comic predecessors transmutes itself into license. Pryor's comedy (as does Bill Cosby's) interrogates adulthood, but Murphy's license is indicative of youth, his comedy represents a coming-of-age narrative. Because he has portrayed young, virile black men whose dilemma lies in the attempt to manifest potency and solitude, Murphy has avoided portraying characters who are encumbered by children, wives, or filial responsibility. To be cool is also to be mobile, free to aim the comic gaze outward in all directions. Unlike Pryor, who indicts the status quo by invoking the "crazy nigger" who is pushed until he loses control, Murphy's comedy adopts an antiracist posture because it equates transgression with crossover appeal.

What results are very distinctive revisions of Pryor's routines. In Live in the Sunset Strip, Pryor's body takes on the character of a lion as he describes his trip into the African forest. Murphy's "bush-bitch" drains Pryor's vision of Africa of its political edge. As a face and a voice, Murphy can occupy transgressive space, but he can do so only by constituting the body in one dimension. Thus, when Pryor describes the first bath he receives after being burned, it is a moment where the humor is generated by his ability to represent, through the use of his body, the pain that issues from having the burnt skin, and thus a former self, scrubbed away. Again, Murphy revises this trope. In Coming to America, Prince Akeem is bathed by three women, one of whom emerges from the water to announce, "The Royal penis is washed, your highness." Murphy's revision of Pryor rests on notions of safety and security, but most of all on the manifestation of invincibility.

Pryor's comedy emanates from an articulation of injury, or the numerous ways the black male body can be ruptured—either from within or without. Murphy's comedic presence is one that manifests itself as impenetrable surface. In establishing a voice that can occupy the icons of 1950s and 1960s television and thus transgress the racial boundaries that it took the Civil Rights and Black Power movements to make visible, Murphy must finally give up the body altogether. The confluence of technology and race, as Harryette Mullen observes, "encodes racial integration so powerfully that it accomplishes otherwise unachieved racial integration through a synthesized synchronicity of images and voices drawn from disparate sources, the media equivalent of gene-splicing" (86). The result of this sound-image, as Murphy engages it, is that the transgressive turns in on itself, the mirror becomes darkly tinted glass.

But *Coming to America* makes it clear that this is so at the expense of any deep interrogation of masculinity. Conceived by Murphy as a "reversed and cleaned up" reworking of *Raw*, the film remains firmly embedded in an endorsement of patriarchy and heterosexuality. Though he insists that he wants a woman who loves him for himself and not what he possesses, Prince Akeem reflects Murphy's inability to loose himself from the Cinderella mythos (where he is both rescuer and rescuee). When Akeem meets the bride chosen for him at birth, he is fascinated by the fact that she must do whatever he tells her to do. Rather than ridiculing this posture and articulating their equality through a refusal to participate in the patriarchal degradation of women, he merely re-situates the domination. Thus, when he makes her jump on one foot while making sounds like an orangutan, he, too, participates in her degradation. Though he claims to disagree with the source of what diminishes her (embodied by his inability to choose a bride and her inability to articulate an identity of her own), he merely wishes to reconstitute it somewhere else. Akeem postulates the desire to encounter the (female) other as subject. However, when he enters a moment when he can implement this desire, what he does is to reinstitute racist stereotypes. But this reinstitution is gender inflected: the female body is used to split off the colonial incarnation of the African body as ape-like and subservient.

That split is redressed, ostensibly, through the agency of heterosexual male desire. Prince Akeem wants "someone who will arouse [his] mind, as well as [his] loins." But this is the same kind of narcissism and hypermasculinity to be found in *Raw*.[25] For when Akeem and his companion, Semmi, leave for America, they do so with the thought that they must find a woman "suitable for a king," leading them to journey to Queens, New York. But this returns the quest to its original parameters: a woman who symbolizes Akeem's royalty, who mirrors his status. Moreover, sexuality obscures the intellect and locates both within male control. This is demonstrated at the end of *Coming to America*, after the wedding, which interestingly brings us back to the beginning of the film, where he began his quest for a wife: we find Akeem in the same position of authority (he will take over his father's throne) with a woman who will be subordinate to him. Thus, the film never challenges the coercive force of patriarchy that is so strongly implied here. Akeem does not challenge his father's wish for him to marry, nor does he (even after a brief foray into working-class life) criticize the inequity of wealth in Zamunda (though the film does send up its extravagance); he merely wants to be involved in the choice of his bride. What this suggests is that black male sexuality itself is coerced. The instrument of coercion is the notion of racial subjectivity the film delineates: the black man as king. Akeem's status as heir locks him into a role that he cannot escape. Despite the fact that he reigns over what is portrayed as an affluent, peaceful African nation, this is a sign of both stable racial identity and confinement of the gendered self.

This reaches its most disturbing level in Murphy's Harlem Nights. In the film, Murphy's character (Quick) has a love interest in the form of one Dominique LaRue. Quick spots her as soon as she enters the club that he runs with his adopted father and business partner, Ray (played, of course, by Richard Pryor). Despite Ray's warnings that he should stay away from Dominique because she is the mistress of Bugsy Calhoun, a white mobster, Quick responds to her invitation to meet her at Bugsy's home. The turn of events that finds him upstairs in the bedroom leads Quick to discover a pistol Dominique has hidden under a pillow and to conclude that it is her intent to kill him after they finish making love. Having placed his own larger pistol under the other pillow, he and Dominique make love and when she attempts to kill him, she finds her pistol has been unloaded. Quick then uses his gun to kill her.

What is disturbing is the manner in which racial and sexual politics intersect here. Right before she reaches for the pistol, Dominique mimics Bugsy (who, as her lover, is also her voice). Earlier in the evening, he attempts to interest Quick in a business arrangement and tells him, "You can't trust anybody. Everybody in this business is a criminal. How can you trust a criminal?" When Dominique repeats this, verbatim, to Quick after making love to him, she is incontrovertibly associated with white male authority. When Bugsy asks her if she'd like to "fuck Mr. Quick," it means that black female sexuality is under white male control and thus becomes an instrument of death for black males. Thus, when Dominique speaks in the voice of the white man, Quick is justified in killing her. As director of the film, Murphy's reliance on stock representations of racial potency resituates this act of violence against a black woman and returns it to the racial sphere. Because black males, as the stereotype runs, are more potent than white males (e.g., Dominique's pistol is smaller than his own pistol; Quick's incredulity that Dominique could be interested in a white man in the first place, expressed through the disparaging comments he makes about Bugsy's body), the lovemaking that occurs between Dominique and Quick cannot be dislodged from the gunshot that kills her. For what occurs between them is a struggle for dominance between Bugsy and Quick that is circulated through Dominique's body. Thus, Quick's violent act is made to appear unstable within the category of misogyny because Quick's real adversary is Bugsy. What appears as a conflict between a black man and a black woman ostensibly masks a purely racial confrontation between a black man and a white man. However, the misogyny does not disappear so much as it is merely part of the process of racial liberation. Thus, Dominique's presence in the film is completely negated, she is a spectral presence whose only function is to serve as the surrogate of white male power.[26]

What this demonstrates is sexual politics' collapse into racial oppositionality; because gender issues fall lower in the hierarchy of oppositionality, black women must either cooperate or be silenced, if not punished outright (sometimes violently). As object, Dominique is centered between two men—one white, one black—attempting to exercise potency in the form of racial identity. Rather than enlisting Dominique's aid against Bugsy by invoking their shared racial status, Quick kills her. Here Quick's sexual prowess—which could be read as a form of racial consciousness—does not lead Dominique to confront the contradiction of working for Bugsy as a black woman. In this instance the black woman is eradicated for her complicity with a white man.

This allows us to decipher another moment in the film, namely when Quick shoots Vera (played by Della Reese) in the foot. During a scene where a fistfight ensues between them, Vera tells Quick, "You hit like a bitch." In Murphy's film, the black woman's violence is proof of the fact that she is a monster to be repressed, by any means necessary. Like the encounter with Dominique, the encounter with Vera suggests a masculine connotation that must be read in a wider context, which can be accessed outside of Murphy's triad of films. In *Another 48 Hours*, Reggie Hammond, in a recapitulation of the bar scene in the first film, shoots a white redneck in the foot and then asserts, "Anyone else wanna limp?!" The word "limp" is important because it works out the intra-gender politics inherent in antiracist discourse: Properly armed, the intersection of blackness and maleness is synonymous with power; a power that is firmly located in the white male psyche (he asserts in *48 Hours*, "I'm your worst motherfucking nightmare!"). The "limp," of course, has to do with the manner in which black masculine power can emasculate its adversaries when it has the proper resources. When joined, the two scenes work out the manner in which black male violence (or the potential for it) renders white men impotent. That this routine is repeated in *Harlem Nights* demonstrates that black women, no less than white men, need to be shown that black men can—and should—exercise control. Quick emasculates Vera, returns her to her "proper" place as a subordinate black woman.

As director of *Harlem Nights*, Murphy creates a world of illegality where male-female conflict is glamorized: black women are whores and mammies and are told by black men to "shut the fuck up!" Not only does Murphy make misogynist practice into a comedic punchline, but ideologically, at a time when black men were reclaiming the "lost territory" of male control, it mirrors the "politically correct" response to a black woman's resistance. We can see Murphy's films as part of the same text as Shahrazad Ali's book, *The Blackman's Guide to Understanding the Blackwoman*. Ali observes: "There is never an excuse for hitting a Blackwoman anywhere but in the mouth. Because it is from that hole, in the lower part of her face, that all her rebellion culminates into words. Her unbridled tongue is a main reason she cannot get along with the Blackman. She often needs a reminder.... [I]f she ignores authority and superiority of the Blackman, there is a penalty. When she crosses this line and becomes viciously insulting it is time for the Blackman to soundly slap her in the mouth." (169). Ali conflates orality and physicality: a black woman speaking is likewise a physical act of transgression that requires an equally aggressive act to restore order and hierarchy. Murphy's films execute this same maneuver: The act of shooting Vera in the foot is the punishment a black woman receives for "crossing the line." What this suggests is that the language of agency, when it takes the form of resistance, is a space reserved for black men and it refers to the situation Michele Wallace describes, wherein black males construct a "status quo" by becoming "the pre-eminent Other." "When the black woman, the 'Other' of the 'Other,'" she writes, "insists on having a voice, [the black male] status quo is profoundly disrupted" (*Invisibility Blues* 149).

This helps us to understand the end of the film, which finds Murphy and Pryor leaving New York. While Pryor's character takes his lover along, Murphy's character is without female companionship, he is alone. While we could characterize this as a homoerotic impulse, what is more aptly argued is that Murphy's character possesses a hypermasculinity capable of reproducing itself. *Harlem Nights* is, finally, a vehicle for men engaged in the black masculine project. It works out the bond between Quick and Ray, as father and son who ride off into the night together.[27] What the ending insists upon is Murphy's representation of cool: women are an encumbrance, men can be valuable allies insofar as they do not counsel gendered self-critique. Within antiracist discourse black men can bond to protect one another from incursions from the outside; in the figurative sense, safely ensconced in their heterosexuality, they can watch each other's backs.[28] But this indicates, in Murphy's case, that the masculine project is characterized on the one hand by its paranoia and on the other by solitude and fecundity.[29] The gaze is never turned inward to consider an inner threat, rather the danger is always externalized.

One finds it unusual, then, that Murphy is so critical of the homoerotic gaze. For, if that gaze is, as Freud asserted, the sign of an interest in self, is not Murphy's construction of his sexuality the same thing? As Michael Warner has argued, what makes Freud's claims so problematic are that they assume that sexuality is the only plane on which one can structure alterity ("Homo-Narcissism" 200). Murphy's deployment of the black male subject argues to the contrary. Because his comic approach is so heavily grounded in racial intervention, the way that issues of gender are rendered static is finally the way by which we can conclude that Murphy's characters and comedy routines fail to dislodge sexual myths about black men.

Because the intersectionality his work displays necessitates that his characters operate in predominantly white surroundings, their sexuality is intact because the spontaneity of the wisecrack is made synonymous with potency; to degrade a white man verbally articulates the potential to best him sexually. But in films such as Beverly Hills Cop and 48 Hours, Murphy's characters imbue the white males that interact with him with potency; the wisecrack becomes a kind of therapeutic force.[30] The static and the conventional are signs of a rigidity that, when aligned with whiteness, prohibits insight. What makes this important is that in all four films Murphy plays a character who, by virtue of his ability to invoke the "natural" state (which comes in the form of being "streetwise"), can lead white characters to a sense of self. White authority is modified, but it remains authority nonetheless.

Thus, we can see the intersection of deficiency and effaceable power at work here: to redress deficiency is likewise to materialize power. Because resistance of a racial sort privileges heterosexuality as a site of enactment, the struggle for racial liberation must be seen as a vehicle that requires the dominant culture to furnish the necessary ingredients. For while one might assume that the word "liberation" is a code word for "paradigm shift," it often serves as the keyword for increased participation in the patriarchal project.

One sees a clear example of this in Murphy's next film, Boomerang, directed and produced by Reginald and Warrington Hudlin. Murphy plays a character more cosmopolitan, suave, and sophisticated than Quick. Rather than the misogynistic tendencies of *Harlem Nights*, we find that Murphy's character, Marcus Graham, is a break from his previous work because he plays the foil. Marcus, an up-and-coming advertising executive in Manhattan, is a man whose womanizing knows no limits. When he meets Jacqueline Broyer (played to "type" by Robin Givens), he sets his sights on commanding her affections. The film's point, that Marcus is a "player who's about to be played," needs to be understood, however, in light of two narratives that predate its premiere: the Hill-Thomas hearings and the recovery narrative. The former brought the issue of sexual harassment into public discourse and connoted the emergence of a new kind of public scrutiny: for men, as it pertained to how they treated women in the workplace, for women, as it pertained to how they "threatened" male hegemony. *Boomerang* must be read as part of Hollywood's response to a perceived infringement on patriarchal control.

The recovery narrative has to do with the process associated with the recovery from substance abuse and the kinds of stories that those experiences generate. But it also needs to be understood within the context of the cult of personality, where stories by a wide variety of public figures—athletes, musicians, movie actors, and others—who claim to be in "recovery," suggest that their improved performance on the court, in the studio, or on the screen, was due to their liberation from the pitfalls of substance abuse. The commingling of these narrative vehicles represents a break from the conventional Hollywood formula for romance: boy meets girl, boy loses girl, boy gets girl back; where women are rescued by men. In its place is a narrative where women are both the substance abused and the site of recovery as well.

Hence, *Boomerang*'s treatment of women needs to be considered as secondary to its dramatization of patriarchal power. Since "turnabout is fair play," one knows that Marcus's outrageous behavior (demonstrated as the film opens, when Marcus is the focus of the female gaze and the object of middle-class female desire) needs to be brought into line, and it will take a "good black woman" to do so. But what makes *Boomerang* intriguing is that the film provides not one, but two, women to challenge Marcus to change. Jacqueline demonstrates what the film characterizes as masculine: she is domineering, manipulative, and insensitive. After Marcus fixes a romantic dinner for two, her response is to ask Marcus if they can take the plates into the living room so that she can watch the Knicks game. Angela (played by Halle Berry), on the other hand, is depicted as being nurturing, sensitive, and domestically inclined. She and Marcus's first night together unfolds after she has cooked Thanksgiving dinner for Marcus and his friends. Hence, Marcus's transformation from "dog" to a man inclined to commitment and monogamy is equated with the domestic sphere. After Angela breaks off their relationship (the result of Marcus's fallback into a sexual liaison with Jacqueline), Marcus leaves his job with the advertising agency in order to win her back. Taking up the role of art teacher at a community center, Marcus's transmogrification coincides with what must be interpreted as a simultaneous rise in his social awareness, where he can think of someone "other than [him]self."

Interestingly, the film never creates a space where Marcus's lack of social awareness can be critiqued. Rather, the film uses his relationships with his two best male friends, Tyler and Gerard, as a way to suggest that Marcus's investment in homosocial bonding signals his progressivity in social and political terms. Once again, Murphy's nationalist roots come to the fore and we must read Boomerang as a film that merely feigns a disinterest in antiracist discourse in favor of the more titillating romantic narrative.

We are offered clues that this is not the sole purpose of the narrative throughout the film, as we see Marcus engaged in conversations about women with Tyler and Gerard. It is Gerard (played by David Alan Grier) who articulates what comes closest to a departure from conventional masculinity. However, his attempt to forge an alternative to Marcus's promiscuity is perpetually ridiculed, both by his friends and by the narrative itself. It is Gerard who attempts to begin a relationship with Angela that is based on friendship and mutuality, but as the film later demonstrates, Angela is not interested in a relationship with a man lacking Marcus's high visibility and charisma, though she clearly wants a relationship that features what Gerard offers. When Marcus walks in on Jacqueline and Angela while they are discussing him, he conjectures that they are discussing the consummation of Angela and Gerard's relationship. But Angela responds, "Gerard couldn't 'hit it' if he had a bat" and thereby suggests that he is neither masculine nor savvy enough to do what is necessary to win her affections. Though the narrative never bears this out, there are intimations throughout the film that Gerard is gay, and he is chided by Tyler because his attempt to articulate less domineering forms of masculinity is equivalent to acting like a "Borderline bitch!"

Conversely, Tyler (played by Martin Lawrence) is working out a masculine identity more reminiscent of that associated with a stereotypical black nationalist perspective. He reads racist intent into every encounter with the dominant culture, ranging from a waitress's description of food to the underlying racism of billiards. At the same time it is clear that women have no place in his world, except as objects of sexual gratification. While he sees male bonding as the keystone arch of any form of societal change, the mastery of black women serves to demonstrate black men's superiority. Tyler and Gerard are very close to being polar opposites, with Marcus providing the mediating force between them, which also demonstrates that his success with women lies in his status as both social and masculine moderate.

These characterizations must be cast against the film's insistence that the relationship between Marcus, Gerard, and Tyler is one of depth and commitment, lacking in macho pretense. But one needs to reposition their relationship against the reality of African American men's inter- and intraracial relationships. This film appears in the early 1990s, at a time when numerous African American males are alienated, by virtue of their participation in gangs or drug culture, from what constitutes mainstream configurations of African American masculinity. By the end of the 1980s, death, both socially and literally, was more likely to occur for African American males through *intraracial*, rather than interracial, strife.

What is interesting is the manner in which *Boomerang* masks this reality. The social death Marcus experiences both during and after his encounter with Jacqueline Broyer suggests that his issues are located solely in the sphere of male-female relationships. In the one instance where Marcus is required to engage the white world, he succeeds by using fear to simultaneously cow the white male (who represents a feminized white world) in charge. But, reading this film as a product of the Hill-Thomas scenario, where a "powerful" black woman attempting to voice her harassment at the hands of a black man chosen for a place in the public sphere was roundly silenced by men and women in both the white and black communities, leads us to a different conclusion. Moreover, the Hudlin Brothers' decision to cast Robin Givens in the film is particularly important, given Givens's stormy marriage to and subsequent divorce from boxer Mike Tyson. While Marcus's treatment at the hands of Jacqueline in no way mirrors Thomas's "high-tech lynching" at the hands of the United States Senate Judiciary Committee, it does reinforce the conclusion that African American women in the public sphere mean their male counterparts no good, and they are willing to achieve success by "any means necessary."

This helps us to understand the film's closing moments. After Marcus breaks off his relationship with Jacqueline once and for all, having recognized that he is in love with Angela, he also experiences a reconciliation with Gerard, who has chastised him for his relationship with Angela. Here, Gerard's hurt results not only because he thinks Angela is a "nice girl" who will be victimized by Marcus's promiscuity, but also because he has not been successful in his attempt to establish a romantic relationship with her. But

Marcus tells him, "You like my brother. . . . I don't wanna go through this no more" and the two reestablish their bond, which is reinforced by Tyler, who asks "Y'all gon let a girl come between us?"

What gets articulated here is the hierarchy established by antiracist discourse, namely, that the more important struggle lies in black men setting aside their differences to combat racism rather than collectively interrogating issues of masculinity; indeed, to combat racism is to engage in a productive, radical form of masculinity where one can assume that women will be treated with respect. Hence, at no point in time does Marcus engage in self-critique regarding Jacqueline. Nor does he conclude that her behavior is what racist patriarchy has laid out as the cultural blueprint for corporate behavior in postindustrial capitalism. Indeed, the film works to formulate the argument that the relationship between Jacqueline and Marcus constitutes an almost complete reversal of power.

There are several moments in the film where the filmmakers attempt to suggest that in a situation where an African American woman exercises power in a professional setting, the reversals of power are complete, as if patriarchy is completely nullified. The first example of this comes after Marcus and Jacqueline agree to end their relationship. The next morning, he arrives to find all the female staff members listening eagerly as Jacqueline openly discusses the details of her intimate encounters with Marcus. Though they try to hold their laughter, when they fail the moment serves to suggest the humiliation women feel when they are the subject of office gossip. However, what the scene obscures is that Marcus's status as an executive, while subordinate to Jacqueline's, continues to hold sway over the majority of the other women in the scene. But the scene proposes that so thorough is Jacqueline's emasculation of Marcus that his power is rendered inert. And yet, we must consider the ways that the silence that results from Marcus's presence is a signifier of his power, not his powerlessness.

The second scene demonstrates an even greater subtlety. After Marcus approves an advertising spot the company owners find offensive, his job is saved by Jacqueline's intervention. However, as she tells him this it is important to observe Murphy's posture, which approximates what we are to interpret as a feminine posture: arms folded across his chest, lips pursed, his movements suggesting restriction, anger that is not just repressed but rather inhibited by an overwhelming sense of impotence. Again, the suggestion is that somehow he has lost all touch with masculine agency. However, what gives this scene away is the fact that when Marcus attempts to leave Jacqueline's office, he walks to a set of double glass doors. The door to the right is locked, and so when he pulls it inward toward him, it does not open. When he moves to his left, he attempts to pull open a door that requires him to push outward. While this moment is meant to suggest entrapment in a female sphere, I would argue that the real significance of this moment is that Marcus is trapped in a space created by patriarchy. That he tries to pull open the door, suggests what white supremacist capitalist patriarchy has always done—open the door for those it wanted to enter, while sending the racial and/or gendered Other to a locked door. But it also speaks to the ways that, Jacqueline Broyer notwithstanding, hegemonic masculinity has located agency on the inside, preventing those outside from accumulating the power necessary to pull the door open. But the film is so thoroughly invested in convincing us that Jacqueline Broyer is a predatory monster, that it never wavers in its representational scheme.

What this suggests is that Boomerang is a film whose first imperative is to provide the viewer with cinematic pleasure as it attempts to occupy a revisionist view of masculine behavior. The black female viewer can take pleasure both in Marcus's demise and his transformation from "dog" to "obedient mate." The heterosexual black male viewer can take pleasure both in the wide range of women with whom Marcus has contact, the innovations he uses to acquire mastery over these women, and the fact that the film ends with his monogamous attachment to Angela, whose lighter complexion makes her a more "attractive" choice than Jacqueline. But more than this, the producers' decision to use Robin Givens coincidentally allows the male viewer to work out his anger over the conviction and subsequent jailing of Mike Tyson after he was charged with raping a beauty pageant contestant. Because of Givens's public image as a "femme fatale," her character fails to constitute the kind of closure usually accorded to fictional characters. Rather, the black male viewer may feel he has access to the "inner workings" of her character because her tempestuous relationship with Tyson (e.g., her "manipulation" of him, followed by their divorce) has been a matter of public discussion.[31]

As a film that partakes of the narrative of reform, Boomerang insists that Marcus's recovery is complete. However, what is not discussed is the manner in which femininity, as per patriarchal convention, is the fulcrum upon which his raised consciousness depends. During their reconciliation, Marcus tells Angela, "I can't breathe without you" as if the whole of his identity requires her presence to be actualized. But in the film's final scene, as Marcus and Angela walk down the street, two women pass them, one young, well-dressed, and alone, the other older, less well-dressed, accompanied by two children. Angela threatens Marcus if he dares to look at the younger woman, while Marcus retorts that, in actuality, his eyes were on the older woman, as if he is "looking at the future." However, what is interesting here is that both women are alone—and both represent the relationship's potential direction: in the case of the former, Marcus's "fall" out of monogamy, and in the latter, Angela's subsequent abandonment as a single parent.

But what is also interesting is that *Boomerang* displaces the negativity, and therefore the source of failure, between black men and women onto American corporate culture, thereby insisting that it is ultimately detrimental to relationships between African American men and women. Though the advertising firm, formed by the merger of two ostensibly black-owned companies, is located in a well-appointed space in a Manhattan office tower, we are still led to believe that such settings are deleterious.[32] At the same time, however, the film does not engage at length those parts of New York City inhabited by the working poor and impoverished classes, in order to suggest alternative spaces for African American corporate know-how. Indeed, the relationships we find in the film are heavily mediated by class and caste politics, which make the film "delightful" to look at largely because of what it does not show.[33]

What makes this problematic, of course, is that it is so heavily grounded in the racial exceptionalist paradigm. Cornel West has articulated the shortcomings of this paradigm, where the subject constructs an image of him- or herself that stands as superior to the other, in any form the other may assume. What drives this notion as a racial paradigm is the presence of white supremacy, to which it is designed as a response, an "attempt to build self-worth upon quixotic myths about the past, exaggerated expectations of the present, and chialastic hopes for the future" (*Prophesy Deliverance!* 75). But this paradigm fails as a response to white supremacy for it reveals that the real roots of the Afro-American exceptionalist tradition lie in "the rise of the Afro-American petite bourgeoisie. The exceptionalist claim of Afro-American superiority can be seen as a cloak for the repressed self-doubts, fears, and anxieties of an emerging Afro-American middle class" (75). The conceptual move enacted here argues that black masculinity functions in the service of the dominant culture's attempt to confront its own repression. In this reading of American society, a racist society attempts to deny black men their privileges as citizens, which is likewise the sign that in order to redress their impotence white men must restructure their racial ideology. By working out the manner in which black masculinity transforms the society, opens it up to its hidden potentialities, the exceptionalist posture that foregrounds it never challenges the concept of supremacy.

But this points to a deeper problem and returns us to where we began: Eddie Murphy as cardboard figure and quiescent force. The high visibility that

Murphy enjoys takes the form of license and mobility. However, as Harry-ette Mullen suggests, this move can be historicized. She locates a shift of the iconic status of the black body, from its representation as a site of unrea-son in the eighteenth century to the nineteenth century where the African American's soul became emphasized over the body. She further observes: "In the twentieth century, the use of the black's image to represent repressed ele-ments of what has been constructed ideologically and semiotically as a 'white psyche,' becomes more pervasive as the very means of expression are tied to technologies highly susceptible to regressive and repressive ideological for-mations" (38). As the sign of both crossover success and the transgressive nature of youth, Murphy offers up the black body as a viable source of cul-tural energy. As Axel Foley, Murphy characterizes the force necessary to yoke together two opposing cultural styles. Though the white men he comes to be partnered with in *Trading Places, 48 Hours, Beverly Hills Cop* (as well as the sequels they generated), begin as plodding and sequential in their movements, Mur-phy's characters, in all their soulfulness, oil the stiffness right out of their joints (H. Mullen 39).

But one thinks of the manner in which Murphy's characters are never allowed to achieve any form of sexual display, until he stars in films directed and produced by African Americans. The deterritorialization, which Diawara describes in Murphy's films, is in large part meant to desexualize him. In his early films, for Murphy's characters to be socially transgressive, he must be sexually inert. The quartet of films I have discussed redress this state: Mur-phy moves from the dangers of heterosexual love in *Raw*, to a masculinized revision of Cinderella in *Coming to America*, to a hypermasculine state in *Harlem Nights*, to the "recovery narrative" of *Boomerang*. As narratives of racial progress, the gaze in each of these films does not turn inward, but instead turns outward to regard a world that needs to loosen up because everything, truly, is "otay."

This distortion seems to make the black male body visible. But in truth, it closes it and makes it viable for consumption. As Easthope has noted, "A hard body will ensure that there are no leakages across the edges between the inner and outer worlds" (*What A Man's Gotta Do* 52). The "leakage" that East-hope describes evokes the dilemma of black male intersectionality. A public figure like Eddie Murphy is a signal of racial progress, a reason to believe that black men are no longer metonyms of threat. Thus, two conditions result: the dominant culture (racist patriarchy) both masks and perpetuates itself while, in the African American community, misogyny and homophobia are valorized as a normative state for anyone who would count himself as cool.

As a discourse constructed around notions of harmlessness, comedy is distinguished by its ability to dismantle the world, then partially reassemble it, for the purpose of challenging the status quo. But it can just as easily serve the more dubious social function of rendering that which we determine to be substantial politically inert. It can reverse the sign function of the most noxious event and make it an icon of safety and quiescence. Eddie Murphy's presence in the public sphere serves a quiescent function, to be sure, but what I also want to suggest is that even as his films allow us to chart the intersection of race and masculinity, it points with great certainty to the hegemony of white supremacist, capitalist patriarchy. For even as African American males continue to offer the mainstream media a means to represent violence and criminality in American culture, what is clear is that this only deflects attention away from violence, criminality, and sexism generated by patriarchal culture at large. Hence, though Eddie Murphy's films offer the viewer an opportunity to delight in the spectacle of public black manhood, what they point to, as Michael Awkward suggests, is "the manner in which marginalized men also participate in patriarchy even as . . . aspects of its socially sanctioned and sanctioning power are denied them" (96).

One needs to consider Eddie Murphy's career in the 1980s as a prelude to the commentary one could make in the 1990s on the requirements of African American masculinity in the public sphere. In the 1980s, Murphy was the incarnation of the classic African American trickster: he was by turns, elusive, outrageous, and irreverent. Flashing what became his trademark grin and engaging in laughter that simultaneously mocked and delighted his audiences, Murphy's box-office success was based on his ability, like Richard Pryor before him, to participate in the mainstream without being permanently affected by it.[34] If he manifested a concern with a "hard body," he did so because he knew African American men were potential targets. But in the present, the trickster has given way to more overt forms of masculine display. Situations that might have been resolved with wit and irony are, in the 1990s, more prone to be resolved through confrontation (often of a physical sort). Moreover, Murphy's solitude, his investment in a masculinity that can reproduce itself, has been replaced by the lure of affiliation—either by the group identity of gang culture or that which springs from the prominent display of a popular brand name. Perhaps the concept of brand names offers us the best way to locate Eddie Murphy in public space. Instantly recognizable, cool beyond reproach. Crossing over to remind us: Watch out! It's a jungle out there!

Notes

I gratefully acknowledge the assistance of Dr. Valerie S. Cade, Vice Provost for University Life, and Dr. Allen Green, Assistant Provost, who provided research support, in the form of a W. W. Smith Post-Doctoral Fellowship and a Minority Permanence Fund Research Grant, to complete this essay. Peter S. Vaughn, Acting Dean of the School of Social Work, was also an indispensable resource, particularly in the area of social work literature regarding masculinity. I also wish to thank Professors Rita Barnard, Craig Saper, Bob Perelman, and Dana Phillips, who provided invaluable insights on an earlier draft and encouraged me to pursue Eddie Murphy as a topic of scholarly inquiry. I am also grateful to Professor Adrienne Davis, who lent her considerable skills to the task of helping me to sharpen the clarity of my ideas. I also want to thank my research assistant, Charles Austin, for compiling a useful collection of articles on Eddie Murphy. Finally, I want to thank my wife, Lisa H. James-Beavers, Esq. for her suggestions on an earlier draft and her ideas on the film *Harlem Nights*, along with the unwavering support she has offered throughout the process of completing this essay, as well as Professor Rudolph Byrd, who served, as he always does, as a necessary sounding board and as a model of masculinity well worth emulating.

1. *Another 48 Hours*, dir. Walter Hill, Paramount Pictures and Eddy Murphy, 1990.

2. Murphy's reputation is, in 1996, somewhat diminished, but I would certainly argue that he is no less a highly recognizable figure in American public life.

3. The term "quiescence," which appears in the title, and throughout this essay, is intended to suggest the idea that it is possible to create both agreeability and satisfaction out of potentially volatile icons through the conscious manipulation of information as it resonates at the level of signs, symbols, myths, and social rituals. My use of the word is foregrounded in the work of political scientist, Murray Edelman. His two books, *The Symbolic Uses of Politics* and *Politics as Symbolic Action* are essential reading in the study of mass arousal and political apathy. As he observes, "Political quiescence . . . can be assumed to be a function either of lack of interest or of the satisfaction of whatever interest the quiescent group may have in the policy in question" (*Symbolic Uses* 22). My use of the term has a great deal to do with how I see a popular-cultural icon like Eddie Murphy functioning in cultural space: his visibility and the manner in which he has achieved and sustained it work out a drama whereby numerous constituencies reach a state of satisfaction within the arena of race relations.

4. *Dirty Harry*, dir. Don Siegel, Warner Brothers, 1971. My reading of Eastwood's films is profoundly influenced by Andrew Ross's reading of the TV Western, which functions in contradistinction to the actual history of "imperialist expansionism" that marked the "way West" in the nineteenth century ("Cowboys" 88).

5. As Kim Crenshaw, Angela Y. Davis, and Patricia Hill-Collins, among others, have argued, black women's oppression operates through the intersection of race, class, and gender. Indeed, Hill-Collins notes, "The assumptions on which full group membership are based—whiteness for feminist thought, maleness for Black social

and political thought, and the combination for mainstream scholarship—all negate a Black female reality" (12).

6. As Angela Y. Davis points out, the slave experience discouraged the notion of male supremacy in black men. What this implies is that the attempt to redress the wounds of slavery has led to a correlation between power and male supremacy, largely because African American males used European males as the paradigmatic vehicle for constructing a viable notion of manhood (Women, Race, and Class).

7. See bell hooks's Yearning: Race, Gender and Cultural Politics. As hooks has pointed out, it is an erroneous notion that racism and sexism are two radically different forms of oppression, where the eradication of racism can occur without a consideration of how sexism supports and sustains it. It is important for me to state here that this project owes its origins to my ongoing dialogue with bell hooks. She has, through writing and example, issued the call to which I here respond. More, her call for the serious interrogation of black masculinity is one which rests squarely within a dialogic space where men and women can challenge, through cooperation, the reified construct that stands for contemporary masculinity.

8. This issue is addressed in the excellent work of Isaac Julien and Kobena Mercer, particularly in an essay entitled "True Confessions: A Discourse on Images of Black Male Sexuality." This essay and others that address issues of sexuality, masculinity, and race can be found in Essex Hemphill and Joseph Beam's very fine collection of fiction, poetry, and essays, Brother to Brother: New Writings by Black Gay Men. It is here that I find voices attempting to reconfigure black masculinity.

9. To borrow from Antony Easthope's examples of the cartoon character's body that continually reconstitutes itself: the black male body, while under assault from racial victimization, can easily remake itself as subject within the spheres of gender or sexuality by either victimizing black women or gay men. Indeed, black masculinity is often formulated around notions of purity, where blackness is indicative of potency—of a social and sexual sort (What a Man's Gotta Do 41).

10. Crenshaw's talk (University of Pennsylvania Law School, 1992) has been extremely helpful because of the manner in which she articulates, through her analysis of the Anita Hill–Clarence Thomas affair, the nature of black women's intersectionality. The Hill-Thomas affair, as spectacle, works out Hill's marginality in the racial sphere because she is not male and is unable to invoke the lynching trope that worked so successfully for Thomas, and she is marginal in the gender sphere because, as a black woman breaking silence about an abusive situation, she does not have the same kind of narrative currency as a white woman who is able to invoke the rape trope. See also Crenshaw, "Mapping the Margins" and "Whose Story." I use Crenshaw's work as a means of opening up the idea of intersectionality in the discussion of black men.

11. See also Richard Majors and Janet Mancini Billson, Cool Pose, which carries the findings of the original article into a wider field and thus to a more pointed conclusion.

12. In her book, The Body in Pain, Elaine Scarry establishes a relation between the

body and the voice that is important to my discussion here. She refers to the "language of agency," which, in its more confusing gestures, "conflates pain with power." What I want to suggest is that black men talking about the wages of racism, as an instance where their bodies are made to suffer, can simultaneously render invisible sexism as a form of bodily recuperation.

13. We have seen in recent years the increase in advertising aimed at the black community that aligns cool with the ability to consume. The marketing of malt liquor, cigarettes, and spirits is often driven by the depiction of upwardly mobile men who are affluent, virile, and sophisticated. These ads often situate the female body within their discourse, where consumption will make the male body the object of the female gaze. Cool, here, is a signifier of potency and resistance.

14. See also Cornel West (with bell hooks), "Black Men and Women" 10.

15. 48 Hours, dir. Walter Hill, Paramount Pictures, 1982; Beverly Hills Cop, dir. Martin Brest, Paramount Pictures; Beverly Hills Cop II, dir. Tony Scott, Paramount Pictures and Eddy Murphy, 1987.

16. Richard Pryor Live in the Sunset Strip, dir. Joe Layton, Columbia Pictures and Raystar, 1982; Richard Pryor in Concert, dir. Jeff Margolis, Special Event Entertainment, 1979.

17. Trading Places, dir. John Landis, Paramount Pictures, 1983. While this is an ironic turn, the film never interrogates this break; Murphy's character feels no dissonance over the break, choosing instead to bond with the white characters in the film. This works out, in the Reagan/Bush 80's, the manner in which blackness was transformed from an icon of collective threat to individual opportunity where one person's accomplishments symbolize racial harmony and progress.

18. As Bogle observes, Pryor's career undergoes a profound change, where he moves from being the "Crazy Nigger, who spoke in the language and idiom of the street" to a more domesticated version, where he was repackaged, and prevented from "[speaking] for America's underclass. [Finally being] removed altogether from that class structure and surrounded by white co-stars" (258, 280).

19. Perhaps the ultimate sign of this is Pryor's current affliction with multiple sclerosis. As a comedian who foregrounded his comedic style via his use of the body, this seems a cruel irony. Though I do not take the issue of Pryor's illness up here, I plan to take the issue up in a later essay devoted to Pryor's recent autobiography, Pryor Convictions.

20. Easthope draws the analogy that the masculine ego is like DaVinci's design for a fortress, one whose impregnability was based on its numerous contingencies against encroachment, rather than its ability to withstand attack from without. Hence, the plan was designed, not to repel, but rather to handle the failure of its defensive postures within (37–40).

21. Clearly African American men are involved in developmental issues than emanate from the notion that a racist society prevents black men from performing adult roles to the same extent as their white counterparts. Control of one's life, accepting

responsibility, are signs of adult status. As the freebasing routine in *Richard Pryor Live in the Sunset Strip* dramatizes, addiction is Pryor's abdication of adult responsibility.

22. One may also think about Pryor's brief, but controversial, foray into commercial television. At the end of one episode, after explaining that he had not had to give up anything of great consequence in order to perform on television, the camera pulled back to reveal Pryor in a body suit that was intended to portray his castration by the network. The show was canceled soon after. But I cite this incident to suggest that Pryor gave black audiences, particularly men, an image of their social status.

23. As Chris Weedon would argue, however, female sexuality, as a discourse that occurs in the presence of the more dominant discourse of male sexuality, functions as a reversal or alternative form of subjectivity for women. But this depends on women's acceptance of this fact, as opposed to their acceptance of patriarchal norms that construct the manner in which the female body functions during the sexual act. Because so many women, Weedon suggests, are unaware of the ways that institutions fix male and female difference as both hierarchical and naturally constituted, it is difficult to dislodge the notion of male superordinance except through the adoption of a radical posture that rejects this notion.

24. *Raw*, dir. Robert Townsend, Paramount Pictures, 1987; *Coming to America*, dir. John Landis, Paramount Pictures, 1988; *Harlem Nights*, dir. Eddie Murphy, Eddy Murphy, 1989.

25. Consider the fact that in *Raw*, Murphy compares the search for the "right woman" with a crap game, ostensibly dangerous because of the AIDS threat, but in actuality dangerous because one might end up with a woman who detracts from his status as a virile sex symbol. At one point in the routine he says, "Come on. I want the perfect woman, now! Intelligent with a mind, nice ass and a body." Murphy suggests, then, that intelligence is meaningful only when it is connected with physicality.

26. It is also important to note that Dominique LaRue identifies herself as Creole. Hence, Murphy suggests that she is not "purely" black because, as such, she rests on the margins of both races. Her status as a racial mongrel justifies Quick's actions.

27. As the film ends, Quick and Ray look at the New York City skyline and express their regret at having to leave Harlem. What is interesting is that Harlem is conflated to become the skyline, which is a geographical and historical distortion. However, within the film's logic, because white men have attempted to infringe upon black space, that black space has retaliated and subsumed total control.

28. A contemporary example of this can be found in the testimony offered during the Anita Hill–Clarence Thomas hearings by John Doggett. Doggett attempted to "close ranks" by suggesting that Hill was, indeed, a black woman out of control.

29. Foucault discusses the evolution of this relation in an essay entitled, "Sexuality and Solitude," in *On Signs*. I find useful Foucault's description of what he calls, "technologies of the self" and his assertion that, with the Augustinian delineation of the struggle between the libido and the will, Western technologies of the self (or subject) have increasingly become invested in a "permanent hermeneutics of oneself."

When we consider Eddie Murphy's *Raw*, for example, the routines are generated, in part, from his dramatization of the struggle between the libido and the will: what results is that the body is fragmented (hence, his declaration that women want "Half!"). The solitude he achieves at the end of *Harlem Nights* represents the successful defense against incursions into the body.

30. Easthope's point that male banter is often the means by which men express their love for one another is well taken here. However, when gender and race intersect, I would argue that banter serves a slightly different function: In this instance, the racial Other (Murphy) is constructed as being highly adept at the wisecrack, which in the films I mention serves the function of transgression. The "therapeutic force" I allude to has much to do with the way the wisecrack brings clarity to a situation, provides a model for whites to emulate. It also works out the manner in which Murphy's characters bear the responsibility of injecting "soul" into an otherwise "impotent" encounter.

31. My intention here is not one of essentializing the black male cinematic gaze, but rather one of suggesting that cinematic vehicles like *Boomerang*, which are directed and produced by African American filmmakers, while perhaps a demonstration of cinematic skill and progress in the area of multicultural filmmaking, are not necessarily invested in a cinematic project whose purpose it is to disrupt the African American nationalist narrative. See Isaac Julien's essay "Black Is, Black Ain't."

32. What makes this so strange is that, as visual representation of African American corporate enterprise that "has it going on," the all-black staff would seem to represent the ideal situation, one that the African American community would regard as positive. However, the presence of women at the head of the company, making decisions that negatively affect men, means that such a corporate endeavor is contaminated, rendered ineffective. In what amounts to "cutting off [our] noses, to spite [our faces]," the Hudlin brothers intimate that patriarchy requires a closing of ranks, a sacrifice of professional accomplishment in order for patriarchal order to be restored.

33. In short, this film works out a romanticized version of African American community that is in keeping with the Hollywood tradition of creating all-black casts in social settings that in banishing whites nonetheless reinscribes the anxiety about racial inferiority so powerfully that the impulse to depict the "best" of the race is too strong to ignore.

34. While I do not go into the matter here, Richard Pryor has abdicated his role as the most visible African American comedian because he has been afflicted by multiple sclerosis. What is ironic is that the very instrument that made his comedy so memorable has failed him. Though Bill Cosby continues to have mass appeal, he has made his comedic mark by portraying the successful patriarch, to the point where he published books on fatherhood and relationships that attempt to transcend racial barriers. Murphy's recent marriage and entry into parenthood have displaced him from his previous place as the wild and cool bachelor, and thus as transgressive figure, making him difficult to locate in the African American comedy spectrum. In an interview in

Gentleman's Quarterly, Murphy talked about wanting to become a "black Cary Grant." As his films, *The Sophisticated Gentleman* and *Beverly Hills Cop 3* would suggest, he is no longer the crossover draw he was in the 1980s, though there is reason to believe that he remains popular with African American audiences.

It would seem that given the weak box-office draw of films like *Vampire in Brooklyn* and *The Nutty Professor,* even though they display Murphy's comedic prowess, they still suggest that Murphy's career will take a turn that one might conjecture will take him to the same place as his nemesis Bill Cosby—that is, into family-oriented entertainment that deemphasizes sex and violence, especially since Murphy's public image is now that of a father and husband as opposed to that of a playboy.

THE WHITE MAN'S MUSCLES

RICHARD DYER

Serge Nubret, now one of the best-known figures in bodybuilding, was around 1960 a very handsome young man with an astonishingly developed champion physique. About the same time, between 1958 and 1965, the Italian cinema produced a cycle of adventure films centered on heroes drawn from classical antiquity played by U.S. bodybuilders, a cycle that has come to be known as the *peplum*.[1] Yet, though he was no less handsome, no less a champion, and no less competent a thespian than, say, Steve Reeves or Reg Park, Serge Nubret never had the starring role in a peplum.

Nubret was a Guadeloupean of African descent, which is to say that he was a black Frenchman.[2] It may seem self evident that such a person would not be the star of Italian films featuring U.S. men, yet neither his nationality nor his color were inevitable barriers. Postwar Italian cinema made frequent use of non-Italian stars; indeed, as Christopher Wagstaff has pointed out,[3] few male Italian film actors became stars in this period (apart from comedians). French stars were often used (notably Henri Vidal in the most successful postwar epic before the peplum cycle, *Fabiola* [1948]), and many pepla were coproductions with, especially, France and/or Spain but also Egypt, Germany, Monaco, Tunisia, and Yugoslavia. Nor did the stars of pepla have in reality to be American, it was enough that they seem so, by virtue of physique, hairstyle, and, above all, name. While many were indeed American—Steve Reeves, Gordon Scott, Gordon Mitchell, Mickey Hargitay—many were not, yet appeared to be. This is not just a question of niceties, such as assuming a Canadian (Samson Burke) or a Briton (Reg Park, Joe Robinson) to be American, but of Italians changing their names (Adriano di Venezia becoming Kirk Morris; Sergio Ciani becoming Alan Steel), and moreover U.S. bodybuilders adopting if need be more American sounding, that is, Anglo names, so that even the Italian-American Lou Degni became Mark Forrest, while Ed Holovchik became Ed Fury.

Being neither Italian nor American need not have prevented Serge Nubret from being cast as a peplum hero. Nor, on the face of it, need his color. Black men had become established bodybuilding competitors during the 1950s, and in 1960 both Nubret and Paul Wynter won (different) Mr. Universe competitions (but both only played secondary roles in pepla); there were champion black physiques around and they were accepted as such. Nor is it unimaginable that an Italian audience could ever accept a black hero. On the contrary: one of the heroes of the enormously popular turn-of-the-century novels of Emilio Salgari was Moko, "the 'coal-black confederate' in sagas of Antillian corsairs, who resolved impossible situations through his strength" (Valperga 68; my translation),[4] while Maciste, when first introduced as a character (in the film *Cabiria* [1914]), was black (albeit played by an Italian, Bartolomeo Pagano). However, in the later films of this cycle, Maciste/Pagano appeared white as did the other musclemen stars (e.g., Luciano Albertini, Carlo Aldini).

Nothing in the production process or, at first glance, the market prohibited the use of a black bodybuilder in a starring role in a peplum in the late 1950s and early 1960s. All the same, the failure to use one (especially ones as otherwise ideal as Nubret and Wynter) indicates that the peplum hero indeed had to be white, that the promotion of his heroic masculinity was a specifically white project. In this, his whiteness, the peplum hero is of a piece with the heroes of two other groups of muscleman films, the Tarzan series and the contemporary run of films with Dolph Lundgren, Arnold Schwarzenegger, Sylvester Stallone, Jean-Claude Van Damme, and others. The peplum hero shares with these figures other, and related, attributes: a built body constantly on display and colonial adventures. Indeed, these kinds of films are the only ones (outside of pornography) where white male bodies are always displayed throughout, whereas non-white male bodies, in these and other genres (Westerns, plantation and jungle films, musicals) are routinely exposed to the view.

My concern in this essay is to consider this exceptional presentation of the white male body as spectacle in film, when the body is a built one and the setting colonial. Why is it only then that white men's bodies have been regularly on show? What does this suggest about the cultural body of white masculinity? I shall concentrate on the peplum on the principle that issues of representation have to be grounded in discussion that respects the historical and textual specificity of cultural production. The differences between muscleman films are important, suggesting different moments in the history of white masculinity: Tarzan movies with their concern over white man's relation to nature; contemporary films springing from anxieties about the role of the male body in bureaucratized, corporatized, technologized worlds, be they "Vietnam" or future dystopias. Yet, while stressing the specificity of

Figure 1. Serge Nubret.

the peplum, I also suggest some characteristics applicable to all muscleman films and even to most constructions of white masculinity. Accordingly I shall begin by discussing some formal and contextual aspects of the peplum as they relate to a construction of white masculinity, before discussing at greater length two aspects — body image, colonial narrativity — which could and should be applied (with an eye to differences as well as similarities) to other images of white men.

This question of specificity and generality has a particular edge in discussing white male cultural production, which still constitutes the vast majority of all cultural production in the West. It is methodologically important to insist on the particularity of white masculinities, but this should not lead one to suppose that there are simply lots of different ways in which white men are represented, that there is no identity and no concomitant position of power to white masculinity. It is the ability to pass themselves off as not particular that allows them to go on being, within the regime of representation that they produce, "invisible." [5] We have to learn to see the generality of white masculinity even while respecting the historicity and textuality of any particular manifestation of it.

In this section, I shall first give a brief account of the peplum genre, and then relate it to two aspects of its historical context: the contemporaneous situation of working-class men, the films' primary addressees, and the fascist period (recent at the time of the films' making) to which the genre makes ambiguous reference. Both contexts yield constructions of white masculinity: the first has to do with the value of male physical power in working class cultures; the second, with the importance of the strong male leader in fascist rhetoric.

Peplum films may be defined as adventure films centered on heroes drawn from classical (including biblical) antiquity played by U.S. bodybuilders. As characters played by these performers, they already embody the white past and future. Classical antiquity was still unchallenged as racially white,[6] and Europeans tend to see the United States as basically a white nation with colorful marginalia. Moreover, classical antiquity, still a material presence in Italy, was also assumed to be the pinnacle of all human achievement, while the United States was widely felt to be the land of the human future. The values associated with classicism and Americanism as they relate to white masculinity will be discussed as I go along.

Most of the peplum heroes figure in ancient texts (Hercules, Spartacus, Theseus, Ulysses, Achilles, Samson, and Goliath [as hero not villain]), but two of the most important are modern inventions: Ursus in the novel and the films of *Quo vadis?* and, most widely used of all, Maciste, created for *Cabiria* in 1914. None of these heroes remain tied to the diegetic place and time of their first appearance: Hercules, Maciste, and the rest appear in numerous other situations, far removed from their own original stories. The whole of the ancient world was drawn upon; new fantasy lands were invented; even the postclassical world was not out of the question, Maciste showing up, for instance, in thirteenth-century Asia (*Maciste alla corte del Gran Khan*),[7] in seventeenth-century Scotland (*Maciste all'inferno*), in China (*Maciste contro i Mongoli*), Arabia (*Maciste contro lo sceicco*), and Russia (*Maciste alla corte dello Zar*), as well as in non-European ancient worlds, for example, Africa (*Maciste nelle miniere del re Salomone*) and Central America (*Maciste il vendicatore dei Mayas, Ercole contro i figli del sole*). Such is the freedom of construction in the cycle that the heroes, originally grounded in different eras and textual traditions (legend, history, romance), can be brought together as comrades (*Ercole, Sansone, Maciste ed Ursus gli invincibili*) or antagonists (*Ulisse contro Ercole, Ercole sfida Sansone*). The coordinates of space and time get looser still when one recognizes how sets and costumes that are prehistoric in one film show up in Roman times in another, or when one sees the films in English-dubbed versions, where distributors often randomly substituted the heroes' names for one another.

This exuberant spirit of collage is undoubtedly explicable in terms of both production and consumption patterns. Although some films were expensive by Italian standards, many were not. Sets tend to look like sets, they and the costumes were reused, rehearsal time was minimal, many of the cast could not understand each other, and the voices one hears are seldom those of the people one sees (even in the original Italian versions). The principal destination of these films were inner-city and rural cinemas and touring film shows, where they were watched, as Christopher Wagstaff has argued of such *terza visione* exhibition in general, more as television is watched, people dropping in and out of the cinema, moving seats, socializing (see Wagstaff). The films drew upon popular traditions of the strongman acts in piazzas, circuses, fairs, and *varietà* that were still familiar to this audience (see Farassino and Sanguineti). Such conditions of production and consumption do not encourage the kind of finished, developmental forms of "classical Hollywood cinema," with its premium on coherence of plot, plausibility of character and setting, consistency of tone. Rather, what can be done and what works are set pieces of action and display, immediately and vividly recognizable characters and settings, and the principle of variety: feats, dances, playlets, slapstick, speeches, tableaux.

This makes a certain kind of cinema possible. I am not thinking here of the kind of abandonment of reason (plausibility, decorum) that the surrealists so much valued in popular cinema and that informs the early French critical championing of the peplum, so much as certain textual consequences relevant to the question of white masculinity.

Given the hero-performers' ignorance (in the main) of Italian, their inexperience as actors, their limited availability, it has clearly often been easier to keep them out of filming that involves interaction with others. The clearest examples of this are two identical sequences in *Maciste contro i mostri* (1962) and *Maciste il vendicatore dei Mayas* (1965), in which a young heterosexual couple in prehistoric times are menaced by a monster until Maciste suddenly appears and throws a spear between its eyes to kill it. The couple, the lake setting, the monster, all the actual shots are the same in both films, except that, through editing, different Macistes (Reg Lewis and Kirk Morris) intervene. He never appears in a shot with the couple or the monster and hence can be substituted at will. This is an extreme instance, but one might note such proceedings as the following: Hercules at the liberation of Thebes in *Ercole e la regina di Lidia* is occupied wrestling a tiger in a pit rather than joining with the other men sacking the city; Maciste's plight, knocked out and buried alive, eclipses the revolt of the people in *Maciste alla corte del Gran Khan*; the climax of *Maciste contro i mostri* consists of a fight between two tribal chiefs with Maciste watching on; the second half of *Le fatiche di Ercole* is devoted to Jason and the Golden Fleece, Hercules going along as indispensable helper but Jason's quest the one that propels the narrative. Time and again the hero is kept to one side of the narrative, whether its detailed unfolding through editing or its larger segmental organization.

There are two points about such narrational devices. One is that they permit the set pieces of posing that follow from casting bodybuilders. The latter are not necessarily agile or acrobatic; the point is their size and shape, frozen in moments of maximum tension. Holding a boulder aloft, in a clinch with a lion, these and many other setups incorporate not only the posing vocabulary of bodybuilding competitions but also the mise-en-scènes of such non-narrative forms as physique photography and the strongman acts. The peplum's collage structure showcases the built body and the values it carries.

Second, keeping the hero to one side of the narrative chain is of a piece with the ambiguity of his ontological status. Is the peplum hero human? Hercules is explicitly and traditionally not entirely so—he is half-god, half-human, a status explored in some films (*Le fatiche di Ercole, Ercole e la regina di Lidia, Ercole alla conquista di Atlantide*); Maciste, a slave in the original *Cabiria*, announces his parents were the sun and the moon in *Maciste contro i mostri*; Crios in *Arrivano i Titani*, is a Titan, a demigod. Even when nothing as explicit is suggested, many of the heroes seem not quite human, not least in their capacity to leap time and space to be where needed, a capacity that is never explained (Maciste's sudden loinclothed appearance at a Scottish witch burning in *Maciste all'inferno* is the most glorious example). Their introduction into the film often has a magical quality. Frequently the hero is discovered by water—the sea, a waterfall—as if he were born of it. In *Le fatiche di Ercole* Hercules asks to be deprived of his immortality, and the granting of this is symbolized in his being drenched in rain, reborn in water as human. The first shot of Maciste in *Maciste nella terra dei ciclopi* has him lying on a stone by the sea in a beam of light in a pose echoing the Adam of Michelangelo in the Sistine Chapel (an image less foreign to anyone who has been through the Italian school system than it might be to others). Such imagery is, of course, Christian (and white)—baptismal water, Genesis. Yet if this insists on the heroes' humanity, other things—their freedom from historical and geographic coordinates, the way they are not fully implicated in the investments of the narrative—make them superhuman. They are both of (male) humanity and above it.

This construction becomes especially interesting in relation to two aspects of the films' historical context: changes in peasant and working-class male labor and the fresh memory of fascism. The class significance of the peplum hero may be understood by considering the significance of male physical strength in the culture of the films' original audiences. The strongman image was rooted, as Giuseppe Valperga shows, in the cultural traditions of rural Italy. In addition to their popularity in entertainments and popular novels, they also had religious and local significance. Veneration and invocation of saints is an important element in Catholic devotion, and in peasant communities there was a special fondness for St. Christopher, the giant who in legend carried Christ on his shoulders. Equally, big, strong men were important figures in peasant communities—giant boy babies were a source of wide interest, seen as a blessing, not least because their strength was of the greatest economic significance in rural labor. In this context big male bodies were a resource of the first importance,[8] and what they could do often suggested props for strongman acts: boulders, tree trunks, carts, and chains.

However, the period of the peplum is also a period of mass internal migration in Italy, from the rural South to the industrial North, from a labor based on strength to one based on skill with machines (or, failing that, shitwork). In the shift away from rural labor, the value of the big, strong body, and the male prestige that went along with it, was undermined. The peplum celebrates that body. The very emphasis on the simple display of muscle, fore-grounded by the films' collage structure, and the heroes' triumphs through their deployment of those muscles, are an affirmation of the value of strength to an audience who was finding that it no longer had such value. Often, too, the hero is shown in conflict with machines, winning against elaborate war gadgetry (*La battaglia di Maratona, Il colosso di Rodi*), freeing people from giant wheels that have to be endlessly, mindlessly turned by hordes of men (*Nel segno di Roma, Sette contro tutti, Maciste l'uomo più forte del mondo*). His triumph over the machine by body alone offers the audience a fantasy of triumph over their new conditions of labor in terms of their traditional resources.

For this audience, there was a significance in these bodies being white ones. People from the South in Italy are pejoratively considered "nero" (black) by those in the North. Awareness of this can only have been intensified by both the experience of South-North migration and the spread of North-centered media (especially television) throughout the country in the postwar years. More generally, the specter of immigrant, that is, Third World labor, and the threat it posed to the indigenous working class, was also beginning to be evoked in Europe: the "race problem" in Britain and France could not but have resonances in a country like Italy with a colonial past and geographical prox-imity to the Third World. (Rightly or wrongly, many in any case considered the South and Sicily virtually Third World countries.) If Maciste, Hercules, and others were to be their primary audience's identification figures, they had to champion both physical labor and its appropriateness to white men.

The peplum heroes are in many ways down-to-earth, good humored, easy-going, fond of a drink, and, at heart, family men. Yet they are also sort-of divine characters played by Americans. If they speak to the realities of their initial audiences and in many particulars seem to be of them, they are also above them. This is one of the structures of feeling that suggests continuities between the peplum and fascism.

Fascism had lasted in Italy over twenty years, twice as long as in Germany; in 1960, when the peplum was at a peak, fascism's demise was only fifteen years past. It was fresh in the memory and a reference point, although not a theme, in cinema. Apart from the brief period of neorealism, itself born of antifascism, it was not until the 1970s that Italy's internationally renowned *autori* (Bertolucci, Cavani, Fellini, Pasolini, Rosi, Wertmüller) started to make films about fascism. Popular cinema, more mindful of the need to address a large national audience where it stood and less inhibited by questions of what the right thing to say was, characteristically did deal with fascism, di-rectly and indirectly in comedy, and in the peplum.

Italian fascism's imagery of masculinity centered on monumentalist imagery and, above all, Mussolini, Il Duce. The regime did produce the kind of massive statuary and painting (especially frescoes and posters) featuring big men in aspirant postures that is also associated with Nazism. One stadium in Rome was surrounded at intervals at the back of the seating by statues three times life-size of muscular naked men in white stone (Felice and Goglia 211). Sportsmen, notably 1932 heavyweight champion Primo Carnera (who appears as an antagonist in Ercole e la regina di Lidia), were promoted as emblematic of the regime and subject matter for artists, including the photographer Elio Luxardo (Milano 21, 413), and increased sporting facilities and gymnastic displays were important aspects of policy (Abruzzese 65; Felice and Goglia 184–87). Yet such imagery, though important, was not saturating and, notably, it was almost absent from the cinema: the one attempt to harness the epic tradition to fascist ends, Scipione l'Africano (1937), did not use a muscleman as hero and was not a great success (Hay 155–61; Dalle Vacche 27–49). Scipione was, however, especially in the attendant publicity and reviews, obvious in its reference to Mussolini, for he was the supreme hero figure of the regime. Indeed, as a child wrote in one of the essays elicited by the film journal Bianco e nero, when Scipione first appeared: "Era bello Scipione sul suo cavallo bianco. Però il Duce è ancora più bello e più bravo di Scipione." [How handsome Scipio was on his white horse. But il Duce is even more handsome and brave than Scipio] (qtd. in Brunetta 77; my translation). Mussolini, as Gian Piero Brunetta and James Hay have both observed, was the Maciste of fascist Italy.[9] He was both, as it were, narratively and iconographically. His role in the story of Italy was that of the strongman (physically, morally, temperamentally) who could sort out the country's problems: unemployment, corruption, inefficiency. It is only in the mid-thirties that this becomes tied up with questions of Italy's greatness measured imperially (realized in the war with Ethiopia) and racially (the passing of anti-Semitic legislation in 1938). Iconographically, as Hay (227–29) details, Mussolini drew his gestures from silent screen heroes and his emblematic roles (warrior, builder, patriarch) from the fascist repertoire. Most significantly here, he promoted these qualities through his body, in his stature and posture (aided by camera angles) when clothed, in the very display of himself when unclothed. He posed for photographs as a swimmer, athlete, or bare-chested skier (Felice and Goglia 82, 88); he appeared stripped to the waist working alongside peasants for photographs (very Maciste-like, in Felice and Goglia 141) and in the newsreel film Il Duce trebbia il grano nell'Agro Pontino (Il Duce threshes wheat in the Pontine Fields) (1938); he was the model for the imperative that everyone should have the body of a twenty-year-old (to the point that he forbade publication of his date of birth [Milano 32]).

The relation of the peplum to this fascist image of the male body is complex and contradictory. A given film may seem to be both denouncing and applauding fascism. *Ercole contro Roma*, for instance, establishes Hercules's Greekness with unusual thoroughness and has him come to the rescue of the ordinary Italian people through the good offices of an Arab merchant-cum-messenger; yet the enemy of the people is a usurper called, unbelievably, Afro, and what Hercules finally restores is a militaristic regime in which the legionaries elect the leader. Thus, he is against Rome in the name of Rome.

Such contradictions are characteristic. In many ways, in explicit allusions and through certain distancing effects, the cycle is a rejection of fascism. Yet in its address and narrative organization it also shows continuities with fascism, or perhaps with even longer continuities, which fascism fed on as much as it promoted. Rather than attempt to side the peplum (and by implication its audience) either with or against fascism, it should be seen as an imaginary working through of the shameful momentousness of the period, shameful because it was fascist and/or because it was defeated.

Where there is explicit reference to fascism in the peplum, it is hostile. This is often expressed iconographically. The obviously fascistic regime of Atlantis in *Ercole alla conquista di Atlantide*, breeding a flaxen-haired master race of men,[10] is emblematized in a vast Atlas-like statue in the queen's underground palace; the giant male statue bestriding the harbor entrance in *Il colosso di Rodi* is an object of hate, serving as a prison for dissidents and aimed at strategic dominance of the Mediterranean; the work camp in *Il trionfo dei dieci Gladiatori* is reminiscent of Nazi concentration camps.[11] References to Rome are often coded references to fascism, because of the importance of Rome in fascist rhetoric (distinctive because, even now, Italy is not a highly centralized country pivoted on a capital city — the fascist emphasis on Rome was both part of its modernizing attempt at centralization and a bid to suggest its continuity with the empire of ancient Rome). Arena displays make oblique reference to the regime's mass spectacles.

More generally, peplum societies are characterized by cruel authoritarianism, with rulers who have usurped power by force and trickery while often (by no means always) having the support of the hoodwinked people. Their aims can be avowedly racial: "Inferior races must be subjugated to us" says the evil ruler in *Maciste il vendicatore dei Mayas*; "If we do not contaminate the purity of our race,[12] one day we will be masters of the world," says his equivalent

Figure 2. Steve Reeves.

in *Sette contro tutti*. Commonly the hero restores "rightful," that is, traditional authority or else leaves the society on the brink of democracy. Significantly, unlike Mussolini, the hero is never himself a ruler.

To this conscious if vague antifascism, we may add two important points that further seem to distance the peplum from fascism. First, the very absence of Maciste and others from the cinema under fascism and hence the revival of these prefascist heroes in the peplum, would suggest that if there was harking back to the past it was to a past that Mussolini had displaced. The "interpretation of fascism as a momentary 'perversion' or 'deviation', as a parenthesis in Italian history," with real Italianness to be found in earlier cultural continuities, was widely canvased at the time (Cannella 12) and would accord with this rediscovery of the prefascist figures of Maciste and others.

Second, the casting of U.S., or U.S.-seeming, bodybuilders is crucial. It should be stressed that it is not just that these performers were presumed to be U.S., but that they looked U.S. The style of the built body was set by U.S. bodybuilders in the postwar period (and especially by Steve Reeves [Sanguineti 88]) and the peplum stars' haircuts are those of Dean, Brando, and Presley. (This is sometimes emphasized in the contrast between the hero and his chief helper among the people: in *Ercole contro i figli del sole*, both Hercules and Maita, the Incan warrior he befriends, are spectacularly well built, but Maita has straight, shoulder-length hair and a headband, whereas Hercules sports the quiff and sheen of a rock star.) The significance of this is, above all, that they were not Italian. Here was the display of the muscular male body, promoted in Italian society only fifteen years previously, stripped at a stroke of its fascist connotations. To this one should add the importance of the United States in the popular imagination in Italy, something that was both exploited by fascism but also served as a talisman on the left. U.S. soldiers had spearheaded the liberation of Italy from Nazi occupation at the end of the war.[13] The United States was a land of modernity, as evident in these technologically honed, scientifically fed, machinelike bodies. It was the land of the Common Man. Not least, it was a land of mass Italian emigration.

Yet for all its explicit antifascism, its heroes who are not rulers and its use of prefascist figures realized in non-Italian bodies, the peplum also deploys fascistic structures of feeling. Some of these were not necessarily invented by the fascists. As Abruzzese argues, "the national socialist use of the body has much deeper roots than the Mussolinian exaltation of the athlete" (65; my translation), reaching back well into the nineteenth century; Maciste in the 1914 *Cabiria* prefigures the monumental incarnations of Primo Carnera and the regime's statuary. The regime had available a repertoire of images very congenial to it and, by the time of the peplum, strongly associated with it. Moreover, though there were no Macistes during the fascist period, the regime had no need of them—it had Mussolini. Key aspects of the peplum— its address, the organization of its narrative world, to say nothing of the hero's body—all suggest continuities with fascism.

These continuities are evident from a consideration of the regime's one epic, *Scipione l'Africano*, even though Scipio is no muscleman and the film's avowedly imperialist narrative is seldom found in the cycle. Nevertheless, he is a hero who is never wrong, never greatly in difficulty, and, like Mussolini, like Hercules or Maciste, the only answer to the problems at hand. Moreover, Scipio is not really offered as a figure for the audience to identify with: for that the spectator has "common man" figures in crowd scenes, lovers in subplots that show the impact of war, or simply the masses. Hay traces this back to prefascist film spectacles, where through "throngs of extras, mass audiences were given a stake in the films' action" but in terms of a presence "for whom the central characters acted" (152). The interests of ordinary people are met, and are only able to be met, by the strongman. The way the peplum keeps the hero to one side of the narrative reinforces this sense that what is at stake in the narrative are the tribulations of the people, solved by the intervention of the hero. The fact that the hero, unlike Scipio or Il Duce, is not a ruler is part of the films' rejection of fascist polity even while it replays fascism's appeal.

Scipione sets up its world in terms of light versus dark, the brilliant forums and bright daylight of the Roman world against the gutteringly lit palaces and thick nighttime darkness of the Carthaginians, "our" invigorating simplicity versus "their" savage barbarianism and Orientalist decadence. In other words, quite apart from its explicit imperialist message, *Scipione* structures its world in colonialist terms. I discuss these in the peplum at greater length below. Here I want to pick up on two of the contradictions in representation that ensue from the peplum's genuine avowed antifascism and its fascist habits of perception.

Peplum societies are often ones of machinating, decadent, and deviant rule, embodied in the person of an evil female ruler. Often this queen may be associated with the fascism of autocracy, eugenics, slaughter of the weak, and mass enslavement, yet the ways in which she is represented are exactly those of the Carthaginian queen Sofonisba in *Scipione* and bad women in fascist ideology in general. The ideal fascist woman was "optimally round and robust"; a "concern with the figure and with thinness" were strongly discouraged (Caldwell 113). In pepla, however, it is these narratively fascist women who display the very characteristics fascists disapproved of in women: elaborate costumes, nipped-in waists, glittery and curlicued makeup and hairdos. Along with this unfascist body ideal and the fact of being rulers, these queens compound their unnaturalness by, sometimes, a readiness to have their children sacrificially slain to further their ambitions and, always, by their expressing overwhelming sexual desire for the hero. In all these ways — body image, (lack of) maternity, libido — they are the antithesis of the hero's woman, whose soft, round shape is enhanced by billowing dresses, who displays maternal care to children and chaste love toward the hero. The gendered moral economy of fascism remains intact in pepla.

This leads to another interesting contradiction, which, I want to stress, does not mean that the peplum is "really" fascist but that it is, precisely, contradictory. In *Ercole alla conquista di Atlantide* wicked Antinea oversees the breeding of a race of ideal men; when she encounters Hercules she, of course, realizes that here is the ultimate specimen of ideal manhood; Hercules is opposed to this fascist regime but Reg Park's muscles embody its very ideals. The appeal of this body type, especially with renewed force in a period of class upheaval, remains throughout the peplum in tension with the memory of its exaltation in the disgraceful recent past.

The peplum deployed a form that promoted the ready and enthusiastic display of the male body, celebrating the worth of the strong white body to an audience for whom its worth was increasingly uncertain, and addressing, in a highly contradictory fashion, the championing of that body in recent political history. These are culturally and historically specific aspects of the peplum's construction of the white male body (though I imagine parallels could be drawn). I turn now to considering, first separately, then together, the two regular conditions for white male body display in mainstream cinema: a built body and a colonial narrative. My instance will continue to be the peplum, but the formulations will suggest generalizable characteristics.

A naked body is a vulnerable body. This is so in the most fundamental sense — the bare body has no protection from the elements — but also in a social sense. Clothes are bearers of prestige, notably of wealth, status, and class: to be without them is to lose prestige. Nakedness also reveals the inadequacies of most bodies by comparison with social ideals of both the female and male body. Paradoxically, it may also reveal the relative similarity of male and female, white and "other" bodies, undo the remorseless insistences on difference and concomitant power carried by clothes and grooming. All of this applies to women as well as men, to non-white as well as white — but white men, far from being displaced from the center of discourse by a myriad of postmodern voices, continue to predominate in the control of the image. It is their bodily vulnerability that matters.

This does not mean that it is surprising that there is any representation at all of the white male body as spectacle. The promulgation of ego ideals, the desire to attract women, the appeal of (acknowledged or not) homoeroticism, the human pleasures in showing off and grooming (not so frowned on in men in Italian culture), the reality of heterosexual women as media consumers, all ensure that a white male heterosexual media industry will nonetheless produce representations of the white male body. Yet for this industry the vulnerability of the body remains disturbing. It is for these reasons that the body must be built.[14]

A built body bears a number of connotations that address both the gender and the racial dimensions of the naked white male body's vulnerability. First, a built body is hard and contoured. Bodybuilding has three goals: mass (muscle size), definition (the clarity with which one muscle group stands out from another), and proportion (the visual balance between all the body's muscle groups). The first two of these present a look of hardness: the skin stretched over pumped-up muscle creates a taut surface; the separation of groups seems, as bodybuilding jargon has it, to "cut" into the body as into stone. Definition and proportion also emphasize contour, of individual muscle groups and of the body as a whole. Posing conventions, maximizing size, tightening for definition, relating muscle groups to one another, further highlight these qualities and are the basis of set pieces in pepla: Steve Reeves in Le fatiche di Ercole straining his lats to a V as he pulls down pillars with the use of a pair of chains; Mark Forrest in Maciste nella valle dei re holding a huge log in his extended arms over his head before hurling it at his antagonists. The use of oil (or often in films water or sweat) on the body emphasizes it as a surface and hence its shape; relatively hard, three-quarter angle lighting brings out muscle shape; shooting against skylines presents the overall body contour—all familiar pepla setups.

Such hardness and contouredness suggests two analogies with masculinity. First, muscles pumped up stiff with blood may be likened to an erect penis, a literal embodiment of phallic potency—the body is not seen for the ordinary thing it is but takes on the aura accorded the penis. (The fact that penises, and "excessive" muscles, are also widely derided, especially by women, does not undermine this argument, since such derision surely has to do with the overvaluation of the penis in patriarchal cultures—the derision is about cutting the phallus down to size, but to do that is to acknowledge that there is cutting down that needs doing.) Second, a hard, contoured body does not

Figure 3. Samson lifting a log. (British Film Institute)

run the risk of being merged into other bodies and in this it is distinguished from the soft, yielding, merging bodies of women (see Chodorow, *Reproduction of Mothering*) and safe from the flooding femininity of both women and the masses (see Theweleit). Hardness and contour protect the male body from the threat posed by the possibility of being mistaken for female or drawn into the state of femininity, both of which would constitute a loss of male power. Such readings assume rather than explain the existence of a gender hierarchy in which to be female is wretched (Segal 83–104), while also indicating ways in which loss of power can be not merely unwelcome to men but psychically terrifying.

Second, a built body not only looks strong enough to fight off attack but its hard contours look like armor, as if it is permanently defended.

Third, the built body is one that is meant to be seen—it is built to show. The peplum revels in the display of the male body. There are shots in *Maciste alla corte del Gran Khan*, where Gordon Scott simply poses center screen to no purpose other than display, and in *Il trionfo dei dieci Gladiatori*, where Dan Vadis stands between two talking characters, giving the camera uninterrupted view of his body while the interlocutors carry the narrative forward; in Steve Reeves's films (notably *La battaglia di Maratona* and *Il figlio di Spartacus*), there is a gradual striptease through the length of the film, sometimes accounted for by the hero having his garments torn in the course of duty, more often inexplicable in terms other than showing off. Yet all of this occupies a safe space of legitimated display. Such a space is needed because the uncovering of the body in a culture that keeps it covered always raises and may even be felt to incite the possibility of libidinal response, which is felt to be dysfunctional in everyday life. Hence the erotic has to have its own spaces (the striptease club, the pinup, pornography, the beach).

Bodybuilding is recognized as a place of display but only ambiguously as a potentially erotic one. It is a space that contains male body display but also, until recently, comes with rhetorics that deny the eroticism of the display. These include the invocation of classical idealism, the virtues of sport, exercise, and health, "Nietzschean" superheroism, and, embracing many of these, the absolute value of competition and winning.[15] These, to varying degrees of inevitability, carry both male and white connotations. The whiteness of classicism has already been discussed, and certainly it has also often been used in the valorization of men over women. Sport, exercise, and health are clearly not white or male prerogatives, though bodybuilding's fondness for U.S., and a fortiori Californian, imagery does carry a white association. Nietzschean imagery, in its Nazi and cryptofascist appropriations, became white and male supremacist. Competition and winning, open to all, nonetheless also inform a widespread model of human history as the story of the winners—white men.

Fourth, built bodies are better bodies. They draw on the rhetorics just discussed: if they are winning bodies, they are the best bodies; if they achieve the ideals of classicism or incarnate the Übermensch, they are superior bodies. It does not matter that many people find built bodies excessive, even hideous. Within its own discourse, wholly transferred to the peplum, bodybuilding sets the terms of bodily excellence, which the hero cannot fail to match up to.

Fifth, a built body is a planned body. A massive, sculpted physique requires forethought and long-term organization; regimes of graduated exercise, diet, and scheduled rest need to be worked out and strictly adhered to; in short, building bodies is the most literal triumph of mind over matter, imagination over flesh. Some pepla (e.g., La schiava di Roma, La guerra di Troia, La battaglia di Maratona) include sequences showing such disciplined physical preparation, but even without these the built body displays the fact that such planning has taken place.

Sixth, built bodies are well-fed bodies, that is, they are wealthy bodies. The huge, firm muscles of Steve Reeves, Gordon Scott, or Reg Park make the simplest contrast with the thin or slack bodies of the native peoples in these films. They also carry a related gender message in the contrast with their slim, sometimes diminutive, definitely weaker white consorts.

Seventh, bodybuilders have hairless (shaved when not naturally so) bodies. Body hair is animalistic. The smooth built body is thus distinguished from those humans who are animalistic, primitives in the peplum who cover themselves in animal hides, have long, straggling hair and beards, daub themselves with mud and blood, crouch among the bushes or live in the earth. The climax of Gli amori di Ercole has Hercules fighting a giant ape, who has previously behaved in a King Kong–like way toward Hercules's beloved Dejanira, stroking her hair and, when she screams, making as if to rape her; close-ups contrast Hercules's smooth, hairless muscles with the hairy limbs of this racist archetype.

Finally, bodybuilders tan their bodies. "To stand out on stage at a physique event, one must be really well tanned," advises Robert Kennedy (139). Tanning, which only white people do, connotes other values associated with both bodybuilding and more typically white privileges: leisure (having the time to lie about acquiring a tan), wealth (buying that time, acquiring an artificial tan or traveling to the sun), and a healthy lifestyle (the California/Australia myth that no amount of melanoma statistics seem to dim). I shall return to the gender and ethnic significance of tanning below.

I have tried in the above account to bring out, where appropriate, the gender and ethnic, the male and white implications of hardness, armoredness, competitive display, classicism, superiority, planning, wealth, hairlessness, and tanning. The built white male body in pepla already carries these potential meanings, but they are further activated by the films' colonialist structures of feeling.

Pepla are seldom explicitly colonialist. They are rarely about the journey to, exploration, conquest, and settlement of foreign lands. Yet the heroes are also not usually inhabitants of the land in which the action takes place. Their relation to this land and the way it is depicted belong to colonialist tradition.

The central narrative motif of the peplum (as indeed of other muscleman films) is intervention. The hero arrives in a foreign land and sorts out its problems. This very often means that he fights on the side of an ethnic other. If need be, he will side with them against bad whites. In Il figlio di Spartacus, the hero, Randus, a Roman, is first won over to the North Africans' plight by seeing a crucified black man and then observing the enslavement of the people. He even goes so far as to observe that "if Rome is for slavery, then I am against Rome." Yet the people suffer as much from barbarian tribes and

Saracens as from Romans; the latter are seen as corrupt individuals, Randus finally bringing about the restoration of the good Caesar's dominion; and the people can only be saved by the intervention of Randus and Vetius, his bleached-blond German comrade-in-arms. At the end of the film, Caesar, aware that Randus's championing of the slaves and natives may be a threat to his own position, orders that Randus be crucified, but a spontaneous, silent mass demonstration makes him change his mind. The film thus affirms imperial rule while at the same time making it appear expressive of the will of the people. This is more commonly the peplum's colonialist structure. The hero does sometimes intervene to free the people to create a new, democratic society, but as often it is to restore traditional rule and enlightened despotism, for the people's own good.

The ideas of intervention and restoration, of acting on behalf of those who cannot act on behalf of themselves, are centerpieces of neocolonialist rhetoric. Colonialism had long claimed that imperial possession brought, and was even done in order to bring, benefits to the natives, and this informed the policy of the Western nations toward their former colonies in the postwar era, headed by the idea of the United States as world policeman, sharpened by Cold War rivalry over political/economic influence.

This complicates the discussion of address above, so that we may say that the peplum hero has a double relation to potential audience identification. Insofar as viewers identify with the characters of the depicted world and their dilemmas, the hero, *Duce*-like, sorts out their problems for them; insofar as they latch onto the foreign otherness of the world, the hero acts on their behalf, or perhaps even as them in bringing order to peoples unable to order themselves.

Pepla are not necessarily set in known historical or mythological nations, but, when they are, those that predominate are the most geopolitically close to Italy and subjects of its most "successful" colonizations (Libya), Arab lands: Egypt (*Maciste nella valle dei re*), Mesopotamia/Iraq (*Ercole contro i tiranni di Babilonia*, *L'eroe di Babilonia*, *Golia alla conquista di Bagdad*, and *Il ladro di Bagdad*), Syria (*Il ladro di Damasco*), across North Africa (*Il figlio di Spartaco*), or just generically "Arab" (*Maciste contro il sceicco*, *Totò contro Maciste*, *Il figlio dello sceicco*, *Le sette fatiche di Ali Babà*, and *Simbad contro i sette Saraceni*). Sub-Saharan, black Africa features only once (*Maciste nelle miniere del re Salomone*), partly because it was not a territory of significant Italian migration, tourism, and diplomacy, but also because of Italy's imperial brush with black Africa. Mussolini's conquest of Ethiopia in 1935 has been seen as the high point of the regime, the moment at which Italy seemed to enter the league of the great white nations by virtue of having an empire; but it lost it in 1941 (to other imperial powers, the Allies). Ethiopia, and thus black Africa generally, was an embarrassing reference point for Italian colonial adventures.

Whether a peplum film is set in known or newly invented lands, the black-white "Manichean delirium" Frantz Fanon (*Black Skin, White Masks* 183) saw as characterizing colonial texts is strongly in evidence. This is often realized in the most literal way through dress and mise-en-scène. *Maciste contro i mostri* depicts warring (racially white) tribes in a prehistoric world. The "bad" tribe is black haired and darker skinned, they wear black clothes, live underground, and worship the moon, the symbol of night; the "good" tribe is fair haired and light skinned, with white clothes, overground dwellings, and worship the sun, the daylight. Other pepla are less unrelenting in their antinomies, but such use of dark and light in clothing, skin color, below/above ground, night and day, bad and good, is nonetheless the rule. It can also have gender and ethnic dimensions.

The contrast between the libidinal bad woman and the chastely loving good woman noted above is also a contrast between a dark- and fair-haired woman, and between nighttime, indoor encounters and daytime, outdoor ones. In *La battaglia di Maratona*, for instance, the hero Philippides first meets the good Andromeda (blond Bardot-look-alike Mylene Demongeot in a loose, white, short tunic) as she and some other women play in the sun with a golden ball in a field; in the next scene he goes at night to the machinating Caris (dark haired in a décolleté, cinched-waist tunic) in her dapple-lit rooms. Whereas he comes across Andromeda because, unaware of him, her ball accidentally falls in the pool he is drinking from, in contrast, Caris has summoned him to her. Where Andromeda only looks at him as little as conversation requires and mainly looks away from him, Caris is twice a voyeur, first looking at him through the window as he approaches, then observing him as he awaits her; throughout the scene she keeps looking at him, walks round him, touches him; when he walks off having defeated one of her bodyguards who was trying to detain him, she gazes admiringly after him.

The spectator is implicated in this contrast. The scene with Andromeda is all in two-shot, she and Philippides always on-screen together; the scene with Caris combines two-shots with shots of him from her point of view—we are invited to contemplate Andromeda and Philippides as a couple, but to look at him through Caris's lustful eyes. He wears the same costume in both scenes, a one-shouldered tunic displaying his arms and right pectoral. In the scene with Andromeda he stands with his left side to the camera, pectoral covered; with Caris he stands with his right to the camera, pectoral

Figure 4. *Samson and the Seven Miracles.* (British Film Institute)

on display. In editing and camera-performer setups, the film invites us both to accept the moral contrast and to enter into the erotic pleasure stimulated by Philippides's body. However, by associating the pleasure with a bad, dark woman, it disavows at a stroke both a transracial and a homoerotic form of desire in the putative straight, white, working-class, male spectator.

Although non-white people do not figure largely in pepla, the ethnic resonances of the black-white antinomies become evident in two ways: racially differentiated mise-en-scènes and the occasional casting of black body-builders.

Ethnically different peoples in pepla are generally played by white actors, but the differences signaled by mise-en-scène are those of racial difference in Eurocentric discourse. On the one hand, there is a use of architecture, clothing, hairstyles, music, and dance gestures to create a broadly Oriental ("Arab" or "Chinese") world, with luxurious court life and devilishly clever modes of torture. This is established in the "Carthaginianism" of forerunners like *Cabiria* and *Scipione l'Africano* and in the depiction of Lidia, all pagodas and tinkling music, in the second film of the cycle, *Ercole e la regina di Lidia*. It is not just a question of such geographical setting, but of the widespread use of Orientalist motifs in the depiction of vicious rule in invented societies, as in, for instance, *Maciste contro i mostri* and *Maciste l'uomo più forte del mondo*. In contrast, in other films or in the same film, there are the primitives, dressed in skins, living in huts or holes, skulking in the undergrowth, crude in their pleasures, brutal in their violence. In *Le fatiche di Ercole*, the tribe that attacks the group on the island of the Golden Fleece are apelike; in *Maciste contro i mostri*, the bad black tribe is accompanied by "jungle" music and seen carrying game suspended from sticks, just like natives in Hollywood African adventure films. There can be variations in the primitives, suggesting degrees of civilization. In *Maciste il vendicatore dei Mayas*, the good white tribe is distinguished from the bad black by wearing cloth, not skins, living in a settlement not underground, and having an elaborated belief system, not just brute instinct.

The hero, who comes from without, is associated with neither the Oriental nor the primitive, though he comes to the aid of the good or rightful elements in either. He is superior to both, cleverer than the Orientals, tougher than the primitives. He contains their strengths, yet is not defined by either cleverness or toughness. On the contrary, often what is explicitly praised in the film is his "simplicity." He is unimpressed by the elaborations of Atlantis in *Ercole all conquista di Atlantide*; some older men in *Le fatiche di Ercole* contrast Hercules's admirable simplicity in sport with the current "fanaticism and cult of the body." The white man both comprehends Orientals and primitives and yet is sublimely straightforward, neither mired in sophistication nor driven by instinct. He is both more than others and yet also less complicated, less problematic, less of a business.

When a black bodybuilder is used, it is as a special case of primitivism (evident in *Maciste nella terra dei ciclopi* in the contrast of Gordon Mitchell's cloth peplum and Paul Wynter's leopard-skin loincloth). Blacks are presented as possessed of a slave mentality: they realize that their best and true place is in subservience to the white man. In *Maciste nella terra dei ciclopi*, the unnamed slave (Wynter) watches a tug-of-war between (racially) black and white teams; when asked which team will win, he says the white one, instinctively (it does not seem cynically) recognizing racial superiority. In *Maciste l'uomo più forte del mondo*, Maciste rescues Banco (Wynter again) from the mole men, and Banco says he will be Maciste's slave forever, for he gave him life; Maciste says that Banco's mother gave him life, that there should be no masters and slaves, yet Banco is unable to accept this and throughout the film acts as a slave. Slavery is thus condemned but shown as what blacks not whites want.

Maciste's refusal of Banco's servitude displays his moral enlightenment. This is often suggested by the hero's behavior in combat with black men. Marco, the chief hero of *Sette contro tutti*, refuses to kill his black combatant in the arena. In *Arrivano i Titani*, Rathor (Serge Nubret) is at first a snarling slave who has run amok; however, in gladiatorial combat Crios defeats him but gets the king to allow him to spare his life; thereafter Rathor is Crios's devoted helper. In the process he changes character—before he meets Crios in combat, he has dispatched another (white) opponent to his death and smiles at his success, his sweating muscles gleaming in the torchlight; after Crios has saved his life, we have no more such shots of exultant physicality. When Maciste and the black slave fight in *Maciste nella terra dei ciclopi*, Maciste is at first under the influence of the slave's black magic potion; there is a very long sequence in which Maciste is viciously beaten by the slave; when the potion wears off and Maciste recovers his superior strength and skill, he dispatches the slave very quickly—while the black slave has lingered over the torment, Maciste just acts with maximum efficiency and minimum pain.

When the black man becomes the white man's slave, he is of limited practical help to him. The hero may occasionally need the black man, either as additional support or as sheer force; but the black man needs the hero even more, because of the latter's ability to size up situations, know right from wrong, do the right thing. This motif of brain versus brawn is explicitly commented on in *Arrivano i Titani*, which insists on its racial dimension by casting the very dark Serge Nubret as Rathor against (as Nubret confirms [61]) bleached-blond Giuliano Gemma as Crios. Before they fight, all the gladiators have to choose swords; while Rathor muscles his way to the front and picks the biggest, Crios stands nonchalantly by and winds up with the smallest. (White mythology's racial penis size obsessions require comment only in this bracket.) Yet in combat it is Crios's skill, his acrobatic swiftness of foot and eye, that wins over Rathor's brute size. When Rathor selected the biggest weapon, Crios shook his head and said, "Tutti muscoli, niente cervello" (all muscles, no brain). A little later, Crios, now favored by the king, watches a contest between a white man and a black bull; the former wins and the queen comments, "L'intelligenza trionfa sempre" (intelligence always wins).

Before finally discussing the relationship between the built body and colonialism in the construction of white masculinity, let me describe an extraordinary scene from *Maciste l'uomo più forte del mondo*, which encapsulates many of the characteristics discussed so far. The queen of the mole people has had Maciste chained with a yoke across his shoulders onto which are lain more and more vast, heavy weights; if Maciste buckles under the strain, prongs beneath the yoke will pierce his two companions who are tied down on either side of him. One of them, Banco, tells him not to hold the weights up on his account, thereby displaying his slavish readiness to sacrifice his life. The

queen watches on and the film cuts to what she sees: close-ups of Mark Forrest's bulged and glistening pectorals and biceps. A point comes at which
Maciste threatens to buckle; the weights slip, a prong enters Banco's chest,
blood seeps out; by a supreme effort, Maciste pushes the weight back up and
then further up and up, till holding it aloft above his head; as the music cli-
maxes, a reaction shot of the queen shows her breathing and gulping with
an excitement that it is hard not to read as orgasmic. The set-piece muscle
display, the lusting bad woman's point of view, the white man's triumph in
the fiendish underground Orientalist test, a triumph spurred on by his moral
compulsion to save the good black primitive, of such elements, here screwed
up to an exceptional pitch of sadomasochistic delirium, is the peplum's construction of the built white male body in colonial enterprise composed.

The construction of white masculinity in the peplum (and other muscleman
movies) as the built body in colonial settings is a particular one. White masculinity is far from being constructed only in built bodies, and the degree to
which its identity is dependent on positing a non-white other needs further
exploration.[16] However, there is at least one aspect of the muscleman construction that is generalizable and this is the way that the hero figure both
establishes white superiority and yet also transcends division. Indeed, it is
perhaps the secret of all power that it both secures things in the interests of
its particularity, while passing itself off as above particularity.

The simplest register of this is in the very skin of the hero's body, for while
unmistakably racially white, it is always darker than that of other whites. This
is in part a function of his being a bodybuilder and therefore, as discussed
above, tanned. Tanning does not suggest a desire or readiness to be racially
black—a tanned white body is always indubitably just that. On the other
hand, the discourse of tanning also implies that white people are capable
of attractive variation in color, whereas blacks who lighten and otherwise
whiten their appearance are mocked for the endeavor and generally held to
have failed (witness the disparagement of Michael Jackson's metamorphoses).

The bodybuilder's body already carries this construction of whiteness as
a particular, yet not restricted, identity, and it is heightened by comparison
with the other bodies in the film. The hero is always darker than all white
women, whether they be good (and blond) or bad (and brunet), a fact encapsulated in the standard pose of the woman's white hand resting against
the broad expanse of the hero's tanned pectorals. He is also darker than other
white men, especially bad ones, Orientalist rulers whose pasty complexions
are of a piece with their decadence, primitives whose underground or cave

dwellings have kept their skins from sunlight. The hero, so often first seen standing in the sun against the horizon or even, as in *Maciste contro i ciclopi*, apparently born in a ray of sunshine, is the antithesis of this whiteness that shrinks from the life-giving sun. Even good white men are seldom as dark as the hero. Yet withal the hero is never equated with racial blackness: as we have seen, the films are at great pains to stress his superior difference from even good, and physically spectacular, black men. This construction of white male superiority as precisely both unmistakably white and yet not particularistically white is characteristic of the representation of white masculinity in general.

More specific to peplum/muscleman constructions is the representation of masculinity and colonialism in terms of relations between bodies. The economic, military, and technological realities of colonialism disappear in a presentation of white bodily superiority as the explanation of the colonizing position. At its simplest this becomes the resolution of colonial conflict as a fight between the hero and an antagonist, be the latter the leading warrior of the society or its ruler (two versions of embodied power). Whatever the narrative specifics of the showdown, the hero's better body wins out over the inferior Oriental or primitive one.

This is very often heightened by pitting the hero's body against the technology of the antagonists. It is they, the object of the hero's colonialist sorting out, who have recourse to elaborate weaponry and massed military, which the hero confronts with his bare body alone. The final confrontation of *L'eroe di Babilonia* has the hero Nipur, the rightful heir, fight for possession of the palace, his bare body, with only a brown cloth peplum and sword to protect him, pitted against soldiers in armored tunics, with plumed helmets, shields, and swords. The contrast is drawn even more sharply in *La battaglia di Maratona*, where Philippides wears only a white loincloth as compared to the heavy armor of his opponents and where he has only a sword to set against their elaborate machineries of war. Yet his built white body triumphs over their black-clad, technologically sophisticated ones. The colonial encounter, and white supremacy, is thus naturalized by being realized and achieved in the body.

The built white body might seem a problematic signifier of the natural body, and certainly it is not the body white men are born with; it is, however, the body made possible by their natural mental superiority. The point after all is that it is built, a product of the application of thought and planning. It is this sense of the spirit at work behind the production of this mere body that defines its whiteness. This makes the built white hero better able to handle his body, to improvise with what is to hand (e.g., boulders, cartwheels, tree stumps used as weapons), to size up situations; no matter how splendid the physiques of the likes of Serge Nubret and Paul Wynter, they can never have this quality. It is a sense of a divine spark within him, suggested by his semi-divine ontological status, his classical inheritance, his Duce-like qualities. The built white physique may be fabulous, but what made it, and makes it effective, is the mind in the body.

This finally suggests the link between the white male body being built and being displayed in colonial fictions, namely, that the built body is analogous to the imperial enterprise. The work of Mary Douglas offers an analytic paradigm based on the proposal that "there are pressures to create consonance between the perception of social and physiological levels of expression," such that "bodily control is an expression of social control" (Natural Symbols 98–99). Different ways of constructing body image have to do with different ways of understanding and practicing social relations. The built body sees the body as submitted to and glorified by the planning and ambition of the mind; colonial worlds are likewise represented as inchoate terrain needing the skill, sense, and vision of the colonizer to be brought to order. The peplum hero has landscaped his body with muscles, and he controls them superbly and sagely; the lands of the peplum are enfeebled or raw bodies requiring discipline. In short, the built white male body and colonial enterprise are mirrors of each other.

Notes

1. The cycle runs from the 1958 Le fatiche di Ercole to 1965, with the odd straggler such as Combate de gigantes (1966); the most complete account is in Cammarota. The term peplum (plural pepla) was coined by French critics in the early 1960s; Siclier uses the term as if his cinéaste readers will obviously understand its meaning. The word is a Latinized Greek word meaning a woman's tunic but here referring to the short skirt or kilt worn by the heroes. Peplum is generally understood to refer to the 1958–65 Italian cycle, but is also sometimes used to refer to an earlier Italian one, from Quo vadis? (1912) and especially Cabiria (1914) to circa 1926, or even to all adventure films set in "ancient times," including Hollywood films such as The Ten Commandments, Ben Hur, Cleopatra, and Conan the Barbarian. In this article however peplum refers only to the 1958–65 cycle. (For an excellent analysis of the genre, see Lagny.)

2. Geography notwithstanding, Guadeloupe is politically and administratively a département of France, its inhabitants full and automatic citizens of France. In fact, in 1960 Nubret was living in Paris and competing for France in bodybuilding championships.

3. In a lecture at the British Film Institute 1991 Summer Conference in Stirling.

4. "Moko, ovvero il 'compare sacco di carbone' nelle saghe dei corsari delle Antille, che risolve grazie alla forza situazioni impossibili."

5. See my discussion (Dyer, "Whiteness"), but also bell hooks's comments ("Representations of Whiteness" in Black Looks 165–78), stressing that whites are far from invisible to black people.

6. The construction by Western culture of Greece as a white forebear and ideal is discussed in Bernal. The Old Testament in the context of hegemonic European cultures should be seen as a gentile source.

7. Translations of Italian film titles and, where appropriate, their titles for distribution in English-speaking countries are given in the filmography.

8. Walkerdine makes a similar point about the class specificity of representations of masculinity in relation to the Rocky films, though stressing the fighting body rather than the purely strong body.

9. Interestingly, Brownlow states that Mussolini was also "much admired in Hollywood, where he was considered the political equivalent of Douglas Fairbanks" (450), another body-displaying male star.

10. This seems, in fact, more like a reference to Nazism than Italian fascism, something that happens elsewhere in pepla, notably in the Teutonic characterization of the dictator-led Gauls in La schiava di Roma, one of the most pro-Roman films of the cycle. One might note that dealing with fascism in terms of Nazism is also common in many of Italy's most internationally renowned films from Roma città aperta (Rome Open City; 1945) to Pasqualino Settebellezze (Seven Beauties; 1976). Italy was, of course, occupied by the Nazis in the final months of the war, facilitating an eclipse of the brutalities of indigenous fascism with the horrors of the German variety.

11. See previous note.

12 The word used is stirpe, most strictly translated as "stock" and a key term in Italian fascist rhetoric.

13. I am grateful to Luciano Cheles for reminding me of this connection.

14. The huge increase in the display of the white male body in recent years has not markedly changed this situation—indeed, we may say that the rest of the white world is only catching up with postwar Italy. The body and performance style of, say, the Chippendales, Marky Mark, Levi's models or, indeed, Schwarzenegger et al. are still informed by the need to defend the vulnerability of the exposed male body. What undoubtedly has changed is the cultural disapproval of male exhibitionism and narcissism.

15. The use in bodybuilding of a posing iconography selectively drawn from classical precedent is detailed in Doan and Dietz; Wyke. Sport and health are emphasized in Webster. "Nietzschean" Übermensch qualities are most obviously evident in the use of Richard Strauss's Also sprach Zarathustra at bodybuilding competitions.

16. Such further exploration was evident at the panel "White Skins, Black Masks" convened by Christopher Looby and Eric Lott for the 1992 MLA meeting in New York,

where it was argued that the construction of normative white masculinity in America is crucially dependent upon the function of the black men in the white male *imaginaire*.

Filmography

The first title in parentheses is a literal translation; any others are the titles by which the film is known in English-language distribution. Only the star playing the hero is listed (his character's name given only when it is not eponymous), except for those films also featuring Serge Nubret or Paul Wynter.

amori di Ercole, Gli (The Loves of Hercules) 1960; Mickey Hargitay.

Arrivano i Titani (Here Come the Titans; Sons of Thunder, My Son the Hero) 1962; Giuliano Gemma (Crios), Serge Nubret (Rathor).

battaglia di Maratona, La (The Battle of Marathon; The Giant of Marathon) 1960; Steve Reeves.

Cabiria 1914; Bartolomeo Pagano (Maciste).

colosso di Rodi, Il (The Colossus of Rhodes) 1961.

Ercole alla conquista di Atlantide (Hercules Conquers Atlantis; Hercules and the Captive Women) 1961; Reg Park.

Ercole contro i figli del sole (Hercules versus the Sons of the Sun) 1964; Mark Forest.

Ercole contro i tiranni di Babilonia (Hercules versus the Tyrants of Babylon) 1965; Rock Stevens.

Ercole contro Roma (Hercules versus Rome; Hercules in Rome) 1965; Alan Steel.

Ercole e la regina di Lidia (Hercules and the Queen of Lidia; Hercules Unchained) 1959; Steve Reeves.

Ercole sfida Sansone (Hercules Challenges Samson) 1964; Kirk Morris (Hercules), Richard Lloyd (Samson).

Ercole, Sansone, Maciste ed Ursus gli invincibili (Hercules, Samson, Maciste and Ursus the Invincible; Hercules, Maciste, Samson and Ursus versus the Universe, Samson and the Mighty Challenge) 1965; Kirk Morris, Red Ross, Nadir Baltimor, Yann Larvor (in eponymous order).

eroe di Babilonia, L' (The Hero of Babylon; Goliath King of the Slaves) 1964; Gordon Scott (Nipur).

fatiche di Ercole, Le (The Labors of Hercules; Hercules) 1958; Steve Reeves.

figlio dello sceicco, Il (The Son of the Sheik) 1962; Gordon Scott.

figlio di Spartacus, Il (Son of Spartacus; The Slave) 1962; Steve Reeves (Randus).

Golia alla conquista di Bagdad (Goliath Conquers Baghdad) 1966; Rock Stevens.

guerra di Troia, La (The Trojan War; The Wooden Horse of Troy); Steve Reeves (Aeneas)

ladro di Bagdad, Il (The Thief of Baghdad) 1961; Steve Reeves.

ladro di Damasco, Il (The Thief of Damascus) 1964.

Maciste all'inferno (Maciste in Hell) 1962; Kirk Morris.

Maciste alla corte del Gran Khan (Maciste at the Court of the Great Khan; Samson and the Seven Miracles) 1959; Gordon Scott.

Maciste alla corte dello Zar (Maciste at the Court of the Czar) 1964; Kirk Morris.

Maciste contro i Mongoli (Maciste versus the Mongols) 1963; Alan Steel.

Maciste contro i mostri (Maciste against the Monsters; Colossus of the Stone Age, Land of the Monsters) 1962; Reg Lewis.

Maciste contro lo sceicco (Maciste versus the Sheik) 1962; Ed Fury.

Maciste il vendicatore dei Mayas aka *Ercole contro il gigante Golia* (Maciste the Mayas' Avenger / Hercules versus the Golia the Giant) 1965; Kirk Morris.

Maciste l'uomo più forte del mondo (Maciste the Strongest Man in the World; The Mole Men Battle the Son of Hercules) 1961; Mark Forrest, Paul Wynter (Banco).

Maciste nella terra dei ciclopi aka *Maciste contro le cyclope* (Maciste in the Land of the Cyclops / Maciste versus the Cyclops; Atlas in the Land of the Cyclops; Monster from the Unknown World; The Cyclops; Atlas against the Cyclops) 1961; Gordon Mitchell, Paul Wynter.

Maciste nella valle dei re (Maciste in the Valley of the Kings; Maciste the Mighty; Son of Samson) 1959; Mark Forrest.

Maciste nelle miniere del re Salomone (Maciste in King Solomon's Mines; Samson in King Solomon's Mines) 1964; Reg Park.

Nel segno di Roma (Under the Sign of Rome; Sign of the Gladiator) 1959; Georges Marchal.

Quo Vadis? 1912; Bruto Castellani (Ursus).

schiava di Roma, La (The Roman Slave Girl; Blood of the Warriors) 1961.

Sette contro tutti (Seven against all) 1966.

sette fatiche di Ali Babà, Le (The Seven Labors of Ali Baba) 1963; Rod Flash Jlush.

Simbad contro i sette Saraceni (Sinbad versus the Seven Saracens) 1965; Gordon Mitchell.

Totò contro Maciste (Totò versus Maciste) 1961; Samson Burke.

trionfo dei dieci Gladiatori, Il aka *Spartacus e i dieci Gladiatori* (Triumph of the Ten Gladiators / Spartacus and the Ten Gladiators; Day of Vengeance) 1965; Dan Vadis (Rocia).

Ulisse contro Ercole (Ulysses versus Hercules; Ulysses against the Son of Hercules) 1962; Georges Marchal (Ulysses), Michael Lane (Hercules).

FISTS OF FURY

Discourses of Race and Masculinity in the

Martial Arts Cinema

YVONNE TASKER

It was undeniably the figure of Bruce Lee who popularized martial arts movies with Western audiences of the 1970s, even before his untimely death made him the stuff of legend. As well as being the first Chinese actor to become a major star in the West, Lee played a significant role in the redefinition of both the Hong Kong and the American action cinema. The martial arts cinema, itself part of the broader action traditions of a popular cinema that is defined by physicality and spectacle, encompasses a vast range of forms and subgenres. Chinese and American martial arts films, from both the 1970s and the present day, offer a fertile ground for an investigation of the play of sexualized racial discourses within the popular cinema.[1] In the pages that follow the operation of these discourses are discussed primarily in relation to the dominating figure of Bruce Lee, but also with reference to the work of recent Western martial arts stars, and the kung fu comedy associated with Jackie Chan. If these traditions have received little sustained critical attention, perhaps this is because critics tend to dismiss the products of the popular cinema as mindless, objecting to the visceral pleasures of physicality that are on offer. This lack of attention, however, will come as no surprise when we consider the marginal audiences with which the films are popular in the West, as well as the relative invisibility of Asian film culture.[2]

The typical action narrative operates around an axis of power and powerlessness, which is complexly articulated through the discourses of race, class, and sexuality that constitute the body of the hero. Themes of activity and passivity are central to all these discourses, as well as to the construction of the action hero. While the hero is, by definition, an active figure, he is also frequently rendered passive, subject to a range of restraints and oppressive forces. The hero is also defined in part by his suffering, which both lends him a certain tragic status, and demonstrates his remarkable ability to endure. The trajectory of tragic suffering is at its most extreme when enacted through the figure of the white male hero of recent Western action movies. While the black protagonists of these films, who usually act as partners to the white hero, are often damaged in some way, this seems to render them symbolically safe. By way of contrast, these same Western movies seem to need obsessively to cut up and punish the body of the white male hero, a body that they, not coincidentally, also offer up as sexual spectacle. In *Cyborg* (1989) the hero, played by Jean-Claude Van Damme, is described as a "walking wound." This phrase comes close to encapsulating the role of the white male hero in the contemporary action movie. He is both massively damaged and yet still functioning. It also indicates the potential purchase of a psychoanalytic discourse in understanding the complex ways in which figures of power and powerlessness are written over the body of a hero who is represented as both invincible and castrated.

"Race," Masculinity, and the Action Tradition

In the action cinemas of both Hong Kong and America, the body of the hero or heroine is their ultimate, and often their only, weapon. A point of distinction between the two traditions lies in the way the Chinese hero often fights for and as part of a community, while within the American tradition the hero has become an increasingly isolated figure.[3] Both, however, tend to find themselves confronting a political system that is almost entirely corrupt, a villain who is the complete personification of evil. In Hong Kong films the use of the colonial past as a setting provides a specific populist point of reference. While some films are set in an unspecified or mythological past, the invocation of Japanese, Russian, or British forces allows for a more historically and culturally located narrative threat.[4] While Western films often tend toward the articulation of narratives centered on class conflict within a context of supposed racial harmony—the interracial male buddies—Hong Kong films are more likely to enact conflict in terms of the figures of colonial oppression, in which the enemy represents a threat from outside. The context of the anticolonial narrative is crucial for thinking about the racial discourses of masculine identity that are worked through in the Hong Kong martial arts cinema. As is evidenced most clearly in Bruce Lee's internationally successful films, the martial arts film of the 1970s deployed a discourse of macho Chinese nationalism that proved popular with a range of audiences. While the assertion of a powerful Chinese hero has an obvious appeal for Asian audiences, both in Asia and America, martial arts films were also hugely popular with black and white working-class audiences in the United States and in Europe during the 1970s. Such popularity can obviously be understood in terms of the production of fantasies of physical empowerment. These fantasies respond to the *constitution of the body through limits*.[5]

The redefinition of the swordplay film into the martial arts format familiar from the 1970s involved the increasing centrality of the fight, and hence the body, as a set piece. The action shifted to settings such as the martial arts school or the tournament, providing a showcase for the skills of the various performers.[6] A typical scenario consists of the fighting schools, in which the hero or heroine, who may be single or plural, fights to defend the honor of their school and the particular style of fighting associated with it against the incursion of a corrupt school, often associated with the Japanese.[7] In *The Chinese Boxer* a rogue Chinese who has been thrown out of the town some years before returns, bringing with him three Japanese karate experts who defeat the good school and take over the town. Only Wang Yu's character survives to take on and defeat these corrupt forces. In the film's final sequence, Wang Yu triumphs over the karate experts despite the machinations of their treacherous Chinese go-between, who has hidden himself under the snow. Within the anticolonial narrative of revenge, the collaborator is an ambiguous enemy. The figure of the traitorous intermediary, who in *The Chinese Boxer* is also a rapist, is interestingly written through sexual imagery in Bruce Lee's *Way of the Dragon* (U.S.: *Return of the Dragon*). A gender dysfunction of some kind comes to define the threat represented by this figure.

Way of the Dragon is set in contemporary Rome, a re-location that does not significantly alter the basic formulation of a Chinese community, here the owners and workers of a restaurant, under threat from an archetypal white capitalist with an army of hired thugs. The European location does allow for an explicit address to issues of Westernization, largely expressed through discourses of sexuality. The treacherous Chinese go-between is styled as a camp gay man who, dressed in outrageously bright Western clothes, minces about the restaurant cooing over Bruce Lee's muscles. Interestingly, he is one of the first characters in the film to realize what Bruce Lee's body is *for*, commenting on its hardness. As in his other movies, Lee's character holds back from fighting for some time and the film teases the audience as to when Lee will "reveal" himself, a double moment in which he both reveals his body, removing his jacket, and his "hidden" strength. The go-between functions not only as a passive figure against which the tough masculinity of Lee's character can be defined, but is also figured here in terms of a specifically (homo)sexual threat associated with Europe. The sexual naiveté of Lee's character, Tang Lung, is indicated through his encounter with a European prostitute who takes him back to her apartment. He happily works out in front of a mirror but is horrified when she appears before him naked, running away in panic. Lee's absorption in his own image here is played off against those characters who have sexual designs on his body.

Set in Shanghai's international settlement, Fist of Fury (U.S.: The Chinese Connection) portrays the struggles of a Chinese school who are powerless against the political power of the Japanese school. A famous image from the film has Bruce Lee as Chen destroying a park sign saying "No Dogs and Chinese." This moment specifically enacts a fantasy that involves the refusal of physical limits. The film militantly champions a muscular Chinese national identity, despite the strictures of the law and against the insults of the Japanese. The go-between in this film acts as a translator for the Japanese — mediating between both language and culture. Disrupting a memorial service for their teacher, the go-between brings the Chinese a challenge, contemptuously referring to them as the "Sick Man of Asia." A close-up shows Chen's fist tightening, with the accompanying soundtrack amplifying and intensifying this physical expression of anger. Finally eschewing his promised restraint, Chen goes to the Japanese, defeating them all and declaring "we are not sick men." This assertion of nationalism is very clearly inscribed through the revelation of Lee's body — as he ritualistically removes his jacket — so that discourses of masculinity and nationhood are complexly bound up together in his star image. It is Lee's body that marks the assertion of a masculine national identity.

The American action cinema is more visibly concerned than other Hollywood forms with discourses of racial difference and masculinity. In a genre defined so much by physicality, black and Asian performers have had more opportunities to take on major roles. The spaces offered by such roles inevitably reinscribe stereotypical definitions of the physical, often further positioning black and Asian characters within a fantasized marginal space of criminality or deviance. Yet the martial arts film is also a genre in which racially overdetermined bodies, spaces for the projection of a range of fantasies, come into intimate physical contact. To this extent, racial difference functions partly within the films as a term that can deflect anxieties around their implicit homoeroticism. A violent physical confrontation, usually between men, forms the climax of the martial arts movie, which can be seen in terms of the staging or the performance of competing masculinities. In the memorable final fight from Way of the Dragon, Bruce Lee takes on karate champion Chuck Norris against the setting of Rome's Coliseum, a location that indicates the grandeur or at least the proportions of the occasion. The film offers competing masculinities and male bodies as a way of speaking about colonial conflict. Ritual images of limbering up, or extended training sequences, as well as the fights themselves, offer the male body as a sexualized spectacle, a spectacle that is inevitably overlaid with the complex meanings of the racially defined body.

The language and images through which the figure of the hero is articulated pose questions of gendered identity in terms of visual and verbal metaphors of hardness and softness. The hero's masculine identity is constructed as hardness. Using a range of methods to fight their opponents, the hero must avoid letting any stray kick or punch through his/her defense, so that the body functions as a sort of armor.[8] In *The Chinese Boxer* Wang Yu must make his hands *like iron*. The film's training sequences detail his disciplined struggle to become invincible, with images of him hardening his hands by placing them in a vat of heated iron filings, running and jumping with iron rods attached to his legs. These images provide a clear, since amplified, instance of the process by which a gendered identity is constituted through the necessary act of imagining, as well as resisting, bodily boundaries. We identify with a masculine identity that is constituted before our eyes, enacted through these narrative images of physical hardening. Judith Butler takes up this point when she suggests that "the body is not a 'being,' but a variable boundary, a surface whose permeability is politically regulated." Butler sees the body as "a signifying practice within a cultural field of gender hierarchy and compulsory heterosexuality," but the purchase of her analysis can also be extended in order to think about the racial constitution of the body (*Gender Trouble* 139). The symbolic centrality of a rhetoric of hardness in the martial arts films finds its parallel in those visual metaphors that express a fear of penetration, or of the softness that would allow it. As we'll see in the case of Bruce Lee, these fears are in part routed through the history of representation in which Chinese men and women have been constituted by the West as "soft."

A metaphoric language of gender that is intimately entwined with issues of place and status, is in operation in the fight film generally. For Western movies of recent years, a fear of softness is more directly connected to the deployment of a sexual, usually homoerotic, imagery of bodily penetration. The terrain of the action cinema is haunted by questions of masculine identity, that are in turn bound up with complex configurations of power and authority. As I've already implied, these ideological figures must be considered not only as they operate textually, but in terms of the audiences' relationship of identification to the figure of the hero. At the most obvious level, the figure

of the graceful and ultimately triumphant martial arts hero offers a more perfect figure of identification for both male and female audiences, and in this
sense our relationship to the image is one of primary narcissism.[9] The hero
performs astounding physical feats with which we can identify — a process in
which identity is *constituted through an identification* with the performance of the
body. The notorious soundtrack of grunts that accompanies martial arts films
forms part of the sensuous assertion of a physicality that transgresses limits.
Our relationship as an audience to the adventures portrayed is also mediated
through an identification with the Oedipal figure of the hero who struggles,
who rebels against, but is subject to, the strictures of the social world.

Martial arts films combine sets of images that define the body in terms
of aggression and sensuousness. It is no accident though that, given a particular understanding of masculinity, Western censors have read the films as
primarily having to do with aggression. The sensuousness of movement is effaced, leaving only the violence of the body, a violence that is then projected
onto a pathologized marginal audience. Yet if we reinstate the eroticized aspects of the graceful movement played out in these films, it also becomes
apparent that the martial arts film has evolved as a cinematic form that allows
men to look at men. In this the films legitimate a taboo look. More than this,
they allow an identification with a male figure who other men will look at
and who will enjoy being the object of that admiring gaze. In understanding
this, the juxtaposition of martial arts and dance is a useful one. In Western
culture, dance is constructed in opposition to fighting. It is also linked to
the feminine, and often explicitly to images of male homosexuality. It is important to note though that this does not mean the *feminization* of the male
dancer, a formulation that operates within a simple gender binary. Rather,
dance offers the possibility of occupying a feminine position that involves,
as with the martial arts film, an explicit location of the male body on display.

While Freud's theorized relationship between primary narcissism and
homosexual desire (love of the self and the same) has proved problematic,
I want to invoke this relationship here as one possible way of talking about
the "regressive" pleasures of the fight films. To some extent psychoanalysis
functions to provide a framework within which terms such as "regressive"
and "childish" do not carry the pejorative connotations that they do in everyday speech. Clearly regressive or childish pleasures are in operation through
our identification with the hero as a more complete figure who triumphs
over adversity. This fantasy of empowerment emerges from and speaks to
those who, like children, find themselves in a position of powerlessness. In
particular, an identification with the physical aspects of the hero's triumph

is crucial—offering a very different set of pleasures to an intellectual identification. The regression at stake in the films can be seen as a resistance to (becoming) the father, a resistance that is radically different but nonetheless present in both the Chinese comedy films and the more earnest, or anxious, products associated with Bruce Lee and with more recent white stars. This resistance relates to the hero's location within a fantasy of omnipotence that is to some extent "outside" the institutions that represent power.

In the revenge narratives around which many martial arts films are structured, the fight has an immense importance. The "shift of the narrative discourse to violence," suggests Chiao Hsiung-Ping, "allows such a particularly intense and coherent statement of conflicts that the fight scenes become the real force carrying the narrative flow" ("Bruce Lee" 35). This understanding is echoed by Stuart Kaminsky who finds a Western point of reference for the films in the Hollywood musical, which has dance as its physical center, expressed in the set-piece musical number (see Kaminsky). Chiao Hsiung-Ping also links the figure of dance to images of physicality and the success of the martial arts films rather more effectively through an image from another hit film of the 1970s, *Saturday Night Fever*. We see the near-naked hero, Tony Manero (John Travolta) alone in his bedroom. On the wall are images of Sylvester Stallone (as Rocky) and Bruce Lee. All three men are figures who have achieved or seek to achieve success through their physicality—dance, boxing, kung fu— escaping the marginal spaces in which they find themselves through their achievements. The bodies of these working-class, marginalized men, which are their only resource, are turned through these forms into a spectacular site of pleasure rather than labor. Such images offer a physical constitution of identity that attempts to escape the policing to which the body is subject. The emphasis on physicality, then, allows the audience to identify with the construction of an oppositional identity sited on the body. This is pleasurable partly because the body is constituted through oppressive physical limitations.

Whilst Chiao's analysis was written retrospectively, critics at the time were not slow to posit links between the Western success of the martial arts films and a "ghetto myth" through which dispossessed groups might identify with the hero's struggle to overcome. B. P. Flanigan's speculation on the success of the films is representative, asserting how it is "obvious" that "people who represent the most oppressed segment of a society would obtain great satisfaction, indeed enjoyment, in watching an antagonist be literally destroyed by the kung fu hero" (10). These equations—between audience and hero— are often rather schematic. The reference to the success of martial arts films with a black urban audience in the United States seems to represent an end point. The lack of further critical work suggests perhaps that the *process of accounting* is all, a process not unlike those regulatory processes of classification familiar from other spheres. An "obvious" explanation can ultimately operate to confirm the marginalized audience in their marginal place, since explaining the appeal of the films somehow exhausts them. Is this because the films, like their audiences, are assumed to be "simple"? By contrast, Chiao's analysis begins to unravel the complex articulation of race, class, and sexuality that is elaborated in the differing Chinese and American reception of these films, as well as within the revenge narratives of the films themselves.

While I am wary of generalization in relation to an area so often characterized precisely as "simple," I wish to risk one at this stage. This is to suggest that while both Hong Kong and American martial arts films are staging fantasies, the primary focus in each tradition is different. Within the Hong Kong cinema the films can be seen as primarily working through fantasies of empowerment that emphasize social relations. By contrast, the Americanized version of the martial arts format has increasingly become used as a space within which to stage homoerotic fantasies, primarily working through issues and anxieties around white male sexuality. Now it is nonetheless the case that both traditions employ a gendered rhetoric through which they articulate their narratives of revenge and struggle.[10]

Bruce Lee and the Remasculinization of the Chinese Body

"Remasculinization" may be a problematic notion within discourses about race and sexuality, potentially implying a return to a mythical gender stability, yet it nonetheless provides a way of situating a discussion of the central figure of Bruce Lee.[11] The significance of Lee's Western success lies partly in his articulation of a tough masculinity within nationalistic films that can be read against a history of "feminizing" Western representations of Chinese men. The significance of this shift becomes even more apparent when we consider the one Western vehicle in which Lee starred, *Enter the Dragon*, a film that gives him an asexual persona and that seeks to rewrite his image into that of a representative of colonial authority. Before moving on to a discussion of Lee's films in this context, I want to make a brief digression into literature. In her novel of Chinese-American womanhood, *The Woman Warrior*, Maxine Hong Kingston writes fantasies of omnipotence precisely in terms of shifting gendered identities. Thus her narrator tells us "[W]hen we Chinese girls listened to the adults talking-story, we learned that we failed if we grew up to be but wives or slaves. We could be heroines, swordswomen." She speculates on whether women "were once so dangerous that they had to have their feet bound" (*Woman Warrior* 25). The polarized terms, of bondage and of the swordswoman's raging freedom, are initially assigned a sex and a gender — female/feminine and male/masculine — from which the text seeks to break free. Kingston uses another opposition — that between China and America — in order to partly deconstruct this gendered binary. Her various narrators are, for much of the text, caught between the two. Kingston's writing invokes a variety of cross-cultural perspectives within an American context, in which China is read, through Orientalist discourses, as a mystical/feminine space.

Kingston's second book, *China Men*, opens with a short fragment, "On discovery," which describes Tang Ao's journey to America, the "land of women." He is captured by women who remove his armor and slowly, painfully "feminize" him. He is made up, his ears are pierced and his feet bound until, when he is serving food at court, we are told that his "hips swayed and his shoulders swivelled because of his shaped feet." He has become a beautiful and painful spectacle: " 'She's pretty, don't you agree?' the diners said, smacking their lips at his dainty feet as he bent to put dishes before them" (*China Men* 10). In this fragment and in the different narratives that follow, King-Kok Cheung sees both the book and its hostile critical reception from Asian critics as revealing "not only the similarities between Chinese men's and Chinese women's suffering but also the correlation between these men's umbrage at racism and their misogynist behaviour" (240). In this she points to the impossibility of tackling questions of gender "in the Chinese American cultural terrain without delving into the historically enforced 'feminization' of Chinese American men, without confronting the dialectics of racial stereotypes and nationalist reactions or, above all, without wrestling with die-hard notions of masculinity and femininity in both Asian and Western cultures" (234). This perception is crucial in enabling King-Kok Cheung to both critique and contextualize the attempts by male literary editors to reproduce and update a heroic masculine tradition of Asian literature. In a footnote Cheung also refers to Bruce Lee, pointing to his significance in representations of Chinese masculinity but also to his rather inhuman characterization in *Enter the Dragon*, the American film that is taken up below.

When Bruce Lee died in 1973 he was given two funerals. Chiao Hsiung-Ping writes of the thirty thousand people who attended his Hong Kong funeral, suggesting though that the event *"was only symbolic"* since the real thing "was held in Seattle, and Steve McQueen and James Coburn were among the

pall-bearers" ("Bruce Lee" 31; emphasis added). What was this double ceremony symbolic of? Perhaps it indicates something of the way in which Lee
was positioned, and positioned himself, as a star in both Asia and America.
Bruce Lee was, and remains, the only Chinese star to achieve an international visibility that included the West. He was also a very *visible* star in that
his films tended to emphasize his physicality in a way that some have characterized as narcissistic. Given that the role of the movie actor is defined by
display, the designation "narcissistic" tends to be invoked only when critics
feel such display is inappropriate or unsettling. In this sense it is significant
that Lee's assertion of a strong, muscular Chinese hero should be so often
dubbed unsettling by contemporary Western critics. Within his films Lee's
lithe muscularity is played off in spectacular film battles against huge, white,
muscular opponents: Chuck Norris in *Way of the Dragon*, Robert Baker in *Fist
of Fury*. I've already noted the way in which Lee's films build up to the moment when he will fight, keeping him clothed up to that point as a form of
disguise. Assuming a variety of disguises in *Fist of Fury*, Lee/Chen uses his invisibility as a Chinese man to spy on the Japanese school. The play of disguise
and revelation is also a play, once more, on an accumulated history of images
of softness and hardness, passivity and masculinity.

   The hardness of Lee's body and of his star image emerges from a history
of softness, a history of images in which both Chinese men and women had
been represented as passive and compliant. In an early film appearance as a
heavy in *Marlowe* (1968), James Garner suggests that Lee's character is gay, thus
leading him to lose his temper and leap to his death. Garner's jibe picks up
on the extent to which the display of Lee's body and physical grace was to be
emphasized in his persona. The display of the male body in action is felt to be
unsettling here, making too explicit as it does the homoeroticism implicit in
these man-to-man showdowns. Later on in his career, Lee was turned down
in favor of David Carradine for the lead role in the television series *Kung Fu*.
Of Carradine, Chuck Norris is reported to have said, with rather disarming
honesty, that he "is about as good a martial artist as I am an actor." Lee himself pondered whether perhaps "they weren't ready for a Hopalong Wong"
(qtd. in Glaessner 91). The earnestness of the Lee persona, along with the
comedic sections of his films, can be situated against this cinematic context.
Lee's struggle within America, which can be contrasted sharply with his success in Hong Kong, has emerged as a key element in the star image that has
developed since his death. Chuck Norris conveys something of this in the following description of Lee, which is taken from Norris's indicatively entitled
autobiography, *The Secret of Inner Strength*: "Bruce lived and breathed the martial

arts. I still recall the night I dropped in on him at home and found him in the den watching television. He was lying on his back in front of the TV set with his young son, Brandon, sitting on his stomach. Bruce had leg weights wrapped around his ankles. He had barbells in his hands. While bouncing Brandon on his stomach, he was inhaling and exhaling, thus tightening the muscles of his abdomen. At the same time, he was doing leg-ups and arm exercises" (67). Such testimonies form part of the mythology surrounding Bruce Lee, a mythos that is constructed through images of an obsessive commitment to training and the struggle to succeed, to become a star.

Lee's image speaks of a struggle to become hard, to negate an imputed softness. Another aspect of this is Lee's reputed refusal to follow any one school of fighting, instead appropriating and adapting a range of styles. Lee is complexly positioned as a star in both, and "in-between," Asia and America. Chiao Hsiung-Ping explores this positioning "in-between" in terms of what she calls Lee's "cross-cultural savvy." Having worked in both industries, she points out, Lee was in a good position to judge what would appeal across the two. He was responsible for moves toward the use of martial artists rather than actors in Hong Kong films, as well as the reduction of rapid editing, camera tricks, the use of trampolines, and so on. Lee "knew the generic importance of the fighting scene, but . . . strove for a 'believable' kung fu. . . . Oriental fantasies were reduced and western realism was emphasized" ("Bruce Lee" 33). In cinematic terms the meaning of this opposition between fantasy and realism is clear, avoiding trick camera work and so on. At an ideological level this opposition echoes a history of racial stereotypes, a history that seeks to represent the kinds of fantasies at work in the Western imaginary as somehow "real." [12]

If a strong masculinity is central to Bruce Lee's image, then this is accompanied by anxieties that prefigure the uncertainties that surround the personae of many white male stars today. That this image of the Chinese man was perceived as problematic within Hollywood is evident in *Enter the Dragon*. The film centers on three men, heroes who are constructed through the use of racial stereotypes. Bruce Lee plays Lee, who is the center of a film that is to a large extent a showcase for his skills. Along with Lee are a white American character called Roper, played by John Saxon (a B movie actor who received equal billing with Lee), and an African American, Williams, played by Jim Kelly, who went on to play the part of "Black Belt Jones." *Enter the Dragon* does not, however, go in for the extensive interracial male bonding that typifies many action pictures of recent years. While the three heroes talk to each other at various points, they do not act together and their stories are kept discrete. There is one key moment of recognizable male bonding in the film, between Williams and Roper when they first meet. Significantly, this moment centers on their shared experiences in Vietnam. Indeed, within the narratives of many American martial arts movies, Vietnam functions as the space/time when the hero acquired his fighting skills. Perhaps because of the very centrality of a "Vietnam" constituted against an Oriental Other in American films, *Enter the Dragon* is clearly uncomfortable with its racial mix, a mix that represents Warner Bros.'s very tentative attempts to promote a Chinese star. Anecdotally, while the film is often seen by Western audiences as Lee's greatest achievement—and it is the film for which he is best known in the West, Asian audiences were suspicious of the film (Chiao, "Bruce Lee" 37; see also Glaessner 93–96).

We are introduced to Lee in the Shaolin Temple, where an English official, Braithwaite, enlists his help against the evil Han (Shek Kin) who is involved in both drugs and sexual slavery. Han holds a martial arts tournament every three years on his fortress island as a way for him to recruit talent to his organization. The struggles against colonial opponents found in *Fist of Fury* and *Way of the Dragon* are replaced by Han who, with his white cat, is very clearly derived from a James Bondian lineage. Such a tradition does not offer a particularly fruitful space for the articulation of a Chinese identity, so that Lee seems to be placed once more in the role of Kato, the sidekick he had played years before in the American television series *The Green Hornet*. After Lee has agreed to act on behalf of the British, he is given a further motivation in a flashback that tells of the death of his sister (Angela Mao Ying). Roper is a compulsive gambler whose debts have led him to fight in the upcoming tournament. Williams's motivation for attending is less clear since we see him saying his good-byes wordlessly in an all-black martial arts school. As he is traveling to the airport Williams is harassed by two white policemen. Williams knocks the men out and steals their police car, signaling an underdeveloped narrative of racial conflict within America—a narrative that is displaced through images of the Orient.

In the complex relationship between the articulation of a Chinese and a masculine identity in Lee's image, the following comments from Robert Clouse, director of *Enter the Dragon*, are indicative:

> He [Lee] had this strut. . . . they showed me his first three films at Warner Bros. and . . . I said the first thing we have to do is kick the strut out of Bruce Lee. We're going to Westernize him to some degree. They wanted an international star. I said we would put him in carefully tailored suits instead of just his Chinese suits. We'll show him both ways. He should

look as though he'd be comfortable in New York or London. . . . [In *Enter the Dragon*] he comes strutting down the field toward the end of the big battle. . . . And I said . . . "You're beyond that now. A Western audience doesn't like the obvious strut. Let's play it straight there." ("Interview with Robert Clause" 43)

Caught up in fantasies of racial and sexual identity, Clouse speaks through oppositions of savagery and civilization, Western suits versus Chinese suits. Gail Ching-Liang Low heads her discussion of cultural cross-dressing with a pertinent statement from Frantz Fanon that the "colonised is elevated above his jungle status in proportion to his adoption of the mother country's cultural standards. He becomes whiter as he renounces his blackness, his jungle" (qtd. in Low 83). Such a logic structures Clouse's desire to put Lee in Western clothes in order that he be "comfortable" in the West, which is really to say that the West would be comfortable with him. Clouse's reference to "playing it straight" in this context unwittingly indicates the homoerotic imaginary that underpins the cinematic performance of Lee's body—a performance in which the body is offered as sexual spectacle, as a site of pleasure rather than subjection.

This same logic is also expressed through Clouse's (failed) intention to kick the strut out of Lee. This phrase signals something of the fear and mistrust that develops around Bruce Lee's star status in the West, fears bound up with the tough nationalistic male identity that is championed in his Hong Kong films. I don't want to suggest that Lee was completely controlled by this discourse, since the parts of *Enter the Dragon* that he directed, and his own performance in particular, do emerge (complete with strut) as to some extent separate from the messy compromise that is the film's attempt to cater to a range of audiences. The confusion of the film is expressly clear in its mobilization of sexualized discourses of race. The three fighters are, in appropriately Bondian-decadent style, offered the choice of a harem of women. Roper selects the white woman who seems to be in charge, while Williams selects four Asian women. Predictably enough, Lee's character absents himself, selecting a woman he knows to be a spy who has been placed on the island.

It is Kelly as Williams who must bear the burden of the film's discourse about race. It is no surprise then that the stereotype of the black stud is invoked or that Williams does not survive to the end of the movie. It is he who also voices the film's social commentary, pointing regretfully to the ghettos of the city. Amidst the general success of Hong Kong action pictures in the America of the 1970s, producers were not slow to notice the appeal of these films to an urban black audience. Black martial arts films, which built on the success of films like Shaft (1971), invoked a hypersexualized image of the black man. By contrast, one of the most enduring Western stereotypes of the East is as a site of a mystical, asexual knowledge. Richard Fung captures this, setting out a representational dichotomy in which Asian men are either an "egghead/wimp" or "the kung fu master/ninja/samurai." He is "sometimes dangerous, sometimes friendly, but almost always characterized by a desexualized Zen asceticism." Fung uses Fanon, who describes how "the Negro is eclipsed. He is turned into a penis. He is a penis," to draw a contrast with Western representations of the Asian man who "is defined by a striking absence down there" (148). In Enter the Dragon Chinese sexuality is erased while blackness, in the figure of Jim Kelly, becomes the overdetermined space through which the film signifies both sexuality and racial difference.

Western Stars and the Martial Arts Cinema

A commentary on the workings of the Western action cinema is useful here in contextualizing the kinds of operation at work in a film like Enter the Dragon or more recent Orientalist fictions, such as Showdown in Little Tokoyo, which I discuss below. The American martial arts film, which is a subsidiary of the big-budget action picture, has very little cultural prestige attached to it. Indeed, Western martial arts stars frequently express the desire to move on from the so-called "chop-socky" action film into more conventional action movies. Jean-Claude Van Damme is no exception, and his films have gradually moved away from showcasing martial arts into more traditional heroics. In any case, the overdeveloped muscular frames of the white Western stars are geared much more toward the sort of static, posed display involved in bodybuilding than the quick-fire action seen in the Hong Kong films. Given this tendency toward static display, it is perhaps not surprising to find that the films are centrally concerned with the sexual commodification of the (usually white) male body. The body is portrayed as sexual spectacle within a narrative that offers a critique of such commodification. Though there is not space here to develop the point fully, the different status of martial arts and other American action pictures can be understood partly through the sense that the martial arts form already carries the kinds of feminized associations that the Western imaginary has long ascribed to the East. The insistent homoeroticism of films featuring stars such as Van Damme, only makes it more important to distance him from such implicit feminization. Thus, it is black characters who once again take up the burden of a pathologized (homo)sexuality in the Western films.

A.W.O.L. (1990) casts Van Damme as Lyon, a soldier who has deserted the legion to visit his dying brother in America. He works his passage stoking the boilers of a ship, a typical plot device in that it both stresses the body as a site of manual labor and allows Van Damme to remove his clothes. Such moments of display are combined with set-piece fights. On his arrival Lyon meets Joshua, a crippled but street-smart black man, who initially seeks to exploit Lyon's fighting skill, though the two soon become buddies. The theme of the commodification of the working-class male body, typical of American fight movies, is also explicitly bound into the sexual implications of that commodification here, as Lyon finds himself working for "The Lady," who runs a high-class bare-knuckle fighting operation. The controlling figure of Cynthia, "The Lady," is a deeply fearful image of the powerful woman who at first seeks to control Lyon and then, when he spurns her sexually, matches him against a vicious white fighter known as Attila, who literally tears his opponents in two. The anxiety attendant on the commodification of the white male body is mediated here through the figure of the powerful (masculine) woman. The version of black masculinity articulated in these films is also crucial to securing the symbolic position of the hero. The recurrent figure of the "damaged" black man is central, with the crippled Joshua fulfilling this role in A.W.O.L., and Hawkins (who has a "dead" eye) befriending Van Damme in Death Warrant (1991). The physical flaws of these initially hostile but ultimately dependable men make them symbolically safe in an anxious representational world. Blackness also functions then as a space within which to deal with fears around homosexual desire.

In Death Warrant Van Damme plays Burke, a cop who goes undercover in a maximum-security jail. The prison narrative is a favorite of the American action cinema, allowing as it does for the free play of homoerotic images and for the repressive mobilization of stock characters, such as the sadistic white warden and guards, dependable black old-timers, and hysterical, knife-wielding Latins. Here the hero is explicitly threatened with rape, an assault that the film's editing implies, though it cannot seem to explicitly state. While Western martial arts and other action movies thrive on interracial same-sex friendships, homosexuality or any notion of gay desire remains almost exclusively expressed in terms of threat and violence. The fight then provides the perfect space for male physical intimacy—since that intimacy is accompanied by a compensatory brutal violence. Serving to highlight the sexual significance of the "castrated" black man in these fictions is another level of blackness conjured up by *Death Warrant* in the figure of Priest. He inhabits a mysterious realm beneath the prison: "The lower you go the funkier it gets in this place," Burke's cell mate tells him cheerfully, adding that he should "cover his ass" and "I mean that literally—it's not a figure of speech." We are told that even the guards won't come here—it is a space then that is both sexual and totally other. Here we find Priest, surrounded by his "ladies," male/female inmates who function as profoundly unstable and hauntingly present figures in the film—images of the subterranean depths that lie beneath the sexual relations as relations of power that structure the prison world. The film both acknowledges and plays to the existence of gay desire, in its images and its narrative, while finally projecting this desire onto a space of pathologized black masculinity, in which sexuality is part of a more general excess.

An earlier Van Damme movie, *Kickboxer* (1989), not only teams the hero with a "damaged" black man—Taylor, a cynical veteran scarred by his experiences in Vietnam—but also employs stereotypical images of the East. Thai kickboxing champion Tong Po embodies the Orient as sexual threat, alongside the figures of the mythic sage and the virginal maiden. The structure of this film is a familiar one in the West. A young white man persuades an ancient "Oriental" man to teach him the skills of a secret martial art. At the same time, he typically meets an "innocent" girl and falls in love. Although he seems to face impossible odds, he ultimately wins out in the final moments of the film. Now this is to some extent a familiar narrative of the Hong Kong cinema in the 1970s. The hero is initially beaten, learns a secret technique that makes him invincible, and, after extended torturous training, is ultimately triumphant—this is roughly the plot of *The Chinese Boxer*. But the version of this narrative that places the white hero at the center represents a significant rewriting.

To think about this further I'll refer briefly to an American cop movie, *Showdown in Little Tokoyo* (1991). Starring Dolph Lundgren and Brandon Lee, this is a rare film in its casting of a Chinese actor in a major heroic role. The film seeks to capitalize on an action-comedy tradition by casting Lee as a thoroughly Westernized Japanese-American, who to some extent undercuts the strong-silent performance of costar Dolph Lundgren.[13] In a perverse colonial logic, Aryan beefcake Lundgren plays a cop brought up in Japan who styles himself as a samurai warrior. His knowledge of Japanese tradition, language, and culture is played off against Lee's Westernized persona. The film's fantasy of cultural cross-dressing operates both to negate the homoeroticism implicit in the buddy relationship and to produce a complex fantasy of white mastery through the appropriation and penetration of the other's culture. Speaking of fantasies of cultural cross-dressing in nineteenth-century imperialist literature, Gail Ching-Liang Low points out that since "the Orient becomes, through western imagination, a site of excess sexuality and deviant behaviour that must be penetrated and controlled," then the "violation of a subject-culture may also be read as a sexualised text" (95).[14] In *Showdown in Little Tokoyo* this fantasy might be directly interpreted in terms of the racist articulation of American fears around Japanization. That these fears are bound up with masculine identity is perhaps most apparent in the "comic" moment when Lee's character compliments Lundgren's on the size of his penis. Recalling Richard Fung's comments on Western myths of Asian sexuality as asexuality, it is clear that Lundgren's superwhite, muscular body functions as a fetish within the film. The body is clearly constituted by "race," and yet it also refuses the limits of that constitution. The freedom to shift, transgress, and adopt racial identities in this way is, of course, as Ching-Liang Low points out, available to different groups differently (98).[15]

Jackie Chan: Masculinity and Kung Fu Comedy

Jackie Chan's combination of action with slapstick comedy is quite distinct from the earnest and anxious suffering of the white stars, and from the dominating figure of Bruce Lee. His films are much more at ease with the hectic heroics of their male protagonists, heroics that are at once offered as spectacle and comically undercut. Comic interludes and punch lines punctuate even relatively tense narratives such as the *Police Story* films. I'd like to make some brief comments on Jackie Chan's films here as a way of talking about a very different kind of Hong Kong filmmaking to that associated with Bruce Lee. The films use a variety of physical set pieces—both comic and violent—drawing on a theatrical tradition that is committed to a different kind of spectacle than the more static bodily display at work in many American films. This is most apparent in the orchestration of group fights of amazing complexity, as in the bar room brawl and the final showdown of *Project A*. The more restrained playground battle in *Police Story 2* pitches Chan against a group of thugs, but even here, when the hero fights alone, the camera work is carefully choreographed around the scene, rather than the individual hero, as spectacle.

Of course, many of the films I've already discussed include comic moments, though I've not focused on this aspect of the action tradition. What distinguishes the quick-fire timing and slapstick comedy for which Chan has become famous is the infiltration of comedy into the fight scenes themselves, fights that as we've seen, form the center of the martial arts movie. In Chan's films, fights are played both seriously and for laughs, as when opponents come to blows and then back off shaking their fists or rubbing their heads in pain. Such moments admit both the possibility of pain and the vulnerability of the body. There is an indicative moment in *Wheels on Meals* when costars Chan and Yuen Biao are involved in a street fight. They look at each other, agree that their opponents are too tough and simply run away. Chan, while at times a very graceful fighter, also plays on the way in which both the body and technology lets its owner down. Thus he often seems to win his fights more by good luck and determination than skill. In the middle of a tense fight at the end of *Wheels on Meals*, Chan frees himself from a hold by tickling his opponent. Similarly, most of the people in a Jackie Chan film are *at some point* a fighter—characters are not written as professional fighters and they are not necessarily students or teachers in a martial arts school. Pauline Yeung, the romantic lead in *Dragons Forever*, who spends most of her time being rescued or wooed, suddenly, and quite inexplicably, produces a short set-piece display of fighting skill, knocking out a bad guy in the films final showdown.

In Chan's movies it is more often the case that women are either explicitly cast as, or ultimately revealed to be, girlish. They increasingly seem to represent a troublesome presence, both an annoying and a fascinating distraction from adventures and from the concerns of male friendship. Heterosexual romance is an important term for the definition of an adult masculine identity in the films, but is also the cause of myriad problems, as in the two *Police Story* films. The chorus of three women who keep getting in Chan's way in *Operation Condor: Armour of God 2* (1991) represents an extreme articulation of women-as-femininity-as-chaos. An inordinate amount of screen time is given over to the comic demonstration of female incompetence, by contrast to Western movies that are much more likely to exclude women altogether. The original *Armour of God* was reviewed and marketed in the West as Chan's attempt to cash in on the success of the *Indiana Jones* films. While these successful films do provide a reference point, there is more than a little naiveté in the assumption that Hong Kong always follows in the wake of Hollywood, especially given Hong Kong's long tradition of producing epic adventure films. So while some critics suggested the film was Westernized, they didn't in turn acknowledge the ways in which *The Armour of God* redefines and undercuts those Hollywood traditions that it does draw on. Indeed, Chan emerges from a changed industrial context in Hong Kong, and the figure of the adventurer is rewritten within its existing traditions. Chan plays Jackie, the "Asian Hawk," an ex–pop star turned adventurer who tracks down ancient artifacts for sale to the highest bidder. The film allows Chan to explore a Europe that is constructed as an alien and exotic territory. The hero is pitted against a fabulously bizarre sect of evil monks who are ensconced in a mountain retreat. A rather camp waiter tells them that the monks come down once a month to fetch supplies and women, establishing both the opponents and the terrain as sexually decadent. The terms of Orientalist fantasies are turned around on themselves, as Europe becomes the site of an exotic adventure for the Chinese heroes and heroine.

The film turns on the relationship between Jackie and his best friend Alan. Though Alan is to some extent a clownish character, this is set up differently to the physical comedy constructed around Chan. Though we see him early on performing in a spectacular stage show before a huge Hong Kong crowd, he lacks masculine competence within the film's terms. He is something of a fashion plate, modeling a series of stylish clothes throughout the film. Given this characterization it is not surprising that Alan is useless in a fight, pointing out hysterically that he doesn't believe in violence while holding onto Jackie for protection, getting them into trouble and needing to be rescued. If the fight bears the narrative discourse of the martial arts film, then a hero who cannot fight is an oddity. Within the film's discourse about masculinity Alan is clearly situated within a feminine position that is played for laughs. The comedy format allows for an articulation of masculinity that is to some extent fluid, not expressed exclusively in terms of a muscular hardness. Ultimately, though, *The Armour of God* falls back on blackness as a space of sexualized deviance. In one of the film's final sequences, when Jackie is attempting to steal the armor, four black furies are turned on him. These fighting women are kitted out in black corsets and stilettos. Both comic and fetishistic, these women represent the displacement of an exaggerated sexuality onto blackness. This image echoes the opening of the film, located in a fantasized Africa, in which Jackie fools a black tribe by talking gibberish. He escapes, stealing the sword that is part of the "armour of god," using a variety of gadgets and stunts. The structures at work here are replicated in the recent sequel, *Operation Condor* (1991), which again begins with Jackie fooling a black African tribe. This time he only narrowly escapes from the threat of marriage. The "Asian Hawk" achieves his heroic identity at the expense of an Africa constructed as primitive and easily fooled.

Unlike Bruce Lee, the struggle for American success is not foregrounded in Jackie Chan's star image, though he also made a rather disastrous American movie with Robert Clouse at one point in his career.[16] "Bruce had that hard tight look whenver he wanted it," observes Clouse, the man who we recall wanted to "kick the strut" out of Lee. Clouse goes on to remark that he "thought Jackie Chan had it but he was soft" ("Interview with Robert Clouse" 9). Chan's "softness" does not consist in a lack of muscularity or an inability to fight, but more in a refusal either to take the male body too seriously or to play the part of Oriental other. Chan's persona is built on the cheerful admission of vulnerability at work in his films—most obviously in the inclusion at the end of the movies of outtakes featuring stunts gone wrong. And while he frequently gets beaten up in his films, he is nonetheless in control. As Chan put it: "In Hong-Kong, I can control everything. In Hollywood I'm just a Chinese actor who speaks bad English" (Rayns 84).

Discourses of race and masculinity are elaborated in vastly different ways in the various martial arts films discussed in this essay. I have sought to comment on some of the many contrasting traditions and subgenres, and to argue that the construction of racial and gendered identities in the genre is not as simple or as easily characterized as it may seem. Though many films work to reinscribe sexual and racial stereotypes, our readings also need to be situated within a historical and a cinematic context. The discussion of the very distinct star images and films of Bruce Lee, Jean-Claude Van Damme, and Jackie Chan emphasizes the radically different ways that the ideas, images, and themes associated with the martial arts genre can be inflected. Indeed, though I have used the term "genre" here, it is probably evident from the range of films discussed that there is no clearly definable set of rules that can encapsulate the martial arts film across either the output of decades or the different industries of Hollywood and Hong Kong.

I have sought to argue, though, that there are certain themes recurring across different films—power and powerlessness, physical limitations and their transgression, narratives of revenge, and so on—that have a clear resonance for the discussion of the construction of masculine identities in the cinema. A central focus for this discussion has been the role of the body in the genre, with the suggestion that we can see the constitution of gendered identities in the cinema as operating through the act of imagining and resisting bodily boundaries. The discussion of various films and stars offered here can only further emphasize the extent to which ideas and images of masculine power—defined through such figures as the "hard" male body, the ability to bear suffering, and ultimately to triumph—are intertwined with discourses of race, class, sexuality, and nationality.

Notes

Thanks to Val Hill, Leon Hunt, and Gwion Jones for their ideas and comments.

1. While the primary focus of this essay is male martial arts stars, Hong Kong cinema has a long tradition of female fighters. Western martial artist Cynthia Rothrock went to Hong Kong to make films such as *Above the Law* (with Yuen Biao), while in Hollywood producers seem more likely to cast her as a "girlfriend."

2. Popular Asian cinema has an extensive circulation in the West through forms such as video. The point I'm making here is that these forms are marginal in comparison to the more widely available and more widely discussed Hollywood material. There are complex links between the popular cinemas of Hong Kong, Taiwan, Japan, and Bombay. These traditions are often ignored by Western criticism, though attention has been paid to more prestigious Asian films. For an excellent industrial survey see Lent.

3. This tendency is most evident in the frequent use of the figure of the Vietnam veteran, portrayed as a slightly unbalanced man who has lost his comrades in battle and been betrayed by his government.

4. I do not know of any Hong Kong action films that deal explicitly with the colonial present, though British figures are very visible, if marginal, in films—for example, the *Police Story* and *Project A* films. Chiao Hsiung-Ping describes *Project A: II* (1987) as "given over to addressing the contradictory situation whereby Hong Kong now fears the 1997 return to the mainland and would rather remain colonised" ("Distinct Taiwanese" 160).

5. In *The Wretched of the Earth* Frantz Fanon writes that "The native is a being hemmed in; apartheid is simply one form of the division into compartments of the colonial world. The first thing which the native learns is to stay in his place and not go beyond certain limits" (40). Fanon also emphasizes that the experience of the world through such oppressive limits generates fantasies of physical empowerment. See also Robins and Cohen, especially *Knuckle Sandwich: Growing Up in the Working-Class City* 94–103, in which they discuss the appeal of the martial arts; and see Walkerdine, for a discussion of class in relation to narratives of fighting. A key reference point for my argument here is Butler's *Gender Trouble*. Butler uses Foucault to discuss the constitution of the body through signs.

6. See Glaessner 54.

7. Glaessner outlines the function of the antagonist school in these films as "a straightforward stand-in for the institutions involved in Japanese imperialism or for their less overt infiltration into Chinese life" (36).

8. The most useful reference point for a consideration of this play of qualities is in the work of anthropologist Mary Douglas, such as *Natural Symbols* and *Purity and Danger*. Theweleit takes up the image of the body as armor in relation to militarist culture in *Male Fantasies*. Theweleit, however, tends toward a pathologization of the ways in which identity is constructed through the establishment of bodily limits.

9. I'm referring here to Freud's essay "On Narcissism" (1914), in which narcissism is situated as part of human development rather than a property of a perverse few.

10. Male buddy relationships are crucial to the Hong Kong action film and have become more explicitly eroticized in some recent films such as *The Killer* (1989). See Chiao, "The Distinct Taiwanese" 163, for what she describes as a "macho/gay feel" to some recent Hong Kong films. The distinction I'm seeking to draw here, though, is around the extent to which recent Western films quite obsessively center on relationships between men.

11. Jeffords interestingly uses the term "remasculinization" in the context of recent representations around Vietnam. See her *The Remasculinization of America*.

12. Though he doesn't discuss China in an extensive way, Said's *Orientalism* is a crucial point of reference here. Bhabha's writings on colonial discourse develop these points within a psychoanalytic framework. See his "Of Mimicry and Man: The Ambivalence of Colonial Discourse" and "Sly Civility."

13. Jackie Chan was also called on to play a Japanese character in the *Cannonball Run* films, part of an early attempt to break into Western markets.

Brandon Lee seems aware that his father's name has given him an access to the American industry denied to other Chinese actors. The publicity machine seems determined to push this line, dubbing him "Son of the Dragon." See, for example, "Interview with Brandon Lee." Since this essay was originally written, Brandon Lee died in unusual circumstances and we have seen the much hyped release of his last film, finished with the help of computer technology. The turn to be taken by media mythology around his death remains to be seen.

14. Bhabha's writings (see note 12) are relevant here in terms of the processes of failed identification at work in the complex fantasies of mastery that structure colonial discourse.

15. Mercer offers an interesting discussion of Michael Jackson's changing image in this context in his "The Boy Who Fell to Earth" 34–35.

16. The film was *The Big Brawl* (1980), which Clouse directed. This is not to suggest that Chan is somehow a more "subversive" figure than Lee. Rather that the two emerged from very different historical moments.

PHOTOGRAPHIES OF MOURNING

Melancholia and Ambivalence in Van Der Zee,

Mapplethorpe, and *Looking for Langston*

JOSÉ E. MUÑOZ

Deciphering A Dream Deferred

Black gay male cultural production is experiencing a boom of sorts. No single type of cultural production is trailblazing the way; this wave of black gay male cultural production is very different from, to cite an obvious example, a tradition of black women writing. Joseph Beam's now classic anthology *In the Life*, the videos of Marlon Riggs, the cultural criticism of Kobena Mercer, the music of Blackberri, the poetry of Essex Hemphill, the fiction of Melvin Dixon, the photos of Rotimi Fani-Kayode, the dance and choreography of Bill T. Jones, and the performance art of Po-Mo Afro Homos, to name a handful of representatives from the black queer diaspora, all inform and help form one another. If one were to describe the unifying concepts, potencies, and tensions that bind the artists listed above as something we might call a movement, beyond and beside the simple fact of their "identities," it would be the complicated task that they accomplish. This task can be summed up as the (re)telling of elided histories that need to be both excavated and (re)imagined over and above the task of bearing the burden of representing an identity that is challenged and contested by various forces, including, but not limited to, states that blindly neglect the suffering bodies of men caught within a plague, the explosion of "hate crime" violence that targets black and gay bodies, and a reactionary media power structure that would just as soon dismiss queer existence as offer it the most fleeting reflection. In this shifting field of artistic performance and production I will examine what might be thought of as a slippery center: Isaac Julien's *Looking for Langston* (1989). In this instance, I use the term "center" to describe the way that film, as a primarily collaborative art form, incorporates and displays other modes of black queer cultural production like music, performance, poetry, prose, cultural criticism, and photography.

In this essay I resist the term "masculinity" as it is examined and deployed elsewhere in this volume. Masculinity has been and continues to be a normative rubric that has policed the sex/gender system. I see very little advantage in recuperating the term masculinity since, as a category, masculinity has normalized heterosexual and male privilege. Masculinity is, among other things, a cultural imperative to enact a mode of "manliness" that is calibrated to shut down queer possibilities and energies. The social construct of masculinity is experienced by far too many men as a regime of power that labors to invalidate, exclude, and extinguish faggotry, effeminacy, and queerly-coated butchness. This is not to discount the possibility that a discourse on masculinity might produce some theoretical traction for scholars working in the field of gender theory. However, I suggest that any such project that fails to consider and interrogate heteronormative and masculinist contours of such a discourse will reproduce the phobic ideology of masculinity.

I hope to offer a reading that will contribute to an understanding of both where this crucial wave of work is coming from and where it currently stands, as well as a decipherment of *Looking for Langston*'s densely layered, aestheticized, and politicized workings. In this analysis I intend to carry out Sylvia Wynter's call for a turn toward *decipherment* as opposed to the dominant scholarly mode of "interpretation," of the "play" of "meanings" and significations a text produces. This decipherment of *Looking for Langston* (and what I see as its influential "co-texts") will attempt to carry out the program for film studies outlined by Wynter in her recent essay "Rethinking 'Aesthetics': Notes Towards a Deciphering Practice":

> Rather than seeking to "rhetorically demystify," a deciphering turn seeks to decipher what a process of rhetorical mystification *does*. It seeks to identify not what texts and their signifying practices can be interpreted to *mean* but what they can be deciphered to *do*, it also seeks to evaluate the "illocutionary force" and procedures with which they do what they do.[1]

This essay will attempt specifically to map out two different tropes or structures of feeling[2]—melancholia and ambivalence—that are central to a comprehension of the inner (textual) and external (social and political) work that the texts under consideration do.

A grand and glowing mytho-text, *Looking for Langston* makes no stale claims of documentary objectivity. It is, in Julien's own words at the beginning of the film, a "meditation" on "Langston Hughes and the Harlem Renaissance." The word "meditation" implies a text that does not deal with clouded imperatives to tell what "really" happened or to give the reader a plastic, "you were there" sensation. The text is instead profoundly evocative, suggestive, and, as I will argue in depth, ambivalent. A meditation like this invites a reader to join the filmmaker in a contemplative position. The invitation reads: imagine, remember, flesh out.

Julien's film is a challenge to more terminal histories that work to dispel and undermine anything but flat, empirical, historiographical facts.[3] An example of this mode of history writing, one that more often than not excludes nonconventional, and especially queer historiography, is Arnold Rampersad's biography of Langston Hughes. Rampersad dismisses considerations of the poet as gay writer due to a lack of empirical evidence: the biographer was unable to find any living person (male or female) who would admit to having had sex with Hughes. Such naive reasoning from such a sophisticated critic is unsettling. This suspicious blindness to both the different economies of desire and the historical and concurrent bonds of gay intertextuality that Hughes shares with other gay cultural workers can only be construed as heterosexist. While it is not my project here, it does bear mentioning that Rampersad's text deserves a long and rigorous inquiry, an inquiry that would examine the heterosexist logic of a study which altogether dismisses the subject's sexual identity before considering a homosexual possibility that, for any attentive reader, is far from opaque.[4] I would argue that a dynamic text like Julien's film offers all the "evidence" one needs to make the case for Langston Hughes as queer.

The evidence that I mention above is not the evidence of rigorous historical fact; it is rather the evidence of revisionary history that meditates on the queer cadences that can be heard in Hughes's life and work. It is a mode of history reading that listens with equal attention to the silences and echoes that reverberate through the artist's production. I understand the historiographical project of *Looking for Langston* to be in line with that called for by Joan W. Scott, the historian of "difference." Scott explains that it is insufficient and risky to propose historiographical salvage operations that troll for some "lost" and essential "experience." The implicit danger of such projects is explicated in a recent essay by Scott:

> History is a chronology that makes experience visible, but in which categories appear as nonetheless ahistorical: desire, homosexuality, heterosexuality, femininity, masculinity, sex and even sexual practices become so many fixed entities being played out over time, but not themselves historicized. Presenting the story this way excludes, or at least understates,

the historically variable interrelationship between the meanings "homo-sexual" and "heterosexual," the constitutive force each has for the other, and the contested nature of the terrain that they simultaneously occupy.[5]

As I argue in the remainder of this essay, Julien's cinematic practice defies the lure of simply propping up a newfound history of what the queer Harlem Renaissance might have been. This cinematic meditation does not confine itself to single meanings but instead works to explain the lack of fixity of such terms as "queer," "Black," and "male" within the temporal space that is represented. Indeed the film works to undermine any static or rigid defini-tions of these concepts.

The first of many "key" Hughes phrases that one catches in the film is "montage of a dream deferred," and the film, in its fluid dimensions, takes up the challenge of this phrase and imagines what it might look like. The classical cinematic theory of montage, first theorized and deployed by the Soviet filmmaker Sergei Eisenstein as "a montage of attractions," speaks quite fluidly to Julien's project. The variation in Julien's interpretation of cinematic montage is his reliance on the juxtaposition of "attractions" that are not merely shots but rather fabrics not traditionally found within the tapestry of montage cinema: materials that include poems, experimental fiction, still photographs, vintage newsreels, and blues songs. Montage cinema creates a certain rhythm in its stark juxtapositions of images that, on the level of tradi-tional narrative logic, clash and set each other off. *Looking for Langston*, though stylistically elegant and apparently seamless, calls upon this tried-and-true calculus of juxtapositions. While the textures of the film's "attractions" are not traditional, they do roughly cluster around two different poles. The poles are connected to the project of black gay male self-representation I have sketched above, a project that is carried out against a heterosexist culture's hegemonic mandate that these lives not be seen, heard, or known. One of the two poles is the "historical self" that is represented chiefly by archival images from the Harlem Renaissance, and the other is the contemporaneous self that produces images that represent an "under-siege" reality. Both poles are em-battled. The historical one is a counterhistory that must constantly define itself against "larger," more official and oppressive histories; the contempo-rary identity pole is populated by images that depict the dangers (and, of course, pleasures) of occupying a black and gay subject position during this particular moment of crisis. I do not wish to reify this dichotomy between "then" and "now" since the film certainly does not commit this error. A suc-cessful montage—and *Looking for Langston* certainly is one—eventually uses the current produced by binary juxtapositions to create what might seem like an autonomous whole. This "wholeness effect" is enacted through the dialectical interplay of conflicting elements.

In his essay "A Dialectic Approach to Film Form" Eisenstein explains that it is not only the visible elements of shots that can be juxtaposed in a montage system. There is also the strategy of emotional combination that produces what the early film theorist has called "emotional dynamization." According to Eisenstein, this brand of montage, if successful, ultimately leads to "liberation of the whole action from the definition of time and space."[6] The transhistorical crosscutting in Julien's film achieves, through its use of evocative and sometimes elusive contrasts and similarities, just such a liberation. The concept of time and space that is generated occupies overlapping temporal and geographical coordinates that we can understand as a queer black cultural imaginary. It is important to also keep in mind that this queer black cultural imaginary is in no way ahistorical. Its filaments are historically specific, and the overall project is more nearly transhistorical. Fredric Jameson, in writing about the triumph of Eisenstein's cinema, sums up the "pay off" that montage can yield when trying to depict history:

> Montage thus assumes the existence of the time between shots, the process of waiting itself, as it reaches back and encompasses the two poles of its former dynamic, thereby embodying itself as emptiness made visible—the line of Russian warriors in the distance, or even more climactically, the empty horizon on which the Teutonic Knights, not yet present, impend.[7]

Looking for Langston resembles Jameson's delineation of "montage" in that the film attempts to represent, make visible, and even champion at least a few different histories that have, due to the strong arm of "official histories," been cloaked.

It would be reductive to account for the dynamic transhistorical referents in the film solely within the terms of the inner working of the formalist montage paradigm. As I mentioned earlier, this runs too high a risk of reifying history and the present. My position in this essay flirts with this problematic, so to resist this trap I will offer another structural model that considers the interplay of transhistorical elements in Looking for Langston. Another mode of understanding the interchange between elements that correspond to different historical moments is the idea of a dialectical interchange between present and past tenses. This seems right in that it speaks to the fact that, as a particular kind of avant-garde film, Looking for Langston is grounded in a complex relation of fragments to a whole. For heuristic purposes, I would like to associate the first pole with a historical black homosexual "tradition" which closes around the images of male Harlem Renaissance queers like Hughes, Countee Cullen, Alain Locke, Wallace Thurman, Bruce Nugent, and Claude McKay. I will associate the other pole with contemporary cultural activists such as Essex Hemphill, Marlon Riggs, and Assotto Saint. It is worthwhile to consider these texts as tangled within a complicated transhistorical dialogue—something akin to Gayl Jones's definition of a traditional African American oral trope known as "call and response," the

> antiphonal back-and-forth pattern which exists in many African American oral traditional forms, from sermon to interjective folk tale to blues, jazz and spirituals and so on. In the sermonic tradition, the preacher calls in a fixed or improvised refrains, while the congregation responds, in either fixed and formulaic or spontaneous words and phrases.[8]

With this pattern in mind, one can hear Essex Hemphill's impassioned poetic voice crying out from one of these historical poles, "Now we think while we fuck," and actually speaking across time to a "forgotten" or "lost" black queer identity painfully embodied in the hushed tones of Langston Hughes's simple, sorrowful, epitaph-like "Poem":

> I loved my friend
> He went away from me
> There is nothing more to say
> This poem ends
> As softly as it began
> I loved my friend.[9]

By pointing to this cross-time dialogue between black gay males, I am suggesting that Julien makes use of call and response to historicize black gay male history and contextualize recent queer African-American cultural production. While rooted in a black vernacular tradition, this technique is innovative in film. The positing of this model as a tool for understanding the transhistorical narrative economy in Looking for Langston does not completely eclipse the notion of the film as a montage. They are, I hope, at least provisionally compatible paradigms that melt into each another.

In general terms, I have discussed how the nontraditional fabrics juxtapose one another in this "montage" or "call and response" weave. Many of these transhistorical pairings bear closer inspection. For example, in a powerful moment early in the film, the voice of bisexual blues singer Bessie Smith is set off by and then briefly mingles with the contemporary song "Blues for Langston," sung by the songwriter/vocalist Blackberri. The resonance of these two voices produces a smooth superimposition that is visually impossible. In an interview, British filmmaker Julien commented upon his need to turn to America to unearth a queer black history—there was no historical icon as provocative as Hughes on his side of the diaspora. The "American" element that factors into the film's hybrid model can be best understood as a "blues aesthetic." In his seminal study on this American form, Houston Baker Jr. describes the blues as a matrix: "The matrix is a point of ceaseless input and output, a web of intersecting, crisscrossing impulses always in productive transit. Afro-American blues constitute such a vibrant network." [10] *Looking for Langston* incorporates the "matrix" function into its own hybridized aesthetic.

While recognizing this matrix function, it is important to maintain that the syncretic incorporation of the blues aesthetic does not overshadow the contemporary black British aesthetic that fills out much of the film. Julien wished to assert his own national identity, hence British locales, actors, and voices are called upon to establish a black British cultural presence that shares a certain symmetry with the African American presence. Coterminous with the American blues aesthetic is the black British diaspora aesthetic of the Black Arts Movement. One can view the film as very much a part of this British movement, which attempts to negotiate representation from a productive space of hybridity, situated between postmodernism and what Paul Gilroy has called "populist modernism." Gilroy describes members of the black British film movement (a movement central to the Black Arts Movement) as enacting a DuBoisian double consciousness: they identify both as cultural producers who are located in modernity and are clearly defenders, producers, and critics of modernism, but who nonetheless feel a moral responsibility to act as the "gravediggers of modernity"—to never forget that they are also the "stepchildren of the West" whose task it is to transform modernity and the aesthetics of modernism to vernacular forms that are "populist," expressive, and not elitist. *Looking for Langston*'s cinematic structure as a transhistorical and transnational "weavelike" texture can be understood as a product of the discomfort caused by traditional Western genre constraints that Gilroy locates in popular modernism: "The problem of genre is there in the desire to transcend key western categories: narrative, documentary, history and literature, ethics and politics." [11]

I will now focus on what I see as the central binary of the film: a binary of photographic images. The juxtapositions and tensions of the photographic binary bear primary responsibility for shaping the film both visually and thematically. The two most crucial and structuring photographic presences in this film are those of Harlem Renaissance portrait photographer James Van Der Zee and New York avant-garde portrait photographer Robert Mapplethorpe.

The Picture of Melancholia

Before discussing mourning and the function of the photographs in Julien's work, I would like to elaborate on my consideration of Looking for Langston as both a photo-centric text and a mytho-text. This populist, modernist mode of "writing" history challenges and confounds traditional historiographies, a point that becomes salient when one reads a passage from Barthes's exquisite book Camera Lucida that considers the relation of the photograph to history:

> A paradox: the same century invented History and Photography. But History is a memory fabricated according to positive formulas, a pure intellectual discourse which abolishes mythic Time; and the Photograph is a certain but fugitive testimony.[12]

While the foundation of Barthes's binary may be somewhat shaky, it serves to illuminate the unique relationship of the photographic document (producing the effect he calls "that-has-been") and the "pure" intellectual discourse of history. The photographs of Hughes and James Baldwin, held up by beautiful queer putti during the film's opening panoramic shots (Figure 1), serve as a fleeting yet powerful testimony to black queer presences within histories that often neglect them. The viewer is left in the position of reading these very vital mythologies and spinning more narratives around them. The photograph in Looking for Langston is a charm that wards off "official histories" and reinscribes necessary mythologies. These mythologies are open spaces of inquiry rather than monolithic narratives full of identity-denying silences.

In 1915 Freud introduced a theory of mourning that is, like most Freud, implicitly heterosexist, tantalizingly thought-provoking, and ultimately unsatisfying. He writes that "[m]ourning is regularly the reaction to the loss of a loved one, or to the loss of some abstraction which has taken the place of one such as one's country, liberty, an ideal, so on."[13] Mourning, unlike melancholia, which he marks as pathological, is a process in which an object or abstraction becomes absent and the withdrawal of libido from the object becomes necessary. But these demands cannot be enacted at once. Libido detaches bit by bit, perpetuating a mode of unreality, because, while the process

Figure 1. Akim Mogaji as the Fallen Angel in *Looking for Langston*, dir. Isaac Julien. (Third World Newsreel)

of libido removal is transpiring, the lost object/abstraction persists. It is, in its simplest formulation, a gradual letting go. This process becomes the work of mourning. Van Der Zee's and Mapplethorpe's pictures, for radically different reasons, symbolically represent and stand in as "works" of mourning.

In Freud's initial definition, melancholia spills into the realm of the pathological because it resembles a mourning that does not know when to stop.[14] Freud used the idea of mourning as a sort of foil to talk about the psychopathology of melancholia. In the *Ego and the Id* he begins to deconstruct his previous binary when he realizes that the identification with the lost object that he at first described as occurring in melancholia is also a crucial part of the work of mourning. The line between mourning and melancholia in this work of cinematic grieving is amazingly thin; it is a fiction that offers itself readily for deconstructing.

Through a highly formalistic route Van Der Zee's and Mapplethorpe's projects are heavily valenced as works of mourning. Van Der Zee and Mapplethorpe are known as master portraitists, and the practice of portraiture suggests another interrelation. Jacques Derrida makes a crucial connection between the work of mourning and prosopopeia, the trope of mourning that Paul de Man wrote about extensively. Prosopopeia was understood by de Man as the trope of autobiography, the giving of names, the giving of face, "the fiction of an apostrophe to an absent, deceased, or voiceless entity, which posits the possibility of the latter's reply and confers upon it the power of speech." [15] The autobiography and the portrait give voice to the face from beyond the grave; prosopopeia is also a way of remembering, holding onto, letting go of "the absent, the deceased, the voiceless." Thus, in the same way that one who writes in a biographical vein summons up the dead, by the deployment of prosopopeia, one who mourns a friend summons her up through elaborate ventriloquism. This contributes to an understanding of how the transhistorical call and response that I proposed above might function: a portrait of Hughes, with his less than perfect mouth smiling a characteristically disarming smile, enacts a strategic flexing of the autobiographical trope that summons back a dead Hughes, gives him voice and permits him to engage in a dialogue with the living black gay male body of Essex Hemphill. The photographic portrait first gives face, then gives voice.

This giving of face and subsequently voice should also be understood as a component of the performative aspect of portrait photography. The portrait photograph is a two-sided performance, one of the photographer who manipulates technology, models, props, and backgrounds behind the camera and the other the model who performs "self" especially and uniquely for the camera. [16] Mourning, in all of its ritualized gestures and conventions, is also performative insofar as the mourner plays a very specific role on a culturally prescribed stage. Viewing both portrait photography and mourning as performative practices, one understands the unique linkage between the two practices—in the case of portraiture a lost object is captured and (re)produced, and in melancholic mourning the object is resurrected and retained. Funeral photography, which grew out of the colonial American tradition of "mourning paintings," is situated at the moment in which both performances blur and take on a crucial role in each other's theater.

In many cultures mourning is highly aestheticized. The scenes of mourning that are enacted in James Van Der Zee's *The Harlem Book of the Dead* are lush and disquieting. In a morbid grammar (that is in no way devoid of wit), Van Der Zee spells out some of the issues that surface when considering mourning and melancholia. The painful attachments that refuse to fade during the process of mourning and the subsequent inability to accept reality are displayed in the section depicting children titled "Children & the Mystery of Birth." In a gesture that might seem macabre today, Van Der Zee posed dead babies with their parents. Asked about this particular artistic strategy, Van Der Zee replied: "It was my suggestion to have them hold the child while the picture was being taken to make it look more natural." [17] This posing of the dead child with the parents succinctly performs the melancholic and gives it a visual presence. This can also be easily read in Van Der Zee's photograph of a man buried with his newspaper because his family wished to imagine that he was not actually dead but instead had once again just fallen asleep reading the paper.

Another photo in the "Children & the Mystery of Birth" section employs a different strategy in its attempt to visualize the process of African American mourning. In this photo an older child is lying in a casket, and a figure that is presumably his father looks on. The child's Boy Scout uniform is draped over the coffin. The twist that Van Der Zee achieves in this photograph is enacted through the technology of superimposition. "Ghosted" over the coffin hovers a family portrait. This portrait shows the lost object in question, the assembled nuclear family. The superimposition includes the lost mother who is absent from the "main" image of the photograph. The viewer wonders where the mother is in the "real time" of the funeral scene. Was she lost before the boy? Did she pass on with the child? Is her grief so great that she could not pose? This image clearly revolves around the subjectivity of the mourning male figure. The act of mourning in this photo frames no single lost object (a child, a mother, a uniform) but rather posits a lost concept, an ego ideal that was contained within the fiction of the nuclear family. This photograph reveals the status of the lost object in this African American imaginary: The lost and dead are not altogether absent. Not only do they exist within the drama of African American life, but they help formulate it.

Another mortuary portrait of a young man in uniform uses the technology of combination printing to tell its story. The portrait is an example of the narrative impulse in Van Der Zee's production. In this image one counts at least four negatives in play. A poem is printed over the image. The poem recounts the sad story of burying a beloved soldier boy. Opposite the text one finds an odd battlefield image. In the upper-left of the image, the subject most closely resembling the corpse holds a pistol. In a nearly cinematic pose, the defeated soldier has drawn his weapon to protect an African American nurse and her dying patient. This melodramatic image is bridged with the equally emotional poem by a smaller image of two medics transferring an injured soldier across a battlefield. The imaginary that Van Der Zee weaves tells the story of a lost, noble soldier. The politics of staging this kind of image betrays one of the political projects of Van Der Zee's photography. This image of the exemplary soldier, beautifully enveloped in a U.S. flag, posits the black male as a war hero in a culture that at the time of its fashioning would not acknowledge him as such. The iconography here is clearly uninterested in mourning an individual, rather the needs, aesthetics, and suffering of a larger community are addressed.

I first encountered a Van Der Zee photo in Barthes's book on photography. On a certain level the work of both men is closely associated for me: both are cultural workers who revel in the most gilded and delicious hypersentimentality, and both realize the influence and limits of the parodic in their work. Granted, this connection is highly unstable, in ways both literal and metaphorical, since these men could never really "speak" to each other. Van Der Zee was never in any position to read Barthes's stylized locutions, and the commentary that Barthes offers on Van Der Zee is flawed by petty racism. When Barthes wrote about Van Der Zee, he contented himself with making a few snide remarks about the middle-class subjects (a traditional-looking African American family) attempting to, in Barthes's own words, "assume the white man's attributes." Van Der Zee's aesthetic utterly undercuts Barthes's writing about photography. Van Der Zee, I would suggest, disrupts the hypersubjective Barthesian approach to the photographic image. His pictures are never just the anticipation/potential occasion for mourning like Barthes's Wintergarden picture which I will discuss below. They are also a phantasmatic illusion that starts from the "end" (death and a communal witnessing of death) and hopes to bring back the dead by a very self-conscious act of prosopopeia. In a strange yet significant way *The Harlem Book of the Dead* beats *Camera Lucida* at its own game.

The photographic text itself, as Barthes has suggested, is already dead. Therefore, as a work of art, the photograph is always already a text of mourning. But if death, as in the case of Van Der Zee, is the obvious or surface subject of the picture, what then might be the role of prosopopeia when considering these pictures? Barthes cathects a photo of his mother as a little girl in the Wintergarden. What fascinates him most about this old photo is the depiction of the time "right before he lived," that is, the historical moment when his mother lived without him. This formula, if expanded to consider group identification as opposed to highly subjective histories, would account for the power of Van Der Zee's photos within the frame of *Looking for Langston*. For a generation of black gay men engrossed in the project of excavating deeply buried histories (as far as "official" historical registers are concerned), these pictures that depict everyday life and death during the (queer) Harlem Renaissance show a very crucial moment: a "right before *we* lived" moment that is as important to this community as the moment in his mother's life before his own birth is for Barthes.

We can understand the importance of this move from the subjective to the communal moment of mourning by turning to Michael Moon's "Memorial Rags, Memorial Rages." Here Moon completes the task of theorizing the significance and crucial differences in collective mourning begun by Freud in *Group Psychology and Ego Formation*. Both Julien and Moon are keyed into the power of collective mourning, and both understand the need to play with potent queer energies that have changed the face of mourning in ways that are paradigm-shaking. The following sentence from Moon's essay illuminates just what kind of tropological revision is at play in Julien's signifying on Van Der Zee:

> I invoke the social in the face of a predominantly privatized, hetero-sexualized, teleologized and "task-oriented" conception of grieving, and mourning because I want to insist on the specifically queer energies at play—or potentially in play—in our experiences of grief and our practices of mourning in the midst of the continuing desolation in our lives caused by AIDS.[18]

Moon calls attention to the characteristic of a dominant cultural logic of mourning that is, by its very premise and foundational principles, hetero-sexist. *Looking for Langston* works to undermine hegemonic constructions of mourning and instead props up an alternate structure that is not pinioned by "privatized and 'task-oriented'" biases but rather posits the necessity for communal practices that speak to the current genocidal crises affecting black and queer communities globally. Julien explains this communal practice as an aesthetic process, explaining in an interview that he "played with the surface" of Van Der Zee's photos so that they would forge an "important relationship" between a contemporary gay scene and a "historical look."[19] A subject does not locate his essential history by researching a "racial" or cultural past. More nearly, and most specifically in the case of *Looking for Langston*'s appropriation and reclamations of Van Der Zee's photographs and photographic aesthetic, what transpires is an insertion of the contemporary "self" into a fiction of the past. This fiction generates in the communal and individual subject an imaginary coherence within the experience of homophobic representational elisions and a general "experience of dispersal and fragmentation, which is the history of all enforced diasporas."[20] Van Der Zee's photos help the queer spectator visualize a past and thus enable an "imaginary" coherence that make the visualization of a present and a future possible.

Disidentifying and Desire in Mapplethorpe

Tony Fischer, in an article on *Looking for Langston*, completely misreads what he calls the "AIDS sub-plot."[21] The hierarchizing gesture of assigning main plots and subplots shows a profound misunderstanding of the film's structural and political formation. The moment of mourning in which we live informs Julien's film in urgent and compelling ways. The best example of the centrality of AIDS mourning in the film would be a consideration of the presence of Robert Mapplethorpe. Mapplethorpe's pictures cannot, after the grim carnival of controversy around them, be seen without a deep consideration of AIDS and the gay and black communities' current crisis of mourning. In a *Vanity Fair* interview, just before his own death, Mapplethorpe commented that most of the black men who appeared in *The Black Book* are now dead due to poverty, lack of insurance, and the high price of health care and medications like AZT (which ultimately proved to be ineffective).[22] While Julien's project is, on one level, the reappropriation of the black gay male body from Mapplethorpe, it is difficult to "read" these images and not be reminded of the terrible plague that robbed us of both the beautiful black men in front of the lens and the troublesome white patron/photographer behind the lens.

In considering the film's aesthetic, one cannot miss the compositional influence of Mapplethorpe's photography. Along with the dramatic and elegant Mapplethorpe lighting, the use and celebration of nude black gay male bodies makes visible the dialectical relationship between Mapplethorpe's and Julien's texts. Perfectly chiseled black male bodies, framed in striking black and white, occupy the central dream sequences of the film. In his signification of Mapplethorpe, Julien introduces a crucial tropological revision: he displays black bodies with black bodies as well as black bodies with white bodies. In this instance he rewrites the Mapplethorpe scene by allowing these men to relate to each other's bodies and not just the viewer's penetrating gaze. Kobena Mercer and Julien's brilliant essay "True Confessions" can be read as the "written" theoretical accompaniment to the praxis which is *Looking for Langston*. In it the subject of black gay male pornography is discussed:

> The convention in porn is to show single models in solo frames to enable the construction of one-to-one fantasy: Sometimes, when porn models pose in couples or groups, other connotations—friendship, solidarities, collective identities—can struggle to surface for our recognition.[23]

This "accidental" identity-affirming effect that takes place in black male porn is "pushed" and performed in Julien's film.[24] And this is only possible through the play with form, convention, and even frame that Julien accomplishes through his cinematic practice. The reading by Julien and Mercer that I cited above casts Mapplethorpe as the exploitative author who only sees these black bodies as meat. But these charges were made early in a debate that, like the current moment of AIDS mourning, has no easy end in sight. Mercer, due in a large part to the homophobic right-wing attacks on Mapplethorpe, has recently reconsidered the images he once denounced as simply reproducing a colonial fantasy. He writes:

> [T]he textual ambivalence of the black nude photograph is strictly undecidable because Mapplethorpe's photographs do not provide an unequivocal yes/no answer to the question of whether they reinforce or undermine commonplace racist stereotypes—rather, he throws the binary structure of the question back at the spectator, where it is torn apart in the disruptive "shock effect."[25]

The ambivalence Mercer speaks about recalls an earlier point I posited regarding the ambivalence toward a lost object bringing about melancholia. That is, melancholia is brought about by the subject's inability to work out the problems or contradictions the object and its loss produce. Hence, the ambivalence brings about a certain "shock effect" that Mercer describes, which is in a striking way structurally akin to the inner workings of melancholia.

I wish to suggest that the pleasure that Mercer, Julien, and other gay men of color experience when consuming Mapplethorpe's images is a disidentificatory pleasure,[26] one that acknowledges what is disturbing about the familiar practices of black male objectification that Mapplethorpe participated in, while at the same time understanding that this pleasure cannot easily be dismissed even though it is politically dangerous. Like melancholia, disidentification is an ambivalent structure of feeling that works to retain the problematic object and tap into the energies that are produced by contradictions and ambivalences. Mercer, Julien, and Jane Gaines have all explicated the ways in which the ambivalence that a spectator encounters with these images is not only a racist exploitation of the black male body but simultaneously a powerful validation of a black male body. Disidentification, as a conceptual model for understanding the "shock effect," acknowledges what is indeed turbulent and troublesome about such images. Peggy Phelan has explained that "objectification" should not be the last word in any appraisal of Mapplethorpe's work:

> Mapplethorpe's photography does "objectify" men, but what is astonishing about his work is how much room there is for dignity despite this

Figure 2. (L-R) John Wilson as Karl, Matthew Biadot as Beauty, and Ben Ellison as Alex in *Looking for Langston*, dir. Isaac Julien. Photograph by Sunil Gupta, Copyright Sankofa Film and Video and Sunil Gupta 1989.

> objectification. His photography demonstrates that love and understanding of a body, while always involving objectification, precisely because it is made over in the mind and eye of the other, do not have to eliminate the private grace and power of the model.[27]

The "making over" in the eye and the mind is a transfiguration. The object that is desired is reformatted so that dignity and grace are not eclipsed by racist exploitation.

Disidentification is this "making over," it is the way that a subject looks at an image constructed to exploit and deny identity and instead finds pleasure, both erotic and self-affirming. Disidentification happens on both the level of production and reception. The glance that cultural critics and workers like Mercer and Julien direct at Mapplethorpe's photographs begins as a disidentificatory transfiguration on the level of reception, and later, when the images are incorporated into different cultural texts (Mercer's cultural critique or Julien's cinematic production), a disidentification is enacted that is linked to artistic process and production.

In the same way that one holds onto a lost object until inner feelings of ambivalence are worked out, Julien sees the importance of collectively hold-

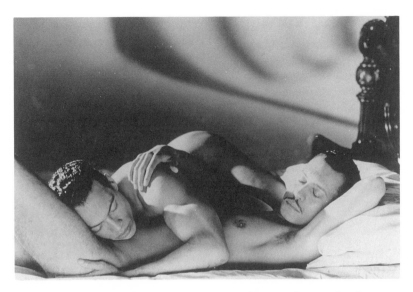

Figure 3. (L-R) Matthew Biadot as Beauty and Ben Ellison as Alex in *Looking for Langston*, dir. Isaac Julien. Copyright Sankofa Film and Video and Sunil Gupta 1989.

ing onto Mapplethorpe's images. These images are invaluable because they speak directly to the complicated circulation of colonial fantasies in our gay communities, both white and of color. Identification in the fantasy narrative (colonial or otherwise), as Judith Butler has shown in her own essay on Mapplethorpe, is never fixed; one can identify not only with characters (occupying either the colonized or colonizer positions) but also with verbs or "acts."[28] This identification, in Mapplethorpe, can perhaps be better understood as a disidentification that refuses to follow the identifying protocols of dominant culture. This brings to mind the scene in *Looking for Langston* in which the white character takes a tour through pages of the *Black Book* that are projected onto the walls of a dark room. Can people who identify as belonging to a once or currently colonized group simply identify with the *Black Book* images projected on the wall of the white "patron's" room, or must they, as Mercer suggests, confront their own identification with the white man, or even with the act of thumbing through this "dangerous" book and taking scopic delight in such images? I am suggesting that for some spectators this confrontation with whiteness does not occlude the pleasure that such images offer, but rather that such confrontations can be part of a disidentificatory project that manages to partially recycle and hold onto these representations.

For me, what binds these very different photographic presences in *Looking for Langston* is a certain quality of mourning intrinsic both to the genre of portraiture and to the specific photographs of Van Der Zee and Mapplethorpe used in the film. In a recent essay, Jeff Nunokawa argues that long before the current epidemic the history of gay men for mainstream culture has been one of death, doom, and extinction. Nunokawa explains the ways in which the AIDS epidemic has been figured in the mainstream (straight) imaginary:

> AIDS is a gay disease, and it means death, because AIDS has been made the most recent chapter in our culture's history of the gay male, a history which, from its beginning, has read like a book of funerals.[29]

Unfortunately, this genocidal wish of the straight mind has been partially fulfilled. Recent queer history, to no small degree, does read like a funeral book. And this is equally true of the history of the African American male, especially the African American gay male. *The Harlem Book of the Dead* and *The Black Book* are both mourning texts that might, at first glance, appear to be such funeral books. I am arguing that there is in fact more to these texts, that when redeployed by cultural producers like Julien they become meditative texts that decipher the workings of mourning in our culture.

Rethinking Melancholia

Above I have tried to explicate the quality of mourning in somewhat abstract terms. If one zooms in on certain cinematic moments a sharper understanding comes into perspective. My argument that *Looking for Langston* is a work of mourning hinges on very specific moments in the film. One of the earliest soundbites heard is the scratchy voice of a radio announcer eulogizing Hughes, and the program he announces is called "In Memoriam Langston Hughes." As I pointed out earlier, the film is billed as a meditation on Hughes and the Renaissance. What I have not mentioned is that the next title screen reads "dedicated to the memory of James Baldwin." Grief is a precondition to this film. Mourning is never far removed from "life" in *Looking for Langston*. In the film, the scene of mourning and the bar scene which represents the transhistorical space of gay life is separated by a winding staircase. Slow pans up and down show the closeness of these spaces. I do not want to view these two scenes, the nightclub and the funeral, as a stark binary. Rather, the layering of different gay spaces shows how varied aspects of our lives always interlock and inform each other.

The establishing shot is the lavishly adorned casket surrounded by elegant mourners—a scene that reconstructs various images from *The Harlem Book of the Dead*. Following is a slow camera movement from an overhead, unmotivated perspective of the filmmaker playing the corpse, seemingly stiff within the coffin. The connection between looker (Julien conducting his cinematic investigation) and the object of the gaze (the figure of Hughes who is, in one sense, "invisible" yet very much present under the revisionary gaze) and the audience are all radically disrupted and destabilized. This destabilizing of traditional cinematic positionalities is a mirroring of the destabilization and ambivalence of identification that is to be found at the center of the communal mourning scene.

Communal mourning, by its very nature, is a complicated text to read. We do mourn for more than one lost object, we also mourn as a "whole," or, put another way, as a contingent and temporary collection of fragments experiencing a loss of its parts. In this context, mourning Hughes, Baldwin, Mapplethorpe, or the beautiful men in the *Black Book* is about mourning for oneself, for one's community, for one's very history. It is not the rather linear line that Freud traces, but a response to the heterosexist and corporate "task-oriented" mourning that Moon describes. While lives that are black and/or queer remain on the line, there is no "normal" teleological end in sight for mourning. Mercer has recently described the achievement of *Looking for Langston* as working

> precisely in the way it shows how desire and despair run together, and thus how desire always entails rituals of mourning for what is lost and cannot be recovered. There is a sense of mourning not just for Langston, buried in the past under the repressive weight of homophobic and eurocentric narratives, but mourning for friends, lovers and others lost to AIDS here and now, in the present. There is mourning but not melancholia: as Langston himself says at the end of the film, "Why should I be blue? I've been blue all night through." [30]

I agree with many of Mercer's conclusions, but I wish to add a corrective to his reading by depathologizing melancholia and understanding it as a "structure of feeling" that is necessary and not always counterproductive and negative. I am proposing that melancholia, for blacks and queers of any color, is not a pathology but an integral part of everyday lives. The melancholia that occupies the minds of the communities under siege in this film can be seen as the revised version of melancholia that Freud wrote about in his later years. It is this melancholia that is part of our process of dealing with the catastrophes that occur in the lives of people of color, lesbians and gays. I have proposed a view of melancholia not as a pathology or as a self-absorbed mood that inhibits activism, but rather as a mechanism that helps us (re)construct identity and take our dead to the various battles we must wage in their names—and in our names. In the end, this analysis does not dismiss the need for and uses of activist militancies but instead helps inform a better understanding of them. Douglas Crimp ends his manifesto "Mourning and Militancy" with this stirring sentence: "Militancy, of course, then, but mourning too: mourning *and* militancy."[31] Julien's melancholic signifying on these two different photographies of mourning supplies a necessary history to a collective struggle. This history comes in the form of identity-affirming "melancholia," a melancholia that individual subjects and communities in crisis can use to map the ambivalences of identification and the conditions of (im)possibility that shape minority identities. Finally, this melancholia is a productive space of hybridization that uniquely exists between a necessary militancy and indispensable mourning.

Notes

This essay benefits from the thoughtful readings of Eve Sedgwick, Michael Moon, Jane Gaines, Karla Holloway, Barbara Herrnstein Smith, Gustavus Stadler, Celeste Fraser Delgado, Brian Selsky, Jonathan Flatley, and Michael Uebel. David Román and Josh Kun offered their helpful phone advice. I am indebted to Paul Scolieri's help with the preparation of this manuscript. Finally, I want to thank Isaac Julien for his gracious support and encouragement.

  1. Wynter, "Rethinking 'Aesthetics': Notes Towards a Deciphering Practice," 266–67.

  2. Raymond Williams first used the phrase "structure of feeling" in his study *Marxism and Literature*, 128–35. For Williams a structure of feeling was a *process* of relating the continuity of social formations within a work of art. Williams explains:

> The hypothesis has a special relevance to art and literature, where true social content is in a significant number of cases of this present and affective kind, which cannot be reduced to belief systems, institutions, or explicit general relationships, though it may include all these as lived and experienced, with or without tension, as it also evidently includes elements of social and material (physical or natural) experience which may lie beyond or be uncovered, or imperfectly covered by, the elsewhere recognizable systematic elements. The unmistakable presence of certain elements in art which are not covered by (though in one mode, might be reduced to) other formal systems is the true source of the specializing category of "the aesthetic," "the arts," and "imaginative litera-

ture." We need, on the one hand, to acknowledge (and welcome) the specificity of these elements—specific dealings, specific rhythms—and yet to find their specific kinds of sociality, thus preventing the extraction from social experience which is conceivable only when social experience itself has been categorically (and at root historically) reduced. (133)

3. For an elaboration of the politics of "queer historiography" see my "Queering Latinidad: Visual Strategies for the Production of Self in Queer Latina/o Video," in my book *Disidentifications* (Minnesota, forthcoming).

4. Rampersad also fails to explore the paths of an orientation that might be primarily autoerotic, in some way "bisexual," or perhaps even non-"traditional" gender identification. In an interview, Nugent refers to Hughes as "asexual." I do not wish to rule out the "asexual" possibility in the same way that Rampersad refuses to seriously consider any sexual option other than compulsory heterosexuality. If one were to envision asexuality as more of a practice than a primary orientation I do not see a contradiction in being both queer and asexual. My intention is not to rule out the asexual as a species but instead to decipher the ways in which asexuality is deployed from a normative heterosexual register as a mechanism to cancel queer possibility. See Rampersad, *The Life of Langston Hughes*. For an excellent example of African American biography writing that engages the queerness of its subject and the Harlem Renaissance, see Wayne F. Cooper.

5. Scott, "The Evidence of Experience" in *Critical Inquiry* 17 (summer 1991): 778.

6. Eisenstein, Film Form: *Essays in Film Theory*, 58.

7. Jameson, *Signatures of the Visible*, 78.

8. Jones, *Liberating Voices: Oral Tradition in African American Literature*, 197. For another useful account of call-and-response in twentieth-century african american cultural production, see John F. Callahan.

9. Hughes's "Poem" was included in the first U.K. version of *Looking for Langston*. It was later edited out of the U.S. film after the Hughes estate demanded that it be deleted. The poem is transcribed from that first version of the film.

10. Baker, *Blues, Ideology, and Afro-American Literature: A Vernacular Theory*, 3–4.

11. Gilroy, "Nothing But Sweat inside My Hand: Diaspora Aesthetics and Black Arts in Britain," 46.

12. Barthes, *Camera Lucida*, 93.

13. Freud, "Mourning and Melancholia," 243.

14. My thinking about melancholia is enabled by the work of Judith Butler who, in *Gender Trouble: Feminism and the Subversion of Identity* describes the melancholic as a subject who "refuses the loss of the object, and internalization becomes a strategy of magically resuscitating the lost object, not only because the loss is painful, but because the ambivalence felt toward the object requires that the object be retained until differences are settled."

15. De Man "Autobiography as De-facement," 75–76.

16. Peggy Phelan has written about this particular ontology of performance in her book *Unmarked: The Politics of Performance*, 33–70.

17. Van Der Zee, *The Harlem Book of the Dead*, 83.

18. Moon, "Memorial Rags, Memorial Rages."

19. See Fischer, "Isaac Julien: Looking for Langston," *Third Text* 12 (1990): 67.

20. Hall, "Cultural Identities and Cinematic Representations," 133.

21. Fischer, "Isaac Julien," 64.

22. See Dominick Dunne, "Robert Mapplethorpe's Proud Finale," *Vanity Fair* (February 1989).

23. Julien and Mercer, "True Confessions," 170.

24. The "black male porn" I am discussing is nothing like lesbian erotica, porn produced for lesbians by lesbians. It is, in fact, just the opposite, porn made by white men for a primarily white audience. One could imagine that the pro-gay, pro-black, pro-sex charge that a black male porn produced by black men might create would indeed be powerful.

25. Mercer, "Looking for Trouble," *Transition* 51 (1991): 189.

26. This is not to imply that only gay men of color can disidentify with Mapplethorpe's images. Jane Gaines has written about the pleasure that straight white women can extract from Mapplethorpe. Gaines narrates her suspicion that "there may be fantasies of defiance as well as fantasies of discovery worked out over these 'borrowed' and shared love objects." The working out that transpires in Gaines's account is then an ambivalent working through, what in the terms of this study would be understood as a disidentification with a complex object. See "Competing Glances: Who is Reading Robert Mapplethorpe's *Black Book*," *New Formations* 16 (spring 1992): 39. Disidentification is not a term that Gaines employs but instead one that I further develop in "Famous 'n' Dandy Like B. 'n' Andy: Race, Pop, and Basquiat" in *Pop Out: Queer Warhol* and in my forthcoming *Disidentifications*.

27. Phelan, *Unmarked*, 51.

28. Butler, "The Force of Fantasy: Feminism, Mapplethorpe, and Discursive Excess," *Differences* 2.2 (1990): 105–125. Butler's formulations in this instance are informed by the work of Jean Laplanche and J.-B. Pontalis, "Fantasy and the Origins of Sexuality."

29. Nunokawa, "'All the Sad Young Men': AIDS and the Work of Mourning," *Yale Journal of Criticism*, 4.2 (1991): 2.

30. Mercer, "Dark and Lovely Too: Black Gay Men in Independent Film," 253–54.

31. Crimp, "Mourning and Militancy," *October* 51 (1989): 18.

 **IV COMING AFTER**

PECS AND REPS

Muscling in on Race and the Subject of Masculinities

DEBORAH E. MCDOWELL

still do I keep my look, my identity . . . Each body has its art, its precious
prescribed pose.
—Gwendolyn Brooks, "Gay Chaps at the Bar"

No joke. Before I read Richard Dyer's "The White Man's Muscles" for this
volume, I thought a peplum was that flared, bias-cut piece of fabric attached
to the lower half of a woman's blouse, or what my great-grandmother used
to call a waist. Designed to drape gracefully over the hips, peplums covered
a multitude of middle-aged women's "figure flaws" in an era before rowing
machines, Stair Masters, and heavy hand-weights could be used to sculpt a
waist long past youthful definition. Thanks to Dyer, I now know that the peplum is a genre of Italian cinema that takes its name from the Latinized Greek
word for a woman's tunic. In the film, what was formerly a woman's tunic
becomes the "brief skirt or kilt" worn by the films' heroes and fashioned to
show off their pulsing muscles. Set in colonial space, the peplum—film and
kilt—cast the white body as spectacle and bound discourses of masculinity
seamlessly to ideologies of race and nationhood.

The language, imaging, and semiotics of the body give to this volume and
to this historical moment a singular energy and focus, and the muscle bids
fair as micrometaphor and icon of the age. Images of muscularity crop up
everywhere in this collection, beginning with Jonathan Dollimore's discussion of the factors that drove André Gide and other sexual tourists to the
arcadian splendor of colonial locales, not least being to fulfill their sexual
desires for the fantasied "muscular physique" and "massive member" of the
"native." Subsequent essays refer to: the "splendid muscular development" of
the soldiers in Colonel Higginson's black regiment, whose bodies appealed
to his "gymnasium-trained eye"; the "perfectly chiseled black male bodies,"
appropriated from Robert Mapplethorpe by Isaac Julien for his film *Looking
for Langston*; the "visual pleasures of physicality" and the "muscular Chinese

national identity" that Bruce Lee's martial arts films display; the hard "impenetrable surface" of Eddie Murphy's body that made him such a box-office draw in 48 Hours, Beverly Hills Cop, and Trading Places.

To press the metaphor even further, the contributors to this collection are engaged in their own form of bodybuilding, building the firm body of cultural criticism, academic style. Make no mistake. This carries its own pressures of rigorous training in contemporary reading protocols—psychoanalysis, film theory, queer theory—and specialized concepts—the gaze, the spectacle, and the fetish, to name but a few. With these conceptual tools, the contributors pulse and flex, flex and point to streamline a very specific form of metaphysical excess run to flatulence and flab: the homogenizing logic of "white bourgeois masculinity." From every angle, they show that white heterosexual males—long granted power and privilege as the unraced, transcendent human norm—"live their whiteness," in Eric Lott's resonant turn of phrase, by impersonating racial "others."

As a collection, Race and the Subject of Masculinities achieves accumulating force and impressive rigor by resisting "normative" identity claims and examining the forces and bodies that secure them. While it is widely acknowledged that ideas of masculinity are constructed as much in relation to the feminine and to sexuality as they are to race, in the economy of this collection, as befits its title, race plays a far more crucial role in these discussions of masculinity and its plural formations. While "race" refers in these essays to Asian, Arab, and Italian men, in the final analysis, it reduces to that familiar duo, at least according to the protocols of U.S. discourse—black and white.

Although the "formation of masculine identity is never strictly, so to speak, a black-and-white issue" (3; this volume), as Michael Uebel puts it eloquently in his introduction to this volume, such turns out to be very much the case. Given this focus, it is not surprising that the contributors find theoretical grounding in such classic texts on the subject as Fanon's The Wretched of the Earth and Black Skin, White Masks, Norman Mailer's "The White Negro," Eldridge Cleaver's Soul on Ice, and Leslie Fiedler's Love and Death in the American Novel. Fiedler immortalized the psychosexual thesis revisited in some form and revised in others by so many of these essays: the American literary tradition rests on a myth of interracial male bonding, at times, homoerotic at its core. Mailer's "The White Negro" extends Fiedler's thesis beyond the parameters of American literature and lends credence to James Baldwin's famous statement in response to "The White Negro." In his essay, "The Black Boy Looks at the White Boy," Baldwin wrote: "to be an American Negro male is also to be a kind of walking phallic symbol, which means that one pays in one's own personality, for the sexual insecurity of others" (290). Fanon theorized similarly that, largely because of that sexual insecurity, the colonizer must transform the colonized into a sexually objectified woman. Some have critiqued Fanon's "neutering" of the black colonial subject as well as his subordination of gender to race. Although he devotes one chapter to the black woman—"The Woman of Color and the White Man"—Fanon admits, without apology: of the woman of color, "I know nothing about her" (Black Skin, White Masks 180). It is perhaps inevitable, then, that with these as grounding texts, the feminine, and specifically the black feminine, would constitute this collection's absence, its unknown.

This is as good a place as any to confront the vexing and perhaps inevitable question about my role as a black feminist commissioned to write the afterword to a volume of essays, which otherwise absents that point of view. Should my words have an ancillary function, granting ex post facto authentication, much like the prefaces William Lloyd Garrison and Wendell Phillips were expected to lend Frederick Douglass's 1845 Narrative? Is it thus my role to have been granted the historical prerogative of white men: to confer validation rather than to seek it? To need it? In a book about "race and the subject of masculinities," these are not idle, frivolous, or entirely "academic" questions —but perhaps a far more pressing question is, Why masculinity now? What in our time compels the bulging industry of studying men? Reshaping men? Watching their rippling biceps or meeting their steady gazes, which burst the frames of mass-market magazine covers, grace the flaps of book jackets, front and back, and span full and half pages in such newspapers as the New York Times and such popular magazines as Newsweek? But more importantly, why are black men so frequently featured on these covers, figured alternatively as "feminized," eroticized objects or as menacing and predatory criminals?

This volume makes clear that answers to the whys and wherefores of masculinity are far-flung and often mutually contradictory, demonstrating that there can (nor should) be no single response to the perceived crisis over masculinity. Taken together, these essays constitute a kind of collective response. But it is difficult to read their critiques of traditional masculinity without contemplating the muscled-tough defenses of masculinity, indeed a hypermasculinity, proliferating from the popular front. Of course, this distinction between the "academic" and the "popular" is a risky simplification, but one that helps to establish manageable boundaries for the scope of this afterword. As polarized as these two realms might seem in their responses to the question of masculinity, both depend for their articulation on traditional sexual politics and lead inevitably to questions about the feminine, questions specifically about the place of the black feminine in public culture and in academic "cultural studies." But first, what do those who study masculinity really want? Of course, much depends on who "they" are. While many women have been attracted to the study, three included here, men are, not surprisingly, its most ardent devotees.

A volume titled *Race and the Subject of Masculinities* would not have been possible even a scant ten years ago, but, thanks to the revitalizing energies of cultural studies, for almost a decade now, the subject has acquired the obsessive force of an *idée fixe*. Given star billing at a variety of conferences and symposia, courses, essay collections and publishing series, the subject of masculinity has found a solid place in the vocabulary and preoccupations of academics. And on the popular front, masculinity has been the featured subject of mass-circulation magazines for the past ten years, ranging from the *Ebony* special issue on "The Crisis of the Black Male," in July 1983, and the *Newsweek* special issue on "Brothers" in 1987, to the "Wild Man" weekends initiated by Robert Bly, the paterfamilias of the men's movement and author of its best-selling guidebook, *Iron John: A Book About Men* (1990).

The *Newsweek* special issue of June 24, 1991, profiles the "men's movement" spawned by *Iron John*. The headline asks, "What Do Men Really Want? Now They Have a Movement of Their Own." Clearly audible is an echo of Freud's infamous question, "What does woman want?" as well as the proprietary rhetoric that many feminists have often summoned in implied, if not direct, response: *something* of "their own." For Virginia Woolf, it was a *room* of her own. Every woman who sought autonomy and the rewards of creative life needed her own sanctuary, her own sacred space. And if she intended to keep on writing, why then she would have to follow Alice Walker's recommendation and have no more than "One *Child* of [Her] Own." For Elaine Showalter, the multiple fruits of that creativity could then lead to a tradition for women, to *A Literature of Their Own*. But even without these examples, it wouldn't be hard to detect (or suspect) that the "movement" that men now have of "their own," even in all its variety, contains the silent, spectral presence of women and of feminism as political movement and cultural force.

Some, like Rosi Braidotti, have put the matter far less delicately, arguing that, at least in the academy, this fixation on masculinity is "nothing more . . . than a contemporary version of the old metaphysical cannibalism: it expresses the male desire to carry on the hegemonic tradition which they inherited; it reveals their attachment to their traditional place of enunciation, despite all" (235; see also Showalter). The appeal of Braidotti's assertion, notwithstanding, let us first take this collection on its own predominantly male-to-male terms, terms not without their own "traditional places of enuncia-tion" regarding matters of race in the United States, matters that inevitably involve subject/object relations.

In titling his response to Norman Mailer, "The Black Boy Looks at the White Boy," Baldwin is most astute. Knowing that blackness is normatively objecti-fied in the white field of vision, Baldwin, as subject, boldly originates a gaze and objectifies Norman Mailer instead. But such reversals are seldom seen in *Race and the Subject of Masculinities*. In its economy of looking, it's not always clear, to borrow the title of Aretha Franklin's hit song, "Whose zoomin' who?"

Whose Zoomin' Who?

Nice tautological body. . . . without external reference, without a risky interior region where roads and tracks may be lost, a model . . . exposing itself to repetition.
—Jean-François Lyotard, *Libidinal Economy*

The scopic preoccupation of U.S. cultural studies partly explains the promi-nent references to bodies and muscles throughout this collection, from Elvis impersonators to Robert Mapplethorpe's photography. Fully half of the essays here focus on film and many of the remainder allude to it. Not surprisingly, then, the concept of the gaze constitutes the central unit of analysis. These essays borrow liberally from feminist film theory, particularly Laura Mulvey's pioneering essay, "Visual Pleasure and Narrative Cinema," which has given critics of culture one of their central axioms: the subject/object dichotomy of seeing/being seen is a gendered accessory to the ideological production of "masculinity" and "femininity." Such an arrangement is the *sine qua non* of Hollywood cinema, which is traditionally predicated on a male viewer and a female who is the object of his gaze.[1] Those essays, which focus on the male body, offer engaging refinements on Mulvey's thesis. Obviously, when men's bodies are put on display, the traditional codes and conventions of who sees and who is seen are contravened.

Not only does the work of exhibitionism, of building muscles, project the white male body outward into the visual field, and thus into a hierar-chical "scopic regime," but it also positions that body squarely in the arena of competition and conquest, domination and control. Thus, it should not go unnoticed that while we read accounts of white male exhibitionism here, the white male never fully relinquishes his hold on spectatorship, nor on its privileges and powers. As Richard Dyer reminds us, although the white male displays his body in the peplum, he is still the mind of the matter, the literal triumph of "imagination over flesh," possessed alone of the privilege and safety of voluntary acts of transgression on colonial soil. In other words, the customary direction of the look of surveillance remains conventionally "raced," as Eric Lott's discussion of Elvis impersonators makes explicitly clear [2] — white men remain alone possessed of the privilege to *contemplate* identity as performative impersonation, to incorporate the "other" into their identity poses. Or as Yvonne Tasker argues, white men alone have the freedom to "shift, transgress, and adopt ["other"] racial identities" (331; this volume). Robin Wiegman and Gayle Wald make similar arguments. In *Adventures of Huckleberry Finn*, notes Wiegman, "Jim does not have access to the multiplicity of roles available to Huck" (62; this volume). Likewise, Gayle Wald observes that the black man *is* Mezz Mezzrow's "racial unconscious" (he lacks an unconscious of his own). While this white blues performer can claim to be a "voluntary Negro," such voluntarism does not work in reverse.

The question of identity formation and the concept of the gaze both hold suggestive implications for the study of race and masculinity in the academic sphere, study that all too often inhabits a traditional place of racial enunciation. Directly and indirectly, the bodies shaping this collection have provided some of the richest and most sophisticated work on race, gender, and sexuality in recent years, but their work is implicated in the reproduction of the very racialized subject/object relations that they so ably critique. By this I mean, there are those who study and those who are the objects of study. Nonwhite men dominate the latter camp. Christopher Looby's concerns with the "meaning of blackness for white men," not the meaning of whiteness for black men, typify this pattern in which black men become mainly the passive, and thus feminized, objects of the white male gaze.

At its worst, this arrangement is the agent of sentimentality, shading toward what Kobena Mercer suggestively terms "negrophilia" or an "aesthetic idealization of racial 'Otherness.'" According to Mercer, negrophilia "merely inverts and reverses the binary axis of the repressed fears and anxieties that are projected onto the Other" in a phobic response. "Both positions, whether they overvalue or devalue the visible signs of blackness, inhabit the shared space of colonial fantasy" ("Looking for Trouble" 187). It is the sentimentalized black male body that figures more prevalently in recent academic discourse, a figure whose function and value are inverted in the popular imaginary, where he is the feared and hated criminal, the bogeyman.

Given the range of possibilities, one would be hard pressed to designate the representative man, for either alternative, but adding to the controversial

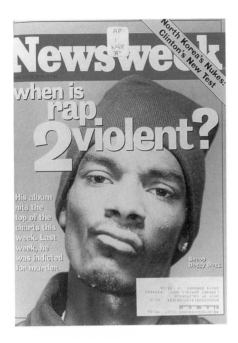

Figure 1. *Newsweek* cover,
"When Is Rap 2 Violent?"
November 29, 1993.

store of Mapplethorpe's "black men," we might propose model Tyson Beck-ford as a more recent example of the feminized/eroticized black body. For its profile on Beckford, the *New York Times* chose the headline: "To Claudia, Naomi, and Cindy, you can add the name Tyson."[3] Tyson becomes *la femme*, one of "the girls," symbolically a kind of "boy-girl." The close-up shot of Snoop Doggy Dogg on the November 29, 1993, cover of *Newsweek* is the proto-typical criminal in knit cap (Figure 1). The accompanying headline reads: "When Is Rap 2 Violent?: His album hits the top of the charts this week. Last week he was indicted for murder."

Without discussing either Snoop Doggy Dogg or his feminized counter-parts, it is clear that the contributors to this collection understand the met-onymic and mimetic function that both figures play in the psychic architec-ture of white masculinity. But, despite the usefulness of this insight, I would still ask, for whose benefit and to what ends do we continue to catalogue, categorize, and critique the desires, aversions, and ego investments of white masculinity? Do we continue to perform endless repetitions of the thesis that views black men as white men's body doubles, or as Wiegman puts it, merely the "symbols and symptoms of the psychodrama of white mascu-linity"? (52; this volume). Where and what does that repetition get us, even if it is put to "oppositional" ends?

To pose such questions is clearly not to suggest that we have exhausted everything there is to say about this charged relationship between black men and white men. Far from it, for as Baldwin puts it, "the relationship . . . of a black boy to a white boy is a very complex thing" ("Black Boy" 290), but I would add, wringing a different twist from Baldwin's term, the "complex" is at the center of the "white boy's" psyche, which remains central after all. Richard Dyer's comments on the peplum cinema admit as much, and they resonate far beyond that genre and beyond the pages of this book: "white men, far from being displaced from the center of discourse by a myriad of postmodern voices, continue to predominate" (299–300; this volume).

That such "centering" risks marginalizing and silencing women, along with many others, is clear, but less apparent is that such centering also risks reinscribing some of the more resilient conceptual givens of racist and racialist discourse. The latter is a point not lost on Jonathan Dollimore. As he notes, "the 'Other' is cited, quoted, framed, illuminated, encased in the shot-reverse-shot strategy of a serial enlightenment" (19; this volume), while at the same time losing its power to signify, to negate, to initiate its desire, to split its sign of identity, to establish its own institutional and oppositional discourse.

The emergence of black males—as filmmakers, actors, cameramen, musicians—in commercial cinema and rap would seem to allay Dollimore's fears that the omnipresent white male gaze denies the "other" the power to look, the power to initiate its own desire, the power to establish its own "oppositional discourse." Black men have seized this power with a violent force and effectively pledged their allegiance to the very privileges of patriarchal and heterosexual masculinity that the contributors to this volume vehemently forswear. In so doing, they join ranks with a diverse movement on the popular front to restore conventional patriarchal prerogatives and arrangements of masculinity, a movement that has found a guru in Robert Bly and a model for living in his best-selling book, Iron John.

That none of the contributors to this collection addressed Iron John is no great matter. But the absence of its broad appeal from consideration, as well as its connections to other patriarchal performances of masculinity from the public stage, raises questions about just what artifacts from public culture are actually usable in academic discourse.

Perhaps at no time in the history of academic production has there been a greater interest in public culture and its industries—commercial cinema, museum and art gallery institutions, mass media, popular music and its supporting videos—but, in this collection, the artifacts of mass culture are clearly colonized for the academy, minted in and for its economy. While these essays break sharply with the traditional canons of academic inquiry, straining, in the process, the very heart of the academy's often tired and flabby body, I leave this collection wondering what might transpire in social space if there were more commerce between academic and popular discourses on masculinity crises and the histories that have created them. Such a discussion would necessarily place the politics of sex and gender front and center and would illustrate the unmistakable place of women, of the feminine, in the struggle for masculine identity.

Perhaps at no time has such emphasis been more urgently needed than now, when dominant ideas of masculinity would press an unquestioned (and unquestionable) return to basic and traditional patriarchal prerogatives of male domination, of fathers/fatherhood that have always necessitated an emotional repudiation of the maternal and have always also held dismal, if not, violent consequences for women. For the rest of this essay, I would like to briefly touch on these issues and thereby see myself less as a commentator specifically on this collection's very suggestive pieces, than as a contributor to its larger project. Let's say that my aim is to muscle in on the subject of race and masculinity as it plays itself out in prominent and highly profiled arenas of contemporary public space—the "men's movement" of Robert Bly, aspects of black male cinema, rite-of-passage programs for black boys, and the lyrics of some gangsta rap. Although they emerge from different sides of familiar race and class divides, what they share sheds a complicating light on race and the subject of masculinities.

See Father: He Is Hard and Strong

The broad appeal of Bly's message is clear from the Newsweek profile, which lists among his followers, construction workers, college professors, computer salesmen, media consultants, marketing consultants, media-marketing consultants, Jungian therapists, substance-abuse counselors, and Unitarian ministers. The "representative man" (Figure 2) on the cover of the magazine is, at first glance, hard to pin down. Except for a pinstriped necktie, he stands naked to the waist, square-jawed, evenly tanned—pectorals and abdominals, triceps and deltoids, clearly defined. No beer belly. No love handles here. Holding a drum in one arm and a naked baby in the other, he is the veritable embodiment of this collection's underlying thesis: masculinity is incoherent, unstable, and in a state of utter convulsion.

For the man on the cover, and others like him who attend Bly's wilder-

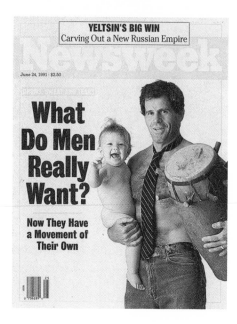

Figure 2. *Newsweek* cover,
"What Do Men Really
Want?" June 24, 1991.

ness retreats, squatting on "naked haunches in the suffocating dark[ness]" of
tepees, and banging drums in the moonlight, the resolution of the crisis lies
in slaying what Bly calls the "soft male," recovering the "warrior" image, and
confronting habitual "father hunger." This process can only be completed
when the "American male" finds a "sword to cut his adult soul away from his
mother-bound soul" (Bly 165).

While few black men have sought refuge in Bly's wilderness weekends,
many express its "warrior" ideals in their own versions of retreat, which have
seen disturbing outcroppings in male-centered programs and educational
initiatives targeted specifically at young black boys. These retreats are planned
by self-appointed father figures who attempt to steer these boys through
the crucial passages to "manhood." For example, in St. Louis, Alderman
Kujaliwa Kennedy runs a rites-of-passage program called Simba Wachanga
(Young Lions), based on African rituals and ceremonies. Chicago community
leaders run a similar program called "Building Black Men."[4] Such programs
are being incorporated into school curricula. At the Marcus Garvey Academy
in Detroit, a central part of the curriculum is a Rites of Passage program,
which includes ceremonies and private rituals designed to mark a boy's passage to manhood. According to Harvey Hambrick, principal of the school,
"If there's no induction into manhood, you get . . . extended adolescence for

males." Such arrested development is owing, Hambrick believes, to female-headed family structures. Hambrick is a part of a growing number of black educators and laypersons who have garnered widespread support for the idea that young black boys become "soft" and "whiny" because they are raised by and thus bound to their mothers. In this regard, Hambrick and his supporters echo Bly's dictum that "only men can change the boy to a man" (16).[5]

To reverse the journey that men have wrongly "taken into softness" by developing their "feminine side," Bly offers these weekend retreats run, ironically, on the model of women's consciousness-raising sessions of the 1970s. He adds to this a universalizing rhetoric concocted from an indigestible mix of anthropology, poetry (much of it Bly's own), pre-Christian fable, and obscure fairy tales, including "Iron John," the title tale. And although he chooses from among the rituals of Hopi and other Native Americans and the Kikuyu in Africa to buttress his program, Iron John, book and myth, is still rooted in a white male heterosexual norm.[6]

If the "masculinity" of that norm is in crisis, that crisis cannot be taken as representative. In other words, the limits, implications, and expressions of social masculinity involve radically different stakes, risks, choices, and privileges, depending on the man on the cover. The man on the *Newsweek* cover, for instance, is part of a movement comprised of men who are white, white-collar, and thirtysomething. Sporting a power tie, a taut, tanned body, a wedding band, he carries a "legitimate" baby on his hip. But more to the point, he can pay the roughly $249 that it costs to drum, sweat, and scream by firelight in the woods. All these signs position him in the upper reaches of the socioeconomic ladder. Of course, it is impossible to contemplate this image in the absence of its spectral counter-image, the denizen of the black "underclass," who is "unwilling" to work, who shirks his family responsibilities, and leaves a trail of babies as wards and burdens of the state.

Those black men who have seized the camera would change this picture, but, according to the dominant symbologies of their films, that change can only be wrought with the restoration of the father. Nowhere is this more apparent than in John Singleton's very popular *Boyz N the Hood*. A story about the possibilities and perils of coming to black manhood in South Central Los Angeles (and by extension, throughout the United States), *Boyz N the Hood* is up-front about its ideological investments in heterosexual masculinity, in the rites of passage to manhood, a state construed as final, terminal, and dependent on a father's direction. Throughout the film, mothers are represented as a neglectful, ineffectual, and abusive lot.[7] Only the presence of fathers can ensure the survival of a black boy and direct his passage to manhood. When Tre's mother delivers him to his father, she concedes, "You're right; I don't know how to teach him to be a man."[8]

The position that black women occupy in the construction of black masculinity has never been more egregiously evident than in this and other recent films, which interpret black political and social life, in their entirety, as a crisis of black masculinity, a crisis allegedly the fault, in large part, of black women, specifically the mother. What Marlon Ross suggests in a forthcoming book about Spike Lee might be applied more broadly to the bumper crop of young black male filmmakers, the most recent exoticized and eroticized black collective of Hollywood cinema: Lee's attempt to "wrestle the camera from white hands is itself a struggle for a kind of black manhood" that persistently relegates black women to the fringes of the frame.

The value of Ross's discussion lies largely in its awareness of how "technology and filmviewing are formally structured *against* the black female faces" on the screen of Spike Lee's film. "Lee's technical mastery of the camera's aim . . . leaves the women stranded together, their most powerful moment in the film expended in feminine complaint." And what more could be expected, given the "technology, structure, rhetoric, and culture of mainstream cinematic tradition." As Ross continues, "what blacks say on film is always hemmed in and unbalanced by the larger apparatus of film technology and viewing itself, and this conflict between empowered voice and marginalizing form is especially intensified when the black characters also happen to be female."

While it would be a mistake to homogenize this current crop of black films, it is safe to say that, taken together, they constitute an aggressive counterdiscourse to critiques of masculinities offered not just by this collection, but by those black feminists have waged for the past two decades, from Toni Cade's astringent critique of the masculinist postures of black nationalism, to Toni Morrison's and Alice Walker's critiques of the equally masculinist priorities of family narratives and obsessions, to Sherley Anne Williams's recent critique of rap lyrics.[9]

A bit of historicizing will be useful here. The prominence of black men in current commercial cinema seems tailor-made to fit the order placed by those black men who bewailed throughout the 1970s and 1980s the perceived dominance of black women writers in the publishing sphere. The single most pervasive charge was that black men were being "emasculated," "castrated" in these writings, which were alleged to be subsidized and underwritten by a white feminist mafia of the U.S. publishing establishment determined to silence black male writers.[10] The line drawing that illustrated Stanley Crouch's review of Morrison's *Beloved* literalized and conjoined the perception and the fear in representing Morrison's as Medusa's head, an image long interpreted as a representation of female genitalia and thus of castration. But more importantly, for this context, Medusa is associated with the power of the gaze, which Craig Owens rightly reads as the principal theme of Ovid's myth, beginning as it does with the theft of an eye shared by the twin daughters of Phorcys.[11] Perseus wants this eye and decapitates Medusa to get it. Without arguing paranoically that these black male filmmakers have "stolen the eye" believed to be held by a black scribbling "sisterhood," many believe that the gaze, in all its objectifying power, is now securely back in black male heads. And what does this eye see?

To repeat, while this spate of films cannot be homogenized, it should nonetheless be noted that many draw unself-consciously on the threat of being feminized, of being made a "pussy" (and subliminally, the threat of being castrated). In Albert and Allen Hughes's *Menace II Society*, that threat is transmitted in the film's dialogue—variations on "Don't be actin' like no pussy" run throughout—but is telescoped most graphically in one of its many cop searches now conventionalized in black male cinema: "Spread your legs," shouts the cop. But permit me first another detour into history.

See the Cat. It Goes Meow-Meow

It is perhaps useful to note that the language of heterosexual erotics can be said to have inaugurated this era of black males as feature filmmakers, an era whose beginnings can be traced to Spike Lee's *She's Gotta Have It*, the story of the insatiable Nola Darling, who suffers only the reprisal of rape for seizing male sexual prerogatives and stances, without apology or shame. The *New York Times* magazine featured eight black male filmmakers on the cover of its July 14, 1991, edition, under the caption " 'They've Gotta Have Us': Hollywood's Black Directors." One plainly hears the echoes of Spike Lee's *She's Gotta Have It*. These eight men are the "us" that "they've" (the white Hollywood film establishment) "gotta have."

The eight men presumably speak in unified quotation as the sexualized, feminized objects implied in the title. But John Singleton, who is much the center of the story's profile, is represented as one who plays at initiating his own desire. Singled out in the group as "poised on the brink of influence," Singleton is cast in a powerful, "manly" role—telescoped by his "silver

Figure 3. John Singleton, *New York Times Magazine*, July 14, 1991.

Peugeot," his "two-car garage," and his large house in the "prosperous" Los Angeles neighborhood of Baldwin Hills. A full-page, close-up shot of Singleton, clothed in the phallic trappings of a black leather jacket, catches him in a threatening pose that, at first glance, seems best read as a defense against the invasiveness of police surveillance captured so brilliantly in *Boyz N the Hood*. But Singleton's enlarged, almost poster-sized body stands in the foreground of Columbia Studios (Figure 3), and we can only wonder at the ambiguities of the pose. Is his index finger, which creates the image of a cocked pistol, aimed at someone threatening his own "endangered" body, or is it aimed at someone threatening trespass on Columbia's grounds? Whose pistol is being cocked? What/whom is being protected?

If this photograph captures what Craig Owens terms "the fundamental duplicity of every pose" ("Posing" 212), the accompanying story completes that picture and studs it with a teasing metaphor. Having covered the material signs of Singleton's success, the writer moves on to describe his home life. He "lives alone," except for an "albino cat who floats down the stairs to greet him." "That's White Boy," Singleton says, "stooping to rub the cat behind his translucent ears." The writer continues, "The metaphor is irresistible: at the moment, John Singleton, a 23-year-old black man, has the notoriously insular and mostly white [and as the story will soon reveal, mostly male]

Hollywood establishment purring." With echoes of Baldwin's "The Black Boy Looks at the White Boy," Singleton has seemingly inverted, if only symbolically, the erotic arrangements of a familiar racial narrative, implied in the story's title, "they've gotta have us." The "Hollywood establishment" is now eroticized, seduced by the likes of John Singleton, who has the power to make it purr. "White Boy" obviously riffs on and reverses that familiar "Boy," the epithet that has historically degraded and infantilized black men. More to the point, the white cat named White Boy is the white male "Hollywood establishment" turned "pussy." But just who is being fucked (or zoomed) here? It's not entirely obvious.

While the writer implies that Singleton has "spread the legs" of the "notoriously insular" world of Hollywood, has penetrated it, if you will, we are left to contemplate the afterimage of Singleton's featured pose. This enlarged, waist-up shot of Singleton—full page, but not full bodied—standing outside the door of Columbia Studios plays paradoxically against a narrative in which he exemplifies "Hollywood's sudden open-door policy toward black filmmakers." And this "new" policy is surely spun from an old principle of economics that seeks to reap the greatest returns on the least investment. Hollywood, cast here as an albino cat named White Boy, has the luxury of such identity-as-impersonation. It might well "gotta have" the "pigmentation" that these filmmakers provide, but what it's "gotta have" more urgently are more profits like the $55 million that Columbia Pictures earned on its $6 million investment in Boyz N the Hood.

When cameras are put in the hands of those without previous professional credits—John Singleton, Matty Rich, and Albert and Allen Hughes, to name just a few—the consequences strike many as a form not just of "shooting back," at the white establishment and its dominant cultural forms, but also at a society that they rightly perceive as denying them the rights and privileges of masculinity. That masculinity—almost always assumed to be heterosexual—includes the right and privilege to render women inessential, superfluous, on the one hand, and to dominate and degrade them, on the other.

Films like Boyz N the Hood have forged a symbiotic partnership with rap groups, the leading signifiers of an aggressively heterosexual black masculinity, a partnership that cannot be overlooked in any effort to understand expressions of black masculinity in contemporary culture. Rap musicians' successful seizure of the reproduction technologies of the white-dominated music industry represents a similar struggle for manhood in an arena from which women—white and black—are largely excluded. But in rap lyrics, as is well known by now, the place and function of women is more complicated. In rap's critiques of institutional racism, black women constitute both the supererogatory and the derogated objects in the grandiose ego investments of most rap musicians.

In a recent interview with Ice Cube, rap artist and costar of *Boyz N the Hood*, Angela Y. Davis was largely unsuccessful in her bid to persuade him of the limitations of focusing exclusively on black men and masculinity in order to wage war on racism.

> *Angela Y. Davis:* What about the women? You keep talking about black men. I'd like to hear you say: black men and black women.
> *Ice Cube:* Black people.
> *AYD:* I think you often exclude your sisters from your thought process. We're never going to get anywhere if we're not together.
> *IC:* Of course. But the black man is down.
> *AYD:* The black woman's down too.
> *IC:* But the black woman can't look up to the black man until we get up.
> *AYD:* Well why should the black woman look *up* to the black man? Why can't we look at each other as equals?
> *IC:* If we look at each other on an equal level, what you're going to have is a divide. (A. Davis, "Nappy Happy" 181–82)

Ice Cube's desire for a silent female partner, who lacks the look—or if you prefer, the gaze—is far from unique to him (or for that matter, unique to black men), but they are widely represented in the gangsta rap of which his lyrics are largely representative.[12]

Given media critics' politically motivated efforts to hold rap to a standard not demanded of other equally masculine-centered and equally violent popular forms, I hesitate to revisit the rap controversy here, lest my remarks be seen as underwriting the media's racist double standard and its ongoing scapegoating of rap. Obviously, to single out rap music in order to decry violence and sexism is patently hypocritical, given the fact that violence and sexism have immemorially given this society perhaps its most distinctive signature. On this matter, Tricia Rose is absolutely justified in condemning the politics of policing and stigmatizing rap. She is right to note that "some responses to sexism in rap music adopt a tone that suggests that rappers have infected an otherwise sexism-free society" (15).

Rose's point can be extended and used to condemn this culture's habitual tendency to use black men to focus the nation's attention on rape, sexual harrassment, and wife battering (substitute your "social disease"). Media culture could clearly lead one to suppose that before gangsta rap there was no violence and misogyny; before Clarence Thomas, no sexual harrassment; before Mike Tyson, no acquaintance rape; and before O. J. Simpson—the largest media icon of them all—there was no wife battering. These, as only the most recent public examples of a generalized form of social scapegoating and hand-washing, should contain any critique that could be said to fuel the problem.

But let me be clear. While rap cannot be held to a higher standard where matters of misogyny are concerned, it is hard to gloss over the lyrics and the videos in which black women are butchered, fragmented, decapitated (castrated?), and metonymized as so many breasts and butts. These open and unabashedly aggressive stances against black women, in order to "secure" black masculinity against racist assault, pose for me a serious problem for studies in masculinity. Even the existence of black female rappers does not forestall critique, especially since in their "tough talking, gunwielding" stances, these women are simply, as Amy Linden argues, "faux men" (Linden 176).[13]

Many readily see that sexual anxiety is, above all else, the real subject of rap. With few exceptions, its lyrics express a fear of being, of becoming a woman, being/becoming feminized. How else to explain this glut of references to bitches, ho's, cunts, and pussies, which have become, in Lisa Jones's pointed language, the "national chant" of rappers?[14] I am not persuaded by Tricia Rose's defense that rap's sexist lyrics "serve to protect young men from the reality of female rejection" and "relieve their lack of self-worth and limited access to economic and social markers for heterosexual masculine power" (15). A male self-worth dependent on the debasement of women is questionable to begin with and cannot be defended. But more to the point, it is precisely the terms of "heterosexual masculine power" that need to be questioned. Although such questions have come from a diverse group of scholars and activists, they have been powerless against the mass marketing of ever more hardened forms of gangsta rap in which rappers like N.W.A. boast of finding a "good piece of pussy and go[ing] up in it" and Dr. Dre fantasizes about killing a black woman and thus leaving the world with "one less bitch." That such lyrics are said to be "real reflections" of black life in the ghetto may be right, but I agree with Sherley Ann Williams that "black people have to ask ourselves why so much of [rap] has become so vehemently misogynistic, violent, and sexually explicit, so soaked in black self-hatred?" (167). Williams does well to note that this shift occurred only when the production, distribution, and promotion of rap ceased to be under black control. Questions such as the ones Williams raises about rap's lyrics (not the genre itself) are seldom listened to and when they are, they are mainly dismissed.[15]

I can add nothing to what has already been said about the place of rap in constructions of black masculinity, and the place of women within those constructions. Rather, I would suggest that such critiques will continue to be dismissed for as long as certain unchallenged keywords and conceptual paradigms are automatically invoked in its defense. Such terms as "racial identity," "class," and "culture" operate as reflexes in much academic cultural studies and public discourse alike, and these terms, in turn, are implicated in the sexual politics of race.

One of the reigning conceptual paradigms is that which tends toward the idealization of the black working class, a tendency that can be traced to the resilient belief in reductive notions about the relation between class position and racial identity.[16] For example, the assumption that the cultural expressions of the black working and lower class are more "authentically" black has long held a kind of sacramental, if largely unexamined, authority. Langston Hughes's famous manifesto, "The Negro Artist and the Racial Mountain," is only one example of that idea. He read black middle-class provincialism as the obstacle to modern, fluid artistic expression, an obstacle that he figured as a black woman.[17]

Such unexamined notions about class are rivaled only by popular, and equally uncritical, assumptions about "culture." While this is not the forum in which to engage such assumptions in detail, I would suggest that "culture" is often crudely invoked to rationalize and reproduce the status quo insofar as patriarchal prerogatives are concerned. You will recall Orlando Patterson's famous chastisement of Anita Hill on the op-ed page of the Sunday New York Times. In his view, Hill and those "neo-Puritan" feminists who supported her, failed to appreciate the "cultural frame" of "most women of Southern working-class backgrounds, white or black, especially the latter." Patterson airs his suspicion that Hill "perfectly understood the psycho-cultural context in which Judge Thomas allegedly regaled her with his Rabelaisian humor." Hill's accusation, he continued "was in no way commensurate with [Thomas's] offense" and was, moreover, "disingenuous because she . . . lifted a verbal style that carries only minor sanction in one subcultural context and [threw] it in the overheated cultural arena of mainstream, neo-Puritan America."[18] And in the ongoing defenses of the aggressively heterosexist lyrics of rap, "culture" is often likewise invoked in their defense.

At the censorship trial of 2 Live Crew, Henry Louis Gates Jr. defended the group's lyrics as part and parcel of a black culture of orality that is a salient component of the black literary tradition. And in his recently published, The New Beats: Exploring the Music, Culture, and Attitudes of Hip Hop, S. H. Fernando writes, in a similar vein, "While it would be folly to justify material that does degrade women, it suffices to say that such attitudes are rooted deeply in the culture of their origin" (277). Tricia Rose concurs, arguing that "rap music is fundamentally linked to larger social constructions of black culture as an internal threat to dominant American culture and social order" (144).

Such notions of "culture" are themselves in need of critique. I agree with Kimberlé Crenshaw that acknowledging the cultural origins of rap in the black oral tradition does not "settle the question of whether such practices are oppressive to women and others within the community" ("Beyond Racism" 130). Such assumptions about the cultural origins of rap clearly rationalize and reproduce the status quo insofar as the prerogatives of heterosexual masculinity are concerned.

The negative place of the feminine, of black women in rap's construction of a radical black hetero masculinity, is a challenge for a model of cultural studies fixated on the relation of race to the construction of masculinity, especially when that model focuses increasingly on these artifacts of youth culture.

What Leerom Medovoi observes about British cultural studies in his essay for this volume applies with equal validity to U.S. cultural studies in the main. Both have had a "long love affair with masculinist youth culture, romanticizing the tough rebelliousness of working-class boys" (165; this volume). The perfect objects of this fantasy are the "bad boys" of gangsta rap.[19] And this romanticization is not just an academic thing. The young white suburban listeners, identified by polls as the leading consumers of rap, live out this generation's incarnation of Norman Mailer's "white Negroes." And they are not alone. Such fantasies extend from the suburbs to the boardroom of the youth-centered corporate culture of MTV, which was profiled in the *New Yorker* by John Seabrook, a self-described "comfortable thirty-five-year-old white man" who listens to Snoop Doggy Dogg on his "way to his office in midtown Manhattan," "digging [Snoop's] murderous styles and poetical techniques" (76).

Anyone who would resist this music is dismissed as bidding to contain the artistic innovation, expressive capacity, and political power of rap. Such characterizations function to override and silence any feminist, political critique, a silencing due, as well, to a persistent emphasis on politics as synonymous with getting physical, with getting violent. Angela Davis is right that the "'essence' of revolutionary commitment today" is considered to be the "image of an armed Black man" (A. Davis, "Black Nationalism" 327), but make no mistake, this arming is "revolutionary" in only the most emptily symbolic sense. It is a form of playing with power, of posing as revolutionaries. This is essentially the power of rap: the power to "discomfit," to provoke, the power to "*pose* a threat" (see Hebdige, "Posing").

On the cover of *By All Means Necessary,* KRS-One poses with an Uzi in what must be read as a photographic quotation of Malcolm X's famous photo following the firebombing of his home in Queens. Malcolm stands at the window with a rifle poised to shoot. His stance, the flexion of his arm, the angle of his body, are all replicated by KRS-One. Meanwhile, down on the streets, black men-in-the-making aim real guns, not at "the police" (Ice T. notwithstanding), but at mirrors of themselves, caught in a perilous stage of development, arrested at boyhood, masculinity but a compensatory fantasy for an all-consuming and unvoiced fear. These are the boys who, despite their postures, are scared stiff, their muscled toughness turned rigor mortis.[20] And their violent self-destruction commands the public's collective, riveted gaze and satisfies its pornographic fascination with violence, with death, and particularly, with the black male body, permanently hardened in death.[21]

This longtime affair with masculinist youth culture has the effect of rendering black girls invisible, a point that Donna Britt makes all too well.[22] In an editorial titled "What About the Sisters?" Britt observes that nobody wants to talk about girls' problems, because they "don't have the thunderclap impact of a gunshot." Because of the repeated thunderclaps of gunshots, the public centers on the black male as "endangered species," and this "rhetoric of extinction," termed here so aptly by Marlon Ross, sets the terms of discourse about contemporary black life. Ross is right to observe that this rhetoric emerges at a moment of feverish visibility.[23] Ross continues, "it is the image of the male, not the female, that dominates this life-and-death argument," and, I would add, it is the image of the male, not the female, that directs and drives initiatives to "save" this "endangered" species.

Among the most controversial of such initiatives is Detroit's three proposed African-centered schools for black boys. In August 1991, a judge ruled that excluding girls from the schools violated both federal and state law, adding that there was no evidence that the school system was failing males *because of the presence of girls.* The schools were founded to reverse the socioeconomic problems that are seen to affect black males disproportionately. That the public school system of Detroit fails girls in almost equal numbers—45 percent dropout rate as compared to 55 percent for boys—is consistently obscured in this initiative to educate boys first. Now taking fire in the larger society, this initiative can be seen, for example, in the "Student's Friend," Inner-City Scholarship

Fund of New York, which uses the image of a young black boy in white shirt and plaid tie for its full-page appeal for tax-deductible contributions.

These girls, who generate their own statistics of school failure followed by ever-escalating rates of teenage pregnancy, are simply written off by those who defend opening all-male academies as a "right" to self-determination and a responsibility to bring black boys to manhood. In the programs of these social engineers, single mothers are openly repudiated and an essential fact is overlooked: the family is not the only player in the identity formation of the child. Harvey Hambrick, principal of Detroit's Marcus Garvey Academy, would disagree in contending that "Single mothers have done a terrible job of raising their boys. . . . Only a man can raise a boy to be a man" (Houppert 31).

The rhetoric will not die. Which bodies matter in discussions of race? That some bodies matter and some do not can be partly blamed again on the inadequacy of existing conceptual paradigms that habitually counterpose race and gender, racism and sexism, that see gender as synonymous with women and thus an afterthought, rather than a factor without which the social construction of masculinity could not be fully understood. Kimberlé Crenshaw speaks for many other black feminists who have repeatedly insisted with her that, "Discursive and political practices that separate race from gender and gender from race create complex problems of exclusion and distortion for women of color" ("Beyond Racism" 112).

Recognition that the two must be read together remains the most serious challenge for current studies in masculinity. Likewise, recognition that the academic and the popular must be "read" more closely together simply adds to that challenge. Meanwhile, I have a fantasy, in which all those who are invested in the plight and perils of masculinity would step off the treadmill that constitutes discourse on the subject, onto much more risky and rugged terrain. Move beyond the safety and security of certain well-conditioned reflexes, whether they be struck in the ivory tower, the night woods, the recording studio, or the cutting-room floor. Move outside what James Baldwin called the "prison" of masculinity in an essay that critiqued those heroes of popular film who cannot "get through to women" and thus become imprisoned by their "muscles, fists, and . . . tommy guns" ("Male Prison" 105). Move beyond a focus on the artistic, sculpted body that "looks hard" and holds its "precious prescribed pose," to one less taut, one less muscle-bound. One less shaped, less secured by the stresses of repetition. One less threatened by the presence and the power of the feminine.

Notes

I would like to thank Matthew Brown and Michael Furlough for providing invaluable research assistance.

1. Since its formulation, Mulvey's theory has been usefully problematized by a range of readers, including Steve Neale, "Masculinity as Spectacle." And in her introduction to *Discourses of Sexuality: From Aristotle to AIDS*, Domna Stanton summarizes still other refinements, including that by John D'Emilio, who "exposes the heterosexism of a gaze theory predicated on a dominant male subject and a passive female object"; Patricia White, who argues that "the desire of the lesbian spectator to look at women does not cast her in the masculine position, but in fact disrupts it"; and Jane Gaines, who examines the "inherent racism of gaze theory from the position of black men who have been historically castrated for looking" (24).

2. Not only is the look of surveillance conventionally raced, but black men, as the objects of the look, are equally conventionalized as physical embodiments, excessively so, of European and Euro-American sexual fantasies. As bodies, they are hypermasculinized and feminized at once. Both registers converge, for example, in Robert Mapplethorpe's *Black Book*, in which an exaggerated masculinity is captured in the excessively large penises of men (one controversially faceless in three-piece suit) and a form of "femininity," in those shots of very young men, surely modeled on the Greek ephebes, caught between boyhood and manhood.

3. See *New York Times*, Sunday, 20 Nov. 1994, p. 6.

4. For a description of such programs, see Bill McAllister, "To Be Young Male and Black: Worsening Problems Confront the Nation's 'Species in Danger'" in the *Washington Post*, Thursday, 28 Dec. 1989, A4.

5. Writer John Edgar Wideman has recently joined this chorus of voices. In his recently published *Fatheralong: A Meditation on Fathers and Sons, Race and Society*, he writes, "Ideas of manhood, true and transforming grow out of private, personal exchanges between fathers and sons. . . . Generation after generation of black men, deprived of the voices of their fathers are, for all intents and purposes, born semi-orphans. 'Mama's baby, Daddy's maybe'" (64–65).

6. Bly freely admits that "most of the language in this book speaks to heterosexual men but does not exclude homosexual men" (x), and that specific address extends implicitly to the book's dominant racial addressee, Bly's golden-haired ephebe.

7. In an essay, otherwise disturbing in many aspects, Orlando Patterson offers a suggestive explanation of the function of the maternal in urban black youth culture, which so much recent black film and rap supposedly reflects: "It is now easy to see the powerful attraction of the violent street gang and 'cool pose' culture for the under- and lower-class youth. The antimaternal abuse and promiscuous sexual and physical violence of the street culture acts as a belated, but savagely effective means of breaking with mother" ("Blacklash" 16–17).

8. Nelson George is right to read this as an "Afrocentric fantasy of child rearing." See

George 39. Singleton's script echoes Robert Bly's account of a woman who "declared that she realized about the time her son got to high school age that he needed more *hardness* than she could *naturally* give" (Bly 17; emphasis added). *Deep Cover*, a New Line Cinema production starring Laurence Fishburne, makes essentially the same point. The opening scene features John, the Fishburne character, as a young boy in a car with his father, who is immediately killed in an armed robbery attempt. In the course of the film, John finds a surrogate father (this time, a police officer, presumably on the right side of the law), and becomes, in turn, a surrogate father to the son of a drug-addicted woman. Coming close to being typecast, Fishburne continues his role as "father figure"—this time, improbably to a young white boy—in *Searching for Bobby Fischer*. There he teaches a young white boy the art and techniques of chess, allegorically, a "game of life." Samuel Jackson plays an almost identical role as chess coach and father figure in *Fresh*. Susan Jeffords sees the relationships between fathers and sons as central to Hollywood's constructions of masculinity during the Reagan era. "Relationships between fathers and sons (or men and their symbolic fathers)" constitute the "chief determinants of masculine identity." She suggests that this pattern is graphically illustrated in the *Star Wars* films, in which "knowledge of the father is such an important part of an individual's identity that, without that knowledge, the individual cannot realize his true skills and abilities" (*Hard Bodies* 86). Obviously, the idealization of father-son relations has extended far beyond the Reagan era.

9. See my "Reading Family Matters." See also Gilroy, "It's a Family Affair," in which he argues that the "discourse of race as community, as family, has been born again in contemporary attempts to interpret the crisis of black politics and social life as a crisis solely of black masculinity. The family is not just the site of cultural reproduction; it is also identified as the mechanism for reproducing the cultural dysfunction that disables the race as a whole. And since the race is nothing more than an accumulation of families, the crisis of black masculinity can be fixed. It is to be repaired by instituting appropriate forms of masculinity and male authority, intervening in the family to rebuild the race" (312). And in a perceptive essay on the Clarence Thomas confirmation hearings, Homi Bhabha sees the rhetoric of family at the heart of Thomas's self-justification and defense: "In Thomas's testimony there is a decisive attempt to obscure the reality of sexual politics in the workplace by way of a spurious familial metaphor that creates the illusion of an identity of interests. . . . Thomas . . . rhetorically reinvents the workplace as the familial space—'My clerks are my family. They're my friends. . . . I don't know why a son or a daughter or a brother or a sister would write some book that destroys a family. I don't know.' This familiarizing, familial discourse associatively picks up the unifying 'black' resonance of a common culture that then explicitly disavows the question of sexuality—Sex within the family? God forbid!—and sanitizes the power relations of the workplace by turning them into filial responsibilities" ("A Good Judge of Character" 236).

10. Here, it might be useful to mention Nelson George's "A Chronicle of Post-Soul Black Culture" in his *Buppies, B-Boys, Bops and Bohos*. This is George's year-by-year

chronicle of the highpoints of black cultural production since 1971. Among those of 1987 is this entry: "Toni Morrion publishes *Beloved* to tremendous acclaim and takes her place as the nation's preeminent African American novelist—a position formerly occupied by Richard Wright, Ralph Ellison, and James Baldwin" (29).

11. See Owens, "The Medusa Effect, or, The Specular Ruse" 191–200. See also Hertz, "Medusa's Head: Male Hysteria under Political Pressure."

12. Much has been made of obscenity and misogyny in the lyrics of rappers like Ice Cube and 2 Live Crew, and while this aspect of their work cannot be explained away merely by invoking "traditions" in black popular culture, it is important to view rap music in the wider context of culture and its products, as Michael Franti is prepared to do. A member of the rap group Hiphoprisy, whose debut album is *Hypocrisy is the Greatest Luxury*, Franti has openly critiqued what he views as the misogyny in hip-hop music, while astutely noting that "misogyny sells records, but I think it's important that we examine why it sells records, young males in particular are fed this stuff in the media every day, in films and in television: males are the dominant gender, women are sex objects. This is not just in rap music. . . . This is in all TV, this is in all film" (157). He also notes that "something like 80 percent of rap is being bought in the white community" (157).

13. I should note that the "beatitude" of Linden's title refers to the religious conversion that Run DMC has undergone. No longer identifying with the debasement of women seen in so much gangsta rap, the group understands that these are the realities of life in the ghetto. Tricia Rose argues that "black women rappers work within and against dominant sexual and racial narratives in American culture" (147).

14. See Lisa Jones, "Genitalia and the Paycheck" 267. See also George, who notes rightly that "misogyny is obviously nothing new. What is new is that a juvenile fascination-fear with women has made bitch, slut, cunt, and ho all too generally accepted parts of the male vocabulary" (130).

15. Sherley Anne Williams draws an important distinction between the lyrics of gangsta rap and rap music in general. She makes clear that her intent is not to "condemn" rap but to "question the content of some rap songs" (171).

16. Stuart Hall makes the similar observation that "dominant ethnicities are always underpinned by a particular sexual economy, a particular figured masculinity, a particular class identity" ("What Is This 'Black'" 31).

17. See Hughes, "The Negro Artist and the Racial Mountain" 95. I am indebted to Dorrie Beam for this observation.

18. Patterson, "Race, Gender and Liberal Fallacies." Patterson has since extended this analysis in a general indictment of the role that feminist thought, especially black feminist thought, plays in obscuring our understanding of gender relations among Black Americans. See Patterson, "Blacklash."

19. George makes the interesting point that "gangsta rap has its strongest antecedents, outside simple reality, in the trash movies stockpiled by ghetto video stores. In both hip hop and urban youth culture the gang concept, the drive-by, the fetish

for automatic weaponry . . . are fantasies of macho potency many African American males first bugged out to via video" (150).

20. Wideman is right to note that they "annihilate themselves in [turf] wars whose only purpose seems to be saving their true enemies the trouble of finishing them off" (27).

21. Nowhere is this fascination more apparent than in the overrepresentation of the black male corpse in contemporary photo journalism. Seen most often laid out in a coffin, his mother standing beside to gaze on his eyes now closed in death, this body becomes a flashpoint in the culture's discourse on "family values" in which black mothers are criminalized.

22. Rabbie and Garber make a similar point about British youth culture. They argue that it is violence that qualifies as newsworthy, an activity from which women have tended to be excluded. See Rabbie and Garber 212.

23. It is useful to consider this overexposure in light of Scarry's observation that "to be intensely embodied is the equivalent of being unrepresented and . . . is always the condition of those without power" (359–60).

WORKS CITED

Abelove, Henry, Michèle Aina Barale, and David M. Halperin, eds. *The Lesbian and Gay Studies Reader*. New York: Routledge, 1993.

Abramowitz, Michael. "All Shook Up in Suburbia." *Washington Post* 10 June 1991: C1, C9.

Abruzzese, Alberto. "Gli uomini forti e le maestre pedoni: Ideologie e pratiche dell'educazione fisica dal risorgimento al fascismo." *Gli uomini forti*. Ed. Farassino and Sanguineti. Milan: Mazzotta, 1983. 57–65.

Ali, Shahrazad. *The Blackman's Guide to Understanding the Blackwoman*. Philadelphia: Civilized, 1989.

Altman, Dennis. *Homosexual Oppression and Liberation*. 1971. London: Allen Lane, 1974.

American Graphic Systems, Inc. *I Am Elvis: A Guide to Elvis Impersonators*. New York: Pocket, 1991.

Anderson, Benedict. *Imagined Communities: Reflections on the Origin and Spread of Nationalism*. London: Verso, 1983.

Anderson, Jervis. *This Was Harlem: A Cultural Portrait, 1900–1950*. New York: Farrar, Straus and Giroux, 1981.

Appiah, Kwame Anthony, and Henry Louis Gates Jr. "Editors' Introduction: Multiplying Identities." *Critical Inquiry* 18 (1992): 625–29.

Aristotle. *Ethica Nicomachea*. Trans. W. D. Ross. *The Basic Works of Aristotle*. Ed. Richard McKeon. New York: Random, 1941. 928–1112.

Aron, Cindy. *Ladies and Gentlemen of the Civil Service: Middle-Class Workers in Victorian America*. New York: Oxford UP, 1987.

Aronowitz, Stanley. *False Promises: The Shaping of American Working-Class Consciousness*. New York: McGraw-Hill, 1973.

———. "Reflections on Identity" and "Discussion." *October* 61 (1992): 91–120.

Ashcroft, Bill, Gareth Griffiths, and Helen Tiffin, eds. *The Post-Colonial Studies Reader*. New York: Routledge, 1995.

Austen, Roger. *Genteel Pagan: The Double Life of Charles Warren Stoddard*. Ed. John W. Crowley. Amherst: U of Massachusetts P, 1991.

Awkward, Michael. *Negotiating Difference: Race, Gender, and the Politics of Positionality*. Chicago: U of Chicago P, 1995.

Bailey, Cameron. "Nigger/Lover: The Thin Sheen of Race in Something Wild." *Screen* 29 (autumn 1988): 28–42.

Baker, Houston A. *Blues, Ideology, and Afro-American Literature: A Vernacular Theory.* Chicago: U of Chicago P, 1984.

Baldwin, James. "The Black Boy Looks at the White Boy." *The Price of the Ticket: Collected Non-Fiction, 1948–1985.* New York: St. Martin's, 1985. 289–303.

———. "The Male Prison." *The Price of the Ticket: Collected Non-Fiction, 1948–1985.* New York: St. Martin's, 1985. 101–5.

Barker-Benfield, G. J. *The Horrors of the Half-Known Life: Male Attitudes Toward Women and Sexuality in Nineteenth-Century America.* New York: Harper and Row, 1976.

Barthes, Roland. *Camera Lucida.* Trans. Richard Howard. New York: Hill and Wang, 1974.

———. *Roland Barthes.* Trans. Richard Howard. London: Macmillan, 1977.

———. *Selected Writings.* Ed. Susan Sontag. London: Fontana, 1983.

Bataille, Georges. "The Sacred Conspiracy." *Visions of Excess: Selected Writings, 1927–1939.* Ed. Allan Stoekl. Trans. Allan Stoekl, Carl R. Lovitt, and Donald M. Leslie Jr. Minneapolis: U of Minnesota P, 1985. 178–81.

———. "The Structure and Function of the Army." *The College of Sociology 1937–39.* Ed. Denis Hollier. Minneapolis: U of Minnesota P, 1988. 137–44.

———. *Theory of Religion.* Trans. Robert Hurley. 1973. New York: Zone, 1989.

"Bathing and Bodies: A Dissertation." *Putnam's Monthly Magazine* 4 (1854): 532–36.

Baym, Nina. "Melodramas of Beset Manhood: How Theories of American Fiction Exclude Women Authors." *American Quarterly* 33.2 (1981): 123–39.

Beame, Thom. "Interview: BWMT Founder—Mike Smith." *Black Men/White Men: A Gay Anthology.* Ed. Michael J. Smith. San Francisco: Gay Sunshine, 1983.

Bechet, Sidney. *The Legendary Sidney Bechet.* RCA, 1988.

———. *Treat It Gentle.* New York: Hill and Wang, 1960.

Beck, Earl R. "The Anti-Nazi 'Swing Youth,' 1942–1945." *Journal of Popular Culture* 19 (winter 1985): 45–53.

Bederman, Gail. *Manliness and Civilization: A Cultural History of Gender and Race in the United States, 1880–1917.* Chicago: U of Chicago P, 1995.

Benjamin, Walter. "The Storyteller." *Illuminations.* Ed. Hannah Arendt. Trans. Harry Zohn. New York: Schocken, 1971. 83–109.

Benson, Thomas. "Rhetoric and Autobiography: The Case of Malcolm X." *Quarterly Journal of Speech* 60 (Feb. 1974): 1–13.

Benston, Kimberly W. "Performing Blackness: Re/Placing Afro-American Poetry." *Afro-American Literary Study in the 1990s.* Ed. Houston A. Baker and Patricia Redmond. Chicago: U of Chicago P, 1989. 164–85.

Bergman, David. "The African and the Pagan in Gay Black Literature." *Sexual Sameness.* Ed. Joseph Bristow. London: Routledge, 1992. 148–69.

Berlant, Lauren. "National Brands/National Body: *Imitation of Life.*" *Comparative American Identities: Race, Sex, and Nationality in the Modern Text.* Ed. Hortense J. Spillers. New York: Routledge, 1991. 110–40.

Berlin, Edward A. *Ragtime: A Musical and Cultural History.* Berkeley: U of California P, 1980.

Berlin, Ira, Joseph P. Reidy, and Leslie S. Rowland, eds. *Freedom: A Documentary History* of Emancipation, 1861–1867. Series 2. *The Black Military Experience*. Cambridge: Cambridge UP, 1982.

Bernal, Martin. *Black Athena*. Vol. 1. *The Fabrication of Ancient Greece 1785–1985*. London: Free Association, 1987.

Bersani, Leo. "Is the Rectum a Grave?" *October* 43 (winter 1987): 197–222.

Berthoff, Werner. "Witness and Testament: Two Contemporary Classics." *New Literary History* 2 (winter 1971): 311–27.

Bhabha, Homi K. "The Commitment to Theory." *New Formations* 5 (1988): 5–23.

————. "A Good Judge of Character: Men, Metaphors and the Common Culture." *Race-ing Justice, En-gendering Power: Essays on Anita Hill, Clarence Thomas, and the Construction of Social Reality*. Ed. Toni Morrison. New York: Pantheon, 1992. 232–50.

————. "Interrogating Identity: The Postcolonial Prerogative." *Anatomy of Racism*. Ed. David Theo Goldberg. Minneapolis: U of Minnesota P, 1990.

————. "Of Mimicry and Man: The Ambivalence of Colonial Discourse," *October* 28 (spring 1984): 125–33.

————. "The Other Question: The Stereotype and Colonial Discourse." *Screen* 24 (Nov.–Dec. 1983): 18–36.

————. "Sly Civility." *October* 34 (1985): 71–80.

"Bill and the King." *New Yorker* 68 (1993): 32–33.

Biskind, Peter. *Seeing is Believing: How Hollywood Taught Us to Stop Worrying and Love the Fifties*. New York: Pantheon, 1983.

"'Blackboard Jungle' Shapes as Top Metro Release in Some Time." *Variety* 1 May 1956. MPAA Archive file on *Blackboard Jungle*, Los Angeles, CA.

Bloch, Ernst. *The Principle of Hope*. Trans. Neville Paice et al. Cambridge, MA: MIT, 1986.

Bly, Robert. *Iron John: A Book about Men*. Reading, MA: Addison-Wesley, 1990.

Bogle, Donald. *Toms, Coons, Mulattoes, Mammies, and Bucks*. New York: Continuum, 1989.

Bold, Christine. *Selling the Wild West: Popular Western Fiction, 1860–1960*. Bloomington: Indiana UP, 1987.

Boone, Joseph A. "Of Me(n) and Feminism: Who(se) Is the Sex That Writes." *Engendering Men: The Question of Male Feminist Criticism*. Ed. Joseph A. Boone and Michael Cadden. New York: Routledge, 1990. 11–25.

————. "Male Independence and the American Quest Genre: Hidden Sexual Politics in the All-Male Worlds of Melville, Twain and London." *Gender Studies: New Directions in Feminist Criticism*. Ed. Judith Spector. Bowling Green, Ohio: Bowling Green State U Popular P, 1986. 187–217.

————. *Tradition Counter Tradition: Love and the Form of Fiction*. Chicago: U of Chicago P, 1987.

Boscaglia, Maurizia. *Eye on the Flesh: Fashions of Masculinity in the Early Twentieth Century*. Boulder: Westview, 1996.

Box, Steven. *Recession, Crime, and Punishment*. Totowa, NJ: Barnes and Noble, 1987.

Braidotti, Rosi. "Envy: or With Your Brains and My Looks." *Men in Feminism*. Ed. Alice Jardine and Paul Smith. New York: Methuen, 1987. 233–41.

Braverman, Harry. *Labor and Monopoly Capital: The Degradation of Work in the Twentieth Century.* New York: Monthly Review, 1974.

Breitman, George. *The Last Year of Malcolm X: The Evolution of a Revolutionary.* New York: Merit, 1967.

———. *Malcolm X: The Man and His Ideas.* New York: Merit, 1965.

Britt, Donna. "What About the Sisters?" *Washington Post* 2 February 1992.

Bronski, Michael. *Culture-Clash: The Making of Gay Sensibility.* Boston: South End, 1984.

Brown, Bill. "Popular Forms II." *Columbia History of the American Novel.* Ed. Emory Elliott et al. New York: Columbia UP, 1991. 357–79.

———. "Science Fiction, the World's Fair, and the Prosthetics of Empire, 1910–1915." *Cultures of U.S. Imperialism.* Ed. Amy Kaplan and Donald Pease. Durham: Duke UP, 1993.

Brown, William Wells. *The Negro in the American Rebellion: His Heroism and His Fidelity.* Boston: Lee and Shepard, 1867.

Brownlow, Kevin. *The Parade's Gone By.* London: Secker and Warburg, 1968.

Brunetta, Gian Piero. *Cinema italiano tra le due guerra: Fascismo e politica cinematografica.* Milan: Mursia, 1975.

Bruynoghe, Yannick. "Mezzrow Talks About the Old Jim Crow." *The Melody Maker and Rhythm* 17 Nov. 1951: 9.

Buell, Lawrence. *New England Literary Culture: From Revolution through Renaissance.* Cambridge: Cambridge UP, 1986.

Burgin, Victor. "Perverse Space." *Sexuality & Space.* Ed. Beatriz Colomina. Princeton Papers on Architecture, 1. New York: Princeton Architectural P, 1992. 219–40.

Burley, Dan. "Whites 'Pass' for Negroes." *New York Age* 24 Sept. 1949: 17.

Burroughs, Edgar Rice. *The Gods of Mars.* 1913. New York: Ballantine, 1963.

———. *The Jungle Tales of Tarzan.* 1916. New York: Ballantine, 1992.

———. *The Outlaw of Torn.* 1914. New York: Ace, 1974.

———. *A Princess of Mars.* 1912. New York: Ballantine, 1985.

———. *Tarzan of the Apes.* 1912. New York: Signet Classics, 1990.

Butler, Judith. *Bodies That Matter: On the Discursive Limits of "Sex."* New York: Routledge, 1993.

———. "Critically Queer." *GLQ: A Journal of Lesbian and Gay Studies* 1.1 (1993): 17–32.

———. "The Force of Fantasy: Feminism, Mapplethorpe, and Discursive Excess." *differences: A Journal of Feminist Cultural Studies* 2.2 (1990): 105–25.

———. *Gender Trouble: Feminism and the Subversion of Identity.* New York: Routledge, 1990.

Caldwell, Lesley. "Reproducers of the Nation: Women and the Family in Fascist Policy." *Rethinking Italian Fascism.* Ed. David Forgacs. London: Lawrence and Wishart, 1986. 110–41.

Callahan, John F. *In the African American Grain: Call-and-Response in Twentieth Century Black Fiction.* Middletown, CT: Wesleyan UP, 1988.

Cammarota, Domenico. *Il cinema peplum.* Rome: Fanucci, 1987.

Cannella, Mario. "Ideology and Aesthetic Hypotheses in the Criticism of Neo-realism." *Screen* 14.4 (1973/4): 5–60.

Cantwell, Robert. *Bluegrass Breakdown: The Making of the Old Southern Sound*. Urbana: U of Illinois P, 1984.

Capeci, Dominic J., Jr. *The Harlem Riot of 1943*. Philadelphia: Temple UP, 1977.

———. *Race Relations in Wartime Detroit*. Philadelphia: Temple UP, 1984.

Carson, Michael. "Home and Abroad." *Gay Times* 129 (June 1989): 42–45.

"Case History of an Ex-White Man." *Ebony* 2.2 (1946): 11–16.

Cayton, Horace, and St. Clair Drake. *Black Metropolis: A Study of Negro Life in a Northern City*. 2nd ed. New York: Harper and Row, 1962.

Chambers, Jack. *Milestones 1: The Music and Times of Miles Davis to 1960*. Toronto: U of Toronto P, 1983.

Cheung, King-Kok. "The Woman Warrior versus the Chinaman Pacific: Must a Chinese American Critic Choose between Feminism and Heroism?" *Conflicts in Feminism*. Ed. Marianne Hirsch and Evelyn Fox Keller. New York: Routledge, 1990. 234–51.

Cheyfitz, Eric. "Tarzan of the Apes: U.S. Foreign Policy in the Twentieth Century." *American Literary History* 1.2 (1989): 339–60.

Chiao Hsiung-Ping. "Bruce Lee: His Influence on the Evolution of the Kung Fu Genre." *Journal of Popular Film and Television* 9.1 (spring 1981).

———. "The Distinct Taiwanese and Hong Kong Cinemas." *Perspectives on Chinese Cinema*. Ed. Chris Berry. London: BFI, 1991. 155–65.

Chibnall, Steve. "Whistle and Zoot: The Changing Meaning of a Suit of Clothes." *History Workshop Journal* 20 (autumn 1985): 56–81.

Chilton, John. *Sidney Bechet: The Wizard of Jazz*. London: Macmillan, 1987.

Chodorow, Nancy. "Mothering, Male Dominance, and Capitalism." *Capitalist Patriarchy and the Case for Socialist Feminism*. Ed. Zillah R. Eisenstein. New York: Monthly Review, 1979. 83–106.

———. *The Reproduction of Mothering: Psychoanalysis and the Sociology of Gender*. Berkeley: U of California P, 1978.

Cixous, Hélène. "Sorties." In *New French Feminisms: An Anthology*. Ed. Elaine Marks and Isabelle de Courtivron. New York: Schocken, 1980. 90–98.

Clark, Kenneth B., and James Barker. "The Zoot Effect in Personality: A Race Riot Participant." *Journal of Abnormal and Social Psychology* 40.2 (Apr. 1945).

Clarke, Cheryl. "The Failure to Transform: Homophobia in the Black Community." *Home Girls: A Black Feminist Anthology*. Ed. Barbara Smith. New York: Women of Color, 1983. 197–208.

Clarke, John Henrik, ed. *Malcolm X: The Man and His Ideas*. New York: Macmillan, 1969.

Clasby, Nancy. "Autobiography of Malcolm X: A Mythic Paradigm." *Journal of Black Studies* 5.1 (Sept. 1974): 18–34.

Cleaver, Eldridge. "Convalescence." *Soul on Ice*. New York: Ramparts, 1972. 176–87.

———. "The White Race and Its Heroes." *Soul on Ice*. New York: Ramparts, 1972. 69–84.

Clover, Carol J. *Men, Women, and Chainsaws: Gender in the Modern Horror Film*. Princeton: Princeton UP, 1992.

Cohen, Philip. "Subcultural Conflict and Working-Class Community." *Culture, Media,*

Language: Working Papers in Cultural Studies, 1972–79. Ed. Stuart Hall et al. London: Hutchinson, 1980. 78–87.

——. "Tarzan and the Jungle Bunnies: Race, Class, and Sex in Popular Culture." New Formations 5 (1988): 25–30.

Cone, James. Martin and Malcolm and America: A Dream or a Nightmare. Maryknoll, NY: Orbis, 1991.

Conn, Peter. The Divided Mind: Ideology and Imagination, 1898–1917. New York: Cambridge UP, 1983.

Cooper, Carol. "Jumping on the Paddy Wagon." Village Voice 8 Sept. 1992: 80.

Cooper, Wayne F. Claude McKay: Rebel Sojourner in the Harlem Renaissance. Baton Rouge: Louisiana State UP, 1987.

Cornish, Dudley Taylor. The Sable Arm: Black Troops in the Union Army, 1861–1865. 1956. Lawrence, KS: UP of Kansas, 1987.

Cosgrove, Stuart. "The Zoot-Suit and Style Warfare." History Workshop Journal 18 (autumn 1984): 78–81.

Craige, Betty Jean, ed. Literature, Language, and Politics. Athens: U of Georgia P, 1988.

Crenshaw, Kimberlé. "Beyond Racism and Misogyny: Black Feminism and 2 Live Crew." Words That Wound: Critical Race Theory, Assaultive Speech, and the First Amendment. Ed. Mari J. Matsuda et al. Boulder: Westview, 1993. 111–32.

——. "Whose Story Is It, Anyway? Feminist and Antiracist Appropriations of Anita Hill." Race-ing Justice, En-Gendering Power: Essays on Anita Hill, Clarence Thomas, and the Construction of Social Reality. Ed. Toni Morrison. New York: Pantheon, 1992. 402–40.

Crimp, Douglas. "Mourning and Militancy." October 51 (1989): 3–18.

Croft-Cooke, Rupert. The Unrecorded Life of Oscar Wilde. New York: David McKay, 1972.

Crowley, John W. "Howells, Stoddard, and Male Homosocial Attachment in Victorian America." The Making of Masculinities: The New Men's Studies. Ed. Harry Brod. Boston: Allen and Unwin, 1987. 301–24.

Cullen, Jim. " 'I's a Man Now': Gender and African American Men." Divided Houses: Gender and the Civil War. Ed. Catherine Clinton and Nina Silber. New York: Oxford UP, 1992. 76–91.

Dalfiume, Richard. Fighting on Two Fronts: Desegregation of the Armed Forces, 1939–1953. Columbia: U of Missouri P, 1969.

——. "The 'Forgotten Years' of the Negro Revolution." Journal of American History 55 (June 1968): 90–106.

Dalle Vacche, Angela. The Body in the Mirror: Shapes of History in Italian Cinema. Princeton: Princeton UP, 1992.

Danto, Arthur C. "Playing with the Edge: The Photographic Achievement of Robert Mapplethorpe." Mapplethorpe. New York: Random, 1992. 311–39.

Davis, Angela Y. "Nappy Happy: A Conversation with Ice Cube and Angela Y. Davis." Transition 58 (1992): 174–92.

——. Women, Race, and Class. 1981. New York: Vintage, 1983.

Davis, Melody D. The Male Nude in Contemporary Photography. Philadelphia: Temple UP, 1991.

Davis, Mike. "Armageddon at the Emerald City." *Nation* 11 July 1994: 46–50.

————. *Prisoners of the American Dream: Politics and Economy in the History of the U.S. Working Class.* London: Verso, 1986.

Davis, Miles, with Quincy Troupe. *Miles: The Autobiography.* New York: Simon and Schuster, 1989.

Delay, J. *The Youth of Andre Gide.* Trans. June Guicharnaud. Chicago: Chicago UP, 1956–57.

Deleuze, Gilles. "Intellectuals and Power: A Conversation between Michel Foucault and Gilles Deleuze." In Michel Foucault, *Language, Counter-Memory, Practice: Selected Essays and Interviews.* Ed. Donald F. Bouchard. Trans. Donald F. Bouchard and Sherry Simon. Ithaca: Cornell UP, 1977. 205–17.

de Man, Paul. "Autobiography as De-Facement." *Rhetoric of Romanticism.* New York: Columbia UP, 1984. 67–81.

DeMarco, Joe. "Gay Racism." *Black Men/White Men.* Ed. Michael J. Smith. San Francisco: Gay Sunshine, 1983.

Demarest, David. "*The Autobiography of Malcolm X:* Beyond Didacticism." *CLA Journal* 16.2 (Dec. 1972): 179–87.

Denning, Michael. *Mechanic Accents: Dime Novels and Working-Class Culture in America.* London: Verso, 1987.

Diawara, Manthia. "Black Spectatorship: Problems of Identification and Resistance." *Screen* 29.4 (1988): 66–76.

Dickinson, Emily. *Letters of Emily Dickinson.* Ed. Thomas H. Johnson and Theodora Ward. 3 vols. Cambridge, MA: Belknap Press of Harvard UP, 1965.

Ditton, Jason. *Part-Time Crime: An Ethnography of Fiddling and Pilferage.* London: Macmillan, 1977.

Doan, William, and Craig Dietz. *Photoflexion: A History of Bodybuilding Photography.* New York: St. Martin's, 1984.

Doherty, Thomas. *Teenagers and Teenpics: The Juvenilization of American Movies in the 1950s.* Winchester, England: Unwin Hyman, 1988.

Dollimore, Jonathan. *Sexual Dissidence: Augustine to Wilde, Freud to Foucault.* Oxford: Clarendon, 1991.

Douglas, Mary. *Natural Symbols.* Harmondsworth: Penguin, 1973.

————. *Purity and Danger.* London: Routledge and Kegan Paul, 1969.

Doyle, Jennifer, Jonathan Flatley, and José Esteban Muñoz, eds. *Pop Out: Queer Warhol.* Durham: Duke UP, 1996.

Du Bois, W. E. B. *Black Reconstruction in America: An Essay Toward a History of the Part Which Black Folk Played in the Attempt to Reconstruct Democracy in America, 1860–1880.* New York: Russell and Russell, 1963.

Duncan, Russell, ed. *Blue-Eyed Child of Fortune: The Civil War Letters of Colonel Robert Gould Shaw.* Athens: U of Georgia P, 1992.

Dunne, Dominick. "Robert Mapplethorpe's Proud Finale." *Vanity Fair* Feb. 1989.

Dyer, Richard. "White." *The Matter of Images: Essays on Representation.* New York: Routledge, 1993. 141–63.

Dyer, Richard, and Ginette Vincendeau, eds. *Popular European Cinema*. London: Routledge, 1992.

Easthope, Antony. *Literary into Cultural Studies*. New York: Routledge, 1991.

———. *What a Man's Gotta Do: The Masculine Myth in Popular Culture*. London: Unwin Hyman, 1986.

Eco, Umberto. *Travels in Hyperreality*. New York: Harcourt Brace Jovanovich, 1982.

Edelman, Murray. *Politics as Symbolic Action*. New York: Academic, 1971.

———. *The Symbolic Uses of Politics*. 1964. Urbana: U of Illinois P, 1977.

Edelstein, Tilden G. *Strange Enthusiasm: A Life of Thomas Wentworth Higginson*. New Haven: Yale UP, 1968.

Ehrenreich, Barbara. *The Hearts of Men: American Dreams and the Flight from Commitment*. Garden City, NY: Anchor, 1983.

Eisenstein, Segei. *Film Form: Essays in Film Theory*. New York: Meridian, 1957.

Eliot, T. S. "Marie Lloyd." 1923. *Selected Prose of T. S. Eliot*. Ed. Frank Kermode. New York: Harcourt Brace Jovanovich, 1975. 172–74.

Elley, Derek. *The Epic Film*. London: Routledge and Kegan Paul, 1984.

Ellison, Ralph. *Shadow and Act*. New York: Vintage, 1972.

Emerson, Ralph Waldo. *Nature. Essays and Lectures*. New York: Library of America, 1983. 5–49.

Emilio, Luis F. *A Brave Black Regiment*. 1894. New York: Bantam, 1992.

Essien-Udom, E. U. *Black Nationalism: A Search for Identity*. Chicago: U of Chicago P, 1962.

Essoe, Gabe. *Tarzan of the Movies*. Secaucus: Citadel Press, 1973.

Evans, Sara. *The Roots of Women's Liberation in the Civil Rights Movement and the New Left*. New York: Vintage, 1979.

Fanon, Frantz. *Black Skin, White Masks*. 1952. Trans. Charles Lam Markmann. New York: Grove Weidenfeld, 1967.

———. *The Wretched of the Earth*. 1961. Trans. Constance Farrington. Harmondsworth: Penguin, 1967.

Farassino, Alberto, and Tatti Sanguinetti, eds. *Gli uomini forti*. Milan: Mazzotta, 1983.

Farber, Jerry. *The Student as Nigger*. New York: Pocket, 1972.

Felice, Renzo De, and Luigi Goglia. *Mussolini. Il mito*. Rome and Bari: Laterza, 1983.

———. *Storia fotografica del fascismo*. Rome and Bari: Laterza, 1982.

Fenton, Robert W. *The Big Swingers*. Englewood Cliffs, NJ: Prentice-Hall, 1967.

Fernando, S. H. *The New Beats: Exploring the Music, Culture, and Attitudes of Hip Hop*. New York: Anchor, 1994.

Fiedler, Leslie. "Come Back to the Raft Ag'in, Huck Honey!" *The Collected Essays of Leslie Fiedler*. 2 vols. New York: Stein and Day, 1971. 1:142–51.

———. *Love and Death in the American Novel*. New York: Stein and Day, 1960.

Filene, Peter Gabriel. *Him/Her Self*. New York: Harcourt Brace Jovanovich, 1974.

Finkle, Lee. "The Conservative Aims of Militant Rhetoric: Black Protest during World War II." *Journal of American History* 60 (Dec. 1973): 692–713.

Fischer, Tony. "Isaac Julien: Looking for Langston." *Third Text* 12 (1990): 59–70.

Fiske, John. *Television Culture*. New York: Methuen, 1987.

Flanigan, B. P. "Kung Fu Crazy, or The Invasion of the 'Chop Suey Easterns.' " *Cineaste* 15.3 (1974).

Flynn, George Q. "Selective Service and American Blacks during World War II." *Journal of Negro History* 69 (winter 1984): 14–25.

Foner, Philip S. *Organized Labor and the Black Worker, 1619–1981*. New York: International, 1981.

Foreman, P. Gabrielle. " 'This Promiscuous Housekeeping': Death, Transgression, and Homoeroticism in Uncle Tom's Cabin." *Representations* 43 (summer 1993): 51–72.

Foucault, Michel. "Body/Power." *Power/Knowledge: Selected Interviews and Other Writings, 1972–1977*. Ed. Colin Gordon. New York: Pantheon, 1980. 55–62.

———. "Sexuality and Solitude." *On Signs*. Ed. Marshall Blonsky. Baltimore: Johns Hopkins UP, 1985. 365–72.

Franti, Michael. "Hiphoprisy: A Conversation with Ishmael Reed and Michael Franti." *Transition* 56 (1992): 152–65.

Frederickson, George M. *The Black Image in the White Mind: The Debate on Afro-American Character and Destiny, 1817–1914*. 1971. Middletown, CT: Wesleyan UP, 1987.

Freud, Sigmund. "Certain Neurotic Mechanisms in Jealousy, Paranoia, and Homosexuality." 1922. *Sexuality and the Psychology of Love*. Ed. Philip Rieff. New York: Collier, 1963. 160–70.

———. " 'Civilized' Sexual Morality and Modern Nervousness." 1908. *Sexuality and the Psychology of Love*. Ed. Philip Rieff. New York: Collier, 1963. 20–39.

———. *Group Psychology and the Analysis of the Ego*. Trans. James Strachey. 1921. New York: Norton, 1989.

———. "Mourning and Melancholia." *The Standard Edition of the Complete Psychological Works of Sigmund Freud*. Ed. James Strachey. 24 vols. London: Hogarth, 1953–1974. 14:243–58.

———. *New Introductory Lectures on Psychoanalysis*. 1933. Trans. James Strachey. New York: Norton, 1965.

———. "On Narcissism." *The Standard Edition of the Complete Psychological Works of Sigmund Freud*. Ed. James Strachey. 24 vols. London: Hogarth, 1953–1974. 14:69–102.

———. "Psychoanalytic Notes Upon an Autobiographical Account of a Case of Paranoia (Dementia Paranoides)." 1911. *Three Case Histories*. Ed. Philip Rieff. New York: Collier, 1963. 103–86.

Fritscher, Jack. *Mapplethorpe: Assault With a Deadly Camera*. Mamaroneck, New York: Hastings House, 1994.

Frow, John. *Cultural Studies and Cultural Value*. London: Oxford UP, 1995.

Fung, Richard. "Looking for My Penis: The Eroticized Asian in Gay Video Porn." *How Do I Look?: Queer Film and Video*. Ed. Bad Object-Choices. Seattle: Bay, 1991. 145–60.

Fusco, Coco. *English Is Broken Here: Notes on Cultural Fusion in the Americas*. New York: The New Press, 1995.

Fusfeld, Daniel R., and Timothy Bates. *The Political Economy of the Urban Ghetto.* Carbondale: Southern Illinois UP, 1984.

Fuss, Diana. *Essentially Speaking: Feminism, Nature and Difference.* London: Routledge, 1989.

———. "Fashion and the Homospectatorial Look." *Critical Inquiry* 18.4 (1992): 713–37.

———, ed. *Inside/Out: Lesbian Theories, Gay Theories.* New York: Routledge, 1991.

Gaines, Donna. *Teenage Wasteland: Suburbia's Dead End Kids.* New York: Pantheon, 1991.

Gaines, Jane. "Competing Glances: Who Is Reading Robert Mapplethorpe's *Black Book?*" *New Formations* 16 (spring 1992): 24–39.

———. "White Privilege and Looking Relations: Race and Gender in Feminist Film Theory." *Screen* 29.4 (autumn 1988): 12–27.

Gaitet, Pascale. "Jean Genet's American Dream: The Black Panthers." *Literature and History* 1.1 (spring 1992): 48–63.

Garber, Marjorie. *Vested Interests: Cross-Dressing and Cultural Anxiety.* New York: Routledge, 1991.

Garfinkel, Herbert. *When Negroes March: The March on Washington Movement in the Organizational Policies for FEPC.* Glencoe, IL: Free, 1959.

Gates, Henry Louis, Jr. *The Signifying Monkey: A Theory of African-American Literary Criticism.* New York: Oxford UP, 1988.

Gay Black Group. "White Gay Racism." 1982. Rpt. in *Male Order: Unwrapping Masculinity.* Ed. Rowena Chapman and Jonathan Rutherford. London: Lawrence and Wishart, 1988. 104–10.

Geduld, Carolyn. *Bernard Wolfe.* New York: Twayne, 1972.

Gehman, Richard B. "Poppa Mezz." *Saturday Review* 16 Nov. 1946: 26.

Genet, Jean. "Interview with Hubertu Fichte." *Gay Sunshine Interviews.* Ed. Winston Leyland. Vol. 1. San Francisco: Gay Sunshine, 1978. 67–94.

———. *Prisoner of Love.* Trans. Barbara Bray. London: Picador, 1989.

George, Nelson. *Buppies, B-Boys, Bops and Bohos: Notes on Post-Soul Black Culture.* New York: Harper Collins, 1992.

Giddins, Gary. *Riding on a Blue Note: Jazz and American Pop.* New York: Oxford UP, 1981.

Gide, André. *Amyntas: North African Journals.* 1906. Trans. Richard Howard. New York: Ecco Press, 1988.

———. *If it Die.* 1920. Private ed., 1926. Trans. Dorothy Bussy. Harmondsworth: Penguin, 1977.

———. *Journals.* 4 vols. London: Secker and Warburg, 1947–51.

———. *So Be It Or The Chips Are Down.* 1952. Trans. Justin O'Brien. London: Chatto, 1960.

———. *Travels in the Congo.* 1927–28. Trans. Dorothy Bussy. Harmondsworth: Penguin, 1986.

Gilbert, James. *A Cycle of Outrage: America's Reaction to the Juvenile Delinquent in the 1950s.* New York: Oxford UP, 1988.

Gill, Gerald R. "Dissent, Discontent and Disinterest: Afro-American Opposition to the United States Wars of the Twentieth Century." Unpub. ms., 1988.

Gillespie, Dizzy, with Al Fraser. *To Be or Not . . . to Bop: Memoirs.* Garden City, NJ: Double-day, 1979.

Gilroy, Paul. "It's a Family Affair." *Black Popular Culture.* Ed. Gina Dent. Seattle: Bay, 1992. 303–16.

———. "Nothing But Sweat Inside My Hand: Diaspora Aesthetics and Black Arts in Britain." *Black Film, British Cinema.* Ed. Kobena Mercer. London: ICA, 1988.

———. "One Nation under a Groove: The Cultural Politics of 'Race' and Racism in Britain." *Anatomy of Racism.* Ed. David Theo Goldberg. Minneapolis: U of Minnesota P, 1990.

"Girls Burn Barn In Memphis; Blame 'Blackboard Jungle.'" *Motion Picture Daily* 17 May 1955. MPAA Archive file on *Blackboard Jungle,* Los Angeles, CA.

Gitler, Ira. *Jazz Masters of the 1940's.* New York: Collier, 1966.

———. *Swing to Bop: An Oral History of the Transition in Jazz in the 1940's.* New York: Oxford UP, 1985.

Gitlin, Todd. *Watching Television.* New York: Pantheon, 1986.

Glaessner, Verina. *Kung Fu: Cinema of Vengeance.* London: Lorrimar, 1974.

Glatthaar, Joseph T. *Forged in Battle: The Civil War Alliance of Black Soldiers and White Officers.* New York: Meridian, 1991.

Glickman, Lawrence B. "I'm All White, Jack." Rev. of *The Wages of Whiteness: Race and the Making of the American Working Class,* by David R. Roediger. *Nation* 17 Feb. 1992: 207–9.

Goldman, Peter. *The Death and Life of Malcolm X.* New York: Harper and Row, 1973.

Gomez, Jewelle, and Barbara Smith. "Talking About It: Homophobia in the Black Community." *Feminist Review* 34 (spring 1990): 47–55.

Goodheart, Lawrence B. "The Odyssey of Malcolm X: An Eriksonian Interpretation." *The Historian* 53 (autumn 1990): 47–62.

Gooding, James Henry. *On the Altar of Freedom: A Black Soldier's Civil War Letters from the Front.* Ed. Virginia M. Adams. Boston: U of Massachusetts P, 1991.

Goodman, Paul. *Growing Up Absurd: Problems of Youth in Organized Society.* New York: Vintage, 1960.

Green, Martin. *The Great American Adventure.* Boston: Beacon, 1984.

Greenberg, Cheryl. *Or Does It Explode? Black Harlem in the Great Depression.* New York: Oxford UP, 1991.

Grossberg, Lawrence. *We Gotta Get Out of This Place: Popular Conservatism and Postmodern Culture.* New York: Routledge, 1992.

Grossberg, Lawrence, Cary Nelson, and Paula Treichler, eds. *Cultural Studies.* New York: Routledge, 1992.

Gruber, Frank. *The Pulp Jungle.* Los Angeles: Sherbourne, 1967.

Guerard, Albert J. *André Gide.* 2nd ed. Cambridge: Harvard UP, 1969.

"Gun Play." *Philadelphia Inquirer* 7 February 1992.

Gurganus, Allan. *White People.* New York: Ivy, 1990.

Hall, Catherine. *White, Male and Middle Class: Explorations in Feminism and History.* New York: Routledge, 1992.

Hall, Stuart. "Cultural Identities and Cinematic Representations." *Ex-Iles: Essays on Caribbean Cinema*. Ed. Mbye Cham. Trenton, NJ: African World, 1992.

———. "Encoding/Decoding." *Culture, Media, Language: Working Papers in Cultural Studies, 1972–79*. London: Hutchinson, 1980. 128–38.

———. "Ethnicity: Identity and Difference." *Radical America* 23.4 (1991): 9–20.

———. *The Hard Road to Renewal: Thatcherism and the Crisis of the Left*. London: Verso, 1988.

———. "New Ethnicities." *Black Film/British Cinema*. Ed. Kobena Mercer. ICA Documents 7. London: Institute of Contemporary Art/British Film Institute, 1988. 27–31.

———. "What Is This 'Black' in Black Popular Culture?" *Black Popular Culture*. Ed. Gina Dent. Seattle: Bay, 1992. 21–33.

———, et al., eds. *Culture, Media, Language: Working Papers in Cultural Studies, 1972–79*. London: Hutchinson, 1980.

———, and Tony Jefferson, eds. *Resistance Through Rituals: Youth Subcultures in Post-War Britain*. London: Hutchinson, 1976.

Hansberry, Elaine. *To Be Young, Gifted, and Black*. Englewood Cliffs, NJ: Prentice-Hall, 1969.

"Hans Massaquoi." *The Good War: An Oral History of World War Two*. New York: Pantheon, 1984.

Haraway, Donna. *Primate Visions: Gender, Race, and Nature in the World of Modern Science*. New York: Routledge, 1989.

Harper, Frederick. "Maslow's Concept of Self-Actualization Compared with Personality Characteristics of Selected Black American Protestors: Martin Luther King, Jr., Malcolm X, and Frederick Douglass." Diss. Florida State U, 1970.

Harpham, Geoffrey Galt. *Getting It Right: Language, Literature, and Ethics*. Chicago: U of Chicago P, 1992.

Harris, William H. *The Harder We Run: Black Workers since the Civil War*. New York: Oxford UP, 1982.

Hatt, Michael. "'Making a Man of Him': Masculinity and the Black Body in Mid-Nineteenth-Century American Sculpture." *Oxford Art Journal* 15.1 (1992): 21–35.

Hay, James. *Popular Cinema in Fascist Italy: The Passing of the Rex*. Bloomington: Indiana UP, 1987.

Hazzard-Gordon, Katrina. *Jookin': The Rise of Social Dance Formations in African-American Culture*. Philadelphia: Temple UP, 1990.

Hebdige, Dick. "Posing . . . Threats, Striking . . . Poses: Youth, Surveillance, and Display." *SubStance* 37/38 (1983): 68–88.

———. "Some sons and their fathers: An essay with photographs." *Ten-8* 17 (1985): 30–39.

———. *Subculture: The Meaning of Style*. New York: Methuen, 1979.

Heins, Henry Hardy, ed. *A Golden Anniversary Bibliography of Edgar Rice Burroughs*. West Kingston, RI: Grant, 1964.

Hemphill, Essex, ed. *Brother to Brother: New Writings by Black Gay Men*. Boston: Alyson, 1991.

Henderson, William McCranor. *Stark Raving Elvis*. New York: Simon and Schuster, 1984.

Hennessey, Mike. "Mezz Mezzrow: Alive and Well in Paris." *Down Beat* 35.11 (1968): 25.

Hentoff, Nat. "Counterpoint." *Down Beat* 11 Feb. 1953: 5.

———. *The Jazz Life*. 1962. London: Panther, 1964.

Hernton, Calvin C. *Sex and Racism in America*. 1965. New York: Anchor, 1992.

Hertz, Neil. "Medusa's Head: Male Hysteria under Political Pressure." *The End of the Line: Essays on Psychoanalysis and the Sublime*. New York: Columbia UP, 1987. 161–93.

Higashi, Sumiko. *Cecil B. DeMille and American Culture: The Silent Era*. Berkeley: U of California P, 1994.

Higginson, Mary Thacher. *Thomas Wentworth Higginson: The Story of His Life*. Boston: Houghton, 1914.

Higginson, Thomas Wentworth. *Army Life in a Black Regiment*. 1869. New York: Norton, 1984.

———. "Barbarism and Civilization." *Atlantic Monthly* 7 (1861): 51–61.

———. "Denmark Vesey." *Atlantic Monthly* 7 (1861): 728–44.

———. "Fayal and the Portuguese." *Atlantic Monthly* 6 (1860): 526–44.

———. "Gabriel's Defeat." *Atlantic Monthly* 10 (1862): 337–45.

———. "Going to Mount Katahdin." *Putnam's Monthly Magazine* 8 (1856): 242–56.

———. "Gymnastics." *Atlantic Monthly* 7 (1861): 283–302.

———. *Letters and Journals of Thomas Wentworth Higginson: 1848–1906*. Ed. Mary Thacher Higginson. Boston: Houghton, 1921.

———. "A Letter to a Dyspeptic." *Atlantic Monthly* 3 (1859): 465–74.

———. Letter to [Sylvester] Baxter. 6 Mar. 1887. Houghton Library, Harvard University.

———. *Malbone: An Oldport Romance*. Boston: Fields, Osgood, 1869.

———. "The Maroons of Jamaica." *Atlantic Monthly* 5 (1860): 213–22.

———. "The Maroons of Surinam." *Atlantic Monthly* 5 (1860): 549–57.

———. "The Moral Results of Slavery." *Hunt's Merchants' Magazine and Commercial Review* 28 (Jan.–June 1853): 706–9.

———. "The Murder of the Innocents." *Atlantic Monthly* 4 (1859): 345–56.

———. "Nat Turner's Insurrection." *Atlantic Monthly* 8 (1861): 173–87.

———. "The Ordeal by Battle." *Atlantic Monthly* 8 (1861): 88–95.

———. "Physical Courage." *Atlantic Monthly* 2 (1858): 728–37.

———. "Recent Poetry." *Nation* 7 Apr. 1892: 262–64.

———. "Saints, and Their Bodies." *Atlantic Monthly* 1 (1858): 852–95.

———. "Unmanly Manhood." *Woman's Journal* 13.5 (4 Feb. 1882): 33.

———. "Walt Whitman." *Nation* 15 Dec. 1881: 476–77.

———. War Diary. MS Am 784. Houghton Library, Harvard University.

———. War Letters. MS Am 784. Houghton Library, Harvard University.

Higham, John, ed. *Writing American History: Essays in Modern Scholarship*. Bloomington: Indiana UP, 1970.

Hill-Collins, Patricia. *Black Feminist Thought: Knowledge, Consciousness, and the Politics of Empowerment*. New York: Routledge, 1991.

Hocquenghem, Guy. *Homosexual Desire*. Trans. Daniella Dangoor with preface by Jeffrey
Weeks. London: Allison and Busby, 1978.

Hodges, John. "The Quest for Selfhood in the Autobiographies of W. E. B. Du Bois,
Richard Wright, and Malcolm X." Diss. U of Chicago, 1980.

Hofstadter, Richard. *The Age of Reform: From Bryan to FDR*. New York: Vintage, 1955.

———. *The Paranoid Style in American Politics and Other Essays*. New York: Knopf, 1965.

Hoggart, Richard. *The Uses of Literacy: Changing Patterns in English Mass Culture*. Fair Lawn,
NJ: Essential, 1957.

Hollinger, Richard C., and J. P. Clark. *Theft by Employees*. Lexington, MA: Lexington, 1983.

Homer. *The Odyssey of Homer*. Trans. Richmond Lattimore. 1965. New York: Harper Colo-
phon, 1975.

Honour, Hugh. *The Image of the Black in Western Art*. Vol. 4, *From the American Revolution to
World War I*. Part 1, *Slaves and Liberators*. Part 2, *Black Models and White Myths*. Houston:
Menil Foundation, 1989.

hooks, bell. *Black Looks: Race and Representation*. Boston: South End, 1992.

———. *Yearning: Race, Gender, and Cultural Politics*. Boston: South End, 1990.

Houppert, Karen. "Separatist But Equal?" *Village Voice* 19 May 1992: 27–31.

Howells, William Dean. *Selected Letters*. Vol. 2: 1873–1881. Ed. George Arms, Christoph K.
Lohmann, and Jerry Herron. Boston: Twayne, 1979.

Hudson, Julius. "The Hustling Ethic." *Rappin' and Stylin' Out: Communication in Urban Black
America*. Ed. Thomas Kochman. Urbana: U of Illinois P, 1972.

Hughes, Langston. "The Negro Artist and the Racial Mountain." *The Portable Harlem Renaissance Reader*. Ed. David Levering Lewis. New York: Viking, 1994. 91–95.

———. "Poem." *Black Men/White Men: A Gay Anthology*. Ed. Michael J. Smith. San Francisco: Gay Sunshine, 1983.

Hunter, Evan. *The Blackboard Jungle*. New York: Arbor House, 1984.

Hunter, Tera. "Household Workers in the Making: Afro-American Women in Atlanta
and the New South, 1861–1920." Diss. Yale U, 1990.

"Interview with Brandon Lee." *The Face* 37 (Oct. 1991).

"Interview with Robert Clouse." *Inside Kung Fu* Aug. 1988.

Jackson, George. *Soledad Brother: The Prison Letters of George Jackson*. Intro. by Jean Genet.
Harmondsworth: Penguin, 1971.

James, C. L. R., George Breitman, Edgar Keemer et al. *Fighting Racism in World War II*.
New York: Pathfinder, 1980.

James, William. "What Makes a Life Significant." *The Writings of William James: A Comprehensive Edition*. Ed. John J. McDermott. Chicago: U of Chicago P, 1977.

Jameson, Fredric. *The Political Unconscious: Narrative as a Socially Symbolic Act*. Ithaca: Cornell
UP, 1981.

———. *Signatures of the Visible*. New York: Routledge, 1991.

Jardine, Alice, and Paul Smith, eds. *Men in Feminism*. New York: Methuen, 1987.

Jeffords, Susan. *Hard Bodies: Hollywood Masculinity in the Reagan Era*. New Brunswick, NJ:
Rutgers UP, 1994.

─────. *The Remasculinization of America*. Bloomington: Indiana UP, 1989.

Johnson, James Weldon. *The Autobiography of an Ex-Colored Man. Three Negro Classics*. New York: Avon, 1965.

Jones, Gayl. *Liberating Voices: Oral Tradition in African American Literature*. Cambridge: Harvard UP, 1991.

Jones, LeRoi. *Blues People: Negro Music in White America*. New York: William Morrow, 1963.

Jones, Lisa. "Genitalia and the Paycheck." *Bullet Proof Diva: Tales of Race, Sex, and Hair*. New York: Doubleday, 1994.

Julien, Isaac. "Black Is, Black Ain't: Notes on De-Essentializing Black Identities." *Black Popular Culture*. Ed. Gina Dent. Seattle: Bay, 1992. 255–63.

Julien, Isaac, and Kobena Mercer. "True Confessions: A Discourse on Images of Black Male Sexuality." *Male Order: Unwrapping Masculinity*. Ed. Rowena Chapman and Jonathan Rutherford. London: Lawrence and Wishart, 1988. 131–53.

─────. "True Confessions: A Discourse on Images of Black Male Sexuality." Revised. *Brother to Brother: New Writings by Black Gay Men*. Ed. Essex Hemphill. Boston: Alyson, 1991. 167–73.

Kaminsky, Stuart M. "Kung Fu Film as Ghetto Myth." *Journal of Popular Film* 3 (1974): 129–38.

Kaplan, Amy. "Romancing the Empire: The Embodiment of American Masculinity in the Popular Historical Novel of the 1890s." *American Literary History* 2.4 (1990): 659–90.

Kater, Michael H. *Different Drummers: Jazz in the Culture of Nazi Germany*. New York: Oxford UP, 1992.

─────. "Forbidden Fruit? Jazz in the Third Reich." *American Historical Review* 94 (Feb. 1989): 11–43.

Kellogg, Peter J. "Civil Rights Consciousness in the 1940's." *The Historian* 42 (Nov. 1979): 18–41.

Kennedy, Robert. *Beef It! Upping the Muscle Mass*. New York: Sterling, 1983.

Kingston, Maxine Hong. *China Men*. London: Picador, 1981.

─────. *The Woman Warrior*. London: Picador, 1977.

Kocka, Jurgen. *A History of White Collar Workers in the United States*. Trans. Maura Kealy. London: Sage, 1980.

Kofsky, Frank. *Black Nationalism and the Revolution in Music*. New York: Pathfinder, 1970.

Kolodny, Annette. *The Lay of the Land: Metaphor as Experience and History in American Life and Letters*. Chapel Hill: U of North Carolina P, 1975.

Korstad, Robert, and Nelson Lichtenstein. "Opportunities Found and Lost: Labor, Radicals, and the Early Civil Rights Movement." *Journal of American History* 75 (Dec. 1988): 786–811.

Kroker, Arthur, Marilouise Kroker, and David Cook. *Panic Encyclopedia*. New York: St. Martin's, 1989.

Lagny, Michèle. "Popular Taste: The Peplum." *Popular European Cinema*. Ed. Dyer and Vincendeau. London: Routledge, 1992. 163–80.

Lambert, G. E. "Mezz Mezzrow—An Assessment." *Jazz Monthly* 6.10 (1960): 10–11.

Laplanche, J., and J.-B. Pontalis. "Fantasy and the Origins of Sexuality." *Formations of Fantasy.* Ed. Victor Burgin, James Donald, and Cora Kaplan. New York: Methuen, 1986. 5–34.

———. *The Language of Psychoanalysis.* Trans. Donald Nicholson-Smith. New York: Norton, 1973.

Lawrence, T. E. *Seven Pillars of Wisdom.* London: Penguin, 1976.

Lears, T. Jackson. *No Place of Grace: Antimodernism and the Transformation of American Culture.* New York: Pantheon, 1981.

Lent, John A. *The Asian Film Industry.* London: Christopher Helm, 1990.

Levine, Lawrence. *Black Culture and Black Consciousness: Afro-American Thought from Slavery to Freedom.* New York: Oxford UP, 1977.

Lewis, R. W. B. *The American Adam: Innocence, Tragedy, and Tradition in the Nineteenth Century.* Chicago: U of Chicago P, 1955.

Leyland, Winston, ed. *Gay Sunshine Interviews.* Vol. 1. San Francisco: Gay Sunshine, 1978.

Lichtenstein, Nelson. *Labor's War at Home: The CIO in World War II.* New York: Cambridge UP, 1982.

Liebow, Elliot. *Tally's Corner: A Study of the Negro Streetcorner Men.* Boston: Little, Brown, 1967.

Lighter, J. E., ed. *The Random House Historical Dictionary of American Slang.* New York: Random, 1994.

Linden, Amy. "Niggas with Beatitude: A Conversation with Run-DMC." *Transition* 62 (1993): 176–87.

Linebaugh, Peter. *The London Hanged: Crime and Civil Society in the Eighteenth Century.* London: Allen Lane, Penguin, 1991.

Lipsitz, George. "Introduction: Creating Dangerously: The Blues Life of Johnny Otis." *Upside Your Head! Rhythm and Blues on Central Avenue,* by Johnny Otis. Hanover, NH: Wesleyan UP, 1993.

———. *"A Rainbow at Midnight": Labor and Culture in the 1940s.* Urbana: U of Illinois P, 1994.

Living Colour. "Elvis Is Dead." *Time's Up.* Epic, 1990.

Lloyd, Genevieve. "Selfhood, War and Masculinity." *Feminist Challenges: Social and Political Theory.* Ed. Carole Pateman and Elizabeth Gross. Boston: Northeastern UP, 1987. 63–76.

Looby, Christopher. "Bachelorhood, Reverie, and the Odor of Male Solitude." Unpub.

———. "Flowers of Manhood: Race, Sex and Floriculture from Thomas Wentworth Higginson to Robert Mapplethorpe." *Criticism* 37 (winter 1994): 109–56.

———. "Race and Eros in Mapplethorpe's Black Book." Unpub.

Loomba, Ania. "Overworlding the 'Third World.'" *Oxford Literary Review* 13 (1991): 164–91.

Lorimer, George Horace. *Letters from a Self-Made Merchant to His Son.* London: Methuen, 1904.

Lott, Eric. "Double V, Double-Time: Bebop's Politics of Style." *Callaloo* 11.3 (1988): 597–605.

————. *Love and Theft: Blackface Minstrelsy and the American Working Class.* New York: Oxford UP, 1993.

————. " 'The Seeming Counterfeit': Racial Politics and Early Blackface Minstrelsy." *American Quarterly* 43 (1991): 223–54.

————. "White Like Me: Racial Cross-Dressing and the Construction of American Whiteness." *Cultures of U.S. Imperialism.* Ed. Amy Kaplan and Donald Pease. Durham: Duke UP, 1993. 474–95.

Low, Gail Ching-Liang. "White Skin/Black Masks: The Pleasures and Politics of Imperialism." *New Formations* 9 (winter 1989): 83–103.

Lupoff, Richard A. *Edgar Rice Burroughs: Master of Adventure.* New York: Canaveral, 1965.

Macleod, David I. *Building Character in the American Boy: The Boy Scouts, the YMCA, and Their Forerunners, 1870–1920.* Madison: U of Wisconsin P, 1983.

Madrid-Barela, Arturo. "In Search of the Authentic Pachuco: An Interpretive Essay." *Aztlan* 4.1 (spring 1973): 31–60.

Mailer, Norman. "The White Negro." *Advertisements for Myself.* New York: Signet, 1960. 298–322.

Majors, Richard. "Cool Pose: The Proud Signature of Black Survival." *Changing Men: Issues in Gender, Sex, and Politics* 17 (winter 1986).

Majors, Richard, and Janet Mancini Billson, eds. *Cool Pose: The Dilemmas of Black Manhood.* New York: Lexington Books, 1992.

Mapplethorpe, Robert. *Black Book.* New York: St. Martin's, 1986.

————. *Mapplethorpe.* New York: Random, 1992.

————. *The Perfect Moment.* Philadelphia: Institute of Contemporary Art, U of Pennsylvania, 1988.

Marable, Manning. *Race, Reform, and Rebellion: The Second Reconstruction in Black America, 1945–1990.* 2nd ed. Jackson: U of Mississippi P, 1991.

Marcus, Greil. *Dead Elvis: A Chronicle of a Cultural Obsession.* New York: Doubleday, 1991.

————. *Mystery Train: Images of America in Rock 'n' Roll Music.* 1975. New York: Dutton, 1982.

Marowitz, Charles. "The Revenge of Jean Genet." 1961. *The Encore Reader: A Chronicle of the New Drama.* Ed. Charles Marowitz et al. London: Methuen, 1965.

Martin, Robert K. *Hero, Captain, and Stranger: Male Friendship, Social Critique, and Literary Form in the Sea Novels of Herman Melville.* Chapel Hill: U of North Carolina P, 1986.

————. "Knights-Errant and Gothic Seducers: The Representation of Male Friendship in Mid-Nineteenth-Century America." *Hidden from History: Reclaiming the Gay and Lesbian Past.* Ed. Martin Duberman, Martha Vicinus, and George Chauncey Jr. 1989. New York: Meridian, 1990. 169–82.

Mathiews, Frank. "Blowing out the Boy's Brains." *Outlook* 108 (1914): 652–45.

Mayer, Arno. "The Lower Middle Class as a Historical Problem." *Journal of Modern History* 47.3 (1975): 409–36.

Mazon, Mauricio. *The Zoot-Suit Riots: The Psychology of Symbolic Annihilation.* Austin: U of Texas P, 1984.

McCann, Sean. "'A Roughneck Reaching for Higher Things': The Vagaries of Pulp Populism." *Radical History Review* 61 (1995): 4–34.

McDowell, Deborah E. "Reading Family Matters." *Changing Our Own Words: Essays on Criticism, Theory and Writing by Black Women*. Ed. Cheryl A. Wall. New Brunswick, NJ: Rutgers UP, 1990. 75–97.

McElroy, Guy C. *Facing History: The Black Image in American Art 1710–1940*. San Francisco: Bedford Arts Publishers in association with The Corcoran Gallery of Art, 1990.

McGee, Mark, and R. J. Robertson. *The J. D. Films: Juvenile Delinquency in the Movies*. Jefferson: McFarland, 1982.

McNeill, William H. *Keeping Together in Time: Dance and Drill in Human History*. Cambridge, Massachusetts: Harvard UP, 1995.

McPherson, James M. *The Negro's Civil War: How American Blacks Felt and Acted during the War for the Union*. 1965. New York: Ballantine, 1991.

McRobbie, Angela. "Settling Accounts with Subcultures: A Feminist Critique." *On Record: Rock, Pop, and the Written Word*. Ed. Simon Frith and Andrew Goodwin. New York: Pantheon, 1990. 66–80.

Medovoi, Leerom. "Mapping the Rebel Image: Postmodernism and the Masculinist Politics of Rock in the U.S.A." *Cultural Critique* 20 (winter 1991–92): 153–88.

Mercer, Kobena. "Black Hair/Style Politics." *New Formations* 3 (1987): 33–54.

———. "The Boy Who Fell to Earth." *Marxism Today* (July 1988).

———. "Dark and Lovely Too: Black Gay Men in Independent Film." *Queer Looks: Perspectives on Lesbian and Gay Film and Video*. Ed. Martha Gever, John Greyson, and Prathiba Parmar. New York: Routledge, 1993. 238–56.

———. "Looking for Trouble." *Transition* 51 (1991): 184–97.

———. "Skin Head Sex Thing: Racial Difference and the Homoerotic Imaginary." *How Do I Look?: Queer Film and Video*. Ed. Bad Object-Choices. Seattle: Bay, 1991. 169–210.

———. "Welcome to the Jungle: Identity and Diversity in Postmodern Politics." *Identity: Community, Culture, Difference*. Ed. Jonathan Rutherford. London: Lawrence and Wishart, 1990. 43–71.

Mercer, Kobena, and Isaac Julien. "Race, Sexual Politics and Black Masculinity: A Dossier." *Male Order: Unwrapping Masculinity*. Ed. Rowena Chapman and Jonathan Rutherford. London: Lawrence and Wishart, 1988. 97–164.

Merck, Mandy. "Difference and Its Discontents." *Screen* 28.1 (1987): 2–9.

Metz, Christian. *The Imaginary Signifier: Psychoanalysis and the Cinema*. Trans. Celia Britton, Annwyl Williams, Ben Brewster, and Alfred Guzzetti. 1977. Bloomington: Indiana UP, 1982.

Meyer, Howard N. *Colonel of the Black Regiment: The Life of Thomas Wentworth Higginson*. New York: Norton, 1967.

Mezzrow, Mezz. *Really the Blues*. 1946. New York: Citadel Underground, 1990.

Michaels, Walter Benn. "The Souls of White Folk." *Literature and the Body: Essays on Populations and Problems*. Ed. Elaine Scarry. Baltimore: Johns Hopkins UP, 1988. 185–209.

Milano, Comune di. *Gli annitrenta*. Milan: Mazzotta, 1981.

Miller, Christopher L. Blank Darkness: Africanist Discourse in French. Chicago: U of Chicago P, 1985.

Mills, C. Wright. White Collar. New York: Oxford UP, 1956.

Milner, Christina, and Richard Milner. Black Players: The Secret World of Black Pimps. New York: Little, Brown, 1972.

Mingus, Charles. Beneath the Underdog. Harmondsworth: Penguin, 1969.

Mitchell, Reid. The Vacant Chair: The Northern Soldier Leaves Home. New York: Oxford UP, 1993.

Modell, John, Marc Goulden, and Magnusson Sigurdur. "World War II in the Lives of Black Americans: Some Findings and an Interpretation." Journal of American History 76 (Dec. 1989): 838–48.

Modleski, Tania. Feminism Without Women: Culture and Criticism in a "Postfeminist" Age. New York: Routledge, 1991.

Mohanty, S. P. "Us and Them: On the Philosophical Bases of Political Criticism." New Formations 8 (summer 1989): 55–80.

Montgomery, David. Workers' Control in America: Studies in the History of Work, Technology, and Labor Struggles. Cambridge: Cambridge UP, 1979.

Montrose, Louis. " 'Eliza, Queene of shepheards,' and the Pastoral of Power." English Literary History 10 (1980): 153–82.

———. " 'The Place of a Brother' in As You Like It: Social Process and Comic Form." Shakespeare Quarterly 32 (1981): 28–54.

———. "Of Gentlemen and Shepherds: The Politics of Elizabethan Pastoral Form." English Literary History 50 (1983): 415–59.

Moon, Bucklin. "The Real Thing." The New Republic 115 (4 Nov. 1946): 605.

Moon, Michael. Disseminating Whitman: Revision and Corporeality in Leaves of Grass. Cambridge: Harvard UP, 1991.

———. "Memorial Rags, Memorial Rage." Unpub.

Moore, William. "On Identity and Consciousness of El Hajj Malik El Shabazz (Malcolm X)." Diss. U of California, Santa Cruz, 1974.

Moraga, Cherrie. "From A Long Line of Vendidas." Feminist Studies/Critical Studies. Ed. Teresa de Lauretis. Bloomington: Indiana UP, 1986. 173–90.

Morley, Dave. The Nationwide Audience: Structure and Decoding. London: British Film Institute, 1980.

Morrison, Toni. Playing in the Dark: Whiteness and the Literary Imagination. Cambridge: Harvard UP, 1992.

Morrisroe, Patricia. Mapplethorpe: A Biography. New York: Random, 1995.

Mosse, George L. Nationalism and Sexuality: Respectable and Abnormal Sexuality in Modern Europe. New York: Howard Fertig, 1985.

Mullen, Harryette. "Miscegenated Texts & Media Cyborgs: Technologies of Body and Soul." Poetics Journal 9 (June 1991): 36–43.

Mullen, R. D. "From Standard Magazines to Pulps and Big Slicks: A Note on the History of U.S. General and Fiction Magazines." Science-Fiction Studies 22 (1995): 144–56.

Mulvey, Laura. Visual and Other Pleasures. Bloomington: U of Indiana P, 1989.

————. "Visual Pleasure and Narrative Cinema." *Feminism and Film Theory*. Ed. Constance Penley. New York: Routledge, 1988. 57–68.

Muñoz, José E. "Famous and Dandy Like B. 'n' Andy: Race, Pop, and Basquiat." *Pop Out: Queer Warhol*. Ed. Jennifer Doyle, Jonathan Flatley, and José Esteban Muñoz. Durham: Duke UP, 1996. 144–79.

Naipaul, V. S. *A Turn in the South*. New York: Knopf, 1989.

Neale, Steve. "Masculinity As Spectacle: Reflections on Men and Mainstream Cinema." *Screen* 24.6 (1983): 2–16.

Nero, Charles I. "Toward a Black Gay Aesthetic: Signifying in Contemporary Black Gay Literature." *Brother to Brother: New Writings by Black Gay Men*. Ed. Essex Hemphill. Boston: Alyson, 1991. 229–52.

Newfield, Christopher. "The Politics of Male Suffering: Masochism and Hegemony in the American Renaissance." *differences* 1.3 (fall 1989): 55–87.

Newsinger, James. "Lord Greystoke and Darkest Africa." *Race and Class* 28 (1986).

Nietzsche, Friedrich. *On the Genealogy of Morals*. Trans. Walter Kaufmann and R. J. Hollingdale. New York: Vintage, 1967.

Norris, Chuck, with Joe Hyams. *The Secret of Inner Strength*. London: Arrow, 1990.

Nubret, Serge. "Rathor parle, ou comment on devient Titan." *Cinéma* 64 (Apr. 1964): 59–65.

Nunokawa, Jeff. "'All the Sad Young Men': AIDS and the Work of Mourning." *Yale Journal of Criticism* 4.2 (1991): 1–12.

Oakley, J. Ronald. *God's Country: America in the Fifties*. New York: Dembner Books, 1990.

O'Brien, Justin. *Portrait of Andre Gide: A Critical Biography*. New York: Knopf, 1953.

O'Connor, Richard. *Jack London: A Biography*. Boston: Little, Brown, 1964.

Ohmann, Carol. "The Autobiography of Malcolm X: A Revolutionary Use of the Franklin Tradition." *American Quarterly* 22.2 (1970): 131–49.

Oliver, Paul. *Blues Fell This Morning*. 1960. London: Cambridge UP, 1990.

Ottley, Roi. *'New World A-Coming': Inside Black America*. Boston: Houghton Mifflin, 1943.

Owens, Craig. "The Medusa Effect, or, The Specular Ruse." *Beyond Recognition: Representation, Power, and Culture*. Ed. Scott Bryson, Barbara Kruger, Lynne Tillman, and Jane Weinstock. Berkeley: U of California P, 1992. 191–200.

————. "Posing." *Beyond Recognition: Representation, Power, and Culture*. Ed. Scott Bryson, Barbara Kruger, Lynne Tillman, and Jane Weinstock. Berkeley: U of California P, 1992. 201–17.

Painter, George D. *André Gide: A Critical and Biographical Study*. London: Baker, 1951.

Palmer, Ken. "Mezz Mezzrow at Sixty-five." *Jazz Monthly* 10.9 (1964): 4–6.

Parker, Charlie. "Romance without Finance." *Bird/The Savoy Recordings [Master Takes]*. Savoy, 1976.

Parry, Benita. "Problems in Current Theories of Colonial Discourse." *Oxford Literary Review* 9 (1987): 27–58.

Pateman, Carole. *The Disorder of Women: Democracy, Feminism and Political Theory*. Stanford: Stanford UP, 1989.

Patterson, Orlando. "Blacklash: The Crisis of Gender Relations among African Americans." *Transition* 62 (1993): 4–26.

———. "Race, Gender, and Liberal Fallacies." Editorial. *New York Times* 20 Oct. 1991.

Paz, Octavio. *The Labyrinth of Solitude: Life and Thought in Mexico.* New York: Grove, 1962.

Perry, Bruce. "Escape from Freedom, Criminal Style: The Hidden Advantages of Being in Jail." *Journal of Psychiatry and Law* 12.2 (summer 1984): 215–30.

———. *Malcolm: The Life of a Man Who Changed Black America.* Barrytown, NY: Station Hill, 1991.

———. "Malcolm X and the Politics of Masculinity." *Psychohistory Review* 13.2–3 (winter 1985): 18–25.

———. "Malcolm X in Brief: A Psychological Perspective." *Journal of Psychohistory* 11.4 (spring 1984): 491–500.

Peterson, Theodore Bernard. *Magazines in the Twentieth Century.* Urbana: U of Illinois P, 1964.

Pfeil, Fred. "From Pillar to Postmodern: Race, Class, and Gender in the Male Rampage Film." *Socialist Review* 23.2 (1993): 123–52.

Phelan, Peggy. *Unmarked: The Politics of Performance.* New York: Routledge, 1993.

Pieterse, Jan Nederveen. *White on Black: Images of Africa and Blacks in Western Popular Culture.* New Haven: Yale UP, 1992.

"Police Seek to Finger 'Blackboard Jungle' As Root of Hooliganism." *Variety* 18 May 1955. MPAA Archive file on *Blackboard Jungle*, Los Angeles, CA.

Porges, Irwin. *Edgar Rice Burroughs: The Man Who Created Tarzan.* Provo, UT: Brigham Young UP, 1986.

Poulantzas, Nico. *Classes in Contemporary Capitalism.* Trans. David Fernbach. London: Verso, 1978.

Pratt, Mary Louise. *Imperial Eyes: Travel Writing and Transculturation.* New York: Routledge, 1992.

Public Enemy. "Fight the Power." *Fear of a Black Planet.* Def Jam/CBS, 1990.

Quarles, Benjamin. *The Negro in the Civil War.* Boston: Little, Brown, 1953.

Rabbie, Angela, and Jenny Garber. "Girls and Subcultures." *Resistance Through Rituals: Youth Subcultures in Post-War Britain.* Ed. Stuart Hall and Tony Jefferson. London: Hutchinson, 1976.

Radway, Janice. *Reading the Romance: Women, Patriarchy, and Popular Literature.* Chapel Hill: U of North Carolina P, 1984.

———. "Reception Study: Ethnography and the Problems of Dispersed Audiences and Nomadic Subjects." *Cultural Studies* 2.3 (1988): 359–76.

Rampersad, Arnold. *The Life of Langston Hughes.* 2 vols. New York: Oxford UP, 1986–88.

Rayns, Tony. "Entretien avec Jacky Chan." *Cahiers du cinéma* Sept. 1984.

Redkey, Edwin S., ed. *A Grand Army of Black Men: Letters from African-American Soldiers in the Union Army, 1861–1865.* Cambridge: Cambridge UP, 1992.

Reed, Lou. *Street Hassle.* Arista, 1978.

Reisner, Robert. *Bird: The Legend of Charlie Parker.* New York: Citadel, 1962.

Robbins, Bruce. "Men in Feminism." *Camera Obscura* 17 (May 1988): 206–14.

Robins, David, and Philip Cohen. *Knuckle Sandwich: Growing Up in the Working-Class City.* Harmondsworth: Penguin, 1978.

Robinson, Cedric J. "Malcolm Little, as a Charismatic Leader." *Afro-American Studies* 3 (1972): 81–96.

Robinson, Cyril. "Exploring the Informal Economy." *Crime and Social Justice* 15.3–4 (1988): 3–16.

Rodman, Gilbert. *Elvis After Elvis: The Posthumous Career of a Living Legend.* New York: Routledge, 1996.

Rodowick, D. N. "The Difficulty of Difference." *Wide Angle* 5.1 (1981).

Roediger, David R. *Towards the Abolition of Whiteness.* London: Verso, 1994.

———. *The Wages of Whiteness: Race and the Making of the American Working Class.* London: Verso, 1991.

Rogers, Seth. "A Surgeon's War Letters." *Proceedings of the Massachusetts Historical Society* 43 (1909–10): 337–98.

Rogin, Michael. "Black Masks, White Skin: Consciousness of Class and American National Culture." *Radical History Review* 54 (1992): 141–52.

———. "Making America Home: Racial Masquerade and Ethnic Assimilation in the Transition to Talking Pictures." *Journal of American History* 79.3 (1992): 1050–77.

———. *"Ronald Reagan," the Movie: And Other Episodes in Political Demonology.* Berkeley: U of California P, 1987.

Rose, Tricia. *Black Noise: Rap Music and Black Culture in Contemporary America.* Hanover, NH: Wesleyan UP, 1994.

Ross, Andrew. "Ballots, Bullets or Batmen: Can Cultural Studies Do the Right Thing?" *Screen* 31.1 (1990): 26–44.

———. "Cowboys, Cadillacs, and Cosmonauts: Families, Film Genres, and Technocultures." *Engendering Men: The Question of Male Feminist Criticism.* Ed. Joseph A. Boone and Michael Cadden. New York: Routledge, 1990. 87–101.

———. "The Gangsta and the Diva." *The Nation* 259, 6 (22/29 Aug. 1994): 191–94.

———. *No Respect: Intellectuals and Popular Culture.* New York: Routledge, 1989.

Ross, Marlon. "Modeling Manhood: Black Masculinities and the Cultures of Racial Uplift." Forthcoming.

Rubin, Lillian B. *Worlds of Pain: Life in the Working-Class Family.* New York: Basic, 1976.

Rutherford, Jonathan, ed. *Identity: Community, Culture, Difference.* London: Lawrence and Wishart, 1990.

Safouan, Moustapha. "Is the Oedipus Complex Universal?" *m/f* 5/6 (1981).

Said, Edward. *Orientalism.* 1978. Harmondsworth: Penguin, 1985.

Sánchez-Eppler, Karen. *Touching Liberty: Abolition, Feminism, and the Politics of the Body.* Berkeley: U of California P, 1993.

Sanchez-Tranquilino, Marcos. "Mano a mano: An Essay on the Representation of the Zoot Suit and Its Misrepresentation by Octavio Paz." *Journal of the Los Angeles Institute of Contemporary Art* (winter 1987): 34–42.

Sanchez-Tranquilino, Marcos, and John Tagg. "The Pachuco's Flayed Hide: Mobility, Identity, and Buenas Garras." *Cultural Studies*. Ed. Lawrence Grossberg, Cary Nelson, and Paula Treichler. London: Routledge, 1992. 566–70.

Sanguineti, Tatti. "Mitologico, Muscle Man Epic, Peplum." *Gli uomini forti*. Ed. Farassino and Sanguineti. Milan: Mazzotta, 1983. 87–99.

Sartre, Jean-Paul. *Black Orpheus*. Trans. S. W. Allen. Paris: Editions Gallimard, 1963.

Saxton, Alexander. *The Rise and Fall of the White Republic: Class Politics and Mass Culture in Nineteenth-Century America*. London: Verso, 1991.

Scarry, Elaine. *The Body in Pain: The Making and Unmaking of the World*. New York: Oxford UP, 1985.

Scott, Joan W. "The Evidence of Experience." *Critical Inquiry* 17 (summer 1991): 773–97.

———. "Multiculturalism and the Politics of Identity." *October* 61 (1992): 12–19.

Seabrook, John. "Rocking in Shangri-La." *New Yorker* 10 October 1994: 64–78.

Sedgwick, Eve Kosofsky. *Between Men: English Literature and Male Homosocial Desire*. New York: Columbia UP, 1985.

———. *Epistemology of the Closet*. Berkeley: U of California P, 1990.

———. "Gender Criticism." *Redrawing the Boundaries: The Transformation of English and American Literary Studies*. Ed. Stephen Greenblatt and Giles Gunn. New York: Modern Language Association of America, 1992. 271–302.

Segal, Lynne. *Slow Motion: Changing Masculinities, Changing Men*. London: Virago, 1990.

Sennett, Richard, and Jonathan Cobb. *The Hidden Injuries of Class*. New York: Knopf, 1972.

Server, Lee. *Danger is My Business: An Illustrated History of the Fabulous Pulp Magazines, 1896–1953*. San Francisco: Chronicle, 1993.

Shapiro, Herbert. *White Violence and Black Response: From Reconstruction to Montgomery*. Amherst, MA: U of Massachusetts P, 1988.

Shaw, Arnold. *Black Popular Music in America*. New York: Schirmer, 1986.

Showalter, Elaine. "Critical Cross-Dressing: Male Feminists and the Woman of the Year." *Men in Feminism*. Ed. Alice Jardine and Paul Smith. New York: Methuen, 1987. 116–32.

Siciliano, Enzo. *Pasolini: A Biography*. Trans. John Shepley. London: Bloomsbury, 1987.

Siclier, Jacques. "L'age du péplum." *Cahiers du cinéma* 22.131 (1962): 26–38.

Sidran, Ben. *Black Talk*. 1971. New York: Da Capo, 1981.

Silverman, Kaja. *Male Subjectivity at the Margins*. New York: Routledge, 1992.

———. "White Skin, Brown Masks: The Double Mimesis, or With Lawrence in Arabia." *differences* 1.3 (1989): 3–54.

Simmel, Georg. "Adornment." 1905. *The Sociology of Georg Simmel*. Ed. Kurt H. Wolff. Glencoe, IL: Free, 1950. 338–44.

Sitkoff, Harvard. "The Detroit Race Riot of 1943." *Michigan History* 53 (fall 1969): 183–206.

———. *A New Deal for Blacks: The Emergence of Civil Rights as a National Issue*. New York: Oxford UP, 1978.

———. "Racial Militancy and Interracial Violence in the Second World War." *Journal of American History* 58 (Dec. 1971): 661–81.

Slack, Jennifer Daryl, and Laurie Anne Whitt. "Ethics and Cultural Studies." *Cultural Studies*. Ed. Lawrence Grossberg, Cary Nelson, and Paula Treichler. New York: Routledge, 1992. 571–92.

Slim, Iceberg [Robert Beck]. *Pimp: The Story of My Life*. Los Angeles: Holloway House, 1969.

Smith, Michael J., ed. *Black Men/White Men: A Gay Anthology*. San Francisco: Gay Sunshine, 1983.

Smith, Paul. "Vas." *Camera Obscura* 17 (1988): 89–111.

Spencer, Jon Michael, ed. *The Emergence of Rap and the Emergence of Black*. A special issue of *Black Sacred Music* 5 (1991).

Spigel, Lynn. "Communicating with the Dead: Elvis as Medium." *Camera Obscura* 23 (1990): 177–204.

Spillers, Hortense J. "Mama's Baby, Papa's Maybe: An American Grammar Book." *Diacritics* 17.2 (summer 1987): 65–81.

Spivak, Gayatri. "Can the Subaltern Speak?" *Marxism and the Interpretation of Culture*. Ed. Cary Nelson and Lawrence Grossberg. Urbana: U of Illinois P, 1988. 271–313.

Stack, Carol B. *All Our Kin: Strategies for Survival in a Black Community*. New York: Harper and Row, 1974.

Stansell, Christine. *City of Women: Sex and Class in New York, 1789–1860*. New York: Knopf, 1986.

Stanton, Domna. *Discourses of Sexuality: From Aristotle to AIDS*. Ann Arbor: U of Michigan P, 1992.

St. Armand, Barton Levi. *Emily Dickinson and Her Culture: The Soul's Society*. Cambridge: Cambridge UP, 1984.

———. "Fine Fitnesses: Dickinson, Higginson, and Literary Luminism." *Prospects* 14 (1989): 141–73.

Stearns, Marshall. *The Story of Jazz*. New York: Oxford UP, 1956.

Stoekl, Allan. Introduction. *Visions of Excess: Selected Writings, 1927–1939*. By Georges Bataille. Ed. Allan Stoekl. Trans. Allan Stoekl, with Carl R. Lovitt and Donald M. Leslie Jr. Minneapolis: U of Minnesota P, 1985. ix–xxv.

Stowe, Harriet Beecher. *Uncle Tom's Cabin; or, Life Among the Lowly*. 1852. New York: Penguin, 1981.

Szwed, John F. "Race and the Embodiment of Culture." *Ethnicity* 2 (1975): 19–33.

Taylor, Susie King. *A Black Woman's Civil War Memoirs*. [*Reminiscences of My Life in Camp with the 33rd U.S. Colored Troops, Late 1st South Carolina Volunteers.*] 1902. Ed. Patricia W. Romero and Willie Lee Rose. New York: Markus Wiener, 1988.

Theweleit, Klaus. *Male Fantasies*. Trans. Erica Carter, Chris Turner, and Stephen Conway. 2 vols. 1977, 1978. Minneapolis: U of Minnesota P, 1987, 1989.

Thompson, E. P. *The Making of the English Working Class*. New York: Vintage, 1963.

Tolson, Andrew. *The Limits of Masculinity*. London: Tavistock, 1977.

Toop, David. *The Rap Attack: African Jive to New York Hip Hop*. Boston: South End, 1984.

Torgovnick, Marianna. *Gone Primitive: Savage Intellects, Modern Lives.* Chicago: U of Chicago P, 1990.

"Toronto Hubbub Over 'Blackboard.' " *Variety* 25 May 1955. MPAA Archive file on Blackboard Jungle, Los Angeles, CA.

Trachtenberg, Alan. *The Incorporation of America: Culture and Society in the Gilded Age.* New York: Hill and Wang, 1982.

Turner, Ralph H., and Samuel J. Surace. "Zoot Suiters and Mexicans: Symbols in Crowd Behavior." *American Journal of Sociology* 62 (1956): 14–20.

Tyler, Bruce M. "Black Jive and White Repression." *Journal of Ethnic Studies* 16.4 (1989): 32–38.

U.S. Senate. *Motion Pictures and Juvenile Delinquency: Interim Report of the Subcommittee to Investigate Juvenile Delinquency to the Committee on the Judiciary.* Washington: U.S. Government Printing Office, 1956.

Valentine, Betty Lou. *Hustling and Other Hard Work: Life Styles in the Ghetto.* New York: Free, 1978.

Valperga, Giuseppe. "Mitologie popolari dell'uomo forte." *Gli uomini forti.* Ed. Farassino and Sanguinetti. Milan: Mazzatto, 1983. 67–68.

Van Der Zee, James. *The Harlem Book of the Dead.* New York: Dutton, 1974.

"Vipers, Tea, and Jazz." *Newsweek* 28 Oct. 1946: 88–89.

Wagstaff, Christopher. "A Forkful of Westerns: Industry, Audiences and the Italian Western." *Popular European Cinema.* Ed. Dyer and Vincendeau. London: Routledge, 1992.

Wald, Gayle. " 'I'm a Loser, Baby': Whiteness and Popular Music Studies." *Whiteness: A Critical Reader.* Ed. Michael Hill. New York: New York UP, 1997. 175–93.

Walker, Alice. "Nineteen Fifty-five." *You Can't Keep a Good Woman Down.* New York: Harcourt Brace Jovanovich, 1981.

———. *The Temple of My Familiar.* New York: Dell, 1989.

Walkerdine, Valerie. "Video Replay: Families, Films and Fantasy." *Formations of Fantasy.* Ed. Victor Burgin, James Donald, and Cora Kaplan. London: Methuen, 1986. 167–89.

Wallace, Michele. *Black Macho and the Myth of the Superwoman.* New York: Verso, 1990.

———. *Invisibility Blues.* New York: Verso, 1991.

Walters, Ronald G. "The Erotic South: Civilization and Sexuality in American Abolitionism." *American Quarterly* 25 (1973): 177–201.

Warner, Michael. "Homo-Narcissism, or Heterosexuality." *Engendering Men: The Question of Male Feminist Criticism.* Ed. Joseph A. Boone and Michael Cadden. New York: Routledge, 1990. 190–206.

———, ed. *Fear of a Queer Planet: Queer Politics and Social Theory.* Minneapolis: U of Minnesota P, 1993.

Webster, David. *Barbells and Beefcake: An Illustrated History of Bodybuilding.* Irvine, Great Britain: Webster, 1979.

Weedon, Chris. *Feminist Practice and Post-Structuralist Theory.* New York: Basil Blackwell, 1987.

Weeks, Jeffrey. *Sexuality and Its Discontents: Meaning, Myths and Modern Sexualities.* London: Routledge, 1985.

Wells, Anna Mary. *Dear Preceptor: The Life and Times of Thomas Wentworth Higginson.* Boston: Houghton, 1963.

Wentworth, Harold, ed. *Dictionary of American Slang.* New York: Crowell, 1960.

West, Cornell. *Prophesy Deliverance!* Philadelphia: Westminster, 1982.

West, Cornell, with bell hooks. "Black Men and Women: Partnership in the 1990's." *Breaking Bread: Insurgent Black Intellectual Life.* Boston: South End, 1991.

Whitfield, Stephen. "Three Masters of Impression Management: Benjamin Franklin, Booker T. Washington, and Malcolm X as Autobiographers." *South Atlantic Quarterly* 77 (autumn 1978): 399–417.

Wideman, John Edgar. *Fatheralong: A Meditation on Fathers and Sons, Race and Society.* New York: Pantheon, 1994.

Wiegman, Robyn. "Melville's Geography of Gender." *American Literary History* 1.4 (1989): 735–53.

Wilber, Bob, with Derek Webster. *Music Was Not Enough.* London: Macmillan, 1987.

Wilde, Oscar. *More Letters of Oscar Wilde.* Ed. Rupert Hart Davis. London: Murray, 1985.

Wilentz, Sean. *Chants Democratic: New York City and the Rise of the American Working Class, 1788–1850.* New York: Oxford UP, 1984.

Williams, Raymond. *Marxism and Literature.* New York: Oxford UP, 1978.

Williams, Sherley Anne. "Two Words on Music: Black Community." *Black Popular Culture.* Ed. Gina Dent. Seattle: Bay, 1992. 164–72.

Willis, Paul. *Learning to Labour: How Working-Class Kids Get Working-Class Jobs.* 1977. New York: Columbia UP, 1981.

———. "Notes on Method." *Culture, Media, Language: Working Papers in Cultural Studies, 1972–79.* Ed. Stuart Hall et al. London: Hutchinson, 1980. 88–95.

———. "Shop Floor Culture, Masculinity and the Wage Form." *Working-Class Culture: Studies in History and Theory.* Ed. John Clarke, Chas Critcher, and Richard Johnson. London: Hutchinson, 1979. 185–98.

Wilson, Christopher. *White Collar Fictions: Class and Social Representation in U.S. Fiction, 1880–1925.* Athens: U of Georgia P, 1992.

Wilson, Edmund. *Patriotic Gore: Studies in the Literature of the American Civil War.* 1962. Boston: Northeastern UP, 1984.

Wilson, John. *Jazz: The Transition Years, 1940–1960.* New York: Appleton-Century-Crofts, 1966.

Winthrop, Theodore. *Cecil Dreeme.* Boston: Ticknor and Fields, 1861.

Wister, Owen. *The Virginian: A Horseman of the Plains.* New York: Macmillan, 1940.

Wolfe, Bernard. "Ecstatic in Blackface: The Negro as a Song-and-Dance Man." *Really the Blues,* by Mezz Mezzrow. New York: Citadel Underground, 1990.

———. "Uncle Remus and the Malevolent Rabbit." *Commentary* 8.1 (July 1949): 31–41.

Wolfenstein, Eugene Victor. *The Victims of Democracy: Malcolm X and the Black Revolution.* Berkeley: U of California P, 1981.

Wolff, Cynthia Griffin. *Emily Dickinson*. 1986. Reading, MA: Addison-Wesley, 1988.

Worley, Sam. "Army Life in a Black Regiment and Reconstruction." *ESQ* 34 (1988): 159–79.

Wright, Erik Olin. *Classes*. London: Verso, 1985.

Wyke, Maria. "Herculean Muscle: The Classizing Rhetoric of Bodybuilding." Forthcoming.

Wynn, Neil A. *The Afro-American and the Second World War*. New York: Holmes and Meier, 1975.

Wynter, Sylvia. "Rethinking 'Aesthetics': Notes Towards a Deciphering Practice." *Ex-Iles: Essays on Caribbean Cinema*. Ed. Mbye Cham. Trenton, NJ: African World, 1992.

X, Malcolm. *Malcolm X Speaks: Selected Speeches and Statements*. Ed. George Breitman. New York: Merit, 1965.

———. "Not Just an American Problem, but a World Problem." *Malcolm X: The Last Speeches*. Ed. Bruce Perry. New York: Pathfinder, 1989.

X, Malcolm, with Alex Haley. *The Autobiography of Malcolm X*. New York: Grove, 1964.

Yacovone, Donald. "Abolitionists and the 'Language of Fraternal Love.'" *Meanings for Manhood: Constructions of Masculinity in Victorian America*. Ed. Mark C. Carnes and Clyde Griffen. Chicago: U of Chicago P, 1990. 85–95.

Yellin, Jean Fagan. *Women and Sisters: The Antislavery Feminists in American Culture*. New Haven: Yale UP, 1989.

Yingling, Thomas. "How the Eye is Caste: Robert Mapplethorpe and the Limits of Controversy." *Discourse* 2.2 (1990): 3–28.

Žižek, Slavoj. "Eastern Europe's Republics of Gilead." *New Left Review* 183 (1990): 50–62.

———. *The Sublime Object of Ideology*. New York: Verso, 1989.

INDEX

CONTRIBUTORS

Herman Beavers is Associate Professor of English at the University of Pennsylvania.

Jonathan Dollimore is Professor in the School of American and English Studies at the University of Sussex.

Richard Dyer is Professor of Film in the Department of Film and Television, University of Warwick.

Robin D. G. Kelley is Professor of History at New York University.

Christopher Looby is Associate Professor of English at the University of Pennsylvania.

Eric Lott is Associate Professor of English at the University of Virginia.

Deborah E. McDowell is Professor of English at the University of Virginia.

Leerom Medovoi is Adjunct Assistant Professor of English at the University of Utah.

José E. Muñoz is Assistant Professor of Performance Studies at New York University.

Harry Stecopoulos is a graduate student at the University of Virginia.

Yvonne Tasker is Senior Lecturer in Film and Media Studies at the University of Sunderland.

Michael Uebel is Assistant Professor of English at the University of Kentucky.

Gayle Wald is Assistant Professor of English at George Washington University.

Robyn Wiegman is Associate Professor of Women's Studies at the University of California-Irvine.

Library of Congress Cataloging-in-Publication Data
Race and the subject of masculinities / Harry Stecopoulos and
Michael Uebel, editors.
p.   cm. — (New Americanists)
Includes bibliographical references and index.
ISBN 0-8223-1958-6 (cloth : alk. paper). —
ISBN 0-8223-1966-7 (paper : alk. paper)
1. Sex role.   2. Race.   3. Gender identity.   4. Masculinity
(Psychology)   5. Men—Psychology.   I. Stecopoulos, Harry.
II. Uebel, Michael.   III. Series.
HQ1075.R33   1997
305.32'089—dc21   96-49942   CIP